The Journey of Adulthood

Ninth Edition

Barbara R. Bjorklund
Wilkes Honors College of Florida Atlantic University

Julie L. Earles
Wilkes Honors College of Florida Atlantic University

 Pearson

Portfolio Manager: *Tanimaa Mehra*
Portfolio Manager Assistant: *Anna Austin*
Product Marketer: *Marianela Silvestri*
Content Developer: *Nic Albert*
Art/Designer: *SPi Global*
Digital Studio Course Producer: *Elissa Senra-Sargent*
Full-Service Project Manager: *Vinodhini Kumaraswamy, SPi Global, Inc.*
Compositor: *SPi Global*
Printer/Binder: *LSC Communications, Inc.*
Cover Printer: *LSC Communications, Inc.*
Cover Design: *Lumina Datamatics, Inc.*
Cover Art: *Tijana Nikolovska/123RF*

Acknowledgments of third party content appear on page 321, which constitutes an extension of this copyright page.

Library of Congress Cataloging-in-Publication Data
Names: Bjorklund, Barbara R., author. | Earles, Julie L., author.
Title: The Journey of adulthood / Barbara R. Bjorklund, Wilkes Honors College of Florida Atlantic University, Julie L. Earles, Wilkes Honors College of Florida Atlantic University.
Description: Ninth edition. | Hoboken, NJ : Pearson, [2020] | Includes
  bibliographical references and index. |
Identifiers: LCCN 2019024590 (print) | LCCN 2019024591 (ebook) |
  ISBN 9780135705117 (Rental Edition) | ISBN 0135705118 (Rental Edition) |
  ISBN 9780134811710 (Instructor's Review Copy) | ISBN 0134811712 (Instructor's Review Copy) |
  ISBN 9780134811703 (Loose-Leaf Edition) | ISBN 0134811704 (Loose-Leaf Edition) |
  ISBN 9780134792897 (Revel Access Code Card) | ISBN 0134792890 (Revel Access Code Card) |
  ISBN 9780135694619 (Revel Combo Card) | ISBN 0135694612 (Revel Combo Card)
Subjects: LCSH: Adulthood--Psychological aspects. | Aging--Psychological aspects. | Adulthood. | Aging.
Classification: LCC BF724.5 .B44 2020 (print) | LCC BF724.5 (ebook) | DDC 155.67--dc23
LC record available at https://lccn.loc.gov/2019024590
LC ebook record available at https://lccn.loc.gov/2019024591

2 2019

	Revel Access Code Card	Loose-Leaf Edition
ISBN-10:	0-134-79289-0	0-134-81170-4
ISBN-13:	978-0-134-79289-7	978-0-134-81170-3

	Revel Combo Card	Instructor's Review Copy
ISBN-10:	0-135-69461-2	0-134-81171-2
ISBN-13:	978-0-135-69461-9	978-0-134-81171-0

	Rental Edition	
ISBN-10:	0-135-70511-8	
ISBN-13:	978-0-135-70511-7	

For my new grandchildren: Jane and Wesley Zeman, Sage Zeman, and Amelia Tobiaz.

You light up my life! BRB

For my father, Dr. Tom Earles, who taught me to appreciate human complexity and search for the good in every person.

I love you dad. JLE

Brief Contents

1 Introduction to Adult Development   1

2 Physical Changes   22

3 Health and Health Disorders   50

4 Cognitive Abilities   77

5 Social Roles   103

6 Social Relationships   127

7 Work and Retirement   156

8 Personality   181

9 The Quest for Meaning   205

10 Stress, Coping, and Resilience   226

11 Death and Bereavement   246

12 The Successful Journey   262

Contents

Preface   viii
About the Authors   xv
Acknowledgments   xvi

1 Introduction to Adult Development   1

1.1 Basic Concepts in Adult Development   2
   1.1.1 Differences and Commonalities   3
   1.1.2 Stability and Change   3
   1.1.3 A Word About "Age"   5
1.2 Sources of Change   5
   1.2.1 Normative Age-Graded Influences   6
   1.2.2 Normative History-Graded Influences   6
   1.2.3 Nonnormative Life Events   8
   1.2.4 Genetics, the Environment, and Their Interactions   8
1.3 Guiding Perspectives   9
   1.3.1 Lifespan Developmental Psychology Approach   10
   1.3.2 Bioecological Model of Development   10
1.4 Developmental Research   11
   1.4.1 Methods   12
   1.4.2 Measures   15
   1.4.3 Data Analysis   15
   1.4.4 Designs   17
Summary: Introduction to Adult Development   **20**

2 Physical Changes   22

2.1 Theories of Primary Aging   23
   2.1.1 Oxidative Damage   23
   2.1.2 Genetic Limits   24
   2.1.3 Caloric Restriction   24
   2.1.4 Turning Back the Clock   25
2.2 Physical Changes in Outward Appearance   26
   2.2.1 Weight and Body Composition   27
   2.2.2 Skin Changes   29
   2.2.3 Hair   30
2.3 The Changing Senses   31
   2.3.1 Vision   31
   2.3.2 Hearing   33
   2.3.3 Taste and Smell   34
2.4 How Age Changes Internal Structures and Systems   35
   2.4.1 Bones and Muscles   35
   2.4.2 Cardiovascular and Respiratory Systems   37
   2.4.3 Brain and Nervous System   37
   2.4.4 Immune System   38
   2.4.5 Hormonal System   38

2.5 Changes in Physical Behavior   40
   2.5.1 Athletic Abilities   40
   2.5.2 Stamina, Dexterity, and Balance   40
   2.5.3 Sleep   41
   2.5.4 Sexual Activity   42
2.6 Individual Differences in Primary Aging   45
   2.6.1 Genetics   45
   2.6.2 Lifestyle   45
   2.6.3 Race, Ethnicity, and Socioeconomic Group   46
Summary: Physical Changes   **48**

3 Health and Health Disorders   50

3.1 Mortality, Morbidity, and Disability   51
   3.1.1 Mortality and Morbidity   52
   3.1.2 Disability   53
3.2 Specific Diseases   54
   3.2.1 Cardiovascular Disease   55
   3.2.2 Cancer   55
   3.2.3 Diabetes   57
   3.2.4 Alzheimer's Disease   58
3.3 Psychological Disorders   59
   3.3.1 Anxiety Disorders   60
   3.3.2 Depressive Disorders   60
   3.3.3 Substance-Related and Addictive Disorders   61
   3.3.4 Treatment of Mental Health Disorders   63
3.4 Assistance Solutions   63
   3.4.1 Assistive Technology   64
   3.4.2 Assistance Animals   64
3.5 Individual Differences in Health   65
   3.5.1 Genetics   65
   3.5.2 Sex and Gender   65
   3.5.3 Socioeconomic Class   66
   3.5.4 Race and Ethnicity   69
   3.5.5 Discrimination   70
   3.5.6 Personality and Behavior Patterns   72
   3.5.7 Developmental Origins   73
   3.5.8 Lifestyle   74
Summary: Health and Health Disorders   **75**

4 Cognitive Abilities   77

4.1 Attention   78
   4.1.1 Divided Attention   78
   4.1.2 Visual Search   79

4.2   Memory   79
    4.2.1   Short-Term and Working Memory   80
    4.2.2   Episodic Memory   81
    4.2.3   Prospective Memory   83
    4.2.4   Slowing Declines in Memory
            Abilities   84
    4.2.5   Memory in Context   85
4.3   Intelligence   86
    4.3.1   Age Changes in Overall Intelligence   87
    4.3.2   Components of Intelligence   88
    4.3.3   Reversing Declines in Intellectual
            Abilities   90
4.4   Decision Making and Problem Solving   91
    4.4.1   Making Choices   91
    4.4.2   Problem Solving and Emotional
            Information   92
    4.4.3   Positivity Bias   92
4.5   Individual Differences in Cognitive Change   93
    4.5.1   Health   94
    4.5.2   Genetics   94
    4.5.3   Demographics and Sociobiographical
            History   95
    4.5.4   Education and Intellectual Activity   95
    4.5.5   Physical Exercise   96
    4.5.6   Subjective Evaluation of Decline   97
4.6   Cognitive Assistance   97
    4.6.1   Medication Adherence   97
    4.6.2   Social Networking   98
    4.6.3   E-Readers and Electronic Games   98
    4.6.4   Safe Driving   99
Summary: Cognitive Abilities   **101**

5   Social Roles   **103**

5.1   Social Roles and Transitions   104
    5.1.1   The Effect of Variations in Timing   104
    5.1.2   Gender Roles   106
5.2   Social Roles in Young Adulthood   107
    5.2.1   Leaving and Returning Home   107
    5.2.2   Becoming a Spouse or Partner   109
    5.2.3   Becoming a Parent   111
5.3   Social Roles in Middle Adulthood   115
    5.3.1   The Departure of the Children   115
    5.3.2   Gender Roles at Midlife   116
    5.3.3   Becoming a Grandparent   116
    5.3.4   Caregiving for Aging Parents   118
5.4   Social Roles in Late Adulthood   119
    5.4.1   Living Alone   120
    5.4.2   Becoming a Care Receiver   121
5.5   Social Roles in Atypical Families   122
    5.5.1   Lifelong Singles   122
    5.5.2   The Childless   123
    5.5.3   Divorced (and Remarried)
            Adults   124
Summary: Social Roles   **125**

6   Social Relationships   **127**

6.1   Theories of Social Relationships   128
    6.1.1   Attachment Theory   128
    6.1.2   The Convoy Model   129
    6.1.3   Socioemotional Selectivity Theory   130
    6.1.4   Evolutionary Psychology   130
6.2   Establishing an Intimate Partnership   131
    6.2.1   Lust   132
    6.2.2   Attraction   132
    6.2.3   Attachment   135
6.3   Living in Intimate Partnerships   137
    6.3.1   Happy Marriages   137
    6.3.2   Cohabitation and Marriage   138
    6.3.3   Same-Sex Marriages and Partnerships   140
6.4   Relationships with Other Family Members   142
    6.4.1   General Patterns of Family Interaction   142
    6.4.2   Parent–Child Relationships in Adulthood 143
    6.4.3   Grandparent–Grandchild Relationships   146
    6.4.4   Relationships with Siblings   148
6.5   Friendships in Adulthood   149
    6.5.1   Friendship Networks   149
    6.5.2   Social Media Friends   150
Summary: Social Relationships   **153**

7   Work and Retirement   **156**

7.1   The Importance of Work in Adulthood   157
    7.1.1   Theories of Career Development   157
    7.1.2   Gender Differences in Career Patterns   158
7.2   Selecting a Career   160
    7.2.1   The Effects of Gender   160
    7.2.2   Family Influences   162
7.3   Age Trends in the Workplace   162
    7.3.1   Job Performance   164
    7.3.2   Job Training and Retraining   164
    7.3.3   Job Satisfaction   165
7.4   Work and Personal Life   165
    7.4.1   Work and the Individual   165
    7.4.2   Work and Family Life   168
7.5   Retirement   171
    7.5.1   Preparation for Retirement   171
    7.5.2   Timing of Retirement   172
    7.5.3   Reasons for Retirement   173
    7.5.4   Effects of Retirement   174
    7.5.5   Alternatives to Full Retirement   176
    7.5.6   Retirement and Well-Being   177
Summary: Work and Retirement   **178**

8   Personality   **181**

8.1   Personality Structures   182
    8.1.1   Personality Traits and Factors   182
    8.1.2   Differential Continuity   183
    8.1.3   Mean-Level Change   184

8.1.4 Intra-Individual Variability 185

8.1.5 Continuity, Change, and Variability Coexist 187

8.2 What Do Personality Traits Do? 188

8.2.1 Personality and Relationships 188

8.2.2 Personality and Achievement 188

8.2.3 Personality and Health 189

8.3 Explanations of Continuity and Change 190

8.3.1 Genetics 190

8.3.2 Environmental Influences 191

8.3.3 Evolutionary Psychology Explanations 193

8.3.4 Cultural Differences 193

8.4 Theories of Personality Development 194

8.4.1 Psychosocial Development 194

8.4.2 Ego Development 198

8.4.3 Mature Adaptation 199

8.4.4 Gender Crossover 200

8.4.5 Positive Well-Being 201

Summary: Personality **203**

9 The Quest for Meaning 205

9.1 Why We Study the Quest for Meaning 206

9.1.1 Meaning Matters 206

9.1.2 The Quest for Meaning is Human 207

9.1.3 Cultures Support Gerotranscendence 207

9.2 The Study of Age-Related Changes in Meaning Systems 207

9.2.1 Changes in the Quest for Meaning 208

9.2.2 Religion, Spirituality, and Health 210

9.3 Theories of Spiritual Development 212

9.3.1 Development of Moral Reasoning 212

9.3.2 Development of Faith 216

9.4 Integrating Meaning and Personality 218

9.4.1 A Synthesizing Model 219

9.4.2 Stages of Mystical Experience 220

9.5 The Process of Transition 220

9.5.1 Transition Theory 221

9.5.2 Triggering a Transition 221

9.5.3 The Impact of Life Changes 222

9.6 Shapes of the Quest 222

9.6.1 Life as Journey 222

9.6.2 Choosing a Metaphor 223

Summary: The Quest for Meaning **224**

10 Stress, Coping, and Resilience 226

10.1 Stress, Stressors, and Stress Reactions 227

10.1.1 Stressors and Stress Reactions 227

10.1.2 Types of Stress 228

10.2 Effects of Stress 229

10.2.1 Physical Disease 230

10.2.2 Mental Health Disorders 231

10.2.3 Individual Differences in Stress-Related Disorders 233

10.2.4 Stress-Related Growth 236

10.3 Coping with Stress 236

10.3.1 Types of Coping Behaviors 237

10.3.2 Social Support 239

10.4 Resilience 240

10.4.1 Reactions to Trauma 241

10.4.2 Personality Traits and Resilience 241

10.4.3 Resilience in Military Deployment 243

Summary: Stress, Coping, and Resilience **244**

11 Death and Bereavement 246

11.1 Understanding Death 247

11.1.1 Meanings of Death 247

11.1.2 Death Anxiety 248

11.1.3 Accepting the Reality of One's Eventual Death 249

11.2 The Process of Death 250

11.2.1 Stages of Reactions to Death 250

11.2.2 The Importance of Farewells 251

11.2.3 Individual Adaptations to Dying 252

11.2.4 Choosing Where to Die 252

11.2.5 Choosing When to Die 254

11.3 Rituals and Grieving 256

11.3.1 Funerals and Ceremonies 256

11.3.2 The Process of Grieving 256

Summary: Death and Bereavement **260**

12 The Successful Journey 262

12.1 Themes of Adult Development 263

12.1.1 Emerging Adulthood (Ages 18–24) 265

12.1.2 Young Adulthood (Ages 25–39) 266

12.1.3 Middle Adulthood (Ages 40–64) 268

12.1.4 Older Adulthood (Ages 65–74) 269

12.1.5 Late Adulthood (Age 75 and Older) 271

12.2 Variations in Successful Development 273

12.2.1 Individual Differences in Quality of Life 274

12.2.2 Other Measures of Life Success 275

12.3 A Model of Adult Growth and Development 278

12.3.1 Proposition 1 278

12.3.2 Proposition 2 279

12.3.3 Proposition 3 280

12.3.4 Proposition 4 282

12.4 Successful Aging 283

12.4.1 Physical and Mental Exercise 284

12.4.2 Social Engagement 285

12.4.3 Diet and Nutrition 285

12.4.4 Complementary and Alternative Medicine 286

Summary: The Successful Journey **286**

Glossary 288

References 294

Credits 321

Author Index 327

Subject Index 340

Preface

Now in its ninth edition, *The Journey of Adulthood* continues to capture the dynamic process of adult development from early adulthood to the end of life. Its core is made up of research findings from large-scale projects and major theories of adult development, but it also reflects smaller studies of diverse groups, showing the influences of gender, culture, ethnicity, race, and socioeconomic background on this journey. I have balanced new research with classic studies from pioneers in the field of adult development. And I have sweetened this sometimes medicinal taste with a spoonful of honey—a little personal warmth and humor. After all, I am now officially an older adult who is on this journey along with my husband, looking ahead at the examples our parents' journeys gave us, and back toward our children who are blazing their own trails. And as of this edition, we have 14 grandchildren—seven of whom are beginning their own journeys of adulthood either as college students or starting their careers.

Not only have I changed over the course of this book, but I have taken on a co-author and have truly enjoyed having her input. She is Dr. Julie Earles, a long-time friend and colleague at the Wilkes Honors College of Florida Atlantic University. She has a little different spin on things, and I think it will make this an even better book as she adds more and more to the chapters.

The first chapter contains the basics for the course—definitions, methods, and guiding perspectives for the study of adult development. Chapters 2 through 8 cover traditional developmental topics, featuring recent research, classic studies, current theories, new directions, and practical applications. Chapters 9, 10, and 11 cover topics not traditionally found in adult development texts, but which we feel are important to round out a student's experience in this course: the quest for meaning; the inevitability of stress, coping, and resilience in adult life; and the way we face our own deaths and those of our loved ones. The final chapter takes a chronological look at adult development, in contrast to the topical theme in the earlier chapters, and also suggests a model of adult development that will "pull the threads together and tie up loose ends."

New in This Edition

The ninth edition of *The Journey of Adulthood* features a comprehensive update of all chapters. Almost one-third of the references are new to this edition, as are many of the figures and tables. The field of adult development is

changing quickly, and this edition of *The Journey of Adulthood* gives a thorough coverage of the changes that have taken place since the previous edition was written 4 years ago. Ultimately a text on development, *The Journey of Adulthood* has itself developed through numerous editions over the past two decades. This ninth edition features several types of change; some reflect change in the field of adult development and some reflect change in the world around us, specifically, the academic settings in which this text is used.

Changes in the Field of Adult Development

The study of adult development is a fairly new field and it expands exponentially from year to year. It began as a field of psychology, but more and more disciplines have shown an interest in the changes that take place over the adult years. This book includes research from scientists who identify themselves as psychologists, sociologists, anthropologists, neuroscientists, epidemiologists, behavioral geneticists, cellular biologists, biogerontologists, and many more. The terminology and methods in these fields have become more and more similar, and many researchers publish in the journals of a variety of fields. This edition of *The Journey of Adulthood* reflects this wonderful collaboration and the richness of a number of multidisciplinary projects. It is an exciting time in developmental science, and this text reflects that energy.

Some of the projects that have been tapped for this text are the Midlife in the U.S. Study (MIDUS), the Berlin Study of Aging, the Grant Study of Harvard Men, the National Comorbidity Study, the Nun Study of the School Sisters of Notre Dame, the Victoria Longitudinal Study, the Swedish Twin Study, the National Survey of Sexual and Health Behavior, The Women's Health Study, and the National Longitudinal Mortality Study.

To emphasize these collaborations, we have identified each major researcher or theorist with his or her field of study. Two editions ago, I was struck with the diversity of scientific fields contributing to the adult development literature. We want this text to reflect that diversity. When we discuss some work in detail, we give the full names of the researchers and how they identify their field of study. We hope that the students who are interested in adult development will take note and consider these areas when they declare their majors or make plans for graduate school. As professors, we all need to remember that we not only teach the content of the courses, but also guide our students in career decisions—in life decisions.

Another change in the field of adult development is that more and more research projects reported in major journals are done by international groups of researchers in settings all over the developed world. We are no longer limited to information on adults in the United States, we also have research being done by Swedish, Japanese, and Egyptian scientists using Swedish, Japanese, and Egyptian participants. When the findings are similar to studies done in the United States, we can be more confident that the developmental phenomenon being studied is an integral part of the human experience and not something particular to people in the United States. When the findings are different from studies done in the United States, we can investigate these differences and find their roots. We have identified these international research teams and the nationalities of their participants. We hope this accentuates the global aspects of our academic community and, as seasoned travelers ourselves, we hope it inspires students to consider "study-abroad" programs and to consider the world outside their own.

We include full names of major researchers and theorists when we discuss their work in detail. Seeing the first and last names makes the researchers more real to the students than conventional citations of "last names, comma, date." Full names also reflect the diversity of scientists—often their gender and their national or ethnic backgrounds. Our students represent a wide range of races and ethnicities, and the time of science being the sole domain of an elite group most of us cannot identify with is gone.

One of the most exciting changes in the field of adult development has been its expansion to emphasize a wider and wider range of age groups. In the early editions of this text, the focus of interest was older adults. The last three editions have featured more and more studies of young adults, middle-aged adults, and emerging adults. This edition features additional research on the opposite end of the age spectrum: those who are 75, 80, 90 years of age and older. Although having people in this age group is nothing new, the growing numbers of them have made it important (and relatively easy) to include them in studies of adult development. Clearly the study of adult development is no longer the study of certain specific age groups, it is now truly a study of every aspect of adulthood. We have tried to capture this inclusion by choosing topics, examples, opening stories, photos, suggested reading, and critical thinking questions that represent the entire adult lifespan.

Changes in the World Around Us

Since the last edition of this book, the world has changed in many ways. As we write this preface, we seem to have recovered from the financial setbacks many families experienced a decade ago and unemployment numbers are low. However, technology and outsourcing have replaced workers in many areas, and those replaced workers are often underemployed in fields that have lower wages. Many students are graduating from college with student loan debt and poor job prospects in their areas of study. Opioid abuse has become a public health crisis, taking a toll on every part of the country and every level of society. Cutbacks in government funding and the weakening of regulations threaten our environment and our planet's future. There is a large political divide. More troops are coming home from overseas deployment, but many have war-related disabilities that include posttraumatic stress disorder (PTSD) and traumatic brain injury (TBI). Single-parent families and dual-earner families in the United States (and in many other developed countries) are having a rough time; they receive little cooperation from the government, the workplace, or the community to assist them in caring for both job and family. Many older women, especially those who live alone, are living below the poverty line. The United States has the highest rates of mental health disorders of any developed country and most of the people experiencing these symptoms do not get adequate treatment. Unhealthy lifestyles are resulting in increased health problems for many adults in the developing world, and the ages of those affected are extending to both the younger and older end of the spectrum. Although we try to maintain a positive tone, these topics are part of the reality of adult life, and we have included them in *The Journey of Adulthood*.

Other changes in the world around us are more positive. Health awareness is increasing at all ages; advances are being made in many areas of disease prevention, detection, and treatment; and a greater percentage of people in developed countries are living into old age. The rate of cancer deaths continues to decline as advances are made in early detection and treatment. Although there is still no "cure" for aging and no sign of a way to increase the existing maximum lifespan, people are increasing the number of healthy years in their lives. Programs such as hospice are making it possible for an increasing number of people to choose to have "a good death" when that time comes. Women are making great strides in professional careers and in their positive adjustment to children leaving home and widowhood. Communication technology has made it easier for families to stay in touch and for older adults to live independently. The average age of people using social media, cell phones, and e-games is increasing. These are also among the topics selected for this text.

Changes in the Classroom

Courses in adult development are offered in all major colleges and universities in the United States and are becoming popular around the world. It is safe to say that graduates in almost all majors will be working in fields that deal with the changes that occur during adulthood. It is also safe to say that students in all majors will be dealing with the topic on a personal level, both their own progress through adulthood and that of their parents. The students at the Wilkes Honors College at Florida Atlantic University this semester are majoring in psychology, counseling, nursing, criminal justice, premedical sciences, prelaw, social work, occupational therapy, sociology, and education. About one-half are bilingual and about one-third speak English as a second language. The majority will be the first in their families to graduate from college. We no longer assume that they have the same academic backgrounds as students a decade ago. For these reasons, we include basic definitions of key terms in the text of each chapter, clear explanations of relevant statistical methods, and basic details of major theories. We meet the readers knowing that the "typical student" is an outdated stereotype, but we meet them with respect for their intelligence and motivation. We firmly believe that it is possible to explain complex ideas clearly and connect with students from a variety of backgrounds and experiences. We do it every week in our classes, and we do it in this text.

Features

Learning Objectives distill the major takeaways of each chapter, stimulating interest in the main topics, helping focus student attention on the most salient points, and serving as a preview of what is to come. Learning Objectives also are linked to the content of the Chapter Summaries and to all questions in the Test Item File.

A Word from the Author—a sometimes funny, sometimes personal, and often introspective look at the main themes of a chapter, illustrated through lived experience and other relevant stories—begins each chapter. This feature helps to ground what can be abstract and theoretical concepts in the real world.

Interactive figures give students the opportunity to take a closer look at the data behind the graphics, allowing them to dive deeper into studies on topics as varied as mortality rates around the world, the top plastic surgery procedures in the United States, and how "in love" long-term couples are at different times in their relationships.

Journal questions encourage students to reflect on the content and relate it to their own experiences.

Shared Writing prompts allow students to write their own essays and then to read and comment on fellow students' essays, giving them a broader understanding of different experiences and perspectives.

Key terms are set in boldface type and defined immediately in the text. We believe we learn best by seeing a term in context. Definitions are also offered in the Glossary.

Highlights of Chapters in This Edition

Chapter 1 serves as an introduction to the study of adult development, beginning with the concept of development being both stable and changing. I use my own journey of adulthood as an example of these concepts and invite students to think of their own lives in these terms. Two guiding perspectives are introduced: Baltes's lifespan developmental approach and Bronfenbrenner's bioecological model. The next section covers developmental research. We don't assume that all students have taken a research methods class, so we limit the methods, measures, analyses, and designs to those that are used in later chapters. In fact, we use some of these studies as examples, hoping that students will feel comfortable with them when they encounter them later in the text.

New in this chapter:

- Studies comparing Eastern and Western cultures on their attitudes toward aging adults.

- New research on age-related changes in olfactory abilities.

- New research on the development of perceived control in emerging adults as they undergo the transition to adulthood.

The theme of **Chapter 2** is *primary aging*, the physical changes that take place predictably in most of us when we reach certain milestones in our journeys of adulthood. Again we begin with some basic theories including Harmon's theory of oxidative damage, Hayflick's theory of genetic limits, and the theory of caloric restriction. Then we cover age-related physical changes including outward appearance, the senses, the bones and muscles, the cardiovascular and respiratory systems, the brain and nervous system, the immune system, and the hormonal system. Most of the age-related change in these systems is gradual, but much can be done to avoid premature aging (and much of that can be done in early adulthood, such as avoiding excessive exposure to sunlight and tobacco use). Next, we cover four areas of more complex functioning: (1) athletic abilities; (2) stamina, dexterity, and balance; (3) sleep; and (4) sexual activity, all of which decline gradually with age. We cover some of the ways these declines can be slowed, but end the chapter with the caution that so far, we have no proven way to "turn back the clock."

New in this chapter:

- Evidence of psychological problems that arise with hearing loss.

- News that hearing loss has decreased in the past two decades, probably because of workplace noise restrictions.

- Studies that show increased risk of hip osteoarthritis for men who play handball, soccer, and hockey. Other studies show that professional ballet dancers have increased risk of hip osteoarthritis, especially women.

- More evidence that physical exercise can promote brain health.

- New research findings on sleep and insomnia.

- On the horizon—lab-grown replacement organs, transfusions of "young" blood components to older people, and identification of gene segments in people 100+ years of age and insertion into the DNA of younger people.

- Ethical and practical implications of extending the maximum lifespan.

Chapter 3 is about age-related disease, or *secondary aging*. We try to keep this separate from the normal changes discussed in the previous chapter. Not everyone suffers from these diseases no matter how long they live, and many age-related conditions can be prevented or cured. We start with data of mortality rates by age because we think it helps students put the risk of death and disease into perspective. For most of our students, the risk of premature death is very low, and the top cause is accidents. We then discuss four of the top age-related diseases and explain their causes, their risk factors, and some preventative measures. These are heart disease, cancer, diabetes, and Alzheimer's disease. We try to balance good news (lower rates of cancer deaths due to early detection and treatment, lower disability rates in the United States) with the bad (rising rates of diabetes at all ages, still no cure for Alzheimer's disease). The second part of the chapter is about mental health disorders. We try to impress upon the students that most of these disorders begin early in adulthood (or even in adolescence) and that most can be treated. However, the individuals suffering from these disorders (or their families) need to seek help and seek competent help. We end the chapter by telling that these physical and mental health disorders are not distributed randomly. Some groups are more apt to suffer than others, depending on one's genes, socioeconomic background, gender, lifestyle, personality patterns, and events that happened to them in very early childhood or even before birth.

New in this chapter:

- Completely updated mortality and morbidity statistics.

- Decreasing rates of disability for adults in the United States and the increasing rates of older adults "aging in place" around the world.

- New findings on the difference in heart disease in women and men.

- Continued decline in cancer deaths in the United States.

- New information about type 2 diabetes rates leveling off and even declining in some age groups.

- New diagnosis techniques for Alzheimer's disease.

- Updated statistics on mental health in the United States.

- New categories of mental disorders to fit DSM-5 classifications (anxiety disorders, depressive disorders, substance-related and addictive disorders).

- Extended discussion about the opioid problem in the United States.

- New information on robotic assistance and assistance animals.

- Bad news about continued poor diets and sedentary lifestyles among most age groups; good news about a drop in tobacco use.

- LGBTQ community faces more isolation and discrimination by the healthcare system than other minority groups, but have more need for physical and mental health assistance due to higher rates of victimization, homelessness, and job discrimination.

- New research on how adversity affects the immune system.

- New findings about intergenerational effects and how they affect our health.

Cognitive aging is discussed in **Chapter 4**. This chapter is about age-related changes in cognitive abilities, including attention, memory, intelligence, and problem solving. We explain how flaws in early research led to the conclusion that cognition declines sharply with age, and we present new research with better methodology that shows different patterns of age-related changes for different cognitive abilities. We demonstrate that some abilities, such as cognitive speed, do decline with age, whereas other cognitive abilities, such as those involving knowledge and expertise, improve with increased age. We begin the chapter with a discussion of research on attention, including research on divided attention tasks. The second part of the chapter is focused on memory and shows students the effects of age on different components of and different types of memory. We include a demonstration of the negative effects that stereotypes of cognitive aging can have on memory performance. We then turn to a discussion of intelligence, including differences in results for longitudinal and cross-sectional studies and differential effects of aging on separate components of intelligence. We also talk about individual differences in cognitive aging and mechanisms for improving cognitive abilities as one ages, and we hope students will be able to apply the research findings to their own cognitive health.

New in this chapter:

- New section on attention that includes research on divided attention and visual search.

- Reorganization of the chapter so that students can see how changes in attention and memory influence intelligence and problem solving.

- New research on the positive effects of physical exercise and cognitive engagement on cognitive abilities.

- Expanded discussion of the use of technology to assist adults with cognitive impairments.

Chapter 5 is about social roles and the change that takes place during adulthood. Social roles refer to the attitudes and behaviors we adopt when we make a transition into a particular role, such as worker, husband, or grandmother. This chapter covers changes within a person due to these life transitions. Gender is a major part of social roles, and several theories suggest how we learn what attitudes and behaviors fit the gender roles we fill. Bem's learning schema theory, Eagly's social role theory, and Buss's evolutionary psychology theory are presented. Various social roles, arranged chronologically, are discussed, including the transition from living in one's parents' home to living independently to living with a romantic partner in a cohabitation relationship or a marriage. Being part of a committed couple is related to good mental and physical health. Another role transition is from being part of a couple to being a parent. Social-role transitions in middle adulthood involve going from having children living in your home to having children who are independently living adults to becoming a grandparent. Another role in middle adulthood is often as caregiver for one's own parents. In late adulthood, many move into the role of living alone and becoming a care receiver. Not everyone fits these role transitions. Some adults never marry and some never have children but still have happy and productive lives. Lots of new social roles appear when there is a divorce in a family and then a remarriage, as most students know firsthand.

New in this chapter:

- Increased proportion of emerging adults and young adults who live in their parents' home. Decreased proportion of emerging adults and young adults who are married or cohabiting.

- Record low birthrates for teens and higher birthrates for women over age 40.

- New research comparing time use of mothers versus fathers when they are employed full time, part time, or not at all.

- Research on how couples divide up housework before and after becoming parents.

- Research that working mothers raise egalitarian sons.

- Increase in proportion of children living in grandparent-headed households, especially African American, Hispanic, and Asian families.

- More detailed look at young and middle-aged adults who spend time as caregivers for older adults. Most report a stressful but positive experience.

- Decreased proportion of older adults who live in nursing homes.

- New research on infertility and the effect it can have on couples.

Social relationships are covered in **Chapter 6** and differ from social roles because they involve two-way interactions between individuals, not just the behavior a person performs in a certain role. This is a difficult distinction, but there is just too much material on social-related topics for one chapter, so it's the division we have chosen. It also roughly fits the division between sociology studies (roles) and psychology studies (relationships). I begin this chapter with Bowlby's attachment theory, Ainsworth's model of attachment behaviors, Antonucci's convoy model, Carstensen's socioemotional selectivity theory, and Buss's evolutionary psychology approach. Then we start with various relationships in which adults participate, beginning with intimate partnerships, which include opposite-sex cohabitation, marriage, and same-sex partnerships. Next are parent–child relationships in adulthood, grandparent–grandchild relationships, and sibling relationships in adulthood. The chapter ends with a section on friendship. Students of all ages relate to this chapter personally and it works well in the middle of the text.

New in this chapter:

- New material on social contacts across the lifespan.

- New findings on what traits men and women find desirable in potential long-term partners.

- New findings on online dating.

- Meta-analyses of longitudinal studies of attachment styles.

- Cross-cultural studies of the acceptance of cohabitation.

- New research on cohabitation in the over-50 age group.

- Research on same-sex couples' counseling.

- Increased contact between parents and adult children, both face-to-face and via telecommunications.

- Increase in divorce for couples age 50 and older and the effect it has on their adult children.

- Older adults dealing with the life crises of adult children—a major source of distress.

- Importance of sibling relationships in middle and older adulthood.

- Benefits of giving social support.

- Social networks in later life.

- Social media and mental health across the lifespan.

- Social media's role in reducing interethnic prejudice.

The topics of work and retirement are covered in **Chapter 7**. In the early editions of this text, students applied the information in this chapter to their futures or to their parents' careers, but recently many apply it to themselves because they are part of the labor force and some are retraining for a second career. A few are even retired and attending college as a pastime. We start the chapter with Super's theory of career development and Holland's theory of career selection. Students are usually familiar with vocational preference tests and interested in finding out what type of work they would enjoy most. Gender differences are an important part of career selection and we question the reasons that even though women are found in almost every line of work and attend college in greater numbers than men, they still make less money and are not equally represented in top-paying, high-prestige jobs. The next section deals with age differences in job performance and job satisfaction. The section on work and personal life includes how jobs can affect individuals, intimate relationships, and responsibilities for other family members, including how household chores are divided up. The section on retirement includes reasons a person decides to retire or not, the effects of retirement, and some middle ground between full-time work and full-time retirement. We try to impress upon the young student that much of one's quality of life in retirement depends on planning ahead, and we hope they take that more seriously than we would have at his or her age.

New in this chapter:

- The concepts of careers that have no boundaries, are versatile, and are open to change.
- New data on women in the labor force.
- Longitudinal study of older adults in the labor force.
- How pre-retirement work complexity contributes to successful cognitive aging.
- How job strain contributes to cognitive changes and health.
- The worldwide problem of young people who are not working and not in school.
- New research on the paid work/family divide by gender and employment status.
- Longitudinal studies of caregivers.
- New research findings on volunteer work.

The topic of **Chapter 8** is personality. We divide the chapter into two parts: first, the research on personality structures, featuring Costa and McCrae's five-factor model, and, second, the grand old theories of personality, including Erikson's theory of psychosocial development, Loevinger's theory of ego development, Vaillant's theory of mature adaptation, Gutmann's theory of gender crossover, and Maslow's theory of positive well-being. We selected these from many because they have continued to inform research into age-related personality stability and change.

New in this chapter:

- New section on stereotypes of personality change.
- New longitudinal research on changes in dependability.
- New discussion of the effects of major life events on personality.
- New research on the relationship between openness and achievement.
- Increased discussion of the relationship between personality and health.
- New research on the effects of discrimination on personality.

Chapter 9 presents information on the quest for meaning and how it is manifest at different stages of adult life. This continues to be the most controversial chapter, with some adopters rating it as the best chapter and others questioning why it is included. Our belief is that it fills an important place in the journey of adulthood as we question how this journey started and where, exactly, we are going. It's a chance to look a little further up the road and a little further back than the other chapters give us. I start by showing how the topic of religion and spirituality has ballooned in empirical journals over the last four decades and the importance of having a sense of the sacred in our lives. Then I cover some diverse theories, including Kohlberg's theory of moral reasoning and Fowler's theory of faith development, showing the similarities in those and two theories from the personality chapter we just covered, Loevinger's theory of ego development and Maslow's theory of positive well-being. Then we conclude the chapter with material about mystical experiences and transitions, which William James, one of the founding fathers of psychology, wrote about in 1902.

New in this chapter:

- Increase in the percent of people in the United States who report belief in God.
- Argument that spirituality is an evolved trait in humans.
- Research on the relationship of religious beliefs and sound mental health, even when socioeconomic status, health behaviors, and specific religious practices are considered.

The related topics of stress and resilience comprise the subject matter for **Chapter 10**. This type of research is usually done by health psychologists and medical researchers but has recently been of interest to social psychologists, sociologists, forensic psychologists, and military leaders. This is another chapter that students take very personally because most are dealing with more than their fair share of stressors. We begin with Selye's concept of the general adaptation syndrome and then present Holmes and Rahe's measurement of life-change events. Research is cited to show that high levels of stress are related to physical and mental disorders. The timely topic of PTSD is covered and individual differences, such as gender and age, are included. We cover racial discrimination as a source of chronic stress and talk about stress-related growth—the idea that what doesn't kill you makes you stronger. Types of coping mechanisms are presented followed by the topic of resilience. Recent studies have shown that the most frequent reaction to trauma is resilience and that some people are more apt to be resilient than others.

New in this chapter:

- Longitudinal study of stress and mortality.
- New APA guidelines on PTSD.
- Research on PTSD in the children of Holocaust survivors.
- Research findings on perceived discrimination and psychological well-being.
- Studies of stress experienced by the LGBTQ community mediated by social support and gay identity.
- Longitudinal study of optimism and whether it acts as a buffer to trauma.
- Use of virtual therapists in military settings.

Chapter 11 covers death: how we think about it at different ages, how we cope with the death of loved ones, and how we face the reality of our own deaths. We begin the chapter with a discussion of how we acquire an understanding of death, both the deaths of others and the eventual death of oneself. This includes abstract methods like overcoming the fear of death as well as practical methods, like making a living will and becoming an organ donor. The place of one's death is important to many people, and most want to die at home with their families. That is becoming more feasible because of the hospice approach, and we explain that in detail. Others who are terminally ill would like to choose the time of their deaths, and that has become possible in several states that have legalized physician-assisted suicide, and we explain how that is arranged and how people make that decision. For the next section we have compiled numerous mourning rituals that take place in different cultures in the United States. It is not an exhaustive list and there may be many exceptions, but it is a good way to start a discussion about our multi-cultural society and about respecting and understanding each other at these most personal times. The chapter ends on a hopeful note with a study of bereavement that shows that the most common response to the loss of a spouse in older adulthood is resilience.

New in this chapter:

- New cross-cultural studies of death anxiety.
- Research suggesting new ways of communicating with dementia patients using classic baseball games and antique cars.

- Updated figures on hospice care and physician-assisted suicide.

In **Chapter 12**, the final chapter, we wrap up everything in chronological order. We add in the relevant new material and present my own model of adult development complete with a flow chart of how we move from disequilibrium to equilibrium in several areas of our lives. We also include a master table of age-related changes throughout adulthood.

Revel™

Educational technology designed for the way today's students read, think, and learn

When students are engaged deeply, they learn more effectively and perform better in their courses. This simple fact inspired the creation of Revel: an interactive learning experience designed for the way today's students read, think, and learn. Built in collaboration with educators and students nationwide, Revel is a fully digital and highly engaging way to deliver respected Pearson content.

Revel enlivens course content with media interactives and assessments—integrated directly within the authors' narrative that provide opportunities for students to read, practice, and study in one continuous experience. This interactive educational technology boosts student engagement, which leads to better understanding of concepts and improved performance throughout the course.

Learn more about Revel

http://www.pearsonhighered.com/revel

Available Instructor Resources

The following resources are available for instructors. These can be downloaded at https://www.pearsonhighered.com. Login is required.

PowerPoint—provides an ADA compliant template of the main ideas, concepts, and select images covered throughout the text. These can easily be customized for your classroom.

Instructor's Manual—includes outcome-based chapter outlines along with questions for discussion and research assignments.

Test Bank—includes additional questions in multiple-choice and open-ended—short and essay response—formats. Each question includes a corresponding skill, difficulty level, text reference, and learning objective.

MyTest—an electronic version of the Test Bank to customize in-class tests or quizzes.

About the Authors

Dr. Barbara Bjorklund has authored the last six editions of Journey of Adulthood, and is pleased to co-author this edition with Dr. Julie Earles. Dr. Bjorklund has taught psychology classes at colleges and universities around south Florida for over 40 years and has conducted research in both child and adult development. In addition to publishing research in academic journals, she has also written for the popular press and been a columnist for Parents magazine. Earlier editions of this book have been written in Germany, Spain, and New Zealand where she was living as a visiting scholar. Currently, Dr. Bjorklund is an Affiliate Professor at the Wilkes Honors College of Florida Atlantic University.

Dr. Julie Earles is a Professor of Psychology at the Wilkes Honors College of Florida Atlantic University where she teaches Lifespan Human Development, Adult Development and Aging, and Research Methods in Psychology. Her research program involves understanding how cognition changes with age, with an emphasis on developmental changes in memory for events. She has published over 30 articles and given over 100 presentations on her work. Her proudest accomplishment is her supervision of over 80 honors thesis projects by undergraduate students. She is also the Faculty in Residence for the Wilkes Honors College and enjoys enhancing connections between faculty and students as part of an engaged learning environment.

Acknowledgments

We are deeply grateful to Helen Bee, who authored the first three editions of this book. We have worked with a variety of talented people while revising this text. Some of them are Ashley Dodge, Sutapa Mukherjee, and Tanimaa Mehra at Pearson's end, our editorial project manager, Michelle Hacker, our developmental editor, Nic Albert, and the entire design and production team at SPi Global. We would also like to thank the many reviewers who offered valuable suggestions for this revision and previous editions.

We greatly appreciate the interest and patience of our family and friends over the long course of updating this edition of *Journey of Adulthood*, especially our husbands, David Bjorklund and Alan Kersten.

Barbara R. Bjorklund

Julie L. Earles

Jupiter, Florida

Chapter 1
Introduction to Adult Development

A multigenerational family.

 ## Learning Objectives

1.1 Explore major themes in developmental psychology

1.2 Explain the major sources of development

1.3 Differentiate between the perspectives of psychological and bioecological models

1.4 Evaluate developmental research methods

A Word From the Author

My Journey of Adulthood

MY JOURNEY OF adulthood began early, as did that of many women of my generation, when I married shortly after high school and began a family. But unlike many women in my peer group, I spent more time reading than I did having morning coffee with the other moms. I always took a book along to read while the kids had music lessons, baseball practice, and orthodontist appointments. The library was important to me. It was as much a weekly stop as the grocery store. By the time my youngest child began kindergarten, I enrolled in college as a freshman—at the age of 29, which was much older than the average at that time. For the next 7 years, my children and I did our homework together at the kitchen table, counted the days to the next holiday break, and posted our grade reports on the refrigerator. Today, as adults, they tell me that they can't remember a time in their childhood when I wasn't in school. Just before I earned my master's degree in developmental psychology, the marriage ended, and I spent some time as a single mother. I abandoned plans for a PhD and took a job at the university, teaching psychology courses and doing research on children's memory development. And just as my children began to leave the nest, I married a man whose own journey of adulthood had brought him to fatherhood rather late, making me stepmother of a 5-year-old, who quickly became an important part of my life. Not too much later, the grandchildren began to arrive, and life settled into a nice routine. It seemed I had done it all—marriage, parenthood, career, single parenthood, stepparenthood, and grandparenthood; my life was full.

Suddenly, my 50th birthday loomed. It seemed to represent much more than turning "just another year older" and caused me to reevaluate my life. I realized that I wasn't ready to ride slowly into the sunset for the next several decades; I needed to get back on track and move forward with my education. The next fall, I entered a PhD program in lifespan developmental psychology at the University of Georgia. It was an invigorating and humbling experience. Instead of being the teacher, I was the student. Instead of supervising the research project, I was being supervised. Instead of giving advice, I was asking where the bookstore was, where to park, and how to use the copy machine. But 3 years later I was awarded a red-and-black hood in a formal graduation ceremony with my children and grandchildren, parents, and siblings cheering for me from the audience.

Now I have an affiliate position at the Wilkes Honors College of Florida Atlantic University, and I write college textbooks. My husband and I live in a rural community in southeastern Florida with a cypress stand in the front yard and a small pine forest in the back. Our neighbors have horses, and we wake to roosters crowing in the morning. The book club I started 13 years ago is still going strong, and I enjoy attending community lectures at the university.

One son and daughter-in-law live nearby with three of our grandchildren, and my typical day consists of early-morning writing followed by a water aerobics class. Afternoons I am on homework-help duty or driving grandkids from school to music lessons to home. One grandson is a budding chef at 15, and he comes to our house after school to cook with my husband. Recently, they have been trying to create the perfect French baguette. Another son and daughter-in-law live with their three children just an hour down the coast, and we visit each other often. Despite some typical family drama, in general, life is good.

Seven years ago, with three children and eight grandchildren ranging in age from 8 to 25, my husband and I felt that our lives had settled down. But then both sons, who had been divorced for some time, remarried and started new families. Within the last 5 years, we have added Lily Pearl (age 5), twins Wesley and Jane (age 4), and Sage (age 2). Our younger son married a woman with a 15-year-old son, Andrés, and we quickly added him to our list. As I write this, our 14th grandchild, Amelia, is getting ready to come home from the NICU, after making her entrance into our family a month ago at 3-1/2 pounds. Looking back, we can't imagine how we felt our lives were complete without these six additions!

If there is a message to take from this text it is this: development doesn't stop at 21, or 40, or 65. Your life will never stop surprising you until you breathe your last breath. My wish for you is that the surprises are mostly happy ones.

I approach the topic of this text both as a developmental psychologist and on a more personal level. Like many people, I am on this journey of adulthood with my sisters, my husband, my friends, my adult children, and my college-aged grandchildren who are in emerging adulthood, so my interest is both scientific and personal. I want to understand how it all works and why, both because that is what I have chosen for my career and also because it is what I think about a good deal of the time when I am not at work. My journey through adulthood is no doubt similar to yours, but it is also different in other ways. What I am searching for in this text are the basic rules or processes that account for both the similarities and the differences. I hope you can share with me the sense of adventure in the scientific search as well as in the personal journey.

1.1: Basic Concepts in Adult Development

OBJECTIVE: Explore major themes in developmental psychology

Developmental psychology is the field of study that deals with the behavior, thoughts, and emotions of individuals as they go through various parts of the lifespan. It includes child development, adolescent development, and **adult development**—the particular concern of this book. We are interested in the changes that take place within individuals as they progress from emerging adulthood (when adolescence is ending) to the end of life. Although many autobiographies give first-person accounts of people's lives and many interesting stories about people's experiences in adulthood, this book is based on **empirical research**—scientific studies of observable events that are measured and evaluated objectively. When personal accounts and examples are used (including the opening story about my life), they are chosen to illustrate concepts that have been carefully researched.

⋁	**By the end of this module, you will be able to:**

1.1.1 Describe differences and commonalities in experiences of adulthood

1.1.2 Identify constants and changes that impact adult development

1.1.3 Differentiate among the various types of age

1.1.1: Differences and Commonalities

OBJECTIVE: Describe differences and commonalities in experiences of adulthood

Some of you are just beginning the journey of your own adult life; some of you are partway along the road, having traveled through your 20s, 30s, and perhaps 40s, 50s, and beyond. Whatever your age, you are traveling, moving through the years and the transformations that come along the way. We do not all follow the same itinerary on this journey; you may spend a long time in a location that I do not visit at all; I may make an unscheduled side trip. Or we may visit the same places but experience them very differently. Every journey has **individual differences**, aspects that are unique to the individual. You may not have experienced the trials of single parenthood as I have or the joys of grandparenthood, and I cannot relate to the independence you must feel when living alone or the confusion you experience when your parents divorce. Likewise, there are also some **commonalities**, typical aspects of adult life that most of us can relate to (either now or in the future). Most of us have moved out of our parents' homes (or plan to), experienced romantic relationships, entered college with some plans for the future, and either started a family or given some serious thought to parenthood. My goal for this book is to explore with you both the uniqueness and the common grounds of our adult lives.

WRITING PROMPT

What Makes You You?

Think about some of the things you have experienced individually that make you the same or different from some of your peers. What are they? How do they impact how you experience adulthood?

 The response entered here will appear in the performance dashboard and can be viewed by your instructor.

Submit

1.1.2: Stability and Change

OBJECTIVE: Identify constants and changes that impact adult development

Two of the concepts featured in this text are stability and change during the developmental process. **Stability** refers to the important parts of ourselves that make up a consistent core. It is the constant set of personality traits, preferences, and typical ways of behaving that make each of us the individuals that we are throughout our lifetimes. In other words, your 40-year-old self will be similar to your 20-year-old self in some ways, as will your 60-year-old self. For example, one of the stable themes of my adult life is a love for books. In fact, it goes back to my childhood. Some of my most prized possessions are the books in my library. I always have several books that I am in the process of reading, and an audiobook that plays in my car via Bluetooth. Thirteen years ago, I started a book club in my neighborhood that has become a big source of joy for me. Another theme that keeps popping up in my life is children, beginning early on with three younger sisters, then my own children, then my stepdaughter, nieces and nephews, then grandchildren. I have always had a toy box in my living room and sippy cups in the kitchen cabinet. In fact, the two themes of books and children often mix. I send books on birthdays for the children on my gift list, and when visiting children spend the night, I have a shelf of children's books in the guestroom, some that belonged to their own parents many years ago. Perhaps you find stability in your life in terms of playing a musical instrument or participating in sports. The genre of books I read may change over the years, and your choice of musical selections or sporting events may be different from time to time, but the core essence of these stable themes remains an integral part of our lives.

Change is the opposite force to stability. It is what happens to us over time that makes us different from our younger (and older) selves. An example from my life is travel. As a child, I never traveled too far out of my home state of Florida. Almost all my relatives lived nearby, and those who didn't were more than happy to visit our warm climate during winter. In fact, at the age of 35, I had never been on an airplane. But when I married my current husband (and no longer had children living at home), I had the opportunity to travel to national conferences and accompany him on international trips as he collaborated with colleagues and worked as a visiting professor around the world. In the last 20 years, we have spent extended periods of time in Germany, Spain, and New Zealand. We have made shorter trips to Japan, China, Italy, Sweden, Norway, Denmark, England, Scotland, Wales, Austria, Switzerland, and Egypt. Last year we made it to Paris! I am an expert packer, and my office is filled with framed photos I have taken in many exotic locations. To compare myself at 30 and 50, my travel habits would constitute a dramatic change. Other examples of change in the adult developmental process occur when one becomes a parent, switches careers, or decides to move to another part of the country (or to an entirely different country). One way to view the journey of adulthood is to consider both the stability and the change that define our lives.

Photo of the author, Barbara Bjorklund, visiting a Roman aqueduct on a recent trip to Pont du Gard, France.

CONTINUITY AND STAGES   Still another way of looking at this journey is gauging how straight the road is. Some stretches of our lives are **continuous**—slow and gradual, taking us in a predictable direction. My gardening certainly fits this definition. In my earliest apartments I had potted plants, and when we rented our first house, I persuaded the landlord to let me put in a small flower garden. As our yards have grown bigger, so have my garden projects. I enjoy plant fairs, trade plant cuttings with friends, and of course, read books about gardening. I find it relaxing to spend time "digging in the dirt." I have increased my knowledge and skill over the years. Now that our yard is measured in acres instead of square feet, I'm in heaven. So far, I have a butterfly garden in the front yard, and I'm working on a vegetable garden in the back. Hopefully I will continue to "develop" as a gardener for many years.

In contrast, our lives also have **stages**, parts of the journey where there seems to be no progress for some time, followed by an abrupt change. Stages are much like driving on a quiet country road for a long time and then getting onto a busy interstate highway (or vice versa). In my adult life I view the years of being home with my young children as a stage that was followed by the abrupt change of the youngest entering school and me starting college. I suddenly went from having minute-to-minute, hands-on parenting duties to the type that involve preparations the night before and then dropping the children off at school in the morning. I also went from having mostly tasks that involved physical work and concrete thinking skills (e.g., how to get crayon marks off the walls) to those that required abstract thinking (e.g., Psychology 101). This mother/student stage continued for many years until I reached the single-mother/researcher stage. An interesting question in the study of adulthood is exploring how **typical** these stages of adult life are: Do most adults go through them along their journeys and, if so, do they go through them in the same order and at the same age? Or are they **atypical**, unique to the individual? I think that sending one's youngest child off to school is probably a universal event in a parent's life, signaling the end of one stage and the beginning of another, but I don't think that the transition from full-time mother to full-time student is typical, though it is more common today than it was a generation ago.

EXTERNAL AND INTERNAL CHANGE   A final theme of this text has to do with internal versus external changes. As we proceed along the journey of adulthood, many **external changes** are visible and apparent to those we encounter. We enter early adulthood and become more confident in our step and our carriage; we fill out and mature; some of us become pregnant; some begin to lose their hair. In middle age many of us lose and gain weight, increase and decrease in fitness. **Internal changes** are not as apparent to the casual observer. We fall in and out of love, hold our children close, and then learn to give them space. We look to our parents for guidance at the beginning of our journeys and then assist them at the end of theirs. And we grow in wisdom and grace. Of course, the internal and external changes are not independent of one another. External changes can affect the way we feel about ourselves, and vice versa. They also affect the way others perceive us, and this, in turn, affects our self-perceptions. Untangling this conceptual ball of yarn is another goal of this text.

WRITING PROMPT

Describe Your Own Life Experience

Think about your current lived experience. What are some things you might characterize as stable? As changing? As continuous or a stage? As external or internal?

► The response entered here will appear in the performance dashboard and can be viewed by your instructor.

 Submit

1.1.3: A Word About "Age"

OBJECTIVE: Differentiate among the various types of age

Most people know that age is just a number. Perhaps ages in childhood give valid information about what to expect in the way of appearance or behavior, but once a child reaches adolescence, many more factors are involved. In fact, the further we venture on the journey of adulthood, the more variability there is among people our "own" age.

Several types of age have been identified, and they illustrate the many dimensions of adult development.

Types of Age

Chronological Age—The number of years that have passed since your birth or the number of candles on your last birthday cake is your **chronological age**. While this may be important in childhood, when all 7-year-olds look relatively similar and have similar interests and abilities, in adulthood, this number is seldom relevant, except during young adulthood when driving, purchasing alcohol, and voting are determined by chronological age, and in older adulthood when eligibility for Social Security and Medicare are determined by chronological age. However, your development in adulthood does not occur because the clocks have struck a certain number of times or the heat from your birthday candles reaches a certain temperature. It may be related, but chronological age does not *cause* developmental changes.

Biological Age—**Biological age** is a measure of how an adult's physical condition compares with others. "He has the memory of a 50-year-old" and "She runs like a 30-year-old" are examples of informal measures of biological age. Of course, biological age is related to the person's chronological age. Having the memory of a 50-year-old means one thing if the person is 70, a much different thing if 30! And riding a bicycle like a woman in her 40s may not seem exceptional unless that woman is Kristin Armstrong, 42-year-old Gold Medal cyclist in the Rio Olympics. Biological age is used to evaluate aging of physical systems, such as with bone density scans, in which patients' bones are compared to those of a healthy 20-year-old. Biological age can often be affected by lifestyle changes.

Psychological Age—Another type of age is **psychological age**, which is a measure of how an adult's ability to deal effectively with the environment compares to others. A 30-year-old woman who can't pay her electric bill because she couldn't resist buying designer jeans and is often late for work because she oversleeps is functioning like many teenagers. Her psychological age is much below her chronological age. In addition, a 25-year-old man who starts his own business and is successful 3 years later, having expanded to several cities and increasing his workforce, is showing the organizational skills and problem-solving abilities of someone twice his age.

Social Age—**Social age** is based on the expected roles a person takes on at a specific point in his or her life. A 23-year-old who works full time, goes to school full time, and sends money home to help support her grandmother has a social age much greater than her years. A middle-aged woman who enrolls in college is taking on the social role of a person who is younger.

Sometimes biological age, psychological age, and social age are considered in a package as **functional age**, or how well a person is functioning as an adult compared to others. But it seems clear that the question "How old are you?" has a number of answers.

As developmental psychologists, we try not to depend solely on chronological age when investigating some aspect of adult behavior. As you will see, many studies use age groups (young adults compared with middle-aged adults) or roles (people without children compared with people with children). Often, they avoid the chronological age question by comparing the same people before and after they take on a role, such as parenthood or retirement. It is important to keep in mind that development and chronological age do not travel hand in hand, and this becomes more and more apparent the older we get.

1.2: Sources of Change

OBJECTIVE: Explain the major sources of development

There are many potential influences on adult development. In fact, the types of influences that result in change have been classified as: (1) normative age-graded influences, (2) normative history-graded influences, and (3) nonnormative life events. In the following section I explain these various influences and give you some examples so you can see them at work in your own lives.

☑ By the end of this module, you will be able to:

1.2.1 Identify normative age-graded influences on development

1.2.2 Describe how historical events impact development

1.2.3 Evaluate the ways that nonnormative events affect adulthood

1.2.4 Explain the interactionist view on the influences of nature and nurture on development

1.2.1: Normative Age-Graded Influences

OBJECTIVE: Identify normative age-graded influences on development

When you hear the phrase "sources of change," your first thought is probably of **normative age-graded influences**, those influences that are linked to age and experienced by most adults as they grow older.

BIOLOGY Some of the changes we see in adults are shared by all of us because we are all members of our species undergoing natural aging processes. This is often represented by the idea of a **biological clock**, ticking away to mark the common changes that occur with time. Many such changes are easy to see, such as hair gradually turning gray or skin becoming wrinkled. Others are not visible from the outside but occur internally, such as the loss of muscle tissue, which results in a gradual loss of physical strength. The rate at which such physical changes occur varies quite a lot from one person to another.

SHARED EXPERIENCES Another normative influence that is dictated for most of us by our ages can be envisioned by a culturally determined **social clock** defining a typical sequence of adult life experiences, such as the timing of college graduation, marriage, and retirement. Even though our society has expanded the choices we have in the timing of these experiences, we still are aware of the "normative" timing of these events. Where we stand in relation to the social clock can affect our own sense of self. The middle-aged man still living at home, the "perpetual student," the older working woman whose friends have retired—all may be doing well in important aspects of their lives, but if those lives are out of sync with what society expects in the way of timing, it may lead to some personal doubts. In contrast, the young adult who is CEO of his own high-tech company, the middle-aged woman who completes law school, and the octogenarian who finishes the Boston Marathon may have reason to celebrate over and above the face value of their accomplishments. Of course, the normal sequence of adult life differs by culture and even subculture. For example, the average age of marriage in India and many African countries is the early 20s, while in most of Europe and Australia it is the early 30s.

Another effect the social clock can have is **ageism**, a type of discrimination in which opinions are formed and decisions are made about others based solely on the fact that they are in a particular age group. Older adults are sometimes stereotyped as cranky, sexless, forgetful, and less valuable than younger people. Television sitcoms, commercials, birthday cards, and jokes on social media all perpetuate these stereotypes. Emerging adults can also be targets of ageism, when they are perceived as being less capable than their older coworkers or when they are stereotyped as delinquents because of their style of clothes and speech. One of my goals for this text is to give a realistic and respectful look at adults of every age.

Another manifestation of the influence of the social clock in virtually all cultures is the pattern of experiences associated with family life. For example, the majority of adults experience parenthood, and once their first child is born, they begin a fixed pattern of shared social experiences with other parents that move along with their children's stages of life—infancy, toddlerhood, the school years, adolescence, and preparation to leave home. Each of these periods in a child's life makes a different set of demands on parents—attending childbirth classes, setting preschool playdates, hosting scout meetings, coaching Little League baseball, visiting potential colleges—and this sequence shapes 20 or 30 years of most adults' lives, regardless of their own biological ages.

Obviously, shared developmental changes based on the social clock are much less likely to be universal than those based on the biological clock. But within any given culture, shared age-graded experiences can explain some of the common threads of adult development.

1.2.2: Normative History-Graded Influences

OBJECTIVE: Describe how historical events impact development

Experiences that result from historical events or conditions, known as **normative history-graded influences**, also shape adult development. These influences are helpful for explaining both the similarities found among people within certain groups and also the dissimilarities among people in those same groups. Both are important parts of a course on adult development.

The large social environments in which development takes place are known as **cultures**, and the ways they influence the adult life pattern can vary enormously: the expected age of marriage or childbearing, the typical number of children (and spouses), the roles of men and women, class structures, religious practices, and laws. I was reminded of this on a trip several years ago, when a young Chinese mother in Beijing struck up a conversation with me, and we began talking about our families. She had a toddler daughter with her who was 2-1/2, just the age of my youngest grandson, I told her. "*Youngest* grandson?" she asked, "How many grandchildren do you have?" I told her I had eight, then realized from her expression of surprise that this was very unusual in China. She explained to me that since 1979 there has been a one-child policy in China. Almost all Chinese parents in urban areas limit their families to one child. She was an only child; her daughter was an only child (and the only grandchild of both sets of grandparents). The typical person in her culture has no siblings, no aunts or uncles, and no cousins. She asked to see pictures of my grandchildren and wanted to know their ages and details about them. We had a very friendly visit, but I could not help but wonder how different my life would be in that culture, and what her life will be like when she is my age. When I learned that China had begun phasing out this policy in 2015, I immediately thought of the nice woman in Beijing, whose daughter might be an adult now. I wondered how this cultural change would affect her and her family.

COHORTS A **cohort** is a more finely grained concept than a culture because it refers to a group of people who share a common historical experience at the same stage of life. The term is roughly synonymous with generation, but narrower—a generation refers to about 20 years, whereas a cohort can be a much shorter period. And a generation can refer to a much larger geographic area, whereas a cohort can be just one country or one region of one country. For example, Cuban Americans who came to the United States in the 1960s to flee Fidel Castro make up an important cohort in south Florida.

One of the most studied cohorts in the social sciences is the group of people who grew up during the Great Depression of the 1930s. This was a time in the United States (and in most of the world) that crops failed, factories closed, the stock market crashed, unemployment skyrocketed, and without unemployment benefits and government social programs, the only help available was from family, neighbors, or churches (none of whom had much to share). Almost no one escaped the effects of this disaster. But what were its effects, and were people affected differently depending on what age they were when the Great Depression hit? That was the thrust of the research on growing up in the Great Depression conducted by sociologist Glen H. Elder, Jr. (1979). He found that the cohort of people who were teenagers during the Great Depression showed fewer long-term effects than those who had been in early elementary school at the same time. The younger cohort spent a greater portion of their childhood under conditions of economic hardship. The hardship altered family interaction patterns, educational opportunities, and even the personalities of the children, so that the negative effects could still be detected in adulthood. Those who were teenagers during the Great Depression did not show negative effects in adult life; on the contrary, some of them seemed to have grown from the experience of hardship and showed more independence and initiative in adulthood as a result. Thus, two cohorts, rather close in actual age, experienced the same historical event differently because of their ages. The timing of events interacts with tasks, issues, and age norms, producing unique patterns of influence for each cohort and helping to create common adult-life trajectories for those in the same cohort.

Although the era of the Great Depression is past, this research should remind us that every one of us, as an adult, bears the marks of the events we have lived through and the age-specific ways we reacted to those events. The recession of 2008 affected many families, and although the economy is doing much better, young adults who grew up in those times will be different in their outlooks toward job security than those who grew up a decade before or a decade afterward.

Although there are no definite ages for the cohorts living today, several general groupings have been suggested. Figure 1.1 shows one such grouping.

Figure 1.1 Primary Cohorts Today

Which cohort do you belong to? Your parents? Your grandparents?

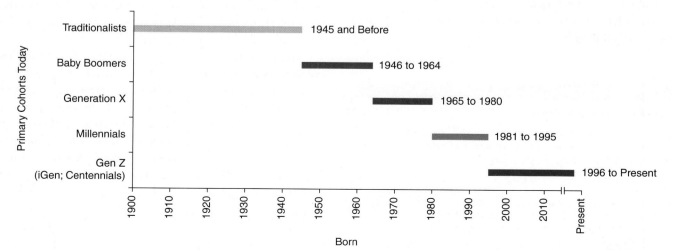

1.2.3: Nonnormative Life Events

OBJECTIVE: Evaluate the ways that nonnormative events affect adulthood

Along with the aspects that you share with most other adults your age and in your culture, there are **nonnormative life events**, aspects that influence your life that are unique to you and not shared with most others. These can have an important effect on the pathway of your life. Examples of nonnormative life events are having one's spouse die in early adulthood, inheriting enough money to retire at age 40, taking over parental responsibility for one's grandchildren, and starting one's own business at 65.

Some of these events are nonnormative for anyone at any age, such as inheriting a large amount of money, but others are nonnormative because of the timing. The death of a spouse is, unfortunately, a normative event in older adulthood, but not so in the earlier years. And starting one's own business may be remarkable in early adulthood, but it is highly nonnormative at the age of 65. As pioneering developmental psychologist Bernice Neugarten advised us back in 1976, we have to pay attention not only to the event itself, but also to the timing. Events that are on time are much easier to cope with (even the death of a spouse) than those that are off time.

I can speak from experience as one who was off time in several aspects of my life—becoming a parent early, going to college late, becoming a grandparent early, going to graduate school late. It makes for a good chapter introduction, but it was not always easy. One problem is the lack of peers—I was always "the older one" or "the younger one," never just one of the group. You don't fit in with your agemates because you are doing something different, but you don't fit in with your fellow students or other moms either because you are not their age. And if this situation is easy to deal with yourself, sometimes others have problems, such as administrators who don't want to hire beginning professors who are older than they are. So, in the best of all possible worlds, it is probably easier to do things "on time" than march to your own drummer—I've just never lived in the best of all possible worlds.

WRITING PROMPT

Marching to Your Own Drummer

What is an example of an event, perhaps from your own life or someone you know, that might be described as nonnormative? What impact might it have (or did it have)?

 The response entered here will appear in the performance dashboard and can be viewed by your instructor.

Submit

1.2.4: Genetics, the Environment, and their Interactions

OBJECTIVE: Explain the interactionist view on the influences of nature and nurture on development

Each of us inherits, at conception, a unique combination of genes. A very large percentage of these genes is identical from one member of the species to the next. This is why our developmental patterns are so much alike—why children all over the world walk at about 12 months, and why we go through puberty in our early teens and menopause around age 51. But our genetic inheritance is individual as well as collective. The study of **behavioral genetics**, or the contributions genes make to individual behavior, has been a particularly active research topic in recent decades. We now know that specific heredity affects a remarkably broad range of behaviors, including cognitive abilities, such as problem solving; physical characteristics, such as height or body shape or a tendency to fatness or leanness; personality characteristics; and even pathological behavior, such as a tendency toward alcoholism, schizophrenia, or depression (Plomin et al., 2012). The extent to which these traits and tendencies remain in place throughout our lives shows the influence of heredity on stability in development.

In searching for genetic influences on variations in adult behavior, behavioral geneticists rely primarily on **twin studies**. These are studies that compare monozygotic twins with dizygotic twins on some behavior. Such studies are based on the fact that *monozygotic twins* develop from the same sperm and ovum and thus share exactly the same genetic patterning at conception, whereas *dizygotic twins* each develop from a separate sperm and ovum and are therefore no more alike, genetically, than any other pair of siblings. In typical twin studies, measurements of some trait or ability are taken on each twin, and then the pairs are compared to see how similar their scores are. If the monozygotic twin pairs are more similar for that trait or ability than the dizygotic twin pairs, then it is taken as evidence that the trait or ability is influenced by genetics.

Twin studies are difficult because the statistics involved require large numbers of participants, and it is difficult for a researcher to recruit hundreds of pairs of twins. For this reason, several countries that have central databanks of their citizens' birth records and health records have taken the lead in this type of research. The largest databank of twins is in Sweden at the Karolinska Institute in Stockholm. It maintains a database of information on over 85,000 twin pairs.

ENVIRONMENT Our environment also contributes to the parts of ourselves that remain relatively stable over time. Although neither our biology nor our upbringing dictates our destiny, both have long-term effects. The lifelong effect of early family experience has been clearly demonstrated by the Grant Study of Harvard Men. Psychiatrist George Vaillant (2002), the study's current director, has concluded that those who lived in the warmest, most trusting homes as children are more apt to be living well-adjusted lives in adulthood than those who spent their childhoods in the bleakest homes. Men from the warmest homes are more able, as adults, to express emotions appropriately and openly, to see the world and the people in it as trustworthy, and to have friends with whom they enjoy leisure-time activities. Vaillant's interpretation is that parents who provide basic trust to their children (in this case, their sons) instill a sense of self-worth, good coping skills, the ability to form meaningful relationships, and in general construct a solid foundation for the core values the child will take with him or her throughout adulthood. And what's more, subsequent studies show that these data could predict which men at age 75 would most likely be aging success-fully (i.e., be healthy and happy) and which would be aging unsuccessfully (i.e., be sick and sad). Taken together, Vaillant's studies show that at least for extreme situations, the early childhood environment can set the course for a lifetime of either emotional openness, trust, and good health or loneliness, mistrust, and illness.

A more recent study showed the effects of living in an impoverished environment on mental health. In the National Health and Nutrition Examination Survey, adults were asked about their depressive symptoms. When responses were examined by income level, respondents at every age who lived in impoverished environments reported more symptoms of depression.

INTERACTIONS   Of course, there are no simple partitions between genes and environment, and we can't separate their contributions to the stability we experience through-out adulthood. Most developmental psychologists now subscribe to an **interactionist view** in which one's genetic traits determine how one interacts with the environment and even the environment itself (Greenberg et al., 2010). For example, a boy with a genetic makeup that promotes avoiding risks will grow up with a certain pattern of interactions with his parents and siblings and will seek out friends and activities that do not involve high risk. Teachers may view this as stable and sensible and steer him to a career such as accounting. The result is a young adult with risk-avoiding genes working in a low-risk career environ-ment and enjoying low-risk activities with his friends. He will probably marry someone who shares these interests, giving him even more support for this lifestyle. You can imagine the life course of this person, perhaps having one child, living in the same home and working in the same job until retirement. Quiet evenings would be spent at home or at the neighborhood tavern. He would have good health

because of regular checkups, exercise, and sensible eating habits. He would probably wear his seatbelt and drive defensively. Vacations would be carefully planned tours of scenic places, and retirement would bring regular golf games with the same friends each week and volunteer work with the foster grandparent program at the local elemen-tary school. Risk avoidance is the theme of this person's life, but can we really say it was caused by his genetic makeup? Or was it the environment? These kinds of questions make up the interactionist's chicken-and-egg dilemma.

One mechanism for this interaction between genes and environment is **epigenetic inheritance**, a process by which the genes one receives at conception are modified by subsequent environmental events that occur during the prenatal period and throughout the lifespan (Kremen & Lyons, 2011). The process by which genes are modified is known as **DNA methylation** because it involves the chemical modification of DNA through the addition of a methyl group, resulting in reduced gene expression. This type of inheritance explains how the environment can cause permanent, lifelong characteristics that were not part of the original genetic endowment at conception. For example, autopsies of adults who committed suicide show that those who had a history of childhood abuse are more apt to have modified glucocorticoid receptor genes in their brains than both adults who committed suicide but had no history of childhood abuse and a control group of adults who died of other causes (McGowan et al., 2009). Glucocorticoid receptors determine how an individual responds to stress. In this case, it seems that early childhood experiences bring forth changes in the children's genetic expression that have lifelong consequences.

1.3: Guiding Perspectives

OBJECTIVE: Differentiate between the perspectives of psychological and bioecological models

Before any questions about adult development can be asked, we need to determine what platform to stand on—the base from which we set the course of this journey. The remainder of this text covers specific areas of development and includes specific theories to guide that research, but two broad approaches are used throughout, and they define the tone of the book.

⌄   **By the end of this module, you will be able to:**

1.3.1   Describe elements of the lifespan developmental psychology approach

1.3.2   Outline the systems used in the bioecological model of development

1.3.1: Lifespan Developmental Psychology Approach

OBJECTIVE: Describe elements of the lifespan developmental psychology approach

One major approach of this text is the **life-span developmental psychology approach**, which states that development is lifelong, multidimensional, plastic, contextual, and has multiple causes (Baltes et al., 1980). Psychologist Paul Baltes and his colleagues introduced these ideas in 1980, and although this approach sounds very ordinary today, it marked a turning point in developmental psychology, which before that time was focused almost exclusively on child development. The major points of the lifespan developmental approach are illustrated in Table 1.1, along with some examples of each. As you read through, you will see that it opened the door for the study of development at all ages—not just your 12-year-old brother, but also you, your fellow students, your parents, your professor, and even your grandparents.

1.3.2: Bioecological Model of Development

OBJECTIVE: Outline the systems used in the bioecological model of development

A second major approach this text takes is based on the **bioecological model**, which points out that we must consider the developing person within the context of multiple environments. The idea is that development must take place within biological, psychological, and, especially, social contexts that change over time, and that these various influences are in constant interaction (Lerner, 2006; Sameroff, 2009). These ideas were introduced by psychologist Urie Bronfenbrenner in 1979 and have been modified over the last four decades (Bronfenbrenner & Morris, 2006). Bronfenbrenner proposed five systems: the *microsystem*, the *exosystem*, and the *macrosystem*, as shown in Figure 1.2, with the *mesosystem* as the interaction among elements in the microsystem. In addition, there is the *chronosystem*, which reflects the fact

Table 1.1 Lifespan Developmental Psychology: Concepts, Propositions, and Examples

Concept	Proposition	Example
Lifespan development	Human development is a lifelong process. No single age is more important than another. At every age, various developmental processes are at work. Not all developmental processes are present at birth.	A 38-year-old single woman makes plans to adopt a child; a 52-year-old bookkeeper becomes less satisfied with her job now that her kids are grown, and she goes back to school to become a small business owner; a 75-year-old Vietnam veteran loses interest in reunions with his former buddies and begins taking a class in memoir writing. They are all experiencing development.
Multidirectionality	We develop in different directions and at different rates. Developmental processes increase and decrease. At one time of life, we can change in some areas and remain stable in others.	Some intellectual abilities increase with age, and some decline. Young adults show independence when they complete college and start a career, but show dependence at the same time when they remain in their parents' homes.
Development as gain and loss	Development is a combination of gains and losses at every age, and we need to learn how to anticipate and adapt to both.	Middle-aged adults may lose their parents, but gain a new feeling of maturity. Young adults add a baby to their family, but may lose some equality in their marriage. Workers start losing speed and precision as they age, but they gain expertise.
Plasticity	Many aspects of development can be modified. Not much is set in stone, but there are limits.	Young people who enter adulthood with behavior problems or substance-abuse problems can overcome them and become responsible, successful adults. Couples with a lot of conflict in their marriages during the childrearing years can be happy once the children are grown. Fathers can stay home with kids and be nurturing and attentive while mothers work outside the home. Older parents can change their values as a result of their young adult children's lifestyles.
Historical embeddedness	Development is influenced by historical and cultural conditions.	People who grew up in the 1970s have more open attitudes toward legalizing drugs than earlier or later cohorts. Those who lived through the Great Depression have different attitudes toward work than members of other cohorts.
Contextualism	Development depends on the interaction of normative age-graded, normative history-graded, and nonnormative influences.	Each of us is an individual because of the interaction of influences we share with other adults in general, those we share because of the times we live in, and those that are unique to us.
Multidisciplinary	The study of human development across the lifespan does not belong to psychology alone. It is the territory of many other disciplines, and we can benefit from the contributions of all.	Contributions to the study of development come from the field of psychology, but also from sociology, anthropology, economics, public health, social work, nursing, epidemiology, education, and other disciplines. Each brings a different and valuable point of view.

SOURCE: Adapted from Baltes (1987).

Figure 1.2 The Bioecological Model

This figure illustrates Urie Bronfenbrenner's model of the ecological-systems approach to studying development. He suggested that researchers look beyond behavior in laboratory settings and consider how development takes place within multiple environments and through time.

SOURCE: Based on Bronfenbrenner (1979)

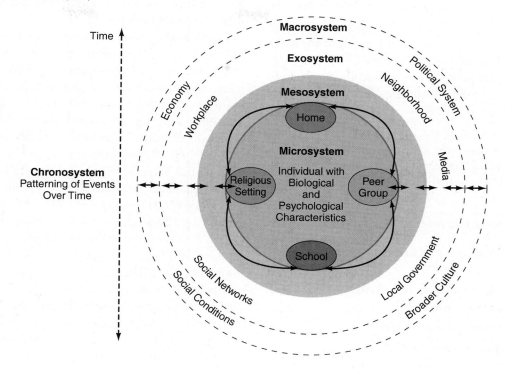

that the other three systems are dynamic—constantly changing over time. This change can be as individual as physical maturation or as encompassing as a large-scale earthquake or an economic recession in one's country.

The major point of Bronfenbrenner's theory, and other developmental contextual approaches in general, is that individuals and their development cannot be studied "out of context." Rather, we must consider the social environment—from family and friends through community and the broader culture, all in interaction—when trying to explain the factors that influence the course of a person's journey to and through adulthood.

As you will see throughout this text, recent research in most areas of the social sciences has reflected this model, investigating the development of adults in the context of their lives as individuals, as partners in relationships, as parents in families, as workers on job sites, and as members of particular cultural groups and cohorts.

1.4: Developmental Research

OBJECTIVE: Evaluate developmental research methods

To understand adult development, it is important to know a little about the research process because information today in the social sciences is, for the most part, science based. I won't attempt to present a whole course on research methods and statistics, but I cover some of the methods that are used in the studies described throughout this text.

All research begins with questions. Suppose, for example, that I want to know something about change or stability in personal relationships over the adult years—relationships with a spouse, with other family members, or with friends. Or suppose that I wanted to study memory over adulthood. Older adults frequently complain that they can't remember things as well as when they were younger. Is this a valid perception? Is there really a loss in memory ability in old age, or earlier? How would I go about designing research to answer such questions? In every instance, there is a set of questions to answer:

- Should I study groups of people of different ages, or should I study the same group of people over time, or some combination of the two? This is a question dealing with basic research *methods*.

- How will I measure the behavior, thought, or emotion I am studying? How can I best inquire about the quality of marriage—with a questionnaire or in an interview? How do I measure depression—is there a set of questions I can use? These are questions of research *measures*.

- What will I do with the data? Is it enough merely to compare the average number of friends, or the average relationship satisfaction described by participants in each age group? What else would I want to do to tease out some of the possible explanations? These are questions of research *analysis*.

- What do the results mean? Depending on the research method, measures, and analysis, what is the overall conclusion? What is the answer to the research question I began with? These are questions of research *design*.

By the end of this module, you will be able to:

1.4.1 Identify methods used in developmental research

1.4.2 Explain the advantages and disadvantages of different measures

1.4.3 Describe forms of data analysis

1.4.4 Differentiate among research designs

1.4.1: Methods

OBJECTIVE: Identify methods used in developmental research

Choosing a research method is perhaps the most crucial decision the researcher makes. This is true in any area of science, but there are special considerations when the topic of study is development. There are essentially three choices:

1. You can choose different groups of participants at each of a series of ages and compare their responses—in other words, the cross-sectional method.

2. You can study the same participants over a period of time, observing whether their responses remain the same or change in systematic ways—the longitudinal method.

3. You can combine the two in any of several ways, collectively called sequential methods.

CROSS-SECTIONAL STUDIES A **cross-sectional study** in developmental psychology describes a study that is based on data gathered at one time from groups of participants who represent different age groups. Each participant is measured or tested only once, and the results give us information about differences between the groups.

One example of a cross-sectional research design was performed by neurobiologist Janina Seubert and her colleagues (2017) to investigate the decline of the sense of smell in participants of different ages. This is an important ability as people get older because without the sense of smell they may not detect gas leaks or other noxious substances in their homes, and because smell is closely related to taste, they may not eat enough to remain healthy or may eat food that is spoiled. The sense of smell is also important for the enjoyment of food and other aromas.

Seubert and her colleagues collected demographic information from 2,848 adults in 11 different age groups between 66 and 99+ years. They were chosen randomly from the participants in a larger study, the Swedish National Study of Aging and Care. The number chosen at each age reflected the population of Sweden at the time. They removed those who reported having allergies, asthma, or just did not want to participate. They also removed any participant who had dementia or several other cognitive impairments, leaving 2,234 healthy participants. Researchers collected demographic information, such as gender, education, physical health, mental health, and whether they had certain genetic markers for diseases, such as the APOE ε4 gene associated with Alzheimer's disease. The participants were also asked about their own evaluations of their senses of smell. Table 1.2 shows the number of participants at each age group and each gender,

The odor test involved 16 items: apple, banana, clove, coffee, cinnamon, fish, garlic, lemon, leather, licorice, peppermint, pineapple, rose, turpentine, mushrooms, and gasoline. Odors were infused into felt-tip pens and each participant was exposed to the odor on the pen for 5 seconds. The researchers recorded how many of the odors each participant was able to identify correctly and how many they identified incorrectly, giving each a score. Those with scores below an established cutoff were considered to have *olfactory dysfunction*, or difficulty with their sense of smell. Figure 1.3 shows what percentage of participating

---

Table 1.2 Number of Participants (*n*) for Each Age and Gender

	60 Years	66 Years	72 Years	78 Years	81 Years	84 Years	87 Years	90 Years
Women	$n = 361$	$n = 272$	$n = 224$	$n = 212$	$n = 89$	$n = 76$	$n = 54$	$n = 65$
Men	$n = 288$	$n = 202$	$n = 156$	$n = 99$	$n = 48$	$n = 43$	$n = 24$	$n = 21$
All Participants	$n = 649$	$n = 474$	$n = 380$	$n = 311$	$n = 137$	$n = 119$	$n = 78$	$n = 86$

SOURCE: Data from Seubert et al. (2017).

Figure 1.3 Prevalence of Olfactory Dysfunction

SOURCE: Data from Seubert et al. (2017).

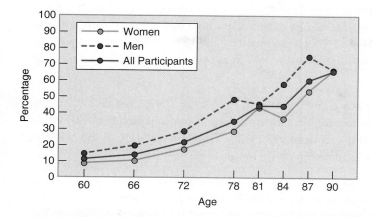

men and women at each age had olfactory dysfunction. As you can see, this problem increases with age from 66 to 90, and it is generally more prevalent in men than in women.

Some cross-sectional studies do not use age groups. Instead, they use stages in life, such as comparing young couples without children to couples who have had their first child to see the effects of parenthood on a marriage. Or comparing young people entering college with those who are graduating to see the effects of education on political views. But all cross-sectional studies are designed to test people from different age groups or stages in life at the same point in time—kind of a shortcut for following one group of people throughout a period of years and charting individual changes. The benefit is that it is quicker, easier, and less expensive than following the same people around the whole time. The downside is that it only shows *age differences*, not change. When cross-sectional studies are conducted with older adults, it is possible that the people in the older groups do not represent the general population as well as those in the younger groups, due to transportation problems, chronic health concerns, and difficulty in recruiting older participants. It is also the case that older participants are those who have survived into old age and may be healthier and wealthier (and perhaps wiser). But again, the minimal time and effort it takes to conduct cross-sectional studies makes them attractive to most researchers, and many of these problems can be predicted and controlled for. At our university, we are able to avoid some of these problems by running studies that compare our students (the young adult group) with students of our Lifelong Learning program (the older adult group). Since the older adults who attend this lecture series tend to be college educated, it gives us an older group that is matched to our younger group.

LONGITUDINAL STUDIES A **longitudinal study** is one in which a researcher follows the same group of people over a period of time, taking measurements of some behavior of interest at regular intervals. In comparison to the cross-sectional study, a longitudinal study might start with a group of people who are 35 to 44, asking how much effort they devote to their health. Then, 10 years later, the researchers could find the same people, now at the ages of 45 to 54, and ask them the same question again. Finally, another 10 years later, the last data could be gathered when the participants are 55–64 years of age. Then comparisons could be made, telling the story of these individuals, at least in regard to *age-related changes* in the time they devoted to their health over their middle years (not just *age-related differences* as are revealed by cross-sectional studies).

An example of a study using the longitudinal method is one conducted by developmental psychologist Dyuma I. Vargas Lascano and her colleagues (2015), who were interested in how the concept of perceived control changes during the transition to adulthood. These researchers were also interested in what factors might affect changes in perceived control. Details of this study are shown in Table 1.3 (see 'Example of a Longitudinal Study').

Some of the most ambitious longitudinal studies are done in large European research centers. For example, the Berlin Study of Aging began in 1990 with 516 participants ranging in age from 70 to over 100. It was the first large-scale multidisciplinary assessment of people in this age group. The initial group was examined on many aspects of their physical, psychological, and social well-being—an examination that took 3 years to complete. Over the next 19 years, the research team repeated key tests on the surviving participants (Baltes & Mayer, 1999). Some of the participants outlived the principle investigator, psychologist Paul Baltes, who died at the age of 67 in 2006. At one point, there were 40 researchers on the staff along with hundreds of students and research assistants. Although the data-gathering ended in 2009, there are still 13 core researchers working on this project and publishing new research articles. Archived data is available for researchers around the world to incorporate into their own projects, and blood samples have been stored for future genetic research.

Another drawback to longitudinal studies is **attrition**, or participant dropout. The Vargas Lascano study began with a fairly general sample of high school students, but as the years went by, each wave of data collection yielded fewer and fewer returns. More than half of the original participants were absent from the last wave of the study. When attrition is present, we need to ask whether those who dropped out might have made a difference in the results. The researchers mentioned this in the discussion section of their journal article. They said that the perceived control scores of those who dropped out and those who remained in the study did not differ in the earlier parts of the survey in which all participated.

Example of a Longitudinal Study

Vargas Lascano and her colleagues began the study in the spring of 1985 with 983 high school seniors from six high schools in Edmonton, Canada. The students' perception of control was assessed by asking them how much they agreed with the statement, "I have little control over the things that happen to me." They responded by rating the statement on a scale of 1 to 6, with the highest level of perceived control scored as 6 and the lowest scored as 1. Data were also collected on their parents' education levels.

The second wave of the study took place in 1986 followed by subsequent waves in 1987, 1989, 1992, 1999, and 2010. The number of participants dropped in each wave, due primarily to problems locating former participants. Between Wave 1 in 1985 and Wave 7 in 2010, the number of participants dropped from 957 to 403, which is just 42% of the original number (Table 1.3). However, this drop is actually less than is found in many longitudinal studies.

Table 1.3 Wave of Longitudinal Study, Years of Testing, Participants' Ages, and the Number (*n*) of Participants

	Wave 1	Wave 2	Wave 3	Wave 4	Wave 5	Wave 6	Wave 7
Year of Survey	1985	1986	1987	1989	1992	1999	2010
Age of Participant	18	19	20	22	25	32	43
Number of Participants	957	662	547	500	403	506	403

SOURCE: Data from Vargas Lascano et al. (2015).

Vargas Lascano and her colleagues computed the average scores of the participants on the perceived control question at each wave and found that the scores increased from 18 to 25 years, then decreased by age 32, with a smaller and slower decrease by 43. These findings are shown in Figure 1.4 on the middle line, labeled "Average trajectory." Researchers then divided the participants into those whose parents had no college degree and those who had at least one parent with a college degree. The scores for these two subgroups are shown in Figure 1.4 in the upper and lower lines. These data show that the participants with college-educated parents had higher perceptions of control and that this perception of control increased throughout the transition to adulthood and beyond. Those whose parents had no college degrees increased somewhat until age 25, then showed a steady decline in perceived control.

Education level of parents is one way of computing the socio-economic status (SES) of a family, and this study indicates that higher-SES parents are able to transmit certain advantages to their children in terms of parenting styles that promote self-reliance and responsibility and also have family resources that foster healthy lifestyles and higher education. High levels of perceived control have been associated with better mental and physical health and lower mortality risk.

The longitudinal method used by Vargas Lascano and her colleagues truly demonstrates *change* because the same participants were tested at each age. There were only 403 participants compared to 2,234 in the cross-sectional study described earlier, but the data points on the graph show increases in perceived control for the same participants over the course of 25 years. Another plus for longitudinal studies is that the participants are from the same cohort, which increases the probability that the changes in perceived control are age related and not the result of some normative history-graded influence on that cohort. However, the minuses of longitudinal studies should be apparent. From the first wave of testing to the published article, the study took 30 years! This method is time-consuming and expensive.

Figure 1.4

Emerging adults (solid line) show a mean average increase in perceived control between the ages of 18 and 25, then decrease until their 40s. When divided by educational attainment of parents, those with college-educated parents (top line) show higher levels and little decline: those with parents who did not attend college (lower line) begin declining at age 25.

SOURCE: Adapted from Vargas Lascano et al. (2015).

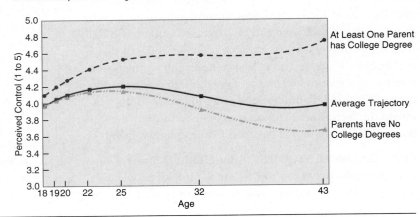

SEQUENTIAL STUDIES One of the ways to combine the positive aspects of the cross-sectional design with those of the longitudinal design is to use the **sequential study**, which is a series of longitudinal studies begun at different points in time. In the simplest form, one longitudinal study (Cohort 1) is begun with participants who are in one age group. Several years later, a second longitudinal study (Cohort 2) is begun with participants who are the same age as the Cohort 1 participants were when the study began. As the two studies progress, they yield two sets of longitudinal data, and they also give cross-sectional data. For example, a sequential study was conducted by psychologist Susan Krauss Whitbourne and her colleagues (Whitbourne et al., 1992) to answer the question of whether young adults' personalities change or remain stable as they moved into middle age (see 'Example of a Sequential Study').

1.4.2: Measures

OBJECTIVE: Explain the advantages and disadvantages of different measures

Once the research design is determined, the next major set of decisions has to do with how to measure the behavior of interest. Each method has its own set of advantages and disadvantages, and I discuss them here briefly.

One of the most common instruments used to gather data is a **personal interview**, that is, having the experimenter ask the participant questions, one-on-one. Personal interviews can be *structured*, like a multiple-choice test, or *open ended*, like an essay test, or a combination of both. While personal interviews have the advantage of allowing the interviewer to clarify questions and ask follow-up questions, and might make participants feel more comfortable than they might simply writing answers on an impersonal questionnaire, one drawback is that the participants might provide responses they feel are socially acceptable to the interviewer. Similarly, the interviewer's feelings toward the participant might cloud the recording or coding of responses, especially with very long interviews. Building rapport between interviewer and participant can be a plus or a minus.

This problem is avoided by using the **survey questionnaire**, consisting of structured and focused questions that participants can answer on their own. Survey questionnaires are often given out on a large scale, such as online or at large gatherings, allowing researchers to reach a large number of people in a wide geographic range. Participants may be more truthful and forthcoming about sensitive topics with a survey than if talking face-to-face with an interviewer. Survey questionnaires are much less expensive and time-consuming than personal interviews. One drawback of survey questionnaires is that there is often a low return rate (an average of 30% of participants return the first questionnaire). Group-administered questionnaires have fewer lost participants, but can be affected by peer influence (especially if given out in the social environment of high school auditoriums or retirement condominium recreation rooms). Good survey questionnaires are also incredibly difficult to construct.

Some of the problems of survey questionnaire construction can be avoided by using **standardized tests**. These are instruments that measure some trait or behavior and have already been established in your field of interest. Drawbacks are that many of these tests are owned by publishing companies, and you have to purchase the right to use them in your research. An example is measuring IQ using the Wechsler scales or personality using the MMPI or the Myers-Briggs Type Indicator. However, a number of tests are also available at no charge that have been standardized and published in research articles, along with instructions for administering and scoring them. For example, researchers in a number of studies in this text measure depression in their participants with an instrument known as the CES-D-10, or the Center for Epidemiological Studies Short Depressive Symptoms Scale (Radloff, 1977). This test is easily available on the Internet. It is a good example of a standardized test that is easily scored and has a good record of **validity** (it measures what it claims to measure) and **reliability** (it would yield a similar score if the person took it again). How would you select a standardized test for your own research? There are reference books that review tests periodically, such as the *Mental Measurements Yearbook* (Carlson et al., 2017), but the advice I give students is to read similar studies published by other researchers and see what they use.

These are by no means the only research measures available. There are many ways to measure human behavior, from complex brain-imaging techniques to one-item questionnaires ("How would you rate your health? Circle one of the following: Very Poor, Poor, Average, Good, Very Good"). Depending on the research question, it's important to find the most appropriate way to measure the behavior of interest.

1.4.3: Data Analysis

OBJECTIVE: Describe forms of data analysis

Once the research method has been chosen and the measure of behavior has been selected, researchers must make another set of decisions about how to analyze the data they will collect. Some of the statistical methods now being used are extremely sophisticated and complex. For now, let's talk about the most common ways of looking at adult development.

COMPARISON OF MEANS The most common and the simplest way to describe age-related differences is to collect the data (scores, measurement results) for each group, find the means (averages), and determine whether the differences in the means are large enough to be significant, a process known as **comparison of means**. With cross-sectional

Example of a Sequential Study

The study began in 1966 with a group of 347 undergraduate students at the University of Rochester whose average age was 20. They were given a personality inventory questionnaire asking them, among other things, to rate statements about their work ethic (or industry) according to how well each described them. In Table 1.4, this group is shown in the top left box labeled Cohort 1, 1966. In 1977, this group was on average 31 years old, and the researchers sent out questionnaires again, receiving 155 in return, as shown in the box labeled Cohort 1, Year of Testing 1977. Also in 1977 a new group of 20-year-old students from the University of Rochester were given the personality inventory questionnaire (Cohort 2, 1977). In 1988

Table 1.4 Year of Testing, Age of Participants, and Number of Participants for Two Cohorts of a Sequential Study

	Year of Testing 1966	Year of Testing 1977	Year of Testing 1988
Cohort 1	Age = 20 Number of Participants = 347	Age = 31 n = 155	Age = 42 n = 99
Cohort 2		Age = 20 n = 296	Age = 31 n = 83

SOURCE: Data from Whitbourne et al. (1992).

the process was repeated for the participants in Cohort 1, who were now 42 years of age, and Cohort 2, who were now 31 years of age. As you can see, 99 of the original 347 in Cohort 1 returned questionnaires, and 83 of the original 296 in Cohort 2 returned questionnaires.

Comparing longitudinal results, Cohort 1 shows a sharper increase in industry (work ethic) scores between age 20 and 31 than does Cohort 2, though both have similar scores at age 31. Cross-sectional results suggest that the normative history-graded influences (Vietnam War, civil rights movement) lowered the young adults' scores in 1966.

At this point, there are two longitudinal studies going on, Cohort 1 with data available for the ages of 20, 31, and 42 and Cohort 2 with data available for the ages of 20 and 31. There is also a cross-sectional study going on, with a group of 20-year-olds, a group of 31-year-olds, and a group of 42-year-olds. Figure 1.5 shows how Whitbourne and her colleagues analyzed the results. The top line shows the work ethic (industry) scores for Cohort 1 at ages 20, 31, and 42. The scores increase sharply between 20 and 31, and the increase becomes more gradual from 31 to 42. This definitely shows change in personality traits during adulthood, but does the same hold for other cohorts? The lower line in the figure shows the pattern for Cohort 2, tested at 20 years and 31 years of age. The pattern is different than for Cohort 1. First, the work ethic (industry) scores are much higher at age 20 for Cohort 2 (6.54 for Cohort 1 and 9.19 for Cohort 2) and, second, the rate of increase is much slower for Cohort 2. Still, both groups had similar work ethic (industry) scores at the age of 31 (13.58 for Cohort 1 and 14.32 for Cohort 2).

The researchers suggest that the 20-year-olds in Cohort 1 were in college during the 1960s, when the work ethic of the establishment was being questioned and rejected, and their low scores on industry were reflections of that era. Once out of school and in the workplace, this group had some catching up to do. Their catching up is represented by the sharp increase in industry scores, which at 31 are very close to the scores of Cohort 2, who were not part of the protest era. Clearly there are nonnormative history-graded influences going on here. Perhaps the normative age-graded pattern of change in the personality trait of industry is more like that of Cohort 2, but when history (e.g., the Vietnam War, civil rights issues) brings about a large student protest movement, it causes a detour in the journey of adulthood for many in that cohort, although in the case of the personality trait of industry, these college students were able to catch up to speed and be back on track by the time they were age 31.

Figure 1.5 Results from A Sequential Study of Two Cohorts Tested at Three Ages and at Three Different Points in Time

SOURCE: Adapted from Whitbourne et al. (1992).

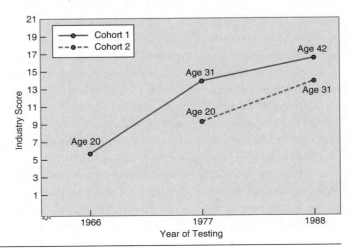

studies, the means of the age groups are compared. With longitudinal studies, the means of the scores for the same people at different ages are compared. With sequential studies, both comparisons are possible. However, the similarity remains—we are looking for an age-related pattern of change.

If the group of participants is large enough, it is often possible to divide it into smaller groups and look for age differences or continuities in the subgroups, such as women versus men, rural dwellers versus urban dwellers, those with young children versus those without young children. If the same pattern appears in all subgroups, we'd be more likely to conclude that this is a significant age-related pattern. However, if the change is different for the subgroups (as is often the case), it opens the door for follow-up questions. For example, in the cross-sectional study described earlier (Seubert et al., 2017), the mean scores for all participants in each age group showed an age-related increase in the percentage of participants who suffered from olfactory dysfunction. (This is shown by the "All Participants" column in Table 1.2.) When the researchers divided the participants into groups by gender, it showed that not only did the prevalence of olfactory dysfunction increase with age, but it was also higher for men than for women in almost every age group (as shown by the rows in Table 1.2 labeled "Women" and "Men").

CORRELATIONAL ANALYSIS   Comparisons of means for different age groups, either cross-sectionally or longitudinally, can give us some insights into possible age changes or developmental patterns, but they cannot tell us whether there has been stability or change within individuals. For this information, a different type of analysis is required: a **correlational analysis** (see 'Implementations of Correlational Analysis').

META-ANALYSIS   Another way of analyzing data is the **meta-analysis**. This approach combines data from a large number of studies that deal with the same research question. A researcher conducting a meta-analysis selects a research question, such as, "Are older adults viewed differently in different cultures?" It is a common belief that people in Eastern cultures have more positive attitudes toward aging and older adults than do people in Western cultures, but is this belief actually true? Michael North and Susan Fiske (2015) conducted a meta-analysis of existing research in an attempt to find out. The first step in a meta-analysis is to find all of the research articles addressing the question of interest. The researchers conducted a literature search and found 37 articles published between 1984 and 2014 that directly compared the attitudes of people from Eastern and Western cultures toward older adults. There were data from a total of 21,093 people. They calculated the size of the difference in attitudes expressed by people from Eastern and Western cultures on every attitude measure from every article. A striking pattern emerged. People from Western

cultures actually held older adults in higher esteem than did people from Eastern cultures. It turns out that only one article found that attitudes toward older adults were significantly more positive in Eastern than in Western cultures.

WRITING PROMPT

To Sleep or Not to Sleep?

It is a common belief that students who get more sleep earn higher grades. How would you design a study to support or refute this belief? What do you predict your results would be?

 The response entered here will appear in the performance dashboard and can be viewed by your instructor.

Submit

1.4.4: Designs

OBJECTIVE: Differentiate among research designs

The closing statement researchers are allowed to make depends on what kind of research design has been used, experimental or nonexperimental. If it is experimental, researchers are able to say their findings show that their factor of interest *caused* the change observed in their participants. If it is not experimental research, they must limit themselves to saying that their results show a relationship or an association with the change.

The distinctions between experimental and nonexperimental designs could fill a whole book (and there are a number of good ones available), but for now, let me just say that the feature that distinguishes experimental from nonexperimental designs is how much control the experimenter has over the way the study is conducted. In the strictest sense of the word, an **experimental design** has a control group, the participants are selected randomly from the population of interest, they are assigned randomly to groups, there is random assignment of groups to treatment and control conditions, and there is a high degree of control over any outside factors that might affect the outcome.

The more of these features that are present, the stronger the case the researcher can make for causality. Table 1.5 shows two types of experimental designs and the presence or absence of these controls.

Experimental designs include true experiments and quasi-experiments, depending on which of the controls listed in the table are present. True experiments are often not possible in answering developmental research questions because when comparisons are made between age groups (or between groups of people at different stages of life, such as preretirement versus post-retirement), the participants cannot be assigned to groups; they are already in one group or the other. That automatically takes a large

Implementations of Correlational Analysis

A correlation is simply a statistic that tells us the extent to which two sets of scores on the same people tend to vary together. Correlations (*r*) can range from +1.00 to –1.00. A positive correlation shows that high scores on the two dimensions occur together. A negative correlation tells us that high scores on one dimension occur with low scores on the other. The closer the correlation is to 1.00 (positive or negative), the stronger the relationship. A correlation of 0.00 indicates no relationship.

For example, height and weight are positively correlated: taller people generally weigh more, shorter people less. But the correlation is not perfect (not +1.00) because there are some short, heavy people and some tall, light people. If you are on a diet, the number of pounds you lose is negatively correlated with the number of calories you eat: high calories go with low weight loss. But this correlation, too, is not a perfect –1.00 (as any of you who have dieted know full well!).

Correlations are also used to reveal patterns of stability or change.

For example, researchers interested in personality traits might give personality assessments to participants over a number of years and then correlate the early scores with the later scores for each person. A high positive correlation would show stability for that trait.

Ultimately, however, correlations can tell us only about relationships; they cannot tell us about causality, even though it is often very tempting to make the conceptual leap from a correlation to a cause. Some cases are easy. If I told you that there was a negative correlation between the per capita incidence of television sets in the countries of the world and the infant mortality rates in those countries, you would not be tempted to conclude that the presence of TV *causes* lower infant mortality. You'd look for other kinds of societal characteristics that might explain the link between the two facts such as income level. But if I tell you there is a correlation between the amount of time adults spend with friends and family and the overall life satisfaction those adults report, you would be much more tempted to jump to the conclusion that greater happiness is *caused* by contact with friends and family. And it may be. But the correlation, by itself, doesn't tell us that; it only tells us that there is a relationship. It remains for further research and theorizing to uncover the causal links, if any. Perhaps the greater life satisfaction people have, the more time their friends and family want to spend with them.

One unique way correlational analyses are used in developmental research is to determine the genetic contributions to various behaviors and abilities. For instance, the typical twin study involves comparing two types of twins, monozygotic and dizygotic, on the behavior you are interested in. For a simple example, let's use height (and twins of the same sex to rule out sex differences). Each twin would be measured and the height recorded. Then two correlations would be computed comparing the twins—one for monozygotic twins and one for dizygotic twins. Which do you think would be more similar in height? Of course, the monozygotic twins would be more similar because they have the same genes, and height is something that is determined by inheritance to a great extent. But what about other characteristics, like IQ, the tendency toward alcoholism, or religiosity?

Those are all characteristics that have been shown to be influenced by heredity to a significant extent. And the research that revealed this involved correlational analyses.

For example, in a study using data from the Swedish Twin Registry, epidemiologist Erica Spotts and her colleagues (2004) investigated whether marital happiness is influenced by heredity. They gave a test of marital happiness to over 300 pairs of twins (all women) and their husbands. About half of the women were monozygotic twins and half were dizygotic twins. When the scores were analyzed, the monozygotic twin pairs were more alike than the dizygotic twin pairs. As you can see in Figure 1.6, if one monozygotic twin wife was happy in her marriage, the other twin tended to be happy too—and if one was unhappy, there was a good chance that the other was too. Their marital happiness scores were positively correlated. This was not the case for the dizygotic twin wives, whose correlations were about half what the monozygotic twins' correlations were. Comparing the two types of twins' correlations shows the

Figure 1.6 Marital Happiness in Twin Pairs

Wives who are monozygotic twin pairs are more similar in their marital happiness than wives who are dizygotic twin pairs. Interestingly, this genetic effect carried over to their husbands who were not related (compare striped columns).

SOURCE: Data from Spotts et al. (2004).

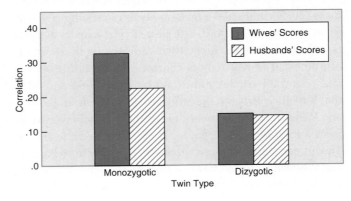

extent of the genetic contribution to marital happiness because the monozygotic twins share the same genes, whereas the dizygotic twins share only half, and as in the case of height, we would not expect them to be as similar. (Of course, parents may be more apt to treat monozygotic twins more similarly than dizygotic twins, thus providing a more similar environment for them.)

In a surprise twist, the researchers also gave the marital happiness questionnaires to the husbands of the twins, who were not related to each other or to anyone else in the study. As you can see in the figure, the husbands of the monozygotic twins also were more similar in their marital happiness scores than the husbands of the dizygotic twins. It may be that the genetic endowment of the monozygotic twins not only gave the women similar outlooks on marriage, but that the women, in turn, influenced the marital happiness of their husbands.

Table 1.5 Experimental Designs and Their Comparative Features

	True Experimental Design	Quasi-Experimental Design
Presence of a control group?	Always	Often
Random selection of participants from a population?	Yes	Some
Random assignment of participants to groups?	Yes	No
Random assignment of treatment to groups?	Yes	No
Degree of control over extraneous variables	Yes	Some

SOURCE: Salkind (2011).

amount of control out of the hands of the researcher and opens the door for a number of problems. As such, most developmental research is quasi-experimental.

DESCRIPTIVE AND QUALITATIVE RESEARCH   Other designs include descriptive research and qualitative research. **Descriptive research** tells the current state of the participants on some measure of interest. The number of people of different ages who die of suicide each year is descriptive research. The rate of births to unmarried women over the past 50 years is descriptive research, and the cross-sectional, longitudinal, and sequential studies discussed earlier are descriptive research. What they have in common is the lack of a high level of experimenter control. They are still valuable sources of information on development.

Qualitative research uses less structured data collection techniques, such as case studies, interviews, participant observations, direct observations, and exploring documents, artifacts, and archival records. If you have ever done genealogy research to find your family history in old records and documents, you have done a form of qualitative research. It is a very old tradition that has only recently been included in developmental sciences. Although research without numbers may sound very enticing to students who have just completed a statistics course, it is not really a replacement for **quantitative research** (research with measurable data), but a different approach that is used to supplement quantitative research.

An example of qualitative research is a study by sociologists Amy Hequembourg and Sara Brallier (2005).

They were interested in the role transitions among adult siblings when their parents need care in old age. We have long been aware that daughters are most likely to be the major caregiver of an aging parent, but these researchers found eight brother–sister pairs and interviewed them at length about their roles and feelings about their caregiving responsibilities. They recorded the answers in detail and then spent many months analyzing them. The finished product was a very interesting view of these families. Yes, the sisters did more, but sometimes they were pleased to be in that role. And other times the brothers stepped in and took over. There was evidence of adult sisters and brothers growing closer to each other as they shared the care for their parents. Although it was a study of only 16 participants, it gave more depth than a questionnaire sent out to 5,000. Clearly there is a place in developmental psychology for this type of research, and I am pleased to see it being discussed in research methods books.

Qualitative research is not easy. It needs to be carefully planned, the sources need to be wisely chosen, and questions need to be designed to focus on the topic at hand. If the research involves spending a lot of time with the people being interviewed, the experimenter needs to be able to remain as objective as possible. Data must be recorded precisely and completely. And then the findings need to be organized and written up to share with others.

Qualitative research is an excellent way to begin a new line of research. Epidemiologist David Snowden, former director of the Nun Study of the School Sisters of Notre Dame, started his research by visiting with the older nuns in a convent in Minnesota. As a beginning professor, he had no idea what he wanted to do for a research program, but one day he stumbled onto a room that contained the archives of the convent. Each sister had a file going back to her first days as a nun, often 50 or 60 years before. They had all written essays about their childhoods and why they wanted to be nuns. Snowdon (2001) wrote that "for an epidemiologist, this sort of find is equivalent to an archaeologist's discovering an undisturbed tomb or a paleontologist's unearthing a perfectly preserved skeleton" (p. 24). From this beginning, he began the research that became his career. For example, he and his colleagues (Riley et al., 2005) found that the more complex the language in the essays the nuns had written as young women, the less likely they were to have Alzheimer's disease in late adulthood. Some of Snowdon's other research findings are discussed later in this text, but for now, this serves as a good example of qualitative research based on archival records.

Summary: Introduction to Adult Development

1.1 Basic Concepts in Adult Development

OBJECTIVE: Explore major themes in developmental psychology

- Developmental psychology includes the study of change and stability over time during childhood, adolescence, and adulthood. The study of adult development covers the time from emerging adulthood to the end of life and is based on empirical research.

- This text covers individual differences among people and also the commonalities they share. It looks at stability and change, continuity and stages, typical development and atypical development, and the external and internal changes that occur over the years of adulthood.

- The word *age* has many more meanings than how many years one has been alive (chronological age). In various usages it also designates estimates of a person's physical condition compared to others (biological age), the abilities one displays in dealing effectively with the environment (psychological age), and the roles one has taken on (social age). Functional age is a combination of biological, psychological, and social ages.

1.2 Sources of Change

OBJECTIVE: Explain the major sources of development

- Sources of change in adulthood are classified into three types. Normative age-graded influences are linked to age and happen to most people as they grow older. They come from both biological and environmental causes and also from interactions between genes and the environment.

- Normative history-graded influences are environmental factors that affect people within a group. These changes include cultural conditions and cohort experiences. One of the best-studied cohorts is the group of people who lived through the Great Depression.

- Nonnormative life events are unique to the individual and cause developmental changes that are not shared by most people.

- Genes and the environment also contribute to change. They usually interact, and one mechanism for this interaction is epigenetic inheritance, in which genes are modified through DNA methylation.

1.3 Guiding Perspectives

OBJECTIVE: Differentiate between the perspectives of psychological and bioecological models

- This text will approach the topic of adult development using the tenets of lifespan developmental psychology, a set of ideas introduced by Baltes in 1980 that encouraged psychologists to study development at many ages and to view development in a broader scope than they had before.

- A second approach this text will take is based on the ecological systems view introduced by Bronfenbrenner in 1979. This set of ideas inspired psychologists to consider the whole person, not just the isolated behavior of a participant in a laboratory experiment.

1.4 Developmental Research

OBJECTIVE: Evaluate developmental research methods

- The first step in conducting developmental research is to select a research method. There are three possibilities: (1) cross-sectional studies gather data on a group of people representing different age groups, (2) longitudinal studies follow the same people over a longer period of time, gathering data at several points along the way, and (3) sequential studies combine the preceding methods by conducting two longitudinal studies during different time periods, thereby making it possible to do both longitudinal and cross-sectional comparisons. There are pros and cons to each method.

- After a method is chosen, a researcher needs to choose an appropriate measure. Some of the most common ones in developmental research are personal interviews, survey questionnaires, and standardized tests.

- The next step in developmental research is selecting analyses. Most research uses either comparison of means, which involves computing the means of the measurement scores for each group and testing them statistically to see if they are significantly different, or correlational analysis, in which the researcher compares scores on several measurements for the participants to see if there is a relationship between the characteristics being measured. Correlations are used to show both change and stability. They are also used to demonstrate heritability by comparing scores of monozygotic twin pairs with scores of dizygotic twin pairs. The meta-analysis combines data from a number of previously published studies that focus on the same research question and reanalyzes it as a larger, more powerful study.

- The final step in developmental research involves stating conclusions, and this depends on whether the research design was experimental or not. If the design was experimental, it is possible to conclude that the results of the study were caused by the factor of interest. Experimental designs include true experiments, and quasi-experiments, and they differ in the amount of control the experimenter has over the conditions of the study and the outside factors that might also cause similar results. True experimental designs are not often used in developmental research. Research designs that are not experimental provide valuable knowledge about development even though researchers cannot conclude that their factor of interest caused the results. These designs include descriptive research and qualitative research.

SHARED WRITING

Introduction to Adult Development

Consider this chapter's discussion of research methods. Using what you've learned in this chapter, design a research study. Be sure to include the goal of your study, as well as methods, measures, controls, and any other pertinent information.

▶ | A minimum number of characters is required to post and earn points. After posting, your response can be viewed by your class and instructor, and you can participate in the class discussion.

Post   0 characters | 140 minimum

Chapter 2
Physical Changes

While everyone ages physically, not everyone ages on the same timeline.

Learning Objectives

2.1 Evaluate theories of primary aging

2.2 Analyze how adults deal with age-related changes in appearance

2.3 Summarize how the senses change with age

2.4 Analyze the social impact of age-related changes to the body

2.5 Determine how age-related physical changes impact life as an older adult

2.6 Relate aging experiences to demographic influences

A Word from the Author

A Short Lesson on Child Development

WHEN MY GRANDSON, Nicholas, was 5 years old, I was writing a book on child development. I wanted to open each chapter with a warm and personal story that would introduce the topic (much as I am doing now). Nicholas was a rich source of material. I was writing about children's cognitive processes, and I knew that at 5, children tend to judge everything at face value.

They are convinced that the glass with the highest level of lemonade holds the most, regardless of its diameter. The longest line of M&Ms has the most candy, regardless of how far apart they are spaced. And people who are taller are older, period.

So I asked Nicholas who was older, Grandma or Dad. He quickly answered that Dad (who is 5' 11") is certainly older than Grandma (who is 5' 7"), although he also knew that Dad was Grandma's son. He knew that Dad was 30 and Grandma was 54, and that 54 is more than 30, but logic is not important at 5. I was pleased—so far, he was perfectly illustrating the important concepts in my text book chapter.

Then I asked, "How do you tell how old a person is?" I expected him to comment on their height or hair color. But I was surprised when he replied, "You look at their hands." Hands? Well, I thought, I guess that's true. The hands of older people have dark spots and larger knuckles. Adolescents have larger hands in proportion to their other body parts. And infants have hands that are closed in reflexive fists. I thought he may be onto something interesting. So I asked, "What do you look for when you look at their hands?"

"Their fingers," he said patiently. He held up one hand with outstretched fingers and said, "You ask someone how old they are and when they hold up their fingers, you count them. See, I'm 5."

Nicholas's hypothesis of determining age by looking at hands may hold up with kids up to the age of 10, but it's not much use in adulthood. In fact, the further we get from "holding up fingers" to tell our ages, the more difficult it is to determine age just by looking at someone. One of the reasons is that there are two processes of aging. **Primary aging**, the topic of this chapter, consists of the gradual, inevitable changes that will happen to most of us as we go through adulthood. Research over the last few decades has given us two major facts about primary aging: first, that it can be differentiated from disease and, second, that there are many different "normal" time lines for primary aging (National Institutes of Health, 2008). **Secondary aging**, the topic of another chapter, refers to the changes that happen more suddenly and that are usually the result of disease, injury, or some environmental event.

I begin this chapter with some of the theories of primary aging and then describe the changes in the major systems of the body most adults experience as they age. Then I discuss the effects of primary aging on complex behaviors like sleep and sexual activity. Finally, I cover some of the individual differences that are found in primary aging patterns and answer the age-old question, "Can we turn back the clock?"

2.1: Theories of Primary Aging

OBJECTIVE: Evaluate theories of primary aging

Why do we age? This question has been the subject of speculation for centuries, but the technology and methodology to investigate it is fairly new. We now have Big Data—huge sets of secondary data such as national health registries that can

be analyzed quickly—as well as major longitudinal data and advances in methods and statistics. These tools make it fairly easy for researchers to "churn out principally descriptive publications" (Bengtson & Settersten, 2016, p. 1), especially when their jobs and livelihood depend so heavily on publications and grants. This work is valuable in describing the primary aging process, but not in answering the "why" of aging. For this, we need theories. We need someone to compile empirical findings so we can integrate what is known, identify what is missing, and point the way to what needs to be investigated next. This is what theories do and why we need them.

In the relatively short life of lifespan development, we have gone from the grand theories of the 1930s and 1940s—theories that were large, inclusive explanations of all aspects of aging—to the minimalist theories of the 1960s and 1970s that were little more than descriptions of the data at hand. Today, the pendulum seems to have swung back to a Goldilocks balance, not too grandiose and not too sparse, but a middle ground that is "just right." Furthermore, the new era of theories are multidisciplinary and focused more on *healthspan* rather than *lifespan*, with a focus on prevention and treatment of age-related changes, whether it be lifestyle change or medical treatment. "Health and well-being are clearly central nodes around which scholars are fostering theories that bridge disciplines and levels of analysis, from cells to society" (Bengtson & Settersten, 2016, p. 8). I have selected a few of the more recent theories to describe here, along with support and criticism for each.

Before we move on, I should caution you not to expect any single theory to be proven to be the one and only correct answer to the question of why we age. As biochemist Brian K. Kennedy explains, "Gone are the days of scientists working on one model for aging or one hypothesis about what causes aging. Instead we are in a new research world that is at once exciting and a bit scary, in which complexity of the aging process is becoming appreciated and a system-level view of aging in an entire organism at least seems theoretically attainable, albeit not in the short term" (2016, p. 108).

∨ | **By the end of this module, you will be able to:**

2.1.1 Explain the idea that cell damage causes aging

2.1.2 Describe how genetics influences aging

2.1.3 Explain the relationship between aging and caloric intake

2.1.4 Identify challenges in prolonging human life

2.1.1: Oxidative Damage

OBJECTIVE: Explain the idea that cell damage causes aging

One theory of primary aging is based on random damage that takes place at the cellular level. This process, first identified by biogerontologist Denham Harmon in 1956, involves the release of **free radicals**, molecules or atoms that possess an unpaired electron and are by-products of normal body metabolism as well as a response to diet, sunlight, X-rays, and air pollution. These molecules enter into many potentially damaging chemical reactions, most of which the healthy body can resist or repair. One consequence of oxidative stress is mutations in mitochondrial DNA. Mitochondria are organelles in most cells that produce energy, so mutations can lead to cellular dysfunction (Gredilla, 2011). According to this theory, our resistance and repair functions decline as we age, and the oxidative damage increases. The result is primary aging.

A number of vitamins and vitamin-like substances have been identified as **antioxidants**, substances with properties that protect against oxidative damage. Some of these are vitamins E and C, coenzyme Q10, beta-carotene, and creatine. Many nutritional supplements on the market contain large doses of these substances and advertise themselves as having antioxidant properties. However, there is no evidence that they can delay primary aging in humans or extend the lifespan. Most people in developed countries have adequate supplies of these nutrients in their diets, and no benefit has been shown for higher-than-recommended doses.

2.1.2: Genetic Limits

OBJECTIVE: Describe how genetics influences aging

The theory of genetic limits centers on the observation that every species has a characteristic maximum lifespan. Something between 110 and 120 years appears to be the effective maximum lifespan for humans, whereas for some turtles it is far longer, and for chickens (or dogs, or cats, or cows, or most other mammals) it is far shorter. Such observations led cellular biologist Leonard Hayflick (1977, 1994) to propose that there is a genetic program setting the upper age limit of each species. Hayflick showed that when human embryo cells are placed in nutrient solutions and observed over a period of time, the cells divide only about 50 times, after which they stop dividing and enter a state known as **replicative senescence** (Hornsby, 2001). Furthermore, cells from the embryos of longer-lived creatures such as the Galápagos tortoise double perhaps 100 times, whereas chicken embryo cells double only about 25 times. The number of divisions a species will undergo before reaching replicative senescence is known as its **Hayflick limit**, and there is a positive correlation between that number and the species' longevity. According to the genetic limits theory, primary aging results when we approach the Hayflick limit for the human species, exhausting our cells' ability to replicate.

The suggested mechanism behind the genetic limits theory of aging comes from the discovery that chromosomes in many human body cells (and those of some other species, too) have, at their tips, lengths of repeating DNA called **telomeres**. Telomeres are necessary for DNA replication and appear to serve as timekeepers for the cells. On average, the telomeres in the cells of a middle-aged adult are shorter than those of a young adult; the telomeres of an older adult are shorter still. And once the telomeres are used up, the cell stops dividing.

Telomere length has been related to both primary and secondary aging. People who are at high risk for heart disease or type 2 diabetes have shorter telomere lengths than healthy individuals the same age. Telomere length has also been related to chronic stress conditions. In one study, a group of mothers who were caregivers for children with chronic illnesses were found to have telomere lengths equivalent to women 10 years older who were caregivers for healthy children (Epel et al., 2004). Seemingly, the stress that comes with caring for a child with chronic illness adds 10 years to one's biological age.

IS IT POSSIBLE TO SLOW DOWN THE LOSS OF TELOMERE LENGTH IN ONE'S CELLS? This was the focus of a study by medical researcher Tim D. Spector and his colleagues (Cherkas et al., 2008), who interviewed over 2,400 individuals between 18 and 81 years of age about their leisure-time exercise. Following the interview, a sample of blood was drawn from each participant, and the telomeres from their white blood cells were examined. The researchers found that those in the light, moderate, and heavy exercise groups had cells with significantly longer telomeres than those in the inactive group. Participants in the heavy exercise group had telomere lengths similar to the people in the inactive group who were 10 years younger. It was interesting that the exercise described in this study was "leisure-time exercise." When researchers examined the amount of work-related exercise the participants got (such as stocking shelves in a grocery store), the results were not significant. This suggests that the "leisure" mode is a key feature of beneficial exercise.

It seems that shorter telomere lengths are good predictors of premature aging and age-related diseases. It also seems that shorter telomere lengths go hand in hand with poor health habits such as eating junk food, smoking cigarettes, and maintaining a sedentary lifestyle. None of this research shows that telomere length *determines* the rate of aging, but the relationships are very strong.

2.1.3: Caloric Restriction

OBJECTIVE: Explain the relationship between aging and caloric intake

One of the most promising explanations of why we age is that aging is connected with our diets—not so much what we eat, but how many calories we metabolize per day. This idea was first suggested 60 years ago when researchers studied the effects of **caloric restriction** (CR) on lab animals by feeding them diets drastically reduced in calories (60–70% of normal diets), but containing all the necessary nutrients. Early researchers found that animals put on these diets shortly after weaning stayed youthful longer, suffered fewer late-life diseases, and lived significantly longer than their normally fed counterparts (McCay et al., 1935). More recent studies have supported these findings. For example, studies with rhesus monkeys show that animals on caloric restriction show a lower incidence of age-related disease, including type 2 diabetes, cancer, heart disease, and brain atrophy (Colman et al., 2009).

WOULD CALORIC RESTRICTION INCREASE HUMAN LONGEVITY? One problem is that, to receive maximum benefits, we would have to reduce our caloric intake by 30%. People eating a 2,000-calorie diet would need to cut back to 1,400 calories—difficult enough for a few months, but close to impossible as a lifetime regimen. Limited studies using human subjects on CR have shown some positive health benefits such as protection against type 2 diabetes and heart disease and a reduction in cancer incidence and cancer deaths (Fontana et al., 2011); however, a number of adverse effects have also been documented. These include cold intolerance, increases in stress hormones, decreases in sex hormones, and the psychological effects of extreme hunger—obsessive thoughts about food, low energy, social withdrawal, irritability, and loss of interest in sex. If the goals of caloric restriction are longevity and freedom from disease, this practice seems promising. But if the goals are quality of life, severely restricting calories does not seem to be the answer, especially in the developed countries of the world, where food cues are abundant and attractive (Polivy et al., 2008).

Scientists have now turned to finding a substance that provides the same health and longevity as caloric restriction without reducing normal food intake. Several candidates have been found, such as *resveratrol*, a substance found in red wine that extended the lifespans of yeast, worms, and flies. However, the results on mammals were disappointing. Another substance, *rapamycin*, has been more promising (Kapahi & Kockel, 2011). Originally found in soil collected on Easter Island, rapamycin inhibits cell growth and was first used as an antirejection medication for organ transplant patients. Studies of the effects of rapamycin on mice extended maximum lifespan by about 12% (Miller et al., 2011), including some mice that were the human equivalent of 60 years of age (Harrison et al., 2009). Unfortunately, rapamycin itself has side effects that rule it out for human consumption, but it is some of the most compelling evidence that aging may someday be slowed by a pharmaceutical product.

WRITING PROMPT

From Lifespan to Healthspan

You've read that there was a shift in aging theory from lifespan to healthspan, focusing on the physical experience of life rather than the simple length of life. What are some other quality-of-life issues that aging theory could address? What do you value most when you think about life as an older adult?

 The response entered here will appear in the performance dashboard and can be viewed by your instructor.

Submit

2.1.4: Turning Back the Clock

OBJECTIVE: Identify challenges in prolonging human life

When it comes to primary aging, there are many ideas about what can be done to slow down the process. We can exercise our minds and bodies. We can eat healthy food and keep our weight in the normal range. We can avoid tobacco, excessive alcohol, and exposure to loud noises. There are also things we can do to cover up some types of primary aging, such as cosmetics, hair dye, and plastic surgery. Despite seeing commercials on TV about how to look and feel young again and reading serious scientific articles about ideas to turn back the clock, I have no solid scientific evidence to offer about actually preventing or reversing the effects of primary aging at this time.

The **maximum lifespan** of our species has been about 120 years for some time now. That means that for centuries there have been a few individuals who live to that age, but none who live beyond. What has changed is the **average lifespan**, the number that comes from adding up the ages at which everyone in a certain population dies and then dividing by the number of people in that population. That number has increased each year, mainly due to eradication of infant and early childhood deaths. When there are fewer deaths of 2- and 3-year-old children, the average lifespan goes up dramatically. Currently, some researchers are trying to find ways to expand our maximum lifespan by finding ways to replace our aging organs with new organs grown in a lab (Kretzschmar & Clevers, 2016). Some are trying to rejuvenate old organs with stem cells or transfuse the blood of young mice into old mice in hopes of transferring components that will repair old cells (Apple et al., 2017). Some researchers are searching the DNA of families with many centenarians to find segments of genes that may be responsible for their longevity, hoping to someday insert it into the DNA of people who do not have those longevity genes (Passarino et al., 2016).

While all these attempts to slow down aging sound exciting, there is another side to the life-extension coin. How will we pay for this expensive life-extension treatment?

Will the retirement age increase? What will this do to our workforce? Do we have enough natural resources for a larger population of new, improved senior citizens?

I don't have the answers to these questions, but I think it is important to ask them and to think about what would happen if we could increase our maximum lifespan, because it is clearly a possibility.

WRITING PROMPT

A Question for the Ages

What changes might take place in a society where people died at an average age of 300?

 The response entered here will appear in the performance dashboard and can be viewed by your instructor.

Submit

2.2: Physical Changes in Outward Appearance

OBJECTIVE: Analyze how adults deal with age-related changes in appearance

Other chapters in this text cover changes in thinking abilities, personality, spirituality, and disease patterns during adulthood. This chapter deals with the physical aspect of adult development, from outward appearance to working through the senses, to various systems of the body, to a discussion of individual differences in primary aging. In this section, we look specifically at changes in outward appearance.

I have reviewed the myriad details of primary aging in Table 2.1, showing the physical characteristics of adults at different ages. When you look at the information this way, you can see that adults are clearly at their physical peak in the years from 18 to 39. In the years of midlife, from 40 to 64, the rate of physical change varies widely from one person to the next, with some experiencing a loss of physical function quite early, and others much later. From age 65 to 74, the loss of some abilities continues, along with significant increases in chronic diseases—both trends that accelerate in late adulthood. But here, too, there are wide individual differences in the rate of change and effective compensations. Many adults maintain perfectly adequate (or even excellent) physical functioning well past 75 and into their 80s. In the oldest group, however, all these changes accelerate, and compensations become more and more difficult to maintain.

∨ By the end of this module, you will be able to:

2.2.1 Outline changes to body composition over time

2.2.2 Characterize how skin changes with age

2.2.3 Describe issues associated with hair and the aging process

---

Table 2.1 An Overview of Physical Changes in Adulthood

Age	Weight and Body Mass	Facial Features	Vision and Hearing	Bone Mass	Neuronal Development	Hormones	Sexual Response
18–24 Years	Weight and body mass are optimal for most. About 17% are obese.	Facial features and skin tone are youthful; hair is full.	Vision is at peak acuity; hearing may start to decline for some due to loud sports and leisure-time activities.	Bone mass is still building.	Neuronal development is mostly completed.	Hormones are fully functioning; fertility is at optimal level.	Sexual response is at optimal level.
25–39 Years	Weight and girth begin to increase around age 30. About one-third are obese.	Facial features remain youthful for most; some men begin hair loss.	Beginning of vision and hearing losses, declines in taste and smell, but not generally noticeable.	Peak bone mass reached at age 30.	Some neuronal loss, but not noticeable.	Production of major hormones begins to decline, but not noticeable.	Sexual responses begin slow decline.
40–64 Years	Weight continues to increase until 40s, remains stable until 60; girth continues to increase and fat moves from extremities to abdomen. About 40% are obese.	Skin begins to wrinkle and lose elasticity. Thinning of hair for men and women, more extreme for men. Largest group for cosmetic surgery.	Near vision loss around age 45; dark adaptation decrease becomes apparent in 60s; cataracts begin in 40s. Slight losses in taste and smell. Hearing loss is more noticeable.	Bone mass begins to decline gradually for men and more sharply for women, especially after menopause.	Neuronal loss continues, especially in brain centers related to memory.	Hormones continue to decline, fertility declines gradually for men; sharply for women after menopause.	Sexual responses become slower, less intense.

Table 2.1 *(Continued)*

Age	Weight and Body Mass	Facial Features	Vision and Hearing	Bone Mass	Neuronal Development	Hormones	Sexual Response
65–74 Years	Weight and girth begin to decrease in 70s. About 37% are obese.	Wrinkles and loss of skin elasticity increase.	Vision loss continues. Cataracts common. Loss of taste and smell becomes noticeable, especially sweet and salty tastes.	Bone mass continues to decline. Risk for fractures increases, especially for women.	Neuronal loss continues.	Hormones continue to decline.	Sexual responses continue to decline, though lack of partner is top reason for not having sexual relations.
75+ Years	Weight and girth continue to decrease until at least age 80. About 15% are obese.	Wrinkles and loss of skin elasticity increase.	Visual and hearing losses continue.	Bone mass continues to decline. Risk for fractures increases sharply, especially for women.	Neuronal loss continues.	Continued low levels of major hormones.	Sexual responses continue to decline, though many continue to enjoy sexual relations throughout adulthood.

2.2.1: Weight and Body Composition

OBJECTIVE: Outline changes to body composition over time

The U.S. Department of Health and Human Services reports that changes in total body weight follow a pattern over adulthood.

As you can see in Figure 2.1, this pattern takes the shape on a graph of an inverted U (Fryar et al., 2016). The upswing in weight that takes place during young adulthood and middle age can be attributed to our tendency to become more and more sedentary during that time without changing our eating habits to compensate (Masoro, 2011). Much of the downturn in total body weight that takes place in later adulthood is due to loss of bone density and muscle tissue (Florido et al., 2011).

Figure 2.1 Changes in Weight Over Adulthood

Total body weight for men and women rises from the 20s to the 40s, stays fairly level into the 50s and 60s, then declines in the 70s.

SOURCE: Data from Fryar et al. (2016).

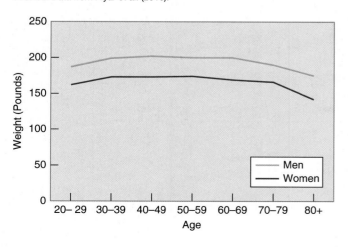

Along with changes in total body weight, there are also changes in where the weight is distributed; starting in middle age, fat slowly leaves the face and extremities and begins to accumulate around the abdomen, resulting in a loss of plump cheeks and lips, a loss of protective padding on the soles of the feet, and a gain in waistline circumference.

When a person's total body weight is more than what is considered optimally healthy for their height, they are considered *overweight*. This is a concern for adults of all ages, and rightly so—almost two-thirds of us in the United States are above optimal weight. Being overweight can impair movement and flexibility, and it can alter appearance. Our society does not generally view overweight individuals as healthy and attractive, and this can result in social and economic discrimination (Lillis et al., 2011).

When the weight-to-height ratio increases to the point that it has an adverse effect on the person's health, it is a medical condition known as **obesity**. The Centers for Disease Control and Prevention (CDC) reports that over one-third of adults in the United States have this condition (Ogden et al., 2015).

How do you stand in the body composition evaluation? Table 2.2 shows how to find your **body mass index (BMI)** by finding your height (in inches) in the far left column and moving across that row to find your weight. The number at the top of the column is your BMI. According to the CDC (2016a), BMIs less than 18.5 are considered underweight, 18.5–24 are considered normal weight, 25–29 are overweight, and 30 and above are obese. This is not a perfect system because some healthy, very muscular people would be assigned the "overweight" label based on their height and weight, but most health organizations and medical researchers around the world use BMI to evaluate body composition.

Adults who are 40–59 years of age are slightly more likely to be obese, but as you can see in Figure 2.2, the proportion

Table 2.2 Find Your BMI

	Body Mass Index (BMI)																						
Weight (Pounds)		Normal						Overweight					Obese										
Height (Inches)	19	20	21	22	23	24	25	26	27	28	29	30	31	32	33	34	35	36	37	38	39	40
58	91	96	100	105	110	115	119	124	129	134	138	143	148	153	158	162	167	172	177	181	186	191
59	94	99	104	109	114	119	124	128	133	138	143	148	153	158	163	168	173	178	183	188	193	198
60	97	102	107	112	118	123	128	133	138	143	148	153	158	163	168	174	179	184	189	194	199	204
61	100	106	111	116	122	127	132	137	143	148	153	158	164	169	174	180	185	190	195	201	206	211
62	104	109	115	120	126	131	136	142	147	153	158	164	169	175	180	186	191	196	202	207	213	218
63	107	113	-118	124	130	135	141	146	152	158	163	169	175	180	186	191	197	203	208	214	220	225
64	110	116	122	128	134	140	145	151	157	163	169	174	180	186	192	197	204	209	215	221	227	232
65	114	120	126	132	138	144	150	156	162	168	174	180	186	192	198	204	210	216	222	228	234	240
66	118	124	130	136	142	148	155	161	167	173	179	186	192	198	204	210	216	223	229	235	241	247
67	121	127	134	140	146	153	159	166	172	178	185	191	198	204	211	217	223	230	236	242	249	255
68	125	131	138	144	151	158	164	171	177	184	190	197	203	210	216	223	230	236	243	249	256	262
69	128	135	142	149	155	162	169	176	182	189	196	203	209	216	223	230	236	243	250	257	263	270
70	132	139	146	153	160	167	174	181	188	195	202	209	216	222	229	236	243	250	257	264	271	278
71	136	143	150	157	165	172	179	186	193	200	208	215	222	229	236	243	250	257	265	272	279	286
72	140	147	154	162	169	177	184	191	199	206	213	221	228	235	242	250	258	265	272	279	287	294
73	144	151	159	166	174	182	189	197	204	212	219	227	235	242	250	257	265	272	280	288	295	302
74	148	155	163	171	179	186	194	202	210	218	225	233	241	249	256	264	272	280	287	295	303	311
75	152	160	168	176	184	192	200	208	216	224	232	240	248	256	264	272	279	287	295	303	311	319
76	156	164	172	180	189	197	205	213	221	230	238	246	254	263	271	279	287	295	304	312	320	328

SOURCE: CDC (2016a).

Figure 2.2 Obesity in the United States

The proportion of people in the United States who are obese is highest for women and for those between the ages of 40 and 59.

SOURCE: Ogden et al. (2015).

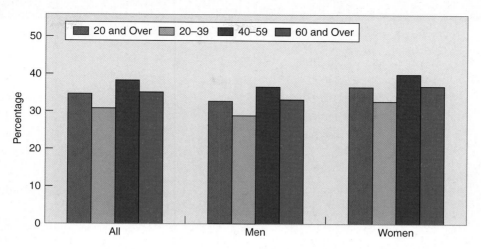

of obese adults in other age groups is not much lower. Still, the fact remains that over one-third of all adults (and 17% of children) have total body weight that is considered a serious medical condition (Ogden et al., 2015).

What can be done about age-related changes in body composition? An active lifestyle in young adulthood and middle adulthood will help minimize age-related weight gain and the amount of fat that accumulates in the abdomen at middle age. Healthy eating habits can reduce excess fat. However, nothing has been found that will totally *prevent* these changes.

2.2.2: Skin Changes

OBJECTIVE: Characterize how skin changes with age

Youth is signaled by smooth skin, but beginning about age 45, wrinkles become evident, resulting in part from redistribution of body fat. Wrinkles also occur because of an age-related loss of elasticity that affects muscles, tendons, blood vessels, and internal organs as well as skin. The loss of elasticity is especially noticeable in skin that has been continually exposed to the sun, such as the skin of the face and hands.

From a quick trip down the beauty aisle of a drugstore or a look at the annual earnings of a cosmetic company, you would get the impression that many miracle cures are available for aging skin. However, the only effective products available over the counter are those that will cover up the wrinkles and age spots. One product available by prescription seems to be effective in reversing skin damage due to exposure to the sun. Several well-designed lab studies have shown that applying Retin-A (tretinoin) to the skin for several months not only changed the appearance

of damaged skin but also reversed some of the underlying changes that had occurred (Rosenfeld, 2005). It is much easier to prevent sun damage by limiting strong, direct sun exposure. When that is not possible, it helps to use sunblock and protective clothing (Porter, 2009).

Skin damage that is too severe to be remedied by prescription creams can be treated by medical procedures, such as chemical peels or microdermabrasion, in which the outer layers of the skin are removed. As you might expect, these minimally invasive procedures are more expensive than skin creams and carry more risks. Nevertheless, many people have been pleased with the results and find that when they look younger, they feel younger. Table 2.3 shows the top procedures performed by plastic surgeons in the United States, along with the average surgeon's fee and the percentage of patients having these procedures in each of five age groups. As you can see, the 40- to 54-year-old age group makes up the largest segment (48%) for plastic surgery procedures (American Society of Plastic Surgeons, 2016).

Men make up about 13% of plastic surgery patients. Surgical procedures that are popular with both genders are nose reshaping, liposuction, and eyelid surgery. Women use it for breast augmentation and tummy tucks; men choose breast reduction and face-lifts. There has been a recent increase in two other surgical procedures for men—buttock lifts and buttock implants (American Society of Plastic Surgeons, 2016).

Several minimally invasive procedures have increased in popularity recently for both men and women. One is injections of Botox, a diluted preparation of a neurotoxin that paralyzes the muscles under the skin and eliminates creases and frown lines. This is now the most frequent procedure done by plastic surgeons for both men and women. Another popular procedure is injections of

Table 2.3 Top Plastic Surgery Procedures in the United States, Prices, Number, and Age of Patients

Procedure	Average Surgeon's Fee	Number of Procedures Performed in 2011	Percent of Patients in Each Age Group				
			13–19 Years	20–29 Years	30–39 Years	40–54 Years	55+ Years
Minimally Invasive Procedures							
Botox	$ 382	6,757,198	0	1	18	57	23
Soft-tissue filler	$ 949	2,440,724	0	3	11	50	36
Chemical peel	$ 636	1,310,252	1	1	13	42	44
Laser hair removal	$ 290	1,116,708	6	22	29	36	7
Microdermabrasion	$ 138	800,340	1	8	23	44	24
Cosmetic Surgery Procedures							
Breast augmentation	$3,822	279,143	3	29	37	29	2
Liposuction	$3,009	222,051	2	15	34	39	10
Nose reshaping	$4,771	217,979	14	32	24	21	10
Eyelid surgery	$2,880	203,934	1	2	6	43	48
Tummy tuck	$5,502	127,967	0	9	35	41	14

SOURCE: American Society of Plastic Surgeons (2016).

hyaluronic acid (Restylane or other products). This is a natural substance found in connective tissues throughout the body, and it cushions, lubricates, and keeps the skin plump. When injected into soft tissue, it fills the area and adds volume, temporarily reducing wrinkles and sagging of the skin. Botox has to be reinjected every few months; Restylane lasts somewhat longer—typically 6 months. Both procedures need to be administered by qualified medical professionals, and they carry slight risks. And needless to say, all are expensive—with Botox at an average of $382 a treatment and hyaluronic acid an average of $949—which is not covered by most health-care insurance plans (American Society of Plastic Surgeons, 2016).

Table 2.3 also shows the proportion of patients having these procedures in each age group. For example, the younger group (13–19 years) favors nose reshaping, whereas the older group (55 and older) tends to have eyelid surgery. It's an interesting picture of what procedures are favored at different ages. It is also interesting to see that almost half of all procedures are undertaken by people from 40 to 54 years of age, probably reflecting the intersection of declining youth and increasing incomes.

2.2.3: Hair

OBJECTIVE: Describe issues associated with hair and the aging process

Hair loss is a common characteristic of aging for both men and women, although it is more noticeable in men. About 67% of men in the United States show some hair loss by the age of 35, and 85% show significantly thinning hair by 50 (American Hair Loss Association, 2010). Graying of hair differs widely among ethnic groups and among individuals within any one group. Asian Americans, collectively, gray much later than Americans of European descent, for example. Figure 2.3 shows the various stages of typical patterns of hair loss.

Figure 2.3 Typical Hair Loss Patterns

There are several typical hair-loss patterns for men, and they proceed in predictable stages.

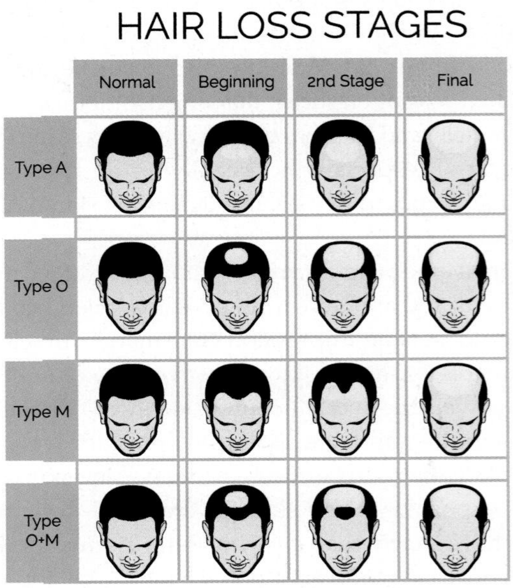

HAIR LOSS STAGES

Men and women have used chemical and natural dyes to conceal gray hair throughout history, and it is still a widespread practice today. Other old solutions in new boxes are wigs, hairpieces, and hair replacement "systems." In addition, drugs are available that slow down or reverse hair loss, some over the counter for men and women, such as Rogaine (monoxidil), and others by prescription for men only, such as Propecia (finasteride). The most extreme solution to hair loss is hair transplant, a surgical procedure in which small plugs of hair and skin are transplanted from a high-hair-growth area of the body to the hairless part of the scalp. Over 15,000 people in the United States underwent this procedure in 2015, about 70% of them men and most of them over the age of 55 (American Society of Plastic Surgeons, 2016). Again, none of these antiaging measures actually turns back the clock, but when they are done by experienced professionals and patients have realistic expectations, they can give a good morale boost for those who need one.

WRITING PROMPT

Looking Younger

Do you plan to (or have you) take(n) measures to influence your age-related appearance? Why or why not?

▶ The response entered here will appear in the performance dashboard and can be viewed by your instructor.

Submit

2.3: The Changing Senses

OBJECTIVE: Summarize how the senses change with age

Another series of body changes noted by many adults as they age affects the senses of vision, hearing, taste, and smell. Vision is by far the most researched, followed by hearing, with taste and smell trailing far behind.

∨ By the end of this module, you will be able to:

2.3.1 Describe age-related vision changes

2.3.2 Relate hearing to the experience of aging

2.3.3 Explain how taste and smell change with age

2.3.1: Vision

OBJECTIVE: Describe age-related vision changes

Vision is the last sense to develop in infants and the first to show signs of decline in middle age. It is also the sensory system that has the most complex structure and function and, as you might guess, has the most to go wrong.

Figure 2.4 Diagram of Eye with Labels
Cross section view of the human eye.

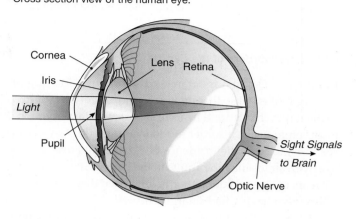

A diagram of the parts of the eye is shown in Figure 2.4. During normal aging, the **lens** of the eye gradually thickens and yellows, and the **pupil** loses its ability to open efficiently in response to reduced light. The result is that the older we get, the less light gets to our **retina**, the site of visual receptor cells. In fact, by age 60, our retinas are getting only one-third of the light they did in our 20s (Porter, 2009). One of the changes we experience as a result is a gradual loss of **visual acuity**, the ability to perceive detail in a visual pattern. To test this yourself, try reading a small-print book both indoors where you usually study and outdoors in full sunlight. If you are like most adults, you will notice that the clarity of the print is better in bright sunlight.

Around the age of 45, the lens of the eye, which has been accumulating layers of cells since childhood and gradually losing elasticity, shows a sharp decrease in its ability to **accommodate**, or change shape to focus on near objects or small print. This loss further reduces overall visual acuity in middle-aged and older adults. Most people with reduced visual acuity or loss of near vision, a condition known as **presbyopia**, can function quite well with prescription glasses or contact lenses.

Another visual change that takes place throughout adulthood is a gradual loss of **dark adaptation**, the ability of the pupil to adjust to changes in the amount of available light. This begins around age 30, but most people experience a marked decline after the age of 60. This causes minor inconveniences, such as difficulty reading menus in dimly lit restaurants or finding seats in darkened movie theaters. It also causes more dangerous situations, such as problems seeing road signs at night or recovering from the sudden glare of oncoming headlights. This is one of the reasons older people prefer attending matinee performances, making "early-bird" dinner reservations, and taking daytime classes at the university instead of participating in nighttime activities.

AGE-RELATED EYE DISORDERS Three more age-related conditions in the visual system may or may not be part of normal aging, but they are so common that I include them here.

Common Disorders of the Eye

Cataracts—The first is **cataracts**, the gradual clouding of the lens of the eye so that images are no longer transmitted to the retina sharply and in accurate color. Cataracts are the most common eye disorder found in adulthood. As you can see in Figure 2.5, the incidence of cataracts increases with age, with almost half the adults in the United States who are 75 years of age or older either having been diagnosed with cataracts or having had cataract surgery.

This outpatient procedure is done quickly and safely under local anesthesia. It involves removing the cloudy part of the lens and implanting an artificial lens that can even be designed to correct for loss of visual acuity and, in some cases, loss of near vision. Cataract surgery has become the most common surgical procedure in the United States; over 3 million are done each year. However, despite the ease of surgery and the fact that the procedure is covered under Medicare, cataracts remain a major cause of vision loss in the United States (Centers for Disease Control and Prevention, 2015b) and the leading cause of blindness in developing countries (World Health Organization, 2016).

Risk Factors for Cataracts

- Increased age
- Diabetes
- Family history
- European ancestry
- Extensive exposure to sunlight.*
- Smoking*
- Obesity*

*Can be controlled or prevented.

SOURCES: American Academy of Ophthalmology (2018); National Eye Institute (2015).

Glaucoma—A second common age-related condition of the visual system is **glaucoma**, a buildup of pressure inside the eye that ultimately can destroy the optic nerve and lead to blindness. Glaucoma is the third leading cause of blindness for all people in the United States and the second leading cause of blindness for people with African ancestry. Glaucoma can be treated with eye drops, laser treatment, or surgery, but first it has to be detected. What are the warning signs of glaucoma? Like other hypertension problems, there are not many. It is estimated that almost 3 million people in the United States currently have glaucoma, but only half are aware that they have it. Glaucoma can be detected as part of a routine eye examination, and it is recommended that people

Figure 2.5 2010 U.S. Prevalence Rates for Cataract by Age and Race

The risk of developing cataracts increases, beginning about age 40 years, for all racial and ethnic groups in the United States, but the increase for white individuals is greater after 70 years.

SOURCE: National Eye Institute (2015).

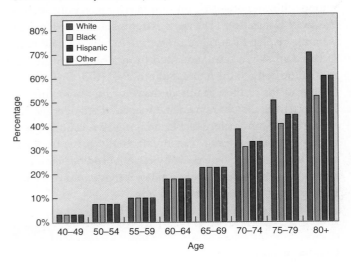

in high-risk groups be screened at age 40. Everyone should be screened at 60 (Glaucoma Research Foundation, 2016).

Risk Factors for Glaucoma

- Increased age
- Family history
- African or Mexican ancestry
- Diabetes

SOURCES: American Academy of Ophthalmology (2018); Glaucoma Research Foundation (2016); National Eye Institute (2015).

Age-Related Macular Degeneration—A third common condition of the visual system is **age-related macular degeneration**, a disorder that affects the retina, causing central vision loss. The cause of this disorder is not clear, but the prevalence is; the risk stays low for all groups until the age of 75, when it increases dramatically for white individuals. Vitamin therapy and laser treatment have shown hopeful results for some types of this disorder, and rehabilitative interventions have helped people with low vision to function independently and increase their quality of life (National Eye Institute, 2015).

Risk Factors for Age-Related Macular Degeneration

- Increased age
- Family history
- European ancestry
- Smoking*

*Can be controlled or prevented.

SOURCES: American Academy of Ophthalmology (2018); Glaucoma Research Foundation (2016); National Eye Institute (2015).

THE IMPACT OF OCULAR CHANGES The overall result of declining visual ability over middle and late adulthood can be limiting in many ways. Often older adults give up driving, which means they are no longer able to do their shopping and no longer as able to visit friends, participate in leisure activities, attend religious services, or go to doctors' offices on their own. There is also a loss of status for some older adults when they must stop driving. Decreased vision is associated with many other problems in older adults, such as falls, hip fractures, family stress, and depression.

The World Health Organization (2015) estimates that over 80% of visual impairments worldwide can be prevented or cured. Problems involve lack of information about diagnosis and treatment, such as the mistaken belief many adults have that the eye exam given to renew drivers' licenses will screen for these visual conditions. Another problem is that many people in the United States and around the world live in areas without access to eye-care specialists. And still another problem arises when older adults and their family members believe that failing eyesight is an unavoidable part of aging.

2.3.2: Hearing

OBJECTIVE: Relate hearing to the experience of aging

Around age 30, many adults begin to experience some hearing loss, mainly of higher-pitched tones. There is also shortening of the *loudness scale*—that is, there is confusion between loud tones that are not being heard as well as before and softer tones that are still being heard accurately. Without the loud–soft discrimination, it is difficult to perceive which sounds are coming from nearby and which

are from across a noisy room—which words are coming from your dinner partner and which from the server taking an order two tables over. This condition is known as **sensorineural hearing loss**, and it is caused by damage to the tiny hairs inside the **cochlea**, a small shell-shaped structure in the inner ear. This mechanism is responsible for picking up sound vibrations and turning them into nerve impulses that will be transmitted to the hearing centers of the brain.

Although age-related hearing loss is gradual for most people, it can reach a point that it has serious effects on peoples' lives. The obvious effects are problems in the workplace and in social situations. And at a time of life that medical information becomes more and more important, over half of people over 60 years of age in one study report that they have misunderstood instructions from their doctors (Cudmore et al., 2017). Less obvious effects are feelings of isolation, depression, and paranoia (Hearing Loss Association of America, 2017).

The prevalence of hearing loss increases with age and is more extreme in men than in women (Hoffman et al., 2017). Figure 2.6 shows this increase by age and gender at two time spans. There is some good news. The rate of hearing loss was higher in the 1999–2004 group (Panel A) than in the more recent 2011–2012 group (Panel B). This decrease is probably the result of a reduction in workplace noise, which is regulated by the U.S. Bureau of Labor.

Table 2.4 shows how loud workplace sounds are allowed to be at certain durations of time. For example, constant noise throughout the workday can't be more than 90 decibels.

Although workplace noise is more controlled now, many of our after-hours and weekend activities involve noise that exceeds safe levels of 85 decibels. For example,

---

Figure 2.6 Prevalence of Hearing Loss in Men and Women at Two Time Spans

SOURCE: Hoffman et al. (2017).

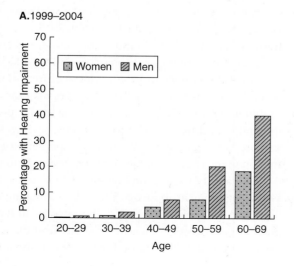
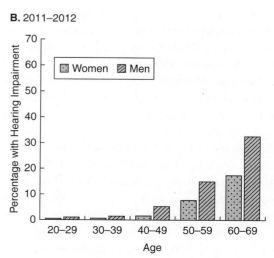

Table 2.4 Permissible Noise Exposure

Duration (Hours Per Day)	Sound Level (Decibels)
8	90
6	92
4	95
3	97
2	100
1½	102
1	105
½	110
¼ or less	115

SOURCE: U.S. Department of Labor (2012).

motorcycles produce 98 decibels of noise, snowmobiles 100 decibels, rock concerts 125 decibels, and a gunshot at 100 feet produces 140 (Hearing Loss Association of America, 2017).

HEARING AIDS AND PSADS What can be done about hearing loss? Hearing aids are effective for some types of hearing loss, but not many people use them. Only 33% of people in the United States diagnosed with hearing loss actually use hearing aids. One reason is the cost; the average hearing aid costs $2,400, and most people need one for each ear. Medicare does not pay for them and neither do most private insurance policies (Grundfast & Liu, 2017). However, the rate of hearing-aid use is low in countries that do pay for them, such as Norway (only 43%), and within groups that provide them for free, such as the Veteran's Administration (less than 50%) (Valente & Amlani, 2017).

Clearly, it is not just the cost that undermines hearing-aid use, but also that it usually requires visiting an audiologist to be examined, being prescribed a particular device, having it fitted to your own specifications, and then returning several times to have it fine-tuned. Recently, many people with hearing loss have been buying personal sound amplification devices (PSADs) that look a lot like hearing aids but cost between $50 and $500. When a team of researchers compared several PSADs with a state-of-the art hearing aid, using a convenience sample of 42 participants with hearing loss, they found that three of the five PSADs improved the understanding of speech accuracy almost as well as the hearing aid. Mean score for the hearing aid was 88% while the three PSADs were 87%, 87%, and 84%. The cost for the hearing aid was $1,910 and the three PSADs were $350, $350, and $300 (Reed et al., 2017). Other people with hearing loss buy over-the-counter hearing aids and electronic devices that amplify sound. None of these are approved by the U.S. Food and Drug Administration

(FDA) for hearing loss, but people seem to like the price and the ability to "unpack a box and plug it in their ear." Several large wholesale companies have begun selling the three most popular hearing aids online. These three hearing aids fit about 85% of the population that has hearing loss. This seems similar to buying over-the-counter reading glasses. In addition, online companies will send prescription hearing aids to people who have seen an audiologist and have an audiogram of the pattern of their individual hearing loss (Grundfast & Liu, 2017).

WRITING PROMPT

Disparities

What are some of the economic and social effects of hearing aids being so expensive and not covered by Medicare or most health-care plans?

 The response entered here will appear in the performance dashboard and can be viewed by your instructor.

Submit

2.3.3: Taste and Smell

OBJECTIVE: Explain how taste and smell change with age

Taste and smell depend on three mechanisms that interact to enable us to enjoy the food we eat and the fragrances in our environment. They also provide survival information that keeps us from eating food that is spoiled and warns us of dangerous substances such as smoke or gas leaks. These mechanisms consist of smell, taste, and common chemical sense. *Smell* takes place in the **olfactory membrane**, a specialized part of the nasal cavity. It consists of 350–400 types of odor receptors, and we perceive the results as subtle and complex scents. In addition, we experience *taste* through the **taste buds**, which are receptor cells found on the tongue, mouth, and throat. The five basic tastes that our species can sense are sweet, salty, sour, bitter, and umami, which is a mouth-filling, savory taste (Owen, 2015). Receptors on the moist surfaces of the mouth, nose, throat, and eyes sense irritating properties of food and odors—things like the spiciness of chili peppers and the coolness of mint (Fukunaga et al., 2005). All three types of receptors take information to different parts of the brain, where the total experience is integrated and translated into messages, such as knowing you are having a pleasurable dining experience or that the milk in your refrigerator has outlived its expiration date.

The ability to taste and smell declines over the adult years, beginning at about age 30 and becoming more noticeable around 65 or 70. Over 2 million people in the United States have disorders of taste or smell, and most of them are older adults. One reason for this is that the amount of mucus in the nasal cavity is reduced so that odor molecules do not bind to the receptors as well as they do in younger people. Similarly, there is a reduction in the amount of saliva produced when chewing food, reducing the release of molecules in food to be sensed by the taste buds. There are fewer receptor cells, both in the sinus cavity and the mouth—about half as many at 70 years of age as at 20. Years of smoking and living in areas with air pollution contribute to the loss of taste and smell. Some diseases have this effect, as well as the use of some medications, both of which are more common in older adults (Douglass & Heckman, 2010).

The results can be minor ones. We prefer salsa to ketchup on our food. We use more salt and spices. We put extra sugar or sweetener in our coffee. Or they can be more serious, when food loses its appeal and older adults skip meals. The reduced sense of smell can cause older people to eat food that has spoiled and may interfere with their ability to smell dangerous odors such as the rotten-egg smell natural gas companies add to their product to signal a leak in the lines.

2.4: How Age Changes Internal Structures and Systems

OBJECTIVE: Analyze the social impact of age-related changes to the body

Most of us are concerned about our outward appearance and how it will change as we navigate the years of adulthood. Many of the most obvious signs of aging belong in this category, and we see them in our parents and grandparents, in our friends, and sometimes in our mirrors. Perhaps less obvious are those changes taking place beneath the surface—in our muscles and bones and heart and lungs and in our ability to fight off disease and infection. In this section, we examine these age-related changes to internal structures and systems.

⌄ **By the end of this module, you will be able to:**

2.4.1 Determine the impacts of age-related bone and muscle changes

2.4.2 Explain how the cardiovascular and respiratory systems change with age

2.4.3 Identify age-related changes to the nervous system

2.4.4 Summarize age-related changes to the immune system

2.4.5 Differentiate how hormone changes affect males and females

2.4.1: Bones and Muscles

OBJECTIVE: Determine the impacts of age-related bone and muscle changes

The major change involved in primary aging of the bones is calcium loss, which causes bones to become less dense. Peak bone mass is reached around the age of 30, followed by a gradual decline for both men and women, but the overall effect of this bone loss is greater for women for several reasons. First, women's bones are smaller and contain less calcium—in other words, even if the decline were equal, women begin at a disadvantage. Second, the decline is not equal; women's bone loss rate shows a marked acceleration between the ages of 50 and 65, whereas men's decline is more gradual. Severe loss of bone mass, or **osteoporosis**, makes the bones more likely to break than those of a younger person. There is controversy over whether or not osteoporosis is a disease because the process is not distinguishable from normal aging of the bones, except in degree of severity.

OSTEOPOROSIS Osteoporosis is based on a measure of **bone mass density (BMD)**, which is easily determined with a test called a DXA (dual-energy X-ray absorptiometry) scan of the hips and spine. The results are compared to those of a young healthy person. BMD measures at either hip or spine that are more than 2.5 standard deviations below normal are considered osteoporosis.

According to the CDC, osteoporosis affects 16% of people over age 65. Women are four times more apt to have osteoporosis than men, and individuals with Mexican American heritage are more likely to have osteoporosis than those of non-Hispanic white or non-Hispanic black heritage (Looker & Frenk, 2015).

The biggest problem caused by osteoporosis is the increased risk of injury after a fall. Diminished eyesight and a decreased sense of balance result in a greater number of falls as we get older. When brittle bones enter the equation, falls can result in serious injury, disability, loss of independent living, and even death. The typical sites of breaks are the wrist, spine, and hip.

New strategies to prevent osteoporosis focus on promoting bone health throughout life, starting with childhood, through proper diet containing required amounts of calcium and vitamin D. Healthy bones also require a regimen of exercise of the weight-bearing muscles, including high-impact exercise such as running and jumping. Peak bone mass is reached in the late teens and early 20s, and the denser the bone mass is at this age, the lower the risk for osteoporosis in later life (National Osteoporosis Foundation, 2016).

Measuring bone mass density is becoming more and more a part of routine examinations by gynecologists, internists, and family physicians. Treatment of bone loss includes vitamin D, estrogen, and drugs that slow down bone loss and increase the rate of bone formation. Recently more emphasis is being placed on *patient adherence* to treatment for bone loss. Patients are being urged to refill their prescriptions before they run out of medication and to follow the instructions carefully to ensure that the drug is being absorbed well into the system and to avoid unpleasant side effects. Medication-delivery systems are available that allow patients to take only one pill a month or one IV treatment a year.

Risk Factors for Osteoporosis

- Increased age
- Family history
- Female gender
- European, Asian, or Latin ancestry
- History of earlier bone fracture
- Sedentary lifestyle*
- Smoking*
- Excessive alcohol consumption*
- Underweight BMI*

*Can be controlled or prevented.

SOURCES: CDC, 2015c; National Institute on Aging, 2013.

OSTEOARTHRITIS Over the adult years, bones also change at the joints. **Osteoarthritis** is a condition that occurs when the soft cartilage that covers the ends of the bones wears away with use and age. This allows the bones to rub together and causes pain, swelling, and loss of motion at the joint. The CDC (2015c) estimates that 34% of people who are 65 years of age or older have osteoarthritis. In older adults this condition is more prevalent in women; in younger adults it is more apt to appear in men and be the result of work and sports injuries.

Researchers are investigating the long-term effects of high-impact sports on bones and joints. Studies have been conducted with male elite athletes, defined as athletes playing at the national or professional levels of high-impact sports, to determine the relationship between participation in various sports and later osteoarthritis of the hip joint. One review of the available literature showed that there was an increase in the risk of hip osteoarthritis for men playing handball, soccer, and hockey, but the evidence for long distance running was not consistent (Vigdorchik et al., 2016).

Women athletes have not been studied enough for review articles, but one recent study involved women (and men) ballet dancers, an art form that can be as physically demanding as high-impact sports (Reider, 2016). Joshua D. Harris, a physician who specializes in orthopedic surgery and sports medicine, along with his colleagues (Harris et al., 2015) examined 47 male and female dancers from an international ballet company using radiographic images of their hip joints. He found evidence of a dysplasia (or deformity) of at least one hip joint in 89% of the dancers. This dysplasia was more apt to be found in female (92%) than male (74%) dancers. I should remind you that all these studies are cross-sectional, and longitudinal studies need to be conducted to determine how (or if) these risk factors and hip dysplasia develop into later-life osteoarthritis and whether some safeguards are possible, such as avoiding certain movements or wearing certain protective gear.

Osteoarthritis, no matter the cause, can lead to depression, anxiety, feelings of helplessness, lifestyle and job limitations, and loss of independence. However, most people with this condition find that the pain and stiffness of osteoarthritis can be relieved with anti-inflammatory and pain-relief medication, and also an appropriate balance of rest and exercise to preserve range of motion. Weight management is also helpful for many.

Some people with osteoarthritis report that they have found help through alternative and complementary medical treatment, such as acupuncture, massage therapy, vitamins, and nutritional supplements. Others have injections of *hyaluronic acid*, which is a natural component of cartilage and joint fluid. Studies are currently being done on all these treatments. For example, researchers recently conducted a meta-analysis of 29 randomized, controlled trials of over 17,000 acupuncture patients who either had needles inserted at traditional acupuncture sites or at sham sites, chosen randomly. When researchers asked patients about the effectiveness of the treatment in alleviating osteoarthritis pain, there was a modest but significant difference in the two treatments, showing that the results patients experience from traditional acupuncture sites are greater than a placebo effect (Vickers, Cronin, Maschino, et al., 2012).

When people with osteoarthritis cannot find relief with these treatments, there is the surgical option of joint replacement. In recent years, over 300,000 hip joints and over 600,000 knee joints have been replaced annually in the United States with high success rates. The vast majority of these surgeries are due to osteoarthritis (American Academy of Orthopaedic Surgeons, 2016a, 2016b).

Risk Factors for Osteoarthritis

- Increased age
- Female gender (after 50)
- Family history
- History of joint injury
- History of repeated joint stress*
- Overweight or obese BMI*

*Can be controlled or prevented.

SOURCES: CDC, 2015c; National Institute on Aging, 2013.

MUSCLE MASS AND STRENGTH With age, most adults experience a gradual decrease in muscle mass and strength. The reason for this is that the number of muscle fibers decreases, probably as a result of reduced levels of growth hormones and testosterone. Another normal, age-related change is that muscles slowly lose their ability to contract as quickly as they did at younger ages. In addition, older people do not regain muscle mass as quickly as younger people after periods of inactivity, such as when recovering from illness or injury. All this being said, most older people have adequate muscle strength to attend to the tasks they need to do, and many athletes stay at high levels of functioning. However, even the most fit will notice some decline as they age.

Two types of exercise help rebuild muscle mass and strength: *resistance training*, which involves contracting muscles by lifting or pushing and holding the contraction for up to 6 seconds, and *stretching*, which lengthens muscles and increases flexibility. Stretches should be held for 5 seconds when beginning, but up to 30 seconds with increased practice. One good way to combine these two types of exercise is water aerobics, and I have used that as part of my exercise plan for many years. Stretching is much easier when the water is supporting much of your weight, and the water also provides more resistance than doing the same exercises on land. I'm lucky enough to live in south Florida and can attend the outdoor classes year-round. (But to be honest, they do heat the pool in the winter, and I stay home when the air temperature is below 60 degrees.)

2.4.2: Cardiovascular and Respiratory Systems

OBJECTIVE: Explain how the cardiovascular and respiratory systems change with age

The cardiovascular system includes the heart and its blood vessels. You may be glad to hear that the heart of an older person functions about as well as a younger person on a day-to-day basis, unless there is some disease present. The difference arises when the cardiovascular system is challenged, as happens during heavy exercise: The older heart is slow to respond to the challenge and cannot increase its function as well as a younger heart.

Another age-related change is that the walls of the arteries become thicker and less supple, so they do not adjust to changes in blood flow as well as younger arteries. This loss of elasticity can cause hypertension, or high blood pressure, which is more prevalent in older people than in younger people. Figure 2.7 shows the proportion of men and women of different ages in the United States who have been diagnosed with high blood pressure. As you can see, the proportion increases with age for both men and women, with the proportion of women being lower than men until the 45–64 age group, then similar to men until the 75+ age group, when it exceeds the proportion for men (CDC, 2016c).

The respiratory system is made up of the lungs and the muscles involved in breathing. This system weakens slightly with age, but in healthy people who don't smoke, the respiratory function is good enough to support daily activities. As with the cardiovascular system, the difference is noticed when the system is challenged, as it is with vigorous exercise or at high altitudes (Beers, 2004).

One good piece of news is that regular exercise can reduce some of the effects of aging. Exercise can make the heart stronger and lower blood pressure; well-toned muscles can aid in circulation and breathing. Aerobic exercise, which includes brisk walking, running, and bicycling, is recommended for the cardiovascular and respiratory systems.

2.4.3: Brain and Nervous System

OBJECTIVE: Identify age-related changes to the nervous system

Many people believe that aging means deterioration of the brain, and research in the past seemed to support this, but more recent studies using new technology have shown that loss of **neurons**, or brain cells, in primary aging is much

---

Figure 2.7 Percentage of U.S. Men and Women by Age Group Who Have Been Diagnosed with High Blood Pressure
High blood pressure increases with age for both men and women.

SOURCE: CDC (2016).

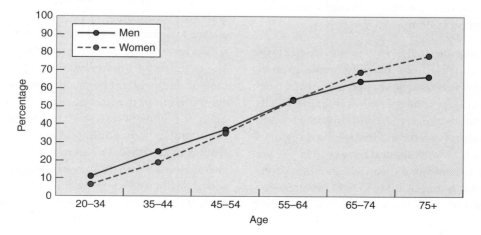

less severe than once thought. Evidence now shows that the nervous system is characterized by lifelong **plasticity**, meaning that neurons are capable of making changes with age. For example, neurons form new connections with other neurons, change thresholds and response rates, and take over the functions of nearby neurons that have been damaged (Beers, 2004).

Along with neuronal loss and plasticity, the role of **neurogenesis**, which is the production of new neurons from neural stem cells, takes place throughout the adult years in two parts of the brain. One is the *dentate gyrus*, a small area of the hippocampus that is crucial for forming memories; the other is the *subventricular zone*, which is part of the lining of the cavities in the brain where cerebrospinal fluid is produced (Apple et al., 2017). **Stem cells** are immature undifferentiated cells that can multiply easily and mature into many different kinds of cells, including neurons. Although neurogenesis continues well into older adulthood, the rate at which neurons are produced slows down as we age, presumably leading to age-related cognitive loss. Researchers are trying to find ways to boost the rate of neurogenesis in the later years either by increasing stem cell production or by identifying factors that lead to the slowdown and finding ways to reduce their effects. One promising line of research is caloric restriction, which preserves the production of stem cells and new neurons in the hippocampus of aged mice (Park et al, 2013) and memory function in adult mice (Hornsby et al., 2016). A growth factor found in the blood of young mice can promote neurogenesis and improve learning and memory when injected into old mice (Valleda et al., 2014).

Molecular neurobiologists Désirée Seib and Ana Martin-Villalba (2015) recommend an alternative method for maintaining brain health – exercise. It has been demonstrated in many research studies that exercise restores cognitive functioning and physical health in human research participants with few side effects. If you add some mentally challenging tasks, the result is increased neurogenesis and brain plasticity in older adulthood.

2.4.4: Immune System

OBJECTIVE: Summarize age-related changes to the immune system

The immune system protects the body in two ways: (1) the **B cells**, produced in the bone marrow, make proteins called **antibodies**, which react to foreign organisms (such as viruses and other infectious agents), and (2) the **T cells**, produced in the thymus gland, reject and consume harmful or foreign cells, such as bacteria and transplanted organs. B cells show abnormalities with age and have been implicated in the increase of autoimmune disorders in older adults. With age, T cells show reduced ability to fight new infection. It is difficult to establish that the aging body's decreasing ability to defend itself from disease is a process of primary aging. It is possible, instead, that the immune system becomes weakened in older adulthood as chronic diseases become more prevalent and exercise and nutrition decline.

Taking nutritional supplements to boost immune function is a topic of controversy. On one side are warnings from the FDA that supplements are not intended to treat, prevent, or cure disease. On the other side are research findings that various antioxidant supplements (vitamins C, E, and others) increase immune function in lab animals (Catoni et al., 2008) and the nutritional supplement manufacturers, who claim that their products will prevent (and reverse) many aspects of primary aging. My personal conclusion is that that unless your physician tells you otherwise, middle-aged adults (and younger adults) with relatively healthy diets and lifestyles don't need to take vitamin supplements. For older adults, especially those with appetite loss or who don't get outdoors much, a daily multivitamin may help and can't hurt—except for the cost (Porter, 2009).

2.4.5: Hormonal System

OBJECTIVE: Differentiate how hormone changes affect males and females

Both men and women experience changes in their hormonal systems over the course of adult life, beginning around the age of 30. Growth hormone decreases with age, reducing muscle mass. *Aldosterone* production decreases, leaving some older adults prone to dehydration and heatstroke when summer temperatures soar. However, as with many other aspects of primary aging, most of these changes are not noticeable until late adulthood (Halter, 2011). One more obvious change is the reduction of hormones that results in loss of reproductive ability, a time of life known as the **climacteric**. The climacteric takes place gradually for men over middle and late adulthood and more abruptly for women around the late 40s and early 50s.

Climacteric in Men and Women

The Climacteric in Men—Research on healthy adults suggests that the quantity of viable sperm produced begins to decline in a man's 40s, but the decline is not rapid, and there are documented cases of men in their 80s fathering children. The testes shrink gradually, and after about age 60, the volume of seminal fluid begins to decline. These changes are associated in part with testicular failure and the resulting gradual decline in **testosterone**, the major male hormone, beginning in early adulthood and extending into old age (Fabbri et al., 2016). Declining hormone levels in men are also associated with decreases in muscle mass, bone density, sexual desire, and cognitive functions and with increases in body fat and depressive symptoms (Almeida et al., 2004).

The Climacteric in Women—During middle adulthood, women's menstrual periods become irregular, then further apart, and then stop altogether. **Menopause** is defined as occurring 12 months after a woman's final menstrual period. The main cause of menopause is ovarian failure, leading to a drop in **estrogen** and complex changes in **progesterone**, both important hormones in women's reproductive health.

Menopause has not been a topic of vast research until the last few decades (Oertelt-Prigione et al., 2010). Common knowledge came from old wives' tales or advice passed down from mother to daughter. Fortunately, several large-scale longitudinal studies have contributed accurate, scientific-based information on the timing of menopause and the changes that most women experience during this process. One of the best-known and largest of these studies is the Women's Health Study (WHS), which has gathered data from almost 40,000 women health professionals over the age of 45. Although the initial study lasted only 10 years, researchers continue to gather data annually from the participants, and this has been the basis for valuable findings about women's health from middle age to the end of life (Buring & Lee, 2012). From studies such as the WHS, we know that the average age of menopause for women in the United States is 51.3 years, the most common range being from 47–55 years of age. Considering that women today can expect to live well into their 70s, most will spend about one-third of their lives in the postmenopause years.

As with men, this series of hormone changes is accompanied by changes in more than reproductive ability. There is some loss of tissue in the genitals and the breasts, and breast tissue becomes less dense and firm. The ovaries and uterus become smaller, the vagina becomes shorter and smaller in diameter with thinner and less elastic walls, and there is less lubrication produced in response to sexual stimulation.

The most frequently reported and most distressing physical symptom that comes with the menopausal transition is the *hot flash*, a sudden sensation of heat spreading over the body, especially the chest, face, and head. It is usually accompanied by flushing, sweating, chills, and often heart palpitations and anxiety. The duration of a hot flash averages about 4 minutes. About three-quarters of women reported experiencing hot flashes and about one-third of women in the WHS reported that they had consulted their doctors for treatment because the hot flashes were frequent and severe. Hot flashes continue for 1 or 2 years for most women.

About 20% of women report symptoms of depression around the time of menopause, especially those who have a history of depression earlier in their lives. The risk of depression declines after menopause (Dalal & Agarwal, 2015).

HORMONE REPLACEMENT *If primary aging is due to a decline in hormone production in men and women, why not replace the lost hormones and reverse the process?* This is not a new suggestion; it has been the impetus behind many failed "fountain-of-youth" therapies throughout history, including the injection of pulverized sheep and guinea pig testicles into patients in the 1890s and chimpanzee testicle and ovary implants into elderly men and women in the 1920s (Epelbaum, 2008). Needless to say, none of these measures restored youth, but more recent attempts to replace diminished hormone supplies in aging adults have met with some success. Although none reverse the aging process, they may alleviate some of the symptoms.

The most-used hormone replacement regimen is a combination of estrogen and progesterone prescribed for women at menopause. This **hormone replacement therapy (HRT)** provides women with the hormones once produced by their ovaries and can reduce some of the adverse symptoms of the climacteric. Hormone replacement therapy can alleviate hot flashes, vaginal dryness, and risk of bone fractures; however, research findings on the negative effects of HRT are mixed. According to the American Cancer Society (2015), some studies have shown that HRT can increase the risk of cancer of the breast, the ovaries, and the endometrium (lining of the uterus). The risk of HRT seems to depend on which hormones are replaced, how long the treatment continues, and the woman's overall medical history (Dalal & Agarwal, 2015). Some nonhormone treatments have been found effective, such as cognitive-behavioral therapy, hypnosis, antidepressants, and paroxetine salt, whereas others have not, such as paced respiration therapy and lifestyle changes that include wearing layers of clothing and avoiding spicy food. Exercise and yoga are also not very effective for alleviating hot flashes, but are helpful for overall good health (Jacob, 2016). Women are advised to talk to their physicians about their menopausal symptoms to decide on the best course of action for them.

Although controversial, testosterone replacement therapy is popular among middle-aged and older men in the form of injections, skin patches, and gels applied to the underarms. Although only about 20% of men over age 60 have lower-than-normal testosterone levels, prescriptions for testosterone replacement in the United States increased from 692,000 in 2000 to over 2 million in 2013, the majority being written by primary care physicians. Despite this increase in use, the benefits and risks of long-term testosterone replacement therapy are unknown at this time, and one of the side effects is the increased rate of division of cancer cells. Several medical associations including the FDA and the American Urological Association have called for more research into the health benefits and risks of this hormone treatment (Garnick, 2015).

DHEA and GH   Age-related declines in both sexes have been documented for two other hormones: **DHEA** (dehydroepiandrosterone) and **GH** (growth hormone). Not only do these hormones decline naturally with age, but animal studies suggest that replacing these hormones reverses aging and provides protection against disease. What about humans? Results have been mixed. An early study using DHEA with a small group of older men and women showed promise, but large clinical trials using placebo controls have failed to demonstrate that it has any effect on body composition, physical performance, or quality of life (Nair et al., 2006). A meta-analysis of 31 randomized, controlled studies of GH's effects on healthy adults over age 50 showed that there were small decreases in body fat and small increases in lean body mass, but increased rates of adverse effects such as increased fluid in soft tissues and fatigue (Liu et al., 2007). A later study showed that GH has little effect on healthy adults and that any increase in lean body mass is possibly due to fluid retention (Birzniece et al., 2011).

All that being said, DHEA is widely used by adults of all ages in the United States, where it is considered a nutritional supplement and sold in health food stores and over the Internet. GH is also widely available in the United States, despite the fact that it must be prescribed by a doctor and the FDA has not approved it as an antiaging drug. Products claiming to contain GH account for millions of dollars of Internet sales each year.

2.5: Changes in Physical Behavior

OBJECTIVE: Determine how age-related physical changes impact life as an older adult

The changes in various body systems discussed so far form the foundation for age-related changes in more complex behaviors and day-to-day activities. These changes include a gradual slowing of peak athletic performance; the decline of stamina, dexterity, and balance; changes in sleep habits; and the changes that occur in sexual functioning for both men and women.

∨	**By the end of this module, you will be able to:**

2.5.1   **Summarize how athletic abilities change with age**

2.5.2   **Identify age-related challenges in personal stamina, dexterity, and balance**

2.5.3   **Characterize sleep at different ages**

2.5.4   **Describe changes and continuities in sexual activity with age**

2.5.1: Athletic Abilities

OBJECTIVE: Summarize how athletic abilities change with age

In any sport, the top performers are almost always in their teens or 20s, especially any sport involving speed. Gymnasts peak in their teens, short-distance runners in their early 20s, and baseball players at about 27. As endurance becomes more involved in performance, such as for long-distance running, the peak performance age rises, but the top performers are almost always still in their 20s. Few of us have reached the heights of athletic superstars, but most of us notice some downturn in athletic ability shortly after the high school years.

Cross-sectional comparisons of athletes of different ages show these changes dramatically. Figure 2.8 shows the oxygen uptake for three groups of men ranging in age from 20 to 90 (Kusy et al., 2012). The group represented by the set of bars on the left consists of professional athletes and master athletes in Poland who trained for endurance sports (cyclists, triathletes, and long-distance runners). The group represented by the bars in the center is their countrymen who have trained for speed-power sports (sprinters, jumpers, and throwers). The set of bars on the right shows the oxygen uptake for untrained men, defined as those who do not have more than 150 minutes of vigorous activity per week. As you can see, the athletes trained for endurance sports have significantly higher levels of oxygen uptake than those trained for speed-power sports. And both types of athletes have significantly higher oxygen uptake levels than the nonathletes at all age levels. Furthermore, although the oxygen uptake of all the men declines with age, the differences in the three groups continue, with some trained athletes in their late 80s still testing higher than some nonathletes in their 20s. The lesson is clear: We slow down as we get older, but when we start out in better shape and keep exercising, we are still ahead of those who never trained at all.

2.5.2: Stamina, Dexterity, and Balance

OBJECTIVE: Identify age-related challenges in personal stamina, dexterity, and balance

In addition to loss of speed, all the physical changes associated with aging combine to produce a reduction in stamina, dexterity, and balance. The loss of **stamina**, which is the ability to sustain moderate or strenuous activity over a period of time, clearly arises in large part from the changes in the cardiovascular and respiratory systems, as well as from changes in muscles. **Dexterity**, the ability to use the hands or body in a skillful way, is lost primarily as a result of arthritic changes in the joints.

Figure 2.8 Age Differences in Oxygen Uptake

The ability to utilize oxygen is greater in endurance trained athletes than in speed-power trained athletes. Both types of training provide better oxygen uptake than no training at all. However, all groups show a decline with age.

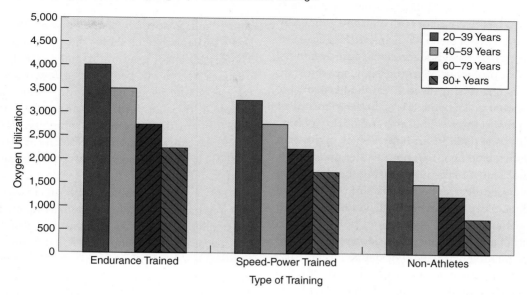

Another significant change, one with clear practical ramifications, is a gradual loss of **balance**, the ability to adapt body position to change. Older adults are likely to have greater difficulty handling uneven sidewalks or snowy streets or adapting the body to a swaying bus. All these situations require flexibility and muscle strength, both of which decline in old age. One result of less steady balance is a greater incidence of falls among older adults. As mentioned previously, declining eyesight and brittle bones combine with the decline in balance to produce a hazardous situation for older adults.

One remedy for loss of balance is regular exercise, including strength and flexibility training such as tai-chi, a gentle form of martial arts that emphasizes fluid movements and balance. Tai-chi is a traditional pastime of groups of older adults in China, now taught in many community centers in the United States and other countries as a type of "meditation in motion." Other suggestions include "fall-proofing" the home, for example, have well-lit stairs and no throw rugs, avoid loose-fitting shoes, and mark the edges of steps (CDC, 2015a).

2.5.3: Sleep

OBJECTIVE: Characterize sleep at different ages

Most of us think of sleep as simply the absence of conscious thought and purposeful activity, and this is true to some extent. It is a period of time set aside for cellular restoration, energy conservation, and consolidation of newly formed memories and learning. But sleep also has an active component. There are important processes going on while we sleep. We find new answers to problems we have mulled over during the day, our creativity is fired up after a good

night's sleep, and mental roadblocks have been circumvented during the night ranging from how to end the opera we are writing to how to solve a family relationship problem that seemed hopeless the night before (Lockley & Foster, 2012). So it stands to reason that it is important for us to get a healthy dose of sleep on a regular basis.

Adults typically need 7–8 hours of sleep per night, and this includes older adults, yet the CDC (2016d) finds that over a third of adults in the United States report getting less than that on a regular basis. This chronic lack of sleep can lead to increased accidents, heart disease, obesity, diabetes, cancer, and mental disorders and decreased immune function.

Sleep problems differ by age in adulthood. Emerging adults have sleep–wake cycles that are about 2 or 3 hours behind that of other adults, making them "night owls" who don't get sleepy until late at night and then don't feel wakeful until midmorning. This has been interpreted by generations of parents (and college professors) as laziness or lack of discipline, but sleep researchers come down on the side of the younger generation, stating that this is a normal developmental phenomenon and that parents and educators should be more understanding and let them sleep later (Carskadon, 2009).

SLEEP PATHOLOGIES Young adults continue to have sleep–wake cycles that are slightly behind their older counterparts, but most of their sleep problems are related to work schedules, family obligations, and stress. In middle age, lack of sleep due to health problems becomes a factor, especially if weight has increased and activity level has decreased. Stress also contributes to sleep problems at this age, when children are entering adulthood and careers are demanding (or uncertain). Menopause affects sleep with hot flashes, and there is also an increase in **sleep apnea**, which is a pause in breathing during sleep due to a constriction of the airway (Lockley & Foster, 2012). Sleep apnea has been declared a hidden health crisis for both men and women by the American Academy of Sleep Medicine (2016) because it is an underlying cause for work accidents, auto accidents, and major health problems. Warning signs are snoring, choking, and gasping during sleep. Treatment is available and about three-quarters of patients who undergo treatment for sleep apnea report improved health and quality of life.

Older adults sleep about an hour less at night than younger adults, waking about an hour earlier on average, but also are more apt to take naps during the day. Sleep problems in older adults can be the effect of physical and mental disorders. Sleep researchers believe that although sleep patterns change in old age, it does not mean that insomnia is part of aging—it's just that health problems and medication use increase with age (Lockley & Foster, 2012) and time spent exercising decreases (Buman et al., 2011).

Insomnia—the inability to sleep—increases with age and affects women more than men. There are three major causes. First, some people seem to be inherently predisposed to insomnia. Second are outside factors such as disease, medication, depression and anxiety, and stress. Third are lifestyle factors such as alcohol use, overuse of caffeine, lack of exercise, daily napping, and the use of blue-screen electronic devices before bedtime (and during the night). Besides not allowing us to clear our minds and relax, the light from tablets and phones mimics daylight and confuses the circadian rhythms much like jet lag does. Some people, especially adolescents and emerging adults, are extremely sensitive to this, and it results in insomnia.

As you can see, some of these factors can be changed easily and others not at all. It is relatively easy to monitor caffeine intake and get regular exercise, but dealing with health problems and medication requires working with your physician (Punnoose, 2012). However, making lifestyle changes is the best place to start before moving on to medication, which has not proven to be as safe and effective as it would seem on TV commercials.

WRITING PROMPT

How Do You Sleep?

Take a moment to reflect on how much sleep you tend to get. Are you a night owl or a morning lark? Have you always been that way? Do you ever have to deal with insomnia? If so, what do you do?

 The response entered here will appear in the performance dashboard and can be viewed by your instructor.

Submit

2.5.4: Sexual Activity

OBJECTIVE: Describe changes and continuities in sexual activity with age

As a result of normal changes in various systems of the body, sexual behavior shows the effects of primary aging. The key indicator used in research is the average number of times per month people of different ages have intercourse. A number of early studies showed that among people in their 20s with regular partners, the number is high—as much as 10 times or more per month, dropping to about 3 times per month for people in their 60s and 70s, and this is found in both cross-sectional and longitudinal studies.

However, one problem with this research question is that it reduces a very complex human interaction into a simple frequency count. Few studies tell us about the quality of the sexual relations people have at different ages or about types of sexual expression that don't involve intercourse. An exception was a study by social psychologists John DeLamater and Sara Moorman (2007) using data collected by the AARP in their Modern Maturity Sexuality Survey. In this survey, over 1,300 men and women from the ages of 45 to 94 were asked about sexual activities such as kissing and hugging, sexual touching, oral sex, and masturbation, as well as sexual intercourse. Although participation in all these sexual activities was related to age, other factors were important, too, such as physical ability, sexual desire, social surroundings, and environmental aspects of life at different points in adulthood. Let's look at some of these factors in more detail.

PHYSICAL ABILITY Studies of the physiological components of the sexual responses of younger men and women (age 20–40) compared to older men and women (age 50–78) show that there are differences in all four stages of sexual response (Medina, 1996; Shifren & Hanfling, 2010). These changes, which are described in Table 2.5, show that sexual responses of younger men and women are a little faster and a little more intense than in the older group. Although many changes may result in less sexual activity with age, some can have the opposite result, such as lack of concerns about pregnancy, more privacy in the home, greater experience, fewer inhibitions, and a deeper understanding of one's personal needs and those of one's partner (Fraser et al., 2004; Shifren & Hanfling, 2010).

One of the most prevalent sexual problems for men is **erectile dysfunction (ED)**, which is defined as the inability to have an erection adequate for satisfactory sexual performance. This problem occurs in about 30 million men in the United States and the incidence increases with age. About 12% of men younger than age 60 are affected, as

Table 2.5 Sexual Response in Older Adults (50–78 Years of Age) Compared to Younger Adults (20–40 Years of Age)

Phase	Women	Men
Physical changes	Decreased blood flow to genitals. Lower levels of estrogen and testosterone. Thinning of vaginal lining. Loss of vaginal elasticity and muscle tone.	Decreased blood flow to the genitals. Lower levels of testosterone. Less sensitivity in the penis.
Desire	Decreased libido. Fewer sexual thoughts and fantasies.	Decreased libido. Fewer sexual thoughts and fantasies.
Excitement	Slower arousal. Vaginal lubrication takes 1–5 minutes (compared to 15–30 seconds in younger women).	Greater difficulty achieving an erection. Erection after stimulation takes 10 seconds to several minutes (compared to 3–5 seconds in younger men). Erections not as rigid.
Plateau	Vagina does not expand as much. Less blood congestion in the clitoris and lower vagina. Diminished clitoral sensitivity (compared to the response of younger women).	Pressure for ejaculation is not felt as quickly (compared to younger men).
Orgasm	Less intense orgasms. Vagina contracts and expands in four to five smooth, rhythmic waves occurring at 0.8-second intervals (compared to 8–10 waves occurring at 0.8-second intervals in younger women). Uterus contracts and is sometimes more painful (compared to younger women).	Less intense orgasms. Urethra contracts in one to two waves at 0.8-second intervals (compared to three to four waves at 0.8-second intervals for younger men), and semen can travel 3–5 inches after expulsion (compared to 12–24 inches in younger men). Smaller volume of semen.
Resolution	Return to prearousal stage is more rapid (compared to younger women).	Return to prearousal stages takes only a few seconds (compared to return in younger men, which takes from minutes to hours). More time between erections.

SOURCES: Medina (1996); Shifren and Hanfling (2010).

are 22% of men age 60–69. Thirty percent of men over age 70 experience erectile dysfunction. Although ED occurs for many reasons (high blood pressure, diabetes, heart disease, side effects of medication, treatment for prostate cancer or bladder cancer), the underlying mechanism seems to be similar in many cases—a shortage of **cyclic GMP**, a substance that is released by the brain during sexual arousal. Part of the job of cyclic GMP is to close down the veins of the penis that normally drain away blood so that the blood supply increases and the tissues become engorged and erect. When cyclic GMP is in short supply, regardless of the reason, the result can be erectile dysfunction. In the last few decades, drugs have been developed—such as Viagra (sildenafil), Levitra (vardenafil), Cialis (tadalafil), and Stendra (avanafil)—that magnify the effects of cyclic GMP, making erections possible if even a small amount of the substance is present. In addition, men with erectile dysfunction are encouraged to make some lifestyle changes, such as not smoking, limiting or avoiding alcohol, increasing physical activity, and avoiding illegal drug use (National Institute of Diabetes and Digestive and Kidney Disorders, 2017).

As mentioned before, one of the effects of menopause for some women is vaginal dryness and the reduced ability to lubricate when sexually aroused. This is often alleviated by estrogen treatment, either pills, patches, or creams, or the use of an artificial lubricant. However, as

is discussed later in this section, sexual behavior involves more than erectile functioning and vaginal lubrication; there is also general health and well-being, relationship quality, conducive surroundings, and the perception of oneself as a sexual being, regardless of age. So far there is no "little blue pill" that will correct problems in all these areas.

SEXUAL DESIRE The desire to participate in sexual activity waxes and wanes throughout adulthood. For example, young adults report loss of desire when career pressures and parental responsibilities are at a peak. Middle-aged adults report increased sexual desire when the day-to-day responsibilities of parenthood end. Older adults report loss of desire because they believe that sex is only for the young or those with youthful bodies. But all in all, the desire to have sex is highest in emerging adulthood and declines with age as part of primary aging. Although lack of physical ability is the major sex-related complaint of men, clinicians report that lack of desire is by far the most common complaint of women (Tomic, Gallicchio, Whiteman, et al., 2006).

Sexual desire is driven by testosterone in women as well as in men. By menopause, women have about half of the amount of testosterone as they did in their 20s, and that decline can contribute to reduced desire for sex and briefer, less pleasurable orgasms for some women.

Testosterone replacement therapy for women is fairly recent and controversial. Several studies have shown that daily testosterone, delivered via a skin patch, can boost sexual desire and increase orgasms for postmenopausal women, but questions remain about the side effects, which can include excess hair growth, acne, liver problems, and lower levels of high-density lipoprotein cholesterol (the "good" cholesterol). The FDA has not given approval for the use of testosterone replacement for women with low sexual desire and will not until further long-term studies are completed (Shifren & Hanfling, 2010), though it is widely prescribed "off label."

In 2015, the FDA approved flibanserin (Addyi) as a treatment for low sexual desire in women. The manufacturer introduced it as a product to "even the score," in other words, to give women the same opportunities as men have with Viagara (Woloshin & Schwartz, 2016). The following year, researchers performed a meta-analysis on data from eight studies of the effects of flibanserin, which included almost 6,000 women. Participants were premenopausal or postmenopausal women who had been in monogamous relationships for at least 1 year and who had experienced a recent decrease in sexual desire. They had been randomly assigned to either a flibanserin group or a placebo group. After the course of treatment, women in the flibanserin group reported having 0.5 more "satisfying sexual experiences" per month than those in the placebo group. Although the difference was statistically significant, it was minimal. In addition, the women in the flibanserin group experienced significantly more side effects, such as dizziness, sleepiness, nausea, and fatigue (Jaspers et al., 2016).

Nearly 90% of U.S. physicians report that they would prescribe an approved drug for women reporting decreased sexual desire in middle age, but it doesn't seem that this particular drug is the answer. It should be noted that there are safe and proven remedies for sexual dysfunction that have been helpful to many couples, such as reducing alcohol consumption and stress, increasing exercise and quality time together as a couple, and consulting a professional sex therapist. Of course, physical ability and sexual desire are not the only considerations when it comes to adults having sex. Here are a few other sexual considerations.

Other Sexual Considerations

Sexual Partner—Regardless of age, the main reason most people do not have sexual relations is that they don't have a partner. Emerging adults may be new to the dating scene or busy with studies, not to mention living in their parents' homes. Young adults may be between partners or recovering from a bad breakup and just not ready to put themselves "out there" again. Middle-aged adults could be divorced after a long-term marriage and uncomfortable with the changes in the dating culture (and changes in themselves) since they were last single. And older adults, divorced or widowed, may have problems finding suitable sexual partners. This is especially true for women, who are more plentiful than men at this age. Whatever the reason, being without a suitable partner is a bigger factor in people's sex lives than their lack of physical abilities and desire.

For example, in a nationally representative sample of women from 28–84 years of age, medical researcher Holly N. Thomas and her colleagues (Thomas et al., 2015) asked over 2,000 women about their sexual activity. The proportion who said they had been sexually active in the past 6 months ranged from 90% of those under 40 to 15% of those in their 80s. One of the most important factors in whether they were sexually active or not was whether they lived alone or had a partner (were married or cohabiting). Those who had a live-in partner were eight times more likely to be sexually active than those who did not.

Privacy—For the older adults who are in nursing homes and for those who live with their adult children, privacy is a major stumbling block to sexual relations, even if they have the desire, the ability, and a willing partner. Nursing homes and other residential facilities for older adults can be problematic for sexually active residents, married or single. Courses in gerontology for nursing home directors and staff often include information on sexuality in older adults and how to structure the environment to be conducive to their activities (Mahieu & Gastmans, 2012). Homophobic attitudes make it very difficult for older lesbian, gay, bisexual, and transgender adults to establish or maintain relationships in nursing homes or the homes of their adult children. For many the answer has been retirement homes and assisted-living centers specifically for the LGBT+ community.

Other Forms of Sensual Activity—There are sources of arousal and sensual pleasure for older adults who lack partners or the physical capability to have intercourse. The National Survey of Sexual Health and Behavior found that almost half of men and almost a third of women 70–94 years of age reported engaging in masturbation in the past year (Laumann et al., 2008). A substantial number of men and women over age 50 report having oral sex in the past year, including about 25% of men and 8% of women over age 70 (DeLamater, 2012). We don't know if this was in place of vaginal intercourse or along with vaginal intercourse, and we don't know the statistics for same-sex couples. However, it seems clear that sexual interest and activity remain a significant part of life and relationships throughout the adult years.

Treatment for Sexual Problems—We previously discussed several treatments for sexual problems, such as medication for erectile dysfunction and various hormone replacement therapies. Studies have shown that somewhere between 10 and 40% of middle-aged and older adults have sought treatment from a professional for a problem related to sexual functioning. Although that is a pretty wide range, one thing is common among all the studies—over half of those who sought help did so from their primary care physician. This points out the need for these medical personnel (family practice physicians, nurse practitioners, and physician assistants) to possess an understanding of the treatment of sexual problems for patients of all ages. They also need to feel comfortable discussing the topic with even their oldest patients. Interestingly, the participants in this study who did seek treatment for sexual problems reported no increased frequency of intercourse after the treatment, but the majority of them did experience an increase in sexual satisfaction (DeLamater, 2012).

2.6: Individual Differences in Primary Aging

OBJECTIVE: Relate aging experiences to demographic influences

There is often a big difference between group means and individual measurements in research findings. In fact, the older we get, the more differences there are between us and our own agemates. If you have had the opportunity to attend a high school reunion, you will know what I mean. Seniors in high school are very similar, and they look and behave in much the same manner, but at your 10-year reunion—at the age of 28 or so—differences are already apparent. Some have not changed much from their 18-year-old appearances, but others have begun to show changes in body shape and thinning of hair. By the time you reach your 30-year reunion—at the age of 48 or so—the differences will be even more dramatic. What factors are involved in this diversity? And, more specifically, you may ask, "What factors might affect the aging process for *me*?"

	By the end of this module, you will be able to:
2.6.1	**Explain the heritability of aging**
2.6.2	**Relate lifestyle to how a person ages**
2.6.3	**Describe racial and socioeconomic impacts on the experience of aging**

2.6.1: Genetics

OBJECTIVE: Explain the heritability of aging

Twin studies and other family studies show that the number of years a person lives is moderately heritable (McClearn et al., 2001), but this may be primarily due to the absence of genetic predispositions for certain diseases. Still, living a long life doesn't tell us much about the rate of primary aging. Do genes influence the rate at which we age? Would a pair of identical twins start showing wrinkles at the same age and have their hair start turning gray together? In one study, researchers gathered data about the aging of skin at the annual Twins Festival in Twinsburg, Ohio, and compared identical twins' faces and those of fraternal twins. For 130 pairs of twins ranging up to 77 years of age, they found that the identical twin pairs were more alike in their facial skin aging patterns than the fraternal twin pairs and that the genetic contribution to facial skin aging is about 60%. This means that 40% of our facial skin aging is due to other causes, such as smoking and UV radiation exposure from the sun (Martires et al., 2009), as well as the use of tanning beds (Robinson & Bigby, 2011). In addition, about 60% of the variation in total body weight, as well as the pattern of age-related weight change, are influenced by genetics (Ortega-Alonso et al., 2009), though physical exercise can modify the genetic influence on both total body weight and waist circumference (Mustelin et al., 2009).

2.6.2: Lifestyle

OBJECTIVE: Relate lifestyle to how a person ages

Another broad category of factors that affect the rate of primary aging involves the lifestyle choices we make. This involves exercise, diet, and use of alcohol, tobacco products, and other substances. One of the most frequently mentioned risk factors for various age-related conditions is sedentary lifestyle. All experts on healthy aging emphasize the importance of an active lifestyle. I try to follow my own advice and get a balance of aerobic exercise, strength and flexibility training, and yoga. I attend early-morning classes almost every weekday before settling down at my desk to write. It does wonders for my back and gives me an energy boost. The social aspects of visiting with others in my classes are important to my mood, too.

Although I have never been a competitive athlete, I do take inspiration from master athletes. These people, who are 35 to 90 years of age (and older), train for athletic events and have better aerobic fitness, higher levels of "good" cholesterol, fewer risk factors for diabetes, and better bone density than their peers who are not master athletes. They also are able to consume more calories while weighing less than people of comparable ages who have more sedentary lifestyles (Rosenbloom & Bahns, 2006). This doesn't make them immune from primary aging, but their appearances and physical abilities are much "younger" than their chronological agemates.

For those who dread the idea of starting an exercise program, there is some encouraging news. Researchers have found that people typically think negatively about *starting* a physical workout regimen, but feel more positive about it once they get started. In other words, even if it seems difficult and unpleasant ahead of time, just do it. You will be happier once you get involved in it (Ruby et al., 2011).

Another important factor in primary aging is diet. I recently bit the bullet (and a lot of celery sticks) and lost 20 pounds that had crept up on me slowly over the last few years. Losing that 20 pounds increased my energy level and made me a little happier about exercising. I noticed when traveling that my knees didn't hurt after a long day of sightseeing, and I was not out of breath when I climbed stairs or hills (both a rarity in south Florida).

Adopting a healthy diet has multilevel benefits. But what is a "healthy diet?" We are all familiar with the recommended daily allowances of calories and various nutrients, but these recommendations often do not take age into account, giving recommendations only for children, adults, and pregnant or lactating women. Recently, the recommended daily requirement of vitamin D and protein were raised for older adults. Other research has shown that the reduced amount of stomach acid that comes with age can contribute to lower levels of vitamin B12 in older adults (Kritchevsky, 2016). It seems clear that "healthy diet" means different things for adults of different ages.

Another lifestyle factor that contributes to accelerated primary aging is exposure to UV radiation from the sun. This is a major cause of aging of the skin, specifically coarse texture, dark and white "age spots," and spider veins—those red webs that appear on the face and legs near the knees and ankles. Although aging of the skin is unavoidable in the long run, we can avoid premature aging by limiting the time we spend outdoors during peak sun exposure, wearing protective clothing, avoiding tanning beds, and using sunscreen.

2.6.3: Race, Ethnicity, and Socioeconomic Group

OBJECTIVE: Describe racial and socioeconomic impacts on the experience of aging

Race and ethnicity are risk factors for many conditions involved with primary aging such as obesity, glaucoma, macular degeneration, and osteoporosis, as we discussed earlier. But when socioeconomic factors are added to race and ethnicity, more differences emerge. Many factors that determine the rate of primary aging depend on education and income levels. Healthy eating requires information about nutrition, exercise takes time, and early screening and treatment for conditions such as glaucoma and osteoporosis are difficult unless families can afford medical care.

Some low-income neighborhoods are *food deserts*, meaning that residents have limited access to fresh fruits and vegetables, food is relatively expensive, and residents have little access to transportation so they can shop elsewhere. The American Nutrition Association (2011) points out that food deserts not only lack healthy food, but they are also usually areas that have a high density of fast-food restaurants and quickie marts offering processed food that is high in sugar and fat. Figure 2.9 shows the prevalence of food deserts in the United States. For this map, food deserts are defined as urban areas with no grocery stores within walking distance (1 mile), or rural areas with no grocery stores within 10 miles.

The CDC (2016b) has found that people who have lower levels of education and lower incomes are more apt to have limited access to medical care, dental care, and prescription drugs. Add to that findings that black Americans are more likely to be shut out of these forms of health care than Hispanic Americans, who are more likely to be shut out than white Americans, and you have a perfect storm that explains why primary aging is more rapid for some racial and ethnic groups than others (Olshansky et al., 2012).

Figure 2.9: Locations of Food Deserts in the United States

SOURCE: U.S. Department of Agriculture, https://www.ers.usda.gov/data-products/food-access-research-atlas/go-to-the-atlas.aspx

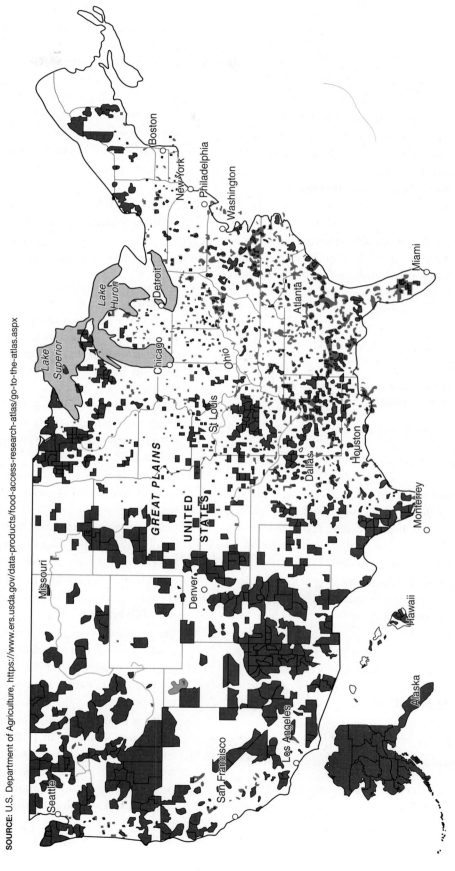

Summary: Physical Changes

2.1 Theories of Primary Aging

OBJECTIVE: **Evaluate theories of primary aging**

- The oxidative damage theory of primary aging says that we age as a result of damage from free radicals that are released during normal cell metabolism.
- The genetic limits theory says that we age because our cells are programmed to stop dividing once we have reached a certain age.
- The caloric restriction theory says that our longevity is controlled by the number of calories we metabolize in our lifetime.
- Although scientists have identified several candidates for being the cause of aging, they have not been able to extend the lifespans of human participants. Most experts agree that there is as yet no way to "turn back the clock" of primary aging.

2.2 Physical Changes in Outward Appearance

OBJECTIVE: **Analyze how adults deal with age-related changes in appearance**

- Weight increases gradually, starting toward the end of young adulthood, remains stable in middle adulthood, and then begins to decline in later adulthood. Obesity rates are high and increasing steadily for adults of all ages in the United States and other developed countries. This condition is linked to a number of diseases, and it also affects self-perceptions of health, ability to exercise, and social interactions. The main causes are eating an unhealthy diet and leading a sedentary lifestyle.
- Skin begins to wrinkle toward the end of young adulthood and becomes more noticeable in the middle years. "Remedies" sold over the counter for aging skin only cover the signs of aging.
- An increasing number of men and women are having cosmetic surgery and other medical procedures to change their appearances, and it is most common for those from 40 to 54 years of age.

2.3 The Changing Senses

OBJECTIVE: **Summarize how the senses change with age**

- Vision begins to decline in early adulthood, but is not noticeable until middle age. Around age 45, near vision is lost more suddenly, but can be corrected with reading glasses or contact lenses. The incidence of cataracts, glaucoma, and macular degeneration increases beginning in middle age.
- Hearing loss begins in the 30s, but is not noticeable until middle age, when adults have problems hearing higher and softer tones.
- Taste and smell begin to decline in the 30s, and this becomes more noticeable in the late years of middle age.

2.4 How Age Changes Internal Structures and Systems

OBJECTIVE: **Analyze the social impact of age-related changes to the body**

- Bone mass density peaks around age 30 and then begins to decline for both men and women. The decline is gradual for men and sharp for women at menopause. Women are at greater risk for osteoporosis and fractures. Osteoarthritis is a common condition in older adults and can lead to decreased activity and depressive symptoms.
- Muscle mass and strength decline slowly and do not affect the daily activities of most adults. Resistance training and stretching exercises can help slow down the decline.
- Changes in the heart and respiratory system are gradual and do not affect the daily activities of most adults, but heavy exercise brings slower responses in the later years. Aerobic exercise can help.
- The brain loses neurons with age, but not at the high rate once believed. However, the nervous system is capable of making adjustments to the losses, and there is evidence that new neurons can be created in parts of the adult brain.
- The immune system does not function as well in later adulthood as it did in earlier years, possibly due to the greater prevalence of chronic diseases and susceptibility to stress. Vitamin supplements may help in later adulthood.
- There is a gradual decline in hormone production and reproductive ability in both men and women from early adulthood into middle age, with a sharp decrease for women at menopause. Hormone replacement is possible, but should be approached with caution and in consultation with a medical professional.

2.5 Changes in Physical Behavior

OBJECTIVE: **Determine how age-related physical changes impact life as an older adult**

- Sleep becomes lighter as we age, and insomnia is more common. Sleep patterns change to earlier bedtimes and earlier awakenings. Lifestyle changes can help and should be tried before medication.

- Sexual activity is a complex set of behaviors determined by physical ability, desire, availability of a partner, and privacy. New medication is available to help with physical ability in men, but other factors can cause sexual activity to decline with age. Many people remain sexually active throughout their lives.

2.6 Individual Differences in Primary Aging

OBJECTIVE: **Relate aging experiences to demographic influences**

- Primary aging is affected by many individual differences. Genes spare some people from predispositions to certain conditions, such as glaucoma and osteoporosis. Genes also account for about 60% of the timing of skin wrinkling, age-related weight gain, and perceived age.

- Lifestyle factors, such as exercise and healthy diet, promote slower decline.

- Race, ethnicity, and socioeconomic factors affect access to health care and living in neighborhoods where exercise and good nutrition are easily obtained.

SHARED WRITING

Physical Changes

Consider this chapter's discussion of the physical changes that occur as people age. What are some changes that you have noticed (good or bad) about yourself or your parents as you have progressed into adulthood? How can you use awareness of these changes to better prepare for your own changes later in life? Write a short response that your classmates will read. Be sure to discuss specific examples.

> A minimum number of characters is required to post and earn points. After posting, your response can be viewed by your class and instructor, and you can participate in the class discussion.

Post   0 characters | 140 minimum

Chapter 3
Health and Health Disorders

Disease and disability can hit people of all ages, but there are more and more survivors who go on to live meaningful, happy lives.

Learning Objectives

3.1 Predict adult health issues based on data

3.2 Analyze ways in which older adults experience disease

3.3 Evaluate mental health challenges facing adults

3.4 Analyze assistance options for physical and mental disorders

3.5 Compare the physical health issues facing adults from different populations

A Word from the Author

Race for the Cure

EVERY YEAR a race is run in our town, and probably in yours too, called the "Race for the Cure," and it is intended to raise awareness (and money) for breast cancer prevention, detection, treatment, and research. The term *race* is fairly loose—ours is in January, and many people go in groups to enjoy a brisk walk in the Florida sun along the waterway, talking with each other and greeting friends they see along the

route. There are also lots of kids on skateboards, rollerblades, and in strollers. But the theme of the day is on everyone's minds—this form of cancer will strike (or has struck) one of every nine women in the United States. Almost everyone in the crowd has been touched by breast cancer, either by being diagnosed themselves or having a loved one counted among its statistics. Despite the festive atmosphere, one inescapable theme of the day is clear: *A whole lot of women (as well as men and nonbinary people) have had breast cancer and survived to walk in the sun.*

This chapter is about health and disease. I wish it were more about health and less about disease, but in truth, disease is part of adult life, and the longer we live the greater the chance we will have one disease or another. Many diseases, like breast cancer, have better and better detection rates and survival rates. Some, like lung cancer, can be prevented to a great extent through lifestyle decisions. And others, like Alzheimer's disease, are more difficult to prevent or to treat at present. In this chapter, I cover some general statistics about disease patterns and the most prevalent physical and mental health disorders. I also review the research on individual differences in health and disease.

3.1: Mortality, Morbidity, and Disability

OBJECTIVE: Predict adult health issues based on data

Secondary aging involves changes that happen to some people as they move through adulthood. Examples of secondary aging are cardiovascular disease and cancer, which become more prevalent with age. These changes are different than those of *primary aging*, which tend to happen to almost everyone, such as hair loss and cataracts. The changes of secondary aging can be caused by external factors, such as infection, or internal factors, such as a disease of a particular organ or system. They can also be caused by accidents. The truth is, the further a person journeys into adulthood, the higher the chances one or more of these conditions will crop up, cause some degree of disability, and eventually, cause death.

On a brighter note, the changes involved in secondary aging are often preventable, or if diagnosed early, curable. This type of aging is more under our control than hair loss or cataracts. In this module, I discuss death rates, different causes of death for different age groups, major age-related diseases, mental illnesses, and individual differences in the prevalence of these conditions. But I also offer ways to prevent many of these diseases and sources of disability, along with research showing how valuable early detection can be.

The World Health Organization (WHO, 2009) released a report on number of deaths by risk factors, which are characteristics of our behavior, environment, metabolism, and occupation that lead to disease. As you can see in Figure 3.1, the top risk factor is high blood pressure, accounting for over 10 million deaths a year. Second is smoking. Many of these risk factors are under the control of the individual, especially in developed countries where healthy food choices and opportunities for safe exercise are readily available. Although the topic of this module is death and disease, the main take-away is hope.

∨	**By the end of this module, you will be able to:**

3.1.1 Distinguish between mortality and morbidity rates

3.1.2 Describe current experiences of adulthood disability

Figure 3.1 Number of Worldwide Deaths by Risk Factor

SOURCE: Based on Ritchie & Roser (2018).

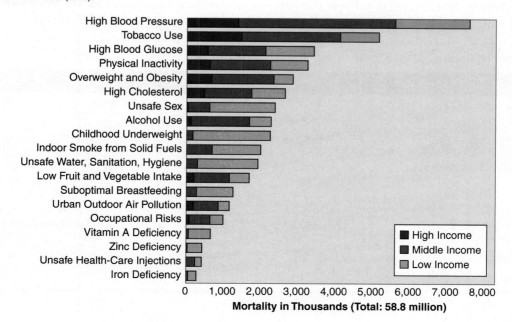

3.1.1: Mortality and Morbidity

OBJECTIVE: Distinguish between mortality and morbidity rates

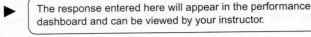

WRITING PROMPT

Critical Thinking

Before you read on, which age group would you predict has the highest rate of acute short-term health problems such as colds and flu, college students or their grandparents? Why?

> The response entered here will appear in the performance dashboard and can be viewed by your instructor.

Submit

You might assume that an age-related pattern would emerge for the **morbidity rate**, or illness rate, with older adults suffering from more of all types of health conditions than do younger adults. But that is not the case. Younger adults are actually about twice as likely as are those over age 65 to suffer from short-term health problems, which physicians call **acute conditions**, including colds, flu, infections, or short-term intestinal upsets. While younger adults are more likely to suffer from acute conditions, older adults are more likely to experience complications when they do suffer from acute conditions.

It is only the rates of **chronic conditions**, longer-lasting disorders such as heart disease, arthritis, or high blood pressure, that show an age-related increase. Older adults are two to three times more likely to suffer from such disorders than adults in their 20s and 30s.

You might also assume there to be an age-related pattern in **mortality rate**, or the probability of dying in any one year. In this instance, your assumption would be correct. Figure 3.2 shows the mortality rate for Americans in various age groups. You can see that fewer than one-tenth of 1% of emerging adults age 15 to 24 die in any

Figure 3.2 Mortality Rates across Various Age Groups

The mortality rate for adults in the United States increases slowly with age well into the 60s, then rises more sharply.

SOURCE: CDC (2016).

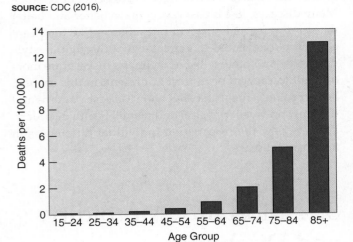

given year, whereas about 13% of adults over 85 die each year (Centers for Disease Control and Prevention [CDC], 2017b). The fact that older people are more likely to die is surely no great surprise (although you may be comforted to see how small the increases are in young adulthood and middle age).

Of course, there are also different causes of death for people at different ages. Table 3.1 gives the major causes of death for people in the United States by age. Three of the top five causes of death for adults from 15 to 34 aren't even diseases; they are accidents, suicides, and homicides. For the age group from 35 to 44, accidents are still in first place, followed by cancer and heart disease. Middle-aged adults (age 45 to 64) have cancer and heart disease in first and second place, and for older adults (age 65 and over) these two diseases are reversed in first and second place, and Alzheimer's disease makes its first appearance in the top five causes of death (CDC, 2017a).

Table 3.1 Leading Causes of Death in the United States by Age Group

	15–24 Years	25–34 Years	35–44 Years	45–54 Years	55–64 Years	65+ Years
1	Accidents (11,836)	Accidents (17,357)	Accidents (16,048)	Cancer (44,834)	Cancer (115,282)	Heart disease (489,722)
2	Suicide (5,079)	Suicide (6,569)	Cancer (11,267)	Heart disease (34,791)	Heart disease (74,473)	Cancer (413,885)
3	Homicide (4,144)	Homicide (4,159)	Heart disease (10,368)	Accidents (20,610)	Accident (18,020)	Chronic lower respiratory disease (124,693)
4	Cancer (1,569)	Cancer (3,624)	Suicide (6,706)	Suicide (8,767)	Chronic lower respiratory disease (16,492)	Stroke (113,308)
5	Heart disease (953)	Heart disease (3,341)	Homicide (2,588)	Liver disease (8,627)	Diabetes mellitus (13,342)	Alzheimer's disease (92,604)

SOURCE: Data from CDC (2017a).

3.1.2: Disability

OBJECTIVE: Describe current experiences of adulthood disability

Psychologists, epidemiologists, gerontologists, and even lawyers who deal with guardianship cases all define *disability* as the extent to which an individual is unable to perform two groups of activities:

1. Basic self-care activities, such as bathing, dressing, getting around inside the home, shifting from a bed to a chair, using the toilet, and eating, collectively called **ADLs (activities of daily living)**.

2. More complex everyday tasks, such as preparing meals, shopping for personal items, doing light housework, doing laundry, using transportation, handling finances, using the telephone, and taking medications, referred to as **IADLs (instrumental activities of daily living)**.

Another way of measuring health, instead of evaluating activities of daily living, is to ask adults of different ages to rate their own health on a simple scale, such as (1) excellent/very good, (2) good, or (3) fair/poor. These types of rating scales have compared well to more objective measures of physical and mental health. One such study was included in the U.S. National Health Interview Survey, and not surprisingly, young adults rated their health better than older adults. However, 40% of adults over the age of 75 rated themselves as being in excellent or very good health (Blackwell et al., 2014). This does not mean, of course, that an 85-year-old who describes him- or herself as being in "excellent or very good" health has the same physical functioning as a 25-year-old who chooses the same description.

Although disabilities occur in all age groups, the incidence increases with age. As you can see in Figure 3.3, the U.S. Census Bureau reports that up until the age of 20, about 1 in 20 emerging adults report having a disability. During young adulthood and middle age, about 1 in 10 report having a disability, but the percentage goes up after age 65 and then again after 75, when almost half of adults report disabilities (Erikson et al., 2016). Among working-age adults with disabilities, 34% are employed (Kraus, 2015). As you can imagine, older adults spend more time on ADLs and IADLs than younger adults, and their ability to perform them is a key indicator of their quality of life.

Having a chronic illness or health condition does not translate directly into being disabled. It is quite possible to have one or more chronic conditions without experiencing significant impairment. One person may have high blood pressure that is controlled with medication and exercise; another may have arthritis that responds well to medication

Disability does not automatically mean "unemployment." About one-third of disabled adults of working age hold jobs.

Figure 3.3 Prevalence of Disability by Age Group in the United States

Disability rates increase with age during the adult years.

SOURCE: Erikson et al. (2016).

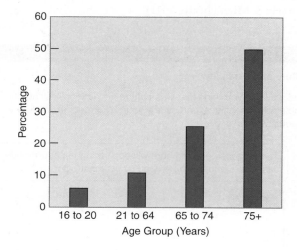

and places no limitation on major activities. For most adults, the crucial issue is not whether they have a chronic condition but whether that condition has an impact on their daily lives, requiring restriction in daily activities or reducing their ability to care for themselves or participate in a full life without assistance.

In the past 20 years, the disability rates among older adults in the United States have declined substantially for a number of reasons. According to population epidemiologist Vicki A. Freedman (2011), this decline is likely due to advances in medical care and changes in attitudes toward health. People are healthier today in all age groups, and this translates into less disability in old age. New surgical procedures and medications help manage diseases such as cardiovascular disease, cataracts, and arthritic knees and hips. Another factor in the decrease of disability rates is assistive technology, which has increased over the last two decades. People who would have been considered disabled in the past are able to function well because of items such as personal computers, cell phones, motorized wheelchairs, and portable oxygen tanks. Older people today have higher incomes and more education, which often results in healthier diets, less stress, and better medical care. Increases in income and education have indirect effects, too. For example, people with more education are less apt to have strenuous jobs that can lead to disabilities in later years.

As a result of these various factors, only about 3% of people over age 65 live in nursing homes or skilled care facilities. About 81% of women and 90% of men over 65 are **community dwelling**, living in their own homes either with their spouses or alone. The remaining people this age live in senior residences or assisted-living facilities that provide limited help or live in the homes of family members (National Institute on Aging, 2011). Even at the age of 90 years and older, almost three-fourths of older adults are living in their own homes or in the homes of family members (He & Muenchrath, 2011).

WRITING PROMPT

Culture and Disability

What way can you think that U.S. culture impacts daily living of people with disabilities, particularly yourself or people you know personally?

 The response entered here will appear in the performance dashboard and can be viewed by your instructor.

Submit

3.2: Specific Diseases

OBJECTIVE: Analyze ways in which older adults experience disease

Chances are that you have people living with age-related diseases or disabilities in your family or among your friends and neighbors. I do. Living in south Florida,

where the proportion of older adults is higher than most places in the country, people with age-related diseases and disabilities have become increasingly common. For example:

> In my yoga class are two women with Alzheimer's disease. One comes with a professional caregiver (who does yoga alongside her), and the other comes with a long-time friend, who drives her to class and then takes her out to lunch afterward, giving her caregiver husband a break twice a week.

> On our highways are digital signs for posting messages about accidents or other public service announcements. Now, along with Amber Alerts for missing children, we frequently have Silver Alerts for older adults with dementia who are missing from their homes.

> The golf club where some of my friends play has a golf pro who takes people living with disabilities out to play golf on Thursday afternoons. Most have cardiovascular disease and can't play all 18 holes, some have Alzheimer's disease but are able to play with some assistance, but all enjoy being out on the course in the golf cart and being with fellow golfers.

> My water aerobics class of about 50 women almost always has one or two with colorful headscarves covering bald heads—the temporary side effect of cancer treatment. After class there is conversation among the current patients and the survivors, exchanging words of encouragement, and talking about wigs, tattooed eyebrows, and care for damaged skin.

This section covers four diseases in detail—cardiovascular disease, cancer, diabetes, and Alzheimer's disease. I certainly don't intend to turn you into medical experts; my aim is to offer a picture of how health affects our daily lives (and also how our daily lives affect our health). While we do need to look at the symptoms and statistics, we must also learn to see the *people* living with age-related diseases. Being diagnosed with Alzheimer's disease or cancer or heart disease is not the end of personhood. There are often many years between the diagnosis and the end of life, and family members, friends, professional caregivers, and even golf pros can help make those years pleasurable and meaningful. If it takes a village to raise a child, it takes the same village to care for its elders.

⌄   By the end of this module, you will be able to:

3.2.1   Differentiate the experiences of cardiovascular disease by sex

3.2.2   Explain how the experience of adulthood cancer has changed over time

3.2.3   Summarize the impact of diabetes on the adult population

3.2.4   Describe the development and progression of Alzheimer's disease

3.2.1: Cardiovascular Disease

OBJECTIVE: Differentiate the experiences of cardiovascular disease by sex

Disease of the heart and blood vessels, or **cardiovascular disease**, covers a number of physical deteriorations; the key change is in the coronary arteries, which slowly develop a dangerous accumulation of **plaques**, or fat-laden deposits. This process is known as **atherosclerosis**, and it is caused by inflammation, which is normally a protective process of the immune system. Chronic inflammation causes plaques to form in the artery walls, which can rupture and form blood clots that block the arteries, leading to heart attack or stroke (Smith et al., 2009).

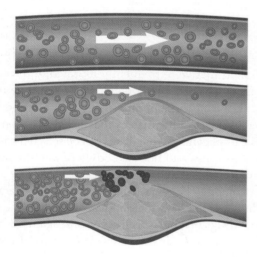

Cardiovascular disease involves the buildup of fat-laden deposits, or plaques, in the coronary arteries.

The death rate from cardiovascular disease has been dropping rapidly in the past two decades in the United States and most other industrialized countries, yet it remains the leading cause of death and disability in the United States (Hoyert & Xu, 2012) and throughout the developed world (WHO, 2012). Some people are at greater risk for cardiovascular disease than others.

Risk Factors for Cardiovascular Disease

Here are some risk factors associated with cardiovascular disease. As you will notice, some of these factors are under our control, such as sedentary lifestyle, and others are not, such as being older than 50.

- Age 50 or older
- Family history of cardiovascular disease
- Tobacco use and environmental exposure to tobacco smoke*
- Obesity*
- Sedentary lifestyle*
- Diabetes*
- High cholesterol*
- High blood pressure*

*Can be modified or prevented.
SOURCE: CDC (2012f).

WRITING PROMPT

Reasons for Cardiovascular Disease Decline

What are some of the reasons that the rate of cardiovascular disease is declining in the United States?

> The response entered here will appear in the performance dashboard and can be viewed by your instructor.

Submit

I feel I should emphasize something here: *Cardiovascular disease is the number-one killer of women throughout the developed world* (CDC, 2017c). The numbers can be misleading because the average age that men have heart attacks and die from cardiovascular disease is younger than the average age for women. Comparing cardiovascular disease rates by age can give the impression that it is a men's health problem; however, it can be just as dangerous for women.

In some ways, cardiovascular disease is even more dangerous for women because the early symptoms can be different. When we think of a heart attack, we think of crushing chest pain, but for women, the chest pain may be absent. They may only experience nausea, fatigue, dizziness, cold sweats, shortness of breath, or sharp pain in the upper body, neck, or jaw. When these warning signs are not heeded or are misinterpreted, cardiovascular disease can advance to the point that the first time medical assistance is sought, the disease has progressed much further than would be the case for men. In addition, women's cardiovascular disease often involves smaller arteries of the heart instead of the large coronary arteries that are typically affected in men. In these cases, routine tests on the larger arteries show low risk of cardiovascular disease, when, in fact, the women can be in advanced stages of microvascular disease, which has few symptoms. For this reason, almost two-thirds of women who die suddenly from cardiovascular disease have had no previous symptoms (CDC, 2017c).

3.2.2: Cancer

OBJECTIVE: Explain how the experience of adulthood cancer has changed over time

The second leading cause of death in the United States is **cancer**, a disease in which abnormal cells undergo rapidly accelerated, uncontrolled division and often move into adjacent normal tissues. Cancer can then spread through the bloodstream or lymph vessels to more distant tissues in the body, including the brain.

The incidence of cancer increases with age. Figure 3.4 shows the probability of developing invasive cancer at different ages for men and women. As you can see, developing invasive cancer becomes more probable with age. Another change with age is in the type of cancer one is likely to have. Breast cancer is the most frequent cause of cancer deaths for

Figure 3.4 Probability of Developing Invasive Cancer by Age and Sex

The risk of developing invasive cancer increases with age and is higher for women before the age of 50 and higher for men after the age of 50.

SOURCE: Siegel et al. (2016).

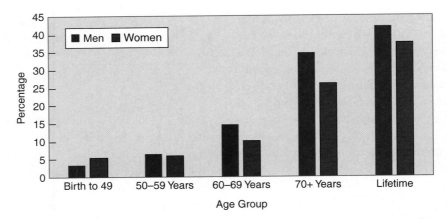

women under age 60, whereas brain and other nervous system cancer is the most frequent cancer death for men under age 40. After 60 for women and 40 for men, the most frequent cause of cancer death is lung cancer. (Siegel et al., 2016).

ADVANCEMENTS IN CANCER RESEARCH The search for a cause of cancer has made dramatic progress recently. It has long been believed that cancer begins with a series of random mutations that turn off tumor-suppressing genes in a cell and turn on tumor-stimulating genes. Once this occurs, the mutated cell divides and replicates excessively, resulting in cancer. Recently, this explanation has been expanded. Although genetic mutations do occur, a major cause of cancer is now thought to arise from **epigenetic inheritance**, in which environmental events cause changes in gene expression (Berdasco & Esteller, 2010). Epigenetic inheritance is thought to go hand in hand with random mutations in causing a number of diseases, including cancer. Genetic characteristics that are caused by epigenetic inheritance are not those that are encoded in the genome at conception, like eye color or dimples. Rather, they are the result of environmental influences during the prenatal period or during the lifespan that affect how existing genes are expressed without altering the genetic code itself. In its desired function, epigenetic inheritance works to *downregulate* (or silence) one gene so that another gene at that location is expressed. While this can produce advantageous effects, it can also produce detrimental effects, such as switching off tumor-supressing genes or turning on tumor-stimulating genes. The difference between this explanation and the traditional "random mutations" explanation is that it may be possible to discover which environmental factors tend to create harmful epigenetic inheritance markers and to work toward preventions.

Advances have also been made in the treatment of cancer, which has evolved from surgery to radiation to chemotherapy. Now the DNA of a tumor can be examined to determine which type of treatment would be most successful. In one study of breast cancer tumors, 18 genes were located that were frequently mutated. Interestingly, five of the genes had been previously linked to leukemia (Ellis et al., 2012). These findings have led to tumors being classified by genes rather than by the tumor's location in the body. The implication is that drugs can be selected based on the mutated genes and not the body location. Researchers have found that one person's breast cancer may be similar in DNA to another person's leukemia and should be treated with similar drugs. This method has opened up the possibility that drugs that have been successful against cancer at one location of the body can be used on genetically similar tumors at other locations.

In 1990, the incidence and death rate from cancer began to decline significantly in the United States for the first time since national recordkeeping began. The most recent statistics from the American Cancer Society show a 25% decline in cancer deaths in the last 20 years (Simon, 2017). This decline is due to advances in prevention, early detection, and treatment. Recent prevention measures include the human papillomavirus (HPV) vaccine, which reduces chances of cervical cancer, and the hepatitis B vaccine, which helps prevent liver cancer (Siegel et al., 2016). Early detection has decreased the number of deaths from cervical, colorectal, and breast cancers. A growing number of people have made lifestyle changes to reduce their risks of cancer.

WRITING PROMPT

HPV Vaccine for Boys?

Why would pediatricians recommend the HPV vaccine for preteen boys as well as girls?

 The response entered here will appear in the performance dashboard and can be viewed by your instructor.

Submit

Risk Factors for Cancer

Here are some risk factors associated with cancer. As you'll see, some are within our control to change, while others are not.

- Age 50 and older
- Family history of cancer
- History of hepatitis C
- Tobacco use (cigarettes, cigars, chewing tobacco, snuff)*
- Exposure to secondhand smoke*
- Unhealthy diet (low in fruits and vegetables)*
- Chemical and radiation exposure in the workplace*
- Sexually transmitted diseases*
- Sedentary lifestyle*
- Obesity*
- Excessive alcohol use*
- Unprotected exposure to strong sunlight or tanning beds*

*Can be modified or prevented.

SOURCE: American Cancer Society (2019).

3.2.3: Diabetes

OBJECTIVE: Summarize the impact of diabetes on the adult population

Diabetes is a disease in which the body is not able to metabolize insulin. Because insulin is required for the utilization of glucose, diabetes results in high levels of glucose in the blood and a reduction of nourishment to the body. Diabetes is related to increased risk of heart disease and stroke and is a major cause of blindness, kidney disease, amputations of feet and legs, complications during pregnancy leading to birth defects, and premature death. Although some diabetes (type 1) appears in childhood or young adulthood, over 90% of diabetes (type 2) is associated with older age, obesity, and physical inactivity. Figure 3.5 shows that the prevalence of type 2 diabetes sharply increased between 1990 and 2008 for middle-aged and older adults. Epidemiologists connect this to the doubling of obesity rates from 1980 to 2000, a decade earlier. The figure also shows that the prevalence of type 2 diabetes has been relatively stable since 2008, perhaps mirroring the recent leveling of obesity rates in the U.S. population. These researchers suggest this is due to the success of various programs undertaken by the U.S. Surgeon General, the National Institutes of Health, and the Centers for Disease Control and Prevention in promoting good nutrition and physical activity (Herman & Rothberg, 2015).

Even though the prevalence of type 2 diabetes seems to be have leveled off in recent years, over 28 million adults and children are still affected, and diabetes has become one of the major causes of disability and death for middle-aged adults in the United States. It is the ninth greatest cause of death worldwide (WHO, 2016).

Because type 2 diabetes seems clearly linked to obesity and sedentary lifestyles, the hopeful news is that most cases are preventable when individuals adopt a healthy diet and lifestyle, especially those in high-risk categories.

Other hopeful news is that people diagnosed with pre-diabetes can slow down the progression to diabetes by losing weight and exercising, even when they are over the age of 60 (Halter, 2011). And a good number of obese people who have diabetes benefit dramatically from gastric bypass and gastric banding surgery, once considered a treatment of last resort (Purnell et al., 2016).

Figure 3.5 Increase in Prevalence of Type 2 Diabetes

The prevalence of type 2 diabetes increased sharply between 1990 and 2008 for adults 45 years of age and older. Since 2008, it has leveled off and shows signs of declining.

SOURCE: CDC (2015).

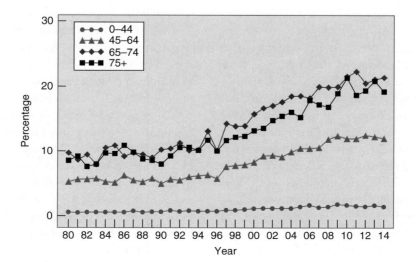

Risk Factors for Diabetes

Here are some risk factors associated with diabetes, most of which are within our control to change.

- Increasing age
- Family history of diabetes
- Obesity*
- High blood pressure*
- High cholesterol*
- Sedentary lifestyle*

*Can be modified or prevented.

SOURCE: International Diabetes Foundation (2015).

3.2.4: Alzheimer's Disease

OBJECTIVE: Describe the development and progression of Alzheimer's disease.

The fifth leading cause of death for people age 65 and over is **Alzheimer's disease**, a progressive, irreversible deterioration of key areas of the brain involved in various cognitive functions. The hallmark loss with Alzheimer's disease is short-term memory, which is important for remembering newly learned information such as recent events or earlier conversations. These deficits increase to affect social, cognitive, and movement abilities and end in death approximately 8 to 10 years after diagnosis (although most patients die of other causes such as pneumonia or complications after a fall). Unlike cardiovascular disease and cancer, which can occur throughout adulthood, Alzheimer's disease is truly a disease of old age, with 90% of the cases developing after the age of 65. Once considered a rare disorder, Alzheimer's disease has become a major public health problem in the United States and throughout the world, primarily because of the increasing proportion of older people in our population. Alzheimer's disease afflicts one out of 10 people in the United States over 65—5.5 million people—and almost half of people 85 and older (Alzheimer's Association, 2017). If you are like 25 million other people in the United States, you are acutely aware of this disease because you have a family member with Alzheimer's disease and are experiencing its effects firsthand.

Alzheimer's disease is the most prevalent type of **dementia**, a category of conditions that involve global deterioration in intellectual abilities and physical function. Other types of dementia can be caused by multiple small strokes, Parkinson's disease, multiple blows to the head (as among professional boxers and football players), a single head trauma, advanced stages of AIDS, depression, drug intoxication, hypothyroidism, some kinds of tumors, vitamin B_{12} deficiency, anemia, and alcohol abuse. I don't expect you to memorize this list, but I do want you to realize that a decline in cognitive functioning is not necessarily Alzheimer's disease; sometimes it is a condition that can be treated and has a more favorable outcome.

The cause of Alzheimer's disease is not clear, but we have known since the early part of the 20th century that autopsies of people who die of dementia often reveal specific abnormalities in the brain tissue. One of these abnormalities, first identified by neuropathologist Alois Alzheimer in 1907, is **senile plaques**. These are small, circular deposits of a dense protein, *beta-amyloid*; another abnormality is **neurofibrillary tangles**, or webs of degenerating neurons.

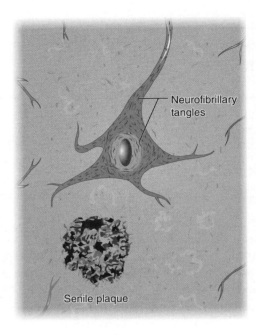

Senile plaque and neurofibrillary tangles.

According to the Alzheimer's Association (2017), several genes have been found to contribute to Alzheimer's disease. One gene, *APOE* E4, increases one's risk for Alzheimer's disease. If you inherit one copy of this gene, you are at higher risk than someone who does not have this form of the gene. If you inherit two copies of this gene, you are at even greater risk, though it is not certain you will have the disease. Three other genes, *APP*, *PSEN1*, and *PSEN2*, determine with certainty that a person will have Alzheimer's disease. The type of Alzheimer's disease caused by all these genes is the early-onset type, occurring in middle age (sometimes as early as 30 or 40) and affecting many family members in each generation. However, this type of Alzheimer's disease accounts for only 5% of the total cases. Scientists have identified a few hundred families in the world with these genes, and they study them in hopes of learning something about the more common forms of the disease. For example, possible vaccines against Alzheimer's disease are tested on these families instead of individuals in the general population because of the higher probability that they will develop the disease in a shorter amount of time.

Genetic Testing: Pros and Cons

What are the pros and cons of being tested for genes that increase the probability that one will develop Alzheimer's disease?

> The response entered here will appear in the performance dashboard and can be viewed by your instructor.

Submit

RISK FACTORS FOR ALZHEIMER'S AND OTHER FORMS OF DEMENTIA The greatest risk factor for Alzheimer's disease is age. Other risk factors are:

Additional Risk Factors for Alzheimer's Disease

Here are some risk factors associated with Alzheimer's disease:

- Age 50 and older
- Head injury*
- Family history of Alzheimer's disease
- High cholesterol levels*
- High blood pressure*
- Sedentary lifestyle*
- Tobacco use*
- Obesity*

*Can be modified or prevented.
SOURCE: Alzheimer's Association (2017).

Some of the risk factors for Alzheimer's disease should seem familiar to you by now because they are the same as those that put us at risk for cardiovascular disease. In fact, people with cardiovascular disease are more apt to get Alzheimer's disease than people with healthy hearts, probably because of the inflammation that underlies both diseases.

One risk factor for Alzheimer's disease and other types of dementia is **traumatic brain injury (TBI)**. Studies have shown that individuals who sustain head injuries severe enough to lose consciousness are two to four times more likely to develop dementia in later life than those who do not have this injury. This applies especially to a type of dementia known as **chronic traumatic encephalopathy (CTE)**. This line of research began in England in the 1960s when the Royal College of Physicians asked medical researcher A. H. Roberts to examine a randomly selected sample of retired boxers. He found that 17% of them fit the diagnosis for CTE (Roberts, 1969). Since that time, autopsies on football, soccer, and ice hockey players have confirmed a high number of cases of CTE, the symptoms of which can include explosive rage, depression, substance abuse, memory impairment, and suicide (Mez et al., 2017).

Of particular concern are military personnel who experience TBI as a result of improvised explosive devices, the weapon of choice of militants in Iraq and Afghanistan

(Hope et al., 2008). TBI has been strongly associated with posttraumatic stress syndrome (PTSD), leading to the hypothesis that many of the combat veterans with PTSD also have CTE (Omalu et al., 2011). Both the professional sports organizations and the Veterans Administration are working on better protection for the young men and women involved and ways to avoid the long-term damage done by these injuries.

DIAGNOSING ALZHEIMER'S Advances are also being made in the diagnosis of Alzheimer's disease. Until the 1990s, it could only be diagnosed with certainty after death with an autopsy. New diagnostic methods include brain imaging and tests for the presence of protein in the blood or cerebrospinal fluid (Alzheimer's Association, 2017).

A pre-Alzheimer's stage is called **mild cognitive impairment (MCI)**, in which patients show some cognitive symptoms, but not all those necessary for a diagnosis of Alzheimer's disease. About half the individuals with mild cognitive impairment will progress to Alzheimer's disease within the next 3 to 4 years (Storandt, 2008).

I end this section with a few words about Alzheimer's disease and normal aging of the brain. The memory of an older adult is not as sharp or as quick as it once was, and it becomes somewhat more difficult for them to learn new information. This might lead you to believe that Alzheimer's disease is just an extreme form of normal aging, but this is not true. Alzheimer's disease is a different creature entirely. With normal aging, we may forget for a minute what day it is, have trouble retrieving a specific name, or misplace our car keys. Cognitive symptoms of Alzheimer's disease include losing track of the season, being unable to carry on a conversation, and being lost in a familiar neighborhood (Alzheimer's Association, 2017).

It is important to attend to personality and cognitive changes in older adults. Although there is currently no cure for Alzheimer's disease, there is treatment available for other conditions with similar symptoms. Medications are now available that may slow down the progression of Alzheimer's disease in its early stages. There is counseling and community assistance for patients with Alzheimer's disease and their caregivers.

3.3: Psychological Disorders

OBJECTIVE: Evaluate mental health challenges facing adults

Compared to physical health disorders, the scientific diagnosis and treatment of psychological disorders is a fairly new topic. Before Freud's time, psychological disorders were the realm of religion or philosophy. Once they became accepted as treatable health conditions, each school of therapy had its own classification system and treatment plan. It was not until

1980 that a standardized system of symptoms and diagnoses was agreed on by mental health professionals in the United States in the form of the *Diagnostic and Statistical Manual of Mental Disorders*, third edition (DSM-III; American Psychiatric Association [APA], 1980). This advance was important for therapists and their patients, but it also made it possible for epidemiologists to compile data and answer questions about our country's mental health. Since that time, several large-scale surveys about the state of the nation's mental health have been conducted. The DSM is now in its fifth edition, reflecting the ongoing changes in our knowledge about mental health disorders and their treatments (APA, 2013).

The proportion of people with mental illness in a particular population is measured in a number of different ways. The **prevalence** is the percentage of people experiencing a disorder within a given period of time, such as *lifetime prevalence* or *12-month prevalence*. Several sources estimate that the lifetime prevalence of mental illness in the United States is just under 50%. That means that almost half of the people in this country will experience some sort of mental disorder that fits the diagnostic description in DSM-5 sometime during their lives. The 12-month prevalence of mental illness in the United States is 25%, meaning that one in four will experience some sort of mental disorder during a given 12-month period (American Psychological Association, 2017; Kessler et al., 2005).

The most prevalent mental health problems for adults in the United States fall into three categories: (1) anxiety disorders, (2) depressive disorders, and (3) substance-related and addictive disorders. In this section, I give more detail about these disorders, along with a brief discussion of treatment.

> ∨   **By the end of this module, you will be able to:**

3.3.1   **Evaluate common anxiety symptoms and treatments**

3.3.2   **Evaluate common depressive symptoms and treatments**

3.3.3   **Characterize addictive disorders**

3.3.4   **Analyze mental health treatment options**

3.3.1: Anxiety Disorders

OBJECTIVE: **Evaluate common anxiety symptoms and treatments**

Anxiety disorders involve feelings of fear, threat, and dread when no obvious danger is present. They are the most common type of mental health disorder for adults in the United States. During a 12-month period, approximately 18% of American adults report experiencing an anxiety disorder that would fit the diagnosis in the DSM-5. The most common anxiety disorders are **phobias**, which are fears and

anxiety out of proportion to the danger presented, and **social anxiety**, which involves feeling fear and anxiety about social situations, such as meeting new people or performing before an audience. Although many adults experience anxiety disorders, they usually begin in childhood. Half the people who have anxiety disorders experience the first one before the age of 11; three quarters of the people who have anxiety disorders have experienced one before the age of 21. About twice as many women than men experience anxiety disorders (American Psychological Association, 2017).

Psychotherapy is very successful in treating anxiety disorders, either in individual therapy, group therapy, or family therapy if the patient is a child or adolescent. The American Psychological Association (2016) states that most people are able to notice improvement in just a few sessions with a therapist and often find the symptoms are reduced or eliminated entirely within 1–2 months of therapy. Symptoms can be relieved with antianxiety medication, antidepressants, and beta-blockers.

Almost everyone has symptoms of anxiety at some point in their lives, but there are a few things we can do to help prevent them from developing into an anxiety disorder. A balanced diet, exercise, and socialization are always a good idea, as well as limiting alcohol and caffeine. Maintaining a regular sleep pattern, keeping a journal to identify triggers of anxiety, and practicing relaxation techniques such as yoga, meditation, and mindfulness are also useful (Anxiety and Depression Society of America, 2016).

Risk Factors for Anxiety Disorders

Here are some risk factors associated with anxiety disorders.

- Shyness in childhood
- Being female
- Family history of anxiety disorder (or other psychological disorders)
- Exposure to stressful life events
- Poverty

SOURCE: NIMH (2017).

3.3.2: Depressive Disorders

OBJECTIVE: **Evaluate common depressive symptoms and treatments**

The most prevalent depressive disorder is **major depressive disorder**, typified by a long-term, pervasive sense of sadness and hopelessness. To be diagnosed with major depressive disorder, the DSM-5 states that for a 12-week period, the patient must be in a depressed mood most of the day and show a loss of interest or pleasure in almost all activities. They may in addition show a change in weight or sleep patterns, fatigue, feelings of worthlessness, problems with decision making, or thoughts of suicide (APA, 2013). In the National Comorbidity Survey, major depressive disorder was the second most prevalent disorder for adults in the United States, affecting over 16% of respondents during their lifetimes (Kessler et al., 2005). The National Institute of Mental Health (NIMH, 2016) reports that the 12-month prevalence for major depressive disorder is about 7% in the United States, with rates high all over the world; it is the leading cause of disability in the world and the leading cause of suicide (WHO, 2017). The median age of onset for this disorder is 30. The prevalence is three times higher in young adults than older adults and twice as high for women as for men (APA, 2013).

Major depressive disorder should not be confused with *depressive symptoms*, which are not as severe or long-lasting and not considered a mental disorder by the DSM-5. These occur more often in older adults and are usually related to chronic disease, bereavement, or loneliness.

Standard treatment for major depressive disorder is medication and psychotherapy. For extreme cases, electro-convulsive therapy (ECT) or transcranial magnetic stimulation (TMS) may be options (NIMH, 2016).

Adults of all ages who feel symptoms of depression can take steps to help prevent it from escalating into major depression. Exercise seems to boost important brain chemicals, as does spending time socializing with others. Confiding in a trusted friend or relative and accepting help from others can help, too. Other advice is to seek out reliable information about depression and avoid alcohol and drugs until you are feeling better. You don't have to have major depressive disorder to talk to a therapist (NIMH, 2016).

Risk Factors for Major Depressive Disorder

Here are some risk factors associated with major depressive disorder.

- Personal or family history of depression
- Being female
- Major life changes
- Trauma and excessive stress
- Certain physical illnesses or medication
- Poverty
- Unemployment
- Alcohol or drug abuse
- Death of a loved one
- Relationship breakup

SOURCE: NIMH (2016); WHO (2017).

3.3.3: Substance-Related and Addictive Disorders

OBJECTIVE: Characterize addictive disorders

Substance-related disorders and **addictive disorders** refer to nine separate classes of drugs plus gambling (APA, 2013).

1. Alcohol
2. Caffeine
3. Cannabis
4. Hallucinogens
5. Sedatives, Hypnotics, and Anxiolytics
6. Stimulants
7. Tobacco
8. Inhalants
9. Opioids

These substances, along with gambling, have one thing in common: They activate the reward system of the brain directly, taking a shortcut to the feelings we ordinarily achieve after a long expenditure of effort. Consider the training and effort put into running a marathon and finishing in the top half of your field. Imagine the rush of euphoria you would feel when you achieved that goal. These substances give that rush of euphoria instantaneously, just for ingesting, smoking, snorting, injecting, or drinking them. And the rush is so much more rewarding than natural rewards like winning a marathon that, over time, the brain circuitry is changed so that the body experiences intense desire for the substance when any related triggers are present. The person with substance use disorder often spends more and more time using the drug and searching for access to the drug that they neglect work, friends, and family, even though the drug use is putting them into high-risk situations. The prevalence of this disorder is highest in young adults from 18 to 24 years of age and the initial drug used is usually alcohol (APA, 2013).

Alcohol use disorder is prevalent in about 9% of adults in the United States in a 12-month period, and it declines with age. The prevalence for younger adults (18–29 years) is 16%, whereas for older adults (65 years or more) it is only 2%. It is higher for Native Americans and Alaskan Natives (12%) than for whites (9%), Hispanics (8%), African Americans (7%), and Asian Americans and Pacific Islanders (5%) (Figure 3.6). Men have more than twice the prevalence of alcohol use disorder than women (12% vs. 5%) (APA, 2013).

Currently, the class of substances with the biggest problem in the United States are *opioids*, which are synthetic drugs that resemble natural opiates, such as morphine. They were developed by pharmaceutical companies to be less dangerous and addictive than the natural opiates, but it has turned out that opioids are just as dangerous and addictive. Some of the opioids are oxycodone, hydrocodone, hydromorphone, methadone, some types of heroin, and, recently, the synthetic opioid fentanyl. Because opioids began as prescribed drugs, they were considered safer than street drugs. They are effective in alleviating pain after surgery and severe injuries, but they also produce euphoria by directly stimulating the brain's reward center. Opioid use—particularly fentanyl, which is 50 to 100 times stronger than heroin—can lead to addiction, respiratory arrest, coma, and death (National Institute on Drug Abuse, 2016).

Figure 3.6 Prevalence of Alcohol Use Disorder for U.S. Adults

About 9% of adults in the United States experience alcohol use disorder in any 12-month period. It is higher in some groups than others, and higher in young adults than in older adults.

SOURCE: APA (2013).

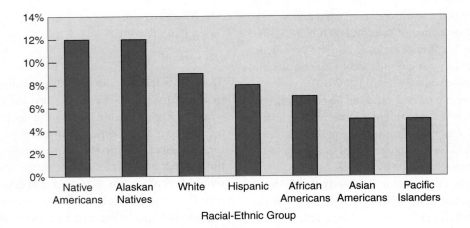

The U.S. is experiencing a drug epidemic with opioid addiction. As you can see in Figure 3.7, deaths from overdoses have increased from over 47,000 at the beginning of 2015 to over 65,000 just 2 years later. This is more than car crashes and gun homicides. Public health officials consider it the worst drug crisis in American history (Bosman, 2017). Opioid use is prevalent in all 50 states and has reduced the life expectancy of the non-Hispanic white population (Dowell et al., 2017).

TREATMENT FOR SUBSTANCE ABUSE Treatment for substance abuse and addictive disorders depends on the drug and the severity of the disorder. Medication is available to reduce the cravings, block the effects of the drug, or induce negative feelings when the drug is taken. Drugs used specifically for mitigating the effects of opioids are naltrexone (Narcan), a drug that can reverse the effects

of an overdose if given soon enough, and buprenorphine (Suboxone) and methadone, two drugs that reduce cravings and withdrawal. Therapy can be given as an outpatient or in a treatment center, and 12-step fellowships, such as Alcoholics Anonymous (AA) or Narcotics Anonymous (NA), can be helpful.

Individuals can do several things to avoid substance abuse and addiction. First, if you are prescribed an opioid pain medication after surgery or an injury, ask if another, less addictive medication is available. If you do take a potentially addictive medication, take it for the fewest number of days possible. If you fit any of the risk factors for this disorder, avoid experimenting with any type of drugs. Don't put yourself in situations where drugs are present. Don't surround yourself with a social group that uses drugs (Substance Abuse and Mental Health Services Administration, 2016).

Figure 3.7 Drug Overdose Deaths: United States

Deaths caused by drug overdoses have increased dramatically in the past few years, mostly due to the increased use of opioid drugs.

SOURCE: CDC (2018).

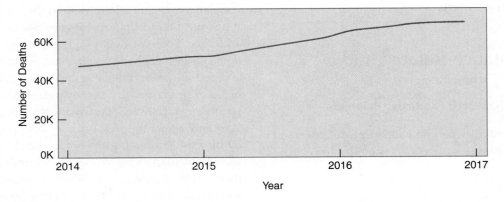

Risk Factors for Substance Abuse Disorders

Here are some risk factors associated with substance abuse disorders.

- Family history of substance abuse or addiction
- Psychological factors such as high impulsivity, sensation seeking, anxiety disorder, eating disorders
- History of physical, sexual, or emotional abuse
- Substance abuse among peers
- Access to addictive substance
- Starting alcohol, nicotine, or other drug use at early age

SOURCE: National Center of Addiction and Substance Abuse (2016).

3.3.4: Treatment of Mental Health Disorders

OBJECTIVE: Analyze mental health treatment options

Only about 40% of adults with mental health disorders seek some sort of treatment. Considering all the recent advances in psychopharmacology and psychotherapy, this shows that the optimistic picture of "curing" mental illness is not a reality for the majority of people who suffer from these disorders. To make matters worse, only about a third of those who seek help actually get treatment that is judged adequate by professional guidelines (Wang et al., 2005).

Another third of the people who seek treatment for mental health disorders go to **complementary and alternative medicine providers,** such as chiropractors, acupuncturists, herbalists, or spiritualists, none of whose methods for treating mental health disorders have been supported by scientific data. Still, patients report that these complementary and alternative medicine providers listen to them and include them in treatment decisions. It is important for mainstream mental health professionals to adopt some of this "bedside manner" and use it to make their conventional treatment more attractive (Wang et al., 2005). Other studies have shown that a brief screening for mental health problems during visits with primary care physicians can be very effective in diagnosing patients at risk for depression and substance abuse disorders and providing counseling or further treatment (Maciosek et al., 2010).

One group that has become the target of concern among educators and mental health professionals is emerging adults. Twenty-one-year-olds who report symptoms of depression are less likely to receive treatment than 16-year-olds. Some of the reasons they give are that they can't afford treatment, they think the symptoms will go away on their own, and they are too busy (Yu et al., 2008). Another reason is that parents can insist that their minor children be treated for health problems, while those who are over 18 are legally adults and must agree to the treatment themselves (unless they pose a danger to themselves or others).

Most mental health disorders first appear in adolescence and emerging adulthood, and if diagnosed and treated early, they are less likely to cause lifelong problems. Research has shown mental health disorders to be responsible for over 10% of high school dropouts and almost 3% of college dropouts (Breslau et al., 2008). Yet few parents, pediatricians, and school officials are trained to identify early symptoms or high-risk variables.

In summary, it seems that the advances in pharmaceuticals and therapy for mental health disorders are not interfacing well with the actual needs of adults of all ages. We need more education about what is a mental disorder and what is not, more information about proven treatment and where to find it, better treatment for people who do seek it, and more people-friendly professionals providing proven, conventional therapies. Let's hope that future waves of studies show some progress in this area.

3.4: Assistance Solutions

OBJECTIVE: Analyze assistance options for physical and mental disorders

Not all the answers to disease and disability involve medication and surgery; some involve assistive technology and assistance animals, and as our population grows older, these "devices" are becoming more and more common.

  By the end of this module, you will be able to:

3.4.1 Describe trends in assistive technology

3.4.2 Summarize the functions of assistance animals

3.4.1: Assistive Technology

OBJECTIVE: Describe trends in assistive technology

When lifespan developmental psychology meets technology, the result can be products that improve the quality of life and independence for adults with age-related conditions or disabilities. These devices can range in complexity from simple reach extenders to complex electronics. For example, wireless personal emergency response systems that transmit information about falls, inactivity, room temperature, fire, and carbon monoxide to remote caregivers or family members, allowing older adults or adults with disabilities to have more independence in their own homes, are widely available. Personal computers run software that translates text to speech or magnifies text for people with vision limitations. Smartphone apps now perform basic medical tests like measuring heart rate, blood pressure, and blood sugar level, keeping a record of the results for the user to monitor or sending the information to a caregiver or physician. Household robots may seem like science fiction to some adults, but they are already present in many homes. (I have one that cleans my pool and another that vacuums my floors.) Other robots can be operated by distant caregivers to communicate with elderly or disabled people via camera, microphone, and speaker. On the horizon are more humanlike robots that cook simple meals, tidy living spaces, and give reminders about medication schedules.

Robot manufacturers in Japan and various European countries that have a large proportion of older adults and too few younger adults to work as caregivers are leading the way in researching and designing robots to provide personal care for older adults who want to live independently for as long as possible (Muoio, 2015). In the United States, there are now voice-activated control systems that will make phone calls, play games, and learn the preferences of their owners to suggest which audiobooks and music they would enjoy (Cuthbertson, 2017).

In addition to doing housework and selecting music, robots also assist in surgical procedures. By 2025, it is estimated that one of three surgeries in the United States will be performed by robotic systems. These systems involve surgeons sitting in front of a computer screen guiding robotic arms, and they are widely used today for hernia repair, bariatric surgery, hysterectomies, and prostate removal. The positive side to this is that robotics give surgeons greater precision and less fatigue. The negative is that they are expensive and actually slow down procedures because of the setup time required for each surgery. Most of the robotic surgery systems are found in developed countries, but plans are for the prices to be reduced so they can also be used in developing countries (Kelly, 2016).

Accessibility for All

Take a look at your campus or home. How accessible is it for people using assistive devices like wheelchairs? What steps could be taken to make your home or campus environment more accessible for everyone, particularly those who rely on assistive technology?

▶ The response entered here will appear in the performance dashboard and can be viewed by your instructor.

Submit

3.4.2: Assistance Animals

OBJECTIVE: Summarize the functions of assistance animals

Much lower-tech help comes from assistance animals. Their roles include guiding the visually impaired, signaling the hearing impaired, or performing services such as flipping on light switches, picking up dropped objects, and alerting their human to alarms, telephone rings, and doorbells. Most of these assistance animals are dogs, but capuchin monkeys can be trained to perform tasks that require fine motor skills like turning the pages of a book and pushing buttons on a microwave oven.

Lower-tech help comes from animals, such as guide dogs that assist the visually impaired.

Another type of assistance animal is a comfort animal, again usually a dog, that is used to calm people in stressful situations, such as in psychotherapy sessions. In fact, Sigmund Freud used his Chow Chow, Jofi, during psychoanalysis sessions to help patients relax (Coren, 2010). Comfort animals are also used to calm people who are institutionalized in nursing homes, mental hospitals, and prisons (Baun & Johnson, 2010). At my university, volunteers bring comfort animals to campus during midterm and final exam weeks, and they receive a very warm reception from students, who are often missing their own "comfort animals" back home.

3.5: Individual Differences in Health

OBJECTIVE: Compare the physical health issues facing adults from different populations

While there's a case to be made for age-linked patterns for various physical diseases and mental health conditions, as you no doubt realize, this is not a matter of "one rule fits all." Within these age patterns are a variety of individual differences caused by factors we are born with, such as sex, and factors we acquire along the way, such as exercise habits. The following is a discussion of some of these factors and how they interact to affect both physical and mental health through the lifespan.

> **By the end of this module, you will be able to:**

3.5.1 Explain the contributions of genetics to adult health

3.5.2 Differentiate health experiences by sex and gender

3.5.3 Describe the ways in which socioeconomic class impacts health

3.5.4 Summarize racial and ethnic differences in health

3.5.5 Explain how discrimination leads to negative health outcomes for women and people from minority groups

3.5.6 Explain how personality influences health

3.5.7 Analyze how prenatal and childhood experiences affect adult health

3.5.8 Determine how lifestyle choices affect health

3.5.1: Genetics

OBJECTIVE: Explain the contributions of genetics to adult health

One's **genotype**, the personal complement of genes that each of us possesses, has a big influence on our health. Most of us are aware of diseases that "run in families," such as breast cancer, heart disease, and substance abuse. Few diseases are determined by a single gene. (One example is early-onset Alzheimer's disease caused by the *APP*, *PS-1*, or *PS-2* genes.) Other diseases, such as depression and cancer, are transmitted by a combination of genes. In these cases, the gene combinations don't cause the disease as much as they predispose the individual to the disease by making him or her more susceptible than others to environmental factors, such as tobacco smoke leading to lung cancer, head injury leading to Alzheimer's disease, or fatty diets leading to cardiovascular disease. Few diseases are determined by a single gene, and genes alone seldom determine our destinies.

Another example of a genetic disorder that has received a great deal of research attention is cystic fibrosis, which appears at birth in a child who has inherited two mutant forms of the *CFTR* gene, one from the mother and one from the father. This disorder causes the normal secretions of the body, such as airway mucus, pancreatic ducts, and bowels, to be unusually thick and dehydrated, leading to breathing and digestive problems. When the disease was first described in the late 1930s, infants born with this disorder did not survive infancy. With each medical discovery, though, the life expectancy increased. Today it is almost 40 years (National Jewish Health Center, 2018)

Other genes have been found that have a protective effect. For example, a mutation of the *APP* gene, which causes early onset Alzheimer's in its nonmutated form, has been found in a small number of Icelanders and seems to serve as protection against Alzheimer's disease. People who carry this mutation also live longer and are less likely to suffer from other types of cognitive decline (Jonsson et al., 2012).

Genetic information can also affect our individual responses to different treatments for diseases. For example, a number of genes have been identified that determine which of several drugs would be most successful in treating leukemia patients. Progress is also being made in identifying genes relating to drug responses for cancer, asthma, and cardiovascular disease (Couzin, 2005). These findings have led to the practice of personalized medicine, in which your own DNA sequence becomes part of your medical record and is used in making decisions about which screening tests you should have for early diagnosis of diseases and, if treatment is necessary, what type is best suited for you.

3.5.2: Sex and Gender

OBJECTIVE: Differentiate health experiences by sex and gender

Men and women have different patterns of health problems. Men have shorter life expectancies than women and develop cardiovascular disease at younger ages. They have higher rates of hypertension, death by accident, and overall cancer rates. Women live longer than men, but when they die, they do so from basically the same diseases that men do; they just develop them later in life (CDC, 2017c).

Women have more chronic health conditions than men, including arthritis, asthma, migraine headaches, thyroid disease, gallbladder problems, irritable bowel syndrome, and urinary and bladder problems, among others (Stöppler, 2015). Women have more visits to doctors, take more medication, and spend more time in hospitals than men (Austad, 2011). In addition, women react differently to many medications than do men (Legato, 2016).

Where might such sex differences come from? The explanations are partly biological, partly environmental. Most investigators agree that the differences in longevity and in later onset of major disease are primarily biological: Women have a genetic endowment that gives them protection in early adulthood against many fatal diseases, such as cardiovascular disease. Why this discrepancy? Many theorists believe that it is because their overall health during the childbearing and early parenting years has been more important to the survival of the species than men overall health (Allman et al., 1998).

A related hypothesis is that men do not live as long as women because, for our ancient ancestors, men had to contend with more dangers in the wild and evolved mechanisms to deal with short-term hazards instead of long-term survival (Austad, 2011; Williams, 1957). Today, men still tend to engage in more high-risk behavior than women and, not surprisingly, are twice as likely to die in accidents (Heron et al., 2009).

Gender differences include behavioral factors, such as health awareness and effort spent on health care, which are higher for women than men throughout adulthood. Perhaps one reason women live longer is because of this vigilance (and also why men with wives live longer than men without them).

There are robust sex differences for specific mental health disorders; women have higher rates of depressive disorders and anxiety disorders, whereas men have higher rates of substance-related and addictive disorders. Men are more likely to commit suicide. The heightened vulnerability to disorders that affects emotional functioning in women is thought to be due, in part, to estrogen levels—the same hormones that provide protection from some physical diseases. Testosterone, on the other hand, tends to protect men against depression by blunting the effect of stress and negative emotions (Holden, 2005).

There are environmental factors for the higher rate of major depression and anxiety disorders in women; women are more apt to be victims of domestic violence and sexual assault than men. In many cultures around the world (and in some parts of the United States) men are in roles that dominate and control many aspects of women's lives.

Being victimized and powerless are risk factors for major depression and anxiety disorders (WHO, 2016). Even when men and women live in relatively egalitarian relationships, women are usually the caregivers of the family and are "on call" when family members have problems, experiencing secondhand stress from the problems of their loved ones (Thoits, 2010).

3.5.3: Socioeconomic Class

OBJECTIVE: Describe the ways in which socioeconomic class impacts health

The United States is one of the wealthiest countries in the world. We spend more on health care than any other country, yet we have one of the lowest life expectancies of any developed country. Figure 3.8 shows that men in the United States can expect to live fewer years than those in 24 other countries, and that women in the United States can expect to live fewer years than those in 27 other countries (CDC, 2017). The largest discrepancy is found in the groups of people with lower incomes and less education. Because people in minority racial and ethnic groups are more prevalent in the lower socioeconomic levels, it is difficult to separate the effects of income, education, and minority status on health, but I attempt to do that in the following section.

SOCIOECONOMIC LEVEL The combined rating of income and education makes up one's **socioeconomic level**. The more income a person has, the more years they can expect to live. Figure 3.9 shows the age of expected death for 40-year-olds, based on their household income ranking. As you can see, the higher the income, the longer the average person is expected to live (Chetty et al., 2016). Furthermore, Blackwell et al., (2014) report that only 54% of people with incomes below $35,000 a year are apt to report being in excellent health or very good health. About 70% of people who make $50,000–74,999 report having excellent or very good health, while over 80% of people who make over $100,000 a year give that favorable response.

Education is also a major factor in health. Figure 3.10 shows how many more years of expected life remain for 25-year-olds with different education levels. As you can see, each step on the education ladder brings more expected years of life (CDC, 2012). Education affects subjective health, too. Only 39% of people with less than a high school education report themselves in excellent or very good health, while 75% of those with a college degree or more give that response (Blackwell et al., 2014).

Socioeconomic status has a large effect also on mental health. In the National Health and Nutrition Examination Survey, adults were asked about their depressive symptoms. When responses were examined by income level, respondents at every age who had lower income levels

Figure 3.8 Mortality: Life Expectancy at Birth, by Country

The average number of years an individual can expect to live depends on their sex and the country in which they live.

SOURCE: CDC (2017).

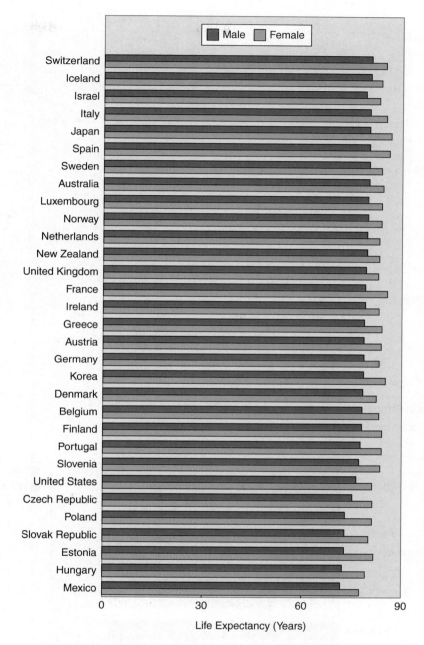

reported more symptoms of depression (CDC, 2012). Figure 3.11 shows those results.

The contributions of age, gender, race, and education to self-rated health were evaluated in a sequential study using longitudinal data from 10 waves of the Health and Retirement Study, consisting of almost 30,000 participants over the age of 50 (Brown et al., 2016). Participants were asked their gender, race, age, and number of years of education.

They were also asked to rate their health on a scale of 1 to 5 with 1 being "poor" and 5 being "excellent." For the men, health ratings decline steadily from age 50 to the end of the study at age 77. White men generally have higher levels of self-rated health than black men, and within those groups, those with higher levels of education have higher levels of self-reported health than those with lower levels. The same is true of black and white women at different education

Figure 3.9 Life Expectancy versus Income in the United States

Men and women's life expectancies are related to their household incomes, with those who have higher incomes having longer life expectancies than those with lower incomes.

SOURCE: Chetty et al. (2016).

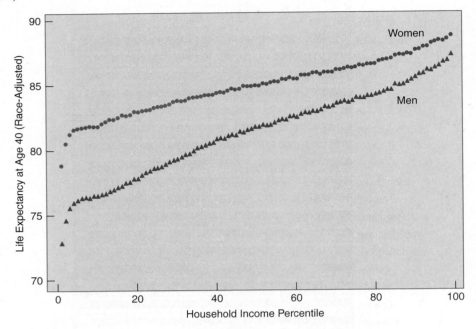

Figure 3.10 Variance in Education in Young Adults

Young adults with more education can expect to live longer, on average, than those with less education.

SOURCE: CDC (2012).

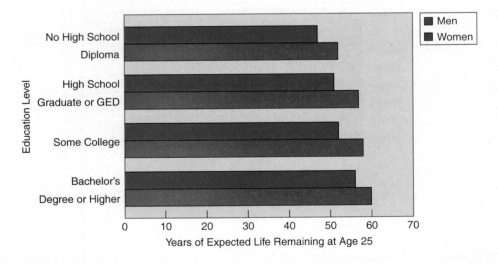

levels. Another notable finding is that there is more variance between the groups at age 50 than later in life. Black men with college degrees start with an advantage over white men with high school educations, but they slowly lose the advantage as they get older. White women without high school educations have a health advantage over black women without high school educations at age 50, but their health ratings decline until they are at the same level at age 77. The general findings of this study are that gender, race, education, and age contribute to self-reported health independently.

Figure 3.11 Effect of Varying Income Levels on Depression

Adults of all ages whose incomes are below the poverty level are more apt to experience depression than those with higher incomes, and the lower the income is, the higher the risk for depression.

SOURCE: CDC (2012).

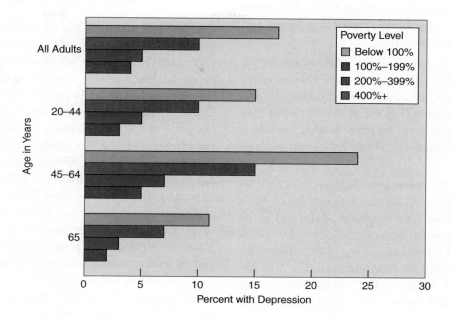

3.5.4: Race and Ethnicity

OBJECTIVE: Summarize racial and ethnic differences in health

There is little agreement on how to categorize people in the United States into racial and ethnic groups, how to define those groups, and what to do with those who don't quite fit into a group (or those who fit into more than one group). In addition, people in minority groups are more apt to have lower incomes and less education, which, as we saw in the last section, contribute to shorter lives and less favorable health outcomes. When this topic was first explored over 20 years ago, the comparisons of interest were black versus white. Then Hispanics were added as a group, although they represent individuals of different races and origins. Since then, Asian and Pacific Islanders have been included, as well as Native Americans, but not as much data has been gathered on these last two groups (Angel et al., 2016). With all that in mind, I summarize the findings here. Be aware: this topic is not as simple as it seems.

Health Outcomes Across Ethnic Groups

Asian Americans/Pacific Islanders—The ethnic group within the U.S. population that seems to have the best health picture is Asian Americans and Pacific Islanders. They have the lowest rates of cardiovascular disease, hypertension, arthritis, cancer, and serious psychological distress (Miller et al., 2007). Members of this group, understandably, are the most likely to rate their health as "excellent." Why the good health? The traditional diets of these groups are healthier than the typical diet in the United States, and the smoking rate for women is lower than for other groups of women as well (CDC, 2017b). However, as with other immigrant groups, the longer they live in the United States, the higher the risk of health problems (Reed & Yano, 1997).

Hispanic/Latinx Americans—Hispanic Americans now have the longest life expectancy at birth than any other group in the United States. They are the least likely to have health insurance (CDC, 2017b), but have lower rates of anxiety disorders, mood disorders (Kessler et al., 2005), and suicides (CDC, 2017b). Similar to Asian Americans and Pacific Islanders, the length of time Hispanic Americans have been in the United States is an important factor, with those who have been here the longest being less healthy (Goel et al., 2004). Country of origin is also a factor; for example, Cuban Americans have substantially better health than other Hispanic American groups (Herd et al., 2011).

The fact that Hispanic Americans have such good health and longevity is surprising to many researchers and has been called the *Hispanic paradox*, which was first described by Markides and Coreil (1986). Some explanations of this paradox have been offered. First, for someone to leave their home and move to the United States (and stay here), they are probably in good health to begin with. Second, because Hispanic immigrants tend to relocate close to family members and others from their home countries, they share a language and provide instrumental help and social support for each other. Third, their traditional culture encourages health-promoting habits and good nutrition (Angel et al., 2016).

Non-Hispanic Whites—Non-Hispanic white adults are the most likely group to have health insurance. They have the highest rates of anxiety disorders, mood disorders, and substance abuse disorders (Kessler et al., 2005) but they are more apt to seek treatment for psychological disorders, especially if they are under age 60 and have good incomes (Wang et al., 2005).

Non-Hispanic Black Americans—Adults classified as non-Hispanic black adults in the United States have shorter life expectancies than Hispanic adults and white adults, and this is especially true for non-Hispanic black men. They have the highest rates of death from heart disease, cancer, stroke, diabetes, HIV, and homicide than any other racial or ethnic group in the United States. Non-Hispanic black people have higher rates of hypertension and lower rates of osteoporosis than other groups and a resulting lower rate of disability from bone fractures (Looker et al., 2017). Women in this group are less likely to commit suicide than any other subgroup, but are more likely to be obese. Non-Hispanic black men and women have lower risks of mood disorders, anxiety disorders, and substance abuse disorders than non-Hispanic white adults (Kessler et al., 2005).

American Indians/Alaskan Natives—The group consisting of American Indians and Alaskan Natives has shorter life expectancies, similar to that of the non-Hispanic black group (Indian Health Services, 2016; U.S. Department of Health and Human Services, 2016). They have the highest rates of diabetes, hypertension, tuberculosis, arthritis, alcohol and substance abuse, smoking, and serious psychological distress, all potentially disabling. Of all racial/ethnic groups in the United States, members of this one are the least likely to rate their health as "excellent." The two leading causes of death for this group are similar to other groups (heart disease and cancer), but the third most common cause of death is accidents (CDC, 2012). These high rates of disease and premature death are due in large part to economic conditions, cultural barriers, and geographic isolation, but sociohistorical factors are at work, too. Still, some progress is being made. For example, the incidence of breast cancer in this group is now the lowest of all racial/ethnic groups (CDC, 2011), but reviewing the overall health data for this group of U.S. citizens, descendants of the original inhabitants of this continent, is disturbing.

3.5.5: Discrimination

OBJECTIVE: Explain how discrimination leads to negative health outcomes for women and people from minority groups

It seems clear that some racial and ethnic minorities have a greater prevalence of early death, physical health problems, and mental health disorders than others. There is also evidence that some groups also receive lower levels of health care, especially African Americans and Hispanic Americans. One study compared mental health care for African American patients and non-Hispanic white patients, finding that the gap between the two groups had increased during the past decade, with fewer African American patients getting adequate treatment for mental health disorders compared to white patients (Ault-Brutus, 2012). Much of this can be explained by socioeconomic factors—the high price of visits to mental health-care providers and the cost of medication. It is also more difficult for people with lower levels of income and education to take time off from work and to travel to medical centers outside their immediate neighborhoods when necessary. It is difficult to know when mental health care is needed or what type of provider is appropriate.

Even so, many individuals also report to researchers that they experience **discrimination**, or prejudicial treatment, from the health-care system because of their gender, race, socioeconomic status, sexual orientation, or ethnicity. For instance, one group that has lower levels of physical and mental health that may be due to discrimination is the lesbian, gay, bisexual, transgender, and related (LGBT+) community. Although there are no nationally representative data on LGBT+ individuals in the United States, smaller studies show that this population has higher rates of tobacco, alcohol, and other drug use than the general population. LGBT+ emerging adults are more likely to be homeless than other youths and are two to three times more likely to attempt suicide. Elderly members of the LGBT+ community don't get adequate health care because of isolation and discrimination by providers. Transgender individuals have higher rates of victimization, mental health issues, and suicide, even when compared to lesbian, gay, and bisexual individuals (U.S. Department of Health & Human Services, 2016).

To test for prejudicial treatment of patients, sociologist Heather Kugelmass (2016) devised an experiment: leaving voicemail messages with 320 psychotherapists, asking for appointments. The callers were actually actors—a black man and a white man along with a black woman and a white woman—who delivered a script in a manner that had been tested on an online crowd-sourcing marketplace to sound either middle class or working class. Each therapist received one voicemail message mentioning the symptoms of depression and anxiety, giving the name of the same insurance plan, and requesting an appointment for a weekday evening. The callers varied by race (black or white), gender (male or female), and social class (working class or middle class). Researchers recorded how many therapists responded to the voicemails and how many agreed to meet with the caller at the requested time. A month later a second, similar call was made, except the therapists who had received an initial call from a white caller received one from a black caller of the same gender and social class.

Out of 640 voicemails, only 287 (44%) were returned, and of those, only 97 (15%) elicited an offer for an appointment at any time. Only 57 (9%) of the calls resulted in appointments at the preferred times (Figure 3.12).

The therapists clearly preferred to make appointments with help-seekers who sounded middle class (28%) compared to those who sounded working class (8%), regardless of perceived race. However, they also preferred help-seekers who sounded middle-class white over those who sounded middle-class black. There were no race differences with working-class help-seekers. Therapists also preferred to make appointments with female help-seekers regardless of perceived race or socioeconomic class. It seems clear that for this group, at least, knowing that one needs help, finding a therapist, and having insurance is not enough. It is also important for therapists to be responsive to help-seekers regardless of perceived race or socioeconomic status.

ADVERSITY AND STRESS The statistics on female and minority health show inequality at all levels of health care—prevention, detection, treatment, and follow-up. However, there is even more to this problem than direct discrimination. The perception that one is being discriminated against can produce stress, which can lead to negative health outcomes. Racial and ethnic minorities (as well as women, people living in poverty, and members of the LGBT+ community) are exposed to different experiences than mainstream society members. These different experiences lead to higher levels of stress, which in turn lead to higher levels of physical and mental health disorders. Stress burdens on women and minorities build up over the life course and result in an increasing health gap between the "haves" and "have-nots." So even if systematic discrimination in health care is not apparent, 40 years of research shows that belonging to a racial or ethnic minority can contribute to early death, more physical and mental health disorders, less treatment (or less-effective treatment), and a lower quality of life than those in the mainstream (Thoits, 2010).

A number of studies over the last decade have shown that inequalities in medical treatment are a reality, but other issues are in play here, too, such as English proficiency, health literacy, neighborhood social cohesion, and cultural distrust of the medical system (Lyles et al., 2011). All of these have an effect on health. For example, help-seekers who perceive that they are discriminated against in medical settings as well as in everyday life are more apt to seek treatment from complementary and alternative medical providers instead of medical providers who use treatments supported by research (Shippee et al., 2012).

Women and members of minority groups can also experience negative health outcomes at times of adversity, when they are experiencing discrimination and still managing to cope and achieve. But there is a cost to coping. Sometimes it takes the form of overeating, smoking or alcohol and drug abuse, which in themselves contribute to poor health (Jackson et al., 2010). Other times it is manifest in lower immune function and susceptibility to infection. In a study that included 150 healthy black adults, those who had higher educational attainment, lower symptoms of depression, and a wider range of social relationships despite a disadvantaged

Figure 3.12 Outcome of Help-Seeking Calls (*n* = 160 per group)

SOURCE: Kugelmass (2016).

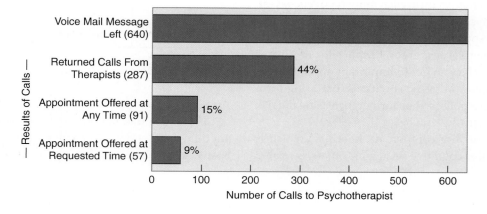

background were also more likely to develop an upper respiratory infection when innoculated with an active rhinovirus culture (Miller et al., 2016). The authors of this study concluded that managing to achieve in spite of adversity can weaken the immune system and lead to physical illness—another way that one's membership in a minority group might lead to less than optimal health status.

3.5.6: Personality and Behavior Patterns

OBJECTIVE: Explain how personality influences health

The idea that one's personality contributes to one's physical health dates back at least to the time of Hippocrates in ancient Greece. Cardiologists Meyer Friedman and Ray Rosenman (1959) made the first empirical demonstration of this relationship when they identified a behavior pattern that predicted risk for coronary heart disease. Since then, this area of research has become well accepted. Specific stable patterns of thinking, feeling, and behaving are indeed associated with increased risk of illness and premature death (Smith & Gallo, 2001).

Individuals classified as having a **type A behavior pattern** are achievement-striving, competitive, and involved in their jobs to excess; they feel extreme urgency with time-related matters and are easily provoked to hostility. People who do not fit this description are referred to as type B. Although the issue has been debated actively for over 50 years, it seems clear that, when careful measures are made, people who fit the type A behavior pattern are at greater risk of coronary heart disease than those with type B behavior (Bokenberger et al., 2014; Smith & Gallo, 2001).

A great deal of research has been done to determine how this effect takes place. Generally, researchers have found both a direct link (type A behavior affects physical health through such mechanisms as increasing stress reactions and lowering immune function) and an indirect link (type A behavior causes the person to create and seek out stressful situations that, in turn, elicit more type A behavior, which leads to physical responses). In other words, people who have this personality style are apt to create other situations that call for similar responses. People who are always racing against the clock to get to important appointments will place themselves in traffic situations that bring forth additional type A responses, thus further increasing the risk for physical problems.

Another personality component, **hostility**, which is defined as a negative cognitive set against others, is related to increased heart rate and blood pressure, direct pathways to cardiovascular disease, premature death (Chida & Hamer, 2008), and peptic ulcers (Lemogne et al., 2015). In addition, there are indirect pathways. For example, people who are high in hostility no doubt have hostile relationships with others, such as in their marriages, and these hostile interactions add more health risk (and subtract the protective effect of social support). Hostile people are also known to engage in more high-risk behaviors, such as smoking, and, as a result, show a higher rate of smoking-related cancer (Lemogne et al., 2013).

In contrast, people who are high in **optimism**, that is, who have a positive outlook on life, believe that good things are going to happen to them, cope with life's problems by taking steps to find direct solutions (instead of hoping that someone will rescue them or placing blame on others), are less apt to suffer from serious physical illness, and are less likely to die prematurely (Seligman, 1991). Since the initial research, the trait of optimism has been linked with positive health outcomes all around the world (Pressman et al., 2013). For example, optimism was related to longevity in a group of older African American women (average age of 77 years) with Caribbean roots (Unson et al., 2008), to better health-care outcomes in a group of Native American elders (Ruthig & Allery, 2008), to successful aging in a group of white and Hispanic women over the age of 60 (Lamond et al., 2008), and to better health during the year following diagnosis in a group of patients with heart disease in Ireland (Hevey et al., 2012). I would be remiss not to add one study that shows the dark side of optimism—college students whose optimism is too high (unrealistic optimism) are more apt to ignore the use of sunscreen protection, even though they are aware of the dangers of ultraviolet radiation exposure, believing that "it won't happen to me" (Calder & Aitken, 2008).

WRITING PROMPT

Effects of Positive Behavior Patterns

If negative behavior patterns such as hostility have both direct and indirect effects on health, how about positive behavior patterns such as optimism? What would the direct and indirect effects be?

▶ The response entered here will appear in the performance dashboard and can be viewed by your instructor.

Submit

If you are like me, you may be wondering whether anything can be done to change people who are type A, hostile, or pessimistic because personality is considered an enduring component of an individual. Many researchers are cautious about using the term *personality* for this very reason; instead, they use other terms, such as *behavior patterns*. But whatever terms are used, the question remains: Is it possible to recognize and modify unhealthy traits in oneself? One meta-analysis of almost 10,000 cardiac patients showed that psychological treatment (including stress management, cognitive-behavioral therapy, and behavioral therapy), when included with the usual medical care, resulted in fewer deaths and recurrences of cardiac events for at least 2 years for male patients (Linden et al., 2007). Another study produced positive affect in a group of college students by asking them to write a short essay about a happy event each week for 4 weeks and also keep a diary of happy events. At the end of the study, they reported better overall health status than a control group of students who had written on neutral topics (Yamanski et al., 2009).

3.5.7: Developmental Origins

OBJECTIVE: Analyze how prenatal and childhood experiences affect adult health

Several researchers have presented evidence suggesting that some diseases of adulthood are determined partly by environmental events earlier in life. Epidemiologist David Barker and his colleagues (Barker et al., 1989) introduced this idea three decades ago when they examined birth and death records for over 5,000 men born within a 20-year period in the same area of England. They found that the men with the lowest weights at birth had the highest likelihood of dying from cardiovascular disease. Later research linked low birthweight to type 2 diabetes and hypertension. Since that time, research with humans and other species has given rise to the **developmental origins hypothesis**, which states that growth during the fetal period, infancy, and the early years of childhood is a significant factor in adult health (Kuh & Ben-Shlomo, 2016).

Environmental factors present in early development that have been studied include maternal nutrition, season of birth, and maternal smoking. The resulting adult health outcomes include hypertension, diabetes, osteoporosis, and mood disorders (Gluckman & Hanson, 2004). A similar study linked family income during very early childhood with adult obesity (Ziol-Guest et al., 2009). Individuals whose parents made less than $25,000 a year during the child's prenatal period and the first year of life were more apt to be obese in adulthood than those whose families had higher incomes. Interestingly, family income during

subsequent years of childhood (from the age of 1 to 15) had no impact on adult obesity.

Furthermore, evidence has been found that if a woman suffers malnutrition during pregnancy, her child is likely to be born at a low birth weight. And if that child is a daughter, *her* children's birth weight and subsequent health could be affected by the malnutrition experienced during the grandmother's pregnancy, even if the daughter did not experience malnutrition herself (Gluckman & Hanson, 2004). The explanation for this is that ova are formed during the prenatal period. Malnutrition of the pregnant woman affects her developing fetus, and if the fetus is female, the malnutrition would affect the development of her ova. Not only can we trace our health status back to our childhood and prenatal experiences, but we can also go back to our *mothers'* prenatal months when half our genetic material was being formed, influences referred to as **intergenerational effects**.

There is also a relationship between childhood infectious disease and adult cardiovascular disease, cancer, and diabetes. One study demonstrating this connection was done by economic historians Tommy Bengtsson and Martin Lindström (2003), who examined 18th-century medical records in four parishes in Sweden for a period of 128 years. They found that the people with the fewest infectious diseases in infancy had the greatest longevity. Even when periods of food shortage were considered, infant infections remained the strongest factor in determining adult longevity. It is suggested that the link between early childhood infections and early death in adulthood is inflammation (Finch & Crimmins, 2004)—a factor implicated in diseases such as heart disease, cancer, and Alzheimer's disease.

In a study using lab animals, neuroscientist Francesca Mastorci and her colleagues (2009) exposed pregnant rats to different types of stressors and investigated the outcomes of the offspring once they reached adulthood. Interestingly, there was no change for any biological structure or function as a result of the prenatal stress alone, but once these adult animals were exposed to environmental stressors themselves, they were less able to regulate their cardiovascular systems and were rendered more susceptible to heart disease than rats that had not experienced the prenatal stress. It seems that the prenatal stress did not produce heart disease itself, but produced a predisposition for heart disease once the animals encountered their own environmental stress.

For those of us in developed countries, the incidence of childhood infectious disease is low, and some researchers suggest that the increase in our lifespans during the 20th century was due to this fact. However, in developing countries, diseases such as tuberculosis, diarrheal illnesses, and malaria are still prevalent. Epidemiologists believe that once these childhood diseases are controlled, there will be a corresponding drop in the rates of life-limiting adult diseases that involve inflammation and a resulting increase in longevity.

3.5.8: Lifestyle

OBJECTIVE: Determine how lifestyle choices affect health

At the risk of repeating myself, I must point out that two of the biggest factors in age-related disease and mental health disorders are sedentary lifestyle and obesity. However, it may surprise you to know that fewer than 20% of adults in the United States get the recommended aerobic and muscle-strengthening exercise each week, and only one in three adults eat the recommended amount of vegetables in their diets (Office of Disease Prevention and Health Promotion, 2016). Over one-third of U.S. adults are obese, due in part to lack of exercise and diets high in calories from sugar and fat.

Other lifestyle factors that contribute to poor health are tobacco and other substance abuse. Tobacco is a risk factor for almost every form of cancer, as well as heart disease and Alzheimer's disease, yet 16% of people in the United States smoke cigarettes, and more use other tobacco products (CDC, 2017b). The good news is that the rate of tobacco use has come down in the last two decades, and the rate of exercise is up.

I have reviewed the changes in health through adulthood in the table below, but I want to end with a reminder that the health disorders and diseases of adulthood don't happen to everyone and don't happen at random. Many can be prevented; others can be detected early and treated successfully, or at least controlled. The best advice is still to eat healthy foods, exercise, get regular checkups, know your family health history, and seek scientifically proven treatment early for whatever disorders occur. Live a balanced life with time for supportive relationships and activities that reduce stress. Don't smoke; if you do smoke, quit. Practice safe sex. Wear your seatbelts and safety helmets. To date, there is still no evidence for magic potions or pills that provide a shortcut to good health and long life.

Review of Health and Illness over the Adult Years

Factors Related to Health and Illness	18–24 Years	25–39 Years	40–64 Years	65–74 Years	75+ Years
Death rate	Very low death rate (0.08%); top causes of death are accidents, suicide, and homicide	Low death rate (0.1%): top causes of death are accidents and suicide	Low death rate (0.6%); top causes of death are cancer and heart disease	Death rate begins to increase (2%); top causes of death are heart disease and cancer; diabetes deaths are fifth	Higher death rate (8%); top causes of death are heart disease and cancer; Alzheimer's disease deaths are fifth
Acute illnesses	Acute illnesses most common	Acute illnesses most common	Some acute illnesses; moderate risk for chronic illnesses; early-onset Alzheimer's can begin, but accounts for only 5% of all cases	Chronic conditions present, but most report having none; almost all are aging in place; Alzheimer's present in 5–10%; other dementias present but some can be treated	Chronic conditions and disability more common; most are community dwelling; 40% report their health as "excellent or very good"
Levels of disability	Lowest levels of disability	Low levels of disability	Moderate levels of disability	Disability levels increase	Increased levels of disability; about 50% over 85 have Alzheimer's disease
Alcoholism and other disorders	Median age of onset of most psychological disorders is 11–13; highest rate of substance-related and addictive disorders	Most mood disorders have their onset before age 30; moderate rates of depressive symptoms	Lower rates of onset for major depression; lower rates of depressive symptoms	Very low rates of onset for major depression. Low rates of alcoholism; higher rates of depressive symptoms	Major depression is rare and often related to disease; higher rates of depressive symptoms, probably due to chronic health problems and bereavement
Rates of treatment for mental health disorders	High rates of treatment before 21, low rates afterward	Higher rates of seeking treatment for mental health problems	Higher rates of seeking treatment for mental health problems	Low rates of seeking treatment for mental health disorders	Low rates of seeking treatment for mental health disorders

Summary: Health and Health Disorders

3.1 Mortality, Morbidity, and Disability

OBJECTIVE: **Predict adult health issues based on data**

- Mortality rates increase with age, especially after 60. Causes of death are different for different ages, with accidents, homicides, and suicides leading the list for emerging adults, heart disease and cancer for older adults.

- Younger adults have a greater incidence of acute illnesses; older adults have a greater incidence of chronic conditions such as arthritis, high blood pressure, and cardiovascular disease.

- Rates of disability also increase with age, although almost half of adults age 75 years or more report having no disability.

- About 81% of women age 65 and older and 90% of men this age are community dwelling. Only 3% are in nursing homes, and most of those are in their 80s or older.

3.2 Specific Diseases

OBJECTIVE: **Analyze ways in which older adults experience disease**

- Cardiovascular disease is the top cause of death among adults throughout the world. It involves the blocking of coronary arteries by plaques in the artery walls and can lead to heart attack. Some risk factors are under our control, such as smoking and leading a sedentary lifestyle. Others are not under our control, such as family history and age. Women get cardiovascular disease at the same rate as men, only later in life and with different symptoms.

- The second leading cause of death for adults in the United States is cancer, which involves rapid division of abnormal cells invading nearby tissue or spreading to other parts of the body. The incidence of cancer increases with age. Risk factors for cancer that are under our control are smoking, obesity, and unprotected exposure to bright sunlight. Factors that are not under our control are age and family history.

- Diabetes is a hormonal condition in which the body does not produce enough insulin to utilize the glucose produced by the digestive system. Type 2 diabetes is increasing in prevalence as a major cause of death and disability for middle-aged adults and older. It is often the result of a sedentary lifestyle and unhealthy eating habits and can be controlled by making changes in these areas of one's life and sometimes by gastric bypass surgery.

- The fifth leading cause of death among older adults is Alzheimer's disease, caused by progressive deterioration of certain parts of the brain. The result is loss of cognitive ability and physical function. Alzheimer's disease is seldom seen before age 50, and 90% of cases occur after age 65. Many of the risk factors for Alzheimer's disease are the same as for cardiovascular disease, and both may be linked to inflammation earlier in life. Some of the risk factors that can be modified are smoking, sedentary lifestyle, and obesity. Factors that can't are age and genetic predisposition. Traumatic brain injuries from contact sports and combat can cause a type of dementia in later life called chronic traumatic encephalopathy.

3.3 Psychological Disorders

OBJECTIVE: **Evaluate mental health challenges facing adults**

- The rate of mental health disorders in U.S. adults has remained stable in the past decade. The most common types are anxiety disorders (phobias, social anxiety), major depressive disorder, and substance-related and addictive disorders. The onset of most mental health disorders is in adolescence and early adulthood. Major depression is more apt to affect young adults than older adults, who are more apt to report depressive symptoms.

- The majority of people who experience symptoms of mental health disorders do not seek treatment, and a third receive treatment that is inadequate or inappropriate. Those who do not seek treatment are more likely to be older adults than younger or middle-aged adults.

3.4 Assistance Solutions

OBJECTIVE: **Analyze assistance options for physical and mental disorders**

- Some solutions for disease and disability involve assistive technology and assistance animals. As our population grows older, these tools are becoming more and more common.

3.5 Individual Differences in Health

OBJECTIVE: **Compare the physical health issues facing adults from different populations**

- Many physical and mental health disorders can be prevented through healthy lifestyles. Others can be detected early and treated successfully. There are no shortcuts to good health and no magic pills.

- Men and women have different patterns of both physical and mental health problems. Men have shorter life expectancies, higher rates of life-threatening physical diseases, more psychological disorders involving alcohol and substance abuse, and more impulse control disorders. Women have more chronic diseases and higher rates of major depression and anxiety disorders. This difference is partly biological and partly sociocultural.

- People in lower socioeconomic groups have lower levels of physical and mental health than higher socioeconomic groups and decline in physical health more quickly. This difference is primarily due to health-care availability, health habits, and the effects of stress.

- Asian Americans and Pacific Islanders have the best health picture of any group in the United States, due in part to their healthy diets and low smoking rates. The lowest level of health in the United States is found in Native American and Alaskan Native groups.

- Discrimination by people in the health-care profession against women, people of color, working-class patients, and members of the LGBT+ community have been reported and demonstrated in investigations by researchers. This discrimination can lead to high levels of stress, which, in turn, can lead to poorer health.

- Another factor that can affect health is behavior patterns (type A, hostility, pessimism) that lead to cardiovascular disease and early death.

- The genetic contribution to disease ranges from actually determining that an individual will have a certain disease (some types of Alzheimer's disease) to providing a predisposition that environmental factors will cause a disease (tobacco and lung cancer). One's genotype may even provide protection against certain diseases. Some medical treatments are now being designed for individuals based on their genotypes.

- Low birth weight, early childhood infections, and low family income during the first year of life have been linked to adult health problems such as diabetes, mood disorders, and obesity.

SHARED WRITING

Individual Differences in Health

Consider this chapter's discussion of individual differences in health as they relate to a variety of factors (genetics, socioeconomic status, race, gender). What are some specific factors that have influenced your health (for better or for worse)? How have they impacted you? Can you make changes? How can you adapt to them? Write a short response that your classmates will read. Be sure to discuss specific examples.

▶ A minimum number of characters is required to post and earn points. After posting, your response can be viewed by your class and instructor, and you can participate in the class discussion.

Post   0 characters | 140 minimum

Chapter 4
Cognitive Abilities

Games can help adults keep their cognitive abilities sharp.

Learning Objectives

4.1 Explain how attention changes with age

4.2 Compare how different forms of memory change over time

4.3 Evaluate the concept of age-related changes to intellectual ability

4.4 Relate decision making and problem solving to age

4.5 Analyze factors that influence individual cognitive change

4.6 Evaluate forms of cognitive assistance

A Word From the Author

Remembering My Dad's Friend, Don Iverson

MY PARENTS TOOK me out to a steakhouse for my 53rd birthday, and when I had trouble getting catsup to pour out of a new bottle onto my fries, Dad showed me a trick he had learned from a catsup salesman—you tap the neck of the bottle sharply against your outstretched index finger and the catsup comes out easily. Then he and Mom reminisced about the catsup salesman, their friend Don Iverson. He lived in Savannah, Georgia, and they had last visited him on the way home from their honeymoon. Don's wife had made a standing rib roast for dinner with peach cobbler for dessert. What a great time they had, eating and playing cards and talking until early morning. What was Don's wife's name? Neither could remember. They talked back and forth a little, trying to come up with the name of the salesman's wife they had not seen in 55 years but finally agreed in desperation: "We just can't remember anything anymore!"

It's true that my parents were growing old—they were 77 and 80 at the time of that birthday dinner—but remembering the catsup salesman's name, the city he lived in, and even what his wife had served for dinner that evening over 50 years before is impressive at any age. Yet one of the most popular stereotypes of aging is cognitive loss, and it is a stereotype that even older adults hold about themselves. The same lost car keys or forgotten phone number that at the age of 30 or 40 is a normal slipup is viewed as a symptom of early senility at 70 or 80. But what is typical of cognitive aging, and what is myth?

A common view of cognitive aging is that people become passive victims of the deterioration of their brains, with a corresponding decline in competent thought and behavior. Some basic cognitive abilities such as attention, the speed with which we process information, and some forms of memory *do* take a turn for the worse as we age. But the picture is not so bleak. Although cognitive decline with advancing age is real, in many cases older adults maintain, and sometimes even increase, their mental skills, and studies using functional brain imaging—which examines not just the structure of the brain but also looks at how the brain functions when performing cognitive tasks—show that the aging brain is a dynamic organ, adapting to cognitive challenges and neural deterioration (Park & McDonough, 2013).

4.1: Attention

OBJECTIVE: Explain how attention changes with age

In the first psychology textbook, William James (1890), defined attention as "the taking possession of the mind, in clear and vivid form, of one out of what may seem several simultaneously possible objects or trains of thoughts. . . . It implies withdrawal from some things in order to deal effectively with others" (p. 404). A good example of a task that requires attention is driving. Many accidents are caused by a driver's failure to attend to the important tasks of driving such as keeping the car on the road and avoiding other cars, road debris, and pedestrians. Younger adults actually have more car accidents than do older adults, but when older adults have accidents, the most common cause is a failure to attend to an important change in the environment, such as the presence of another car, pedestrian, or traffic sign.

In order to drive successfully, we must not only attend to our driving, we also must be able to ignore distractions from things like beautiful scenery, a passenger drinking coffee, a dog in the backseat, etc. Older adults are more susceptible to failures of attention due to distraction than are younger adults.

4.1.1 Describe how the ability to maintain divided attention changes with age

4.1.2 Relate visual search ability to age

4.1.1: Divided Attention

OBJECTIVE: Describe how the ability to maintain divided attention changes with age

When we try to attend to more than one task at a time, this is called **divided attention**. Driving is even more difficult, for example, when a person is simultaneously trying to pay attention to driving and to talking on a cell phone, talking to a passenger, or thinking about work. While both younger and older adults show a decrease in performance on most tasks when dividing their attention, older adults find attending to multiple things at one time particularly difficult. Another good example of a divided attention task that occurs often in everyday life is trying to follow more than one conversation at the same time. In one experiment, researchers simulated the conditions of a cocktail party in which younger and older participants were required to attend to stimuli coming to them from various voices and multiple directions (Getzmann et al., 2016). Figure 4.1 shows the results of this experiment. When the information was being given by a single speaker

Figure 4.1 Younger and Older Adults Attending to Speech in Varied Environments

Younger people and older people attend well to auditory cues from a speaker with no distractions, but there is an age difference when the cues are given by multiple speakers at once. Younger participants attend significantly better than older participants when instructed to divide attention.

SOURCE: Getzmann et al. (2016).

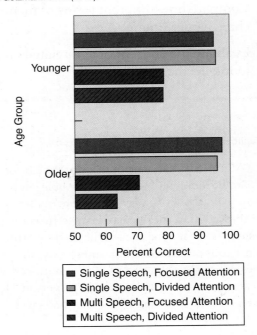

- ■ Single Speech, Focused Attention
- ■ Single Speech, Divided Attention
- ■ Multi Speech, Focused Attention
- ■ Multi Speech, Divided Attention

with no distraction, participants in both age groups attended well, but when the information was being given by multiple speakers at once, the younger group performed better than the older group. Furthermore, when asked to attend only to information coming from one direction or another (divided attention), the younger group was significantly better at the task than the older group.

4.1.2: Visual Search

OBJECTIVE: Relate visual search ability to age

Another attention task that people often perform in everyday life involves **visual search**, the process of searching your environment in an attempt to locate a particular item. Cognitive psychologist Allison A. Brennan and her colleagues (2017) compared the abilities of children, younger adults, and older adults to find certain objects in their environment. The older adults included a group who reported having fallen at least twice in the past year. The research participants were instructed to open the door to a room, walk inside, and visually locate a common item, such as an apple or a ball, on shelves containing many items.

They repeated this task with different items in different locations 16 times. As can be seen in Figure 4.2, the number of times participants failed to locate the object within 20 seconds decreased from childhood to young adulthood and then increased from young adulthood to older adulthood. The group of older adults with a history of falls had the most failed attempts to locate the objects. The researchers concluded that older adults have more difficulty locating objects in their environment, and those who have particular difficulty in visual search tasks may be more likely to fall (Brennan et al., 2017).

4.2: Memory

OBJECTIVE: Compare how different forms of memory change over time

Memory is defined as the ability to retain or store information and retrieve it when needed. Attention is essential to memory because we cannot retain and store information successfully if we do not attend to the information to start with. For example, if we fail to retrieve the name of a person, it may be that we never successfully attended to the information and thus never stored the information into memory. As illustrated in my story about the catsup salesman at the beginning of this chapter, older adults often incorrectly interpret minor memory lapses as signs of serious mental failure, and at the same time they do not give themselves credit for the many accurate and important memory tasks they perform each day. Most adults over the age of 65 report that they have noticed a recent decline in their memory abilities, and most express concern over it, associating it with illness, loss of independence, and their own mortality (Lane & Zelinski, 2003).

Memory, however, is not a single ability, and age does not have the same effect on all memory abilities. **Short-term memory** involves holding information for several seconds and then either discarding the information or moving the information to **long-term memory**, where information can be stored for many years or even forever. **Working memory** expands the definition of short-term memory to include not just the holding of information in memory, but also the processing of that information, which would include strategies for moving information from short-term to long-term memory.

Figure 4.2 Locating Objects in a Visual Search Task

Errors on visual search task decrease from childhood to young adulthood, but increase from young adulthood to older adulthood.

SOURCE: Brennan et al. (2017).

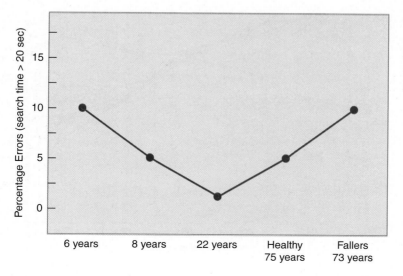

▼	**By the end of this module, you will be able to:**

4.2.1 Differentiate short-term and working memory

4.2.2 Summarize how declarative and nondeclarative memory change with age

4.2.3 Characterize prospective memory

4.2.4 Explain how memory training works

4.2.5 Describe potential issues with age-related memory studies

4.2.1: Short-Term and Working Memory

OBJECTIVE: Differentiate short-term and working memory

Short-term memory (STM) is the passive maintenance of information for a short period of time and is assessed by tests such as the **digit-span task**. In the digit-span task, an examiner reads a series of randomly arranged digits at a rate of about one per second, and at the end of the list the person must repeat the digits back in the same order. Short-term memory shows relatively small declines with age through the 70s and 80s (Gregoire & Van der Linden, 1997) and remains relatively stable through the mid-90s (Bäckman et al., 2000). Declines in verbal short-term memory with increased age may be due in part to hearing loss. Verhaegen and colleagues (2014) found equivalent verbal STM performance when comparing the performance of older adults with younger adults who were matched in hearing thresholds.

Most of the time, however, we are not passively maintaining information for a short period of time. Instead, we are actively processing the information. Working memory (Baddeley, 1986) refers to the amount of information we can hold in mind while performing some type of operation on it. For example, in the backward digit-span test, a common measure of working memory, one hears a series of digits, and then repeats those digits in reverse order. There is a much more substantial decline with age in working memory (Berg & Sternberg, 2003; Hale et al., 2011) than in short-term memory.

This different effect of age on short term and working memory was demonstrated by psychologist Denise Park and her colleagues (Park et al., 2002). They gave a variety of memory tasks to participants in seven groups, ranging in age from the 20s to the 80s. The results of some of these tests are shown in Figure 4.3. Short-term memory tasks included watching the experimenter point to a sequence of colored blocks and then repeating the sequence and listening to the experimenter give a sequence of numbers and repeating them back. As you can see, performance declined with age

Figure 4.3 Age-Related Cross-Sectional Changes on Various Cognitive Tasks

Age-related cross-sectional changes are demonstrated on a variety of cognitive tasks. Note that although both short-term (primary) and working memory decline with advancing age, the decline is steeper for working memory.

SOURCE: Park et al. (2002).

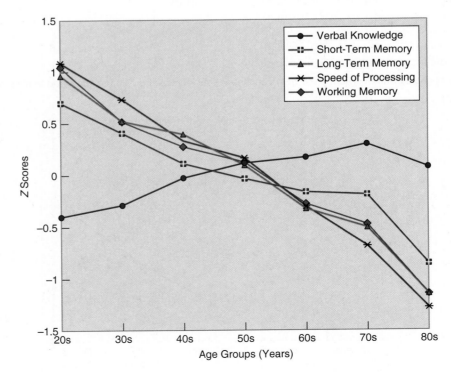

for short-term memory. Declines were sharper, however, for tests of working memory. These tests involved storing information in memory while performing some computation on it. For example, in the reading-span test, participants listened to a sentence ("After dinner the chef prepared dessert"). They were then asked to answer a multiple-choice question about the sentence ("What did the chef prepare? a. fish, b. dessert, c. salad"). Participants were presented a number of different sentences and questions, then asked to remember the last word in each sentence in exact order. The trajectory for these tasks, as you can see, shows a much steeper decline with age than for the short-term memory tasks. But the rate of decline also depends on what people are remembering. For example, age-related declines in working memory are greater for spatial information (e.g., remembering the location of a series of Xs on a grid) than for verbal information (e.g., remembering the last word in each of several sentences) (Hale et al., 2011).

The same pattern of results has been found in longitudinal studies. For example, psychologist David Hultsch and his colleagues (1998) gave various memory tests to a group of 297 older Canadian adults who were participants in the Victoria Longitudinal Study. The average age of one group of participants was 65 when they were first tested, and the average age of the other group was 75. Three years later, both the younger group (now 68) and the older group (now 78) showed significant declines in verbal working memory, and the older group had a significantly greater decline than the younger group.

HOW WORKING MEMORY CHANGES What is the reason for this decline in working memory? One theory is that older people don't have the mental energy, or attentional resources, that younger people do (Craik & Byrd, 1982). A related idea is that older people are not as able to use the strategies required by working-memory tasks (Brébion et al., 1997). Another explanation offered is a decline in processing speed (Salthouse, 1996). Park et al. (2002) measured processing speed in addition to short-term memory and working memory and found that processing speed declines with increased age. Recent research has contrasted the "strategy-use" versus "processing speed" hypotheses and found that although differences in strategy use can account for some individual differences in working memory, this cannot account for all of the age differences in working memory. In contrast, differences in processing speed account for a substantial amount of the age differences in working-memory performance among older adults (Bailey et al., 2009). A fourth hypothesis is that older adults are less able to inhibit irrelevant and confusing information (Samrani et al., 2017). This irrelevant information takes up space in working memory and distracts from the ability to remember the important and relevant information. In addition, researchers have found evidence that older adults took

longer than younger adults to remove no-longer-relevant information from working memory (Yi & Friedman, 2014).

It is also interesting to know that when younger and older adults perform comparably on working-memory tasks, such as when the memory load is small (for example, only two to four items have to be remembered), brain imaging studies reveal that they use different parts of their brains (Reuter-Lorenz, 2013). For example, for small memory loads, older adults show more activation in the frontal regions of the brain, an area associated with higher-order cognition. As the task becomes more demanding, younger adults also show increased activation in these areas (Cappell et al., 2010; Schneider-Garces et al., 2010). This pattern of neural activation suggests that older adults are not the passive victims of a deteriorating brain, but rather are developing alternate neural strategies to maintain their levels of cognitive performance.

Why is working memory, in particular, so important? The primary reason is that working memory is associated with performing almost all other cognitive tasks. The ability to keep information active in one's mind and do something with that information (that is, "think" about it) is central to almost every problem people set out to solve, from the mundane act of preparing one's coffee in the morning to making decisions about buying a new flat-screen TV. Working memory is a central component of what psychologists call **executive function**, which refers to the processes involved in regulating attention and in determining what to do with information just gathered or retrieved from long-term memory (Jones et al., 2003; Miyake & Friedman, 2012). In addition to working memory, executive function includes the ability to inhibit responding and resist interference, the ability to selectively attend to information, and cognitive flexibility, as reflected by how easily individuals can switch between different sets of rules or different tasks. Each of these skills declines in efficiency in older adults (Goh et al., 2012; Passow et al., 2012).

4.2.2: Episodic Memory

OBJECTIVE: Summarize how declarative and nondeclarative memory change with age

Memory is not a single process. In fact, *memories* themselves are not a single thing—a specific event that is retrieved from long-term memory and brought to consciousness. Rather, psychologists have proposed that information is represented in long-term memory in one of two general ways: declarative memory and nondeclarative memory (Tulving, 1985, 2005). **Declarative memory**, sometimes called *explicit memory*, refers to knowledge that is available to conscious awareness and can be directly (explicitly) assessed by tests of recall or recognition memory. Declarative memory comes in two types: **semantic memory**, our knowledge of language, facts, and concepts, and **episodic memory**, the ability to recall events. When you appear on the TV program *Jeopardy* and come up with the correct name of the 15th president of the United States, you are using your semantic memory. When you come home and tell your friends and family about your trip to Los Angeles and the whole game-show experience, you are using your episodic memory.

When older people say, "My memory isn't as sharp as it used to be," they are talking about their episodic memory. In information-processing terms, it would be expressed this way: "My storage and retrieval processes don't seem to be working as efficiently as they once did." Episodic memory is typically studied by presenting people of different ages with lists of words or stories for memorization. Later (anywhere between a few seconds and several days) they are instructed to recall as many of the words or as much of the story as they can. The typical findings are that older adults do not recall as many of the words as younger adults, and that this decline, though relatively slow, is continuous over the adult years; it begins early, perhaps as early as the late teens and early 20s, and is continuous into at least the mid-90s (Hoyer & Verhaeghen, 2006; Ornstein & Light, 2010).

One part of episodic memory that is especially difficult for older adults is binding together individual features of an event. When we try to remember a real-world event, we must remember both the features of the event (such as, the people, the actions, the context) and how these features are connected (for example, who performed which action and in which context). Developmental psychologist Julie Earles and her colleagues demonstrated this by showing younger and older adults a series of video clips of people performing simple actions (a young woman peeling an apple, for example).

They came back later and were shown another series of video clips, some of which were the same clips they saw before and others that were different. Some of the different videos showed a new action that had not been seen before. Others of the new videos, conjunction events, showed a person they had seen before performing an action they had seen before, only being performed by someone else. Older adults were much more likely than younger adults to make these conjunction event mistakes, even when they remembered the people and the actions as well as did the younger adults. Older adults have difficulty forming associations among single units of episodic memory and retrieving them from long-term memory (Earles et al., 2008, 2016; Kersten et al., 2008). This age-related associative deficit is also consistent with the finding that older adults have more difficulty than younger adults learning the names of new acquaintances (Old & Naveh-Benjamin, 2012) and have more difficulty remembering the sources of information (Cansino et al., 2013).

SEMANTIC MEMORY What about semantic memory? We know that IQ subtests that deal with vocabulary and general knowledge show very little, if any, decline with age (Salthouse, 1991), so it seems that semantic memory is fairly stable before the age of 75. In addition, studies of middle-aged adults (age 35–50) show no age changes on semantic memory tasks (Bäckman & Nilsson, 1996; Burke & Shafto, 2008). Studies of participants between the ages of 70 and 103 in the Berlin Aging Study showed a gradual but systematic decline in the performance of tasks that tap this store of facts and word meanings (Lindenberger & Baltes, 1994). Figure 4.4 presents estimates for changes in semantic

---

Figure 4.4 Estimated Changes in Semantic and Episodic Memory

Estimated age-related changes in semantic and episodic memory abilities. Semantic memory abilities show increases over middle adulthood and a slow decline in older age, whereas episodic abilities display a sharper decline in the mid-60s.

SOURCE: Rönnlund et al. (2005).

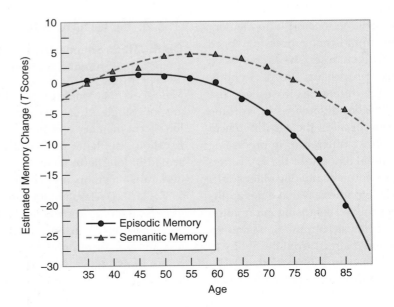

and episodic memory from 35 to 85 years of age (Rönnlund et al., 2005). As you can see, semantic memory abilities actually show increases into middle age before experiencing a moderate decline, whereas episodic memory abilities show a sharp decline beginning in the mid-60s. This was further illustrated by cognitive psychologist Boaz M. Ben-David and his colleagues (2015), who looked at the vocabulary scores of over 2,000 younger and older adults that they had tested over a 16-year period. Across studies, older adults had consistently higher vocabulary scores than younger adults.

The one exception to the rule of semantic memory remaining stable over the years is the case of **word-finding failures**—that feeling many middle-aged and older adults get when they know the word they want to use but just can't locate it at the moment, often referred to as the *tip-of-the-tongue phenomenon* (Shafto et al., 2007). The related semantic memory phenomenon of **name-retrieval failures**, for example, the failure to come up with "the name of that actor who used to be on *Star Trek* and now does hotel commercials," also begins to increase in middle age (Maylor, 1990). Psychologist Fergus Craik (2000) explained these exceptions by suggesting that specificity is the key to whether a long-term memory system component is stable or declines with age—tasks that require a specific word or name as an answer are more difficult and show a decline with age, whereas other tasks that require a more general answer are easier and remain stable up to late adulthood. In the example given earlier of the *Jeopardy* game experience, "James Buchanan" is a very specific item of information, and failure to recall it could not be compensated for by the use of other words. However, the story about the trip to L.A. consists of more general information, and even if some specific items could not be recalled (for example, the name of the host of *Jeopardy*), the story could still be told using "the game-show host" or "the star of the show" instead of "Alex Trebek." Using Craik's explanation, the reason semantic memory is so stable with age is that it is usually general rather than specific. And the reason there are age-related changes in episodic memory is due to the specificity required.

NONDECLARATIVE MEMORY In contrast to declarative memory, **nondeclarative memory** or *implicit memory* is the memory system responsible for skill learning and retention (Tulving, 1985). The skills that depend on this system include many motor systems such as driving a car, tying one's shoes, or riding a bike. Once learned, these skills involve well-learned, automatic mental processes that are not available to conscious awareness. We don't have to remind ourselves how to use a can opener or how to ride a bike, and the fact that these skills are independent of conscious memory seems to protect them from the effects of aging and brain damage. There is little change in implicit memory with age over adulthood, except for tasks that

require speeded performance (Dixon et al., 2001). Further evidence of the durability of implicit memory is found in studies of individuals suffering from various types of amnesia. Although this condition is defined by loss of memory ability in many areas, implicit memory abilities often remain at normal levels (Schacter, 1997).

4.2.3: Prospective Memory

OBJECTIVE: Characterize prospective memory

One other type of memory that is of importance to older adults is **prospective memory**, remembering to do something later on or in the future (Einstein & McDaniel, 2005). This can involve remembering to perform a specific one-time task (remembering to call the golf course for a tee time on Saturday) or performing some habitual routine (remembering to take your medication every day after lunch). Prospective memory requires not only that a person remember to do something in the future, but also to remember what it is that needs to be done. Perhaps some of you can recall staring at your calendar knowing that there was something you were supposed to do on Tuesday at 2:30, but not recalling what that "something" was. Research has consistently reported that older adults perform more poorly on prospective memory tasks than younger adults (Smith & Hunt, 2014), but the magnitude of the difference is usually smaller than for episodic memory (Henry et al., 2004). The exception seems to be when there is interfering material or activities involved. For example, when participants must quickly switch from performing one task to performing another, so that the second task interferes with the first, older adults perform more poorly than young adults, although the differences among the younger and older adults are much smaller or nonexistent when there is no interference (Kliegel et al., 2008). One explanation for this finding is that aspects of prospective memory are dependent on executive function, which shows declines in older adults (Cepeda et al., 2001).

Both younger and older adults show increased prospective memory performance when they use external cues as reminders. This was demonstrated by psychology researcher Julie D. Henry and her colleagues (2012), who used a computerized board game called Virtual Week to assess prospective memory in younger and older adults. In this game, participants moved around a board that is divided into days of the week. As they moved around they saw pop-up screens with descriptions of events and were asked to make decisions, such as what they want to eat when they enter a restaurant. Embedded within the game are prospective memory tasks such as taking medicine with every breakfast and dinner event (event-based prospective memory). Participants are also asked to perform prospective memory tasks at particular times (time-based prospective memory). Participants played the game under three different conditions. In the control condition there were no reminder cues. In the experimenter-initiated condition, participants were given reminders within the game. And in the self-initiated reminder condition, participants saw a "To Do" button on the screen and could click this button for reminders of the prospective memory tasks. As can be seen in Figure 4.5, younger adults performed better on both the event-based and the time-based prospective memory tasks than did older adults, but both groups benefited from external reminders.

4.2.4: Slowing Declines in Memory Abilities

OBJECTIVE: Explain how memory training works

If some types of memory abilities decline with age, is it possible for older adults to be taught special strategies to compensate for their processing problems? This is the idea behind many memory-training studies. For example, older adults have been successfully trained to remember names of people they have just met by using internal memory aids such as mental imagery to form associations between the people's faces and their names (Yesavage et al., 1989). In other studies, older adults have been given training on

encoding, attention, and relaxation strategies to improve word recall (Gross & Rebok, 2011) or to discriminate between old and new items on a recognition test (Bissig & Lustig, 2007; Jennings et al., 2005). And participants in the Berlin Aging Study learned to use the method of loci to improve their recall performances by associating words on the recall list with landmark buildings along a familiar route in their city (Kliegel et al., 1990).

Although training sometimes improves memory function on a specific task, it doesn't do away with the decline completely. In none of these studies did the performance of older adults reach the level of young adults, but all brought significant improvement over the participants' earlier performance or over a control group of older adults who received no training. Moreover, children and younger adults typically benefit more from training than older adults. For example, 9- to 12-year-old children and 65- to 78-year-old adults were trained to use an imagery-based memory strategy to help them encode and retrieve words by using location cues (Brehmer et al., 2007). The researchers reported that although the children and adults had similar performance at the beginning of the study and that each showed improvement as a result of the training, the children displayed greater benefits than the older adults. Unfortunately, there is conflicting evidence for transfer from the improvements on the trained tasks to new tasks. For example, psychology researcher Erika Borella and her colleagues (2017) found evidence that training older adults on working-memory tasks did improve performance not just on the working-memory tasks that were trained but also on other cognitive tasks. However, other researchers found no such evidence of transfer (Guye & von Bastian, 2017; Salthouse, 2016).

While the effects of cognitive exercise on general cognitive abilities may be somewhat limited, physical exercise definitely does have a large effect on cognitive ability. For example, researchers compared the effects of physical exercise, cognitive training, and mindfulness on working memory and found that the physical exercise had a much larger positive effect on working-memory performance and produced a much higher level of brain-derived neurotrophic factor (BDNF) (Håkansson et al., 2017). At the 2018 Cognitive Aging Conference, which is attended by the best cognitive aging researchers in the world, conference attendees were asked to raise their hand if they practiced a particular working-memory task, and no one raised their hand. When asked if they exercised to prevent cognitive decline, almost everyone raised their hand.

Other memory researchers have focused on training older adults to use external memory aids, such as making lists, writing notes, placing items-to-be-remembered in obvious places, and using voice mail, timers, and handheld audio recorders. In one such study, psychologists Orah Burack and Margie Lachman (1996) randomly assigned

Figure 4.5 Age Differences in Prospective Memory Tasks

Young adults performed prospective memory tasks better than older adults, and all participants did better when given cues.

SOURCE: Henry et al. (2012).

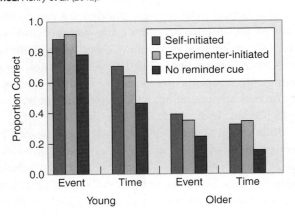

young and older adults to two groups—list-making and non-list-making—and gave them word recall and recognition tests. As expected, in the standard recall condition (non–list makers), the older adults performed less well than the younger adults, but for the list makers, there were no significant differences between the old and young groups. In addition, the older list makers performed better than the older non–list makers.

In an interesting twist, the authors of this study added a condition in which some of the list-making participants were told ahead of time that they would be able to refer to their lists during the recall test but then were not allowed to use them. These participants benefited as much from making the lists and not using them as the participants who made the lists and did use them, suggesting that the activity of list making improves memory, even when the list is not available at recall. (If you have ever made a grocery list and left it at home, you will realize that the act of making the list is almost as good as having it with you.)

Studies such as these show that training on both internal and external memory aids can benefit older adults whose memories are not as sharp as they were in younger years, and physical exercise has powerful positive effects on memory. They may not bring back 100% of earlier abilities, but intervention and improvement are possible.

4.2.5: Memory in Context

OBJECTIVE: Describe potential issues with age-related memory studies

Laboratory studies of age changes in memory have yielded valuable insights into this aspect of adult development. However, their dependence on out-of-context tasks may not tell the complete story of how thinking changes with age. Typical tasks in memory experiments "are relatively stripped down in terms of familiarity or meaningfulness," and little attention is paid to individual characteristics of the participants (Hess, 2005, p. 383).

A number of researchers have adopted an approach to adult cognition known as the **contextual perspective**. Its proponents believe that traditional laboratory studies fail to consider that cognitive processes across adulthood take place in everyday life and appear in a different light when age-related contexts are considered. The contextual perspective considers the **adaptive nature of cognition**, the idea that as we age our lives change and that successful aging depends on how we adapt our cognitive styles to fit those changes. For example, younger adults tend to be involved in education or job training and thus are more apt to focus their cognitive abilities on acquisition of specific facts and skills, often for the approval of authority figures. In contrast, older adults are often involved in transmitting their knowledge to the younger generation and thus may focus

their cognitive abilities on extracting the emotional meaning from information and integrating it with their existing knowledge. Traditional lab tasks that investigate age differences are more similar to the typical cognitive activities of young people (Hess, 2005).

This difference was demonstrated in a study by psychologist Cynthia Adams and her colleagues (2002) in which women in two age groups were given a story to remember and retell either to the experimenter or to a young child. The younger group's average age was 20; the older group's was 68. Those who had been instructed to retell the story to an experimenter resembled a typical laboratory experiment, and the results were not surprising: Younger women recalled more of the story than older women. However, for those who were instructed to retell the story to a young child, older women recalled as much of the story as younger women. In addition, the older women were more apt to adjust the complexity of the story to fit the young listener. Adams and her colleagues (2002) concluded that older people can recall stories as well as younger people when the goals are adjusted to fit the context of their lives—when they are given a task appropriate for a grandmother's goals rather than those of a young student.

STEREOTYPE THREAT Another factor that is not considered in traditional lab studies is the role of negative stereotypes of aging and memory ability. When members of a group are aware of a negative stereotype that is widely held about their group, they can experience anxiety when they are put in a position that might confirm the stereotype. This contextual factor is known as **stereotype threat**, and one example is the negative stereotype of older adults as forgetful. As I mentioned in the beginning of this section, age-related memory loss is a very touchy topic for many adults, and some researchers argue that older adults' cognitive abilities can be compromised just by the knowledge that they are in a memory study (Desrichard & Köpetz, 2005; Levy & Leifheit-Limson, 2009). In fact, when the "memory" part of the study is deemphasized, older adults perform better (Hess et al., 2004). In a study of older adults who were around the age of 78, researchers found that their memory abilities declined as more words describing negative stereotypes were added to the test materials. When asked if they had concerns about their own memory abilities, those who expressed more concerns were the ones whose recall was affected the most by the stereotypes (Hess et al., 2003). Negative stereotypes affect memory performance for older adults, and the size of the effect is related to the amount of concern they express about their own memories.

But why should being reminded of negative age stereotypes cause older adults to remember less? Psychologist Marie Mazerolle and her colleagues (2012) hypothesized that stereotype threat may consume more working-memory resources in older than in younger adults, accounting for the greater decline in memory performance. To test this, younger (average age of 21 years) and older (average age of 69 years) adults were given a working-memory task, in which participants read short sentences and were asked to recall the last word in each sentence in the order they were presented. They were also given a cued-recall task in which they read 40 words displayed one at a time on a computer screen and later were shown the first three letters of those words and asked to recall the entire word. Participants were told that these tasks were "fully validated and diagnostic of memory capacity." Both the younger and older participants were then assigned to one of two conditions. In the stereo-type-threat condition, participants were simply told that both younger and older adults would be performing these tasks, which is usually enough to remind older adults that memory is typically worse in older than younger adults. In the reduced-threat condition, participants were also told that both younger and older adults would be taking the test but further told these were "age-fair" tests in which performance does not vary with age.

As expected, the younger adults performed better than the older adults on the cued-recall task, with the difference being greatest in the stereotype condition. This finding is not new, but simply confirms that older adults perform worse on declarative memory tasks when they are reminded of the negative age stereotype. What is interesting in this study is that this effect was associated with performance on the working-memory measure. Figure 4.6 shows younger and older adults' scores on the working-memory task in both the stereotype-threat and reduced-threat conditions. As you can see, although the younger adults performed the same in the two conditions, the older adults' working-memory scores were significantly reduced in the stereotype-threat condition. The authors interpreted these results as indicating that one reason for older adults' reduced performance on declarative memory tasks when they are reminded of

the negative age stereotype is that such reminders consume working-memory capacity, which in turn affects how well they can remember the task information.

4.3: Intelligence

OBJECTIVE: Evaluate the concept of age-related changes to intellectual ability

Memory is just one component of intelligence. When we think of evaluating age changes in cognitive processes, most of us think immediately of IQ scores. The less capable we feel about ourselves, the more we worry about losing our intellectual abilities as we age (Parisi et al., 2017). Does IQ actually change as we get older? If so, is there a sudden drop at a certain age, or is the change gradual? Are some types of intelligence affected more than others? These types of questions have long been the basis of cognitive aging studies, but let's first say a few words about the concept of intelligence and about IQ tests, the tools we use to measure that concept.

Defining **intelligence** is one of the more slippery tasks in psychology. The typical definition goes something like this: "the aggregate or global capacity of the individual to act purposefully, to think rationally and to deal effectively with his environment" (Wechsler, 1939, p. 3). In other words, intelligence is a visible indicator of the efficiency of various cognitive processes that work together behind the scenes to process information in various ways (Nisbett et al., 2012). The field of psychology that studies the measurement of human abilities such as intelligence is **psychometrics**.

Many psychologists assume that there is a central, general intellectual capacity, often called g, which influences the way we approach a great number of different tasks (Jensen, 1998; Spearman, 1904). The score on an intelligence test is intended to describe this general capacity, known as the **IQ (intelligence quotient)**. As you may know from previous

Figure 4.6 Younger and Older Adults' Performance Under Scores on Stereotype-Threat and Reduced-Threat Conditions

Working-memory scores for older adults decreased sharply when they were reminded of the negative age stereotype. When this reminder was reduced, their scores were more similar to those of the younger group.

SOURCE: Mazerolle et al. (2012).

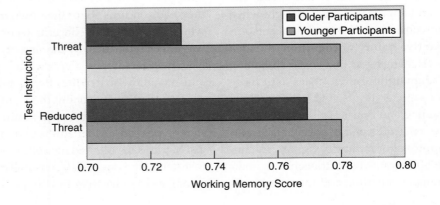

courses, the average IQ score is normally set at 100, with scores above 100 reflecting above-average performance and scores below 100 reflecting below-average performance.

In addition to *g*, some psychologists who study intelligence are interested in the specific components of intellectual capacity. On standard IQ tests, these capacities are measured by the various subtests that make up the total IQ score. For example, the latest version of the Wechsler Adult Intelligence Scale (WAIS-IV; Pearson Education, 2008) provides a Full Scale IQ based on four separate indexes: Verbal Comprehension, Perceptual Reasoning, Working Memory, and Processing Speed, each of which consists of a number of different subtests (for example, vocabulary in Verbal Comprehension; block design in Perceptual Reasoning; backward digit span in Working Memory; symbol search in Visual Perception, and speed in Processing Speed).

⌄ By the end of this module, you will be able to:

4.3.1 Outline changes to intelligence over time

4.3.2 Analyze how the components of intelligence function with age

4.3.3 Determine the effectiveness of intellectual retention exercises

4.3.1: Age Changes in Overall Intelligence

OBJECTIVE: Outline changes to intelligence over time

Do IQ scores decline with age or stay constant? Most of the early information on consistency or change in adult intelligence came from cross-sectional studies (1920s to 1950s), which seemed to show that declines in IQ began in early adulthood and continued steadily thereafter. However, in the decades since then, we have learned a lot more about adult intelligence. Researchers of cognitive aging have developed new designs that do away with some of the problems with traditional methods and have extended longitudinal studies to include healthy, community-dwelling people in their 60s, 70s, 80s, and beyond. Although results continue to show some cognitive decline with age, the news is much more optimistic. Some aspects of adult thought processes function at very high levels into very old age. When decline occurs, it is often much less extreme than once thought, and we often compensate so that it is not noticeable. Moreover, there are precautions we can take that will increase our chances of staying bright and high functioning throughout our lives.

Figure 4.7 shows the contrast between longitudinal and cross-sectional analyses of IQ scores in the Seattle Longitudinal Study. This study used a sequential design that allowed for both longitudinal and cross-sectional comparisons. The numbers are not traditional IQ scores with a mean of 100. Instead, they have been calculated to show the change in scores for each participant over the course of the study, with the beginning score set at 50 and a standard deviation of 10. Thus, two-thirds of all adults should fall between scores of 40 and 60 (one standard deviation on either side of the mean), and about 95% should fall between 30 and 70 (Schaie, 1994; Schaie & Zanjani, 2006).

When you compare the longitudinal and cross-sectional data, you can see that they yield very different answers to the question, "What happens to IQ over the course of adulthood?" The cross-sectional evidence, of which the lower curve is very typical, shows a decline in IQ starting

---

Figure 4.7 Contrast between Longitudinal and Cross-Sectional Analyses

Age changes in total IQ based on cross-sectional data (lower line) and longitudinal data (upper line) can show very different trajectories. Depending on cross-sectional data in the past led to erroneous conclusions that cognitive performance begins to decline around age 40 and that the decline is very fast.

SOURCE: Data from Schaie (1983).

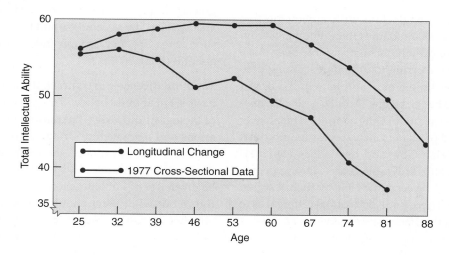

somewhere between ages 32 and 39. In contrast, the longitudinal information actually suggests a slight rise in IQ through middle adulthood. Only in the period from 67 to 74 do the total IQ scores begin to drop, although, even here, the decline is not substantial. In fact, according to developmental psychologist K. Warner Schaie, codirector of the Seattle Longitudinal Project, "The average magnitude of intellectual decline . . . is quite small during the 60s and 70s and is probably of little significance for competent behavior of the young old" (2006, p. 601). Average declines become more substantial, however, in the 80s (Schaie, 1996).

THE FLYNN EFFECT   One explanation for the difference between the cross-sectional and longitudinal comparisons is that there may be differential effects of prior test experience. Cognitive psychology researcher Timothy A. Salthouse (2016) found that when prior test experience was controlled, the results of longitudinal studies more closely resembled the results of cross-sectional studies. Another explanation is that there are cohort effects at work here. As years of education, good health, and the cognitive complexities of life have increased over the past century, the average scores for each successive cohort have gone up. In fact, researchers have found that average verbal IQ scores for groups of older adults are increasing by over four and a half points each decade (Uttl & Van Alstine, 2003). This is related to the **Flynn effect**, named after psychologist James Flynn (1987), who documented that average IQ had increased steadily over the 20th century. Flynn argues that the increase is mainly due to changes in modern life. Advances in education, greater use of technology, and more people being engaged in intellectually demanding work has led to a greater proportion of people with experience manipulating abstract concepts than was the case in decades past, and this, in turn, is responsible for elevated IQ scores for people of all ages. As a result, cross-sectional studies comparing people born decades apart may show lower IQ scores for older people, but they are not accurate predictors of what the future holds in store for young people today.

Although IQ tends to decline with advancing age (and more for some types of abilities than others), overall, intelligence as measured by IQ is highly stable over one's lifetime. By stable, I'm referring to differences among people being similar over time. For example, will the bright 10- or 20-year-old also be the bright 70- or 80-year-old, relative to other people measured in the sample? The answer seems to be yes. Based on data from a 76-year longitudinal study, psychologist Alan Gow and his colleagues (2011) reported that at least 50% of IQ differences among people in late adulthood could be accounted for by their test performance as children. There's still 50% of the differences to be accounted for by other factors, so change is as much a part of the picture as stability. But IQ, from childhood into

older adulthood, is one of the most stable psychological traits behavioral scientists have studied.

To summarize, there is good support for the optimistic view that general intellectual ability remains fairly stable through most of adulthood. But now let's dissect intelligence a little and see what happens with age to some of the specific intellectual abilities that are components of IQ.

WRITING PROMPT

Determinants of IQ

If approximately half of an older adult's IQ is determined by genetics, what kind of factors might determine the other half?

 ▶   The response entered here will appear in the performance dashboard and can be viewed by your instructor.

Submit

4.3.2: Components of Intelligence

OBJECTIVE: Analyze how the components of intelligence function with age

Standardized IQ tests yield more than a single score. They also provide subtest scores, representing different types of cognitive abilities associated with intelligence. One distinction that is widely used by researchers is between crystallized and fluid abilities, initially proposed and developed by psychologists Raymond Cattell and John Horn (Cattell, 1963; Horn & Cattell, 1966).

Crystallized and Fluid Intelligence

Crystallized Intelligence—**Crystallized intelligence** is heavily dependent on education and experience. It consists of the set of skills and bits of knowledge that we each learn as part of growing up in a given culture, such as the ability to reason about real-life problems and technical skills learned for a job and other aspects of life (creating a spreadsheet, counting change, finding the salad dressing in the grocery store). On standardized tests, crystallized abilities are measured by vocabulary and by verbal comprehension, such as reading a paragraph and then answering questions about it (Blair, 2006).

Fluid Intelligence—In contrast, **fluid intelligence** is a more basic set of abilities believed to be more under the influence of biological processes, "requiring adaptation to new situations and for which prior education or learning provide relatively little advantage" (Berg & Sternberg, 2003, p. 105). A common measure of this is a letter-series test. You may be given a series of letters like *F, G, I, L*, and *P* and have to figure out what letter should go next (*U*). This demands abstract reasoning rather than reasoning about familiar or everyday events. Most tests of memory measure fluid intelligence, as do many tests measuring response speed or reproducing designs with blocks.

Whatever labels we apply to these two broad categories of intellectual ability, the results are similar. Nonverbal, fluid tasks decline earlier than verbal, crystallized tasks (Lindenberger & Baltes, 1997). In fact, aspects of crystallized abilities, such as world knowledge, continue to grow into the 60s and show only gradual declines into the 70s (Ackerman, 2008; Ornstein & Light, 2010). In contrast, specific aspects of fluid abilities, such as speed of processing and working memory, show initial declines around 35–40 years of age (Dykiert et al., 2012; Horn & Hofer, 1992).

This pattern of change in crystallized and fluid abilities was demonstrated in research by psychologist Shu-Chen Li and her colleagues (2004). People from 6 to 89 years of age were given a battery of both crystallized and fluid tasks. Performance on the fluid tasks peaked for people in their mid-20s, with declines being obvious by the mid-30s. In comparison, crystallized abilities did not peak until the 40s and remained stable until about age 70, when a decline was seen.

COGNITIVE RETENTION Older adults who "exercise" their crystallized abilities often continue to display improvements on specific cognitive tasks well into their 70s. Consider people who do crossword puzzles regularly. Figure 4.8 shows the combined results of several studies in which participants of different ages were given *New York Times* crossword puzzles to solve (Salthouse, 2004). As shown

in the figure, the number of words participants completed correctly increased with age. The most words were solved by those in their 60s, whereas those in their 20s and 30s solved fewer than those in their 70s. Doing crossword puzzles, as well as identifying synonyms and other verbal tasks, represent components of intelligence that depend more on accrued knowledge than on speed of processing or learning new skills, and they fit hand-in-glove with the cognitive abilities of healthy older adults.

Not only does intelligence decline more slowly than the experts once thought, but we are also finding out that few rules apply to everyone when it comes to cognitive aging. In other words, even when the mean scores are higher for younger people than for older people, there are still a lot of people in the old group who do better than a lot of the people in the young group, and vice versa. Even at 80 years of age and older, 53% of the people were performing comparably to the young people on tests of both fluid and crystallized intelligence (Schaie, 1996). And when older people are tested over time, most remain stable within a 7-year period, some decline, but even in their 80s, a few individuals increase in scores on a Verbal Meaning test (Schaie, 2013).

One interesting finding is that intelligence predicts health and longevity. This is true when intelligence is measured by IQ-type tests (Deary et al., 2008; Gottfredson & Deary, 2004) or by tests assessing everyday cognitive abilities, such as those associated with medication use, financial management, food preparation, and nutrition (Weatherbee & Allaire, 2008). The reason for this connection is not clear,

Figure 4.8 Age Differences in Solving *NYT* Crossword Clues

The ability to correctly complete the *New York Times* crossword puzzle increases with age, showing the effect of mental "exercise" on crystallized abilities.

SOURCE: Salthouse (2004).

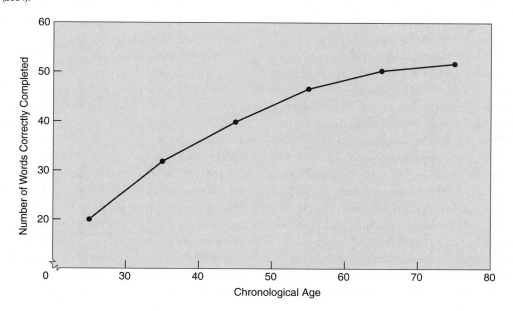

although one possibility is that people with better reasoning and problem-solving skills make better decisions with respect to health care and avoiding accidental injuries (Gottfredson & Deary, 2004).

4.3.3: Reversing Declines in Intellectual Abilities

OBJECTIVE: Determine the effectiveness of intellectual retention exercises

Beginning in the 1970s, when it became apparent that intelligence did not drop off drastically with age, researchers began asking if anything could be done to reverse the moderate decline in IQ shown in longitudinal studies. The answer was yes (Kramer & Willis, 2002). Many studies showed that physical exercise brought about significant improvement in intellectual performance (Chu et al., 2015; Colcombe & Kramer, 2003), as did training in the components specific to the task being tested (Willis et al., 2006) and training in nonspecific aspects of the test, such as willingness to guess when one is not sure of the correct answer (Birkhill & Schaie, 1975).

Sports psychologist Chen-Heng Chu and his colleagues (2015) examined the immediate effects of exercise on executive function in older adults. They measured the physical fitness of the participants and divided them into a low fitness group and a high fitness group. Participants cycled for 30 minutes or read a book on exercise for 30 minutes before testing. Participants were then given a Stroop test, in which they were shown a list of colors, some written in the same color as the word ("RED" in red ink) and some in different colors ("RED" in blue ink). They were told to report the color of the ink as fast as possible. As Figure 4.9 shows, physical exercise resulted in faster response times and greater accuracy.

Schaie and Willis (1986) included a training study in one wave of their ongoing longitudinal project to determine whether training was effective for people who were already showing a decline or just for those who had not yet begun to decline. Participants, age 64–94, received 5 hours of training. About half of the participants had shown a decline over the last 14 years, and about half had not. Some received training on spatial orientation and some on inductive reasoning, both abilities that tend to decline with age and are considered more resistant to intervention. When the results of the training were examined for those who had declined, it was found that about half had gained significantly, and 40% had returned to their former levels of performance. Of those who had not yet shown declines, one-third had increased their abilities above their previous levels.

Seven years later, the same researchers retested about half of these participants and compared them to others in the study who were the same age and had not received

Figure 4.9 Effects of Exercise on Executive Function in Older Adults

Adults who exercised were faster and more accurate with their Stroop test responses.

SOURCE: Chu et al. (2015).

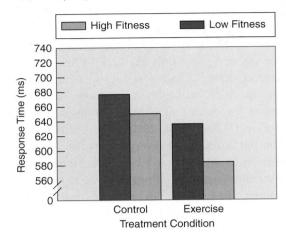

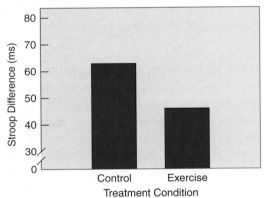

training. The scores of the group that received training had declined from their previous levels, but they still performed better than the controls, even though it had been 7 years since their training. These participants were then given an additional 5 hours of training, which again raised their test scores significantly, but not to the level of 7 years earlier (Willis & Schaie, 1994). Similar results have been found for memory training in a visuomotor task over a 2-year period (Smith et al., 2005), a perceptual-motor task over a 5-year period (Rodrigue et al., 2005), and a strategic memory task over a 5-year period (Gross & Rebok, 2011).

Unfortunately, cognitive training on one aspect of intelligence does not usually seem to improve performance on other measures of intelligence. For example, researchers conducted a meta-analysis in which they looked at the results of 145 experiments on the training of working-memory abilities and found a short-term increase in performance on the working-memory tasks that were in the training but these training effects did not transfer to other cognitive skills (Melby-Lervag et al., 2016).

4.4: Decision Making and Problem Solving

OBJECTIVE: Relate decision making and problem solving to age

Solving problems and making decisions are complex cognitive skills that require the coordinated interplay of various types and levels of thinking. These abilities were important for the survival of the earliest humans and are also important today. Although the study of decision making and problem solving is an established area of cognitive psychology, it has only recently been applied to adulthood and aging. We are all aware that the types of judgments and decisions people are required to make change with age, but the question asked in the following section is whether the quality of the judgments and decisions they make changes—that is, whether there are age-related changes in the underlying cognitive processes (Sanfey & Hastie, 2000).

By the end of this module, you will be able to:

4.4.1 Explain how the process of choosing changes with age

4.4.2 Compare how older and younger adults deal with problem solving and emotional information

4.4.3 Characterize positivity bias in older adults

4.4.1: Making Choices

OBJECTIVE: Explain how the process of choosing changes with age

One type of decision that adults are frequently required to make across the lifespan is *choice*, or choosing among a set of alternatives that have multiple attributes. Which university should you attend when you have been accepted by three, all having different tuition costs, distances from home,

levels of prestige, and amounts offered in scholarships? Or which of two treatments to choose for your illness, when each has different risks, side effects, costs, and probabilities of success?

Many studies of this skill are done in labs using a matrix of attributes known as a *choice board*. Figure 4.10 shows a car-buying dilemma. Key factors in a decision include comparing total price, number of passengers each car will hold, fuel efficiency, and manufacturers' rebates offered for each car. At the beginning, the categories are visible, but the attributes are on cards, placed face-down on the matrix. (Some labs use computer screens.) Participants are told to look at whatever information they need and take the time necessary to make the decision. The cards that the participant turns over, the pattern in which they are turned, and the time each card is studied are all recorded. When the choice-making processes of younger and older adults are compared, we learn something about age differences in this type of judgment and decision making.

Using a choice-board technique, researchers investigated how young adults (mean age 23) and older adults (mean age 68) chose which of six cars to buy after having an opportunity to compare them on nine features. A later study compared the apartment-rental choices of the two groups when five apartments were shown on the choice board with 12 features available for each apartment (Johnson, 1993). Another research group examined decision-making processes of 20-year-olds versus people in their 60s and 70s as they made complex financial decisions (Hershey & Wilson, 1997). In a study of medical-treatment choice, young women, middle-aged women, and older women were compared on their decision-making processes in a simulated situation involving breast cancer treatment (Meyer et al., 1995). Although these studies ran the gamut on decision topics, they all had similar results. Basically, older people used less information and took less time than younger people to make their choices. Regardless, there was essentially no difference between the choices made by the two groups.

Figure 4.10 Example of Choice Board: Car-Buying Dilemma

Example of a choice board used in studies of decision making. This one includes four factors for each of four car choices.

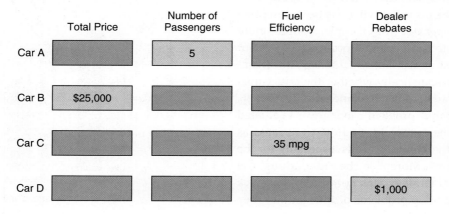

One possible explanation for these findings is that older people recognize their cognitive limitations and make decisions based on less complex thought processes. However, the fact that their decisions are the same as those of younger people in these studies suggests an alternative explanation. This hypothesis is that older people are experts on making choices such as which apartment to rent, which car to buy, or which medical treatment to undergo. By the time most adults reach the older stage of life, they have gone through these thought processes many times, and they approach them much like a chess master approaching a chessboard, using deductive reasoning and tapping their long-term store of experiences. This explanation is supported by the accounts given by some of the participants when asked to "think aloud" while making choices (Johnson, 1993).

These studies affirm that when adults of any age are evaluated in the context of their current lifestyles, interests, and areas of expertise, they show much better cognitive capabilities than on traditional, "one-size-fits-all" laboratory tests.

4.4.2: Problem Solving and Emotional Information

OBJECTIVE: Compare how older and younger adults deal with problem solving and emotional information

One interesting finding about problem solving in older adults is that, despite cognitive declines in executive function, their ability to regulate their emotions, particularly in the context of problem solving, is often as good as in younger adults (Blanchard-Fields, 2007). In fact, older adults often show better decision-making skills than younger adults, especially when interpersonal problems are confronted. For example, researchers gave younger and older adults problems dealing with interpersonal issues (for instance, "Your parent or child criticizes you for some habit you have that annoys him or her") or nonpersonal issues (for instance, "A complicated form you completed was returned because you misinterpreted the instructions on how to fill it out"). Older adults were more apt to solve the nonpersonal problems using what has been described as a *problem-focused approach* (for example, "Obtain more information on how to complete the form correctly"), but were more likely to use an *avoidant-denial strategy* (for example, "Try to evaluate realistically whether the criticism is valid") for interpersonal problems (Blanchard-Fields et al., 2007). When participants' problem solving was evaluated in terms of effectiveness, the older adults were rated as more effective than the younger adults, especially for the interpersonal problems. Moreover, the older adults' use of an avoidant-denial strategy was not due to their lack of energy to actively solve problems or the fact that they

are too emotional. Instead, "they may effectively recognize that not all problems can be fixed immediately or can be solved without considering the regulation of emotions" (Blanchard-Fields, 2007, p. 27).

In fact, older adults in general show better cognitive performance for emotional than for nonemotional information, with age differences being most apparent for positive emotions (Carstensen et al., 2006). One example is a study by psychologists Helene Fung and Laura Carstensen (2003) in which people ranging in age from 20 to 83 were shown advertisements featuring three different types of appeals: emotional, knowledge-related, or neutral. As illustrated in Figure 4.11, the older participants remembered more information from the emotional advertisements than the other two types, and the younger participants remembered more information from the knowledge-related and neutral advertisements. Carstensen and her colleagues suggest that younger people are interested in processing information to acquire knowledge; in contrast, older people are interested in processing information to enhance positive emotions. Unfortunately, most laboratory studies of memory are devoid of emotional content, thus favoring younger participants.

4.4.3: Positivity Bias

OBJECTIVE: Characterize positivity bias in older adults

In related research, young (age 19–29), middle-aged (41–53), and older (65–85) adults were shown a series of positive, negative, and neutral images to examine and remember for later on (Charles et al., 2003). Although the young and

---

Figure 4.11 Memory for Emotional, Knowlege-related, and Neutral Advertisements in Younger and Older Adults

Older participants remember more information than younger participants when material has emotional appeal; younger participants remember more when material has knowledge or neutral appeal.

SOURCE: Fung and Carstensen (2003).

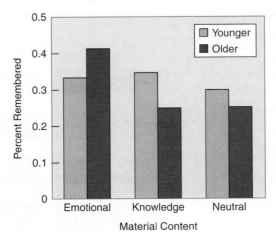

Figure 4.12 Emotion and Memory for Images

The number of positive, negative, and neutral images recalled is a function of age, with older adults showing a distinct positivity bias.

SOURCE: Charles et al. (2003).

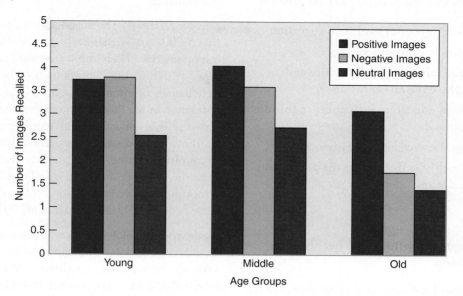

middle-aged adults recalled more images overall than the older adults, there was a significant difference in the pattern of performance, which is shown in Figure 4.12. As you can see, the older adults displayed higher levels of performance for the positive images compared to the neutral and negative images. Differences in recall between the positive and negative images were smaller or nonexistent for the young and middle-aged adults.

This **positivity bias** is not limited to memory, but has been found in a number of situations (Carstensen & Mikels, 2005). For example, older adults are more apt than younger adults to direct their attention away from negative stimuli (Mather & Carstensen, 2003), have greater working memory for positive than for negative emotional images (Mikels et al., 2005), evaluate events in their own lives (positive, negative, and neutral ones) more positively than younger adults (Schryer & Ross, 2012), and are generally more satisfied with the decisions they make than younger adults (Kim et al., 2008). In general, older adults are more emotionally positive than younger adults.

One explanation for older peoples' positivity bias is provided by **socioemotional selectivity theory** proposed by Laura Carstensen and her colleagues (1999; Carstensen & Mikels, 2005). According to this theory, younger people view time as expansive and tend to focus on the future. As such, they invest their time in new activities with an eye to expanding their horizons. Older people, in contrast, view time as more limited and as a result "direct attention to emotionally meaningful aspects of life, such as the desire to lead a meaningful life, to have emotionally intimate social relationships, and to feel socially interconnected" (Carstensen & Mikels, 2005, p. 118). As a result, they tend

to emphasize the positive aspects of experiences and devote more cognitive (and social) effort to them.

WRITING PROMPT

Selecting Weekend Activities

How would you predict a 25-year-old would choose to spend Saturday night? What about a 75-year-old? Explain this using socioemotional selectivity theory.

▶ The response entered here will appear in the performance dashboard and can be viewed by your instructor.

Submit

4.5: Individual Differences in Cognitive Change

OBJECTIVE: Analyze factors that influence individual cognitive change

If cognitive decline with age were the rule, we would all fade away together in a predictable pattern, showing little variation in change from our agemates. As you have surely observed in your family or your community, this is not the case; chronological age is only part of the story. Your grandmother and her best friend, Lillian, may be only a few years apart and may have had similar cognitive abilities in early and middle adulthood, but now, in their early 70s, Grandma may be an honor student at the community college and know the names of all 56 people in her water aerobics class, whereas Lillian needs help managing her finances and making a grocery list. What factors might predict this difference in cognitive change?

▽ **By the end of this module, you will be able to:**

4.5.1 Evaluate the influence of health on cognition

4.5.2 Relate genetics to cognitive change

4.5.3 Determine the role that demographics and sociobiography have on cognition

4.5.4 Determine how education influences cognition in later adulthood

4.5.5 Relate physical exercise to cognitive change

4.5.6 Explain the role of self-doubt in the perception of cognitive decline

4.5.1: Health

OBJECTIVE: Evaluate the influence of health on cognition

As is well known, poor health can affect cognition, but it is important to keep in mind that this is true for people of any age. The reason health is a topic for discussion here is that older adults are more apt to experience health problems that interfere with cognition. Another word of caution is necessary; most of these factors are known only to be predictive of or associated with cognitive change—whether or not they are causes has not been well established.

Factors Associated with Cognitive Change

Vision and Hearing—My first candidate for markers of cognitive change would be vision and hearing difficulties (Lin et al., 2011; Lindenberger & Baltes, 1994; Wingfield et al., 2005). Over a third of people over age 65 have hearing impairment, and most have some visual disability. Frank Lin from the Johns Hopkins Center on Aging and Health has conducted many studies showing a link between hearing thresholds and cognition (e.g., Lin, 2011; Lin et al., 2011). The prevalence of decline in these two sensory systems is further illustrated by psychologists Ulman Lindenberger and Paul Baltes (1994; Baltes & Lindenberger, 1997), who tested the vision and hearing abilities of 156 participants, age 70–103, from the Berlin Study of Aging. Tests of cognitive abilities showed the expected decline with age, but when the vision and auditory evaluations for the participants were added to the equation, the researchers found that these deficits explained 93% of the variance in IQ measures. In a study by psychology researchers Carryl L. Baldwin and Ivan K. Ash (2011), older adults' (60–82 years of age) auditory working-memory span was more influenced by reductions in the intensity of the spoken stimuli than that of younger adults (18–30 years of age). The results of this study show age differences in listening memory span as

a function of the decibel level of the stimuli. The authors interpreted these findings as pointing to *auditory acuity* as an important factor in older adults' working-memory performance.

Chronic Disease—The major diseases contributing to cognitive decline are Alzheimer's disease and other dementias, but others have been implicated also, such as obesity combined with high blood pressure (Waldstein & Katzel, 2006), deficiencies of vitamin B_{12} and folic acid, thyroid disease (Bäckman et al., 2001), clinical depression (Kinderman & Brown, 1997), and subclinical depression (Bielak et al., 2011). Cardiovascular disease is associated with a large proportion of cognitive decline, and it predicts performance on tests of episodic memory and visuospatial skills even when age, education, gender, medication, and mood are controlled for (Emery et al., 2012; Fahlander et al., 2000).

Medication—Related to health is another cause of cognitive decline in later adulthood—-the medication people take for their chronic conditions. Many drugs have side effects that affect cognitive processes in people of all ages, and some drugs affect older people more strongly because metabolism slows with age. Often these side effects are mistaken for signs of normal aging, such as bodily aches and pains, sleep disturbances, and feelings of sadness and loss. Other drug-related problems that can contribute to cognitive decline in older people are overmedication and drug interactions. Many older people see a number of different doctors, and it is important for each to know what drugs are being prescribed by the others.

4.5.2: Genetics

OBJECTIVE: Relate genetics to cognitive change

A factor that undoubtedly underlies many of the health-related differences in cognitive aging is genetics. The strength of genetic influence on a behavior is measured by *heritability scores*. Studies comparing the traits and abilities of pairs of individuals with varying degrees of family relationship have demonstrated that cognitive abilities are among the most heritable of behavioral traits. Meta-analyses of studies involving over 10,000 pairs of twins show that about 50% of the variance in individual IQ scores can be explained by genetic differences among individuals (Plomin et al., 2008). Furthermore, researchers report that for general cognitive ability, heritability increases with age, starting as low as 20% in infancy and increasing to 40% in childhood, 50% in adolescence, and 60% in adulthood (McGue et al., 1993).

To find out about the heritability of cognitive abilities in older adulthood, behavioral geneticist Gerald McClearn and his colleagues (1997) conducted a study of Swedish twin pairs who were 80 years of age or older. In this study, 110 identical twin pairs and 130 same-sex fraternal twin pairs were given tests of overall cognitive ability as well as tests of specific components of cognition. As the graph in Figure 4.13 shows, identical twin pairs, who have the same genes, had scores on the tests that were significantly more similar to each other than did fraternal twin pairs, who share only about half their genes. Because we know that genes are implicated in many diseases and chronic conditions, these findings of a genetic contribution to cognitive decline should come as no surprise.

Another interesting result of this study is the variation in heritability for the different cognitive abilities, ranging from 32 to 62%. Taken together, these findings show not only that cognitive ability is influenced by genetics, but also that different types of cognition are influenced to different extents.

As a final word on this subject, I must point out that even if approximately 60% of the individual differences in general cognitive ability in older adults can be explained by genetics, 40% must be considered environmental in origin. In Figure 4.13, you should note that none of the bars reaches the 100% level. This means that even identical twins with identical genes are not identical in cognitive abilities.

4.5.3: Demographics and Sociobiographical History

OBJECTIVE: Determine the role that demographics and sociobiography have on cognition

Women have a slight advantage over men in several cognitive areas (episodic memory, verbal tasks, and maintaining brain weight), and these gender differences continue into very old age (Bäckman et al., 2001).

Another set of factors is what Paul Baltes calls **sociobiographical history**, the level of professional prestige, social position, and income experienced throughout one's life. It was once thought that people who had led privileged lives in these respects would be less likely to decline in cognitive abilities as they grew older, but most of the research evidence shows otherwise; the *rate* of decline is the same, regardless of what blessings people have received or earned in their lifetime (Lindenberger & Baltes, 1997; Salthouse et al., 1990). The only difference is that the more privileged individuals usually attain higher levels of cognitive ability, so that even if the rate of decline is equal, their cognitive scores are still higher at every age (Smith & Baltes, 1999).

4.5.4: Education and Intellectual Activity

OBJECTIVE: Determine how education influences cognition in later adulthood

Formal education predicts the rate of cognitive decline with age. All other things being equal, people with fewer years of formal schooling will show more cognitive decline as years go by than will their same-aged peers with more years of formal education. This evidence comes from the repeated finding that better-educated adults not only perform some intellectual tasks at higher levels but also maintain their intellectual skill longer in old age, a pattern found in studies in both the United States (Compton et al., 2000; Schaie, 1996) and in Europe (Cullum et al., 2000; Laursen, 1997).

There are several possible explanations of the correlation between schooling and maintenance of intellectual skill. One possibility is that better-educated people remain

---

Figure 4.13 Heritability of Cognitive Abilities in Older Adulthood

Correlations on tests for a number of cognitive abilities are higher for monozygotic twin pairs (who share the same genes) than for dizygotic twin pairs (who share about 50% of their genes), demonstrating significant and separate genetic contributions for those abilities.

SOURCE: McClearn et al. (1997).

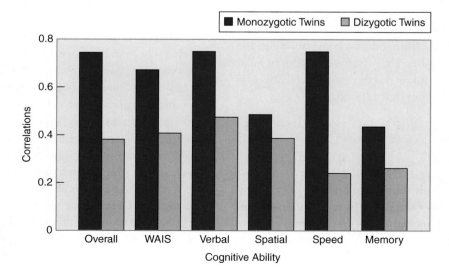

more intellectually active throughout their adult years. It may thus be the intellectual activity ("exercise" in the sense in which I have been using the term) that helps to maintain the mental skills. Another possibility is that it may not be education per se that is involved here, but underlying intellectual ability, leading both to more years of education and to better maintenance of intellectual skills in old age. A related explanation is that some tests used to measure cognitive ability may actually be measuring education level instead (Ardila et al., 2000). Studies with illiterate, non-schooled adults (Manly et al., 1999) have shown that some types of cognitive tests reflect lack of literacy and schooling (comprehension and verbal abstraction), whereas others reflect true cognitive decline (delayed recall and nonverbal abstraction).

INTELLECTUAL ACTIVITY Adults who read books, take classes, travel, attend cultural events, and participate in clubs or other group activities seem to fare better intellectually over time (Schaie, 1994; Wilson et al., 1999). It is the more isolated and inactive adults (whatever their level of education) who show the most decline in IQ. Longitudinal studies have shown that demanding job environments (Schooler et al., 1998) and life with spouses who have high levels of cognitive functioning (Gruber-Baldini et al., 1995) help to ward off cognitive decline. In contrast, widows who had not worked outside the home showed the greatest risk of cognitive decline in the Seattle Longitudinal Study (Schaie, 1996).

A number of studies have shown that cognitive processes are preserved in later adulthood for people who exercise those processes regularly through such activities as playing chess (Charness, 1981) or bridge (Clarkson-Smith & Hartley, 1990), doing crossword puzzles (Salthouse, 2004), or playing the game of Go (Masunaga & Horn, 2001). The sets of highly exercised skills required for such activities are known as *expertise*, and studies have shown that older people who have expertise in specific areas retain their cognitive abilities in those areas to a greater extent than age-mates who do not share this expertise.

However, before you rush out to join a chess club, I must warn you that most of these studies are correlational, which means that other factors may be contributing to the retention of cognitive ability. These individuals might be in better health to begin with or receive more social stimulation and support at the gym or bridge club.

4.5.5: Physical Exercise

OBJECTIVE: Relate physical exercise to cognitive change

Physical exercise has both short-term and long-term positive effects on cognition. Exercise helps to maintain cardiovascular (and possibly neural) fitness, which we know is linked to mental maintenance. And researchers who compare mental performance scores for physically active and sedentary older adults consistently find that the more active people have higher scores.

Aerobic exercise has been targeted specifically because of its role in promoting cell growth in the hippocampus and other brain structures involved in memory. Most of these studies are correlational, so we face the problem of determining whether the memory changes are caused by the aerobic exercise or by other factors, such as higher education level, better health, or more social support. Nonetheless, a meta-analysis of studies that randomly assigned participants to exercise and nonexercise conditions found that exercise has positive effects on cognitive functioning. In fact, the greatest effects were on tasks such as inhibition and working memory, which are directly relevant to normative age differences in memory performance (Colcombe & Kramer, 2003).

In a follow-up study, the researchers used MRIs to compare the brain structures of older people who exercise with those who do not. They found that the biggest difference was in the cortical areas most affected by aging. Although the participants in this study had not been randomly assigned to exercise and nonexercise groups, the combination of studies provides reasonable support for exercise having a positive impact on age-related memory performance. Studies have shown that the effects of physical exercise on cognition are dose dependent. The more an older adult exercises, the better their cognitive ability (Loprinzi et al., 2018; Zhu et al., 2016). The same is true with muscle-strengthening activities (Loprinzi, 2016). Clearly the extent to which an individual exercises (or doesn't) should be considered when assessing memory abilities in later adulthood (Colcombe et al., 2003).

A longitudinal study by psychologist Robert Rogers and his colleagues (1990) points us in the same direction. They followed a group of 85 men from age 65 to 69. All were in good health at the beginning of the study, and all were highly educated. During the 4 years of the study, some of these men chose to continue working, some retired but remained physically active, and some retired and adopted a sedentary lifestyle. When these three groups were compared at the end of the study on a battery of cognitive tests, the inactive group performed significantly worse than the two active groups.

This is by no means an exhaustive review of the research in this very active field. I simply wanted to give some examples of work that supports the argument of those who take the contextual perspective of cognitive aging. Sure, no one argues with the evidence that cognitive abilities decline with age, but there is active debate about how much the decline is and in which areas of cognition. There are also some lessons in the research on individual differences about steps that might be taken to delay or slow down the inevitable decline. Certainly it seems that we would increase the probability of maintaining our cognitive abilities as we grow older if we engage in physically and cognitively challenging activities throughout adulthood.

4.5.6: Subjective Evaluation of Decline

OBJECTIVE: Explain the role of self-doubt in the perception of cognitive decline

One factor that is not implicated in cognitive decline is our own opinion of our cognitive abilities. There is a very strong relationship between age and subjective reports of cognitive decline—the older the group is, the more reports there are of intellectual failure. However, when reports of cognitive decline are compared with actual tests of intellectual functioning, there is virtually no relationship. In a very thorough investigation of this phenomenon, researchers questioned almost 2,000 people in the Netherlands ranging in age from 24 to 86. They asked about various components of cognitive functioning (such as memory, mental speed, decision making) and how they rated themselves compared to their agemates, compared to themselves 5–10 years earlier, and compared to themselves at 25 years of age. Results showed that participants' perceptions of cognitive decline began about age 50 and increased with age, covering all the cognitive domains included in the questionnaire. However, when participants' actual cognitive abilities were measured, there was no relationship between their abilities and their subjective assessments (Ponds et al., 2000). This suggests that adults believe that cognitive decline begins around age 50 and begin to interpret their cognitive failures and mistakes as being due to aging, whereas the same lapses at earlier ages would have been attributed to other causes, such as having too much on their mind or not getting enough sleep the night before.

WRITING PROMPT

Explaining Memory Lapses

Have you forgotten anything recently, or become confused with instructions of some kind? How did you explain these cognitive failings? If you were 20 years older, would the explanation be different?

 The response entered here will appear in the performance dashboard and can be viewed by your instructor.

Submit

4.6: Cognitive Assistance

OBJECTIVE: Evaluate forms of cognitive assistance

If you take notes on your laptop while your professor lectures or make a list of things to do before your weekend trip, you are using cognitive assistance. Here are some solutions to cognitive limitations that help older adults to function well.

By the end of this module, you will be able to:

4.6.1 Describe strategies for dealing with cognitive challenges in medication adherence

4.6.2 Relate social networking to cognitive retention

4.6.3 Determine effective forms of electronic stimulation for cognitive exercise

4.6.4 Analyze the issues involved in driving by older adults

4.6.1: Medication Adherence

OBJECTIVE: Describe strategies for dealing with cognitive challenges in medication adherence

One of our biggest preventable health-care problems is **medication adherence**, or the inability of patients to follow their physicians' instructions about taking their prescribed medication in the right dosages, at the right time, and for the right length of time. It is estimated that about half the people in the United States who suffer from chronic conditions such as high blood pressure and diabetes do not adhere to their physicians' instructions (Sabaté, 2003), leading to poor outcomes, higher death rates, and reduced quality of life. Many reasons have been found for this nonadherence, such as economic circumstances, side effects of the medication, and the doctor–patient relationship quality, but one that has been of interest to cognitive psychologists is memory ability, specifically *prospective memory*, or the ability to remember to do something at a later time. Studies have shown prospective memory problems are linked to medication adherence in adults of various ages suffering from a variety of diseases and chronic conditions, such as HIV, diabetes, and rheumatoid arthritis, independent of economic factors, side effects, and patient–doctor relationships (Zogg et al., 2012). Electronic devices are available that can be set to signal people that it is time to take their medication, what the proper dosage is, and any other instructions necessary. Pharmacies are able to package multiple pills in blister packs, clearly labeled with the date and time they should be taken. Once the medication is taken, the empty place on the card serves as feedback. Automated phone calls can remind people when it is time to take medication, and there are smartphone apps that keep track of medications and also give reminders. There is evidence that new electronic medication packaging (EMP) devices that are embedded in the medication's packaging may be effective in improving compliance.

Medical researcher Kyle D. Checchi and his colleagues (2014) reviewed 37 studies of the effectiveness of these devices and found that the most effective devices included recording when the medication was taken and keeping a record, audiovisual reminders, digital displays, real-time monitoring, and feedback on how well the person is adhering. Although this doesn't solve all the problems of nonadherence, it can help with those cases that are caused by age-related cognitive problems.

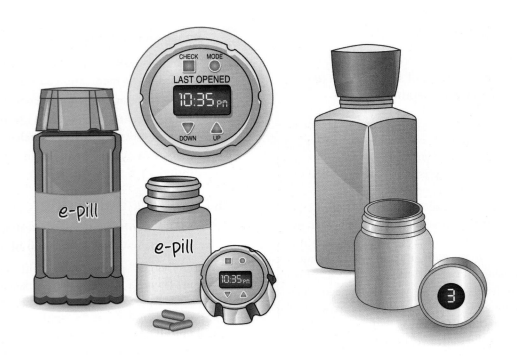

Today, many different devices can help with medication adherence.

4.6.2: Social Networking

OBJECTIVE: **Relate social networking to cognitive retention**

In the later years of adulthood, social groups get smaller as friends and relatives move away or die. The high value of social support enhances memory for social information. Both younger and older adults remember high-value social information better than low-value social information, but this difference is especially large for older adults (Hargis & Castel, 2017).

The use of personal computers for social networking can help older adults stay in touch (Hogeboom et al., 2010). Facebook is the major social networking platform for most adults, but Instagram, Pinterest, Snapchat, LinkedIn, Twitter, and WhatsApp have all dramatically increased in use since 2012 (Smith & Anderson, 2018). According to a 2018 Gallup poll, Facebook use by people age 50–64 increased from 34% in 2011 to 52% in 2018 (McCarthy, 2018).

Almost all of today's adults are long-time telephone users and have made the switch to cell phones. Among people age 64 and older, 85% own a cell phone and 46% have a smart phone. Older adults have more favorable views of their smartphones than do younger adults. According to the Pew Research Center, older adults (82%) are much more likely than younger adults (64%) to say that their smartphone represents "freedom," and younger adults (36%) are much more likely than older adults (18%) to say that their smartphone represents "a leash." Older adults (82%) are also more likely than younger adults (63%) to say their smartphone is "connecting," and younger adults (37%) are more likely than older adults (18%) to say their smartphone is "distracting" (Anderson, 2015).

4.6.3: E-Readers and Electronic Games

OBJECTIVE: **Determine effective forms of electronic stimulation for cognitive exercise**

Intellectual activity is important for cognitive function, but for older adults, there are more barriers to keeping up with newspapers, magazines, and books than with younger adults. Visual problems are more prevalent as we get older, it may be difficult to travel to a bookstore or library, and the cost of reading material may be too high. Many middle-aged and older adults have started using e-books and find this a solution to some of these problems. E-books allow the reader to increase the font size and adjust the back lighting. Some have text-to-speech features so they can be used as an audiobook. It is possible to read a book, newspaper, or magazine at any time or place, and the cost is usually lower than the cost of a conventional book. For avid readers, it is much lighter to carry an e-reader than to weigh oneself down with conventional books. I recently started reading our local newspaper on my tablet because I could increase the size of the font for some of the small print, such as movie theater timetables. Before that realization, I had been one of those people who claimed they would never give up the smell of the newsprint and the rustle of the pages as they turn. Another plus is that the electronic "paper" arrives much earlier on my tablet than the paper one does in the front yard.

Despite all the advantages of e-readers, they are not as popular with older people as are computers and cell phones. In fact, some research has shown that even though older adults read faster and comprehend just as much when reading an e-reader as a book with paper pages, they overwhelmingly prefer to read traditional books (Kretzschmr et al., 2013). In a survey conducted in 2016 by the Pew Research Center, only 10% of younger adults preferred reading newspapers in print form rather than online, while 63% of those over age 65 preferred reading a printed newspaper over reading the news online.

Research also shows that cognitive abilities are sustained by playing games, preferably in a social setting. When one's ability and motivation to go out with friends decline, so do the bridge parties and poker nights. But many people now play the same games using smartphones and computers, allowing them to play chess, bridge, and Scrabble with friends (and strangers) who live around the world. I am currently engaged in a Scrabble tournament with my sister, Rose. We live about 250 miles apart and have very busy lives, but we are "in touch" several times a day through the game apps on our smartphones. My husband has several online chess games going with our grandchildren on various devices. There are also games to play alone, such as crossword puzzles and Suduko.

Some video games are designed to provide both cognitive and physical exercise, and research shows that they accomplish both. These "exergames," such as the ones found on PlayStation, Xbox, and Wii, feature motion sensors that incorporate the gamers' movements within the game. Some of the activities available are bowling, tennis, and dancing. The potential benefits of exergames on physical and cognitive performance were assessed in a study with French adults between the ages of 65 and 78 (Maillot et al., 2012). Participants received pre- and posttest assessments of their physical fitness (for example, heart-rate measures, ratings of perceived effort in doing everyday tasks, BMI) as well as their cognitive performances on a series of tasks measuring executive control, speed of processing, and visuospatial abilities. One group then received 12 weeks of training playing Nintendo Wii games, whereas the control group received no special training. The researchers reported that participants in the exergame training group demonstrated significant gains on most measures of both physical fitness and cognitive abilities, a clear indication that playing video games can be beneficial for older adults' physical and cognitive health.

4.6.4: Safe Driving

OBJECTIVE: Analyze the issues involved in driving by older adults

The topic of older adults and driving brings forth a variety of opinions, most very emotional. In many parts of the United States, the ability to drive a car is synonymous with being an adult. Emerging adults count the days until they can drive, and older adults dread the day they must give it up. One of the biggest problems between middle-aged adults and their older adult parents is "the driving issue," when and how to convince Mom or Dad to give up the car keys. An automobile is a dangerous piece of machinery. Auto accidents are the leading cause of death for people in the United States for emerging adults and young adults, and the 12th highest cause of death for all ages (National Highway Traffic Safety Administration, 2015). The question of whether age-related cognitive changes are detriments to driving safety is an important one, and research has been done trying to pinpoint just what is involved in unsafe driving and if anything can be done to retrain older drivers to make them safer.

About 19% of all drivers in the United States are 65 years of age or older and account for 28% of all auto accident fatalities (U.S. Census Bureau, 2012a). However, these numbers don't give us an accurate picture of older adults' driving records because older adults don't drive as much as younger adults. When the accident rates for different age groups are adjusted for the number of miles driven per year, the results (Figure 4.14) gave a clearer picture of the situation (Insurance Institute for Highway Safety, 2018).

However, the number of fatalities in each age group for the number of miles driven isn't the most accurate picture either because older drivers and their passengers are usually in poorer health than younger drivers and their passengers, and also have more brittle bones and other preexisting problems that make them more at risk for fatal injuries than do younger drivers. Still, we must concede that age is a factor in safe driving and it makes sense to look into the age-related cognitive changes that may be involved.

A USEFUL FIELD OF VIEW Older drivers have problems navigating intersections with flashing signals or yield signs and making left turns at stop signs or traffic signals, among other things. It has been suggested by some that although older adult drivers have the visual acuity to pass the vision tests, they are limited in their **useful field of view**, the area of the visual field that can be processed in one glance. Older drivers who had a reduction in their useful field view of 40% or more were twice as likely to be involved in an auto crash as those with normal visual fields (Sims et al., 2000).

Research has shown that the useful field of view is not a constant perceptual ability; it decreases in lab studies when the individual is attending to other activities. In one study

Figure 4.14 Age of Drivers and Number of Fatal Crashes

Drivers under age 30 and over age 70 are more apt to be involved in fatal two-car crashes, and the rate increases dramatically after the age of 80.

SOURCE: Insurance Institute for Highway Safety (2018).

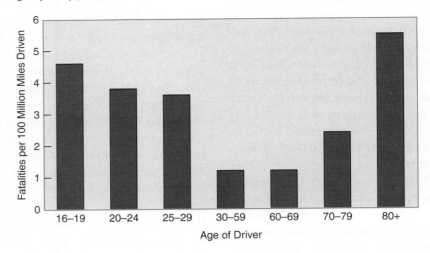

of young, healthy college students, the time it took to detect visual stimuli in the periphery of their visual fields was significantly reduced when a spoken word-selection task was added to the test (Atchley & Dressel, 2004). Although this was a test done in a lab and not on the road, it has serious implications for drivers of all ages who multitask behind the wheel. Driving is a very demanding and complex cognitive activity and should not be combined with competing tasks, such as talking or texting, especially for older drivers who may have reduced functional visual fields.

After this somber message, there is some bright news: It is possible to train people to have larger useful fields of view. For example, in one study, older drivers (average age of 72 years) who had reduced useful fields of view were given either speed-of-processing training or driver-simulator training (Roenker et al., 2003). The speed-of-processing training involved a touch-screen computer on which targets appeared for various durations in the periphery of the visual field. Participants were required to respond to the targets as soon as they were detected until they reached proficiency (about 4.5 hours of training). Two weeks later in a driving simulation test, the speed-of-processing group made fewer dangerous maneuvers than they had at baseline, such as ignoring traffic signals at intersections and misgauging the space between cars when making turns across an intersection, two behaviors that contribute substantially to car crashes. They also had increased their reaction time an average of 277 milliseconds. (In real-life terms, this translates into being able to stop 22 feet sooner when going 55 miles an hour—not a trivial improvement.) The driver-simulator group did not improve on reaction time, but did improve on the specific skills on which they were trained. Eighteen months later, improvements for the speed-of-processing group were, for the most part, still present. The researchers

suggest that the training in speed of processing serves to increase the useful field of view for older drivers, and that this increase translates to improvement in driving ability, specifically the speed with which drivers process and act on complex visual information.

Another study looked at older drivers' failure to scan as effectively at intersections as younger drivers, asking whether it was a result of cognitive aging and physical decline or unsafe driving habits, which could be modified. The latter was concluded when a training group who received feedback on videos of their everyday driving and who spent time in a driving simulator learning to scan more thoroughly at intersections performed better than a control group who only received coaching about the importance of scanning, but no video feedback or simulator training. In fact, the training group performed as well as a control group of younger drivers (Pollatsek et al., 2012). The authors concluded that a major problem with older drivers is the failure to scan adequately for upcoming hazards at intersections. They think that this is more of a bad habit than a result of cognitive or physical deterioration because a short training session involving feedback and practice in a driving simulator led to significant improvement.

WRITING PROMPT

Law and Order

What is the law in your area pertaining to cell phone use or texting while driving? Do you agree or disagree? Why?

▶ The response entered here will appear in the performance dashboard and can be viewed by your instructor.

Summary: Cognitive Abilities

There is no doubt that people become slower and less accurate with age on many types of cognitive tasks, and this is the case even for the healthiest among us. But the best way to view these overall changes in cognitive abilities is in terms of both losses and gains.

Dixon (2000) pointed out that there are gains in terms of abilities that continue to grow throughout adulthood, such as new stages of understanding (Sinnott, 1996) and increases in wisdom (Baltes & Staudinger, 1993; Worthy et al., 2011). There are also gains in terms of doing better than expected. For example, although Schaie (1994) found a general trend of decline in cognitive abilities with advanced age, not all abilities follow that trend. In fact, 90% of all the participants in his study maintained at least two intellectual abilities over the 7-year time period they were studied. Dixon (2000) also pointed to compensation as a gain in the later years, when we find new ways of performing old tasks, find improvements in one skill as the result of losses in another, and learn to use our partners or others around us as collaborators. This viewpoint may be overly rosy, but there is a good deal of truth in it. The process of cognitive aging is not entirely a story of losses, and this gives us a nice balance with which to end the chapter.

4.1 Attention

OBJECTIVE: Explain how attention changes with age

- Cognition begins with attention, and the ability to attend to one thing and not another declines with age. A particular problem with older adults is divided attention, such as talking on a cell phone while driving. The attention task, visual search, involves finding a familiar object in a room full of other objects. Older adults fail to find the objects more than younger adults, and older adults who have experienced falls in the past year have the most failures.

4.2 Memory

OBJECTIVE: Compare how different forms of memory change over time

- Memory consists of short-term memory and long-term memory, which are cognitive storage areas. Working-memory processes information in short-term memory for immediate use and also for storage in long-term memory. Scores on tests of short-term memory, long-term memory, and working memory, as well as speed of processing all decline with age. Verbal knowledge increases with age.
- Information in long-term memory consists of declarative (explicit) memory, which is available to consciousness, and nondeclarative (implicit) memory, which involves skills and automatic processes, such as riding a bike.

Declarative memory has two parts, semantic memory, which is knowledge of language, facts, and concepts, and episodic memory, which is knowledge of recalled events. Episodic memory declines with age, beginning around 60, but semantic memory stays stable over the years except for word-finding failures and name-finding failures.

- Prospective memory is remembering to do something in the future, such as taking medication on a certain schedule or meeting a friend tomorrow. It is stronger in younger people than older people.
- Cognitive training can improve memory performance in older adults for specific tasks, but not bring it back to that of younger adults. Physical exercise has a bigger positive effect on cognitive ability.
- Memory loss can be partially compensated for by external aids (lists, calendars) and training (mental imagery, method of loci).
- Some researchers, using the contextual perspective, show that older people do better on memory tests if the tasks better fit the cognitive styles they have adapted to fit their lifestyles, such as using information with emotional content, proposing a task that involves transmitting knowledge to the next generation, or avoiding stereotype threat.

4.3 Intelligence

OBJECTIVE: Evaluate the concept of age-related changes to intellectual ability

- Early studies of IQ scores for people of different ages showed that intelligence began to decline in the early 30s and continued sharply downward. Later, longitudinal studies showed that the decline didn't start until people reached their 60s, and the decline was moderate. The difference is primarily due to cohort effects.
- Scores of fluid intelligence abilities decline starting in the 60s. Crystallized intelligence abilities remain stable well into the 70s or 80s.
- Declines in intellectual abilities can be reversed using specific training for various abilities, physical exercise, and general test-taking training. This training has long-term effects.

4.4 Decision Making and Problem Solving

OBJECTIVE: Relate decision making and problem solving to age

- In real-world cognition, older people are able to make good decisions and judgments in less time and using less information than younger people, probably drawing on their greater store of experience. In fact, older adults often show better decision-making skills than younger adults, especially when interpersonal problems are confronted. Older adults tend to show a positivity bias, being more attentive to positive than negative events and emotions and performing better on tasks involving positive images or emotions.

4.5 Individual Differences in Cognitive Change

OBJECTIVE: **Analyze factors that influence individual cognitive change**

- Not everyone ages in cognitive abilities at the same rate. Some of the individual differences are in the area of health, including vision and hearing, chronic disease, and medication. Genes play a role, as does one's education and income history. Mental and physical exercise can lead to better cognitive abilities in later years.

- Older people's subjective evaluations of their cognitive abilities are based more on their stereotypes of aging than on any actual decline.

4.6 Cognitive Assistance

OBJECTIVE: **Evaluate forms of cognitive assistance**

- Cognitive assistance involves practical solutions to age-related cognitive decline. Examples are electronic timers and phone apps to help people take their medications as prescribed and new pharmacy packaging that bundles multiple pills onto cards with time- and date-labeled windows.

- Social relationships are assisted by participating in social networking sites. The majority of people over age 65 are regular Internet users and a third are on Facebook or other such sites.

- The number of older drivers on the road is increasing, and they are very safe drivers up until the age of 70, when their involvement in fatal accidents begins to increase, being higher than teenagers at 80 and beyond. Because driving is essential to daily life in many areas, researchers have identified the useful field of view as a critical factor in safe driving. It is possible to retrain older adults to increase this visual ability. It is also possible to reduce distractions (such as cell phone use) that decrease the useful field of view. Other studies point out poor driving habits that can be remedied by instruction with feedback for older drivers.

SHARED WRITING

Cognitive Abilities

Consider this chapter's discussion of individual differences in cognitive abilities as they relate to a variety of factors (health, schooling, physical exercise, etc.). What are some specific factors that have influenced people you have known (family, friends, relatives)? How have these factors impacted these people? How much of an impact do you think these factors have? Write a short response that your classmates will read. Be sure to discuss specific examples.

 A minimum number of characters is required to post and earn points. After posting, your response can be viewed by your class and instructor, and you can participate in the class discussion.

Post   0 characters | 140 minimum

Chapter 5
Social Roles

Newlyweds snap a quick selfie.

Learning Objectives

5.1 Analyze how social roles change over time

5.2 Characterize social roles in young adulthood

5.3 Determine how social roles impact middle adulthood experiences

5.4 Evaluate ways of handling transitions in late adulthood

5.5 Analyze the interactions between atypical families and their cultures

A Word From the Author

Roles and Adjustments

I TEACH DEVELOPMENTAL psychology courses at a university in south Florida, and I enjoy the role of professor. I am fortunate to be at a smaller partner campus of a large university, so I am able to get to know the students. Many of them recognize me around campus and stop to talk to me about the courses they are planning to take, the graduate schools they are applying to, or some point we covered in class. It is especially enjoyable for me because the other part of my career, writing this textbook, is very isolated. For that job I have an office at home where I have little social interaction. Together, the two professional roles provide a pleasant balance.

My husband is a professor on the main campus of the same university, and I find myself on "his" campus from time to time. The difference in my social roles from one campus to the other is striking. On "my" campus, colleagues ask me about my classes, my book, or some bit of academic intrigue; on my husband's campus, I'm asked about the family or our latest vacation. Clearly, I have the role of professor on one campus and the role of professor's wife on the other.

However, being viewed as a professor is not my most prestigious role. The first Friday of the month is Lunch with Family Day at my youngest grandson's elementary school, and after 6 years I know the drill. I pack lunches and wait on the patio outside the cafeteria. When the fifth-grade classes arrive, he scans the group of waiting family members, looking for a familiar face. Then I hear, "Grandma, Grandma!" and he comes running to give me kisses and hugs (and to see what I brought for lunch). We eat together under the trees, and he proudly tells passing friends and teachers, "This is my grandmother! She came to have lunch with me!" Although I am aware that he may not be as pleased to have me hanging around his middle school next year, I am enjoying the fame while I can. I don't think the president of our university gets such accolades—at least not on such a regular basis.

In addition to these roles, I am a wife, a mother, a stepmother, a sister, an aunt, and a friend. Many of these roles, such as textbook author and grandmother, are fairly new, and many of the old ones, such as sister and mother, have changed over the years. Reflecting on the changing roles in my life gives me a good measure of my progress on the journey of adulthood.

This chapter is about the roles we occupy in adulthood, with an emphasis on the adjustments we make as they change over time. I begin with a short discussion of social roles and transitions, and then go on to the roles that are typical in young adulthood, middle adulthood, and older adulthood. Sprinkled among these is a discussion of gender roles and how they change within our other roles. Finally, I talk about those who don't fit the broad categories—the lifelong singles, the childless, and the divorced and remarried. And I want to emphasize, as you may know already, that the transitions from one role to another are often as challenging as the roles themselves.

5.1: Social Roles and Transitions

OBJECTIVE: Analyze how social roles change over time

The term **social roles** refers to the expected behaviors and attitudes that come with one's position in society. One way adult development is studied is by examining the succession of social roles that adults typically occupy over the years. In the early days of social role theory, adulthood was described in terms of the *number* of roles an individual occupied at different stages of life. The theory was that people

acquired a large number of roles in the early years of adulthood and then began shedding them in the later years. In fact, "successful aging" was once measured by how many roles an older person had relinquished and how willingly they had been relinquished (Cumming & Henry, 1961). In the last few decades, this viewpoint has changed to one of **role transitions**. This emphasis acknowledges that, with few exceptions, roles are neither gained nor lost; they change as the life circumstances of the individual change (Ferraro, 2001). The emerging adult moves from the constraints of being a high school student to the relative freedom of a college student's role; the young adult makes the transition from being a spouse to being a new parent; the middle-aged adult moves from being the parent of a dependent teenager to the parent of an independent adult; and the older adult may lose some roles as friends and family members die, but the remaining roles increase in richness and the satisfaction they provide (Neugarten, 1996). Studying role transitions involves finding out how people adjust when they change from one role to another and how the transition affects their other roles.

In the past chapters I have talked about patterns of change over adulthood in health and physical functioning—changes that are analogous to the hours on a **biological clock**. In this chapter I talk about patterns of change over adulthood in social roles—comparable to the hours of a **social clock**. To understand the social role structure of adult life, we need to look at the age-linked social clock and at the varying roles within each period of adult life.

▼ By the end of this module, you will be able to:

5.1.1 Relate life satisfaction to social timing

5.1.2 Explain the existence and impact of gender roles

5.1.1: The Effect of Variations in Timing

OBJECTIVE: Relate life satisfaction to social timing

Social timing refers to the roles we occupy, how long we occupy them, and the order in which we occupy them. It also depends on the culture we live in and what expectations our society has for role transitions (Elder, 1995). For example, to become a parent at age 15 may be expected in some societies (and may even happen frequently in our society), but it is considered "off-time" by mainstream U.S. norms. Similarly, a 45-year-old man who does not want to get involved in marriage or parenthood because he values his independence is also considered off-time. Both behaviors would be more typical, or "on-time," at other ages. The extent that one's roles are on-time or off-time is hypothesized to be of prime importance to one's social development and well-being (McAdams, 2001).

The concept of a social clock becoming important in adulthood was first proposed by sociologist Bernice Neugarten and her colleagues (Neugarten et al., 1965). They viewed this as an important distinction between children and adults in that adults were capable of viewing their lives both in the past and in the future, comparing their past selves with their present selves and anticipating their future selves. It also allows us to compare our own life cycles with those of others. Neugarten believed that we form a mental representation of the "normal, expectable life cycle" and use this to evaluate our own lives and the lives of others.

Young adults who continue living at home with their parents, not having a serious romantic relationship or making efforts to become financially independent are no doubt aware of their off-time development. Middle-aged adults are likewise aware that the time has come to either reach their career goals or disengage. Likewise, older adults fare better when they are able to make age-appropriate role transitions in their lives (such as accepting care from their children). Psychologist Jette Heckhausen (2001) theorizes that the stronger the correlation a person's social role sequence has with developmental norms, the less stress he or she will have in life.

To my thinking, the idea of a social clock adds another dimension to the roles we move into during adulthood.

It's not only important to assume the expected roles and fulfill them well, but also to assume them at the right time and in the right order. This is not always within our control, as exemplified by the 27-year-old woman who is a widow because her husband died in an auto accident, or the 75-year-old grandmother who is raising her school-age grandchildren (and her 77-year-old husband who has gone back to work to support them). However, it is accurate to predict that people who are off-time with the social clock of their culture are more apt to have difficulty in their roles and less apt to report high levels of life satisfaction.

Here, I have pulled together the various patterns of change with age in an overview table (Table 5.1) so that you can begin to build a composite picture of the qualities and experiences of adults in different age groups. The key point is this: Despite all the variations in timing and sequence, the basic shape of the pattern of role transitions seems to be similar for most adults. We move into more roles in early adulthood, renegotiate and make transitions into different roles in middle adulthood, and make still more transitions in late adulthood. Some roles are ruled by the biological clock and some by the social clock, but there is a similar basic itinerary for most adults.

Table 5.1 Overview of Social Roles Throughout Adulthood

18–24 Years	25–39 Years	40–64 Years	65–74 Years	75+ Years
Social roles of emerging adults are a mixture of childhood and adult roles, and transitions are fluid as they move in and out of roles.	Busiest time for role transitions as young adults enter the workforce and establish careers.	Roles become more intense as children get older, jobs become more important, and community involvement often involves leadership responsibilities.	Roles have less content as children become more independent and retirement arrives. Roles of volunteer worker and grandparent become important.	Roles are highly individualized depending on health, marital status, and personal preferences.
Gender role differences are moderate.	Maximum gender role differences occur, especially after the transition to parenthood.	Gender role differences remain strong while children are in the home.	Gender roles expand to allow for more freedom, but do not "cross over."	Gender roles remain expanded.
Most live in parents' home and are financially dependent to some extent.	Roles with parents involve assistance and advice from them.	Roles with parents are more equal than at other times of life. Some move into caregiving role with parents.	Role with surviving parents usually involves some level of caregiving.	Role with parents is over. Role with surviving siblings becomes extremely strong.
Role of partner is usually one of dating or cohabiting.	Most marry during this time, although many cohabit or remain single. Marriages often end in divorce.	Role of spouse is central, though divorce and remarriage may occur.	Role of spouse for many has changed to role of widower or role of remarried widower.	Many are widowed, especially women.
Small percentage take on parental role during this time.	Transition to parent role occurs.	Role with children is central; most become grandparents.	Role with children remains important, though nonparents have social networks with siblings and their children, close friends, stepchildren.	Adjustment to care-receiver role takes place. Role with children is central as they assume caretaking in varying degrees. Those without children receive care from other relatives, friends, or stepchildren.

5.1.2: Gender Roles

OBJECTIVE: Explain the existence and impact of gender roles

Woven through the topic of social roles is the concept of **gender roles**, which describe what men and women actually do in a given culture during a particular historical era. Almost any role we take on during our adult lives is colored by gender. For example, becoming a parent means moving into a different role depending on whether you are becoming a mother or a father. For example, in typical families with male–female parents around the world, the mother is the major caregiver of the children and does the bulk of the housework; the father is the major breadwinner and is in charge of repairs around the house and yardwork, although the roles of men and women have become more and more similar in the past 50 years and many people have chosen not to be limited to one typical gender role or another.

Why would this be? The classic answer comes from **gender schema theory**, which states that children are taught to view the world and themselves through gender-polarized lenses that make artificial or exaggerated distinctions between what is masculine and what is feminine. As adults, they direct their own behavior to fit these distinctions (Bem, 1981, 1993). A similar explanation comes from **social role theory**, stating that gender roles are the result of young children observing the actual division of labor within their culture, thus learning what society expects of them as men and women, and then following these expectations (Eagly, 1987, 1995).

Both of these theories of the origins of gender roles deal with **proximal causes**, factors that are present in the immediate environment. Other theories explain the origins of gender roles using **distal causes**, factors that were present in the past. For example, **evolutionary psychology** suggests that gender roles were solutions our primitive ancestors evolved in response to recurrent problems they faced millions of years ago. This theory proposes that females and males are genetically predisposed to behave in different ways. The genes for these behaviors are present in us today because throughout human history they have allowed men and women in our species to survive and to select mates who help them reproduce and protect children, who, in turn, pass along the genes for these behaviors to the next generation (Geary, 2005). Early forms of this theory seemed to imply that one's genes determine one's behavior, but more contemporary views are that the environment in interaction with evolved dispositions may bias men and women to behave in certain ways that are beneficial to the species' survival (Schmidt, 2017).

GENDER STEREOTYPES A related phenomenon to gender roles is **gender stereotypes**, which are sets of shared beliefs of generalizations about what *all* men and women in a society have in common, often extending to what members of each gender *ought* to do and how they *should* behave.

Although gender stereotypes can be useful, they can also be inaccurate, and they are particularly harmful when they are used to judge how well an individual man or woman is measuring up to some standard of behavior.

Gender stereotypes are surprisingly consistent across cultures. In an early, comprehensive study, psychologists John Williams and Deborah Best (1990) investigated gender stereotypes in 25 countries. In each country, college students were given a list of 300 adjectives (translated into the local language where necessary) and asked whether the word was more frequently associated with men, with women, or neither. The results showed a striking degree of agreement across cultures. In 23 countries, a vast majority of the people agreed that the male stereotype is centered around a set of qualities often labeled **instrumental qualities**, such as being competitive, adventurous, and physically strong, whereas the female stereotype centered around qualities of affiliation and expressiveness, often referred to as **communal qualities**, such as being sympathetic, nurturing, and intuitive.

In addition, gender stereotypes are surprisingly consistent over time. I think most of us would predict that the general view of masculine and feminine roles has changed in the past 30 years, but some recent research shows otherwise. Social psychologist Kay Deaux and her colleagues, who conducted a study of gender stereotypes in the early 1980s, repeated it again 30 years later (Deaux & Lewis, 1984; Haines et al., 2016). They found stability in gender stereotyping over the course of three decades in spite of all the changes that had occurred in men and women's work and family roles. Participants were asked whether a trait or a role referred to a "man," "woman," or "person." Table 5.2 gives some of the traits, occupations, and roles used in these studies.

Table 5.2 Examples of Gender Stereotypes

	Masculine (Instrumental)	Feminine (Communal)
Traits	Independent	Emotional
	Competitive	Able to devote self to others
	Makes decisions quickly	Gentle
	Never gives up easily	Kind
	Self-confident	Aware of the feelings of others
	Stands up well under pressure	Understanding of others
	Feels superior	Warm in relationships with others
		Helpful to others
Roles	Head of household	Source of emotional support
	Financial provider	Manages the household
	Leader	Takes care of the children
	Responsible for household repairs	Responsible for decorating the home

SOURCE: Deaux & Lewis (1984); Haines et al. (2016).

It seems clear from these studies that there is something about gender stereotypes that is ingrained in us and resistant to change, even in the face of conflicting evidence. These participants are no doubt aware of women who are leaders and men who are sources of emotional support in real life, but in the abstract, they still tag those roles as pertaining to a man or a woman, not a person. It is useful to remember the difference between gender roles and gender stereotypes. We need to be aware that these stereotypes may dwell as generalities in our minds and be watchful that they don't creep into our evaluations of others (or of ourselves).

That being said, there are real gender differences for most of us in the content of our social roles, and the strength of these differ with age. The following sections include discussions of the multiple roles people take on in various stages of life and how gender typically affects the contents of those roles.

5.2: Social Roles in Young Adulthood

OBJECTIVE: Characterize social roles in young adulthood

Anyone experiencing young adulthood—and anyone who has been through it—would surely agree that there are more changes in social roles at this time than in any other period of life. Emerging adults are searching for the right paths in life, but their roles are still slight modifications of their adolescent roles (Shanahan, 2000). Young adulthood, by definition, involves leaving the role of student and beginning the role of worker. It also can involve becoming independent of one's parents, becoming a spouse or committed partner, and becoming a parent. The **transition to adulthood**, or the process by which young people move into their adult roles, varies enormously. Some people complete high school, go to college or enter some type of career training, establish themselves economically, and move out of the parental home. Others complete high school, move out of their parents' home, take a series of entry-level jobs around the country for a few years, and then move back with their parents, ready to begin college. A few marry immediately after high school, and others leave the parental home to enter cohabiting relationships as they make this transition. So there are clearly a variety of options open to young people as they navigate their way into the roles of adulthood.

The lack of ironclad rules has its benefits; young people are not necessarily pushed into roles that may not be right for them, such as spending 4 years studying for a career for which they are ill-fitted or rushing into an early marriage with someone who is not a good match. Research suggests that this long period of transition also serves to correct problem trajectories begun in childhood and provides a

discontinuity or turning point toward successful adulthood (Schulenberg et al., 2004). Studies have shown that a number of young people entering adulthood with less-than-optimal mental health outlooks, including antisocial behavior and substance abuse, are able to turn their lives around during the extended transition to adulthood, often after assuming the role of member of the military (Elder, 2001) or spouse (Craig & Foster, 2013).

This time of transition between late adolescence and full-fledged adulthood has become so common in developed countries that it is now considered to be a new stage of adulthood. Developmental psychologist Jeffrey Arnett (2000) proposed the term **emerging adulthood** for this time of life, roughly between the ages of 18 and 25. He described it as a time in which young people try out different experiences and gradually make their way toward commitments in love and work. He later described five features that make emerging adulthood different from either adolescence or adulthood. Emerging adulthood is (1) the age of identity explorations, (2) the age of instability, (3) the self-focused age, (4) the age of feeling in-between, and (5) the age of possibilities (Arnett, 2007).

Although emerging adulthood does not occur in all cultures, it has been noted, with some variations, among American Indian youths (Van Alstine Makomenaw, 2012) and in China (Nelson & Chen, 2007), Argentina (Facio et al., 2007), Japan (Rosenberger, 2007), Latin America (Galambos & Martínez, 2007; Manago, 2012), and some European countries (Douglass, 2007; Tynkkynen et al., 2012). Most of these studies have been conducted with university students in urban settings and suggest that the focus on self and the exploration of individual identity may not be present to the same extent with young people in rural areas and less-privileged families. Adolescents in those areas are more likely to move directly into full-time work and family responsibilities, exhibiting the traditional role transitions found in the United States up until the 1950s.

	By the end of this module, you will be able to:

5.2.1 Identify influences on young adult independence

5.2.2 Describe partnership for young adults

5.2.3 Summarize life changes associated with the role of parent

5.2.1: Leaving and Returning Home

OBJECTIVE: Identify influences on young adult independence

The leaving-home process for emerging adults has a lot of variability today, both in the timing and the destination. Take, for instance, my own family. One of my children moved out immediately after high school into a cohabiting relationship. Another went away to college and came home each summer through graduate school. And my husband's daughter, who never lived with us on a permanent basis during childhood, moved in and out of our "empty nest" several times during her emerging adult years as she attended college or was "between apartments."

What is the most accurate picture of living arrangements for young people? As seen in Figure 5.1, the Pew Research Center shows that 32% of emerging and young adults in the United States between 18 and 34 years of age are living with their parents. This is the highest proportion since 1940, and it is the first time that more young people in this age group are living with parents than living with a spouse or romantic partner (Fry, 2016).

Figure 5.1 shows that 62% of 18- to 34-year-olds were living with a spouse or romantic partner in 1960, but by 2014, only 32% had chosen this living arrangement—a drop by almost half. Another factor is that young people are more likely to be unable to afford their own living arrangements due to unemployment, low wages, or long education processes. Once they graduate, many young people are burdened with student loan debt and must fall back on the safety net of living with parents (Fry, 2016).

There are many other reasons for young adults remaining in their family home. There are more state colleges and online courses, which make it more economical for college students to remain in their family homes. Parents are more affluent and are better able to support their adult children. Parents have larger homes and fewer children. Young men are not drafted into military service as in times past. And the relationships between parents and their adult children are often more egalitarian than in past generations.

What do we know about young adults who remain in their parents' homes? The stereotype is that they are loafing—sitting in their parents' basements playing video games and avoiding adulthood. The facts are quite different. The U.S. Census Bureau has found that about 80% of them are either working or attending school. The others are classified as "idle," but many are taking care of their own young children or are disabled (Vespa, 2017).

Many young adults leave their parents' homes and then return. In a number of countries surveyed, the incidence of these "boomerang kids" has doubled in the last few decades. In the United States, it is estimated that about half of all young people who move out of their parents' homes for at least 4 months will return again. The younger they are when they move out, the more likely they are to return. The reasons young people return to the family home are similar to the reasons for not leaving in the first place and often are precipitated by some misfortune, such as losing a job, filing for bankruptcy, or a relationship breakup. (Sometimes it is the parents' misfortunes, such as poor health or financial reversals, that cause the adult child to return home.)

Figure 5.1 Living Arrangements for Emerging and Young Adults

More 18- to 34-year-olds are living with their parents than since the 1940s

SOURCE: Fry (2016).

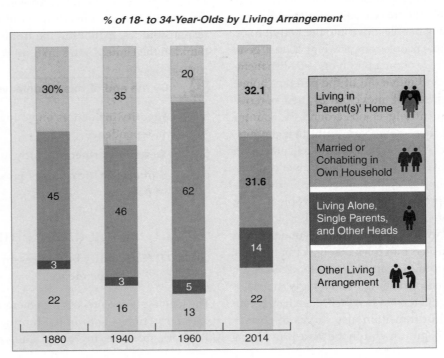

LIFE TRANSITIONS   What is the result of young people remaining in their parents' homes after the "normal" time to leave?

First, we need to remember that the timing of most life transitions is socially created within the specific cultural and historical setting (Hagestad & Neugarten, 1985). When over a third of 18- to 34-year-olds are still living with their parents, the "normal" time to move out has a different meaning.

Sociologist Thomas Leopold (2012) examined this phenomenon in Europe to determine the effects of young adults living with their parents. Using data from over 6,000 families from 14 countries in Europe, he identified a group of young adults as being late leavers relative to others in their country and birth cohort. The ages ranged from just under 20 years in Denmark to just over 26 in Italy. When Leopold investigated the subsequent relationships between the late leavers and their parents, he found that these young adults shared a higher level of solidarity with their parents than their siblings who moved out at a younger age. They lived closer to their parents, maintained more frequent contact, and provided more help to their parents than their siblings. The solidarity went both ways—these late-leaving adult children were also more apt to have received support from their parents after they moved out. He concluded that the practice of remaining in the home of one's parents later than others in that culture and at that time serves to promote generational solidarity for both the adult child and their parents as they grow older.

For some young people, making the transition to adult roles means entering a different culture. Examples of this would be American Indian youths who have attended schools on their reservations and then entered a state university where they are a minority (Van Alstine Makomenaw, 2012), or young people in developing countries who move out of their parents' rural homes to a larger city with changed values, wide choices, and new norms for behavior and gender equality (Manago, 2012). For some emerging adults in developing countries, the drive to be independent is a key factor in their decisions to emigrate to countries with greater opportunities (Azaola, 2012).

GENDER DIFFERENCES IN LEAVING HOME   There are gender differences in whether one lives on one's own or with one's parents, and they might not be what you would expect. Figure 5.2 shows the proportion of men and women living at home every two decades since 1880 (Fry, 2016). This figure shows that for the past 140 years, a larger segment of young adult men has remained in their parents' homes than young adult women. One reason for this is that women are usually younger when they move into a marriage or cohabitation situation than are men. Another reason is that when a partnership fails, and children are involved, young mothers often reside on their own with the children while the fathers move back with their parents and contribute to the children's support. One last reason is that

Figure 5.2 Proportion of Men and Women Living at Home

Young men are more likely to live with a parent than young women.

SOURCE: Fry (2016).

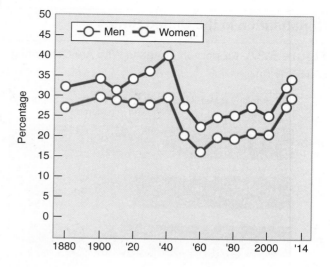

in some cultures in the United States, sons are more "protected" than daughters from cooking, housework, laundry, and other tasks of adulthood. Until the sons get wives to do these tasks for them, the solution is for them to live at home and let their mothers (or sisters) do them. In addition, some cultures are very restrictive of their daughters who live at home, compared to their sons who get more freedom, so the daughters feel more compelled to move out in order to live a less constrained life.

5.2.2: Becoming a Spouse or Partner
OBJECTIVE: Describe partnership for young adults

For many young adults, moving into the role of adult has involved forming an intimate partnership and creating a home with this partner. Marriage remains the traditional form of intimate partnerships in the United States and around the world, but the proportion of people who marry is decreasing, and the age at which they marry is increasing. According to the most recent figures from the U.S. Census Bureau, the age at which most women marry is now 27, and the age at which most men marry is now 29. This has increased by about 4 years over the last three decades (Fry, 2014). When couples marry later, the result is an overall decline in number of marriages each year and fewer married people in the adult population at a given time. Why do young people today delay marriage? Some of the answers are that couples want to enjoy a higher standard of living in their marriages than couples in the past, and there is not as much pressure as in the past for a couple to marry to have a sexual relationship (or even children).

Another reason young adults are marrying at later ages is the increased rate of **cohabitation**, or living together without marriage, which is becoming more and more common in the United States. Although only 7% of all adults in the United States are cohabiting, it varies quite a bit by age (Fry, 2014) (see 'Cohabitation in the United States').

The National Survey of Family Growth (Copen et al., 2013) found that 60% of women and 67% of men between ages 18 and 44 agreed that "living together before marriage may help prevent divorce." When this survey was originally

Cohabitation in the United States

Figure 5.3A Proportion of Adults Who Are Cohabiting

SOURCE: Fry (2014).

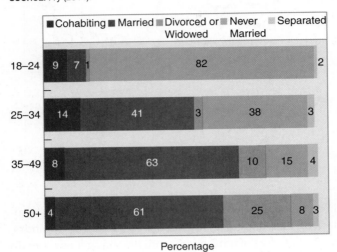

Figure 5.3B Rate of Cohabitation

SOURCE: Copen et al. (2013).

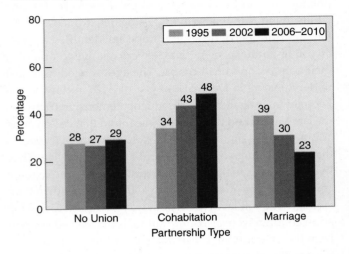

Figure 5.3A shows the proportion of adults in various age groups who are cohabiting compared to other arrangements. As you can see, the group of 25- to 34-year-olds has the highest rate of cohabitation (14%).

When young adults enter into their first romantic partnership, it is more apt to be cohabitation than marriage. A survey of over 12,000 women who were 18 to 44 years of age and who were part of the National Survey of Family Growth showed that almost half (48%) had participated in a cohabitation living arrangement as their first "union" compared to only 23% who married before living together (Copen et al., 2013). Figure 5.3B shows these data as well as those for two previous time periods. As you can see, the rate of cohabitation has gone up since the initial surveys in 1995 and the rate of marriage as a first "union" has gone down. Still, the U.S. Census Bureau predicts that about 86% of young men and 89% of young women will marry at some point in their lives (Vespa et al., 2013).

conducted, it captured responses from approximately 10,000 men and women from 18 to 44 years of age. How do you think you compare? Take the survey on the following page to compare your answers with the survey participants.

GENDER ROLES IN EARLY PARTNERSHIPS Whether a young person cohabits first or moves directly into a marriage, it is clear that the acquisition of this new role as partner brings profound changes to many aspects of his or her life. One of the major hallmarks of this time of life is in gender roles. At the beginning of a marriage or partnership, before children are born, men and women have more **egalitarian roles**, or equal roles, than at any time until late adulthood. Financial contributions to the household are close to equal, both partners usually work full time, and the housework is divided equally. Moving into this new role involves working out how to share the rent, learning how to make financial decisions together, and deciding who takes care of which household tasks. Gender is not the major factor in these adjustments

today as it might have been for their grandparents. Work schedules, interests, abilities, and an egalitarian ideology determine more than traditional gender roles.

A couple shares their household chores.

Survey: Trends and Attitudes about Marriage, Childbearing, and Sexual Behavior

1. Living together before marriage may help prevent divorce.

   a. agree   (women = 60%; men = 67%)
   b. disagree (women = 38%; men = 31%)

2. Divorce is usually the best solution when a couple can't seem to work out their marriage problems.

   a. agree   (women = 38%; men = 39%)
   b. disagree (women = 62%; men = 60%)

3. A young couple should not live together unless they are married.

   a. agree   (women = 28%; men = 25%)
   b. disagree (women = 71%; men = 75%)

4. Marriage has not worked out for most people I know.

   a. agree   (women = 36%; men = 32%)
   b. disagree (women = 63%; men = 67%)

5. It is OK to have children when the parents are living together and not married.

   a. agree   (women = 75%; men = 76%)
   b. disagree (women = 25%; men = 24%)

6. It is OK for an unmarried woman to have and raise a child.

   a. agree   (women = 78%; men = 69%)
   b. disagree (women = 21%; men = 30%)

7. Gay or lesbian adults should have the right to adopt children.

   a. agree   (women = 75%; men = 68%)
   b. disagree (women = 24%; men = 31%)

8. People can't be really happy unless they have children.

   a. agree   (women = 6%; men = 9%)
   b. disagree (women = 93%; men = 90%)

9. It is alright for unmarried 18-year-olds to have sexual intercourse if they have strong affection for each other.

   a. agree   (women = 54%; men = 64%)
   b. disagree (women = 45%; men = 35%)

10. It is alright for unmarried 16-year-olds to have sexual intercourse if they have strong affection for each other.

    a. agree   (women = 15%; men = 21%)
    b. disagree (women = 84%; men = 79%)

11. Sexual relations between two adults of the same sex is alright.

    a. agree   (women = 60%; men = 49%)
    b. disagree (women = 38%; men = 50%)

SOURCE: Data from Daugherty, J., & Copen, C. (2016). *National Health Statistics Report: Trends in attitudes about marriage, childbearing, and sexual behavior: United States, 2002, 2006–2010, and 2011–2014.* Retrieved June 15, 2016, from https://www.cdc.gov/nchs/data/nhsr/nhsr092.pdf.

5.2.3: Becoming a Parent

OBJECTIVE: Summarize life changes associated with the role of parent

One of the major transitions that most adults experience in the years of early adulthood is becoming a parent. Roughly 85% of adults in the United States will eventually become parents, most often in their 20s or 30s (Centers for Disease Control and Prevention [CDC], 2017b). For most, the arrival of the first child brings deep satisfaction, an enhanced feeling of self-worth, and perhaps (as in my case) a sense of being an adult for the first time. It also involves a major role transition, often accompanied by considerable changes in many aspects of one's former life.

Not only are young adults leaving their parents' homes and marrying at later ages, they are also delaying the transition to parenthood. For teenagers and emerging adults, the childbirth rate is currently at a historic low. This is accompanied by declines in teen pregnancy, abortions, and fetal loss rates, and is probably due to the strong pregnancy prevention messages directed at young people and the increased use of contraception. On the other hand, births to women over age 40 have increased, partly as a result of delayed

childbirth at earlier ages, advances in fertility technology, and growing acceptance of single motherhood. These numbers include over 500 births to women over age 50 (Martin et al., 2012).

The average age at which U.S. women give birth for the first time is now 26 years and has increased almost 4 years over the past three decades (CDC, 2017b). The trend toward later childbearing is evident in most developed countries, as you can see in Figure 5.4, which shows the average age women give birth for the first time in 30 developed countries. The average is almost 29 years, and the range is from just under 26 years in Bulgaria to 31 in Korea, with the United States having one of the lowest average ages (Organization for Economic Cooperation and Development [OECD], 2016).

Another trend is that when adults in the United States (and in many countries around the world) do become parents, they often do it without being married first. The old adage of "first comes love, then comes marriage" has been replaced, for many, by "first comes love, then comes the baby carriage." According to the most recent reports, about 40% of all births are to unmarried parents (CDC, 2017c). However, this trend seems to have slowed down since 2008,

Figure 5.4 Average Age Women Give Birth for the First Time in 30 Developed Countries

The average age that women give birth to their first children ranges from almost 26 in Bulgaria to over 30 in Korea.

SOURCE: Organisation for Economic Cooperation and Development (2016).

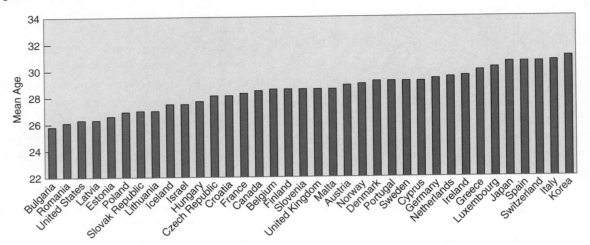

when over 50% of all births were to unmarried parents. This downward trend holds true for couples of all ages and all racial-ethnic groups.

An increasing number of "nonmarital" births (58%) are actually to couples in cohabiting relationships (Martin et al., 2012). The stereotype of "unwed mothers" being young and alone no longer fits the reality of the situation.

GENDER ROLES AMONG COUPLES WITH CHILDREN
The transition from being single to being part of a couple brings a slight shift toward the more traditional or stereotypical male and female roles. The effect of the birth of the first child continues this shift, with new mothers becoming more traditionally female and fathers becoming more traditionally male. In other words, new mothers are more likely to become more nurturant and communal while new fathers are more likely to become more instrumental. The change couples make to a less egalitarian relationship is often studied using the division of housework as an expression of the couples' gender roles. For example, Natalie Nitsche and Daniela Grunow (2015) analyzed data from a longitudinal study of over 12,000 German adults to determine how they divided housework at different stages of life. Participants who were married or in a different-sex cohabiting relationship were asked to rate on a scale of 1 to 5 what proportion of the housework was done by the woman in the partnership. The left-hand side of Figure 5.5 shows the responses for childless couples over the various waves of the study. With a score of 3 meaning that the housework was divided equally between the male and female in the relationship, the average response (3.5) shows that women do slightly more of the housework and that it remains stable throughout the five waves of the panel study. In contrast, the right-hand

side of Figure 5.5 shows the division of housework before and after the birth of the first child, which is denoted with a "0" on the horizontal axis. Before the child is born, the division of housework is similar to that of childless couples, but after the child is born, the woman's share of the housework increases, approaching a score of 4.

EXAMINING THE GENDER ROLE SHIFT   What is it about becoming a parent that causes men and women to shift their gender roles? One explanation comes from **parental investment theory**, which holds that women and men evolved different gender role behaviors and interests because they differ in how much time and resources they invest in each child. Women, who invest 9 months of pregnancy and several years of hands-on care for each child, devote more to the role of caregiver for each child than men, who invest only their sperm at time of conception and could produce a large number of offspring in the same time it takes women to produce one (Trivers, 1972).

Another theory for gender role differences among new parents is the **economic exchange theory**, which says that men and women join together as a couple to exchange goods and services. Women bring to the relationship the ability to bear and care for children and in exchange, men take over the financial responsibility of paid work (Becker, 1981). Recent research (and our own experiences) show that this "exchange" is not absolute. The majority of women (61%) with children under age 18 are now working in paid jobs and their husbands are doing a share of the housework and childcare (Bureau of Labor Statistics, 2017).

It is difficult to judge who does what within a private family home. It is also difficult because "housework"

Figure 5.5 Proportion of Housework by Gender, With and Without Children

Childless men and women (left) report that the woman in the relationship does slightly more housework than the man during 5 years of their relationship. For couples with children, the birth of the child signals an increase in the amount of housework the woman does.

SOURCE: Nitsche and Grunow (2015).

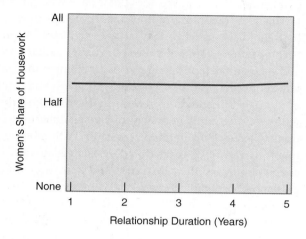 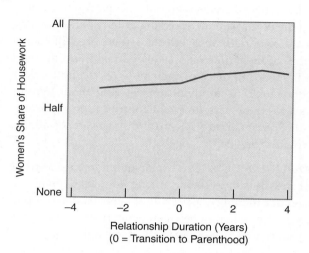

is not easily defined. For example, when yardwork and home repairs are not included, findings show that women do much more than men. But when those typically male tasks are included as "housework," the workload becomes more equal between the genders. It is also difficult because many surveys consider anyone who works for pay, whether full time or part time, to be "employed." Since many women work part time, this tends to show

that, on average, "employed" women do more housework and childcare than men. Figure 5.6 gives a more accurate picture of how much time mothers and fathers with young children report spending on family activities, based on their work status.

As Figure 5.6 shows, mothers with full-time paid jobs do more childcare and housework than husbands with full-time paid jobs (168 minutes per day for mothers vs.

Figure 5.6 Number of Minutes Spent on an Average Day on Family-Related Activities by Parents With Children Under 18 Years of Age for Different Employment Statuses

Using this figure, it is possible to compare what mothers and fathers with full-time jobs report that they do for the family. It is also possible to compare the time spent on household tasks by mothers who work for pay full time, part time, and not at all.

SOURCE: Data from the Bureau of Labor Statistics (2016).

* Insufficient number of fathers working part time to be analyzed.

116 for fathers). However, mothers with full-time paid jobs spend less time on their jobs than fathers (318 minutes per day for mothers vs. 372 for fathers). When these are considered together, there is an 18-minute difference in favor of mothers. Parents with full-time paid jobs are busy during the day, and both are doing a share of housework, childcare, and paid labor, but the fathers are still spending more of their time on job-related tasks and mothers are still spending more of their time on the housework and childcare. Plus, mothers are spending about 18 more minutes a day on activities that contribute to the family instead of personal care, leisure and sports, or socializing with friends (or sleep).

GENDER IDEOLOGY One explanation for this difference is that the division of labor among couples depends on their **gender ideology**, especially the husband's. Couples who believe in equality between genders are more apt to divide household tasks more fairly. One longitudinal study found that the more egalitarian views expressed by a couple early in their relationship, the more equally they will divide the household tasks in years to come. This is true no matter which partner is working or not working and no matter which partner is making the most money (Nitsche & Grunow, 2015).

One study took gender out of the equation by following lesbian couples through pregnancy and the early months of parenthood. Because these were same-sex couples, the researchers were interested to see how the parental roles were divided. They found that the housework was shared equally, but that the biological mothers did more of the primary child care. The nonbiological mothers worked more hours of paid work after the baby was born, and the biological mothers decreased their paid workloads. Biological parenthood seems to affect the child-care/breadwinner aspects of the relationship, whereas gender ideology seems to affect the household chores (Goldberg & Perry-Jenkins, 2007).

A more recent study bypassed the biological roles by examining gay, lesbian, and heterosexual couples who were adopting their first child. Results showed that even among adoptive parents with no biological tasks (pregnancy, childbirth, breastfeeding), housework is not shared equally. Instead, regardless of gender, the parent who worked the most hours outside the home did less childcare (feeding, changing diapers, getting up at night, bathing the child). The parent who contributed the most income to the family did less housework (cooking, cleaning, kitchen cleanup, laundry). This study also showed that same-sex couples (both male and female) shared household tasks more equally than heterosexual couples (Goldberg et al., 2012).

As this field of psychology has developed over the years, I have seen the gender gap in housework grow smaller and smaller. I think this is partly because we have had a large number of mothers in the workforce for several generations now. We know that boys who grow up in families with working mothers are more apt to share the household chores when they marry or cohabit. When they become fathers, they are more apt to have egalitarian views and spend more time taking care of the children than fathers whose mothers did not work outside the home (McGinn et al., 2019). It stands to reason that girls who grow up with working mothers may also have egalitarian expectations when establishing a partnership. With more women involved in paid jobs each decade, this translates into better cooperation from their husbands and partners with childcare and household chores.

Of course most of these studies are surveys and self-reports, and that is different than observing thousands of parents and tabulating how they spend their time on an average day. We all have our own ideas about how we spend our time—for example, my husband and I both believe we do 75% of the housework!

WRITING PROMPT

Gender Ideology and You

What's your gender ideology? In what ways might your own gender ideology impact the way you think about, participate in, and otherwise contribute to your family life?

▶ | The response entered here will appear in the performance dashboard and can be viewed by your instructor.

[Submit]

PARENTHOOD AND MARITAL HAPPINESS Unlike the transition to marriage, which seems to be accompanied by an increase in happiness and satisfaction for a couple, the new role of parent seems to bring a decrease. This decrease is small, but it is reliably found in various age and socioeconomic-status groups and other countries. The general finding is that of a curvilinear relationship between marital satisfaction and family stage, with the highest satisfaction being before the birth of the first child and after all the children have left home.

The decline in new parents' marital happiness is not new. Over 50 years ago, social scientists identified this transition as one of the most difficult adjustments in the family cycle (Lemasters, 1957). A good number of studies over the years have traced this phenomenon for many couples (Belsky & Kelly, 1994; Belsky et al., 1983; Cowan & Cowan, 1995; Gottman et al., 2010). However, this decline is small and not all new parents experience it. And certainly not all new parents end up unhappy and divorced.

Studies have shown that the pregnancy and birth period is associated with increasingly positive feelings for couples, involving joy, happiness, fulfillment, and gratification. After the birth of the first child, there is a decline in the couples' relationship, associated with mood changes, childcare tasks, financial issues, a shift of attention from the self and the partner to the baby, and changes in relationships with friends and family. These fluctuations in relationship quality are experienced by the couple together, not alone by one or the other (Canário & Figueiredo, 2016). The best advice the researchers give is to realize these changes in feelings are common and understandable, considering the drastic changes parenthood brings to a couple. It is also important to remember that there are a lot of positive feelings that come from becoming a parent, too.

To wrap up this section, let me reiterate that young adulthood is the time that the greatest number of social role transitions take place and also a time of extremely complex and demanding adjustments. Adapting to these changes is not simple, even when they are done gradually through extended periods of emerging adulthood, such as living in the parental home longer, moving into a cohabiting relationship instead of marrying, and delaying parenthood. It is a good thing that this time of life usually coincides with peaks in mental and physical well-being. My message for young adults is that it gets easier, and it gets better. And my message to those who are past this time of life is to think back and offer a little help (or at least a few words of encouragement) to the young adults who are navigating these important role transitions.

5.3: Social Roles in Middle Adulthood

OBJECTIVE: Determine how social roles impact middle adulthood experiences

During the middle years, existing roles are redefined and renegotiated. This time of life brings stable levels of physical health and increases in self-reported quality of life (Fleeson, 2004). Between the ages of 40 and 65, the parenting role becomes less demanding as children become more self-sufficient. Women's childbearing years end during this time, and most men and women become grandparents, a role that is, for most, less demanding than parenthood and more pleasurable. Marriages and partnerships become happier (or

people end troublesome ones and either find more agreeable partners or opt to live alone). Relationships with one's parents slowly change as they grow older and begin to need assistance in their daily lives. The work role is still demanding, but most adults have settled into their careers and are usually competent in their jobs. Many experience a role transition from junior worker to senior worker and mentor, taking the time to help younger colleagues learn the ropes of the workplace. This is not to say that the biological and social clocks have stopped, just that they are ticking less loudly than in early adulthood.

⌄ **By the end of this module, you will be able to:**

5.3.1 Describe changes in how parents have adjusted to children leaving the home

5.3.2 Relate midlife to gender roles

5.3.3 Compare grandparenting today to grandparenting in the past

5.3.4 Explain the impacts of caregiving on caregivers

5.3.1: The Departure of the Children
OBJECTIVE: Describe changes in how parents have adjusted to children leaving the home

Middle age is sometimes called "postparental," as if the role of parent stopped when the last child walked out the door, suitcase in hand. Clearly, it does not. Adults who have reared children go on being parents the rest of their lives. They often continue to give advice, provide financial assistance, babysit with grandchildren, and provide a center for the extended family. Many have adult children still living in their homes with varying degrees of dependency. But on a day-to-day basis, the role of parent clearly changes, becoming far less demanding and less time-consuming.

A middle-aged couple whose kids have left home.

Prior to the 1950s, this time of life was considered to be a particularly sad and stressful period, especially for women. The term "empty nest" was used to refer to homes that had once been centered on raising children. Whether this was a falsehood or just a cohort effect, it is not an accurate description of today's middle-aged parents whose roles no longer include the day-to-day care and feeding of children. Research has found that the results of this role transition are more positive than negative for most (Hareven, 2001). Marriages are happier than they have been since before the children were born, and many couples report experiencing this phase of their marriage as a second honeymoon (Rossi, 2004). Women who have fewer family responsibilities often take the opportunity to restructure their lives, moving to a new career, seeking out new interests, or returning to college for the degree they postponed when the children came along.

5.3.2: Gender Roles at Midlife

OBJECTIVE: Relate midlife to gender roles

If gender-stereotypical behavior becomes stronger when young adults make the transition to adulthood, it stands to reason that this behavior will decline once the children are gone, and there have been theories based on this assumption. Psychoanalyst Carl Jung (1971) wrote that a major task of midlife is integrating the feminine and masculine parts of the self. Psychiatrist David Gutmann (1987) wrote that men and women, once they had passed the "parental emergency" stage of life, are free to explore parts of their personalities that had been closed to them, such as traits of the other gender. He suggested that a *gender crossover* takes place after the parenting years, in which women take on more masculine roles and traits and men take on more feminine ones. As logical as this might sound, the research evidence has been mixed, and recent studies have shown that most men and women identify with the gender traits related to their own gender across the lifespan, and that there is no evidence of a gender crossover in middle age (Lemaster et al., 2017).

5.3.3: Becoming a Grandparent

OBJECTIVE: Compare grandparenting today to grandparenting in the past

For today's adults, one of the central roles of middle adulthood is that of grandparent. Today there are over 65 million grandparents in the United States, and it is predicted that by 2020, one-third of the people in the United States will be grandparents. This increase began back in 1990 when the baby boomers reached grandparenting age. Even though people are having children at later ages, with longevity increasing, most men and women can expect to spend over half their lives in the roles of grandparents (Silverstein & Marenco, 2001). There are more grandparents in the world today than at any time in history.

Today's grandparents in the United States are healthy *and* wealthy. The majority of grandparents are under 65, though that age will increase as the baby boomers get older. In the very near future, the majority will be 65 and older. As they head for retirement, today's grandparents have help from Medicare for medical costs and have better pensions and retirement savings than generations before. And they have fewer children (and presumably fewer grandchildren) to spend all that time, energy, and money on. In fact, about one-fourth of grandparents report spending more than $1,000 on their grandchildren in the last year—mostly for gifts and fun activities, but also for educational and medical expenses. Over one-third of the grandparents reported helping out with their grandchildren's everyday living expenses.

A survey conducted by the AARP revealed that most grandparents live within 10 miles of at least one grandchild and see them weekly. They watch TV or videos together, go shopping, play sports and exercise together, cook or bake, and go to outings like movies, museums, and amusement parks. Most grandparents report feeling as close to their son's children as they do to their daughter's children. If they are closer to some grandchildren than others, it is because they live nearby. Even when they do not live nearby, most grandparents reported that they communicate with their grandchildren weekly, mostly by telephone, and they discuss morals, safety, college plans, current events, problems the grandchildren are dealing with, health, bullying, smoking, drugs, and alcohol use. Over one-third of grandparents report talking with their grandchildren about dating and sex (Lampkin, 2012). Most grandparents believe that they play an important role in their grandchildren's lives and that they are doing an excellent or above-average job as a grandparent (Lampkin, 2012).

THE NEW GRANDPARENT At my house, I have a "grandchild room" with books, games, a folding crib, and about a dozen boys' swimsuits in various sizes. (The girls prefer to bring their own.) The garage contains skateboards, bicycles, a pogo stick, and snorkel gear. There is a basketball hoop at the end of the driveway, a swing in the tree by the front door, and a horseshoe pit in the backyard. The pantry and refrigerator contain the grandchildren's favorite foods, and I often find their requests written on my grocery list, such as "dubble choklot ise creem." I buy their school supplies at the beginning of the year, and we contribute financial help to grandchildren in college. It is kind of comforting to know that we are not outliers in this focus on grandchildren. (As I write this, I have a 19-year-old grandson, Brendan, sleeping in my guest room, home from college with his dog, Karma. My adult children complain that I don't like them to bring their dogs over, but this is different. He is my *grandson*.)

Figure 5.7 Grandparents with Grandchildren Living at Home

Although Hispanic, black, and Asian people make up a minority of people 50 years of age or older in the United States, they constitute a majority of grandparents who have grandchildren living in their homes.

SOURCE: Adapted from Krogstad (2016).

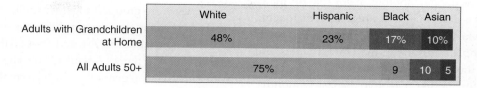

	White	Hispanic	Black	Asian
Adults with Grandchildren at Home	48%	23%	17%	10%
All Adults 50+	75%		9	10	5

Clearly this is not the role that our grandparents or even our parents had. We don't have role models for being today's type of grandparents, and most of us are learning as we go. The role of grandparent depends so much on the age of the grandparents and the grandchildren, the distance between their homes, the relationship between the grandparents and parents, the health and income of everyone concerned, and many other factors.

To be fair, I should include evidence of the less-than-fun side of the grandparent role. There can be problems, and the most frequent stem from disagreements over childrearing between the grandparents and their adult children (the parents of the grandchildren). Some grandparents have trouble making the transition from full-time parent of dependent children to the more egalitarian role of parent to an adult child who has children of his or her own. (And some adult children have had problems in their role transitions, too.)

GRANDPARENTS RAISING GRANDCHILDREN A substantial number of grandparents have taken their grandchildren into their homes and assumed the parental role for them, forming a family referred to sometimes as *grandfamilies*. Usually this takes place when the children's parents are unable (or unwilling) to fulfill their roles as parents due to immaturity, drug use, imprisonment, mental illness, or even death. According to the U.S. Census Bureau (2016), 7% of children live in grandparent-headed homes. About one-third of those have neither parent present in the home, amounting to about 1.5 million children, or 2% of all U.S. children.

Who are these families? The Pew Research Center examined census data and found that grandparents who had grandchildren living in their homes, whether the children's parents were present or not, were more apt to be Hispanic, black, or Asian than white, compared to the race and ethnicity of the general population of Americans over age 50. Figure 5.7 shows this difference. The bottom line shows the proportion of people over the age of 50 in the United States, divided by race or ethnic group; the top line shows the proportion of grandparents who have grandchildren living in their homes divided by race or ethnic group (Krogstad, 2015).

Other grandchildren living with grandparents include recent immigrants, who are more apt to live in multigenerational households, children with unmarried mothers who have no partner present, and children whose parents have become addicted to opioids or other drugs. When children are removed from their parents' custody by social services, the first choice of placement is often the grandparents instead of a foster home. It is understandably stressful for grandparents to reassume the role of parents, but there are other complications for grandparents raising grandchildren.

Problems for Grandparents Assuming the Role of Parents

Lack of Sufficient Funds—First is money: About 20% of grandparents live below the poverty line. If they are licensed as foster parents, they are eligible for government services and support, but many are not. Unless they have legal custody of the grandchildren, they are not able to collect child support from the absent parents, get medical care for the children, or interact with the children's schools. The good news is that some states are beginning to respond to these families and provide some help. And other states are setting up navigation services that help grandparents find financial aid, housing assistance, and counseling.

Problems of Parental Origin—A second problem for grandparents raising grandchildren is found in the reason the parents are unable to take on this role. When the children have been exposed to drug addiction, criminal behavior, or domestic violence, they can have emotional problems themselves. It is difficult for anyone to tackle these problems in children, but especially hard for older adults who may be struggling also with finances and the problems of their adult children (Wiltz, 2016).

Studies of grandparents raising grandchildren have shown that the major sources of stress for the grandparents come from problems with the grandchildren's parents, for example not supporting their children emotionally or financially, adding to the grandparents' stress with their own issues. These grandparents also cite problems with the grandchildren's learning, for example, attention-deficit/hyperactivity disorder or discipline problems.

5.3.4: Caregiving for Aging Parents

OBJECTIVE: Explain the impacts of caregiving on caregivers

As people tend to live longer, another major role for many middle-aged adults is that of unpaid caregiver to their aging parents. The National Alliance of Caregiving (2015) interviewed a large sample of adults in the United States and found that 10% of those between ages 25 and 64 had provided unpaid care for another person in the last 12 months, and most of these were caring for parents or parents-in-law. The majority of caregivers were women. What does the role of unpaid caregiver for one's parents entail? The average middle-aged person caring for an aging parent provides about 24 hours of care a week for 4 years. The caregiver is most likely a daughter or daughter-in-law, and they are usually assisted by other unpaid caregivers, such as their spouse or siblings. The care receiver is usually a mother, mainly because there are more older women than older men, but also because adult children tend not to feel the same obligation to fathers, especially if the parents have divorced (Antonucci et al., 2016). The middle-aged caregiver's role is to arrange for services, such as doctor's visits, and to assist with independent activities of daily living (IADLs), such as transportation, shopping, housework, meal preparation, finances, and management of medications.

About 40% of middle-aged caregivers work full time and report that they have made changes in their jobs because of their caregiving responsibilities, such as cutting back on hours or taking a leave of absence. Most report that their supervisors are aware of their caregiver role and have given them flexible work hours and paid sick days. Unlike almost all countries in the world, the vast majority of workers in the United States do not have paid family leave to help them care for aging parents. About a quarter (26%) of unpaid caregivers have a child under age 18 living in the home (Wolff et al., 2018). What is the result of adding the role of caregiver to the existing roles middle-aged adults occupy? The answer may surprise you.

CAREGIVING AND HEALTH For many years it was thought that caregiving automatically brought stress, which resulted in physical and mental health problems. Early studies had recruited caregivers from medical settings and noncaregivers from social groups or senior centers. These *convenience samples* of noncaregivers were not representative of the general population because they were socially connected and healthy enough to be members of these groups. So it was no surprise to find that the caregivers had more physical and mental health problems than the noncaregivers. More recent research has used better control groups and has found very different results.

Studies that use comparable groups of caregivers and noncaregivers show that only a small number of caregivers report elevated levels of depression and physical health problems compared to the control group of noncaregivers. Medical researcher David L. Roth and his colleagues reviewed data from over 43,000 people concerning their physical and mental health, depressive symptoms, social contacts, and caregiving status (Roth et al., 2009). These four categories were grouped together under the term *quality of life*. Family caregiving responsibilities were reported by 12% of the sample (about 5,171), and about a third of those were taking care of a parent (about 1,700). The respondents who were caregivers in general reported a small but significantly higher incidence of problems with psychological health than noncaregivers, but there was no difference in physical health between the two groups. However, caretakers who said they had a high level of stress as a result of this role were more apt to report more physical and psychological health problems, especially depressive symptoms, and also report fewer social contacts than both the low-stressed caregivers and the noncaregivers. Interestingly, the caregivers who reported lower levels of stress (or none) were in better physical and mental health than the noncaregivers. When the researchers considered the hours of care provided, the relationship between the caregiver and care-recipient, and whether the caregiver lived with the care recipient or not, the amount of stress reported by the caregiver was still the strongest predictor of physical and mental health. This means that the *perception* a caregiver has of the stress involved in the job is more important than the job itself when it comes to quality of life.

The factors that are related to caregivers' perceptions of greater stress are older age, preexisting health problems, caring for a loved one with dementia, being forced to delay their own education or career plans, marital problems, and financial problems (American Psychological Association, 2017a).

POSITIVE CAREGIVING EXPERIENCES I need to mention two possible cautions before we make the direct link from perception of caregiving to health outcomes. First is the *healthy caregiver hypothesis*, the argument that family members who take on the caregiving role and continue to give care over time are often the ones who are in better health themselves to begin with, and also that their prosocial behavior in caregiving may provide the caregivers with further health benefits (Fredman et al., 2006). The second caution is that simply having a parent who has declined to the point that they need care is very difficult emotionally and can lead to stress and depressive symptoms whether you are a caregiver for them or not (Amirkhanyan & Wolf, 2003). It would be nice to see a study comparing the health of middle-aged adults who are serving as caregivers for their aging parents with their noncaregiving siblings.

Another surprising finding about providing care for one's aging parents is that a large majority of caregivers (83%) report that it was a positive experience. They felt that they had a chance to give back something to their parents who had done so much for them. They felt good knowing

Table 5.3 Positive Aspects of Being a Caregiver for a Relative with Alzheimer's Disease

Positive Aspect	Example
Insights about dementia and acceptance of the disease	A daughter caregiver reports that being in this role has made her slowly realize how much she has learned from her father about life and aging.
A sense of purpose and role commitment	The wife of an Alzheimer's patient states that she does not let herself get discouraged. She is determined to care for him, be supportive, and console him as long as needed.
Feelings of gratification and gratitude	A woman says that she feels all her hard work is worthwhile when she sees any improvement in her mother's condition.
A sense of mastery	One wife of an Alzheimer's patient tells about planning a party for her husband so he could see some of his old friends. Although he didn't remember everyone, he had a wonderful time and she felt very happy about the success of the party.
Increased patience and tolerance	A daughter reports that she has become more tolerant as a result of taking care of her mother. She has learned to deal with her mother's repetitive behaviors and it has made her more patient and less short-tempered in other aspects of her life, too.
Cultivating a positive mindset	The son of an Alzheimer's patient told about his mother trying to prepare a meal for him, not realizing that the he had already prepared it. He was irritated at first, but then realized how nice it was that his mother had wanted to cook for him.
Learning to let go	The wife of an Alzheimer's patient said that she learned to control her emotions by letting go of her husband and herself. We were both losing so much, and once the sadness of those losses was gone, we could walk together into whatever future we had left.
Closer bond with the care receiver	One man who was taking care of his wife said that the experience had made them closer. They had always been busy with their own lives, but they have come to know each other better.
Finding people who care	Three adult children of an Alzheimer's patient reported that they have become closer since their mother began to need their care. They have a common topic to talk about and we all show concern for Mom and for each other.
A sense of usefulness for helping other caregivers	A daughter joined a caregiver support group and said that she was able to help other caregivers with their problems. She said it helped her a lot to be useful to them.

SOURCE: Cheng et al. (2015).

that their parents were getting excellent care. Many reported a sense of personal growth and purpose in their lives. This doesn't mean that they don't feel stressed, but that both emotional distress and positive growth can be found in the same experience (American Psychological Association, 2017b).

In a qualitative study, psychologist Sheung-Tak Cheng and his colleagues (2015) asked 57 primary caregivers to make a voice recording each day of positive events that happened during the course of caregiving for their family members with Alzheimer's disease. The researchers found 10 categories of positive events, which are shown in Table 5.3 along with examples in the caregivers' own words.

5.4: Social Roles in Late Adulthood

OBJECTIVE: Evaluate ways of handling transitions in late adulthood

In late adulthood, we make transitions into simplified forms of former roles—we move into smaller homes or retirement communities; we leave our full-time jobs and spend our time on part-time work, volunteer work, or caregiving for our spouse, relatives, or friends; we take pride in the development of our grandchildren and

great-grandchildren; and we watch our children mature and enjoy their success and happiness. Some roles are not of our choosing, such as the role of living alone, usually as widow or widower, and the role of care receiver, but they are also part of the journey of adulthood for many older adults.

At one time, late adulthood was considered a time of role loss. Even when the concept of role transition became popular, the normative results of these transitions for older adults were often considered to be stress, grief, and a sense of loss. More recently, studies have shown that there are no typical ways that adults react to role transitions in late adulthood. Different people experience these transitions in different ways, and even the same person may experience extreme disruption in his or her life during these transitions, only to recover and take on new roles with gusto. Instead of viewing late adulthood as a time of loss, researchers are busily investigating the wide range of outcomes possible and the personal factors that might predict the outcomes for different individuals.

> ∨ **By the end of this module, you will be able to:**
>
> **5.4.1** Identify factors that lead to many older adults living alone
>
> **5.4.2** Describe challenges associated with receiving care

5.4.1: Living Alone

OBJECTIVE: Identify factors that lead to many older adults living alone

One new challenge that comes to many adults in their later years, most frequently to women, is that of learning to live alone, a change brought about by leaving the role of spouse due to widowhood or sometimes divorce. Figure 5.8 shows the living arrangements for people 65 years of age and older in the United States from 1990 to 2014, the most recent data available from the Pew Research Center (Stepler, 2016) (see 'Living Arrangements for People 65 Years of Age and Older in the United States from 1990 to 2014').

Other factors that determine where older adults live are health, finances, the number of adult children they have, the location of the children, and the relationship they have

---

Living Arrangements for People 65 Years of Age and Older in the United States from 1990 to 2014

These two sets of bars represent the living arrangements of men and women from 65 to 84 years of age. As you can see, the proportion of women in this age group living alone (30%) is significantly greater than the number of men living alone (17%). This can be explained by the custom of women marrying older men and the fact that women live, on average, about 3 years longer than men. The reverse side of the coin is seen in the proportion of women living with their spouses (46%) versus that of men (69%).

Figure 5.8A Living Arrangements of Men and Women from 65 to 84 Years of Age

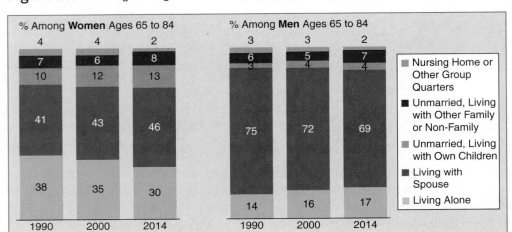

These two sets of bars show the living arrangements of men and women who are 85 years of age and older. Again, there is a big gender difference in the proportion of women (46%) and the proportion of men (27%) who live alone. There is also a matching difference in the proportion of women living with their spouses (12%) versus the proportion of men (49%). Another interesting piece of information in this figure is the proportion of older Americans living in nursing homes, which has declined steadily for all groups since 1990.

Figure 5.8B Living Arrangements of Men and Women 85 Years of Age and Older

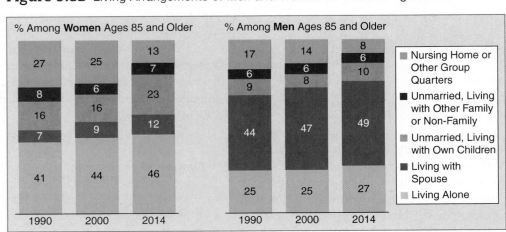

SOURCE: Stepler (2016).

with the children (and their children's spouses). There has been a dramatic decline in the percentage of women over age 65 living alone since 1990, and that can be explained by a similar increase in the percentage who continue to have spouses and who live with their adult children. For most older people in the United States, the wish to live independently is very strong, and if they can afford it and are able to take care of themselves, most without a spouse prefer to live alone. Still, it is not an easy transition.

AGING IN PLACE **Aging in place** refers to the ability of older people to remain in their own homes their whole lives. This doesn't necessarily mean the same home, but to be independent and spend one's later years in a place of their own, either with a spouse or partner or by themselves. Most adults express the wish to age in place (Bayer & Harper, 2000). Factors that influence the ability to age in place are the person's health, finances, attachment to the neighborhood, security of the neighborhood, and distance from family members (Anesensel et al., 2016).

Our family experienced this situation a few years ago when my father-in-law died and left his wife of 64 years living alone in the house they had shared in New England. Although she would technically be classified as "living alone," that was hardly the case. Three adult children lived nearby with their spouses, and there were seven adult grandchildren within easy driving distance. One daughter-in-law called her every morning on her way to work, one son stopped by on his way home from work each afternoon, another son and his wife took her out to dinner every Wednesday and for breakfast every Sunday. A daughter had the whole family over for dinner on Sunday nights. Each day a community volunteer stopped by to bring her lunch, and women from her church picked her up for activities there. My mother-in-law had not driven for years, so she gave her car to a granddaughter who needed one. In exchange, the granddaughter was happy to drive her grandmother on her errands and appointments. My husband and I, who live in Florida, visited often and would have loved for her to come and spend the winter with us, but she always declined. I think this may be the case with many older men and women who are listed as "living alone."

Living alone is not synonymous with being **lonely**, which is defined as the perception of social isolation. When researchers investigate the prevalence of loneliness among people of different ages, they find that young adults and older adults tend to be less lonely when they live alone than when they live with others. The loneliness factors for older adults are the loss of a spouse or partner, limited income, and functional limitations. Because loneliness is very subjective, older people who have lower levels of social engagement may not necessarily be lonely. It all depends on how they perceive their social lives (Luhmann & Hawkley, 2016).

5.4.2: Becoming a Care Receiver

OBJECTIVE: Describe challenges associated with receiving care

One role that few older adults plan to fill is that of care receiver. After spending many years of one's life as an independent adult and caregiver to their children, their own parents, and sometimes their grandchildren, many older adults find themselves unable to live on their own. The solution for many is either moving into a nursing home or moving into the home of an adult child or other family member. Although it sounds like a long-overdue reward, most older adults feel otherwise. In a dissertation study of almost 2,000 adults who were 65 years of age or older, the quality of "remaining independent" was named as important by over 93% of the respondents, second only to "having good health" (Phelan, 2005).

The best-known type of care for older adults is the **nursing home**, which is a place for people to live when they don't need to be in a hospital but can't be taken care of at home. Young adults often think that nursing home care is inevitable if a person lives long enough. As familiar as this arrangement is to us, it is not actually used very much. If you look back at Figure 5.8, you will see that only 2% of men and women between age 65 and 84 live in nursing homes, and only 13% of women and 8% of men who are 85 and older reside there (Stepler, 2016).

A more common living arrangement for older adults is living with their own children. Receiving care from family members has a number of advantages, the most obvious being economic. Nursing homes are expensive and so are home health care services. When family members are willing and able to provide care, it saves money for the older person and the healthcare system. Less obvious benefits are that it gives family members the opportunity to become closer in the time remaining, time for mending fences and deepening feelings for each other.

Being the recipient of care also has its negative effects (Roberto, 2016). We have all heard accounts of **elder abuse**, which is an intentional act by a caregiver or other trusted person that causes harm to an older adult. Elder abuse can be physical, psychological, sexual, or financial; it can also be neglect. Although it is difficult to estimate the prevalence of elder abuse because many cases are not reported, geriatric researchers Mark S. Lachs and Karl A. Pillemer (2015) reviewed a large number of studies of elder abuse and concluded that approximately 10% of noninstitutionalized adults over age 60 in the United States have been victims of elder abuse in the past 12 months. Older adults most at risk for elder abuse are women, individuals with dementia, and those with low levels of social support. Those most likely to abuse elders are husbands or sons and individuals with a history of substance abuse, mental or physical health problems, problems with the police, unemployment, or financial problems (National Center on Elder Abuse, 2016).

CAREGIVING BY OLDER ADULTS Although caregiving for parents is a major role for middle-aged adults, a number of older adults also find themselves in the role of caregiving for their spouse or other older relatives, and this number is growing every year. There are more and more older adults in the United States (and in the world, in general), and many need hands-on care in their daily lives. The Family Caregiver Alliance (2016) estimates that over 3 million adults age 75 and older are caregivers for another person, most of them also 75 or older. About half of the care receivers are spouses, but these older caregivers also assist siblings, friends, and neighbors. About 9% of these caregivers over 75 provide care for *their* parents! The care that older adults provide is usually different from the care middle-aged adults provide. Since many are taking care of spouses, they are usually living in the same home and it is a full-time job. At this age, the care needed is with activities of daily living (ADLs), such as bathing, dressing, eating, using the toilet, and moving around inside the house. Ironically, these require more physical strength and more time than the typical care provided by middle-aged adults. In fact, as shown in Figure 5.9, the older the caregiver, the more hours he or she spends on caregiving responsibilities.

Figure 5.9 Hours Dedicated to Caregiving by Age

The number of hours caregivers spend on giving care increases with their age.

SOURCE: Family Caregiver Alliance (2016).

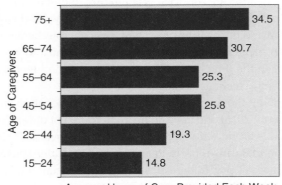

Average Hours of Care Provided Each Week

Researchers have compared changes in the caregiving role over the past 16 years and have found that older people who were caregivers for their spouses are providing fewer hours of care than 16 years ago and are half as likely to report emotional, physical, or financial difficulties. Those caring for spouses with dementia were twice as likely to use respite care than 16 years ago (Wolff et al., 2018). Medicaid officials are beginning to recognize the contribution of family caregivers and there has been some discussion about saving costs on long-term care by directing payments to family members (Newcomer et al., 2012), which has become a reality in France (Doty et al., 2015).

5.5: Social Roles in Atypical Families

OBJECTIVE: Analyze the interactions between atypical families and their cultures

A great many adults do not follow the life patterns of adults who move through the social roles of single young adult, spouse (or cohabiting partner), parent, and grandparent. Some remain single, others marry but have no children, and many start out on the typical path and decide on an alternative journey. So, in fairness to families like mine (and probably yours), I cannot leave this chapter without talking about those whose social role experience in adulthood differs from this mythical "norm."

	By the end of this module, you will be able to:

5.5.1 Describe experiences of lifelong singles

5.5.2 Relate child-free experiences to sociocultural expectations

5.5.3 Summarize experiences of divorced and remarried adults

5.5.1: Lifelong Singles

OBJECTIVE: Describe experiences of lifelong singles

About 28% of households in the United States consist of just one person—no partner, no children, no roommate. This category covers a lot of situations—young people who have not found a partner yet, older people who are divorced or widowed and whose children are grown, or individuals who have chosen living alone as their preferred lifestyle. It is estimated that about 5% of the U.S. population over age 64 has never married, more being men than women. This number has stayed near the same level since the 1960s (U.S. Department of Health and Human Services, 2017).

Reasons for being a lifelong single person range from being focused on a career to being very shy. Women who have never married tend to be more educated and have higher incomes than men who have never married, making it difficult for them to match up with each other. The Pew Research Center finds that the number one quality women want in a potential husband is a secure job. They also want someone close to their own age who has not been married before. This may not be possible for many women who already have secure jobs themselves. There are fewer men in the workforce than in 1960, and the proportion of women has increased dramatically. One solution is for a single woman to marry an older man or one who is divorced or widowed. If that is not acceptable, remaining unmarried is the choice for many (Luscombe, 2014).

Lifelong single people often worry (or are warned by well-meaning friends) that when they get older and need help, there will be no one to care for them because they lack both a partner and, usually, children. However, research shows that most older people who have never married have formed a network of friends and more distant relatives who offer the instrumental and social support they need.

Being single does not always mean being alone. Single people may be involved in various intimate relationships, live with a group of friends, live with children they have decided to raise on their own, or be in a long-term committed relationship but retain their own living arrangements. The latter is a fairly new living situation (at least to researchers), and it is called *living together apart*. It seems most common among older adults who have established their own lifestyles and enjoy their independence while still desiring to share their lives with a significant other (Antonucci et al., 2016).

5.5.2: The Childless

OBJECTIVE: Relate child-free experiences to sociocultural expectations

Despite all the current news about advances in infertility treatment, late-life pregnancies, and women choosing to have children without the benefit of marriage (or even a partner in their lives), the rate of childlessness is increasing for U.S. women. (And we assume the same is true for men, although statistics report only women's fertility rates.) According to the most recent census figures, about 15% of U.S. women end their childbearing years with no children (Livingston, 2015). This is down from 20% in the year 2005. Figure 5.10 shows this trend from 1976 to 2014.

The increase in childlessness has also occurred in other developed countries, with the United Kingdom and Spain having similar rates as the United States, and eastern European countries, Mexico, and Portugal reporting about half the rate as the United States (OECD, 2016).

INFERTILITY Of course, some of the people included in the "childless" category have just decided that being a parent is not the way they want to spend their adult lives, whereas others would like to have children but are unable to for some physical reason. We don't have an accurate figure for these childless adults because it has long been considered a private matter and people were unwilling to disclose this information, even to close friends and relatives. Recently, people have become more open about their infertility and researchers have been compiling data on them. We have some evidence that about 12% of women of

Figure 5.10 Percentage of Childless Women, Ages 40–44

The proportion of women who have reached the age of 40 and who are childless increased steadily until 2006, then began falling.

SOURCE: Livingston (2015).

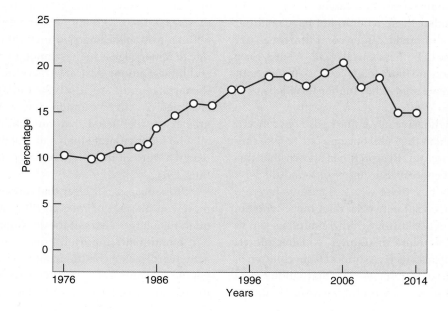

childbearing age are infertile, meaning they have tried to get pregnant for 12 months but remained childless (CDC, 2016). About half of women experiencing infertility seek medical treatment (Boivin et al., 2007), and about 2% of all infants born in the United States last year were the result of artificial reproductive technology (CDC, 2017a).

These numbers don't reflect the psychological experience of being infertile. And even though the technology to assist in reproduction has advanced, the social support for people experiencing infertility has not kept up with it. Filling the role of parent is an almost-universal goal of both men and women, and when faced with the knowledge that this may not be a reality in one's life, for many it can cause feelings of loss, mistrust of one's own body, and absence of hope in the future. In addition, infertility treatment can bring additional problems because it often involves laparoscopic surgery, daily injections of hormones that bring mood swings, seemingly endless medical appointments, high costs, and waiting for results. Even if conception does takes place, anxiety often continues over whether the pregnancy will result in a healthy, full-term baby. To further complicate things, couples may not have each other to lean on because both are experiencing the same stress (Galst, 2017). Recently, psychotherapists have begun specializing in treatment for patients experiencing problems related to their infertility and infertility treatment. These difficulties include shame they can't conceive, guilt that they resent their friends and siblings who have children, disappointment when treatment fails, and differences in coping from one partner to another (Stringer, 2017).

FOCUSES AND CONCERNS OF CHILD-FREE ADULTS For whatever reason they are childless, women without children often choose to focus on their roles as workers. Without children to care for, there is far less of a barrier to a woman's pursuit of a full-time career. Whether women who have made a commitment to a career choose not to have children or whether those who do not have children subsequently make a stronger career commitment is not completely clear. Some of both may well occur. What is clear is that childless women are more likely to work throughout their adult lives, to have somewhat higher-level jobs, and to earn more money.

Similar to those who have never married, a big concern of childless people is that they will have no one to take care of them when they are old. Research has shown that this is usually not a valid concern. Studies of older adults who need assistance show that those who are parents have no more assistance from social networks than those who are not parents (Chang et al., 2010). Childless adults seem to have a strong social network of siblings, cousins, nieces, and nephews and may also receive support from children of neighbors and close friends. It seems clear that childlessness is not an age-related status; older adults who are childless

were also middle-aged childless adults. Most invested in deep friendships and nurtured ties with their siblings and other relatives. The social networks they have in older adulthood are not much different in size and function from older adults who are parents (Zhang & Hayward, 2001). I think it is safe to say that the picture of adults without children is not one of persisting sadness or regret.

One difficulty for childless people is that life in our society seems to be shaped by family milestones. Without children, the rhythm of the family timetable is simply not there to structure the adult's life experiences. For better or for worse, there is no change in relationship or roles when the first child is born, no celebration when the first child starts school, no bar mitzvahs or first dates or leaving home—no empty nests because the nest has never been full (or, perhaps, has always been full).

5.5.3: Divorced (and Remarried) Adults

OBJECTIVE: Summarize experiences of divorced and remarried adults

Taking on the role of spouse does not always end up with living happily ever after—at least not together. About 25% of today's young adults who marry will divorce before they reach their 10th anniversary, and most will remarry, with an average unmarried interval of about 4 years. The rate of remarriage is highest among white men (about 75%) and lowest among African American women (about 32%). Remarriage rates are also linked to age: The younger you are when you divorce and the fewer children you have, the greater the likelihood that you will remarry. And among all who remarry, more than half will divorce a second time. About a third of these will remarry once again (Kreider & Ellis, 2011).

Nonetheless, it is clear that divorce brings a larger and more complex set of roles to fill. The single parent must often fill a larger share of the adult family roles: breadwinner, emotional supporter, housekeeper, child caregiver, activities director, chauffeur, and the rest. And let's not forget the economics of it all. Divorce means that a one-family income may need to be stretched to support two families, a fact that lowers the standard of living for all family members. Many of the detrimental effects of divorce for both parents and children can be traced to the economic loss rather than the divorce itself (Sayer, 2006).

With remarriage, more new roles emerge. One becomes a spouse again and frequently a stepparent. About 90% of men and women in a second marriage have at least one child from a previous relationship. If the new spouse's children are young, one might quickly move from the role of being a childless adult to having children in the home on a daily basis.

Although women who marry men with children may seem to have an easier role because the children often don't live full time with their father (and her), in many ways, being a stepmother can be more difficult than being a stepfather. The role of a stepmother starts out with one of the most threatening false stereotypes found in legends and classic children's literature—the evil stepmother. I doubt if there is a stepmother alive who has not said, "I don't want to seem like a wicked stepmother!" I know I have. Another complication is that our cultural stereotypes allow for only one mother per child, so a stepmother must be careful not to intrude in the special relationship the child has with his or her "real" mother. At the same time, the traditional division of household tasks often means that the stepmother

does the extra cooking, laundry, and nurturing when the stepchildren visit. This ambiguity in role content is no doubt also present in the stepchild's reaction to the stepmother.

Although the role of stepmother is hardly new, it has not been the topic of much research. In one of few studies, family studies researchers Shannon Weaver and Marilyn Coleman (2005) interviewed 11 stepmothers in depth and found them to describe one of three distinct roles. The first role is "mothering, but not mother," in which women describe serving as a responsible and caring adult, a friend, a provider of emotional support, or a mentor. The second is an "other-focused" role in which the women described serving as a liaison or buffer between the biological parents. The third role is that of "outsider," in which the stepmother has no direct role with the stepchildren.

Weaver and Coleman concluded their study by calling for more research into the role of stepmother and how it relates to women's well-being. It is surely one area where the feelings involved in caring for a child who belongs to one's spouse are often in conflict with the expectations of the spouse, the child's biological mother, the stepchildren themselves, the extended family, and the culture. For a role that is so prevalent in today's families and shows no sign of decreasing in the near future, it seems like a much-needed line of inquiry.

Summary: Social Roles

5.1 Social Roles and Transitions

OBJECTIVE: **Analyze how social roles change over time**

- Despite many variations today in the timing and sequence of roles, adulthood is still largely structured by the patterns of roles adults take on and the role transitions they experience.

- Although we have a lot of flexibility today in the timing of social roles, life is still easier when the roles are moved through on-time instead of off-time.

- Gender roles are fairly diverse and describe what people really do within their roles as men and women; gender stereotypes are shared beliefs about what men and women have in common. The stereotypes for women usually center around communal qualities (being nurturing and intuitive); the stereotypes for men usually center around instrumental qualities (being adventurous and competitive).

- Learning-schema theory states that gender roles are based on distorted views that exaggerate gender differences. Social role theory states that gender roles are based on observations of male and female behavior. Evolutionary psychology states that gender roles are

based on inherited traits men and women have that were critical to survival and reproduction for our primitive ancestors.

5.2 Social Roles in Young Adulthood

OBJECTIVE: **Characterize social roles in young adulthood**

- The transition from emerging adult to young adult is a change in roles from dependent child to independent adult. It can include moving out of the parental home, entering college or military service, entering into a marriage or cohabitation relationship, becoming financially independent, and becoming a parent. These roles are not taken on in a single typical sequence, and many young adults move in and out of them several times before viewing themselves as totally adult.

- Adults in the United States are marrying at later ages, and a greater percentage are cohabiting before marriage. This is true in developed countries throughout the world. However, marriage remains the preferred form of committed relationship.

- Adults are delaying the transition to parenthood in the United States and other developed countries. About

40% of all births in the United States are to unmarried parents. However, almost 60% of these are born to parents who are cohabiting at the time of the birth.

- When men and women become parents, their gender roles become more traditional. The amount of childcare and housework that fathers do is increasing, but mothers still do more, even when they have full-time jobs. In two-parent households, fathers usually spend more time doing paid work than mothers.

5.3 Social Roles in Middle Adulthood

OBJECTIVE: Determine how social roles impact middle adulthood experiences

- Gender roles in middle adulthood seem to remain stable. There is no apparent "crossover" after the parenting years, despite long-held theories to the contrary.
- In the middle years of adulthood, the role of parent changes from a day-to-day role to a more distant one as children move out of the house and start their own families, but the role of parent does not end. Most parents find this transition to be positive and use the new freedom to restructure their own lives.
- Middle age is the time of life when most people become grandparents. This role can take many forms. For a growing number of grandparents, it means returning to the role of parent or returning to full-time work to care for their grandchildren.
- Another role in the middle years is that of caregiver for aging parents. About 10% of middle-aged adults have taken on the caregiving role, mostly for parents or parents-in-law. Although spouses are usually the first-line caregivers, many family members help out, especially daughters and daughters-in-law. Many people with multigenerational responsibilities report that their roles are important and satisfying. When the burden of caregiving is extreme and long lasting, it can lead to depression, marital problems, and physical illnesses.

5.4 Social Roles in Late Adulthood

OBJECTIVE: Evaluate ways of handling transitions in late adulthood

- Social role transitions in late life include learning to live alone, more common for women than for men, and becoming the receiver of care, which can be a difficult transition. However, informal care from family, friends, and neighbors can keep older adults living in their own homes and feeling in control of their lives. A small proportion of older adults live in nursing homes. More live with their spouses, their adult children, or other family members. About 10% of noninstitutionalized adults are victims of elder abuse each year.

- A large number of people 75 years of age and older have taken on the role of caregiver themselves. Most of these care for their spouses, but about 10% of them care for their own parents.

5.5 Social Roles in Atypical Families

OBJECTIVE: Analyze the interactions between atypical families and their cultures

- Not everyone fits the preceding discussion. Some people never marry (about 5% of people over age 65 in the United States). Those who have close relationships with friends and relatives report being as happy and fulfilled as their married peers with children. About 20% of women over age 40 have not had children. Among older adults, the childless are as happy as those with children. And among older adults who need assistance, those without children receive as much help from their social networks than those who have children.
- About 12% of women of childbearing age are infertile and this can sometimes cause psychological problems. About half of infertile couples seek treatment. About 2% of babies born today are the result of reproductive technology.
- About one-fourth of couples marrying today will divorce within 10 years. Most will remarry, causing a number of role transitions, such as ex-spouse, stepmother, and stepfather.

SHARED WRITING

Social Roles

Consider this chapter's discussion of role transitions. What role transitions have you experienced in the last few years? What kind of adaptations did they require and why? Write a short response that your classmates will read. Be sure to discuss specific examples.

 A minimum number of characters is required to post and earn points. After posting, your response can be viewed by your class and instructor, and you can participate in the class discussion.

Post   0 characters | 140 minimum

Chapter 6
Social Relationships

Social relationships across the lifespan are dynamic and changing.

 ## Learning Objectives

6.1 Compare theories of social relationships

6.2 Determine how people choose intimate partners

6.3 Evaluate the impact of intimate partnership on adulthood experiences

6.4 Analyze the ways that family interactions influence adulthood experiences

6.5 Evaluate the ways friendship circles affect adulthood

A Word From the Author

When Writing a Book

THERE ARE NOT many developmental psychology jokes, but a student in my human development class told me one many years ago. It goes like this:

A child psychologist was sitting in his office writing a textbook when he heard an annoying squeaking sound. He looked outside and saw a little child on a tricycle riding across his newly surfaced driveway. He ran outside and yelled angrily at the boy to get off his property and take his tricycle with him. A neighbor observed this and said to him, "How can you call yourself a developmental psychologist and write books on child development when you are so intolerant of little children?" The psychologist replied, "Because, madam, I like children in the abstract, not in the concrete."

Besides the bad pun, I like this joke because it helps me keep my priorities straight. I do most of my writing in my home office, and while I am writing this chapter on relationships, a lot of "relating" is going on around me, especially of the family variety. It is spring break, and I have some teenage grandchildren in the pool. In addition, my son is bringing my 6-year-old granddaughter here this afternoon to spend a few days at "Grandma's house." She looks forward to helping me bake cookies, while the teenagers in the pool like to eat them. Just when I am ready to say, "Please leave me alone so I can write this section on grandparent–grandchild relationships," I remember the joke about the developmental psychologist and laugh. If I sound a little authoritative in this chapter on relationships, it is because I am living it as I write—not in the abstract, but smack dab in the concrete.

Social relationships involve dynamic, recurrent patterns of interactions with other individuals and the ways they change over the course of adulthood. In this chapter, I discuss these relationships, particularly changes in the give-and-take interactions among people and how such changes affect them (and the people they give to and take from).

If you think about your own social relationships—with your parents, your friends, your spouse or partner, your coworkers—it's clear immediately that they are not all the same, either in intensity or in quality. And if you think back a few years, it should also be clear that each of your relationships has changed somewhat over time. This is the dynamic quality of social interactions—each give-and-take changes each participant, which, in turn, changes the relationship. The topic is highly personal and complex. A fairly new field, relationships are difficult to study scientifically, but I think you will find it interesting and important on several levels. As one set of researchers put it, social relationships are "the wellspring from which our daily lives emerge, accumulating into our life experiences. These relationships play a major role in how the life course is experienced and evaluated" (Cate et al., 2002, p. 261).

I start this chapter with a discussion of some current theories about the development of relationships, then cover what we know about specific relationships within partnerships, families, and friendships.

6.1: Theories of Social Relationships

OBJECTIVE: Compare theories of social relationships

The study of social relationship development in early childhood is a prominent topic of research and theory, but only recently has attention been focused on social relationships in adulthood. As you will see, attachment theory has been extended from early childhood into adulthood. Evolutionary psychology deals primarily with the young adult years and intimate partnerships, though it has recently expanded

into grandparenthood. Socioemotional selectivity theory addresses older adulthood, and the convoy model seems to apply across the life span.

☑ | **By the end of this module, you will be able to:**

6.1.1   **Explain attachment theory**

6.1.2   **Characterize the convoy model of relationships**

6.1.3   **Explain socioemotional selectivity theory**

6.1.4   **Relate evolution to social relationships**

6.1.1: Attachment Theory

OBJECTIVE: Explain attachment theory

One of the oldest and best-known theories of social relationships is **attachment theory**. The concept of **attachment** is most commonly used to describe the strong bond of affection formed by an infant to his or her primary caregiver. These bonds are considered part of an innate regulatory system that evolved in our primitive ancestors, presumably because they aided survival of young children, who are born with few abilities to care for themselves. Psychiatrist John Bowlby (1969) and developmental psychologist Mary Ainsworth (Ainsworth et al., 1978), two of the major theoretical figures in this area, both made a clear distinction between the attachment itself, which is an invisible, underlying bond, and **attachment behaviors**, which are the ways an underlying attachment is expressed. Because we cannot see the attachment bond, we have to infer it from the attachment behavior. In securely attached infants, we see it in their smiles when their favored person enters the room, in their clinging to the favored person when they are frightened, in their use of the favored person as a safe base for exploring a new situation. The three key underlying features are (1) association of the attachment figure with feelings of security, (2) an increased likelihood of attachment behavior when the child is under stress or threat, and (3) attempts to avoid, or to end, any separation from the attachment figure (Weiss, 1982).

In adults, of course, many of these specific attachment behaviors are no longer seen. Most adults do not burst into tears if their special person leaves the room; adults maintain contact in a much wider variety of ways than those we see in young children, including the use of phone calls, e-mail, text messages, social networking, and imagery. But if we allow for these changes in the attachment behavior, it does appear that the concept of attachment is a useful way to think about many adult relationships.

First of all, we appear to form strong new attachments in adulthood, particularly to a spouse or partner, and we usually maintain our attachment to our parents as well. Social psychologists Mario Mikulincer and Philip R. Shaver (2009) listed three kinds of support that people of all ages seek from attachment figures in time of need: proximity (comfort that comes from the close physical or psychological presence of the attachment figure), a safe haven (help and support when a threat is present), and a secure base (support in pursuing personal goals).

INTERNAL WORKING MODEL OF ATTACHMENT RELATIONSHIPS Attachment theorists propose that each person has formed an **internal working model** of attachment relationships—a set of beliefs and assumptions about the nature of all relationships, such as whether others will respond if you need them and whether others are trustworthy. Based on early childhood experiences, this internal working model has components of security or insecurity. The behavior that reflects the internal working model is an **attachment orientation**—patterns of expectations, needs, and emotions one exhibits in interpersonal relationships that extend beyond early attachment figures.

Adults with secure attachment orientations believe the world is a safe place. They welcome the challenges that life presents. They know they can rely on others when they need protection and support. They are able to explore the world, meet new people, and learn new things without the fear of failure. This doesn't mean that they never feel threatened or discouraged, and it doesn't mean that they will always succeed, but they enter into interactions knowing that they are able to summon help and encouragement from their support system—sometimes in person and sometimes with a phone call or text message. It is also possible to receive comfort by simply recalling the support one has received reliably in the past.

To complement the attachment orientation, theorists believe that we have also evolved a **caregiving orientation**, a system that is activated in adults when they interact with infants and young children. Most adults will respond to the appearance and behavior of younger members of the species (and often other species) by providing security, comfort, and protection. Many evolutionary psychologists believe that we also use this caregiving orientation in our relationships with adult friends, romantic partners, and elderly parents. Some believe it is also used by teachers in their devotion to their students, nurses with their tender loving care of patients, and therapists with their deep concern for clients.

Now if everyone has some degree of secure or insecure attachment orientation and also some degree of caregiving orientation, you can see how it plays out in social relationships in adulthood. There are individual differences in how much support a person needs, how well they are able to ask for support, and how clearly the person asked for help can understand their needs and provide support. All these individual differences have their roots, according to Bowlby (1973), in the parent–child relationship in infancy and childhood. If we had caregivers in infancy and childhood who were available, responsive, and supportive of our needs, we are more apt to have secure attachment orientations and effective caregiving orientations in adulthood. We can solicit social support from our spouses, partners, family members, and friends with confidence that they will provide it. We can tell when important people in our lives need caregiving, and we are able to give that care.

Attachment theory has been backed up by empirical research showing that an infant's attachment classification tends to remain stable into young adulthood (Waters et al., 1995) and studies showing that parents' attachment classifications correspond to their children's attachment classifications (van IJzendoorn, 1995). Attachment theory has also been applied to the formation of intimate relationships.

6.1.2: The Convoy Model

OBJECTIVE: Characterize the convoy model of relationships

Another approach to relationships in adulthood comes from developmental psychologist Toni Antonucci and her colleagues (Antonucci, 1990; Kahn & Antonucci, 1980), who use the term **convoy** to describe the ever-changing network of social relationships that surrounds each of us throughout our adult lives. "Convoy relationships serve to both shape and protect individuals, sharing with them life experiences, challenges, successes, and disappointments" (Antonucci et al., 2004, p. 353). These relationships affect how the individual experiences the world. They are reciprocal and developmental; as the individual changes and develops through time, the nature of the relationships and interactions is also likely to change.

In her research using the convoy model, Antonucci (1986) developed a mapping technique. She asked respondents to report on three levels of relationships and write the names of the people within three concentric circles. The inner circle is for names of people who are so close and important to the respondent that he or she could hardly imagine life without them. The middle circle is for people who are also close, but not as close as those in the inner circle. And the outer circle is for names of people who are part of the respondent's personal network but not as close as the other two groups. The entire structure is referred to as a *social network* (Figure 6.1).

Ongoing research is investigating the role of social networks as buffers against stress and how the support a person perceives that they get from their social network affects their health. Plans have been made for longitudinal studies that may lead to better health through preventative measures and intervention programs. Is it possible to make changes in social networks with the goal of improving

Figure 6.1 The Convoy Model

What names would fill out your own personal convoy model?

SOURCE: Based on Antonucci (1986).

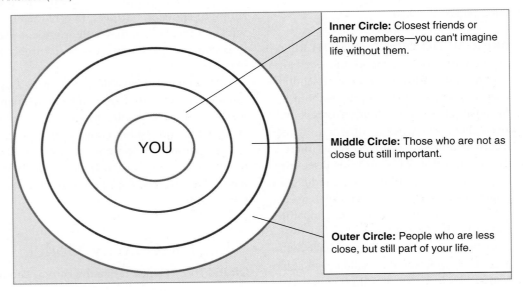

Inner Circle: Closest friends or family members—you can't imagine life without them.

Middle Circle: Those who are not as close but still important.

Outer Circle: People who are less close, but still part of your life.

physical and mental health? These are some of the topics being explored by researchers using the convoy model to explore social networks (Tighe et al., 2016).

6.1.3: Socioemotional Selectivity Theory

OBJECTIVE: Explain socioemotional selectivity theory

Yet another explanation of social relationship changes in adulthood comes from psychologist Laura Carstensen (1995; Carstensen et al., 2006). Known as **socioemotional selectivity theory**, it states that as we grow older, we tend to prefer more meaningful social relationships. This results in our social networks becoming smaller but more selective as we devote our limited emotional and physical resources to a smaller group of relationships that are deeply satisfying emotionally. In other words, the quantity of social relationships declines with age, but the overall quality remains the same (or even better).

Carstensen explains that younger adults perceive time as open-ended, measuring it by how long they have been on this earth. They are motivated to pursue information, knowledge, and relationships. In contrast, older adults perceive time as constrained, measuring it in terms of how long they have left on this earth. They are motivated to pursue emotional satisfaction, deepen existing relationships, and weed out those that are not satisfying. Research findings have backed this up by showing distinct age differences in social relationships and also the topics people are most likely to attend to and remember (Kryla-Lighthall & Mather, 2009).

WRITING PROMPT

The Convoy Model and You

Using the convoy model, map your relationships. How have your relationships changed in the past 5 years?

> The response entered here will appear in the performance dashboard and can be viewed by your instructor.

Submit

6.1.4: Evolutionary Psychology

OBJECTIVE: Relate evolution to social relationships

The final theory to be discussed is based on the belief that social relationships had an important role in human evolution, perhaps the central role in the design of the human mind (Buss & Kenrick, 1998). This is based on the premise that our early ancestors banded together in small social groups as an important survival strategy (Caporeal, 1997). Social relationships provided protection from predators, access to food, and insulation from the cold. Simply put, according to **evolutionary psychology**, individuals who carried genes for cooperativeness, group loyalty, adherence to norms, and promotion of social inclusion were more apt to survive in the primal environment and pass on these genes to their descendants (and ultimately to us). These genes continue to affect our social and cognitive behavior and are reflected in the ways we form and maintain social relationships in today's environment.

According to this theory, today's humans have biological systems that foster the formation and maintenance

Figure 6.2 Frequency of Face-to-face Contact with Social Network Members

Family visits (the solid line) remain fairly stable between the ages of 17 and 85—somewhere between once a month and once a week. On contrast, visits with nonfamily members (friends, neighbors, and acquaintances) started out high in emerging adulthood (at least once a week), declined sharply through young adulthood, and then declined more gradually until late old age (at least once a month).

SOURCE: From Sander et al. (2017).

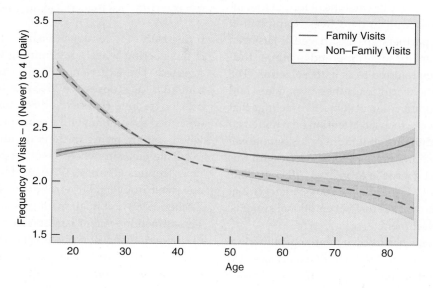

of social relationships manifested in a universal "need to belong." This need drives us to engage in frequent and pleasurable social interactions with a small number of familiar people who care about us and depend on us to care about them. Members of all human societies respond to distress and protest when they are separated from their social group or when a close relationship ends (Baumeister & Leary, 1995). The need to belong is observed in all human societies and in many other primate social species (de Waal, 1996).

A WORD ABOUT THEORIES OF SOCIAL RELATION-SHIPS You have no doubt noticed that these theories have a lot of similarities. In fact, the proponents of convoy theory are now writing about attachment as the "glue" that holds the convoys together. Both evolutionary psychologists and attachment theorists refer to attachment as an evolved mechanism to ensure the survival of infants and children. It seems pretty clear that the theories have more similarities than differences.

Graduate student Julia Sander and her colleagues (Sander et al., 2017) examined data from over 36,000 adults between 17 and 85 years of age who were part of the German Socioeconomic Panel Study. The participants were asked how often they had face-to-face contact with family and nonfamily members in their social networks. A rating of 0 was "never," 1 was "seldom," 2 was "at least once a month," 3 was "at least once a week," and 4 was "daily." You can see the results in Figure 6.2.

Although this study was based on frequency of contact, and both the convoy model and the socioemotional selectivity theory are based on the number of people in one's social network, the basic findings are similar: Adolescence

and young adulthood is the time that we look to the future, seeking information and new relationships, and these results demonstrate that our personal networks and friendship networks expand during those years. In contrast, later adulthood is a time that we reflect back over our lives and concentrate on fewer—but deeper—relationships. These results demonstrate that decrease in personal and friendship relationships. The convoy model explains that we travel along the road of life with a group of fellow travelers, and that is exactly what happens with the family network. The names may change over adulthood, but the size of our family social network remains the same from adolescence to the end of life. This study is also consistent with evolutionary psychology theory, which emphasized the lifelong importance of kinship groups and our lifelong concern with the survival of those with whom we share genes. It also shows that emerging adults and young adults invest more time in nonrelated social contacts because they are important for mating and reproduction (Sander et al., 2017).

6.2: Establishing an Intimate Partnership

OBJECTIVE: Determine how people choose intimate partners

One social relationship that almost all adults experience is the intimate partnership. Most research on this topic involves married couples, but I also discuss cohabiting relationships, both with heterosexual and same-sex partners.

Although it seems like a variety of relationships, you will likely find that romantic partners in all committed relationships share more similarities than differences.

The process of choosing a life partner and formalizing the relationship is found in every known culture; 90% of people in the world will marry or enter into a formal romantic partnership at some point in their lives (Campbell & Ellis, 2005). How such partnerships are arrived at has been the interest of researchers for some time, and in recent studies this process has been referred to as **mate selection**. The majority of people in the world select their own mates and do it on the basis of a combination of subjective feelings that include "euphoria, intense focused attention on a preferred individual, obsessive thinking about him or her, emotional dependency on and craving for emotional union with this beloved, and increased energy" (Aron et al., 2005, p. 327). Anthropologist Helen L. Fisher (2000, 2004) suggests that mate selection depends on three distinct emotional systems: lust, attraction, and attachment.

Each of these systems has its own neurological wiring. The *lust system* causes men and women to experience sexual desire and seek out sexual opportunities. The *attraction system* directs men and women to attend to specific potential mates and to desire an emotional relationship with them. The *attachment system* drives men and women to be close to the target of attraction (and lust) and to feel comfortable, secure, and emotionally dependent with that person. Fisher's theory of relationship formation makes a good model for viewing the components of the process of partnership formation.

▼ **By the end of this module, you will be able to:**

6.2.1   Characterize lust

6.2.2   Analyze the elements of attraction

6.2.3   Differentiate the four kinds of romantic attachment

6.2.1: Lust

OBJECTIVE: Characterize lust

This system should be familiar to all psychology majors, not because of their torrid personal lives but because it was the cornerstone of Freud's classic psychoanalytic theory. Freud believed that **libido**, or sexual desire, was the foundation of all intimate relationships, and that one's experience of such relationships depends on how much sexual desire one feels for the other person, whether one is consciously aware of it or not (Jones, 1981). Lust is certainly part of romantic love, but it can also operate independently. Most adults are familiar with feelings of lust toward someone they have no romantic involvement with and also the inverse—no feelings of sexual desire toward someone they do have a romantic involvement with. The lust system is powered by androgens

in both men and women. Using an automobile analogy, lust could be viewed as the accelerator of mate selection.

6.2.2: Attraction

OBJECTIVE: Analyze the elements of attraction

If lust is the accelerator in Fisher's theory, then attraction is the steering wheel, determining where the lust will be directed. The experience of attraction is also known as romantic love, obsessive love, passion (Sternberg, 1986), passionate love (Hatfield, 1988), and *limerence*, which is described as thinking of the other person all the time, even when you are trying to think of other things, and feeling exquisite pleasure when the other person seems to return your feelings (Tennov, 1979). Mate-attraction behavior is observed in every known human culture (Jankowiak & Fischer, 1992) and in all mammals and birds (Fisher, 2000). The attraction system is associated with increased levels of dopamine and norepinephrine and decreased levels of serotonin, all neurotransmitters in the brain.

In a study of brain activity, young men and women who reported being in love for 1–7 months were shown a photo of their loved one and asked to think about a pleasurable event that had occurred when they were together (Aron et al., 2005). As a control, they were shown a photo of a neutral person in their lives and asked to think about pleasurable events with that person. Results showed that viewing a photo of their loved one and thinking about a pleasant interaction with him or her activated regions of the brain that are rich in dopamine receptors—regions associated with the motivation to acquire a reward. These regions were not activated when the participants turned their attention and thoughts to a neutral person. Furthermore, the length of time a person had been in love caused different activation patterns; the more recent the relationship, the stronger the activation. The authors emphasize that the patterns of brain activation for new romantic love are different from those associated with the sex drive (or lust system, as Fisher calls it), indicating that they are distinct systems. Some evidence suggests that the hormones responsible for attachment may decrease the levels of androgen, causing sexual desire to decline as attachment increases.

Fisher and colleagues (2016) compare this early stage of intense romance to addiction. Both involve "euphoria, craving, tolerance, emotional and physical dependence, withdrawal and relapse" (p. 687). She has conducted brain imaging studies using functional magnetic resonance imaging technology and shown that people in this stage of love show activity in the brain's reward system, which is also activated by drugs or other sources of addiction.

The topic of what attracts one person to another, or two people to each other, was traditionally explained by **filter theory**, which states that we begin with a large pool of potential mates and gradually filter out those who do not fit our specifications (Cate & Lloyd, 1992). An alternative explanation was **exchange theory**, which says that we all have certain assets to offer in a relationship, and we try to make the best deal we can. Research has shown that people tend to have partners who match them on physical attractiveness. However, characteristics such as education level, pleasing personalities, and good grooming can help offset unattractive features (Carmalt et al., 2008). Sense of humor is also "exchanged" for physical attractiveness (McGee & Shevlin, 2009).

AN EVOLUTIONARY PERSPECTIVE ON ATTRACTION

Evolutionary psychologists have a somewhat different explanation of mate selection, although their conclusions are similar. Their explanation is based on our ancient ancestors' need to increase their chances of reproducing and providing for their children until they were old enough to fend for themselves. Men, who needed someone to bear and feed their children, looked for signs of good health and fertility—such as youth, low waist-to-hip ratio, clear skin, lustrous hair, full lips, good muscle tone, sprightly gait, and absence of sores or lesions. Women, who needed someone to care for their needs during pregnancy and to provide for them and their infants during the first few years after birth, looked for men with

qualities that signal economic resources, such as social status, self-confidence, slightly older age, ambition, and industriousness. They also needed someone to contribute healthy genes and protect them and their infants, so they preferred men who were brave, were athletic, and had a high shoulder-to-hip ratio (Buss, 2009). According to evolutionary psychology, these preferences are genetically based, and those members of our species who acted on these preferences were more apt to survive and pass them on to their offspring. Those who did not were less apt to survive or to have healthy offspring.

Psychologist Melissa R. Fales and her colleagues (Fales et al., 2016) examined the results of a large survey—one that included over 22,000 respondents, approximately half women and half men, ranging in age from 18 to 65 years of age. Participants were asked about traits they wanted in a potential partner for a long-term relationship or marriage. Among the possible traits were: is good looking, has a steady income, and makes (or will make) a lot of money. The participants indicated their mating market choices by rating each trait with 1 (very undesirable), 2 (undesirable), 3 (neutral), 4 (desirable but not essential), or 5 (absolutely essential). The results are shown in Figure 6.3.

Figure 6.3 Desirable and Essential Traits in Prospective Partners

The bars indicate the percentage of men and women who rated each trait as either 4 (desirable but not essential) or 5 (absolutely essential). More men consider good looks and a slender body to be desirable or essential; more women consider having a steady income and making a lot of money to be desirable or essential.

SOURCE: From Fales et al. (2016).

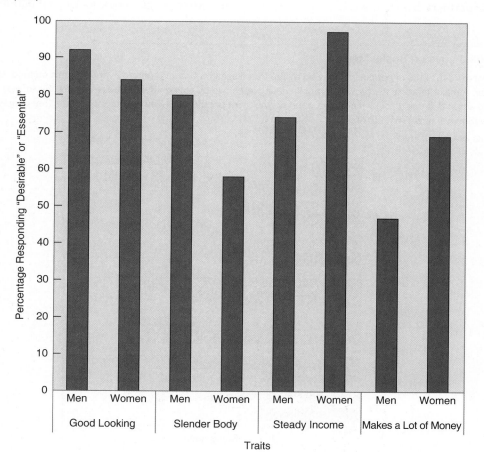

Studies across cultures have demonstrated these same preferences in potential mates. For example, psychologist Todd Shackelford and his colleagues (2005) examined data from over 9,000 young adults living in 37 different cultures around the world and found sex differences on three out of four universal dimensions of mate preference for long-term relationships. As predicted by evolutionary psychology, women value social status and financial resources, as well as dependability, stability, and intelligence more than men do. Men value good looks, health, and a desire for home and children more than women do. Studies of online dating sites show that these preferences are present across the lifespan, even when reproduction is not an issue, with adults age 20 to 75 and older expressing similar preferences—men are more likely to prefer women who are physically attractive, and women are more likely to prefer men with status (Alterovitz & Mendelsohn, 2011).

Other research on mate selection has shown that men and women have different preferences for mates depending on whether they are interested in a long-term or short-term relationship. Women also show different preferences depending on whether they are ovulating or not, their age, their life stage, and their own value as a mate (Buss, 2009). According to evolutionary psychology, all these preferences are explained by our species' drive to survive and to reproduce successfully.

ONLINE DATING SITES In the past few decades, adults of all ages have increasingly used social media to seek out potential romantic partners. See Figure 6.4.

But how successful are online dating sites for finding long-term relationships? In spite of glowing reports from the dating sites themselves, only 5% of Americans who are married or in a committed relationship met using dating sites. And even if you consider those who have been married 5 years or less, the number only goes up to 12%. One explanation for such low numbers is that the researchers are just considering official online dating sites. There are other ways to meet a potential partner online, such as Facebook and Twitter, and it is estimated that for every couple who met through an online dating site, there is another couple who met through other online channels (D'Angelo & Toma, 2017).

Researchers demonstrated another problem with online dating: too many choices. Using a term from behavioral economics, *choice overload*, researchers showed that college students in a situation similar to online dating were more satisfied with their choices a week after selecting them for a potential date if they had been given a small number to choose from rather than a large number (D'Angelo & Toma, 2017). It seems the very opposite of what online dating sites intend when they offer customers large pools of potential partners to choose from.

It is important to remember that online dating sites are usually for-profit organizations. Many employ psychologists or researchers to set up matching algorithms or demonstrate their value. These experts should be taken for who they are: employees of the for-profit dating service. Another important thing to remember is that these Internet dating sites can serve as informal lists of single people looking for partners. Users would be

---

Figure 6.4 Finding Love on Social Media

This figure shows that in 2013, 11% of people interviewed by the Pew Research Center reported ever using this method, and it increased to 15% just 2 years later. A major factor is the growth of mobile dating apps use by young adults. One reason for this increase might be that more and more U.S. adults agree that using social media is a good way to meet people, while fewer and fewer agree that people who use social media are desperate (Smith & Anderson, 2016).

SOURCE: From Smith and Anderson (2016).

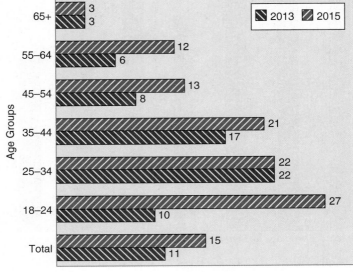

Percentage

wise never to give out any personal information until they feel a trusting relationship is formed and never to send money to anyone they have met on these sites. Research has shown that about half of dating site users in the United States and in England admit to lying on their dating website profile—women about their appearances and men about their income and status (Anderson, 2016). As with any other purchases, you would be wise to heed this advice: "Buyer beware."

6.2.3: Attachment

OBJECTIVE: Differentiate the four kinds of romantic attachment

Fisher's attachment system has some similarity to its namesake, Bowlby's attachment theory. Although Bowlby initially formulated his theory to explain parent–infant relationships, he believed that attachment was a lifelong process and that the quality of relationship one had with parents was the base for later attachments, including romantic partnerships. More recent attachment theorists have suggested that attachment between romantic partners is a mechanism that evolved to keep parents together long enough to raise their children. Men and women who are able to feel secure together and lonely when apart are more apt to be committed to each other and to the task of raising their child safely into adulthood. Interestingly, the hormone oxytocin plays a central role in mother–infant attachment and also in women's romantic attachment to a mate (Campbell & Ellis, 2005).

Another link between early childhood attachment relationships with one's parents and adult attachment relationships with one's intimate partners is the topic of a large portion of adult attachment research. Extensions of Bowlby's attachment theory have been used to suggest that adult romantic relationship styles are reflections of the attachment bond the adults had with their parents in childhood (Bartholomew, 1990; Hazan & Shaver, 1987).

When adults were given questionnaires asking them to choose a description that best characterized the way they felt about romantic relationships, they fell into categories that were similar to Ainsworth's secure and insecure categories, and the proportion of adults falling into each category was similar to that of infants (Feeney & Noller, 1996; Hazan & Shaver, 1990; Mikulincer & Orbach, 1995). Later researchers confirmed these results with participants from the ages of 15 to 54 (Michelson et al., 1997) and over a period of several years (Feeney & Noller, 1996), suggesting that styles of adult romantic attachments reflect internal working models of attachment established in early childhood. In longitudinal research, 2-year-olds who showed secure attachment to their mothers were better able, at age 20 or 21 years, to resolve and rebound from romantic relationship conflicts than former 2-year-olds who were insecurely attached. In addition, the *partners* of securely attached 20-year-olds also rebound faster from relationship conflict regardless of their own attachment history (Simpson et al., 2011). While attachment appears to be relatively stable over time, it's not set in stone (see 'Attachement Across the Lifespan').

Attachment Across the Lifespan

An extension of Hazan and Shaver's (1990) model has been proposed that has four categories of attachment styles based on a person's model of the self and others (Bartholomew & Horowitz, 1991). Based on self-reported ratings of how well different statements describe their own attitudes toward relationships, people are classified as secure (having a positive model of both self and others), dismissing/avoidant (having a positive model of self and a negative model of others), preoccupied/anxious (negative model of self and positive model of others), or fearful (negative model of both self and others). The descriptions used in this study are shown in Table 6.1, along with the attachment classifications that correspond to each. Using this relationship questionnaire with young adults, the researchers found that almost half rated themselves as secure, whereas the other half was equally distributed among the remaining three categories. Some research organizes these four groups into two: secure and insecure, which included preoccupied/anxious, fearful, and dismissing/avoidant (Meuwly & Schoebi, 2017).

Table 6.1 Adult Romantic Attachment Styles

Attachment Type	Description
Secure	"It is relatively easy for me to become emotionally close to others. I am comfortable depending on others and having others depend on me. I don't worry about being alone or having others not accept me."
Preoccupied/Anxious	"I want to be completely emotionally intimate with others, but I often find that others are reluctant to get as close as I would like. I am uncomfortable being without close relationships, but I sometimes worry that others don't value me as much as I value them."
Fearful	"I am somewhat uncomfortable getting close to others. I want emotionally close relationships, but I find it difficult to trust others completely or to depend on them. I sometimes worry that I will be hurt if I allow myself to become too close to others."
Dismissing/Avoidant	"I am comfortable without close emotional relationships. It is very important to me to feel independent and self-sufficient, and I prefer not to depend on others or have others depend on me."

SOURCES: Adapted from Bartholomew and Horowitz (1991); Hazan and Shaver (1990).

Infant Attachment

It is still not clear what direct role infant attachment plays in adult romantic relationships. Some argue that infant attachment affects peer competence in primary school, which affects friendship security in adolescence, which in turn affects romantic relationships (Simpson et al., 2011). Psychologist R. Chris Fraley and his colleagues (Fraley et al., 2013) examined data from over 700 emerging adults who had been participants in an ongoing longitudinal study since shortly after birth. They found that the various adult attachment styles they exhibited at the age of 18 could be traced to their early caregiving environments (early maternal sensitivity, changes in maternal sensitivity, father absence, maternal depression), changes in social competence, and quality of relationships with best friends.

Lifespan Attachment

How does attachment play out over the lifespan? Psychologist William J. Chopik and colleagues (Chopik et al., 2017) combined findings from five longitudinal studies conducted between 1923 and 1969, resulting in data from over 600 individuals between 13 and 73 years of age. All these studies measured the participants' attachment styles at several points in time and, when combined, gave a good picture of how these styles change over the lifespan. Two types of insecure attachment were featured: dismissive/avoidant and preoccupied/anxious. Figure 6.5 shows the mean dismissive/avoidant scores for five studies (listed in the key). As you can see, for example, the Oakland study only

followed participants from the late 30s to 60 years of age. The Guidance study consisted of younger participants, from 13 to 40 years, and the Radcliffe study covered older participants, from 40 to 73 years. Taken together, these five studies show dismissive/avoidant scores decline slowly but steadily through all the years that were studied. In other words, people who feel discomfort with intimacy as emerging adults and young adults gradually feel less discomfort as they move into middle and older adulthood.

A second finding of the study concerns preoccupied/anxious individuals, shown in Figure 6.6. People who tend to feel no need for intimate relationships, preferring to not depend on others or have others depend on them, show high levels of this in adolescence and early adulthood before declining through middle age and older adulthood. The authors of this study point out that the changes on both these attachment styles were significant, but not very large, showing that attachment style is a relatively stable trait across the lifespan. They also explain that these trajectories fit other findings of relationship importance over the lifespan, from the insecurity of new relationships in young adulthood to the need for social belongingness as people start families and become enmeshed in work, to the efforts older adults make to become closer to their good friends and family members. They also point out that participants who were in relationships showed lower levels of dismissive/avoidant and preoccupied/anxious attachment styles than those who were unpartnered.

Figure 6.5 Findings from Five Studies of Attachment Over the Lifespan

SOURCE: Chopik et al. (2017).

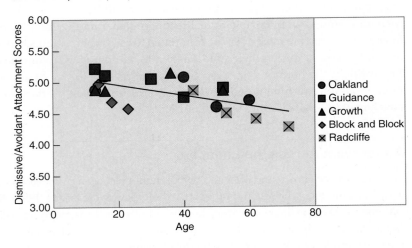

Figure 6.6 Preoccupied/Anxious Individuals

SOURCE: Chopik et al. (2017).

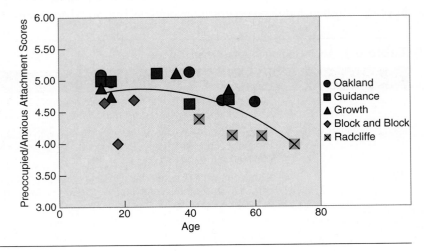

WRITING PROMPT

Attachment and You

Reflect on your attachment relationship with your parents. How has this relationship influenced your relationships with other people?

> The response entered here will appear in the performance dashboard and can be viewed by your instructor.

Submit

6.3: Living in Intimate Partnerships

OBJECTIVE: Evaluate the impact of intimate partnership on adulthood experiences

What happens *after* partners select each other? As you well know, not all couples who marry or otherwise commit to a partnership end up living happily ever after. Some do, but others drift into empty relationships, some divorce, and some live together in a constant war zone. What makes the difference? This section looks at what is both an academic question and a personal one by scrutinizing relationships—whatever form they may take.

 By the end of this module, you will be able to:

6.3.1 Identify elements that increase the chance of happiness in a long-term marriage

6.3.2 Compare cohabitation and marriage

6.3.3 Characterize the long-term relationships of same-sex couples

6.3.1: Happy Marriages

OBJECTIVE: Identify elements that increase the chance of happiness in a long-term marriage

Almost all of us wind up in partnerships of one kind or another, and it's safe to say that almost all of us want them to be happy and long-lasting. But what is the secret to a happy marriage? We have the benefit of several longitudinal studies that provide some answers.

Psychologist Howard J. Markman and colleagues (Clements et al., 2004) studied 100 couples from before marriage until well past their 13th anniversaries. This study was unusual not only because of its duration, but also because it included data from both members of the couples, it did not rely only on self-report data, and it consisted of a group of young couples from the general population rather than couples who were in marriage counseling or otherwise considered at risk.

Before marriage, each couple was interviewed and participated in discussions about problem areas in their relationship. They were given a number of standardized tests of relationship satisfaction, interaction, and problem solving. This was repeated 10 times in the next 13 years, and at the end of that time, the 100 couples were divided into three categories—those who had divorced (20 couples), those who remained happily married (58 couples), and those who had experienced a period of distress at several assessment points (22 couples). Groups were compared based on the data gathered at the beginning of the study, and it was clear that the three groups differed even before their marriages took place. For example, the groups that experienced divorce or marital distress had exhibited negative interactions with each other in their first interviews, expressing insults toward each other, showing lack of emotional support, and making negative and sarcastic comments about their partners. Markman and his colleagues described the process as "erosion" and said that these negative interactions before marriage and in the early years of marriage wear down the positive aspects of the relationship and violate the expectation that one's partner will be a close friend and source of support. Subsequent studies with different groups of couples have yielded similar findings (Markman et al., 2010a, 2010b). Markman and his colleagues concluded that there are a number of risk factors for unhappy marriages and divorce, some of which can be changed and some of which cannot. These risk factors include aspects of personal history that cannot be changed (having divorced parents, different religious backgrounds, children from previous relationships); individual personality traits (being defensive when personal problems arise, having negative styles of interacting with others, not being able to communicate during disagreements); and different ideas about the future (unrealistic beliefs about marriage, different priorities, and less than total commitment to each other).

POSITIVE AND NEGATIVE INTERACTIONS   The eroding power of negative interactions has also been found in the results of longitudinal studies by psychologist John Gottman and his colleagues. For example, Gottman and Notarius (2000) found that couples who will eventually divorce can be identified years ahead of time by looking at the pattern of positive and negative exchanges. In fact, Gottman (2011) claims that he is able to interview a couple for a few hours and predict with 94% accuracy whether they will be divorced or still together 4 years later. Gottman asks couples to tell him "the story of us." He listens for five key components and evaluates whether they are positive or negative. If the positive outweighs the negative, then the couple will almost certainly be together 4 years later.

These are the key components Gottman evaluates during the interview:

- *Fondness and admiration*—Is the couple's story full of love and respect? Do they express positive emotions like warmth, humor, and affection? Do they emphasize the good times? Do they complement each other?

- *"We-ness" versus "me-ness"*—Does the couple express unity in beliefs, values, and goals? Do they use "us" and "we" more than "I" and "me"?

- *Love maps*—Does the couple describe the history of their relationship in vivid detail and with positive energy? Are they open with personal information about themselves and their partner?

- *Purpose and meaning instead of chaos*—Do couples talk about their life together in terms of pride over the hardships they have overcome? Do they talk about shared goals and aspirations?

- *Satisfaction instead of disappointment*—Do couples say that their partner and their marriage have exceeded their expectations? Are they satisfied and grateful for what they have in each other? Do they speak positively about marriage?

Fortunately, negative patterns in marriage can be changed. Therapists who work with couples have found that marital satisfaction can be increased significantly by teaching couples how to understand each other better, increase affection, attend to each other and influence each other more, practice healthy conflict resolution, and create shared meaning within their relationship. It is possible for couples whose relationships have grown distant or hostile to acquire new skills or relearn earlier patterns of interaction through relationship education courses (Markman & Rhoades, 2012), which have been given successfully to high-risk couples online (Loew et al., 2012).

LONG-TERM MARRIAGES   Other researchers have studied couples in long-term marriages to find out how they feel about each other and what the differences are between couples that have positive feelings about each other and those who do not. Although some theories suggest that passionate love occurs mostly in the early years of a relationship and then is replaced by companionate love, little research has been done with long-term married couples to see if this is true. Psychologist K. Daniel O'Leary and his colleagues (2012) surveyed almost 300 adults who had been married an average of 20 years. The central question they asked was, "How in love are you with your partner?" They were asked to rate their love on a scale from 1 to 7, with "Very intensely in love" being 1 and "Not at all in love" being 7. Unexpectedly, the researchers found that the most frequent response was 1—over 46% of the men and women in this sample reported being very intensely in love with their partners. These findings are shown in Figure 6.7. Those who reported intense love for each other were also apt to report high

Figure 6.7 Long-Term Married Couples Rate How Much in Love They Are

SOURCE: Data from O'Leary et al. (2012).

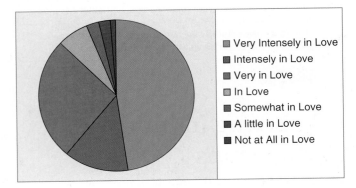

- Very Intensely in Love
- Intensely in Love
- Very in Love
- In Love
- Somewhat in Love
- A little in Love
- Not at All in Love

levels of thinking positively about their partner, affectionate behaviors and sexual intercourse with their partners, sharing novel and challenging activities with their partners, and having a general feeling of life happiness.

Another study looked at unhappy long-term marriages. Sociologists Daniel N. Hawkins and Alan Booth (2005) examined over 12 years of data from couples in low-quality marriages. The study showed that people who remain in unhappy marriages experience a reduction in life satisfaction, self-esteem, psychological well-being, and overall health. Furthermore, people who stay in unhappy marriages are less happy than those who divorce and remarry, and they have lower levels of life satisfaction, self-esteem, and overall health than those who divorced and remained single. A similar study of middle-aged adults showed that women (but not men) in very low-quality marriages at the beginning of the study showed high levels of life satisfaction 10 years later if they have divorced (Bourassa et al., 2015). For these samples of people at least, there was no benefit to remaining in unhappy marriages instead of divorcing.

The lesson from studying various types of marriages is that a happy marriage is a huge plus in the partners' lives, and that an unhappy marriage is a huge minus. Not all beginning marriages are happy and healthy, and not all long-term marriages are cooled down and companionable; a lot still sizzle. So unless you view long-term commitment to your partner primarily as a means to successfully raise children, as evolutionary psychology emphasizes (Salmon, 2017), it might be a good idea to follow some of the advice in this section. Unhappy relationships can be helped with family therapy or relationship education classes.

6.3.2: Cohabitation and Marriage

OBJECTIVE: Compare cohabitation and marriage

Cohabitation has become an increasingly common choice of couples who want to live together in an intimate relationship, and this is true of adults of all ages, as seen in

Figure 6.8. What's the difference between the relationships of married partners and cohabiting partners? And what happens when cohabiting partners marry?

Early research found that couples who marry and then move in together are more likely to stay married than those who move in together and then marry later (Hewitt & de Vaus, 2009). Why would this be true? Some have argued that there is a *selection effect*—those who are more mature and have stronger relationships follow the traditional path to marriage, whereas those with doubts and troubled relationships opt for cohabitation first (Woods & Emery, 2002). Others believe that the experience of cohabiting changes the couple's attitudes about marriage (Magdol et al., 1998). However, studies by psychologist Howard Markman and his colleagues (Kline et al., 2004; Rhoades et al., 2009; Stanley et al., 2010) show that there are two distinct types of cohabitation relationships that lead to marriage: *engaged cohabitation*, in which the couple becomes engaged before moving in together, and *preengaged cohabitation*, in which the couple becomes engaged after moving in together. The former tends to lead to marriages as successful as those of couples who did not cohabit before marriage; the latter tends to lead to less successful marriages. Why? The authors conclude that couples who become engaged before moving in together have made a formal commitment to each other, and their relationships are more similar to those of couples who marry before living together than to those of couples who cohabit without that commitment.

CULTURAL ACCEPTANCE OF COHABITATION Another factor in the success of cohabiting couples is how well it is accepted in one's culture—their family, community, and religion. Sociologist Kristen Schultz Lee and Hiroshi

Ono (2012) investigated the happiness of over 25,000 married and cohabiting couples in 27 countries. They assigned scores to each country indicating the relative strength of traditional gender beliefs (how they view mothers of young children who work outside the home) and religious context (how important religion is in their personal lives). These scores are shown in Table 6.2. Results showed that there was little difference for men's happiness in any country whether they were cohabiting or married, but in countries where traditional gender beliefs and religious context is high, there is a "happiness gap" between married women and cohabiting women. In countries where the traditional gender beliefs and religious context is low, there is no difference in happiness between married and cohabiting women. Apparently, women's relative unhappiness in more gender-restrictive,

Table 6.2 Twenty-Seven Countries with Ratings for Religious Beliefs and Gender Context

Country	Religious Climate	Gender Climate
Australia	0.10	−0.10
Austria	0.18	0.09
Belgium	−0.50	0.01
Brazil	1.51	0.74
Chile	1.28	0.59
Czech Republic	−1.71	0.00
Denmark	−0.92	−0.63
Finland	0.14	−0.25
France	−0.88	−0.22
Germany East	−1.15	−0.71
Germany West	−1.15	−0.18
Hungary	−0.56	0.38
Latvia	−0.17	0.16
Mexico	1.71	0.50
Netherlands	−0.83	−0.15
New Zealand	0.01	−0.07
Norway	−0.58	−0.45
Philippines	2.00	0.16
Poland	1.45	0.07
Portugal	0.94	0.35
Russia	−0.36	0.27
Slovakia	0.48	0.18
Spain	−0.40	−0.03
Sweden	0.11	−0.51
Switzerland	−1.18	0.06
Taiwan	−0.08	−0.05
UK	0.31	−0.20
USA	1.50	−0.24

SOURCE: Data from Lee and Ono (2012).

Figure 6.8 Cohabitation Among Adults of All Ages

SOURCE: Stepler (2017b).

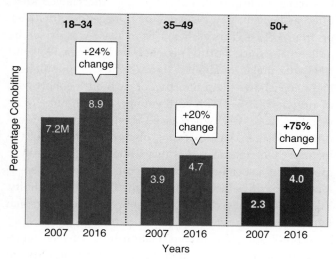

religious countries is a reaction to the negative connotations cohabitation has in their culture. Although these findings were for people living in these countries today, they would also apply to people who were cohabiting in the United States a few decades ago when the practice was not so well accepted (Loving, 2011).

When couples cohabit in cultures that are not accepting of that practice, their eventual marriages are more apt to end in divorce than cohabiting couples in more accepting cultures. This was demonstrated in a study by sociologist Yongjun Zhang (2017), who examined survey data from a nationally representative sample of adults living in China. He found over 17,000 couples who married between 1980 and 2010, and he divided them into two cohorts, those who married at a time that cohabitation was not well tolerated (1980–1994) and those who married when cohabitation was better tolerated (1995–2010), due to economic reforms in the country. Zhang found that cohabitation before marriage was five times higher in the post-reform cohort (5% versus 25%). More interesting was that couples in the pre-reform cohort that cohabited before marriage were more likely to divorce than couples in that cohort who did not cohabit before marriage. This was not true of the couples in the post-reform cohort; cohabitation had no effect on divorce rate. Zhang concluded that when premarital cohabitation is not well tolerated in a culture, couples who cohabit may feel pressure to eventually marry regardless of the quality of their relationship, thus leading to unhappy marriages and subsequent divorce. When cohabitation is better tolerated by a culture, couples may feel free to end the relationship without marrying.

OTHER ISSUES IN COHABITATION On the topic of cohabitation, there are often more people involved in the relationship than just the couple. In the United States today, 25% of babies are born to cohabiting couples. Researchers have begun to look into such matters as the differences between cohabiting families and married families, and the effect the parents' marital status has on the children. Again, the difference seems to be whether the cohabiting couple ultimately marries or not. Those who marry before the child's fifth birthday (when the study ended), reported the same relationship quality as parents who were married when the child was born. Those who continued cohabiting (and those who broke up) during that 5-year period reported lower levels of relationship quality (McClain & Brown, 2017).

My conclusion from this is that the success of a couples' partnership and parenting depends more on commitment than whether they are officially married or not, and life is easier for these couples (and families) when they live in a culture that is accepting of their personal choices to either marry or cohabit.

These studies are focused on young adults—the age group most likely to cohabit—but they are not the only group in the United States to choose living together in intimate partnerships without being married. More and more adults who are 50 years of age and older are joining this group, increasing from 2.3% to 4% in the past decade (Stepler, 2017a). This is partly due to an increase in the divorce rate for this age and also an increase in the number of people who have never married. Interestingly, cohabiting results in a better outcome for older men than for older women. Women over age 50 report the same amount of depressive symptoms and perceived stress whether they are married, cohabiting, dating, or unpartnered, while men who cohabited reported fewer depressive symptoms than those who were dating, unpartnered, or married. Researchers suggested that older women may not get the same benefit from being in any kind of partnership because their gender roles include caregiving, while men this age are more likely to be the care recipients (Wright & Brown, 2017).

WRITING PROMPT

Cultural Effects on Cohabiting Couples

Choose a country in Table 6.2 and predict the happiness of a cohabiting couple in that country, based on Lee and Ono's 2012 study. How might this affect any children they might have?

▶ The response entered here will appear in the performance dashboard and can be viewed by your instructor.

Submit

6.3.3: Same-Sex Marriages and Partnerships

OBJECTIVE: Characterize the long-term relationships of same-sex couples

In a recent Gallup poll, 4.1% of people interviewed identified as lesbian, gay, bisexual, or transgender (LGBT+), up from 3.5% 4 years earlier. This increase was driven by millennials, the cohort of people born between 1980 and 1998 who make up about a third of the U.S. population. Figure 6.9 shows the proportion of each birth cohort who identify as LGBT+. With each younger cohort, more of its members said "yes" when asked if they personally identified as lesbian, gay, bisexual, or transgender. Why the increase? One reason is that this is the first generation to grow up in a social climate where the majority of people reported positive feelings toward the LGBT+ community. Millennials are also more comfortable giving out personal information on surveys.

Long-lasting, committed relationships between same-sex partners are very common today, and gay and lesbian

Figure 6.9 Proportion of Population Self-Identifying as LGBT+, by Birth Cohort

SOURCE: Gates (2016).

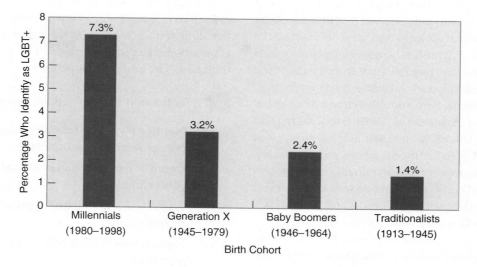

partners have been able to legally marry throughout the United States since 2015. As of this writing, one in 10 LGBT+ Americans is married to a same-sex partner, and the majority (61%) of same-sex cohabiting partners are married (Masci et al., 2017). Researchers have begun to study married and cohabiting couples from the LGBT+ community to compare them with heterosexual couples and also to find effective methods to use with same-sex couples who seek counseling (Filmore et al., 2016). In a landmark longitudinal study of gay, lesbian, and heterosexual married and cohabiting couples, psychologist Lawrence Kurdek (2004) found that the factors that influence relationship quality and stability for the various categories of couples was essentially the same.

More recently, researchers at the Gottman Institute followed over 100 same-sex couples who sought relationship therapy at their institute. Standard couple counseling increased the relationship satisfaction measures significantly, and results were apparent in even fewer sessions than is usually found with heterosexual couples. The researchers suggested that one of the reasons for this difference was that same-sex couples have less gender inequality and fewer gender role differences. They are socialized similarly and share more similar communication styles. They show more humor, kindness, and positivity when discussing disagreements and use fewer hostile and controlling emotional tactics. In addition, same-sex couples continue to keep alive play, fun, and sex in their long-term relationships and report a greater level of satisfaction with their sexual relations and leisure-time activities together. The researchers concluded that although same-sex couples in this study had similar conflict and relationship issues as heterosexual couples, it was possible to restore relationship satisfaction in a shorter amount of time (Garanzini et al., 2017).

SIMILARITIES AND DIFFERENCES BETWEEN SAME-SEX AND HETEROSEXUAL COUPLES Same-sex couples and different-sex couples are similar in many ways. They fall in love, worry about the long-term outcome of their relationships, and enjoy legal status as a recognized couple. Both partners probably work outside the home, and they divide up household chores and financial responsibilities. Regardless of couple type, the one who makes the most money usually does the least around the house. The stereotypes that same-sex partners take on "male" and "female" roles have not been supported by research (Harman, 2011). And although gay-friendly neighborhoods or "gayborhoods" do exist, a recent poll showed that only 12% of LGBT+ Americans report that they live in such a place (Brown, 2017).

There are still differences in the degree of openness same-sex partners express about being gay and being in a relationship. In one study, researchers interviewed gay and lesbian couples about how they presented their relationships to friends, family members, and coworkers and how satisfied they were with their partners. Then they asked the couples to discuss a problem area in their relationships. They found that couples who were more open about their relationships reported greater satisfaction with their partners and also treated each other with more positive emotions when they discussed problem areas in their relationships (Clausell & Roisman, 2009). This research illustrates another way that same-sex couples differ from different-sex couples: Few heterosexual people feel a need to hide their sexual orientation or their intimate partnerships from others. The resulting loss of social support and contact with important friends and family members seemingly takes a toll on same-sex relationships in a way that it often does not affect different-sex couples.

One more difference in same-sex relationships is contending with physical violence. Members of the LGBT+ community are more apt to be victims of violence, especially transgender women. One study showed that in comparison with their heterosexual siblings, gay and lesbian adults reported experiencing significantly more violence over their lifetimes—more childhood psychological and physical abuse by parents, more childhood sexual abuse, more psychological and physical victimization in adulthood, and more sexual assault in adulthood (Balsam et al., 2005). Social stigma and discrimination are still more common for this group, and many face rejection from family, neighbors, and coworkers, the source of social support for most others. These stressors lead to high rates of health problems, as well as high levels of psychiatric disorders, substance abuse, and suicide (U.S. Department of Health and Human Services, 2017).

Although these studies by no means present a complete picture of gay and lesbian partnerships, they feature creative, solid research that gives us valuable information. Perhaps the most important finding is that homosexual relationships are far more similar to heterosexual relationships than they are different. Many last a lifetime. The human urge to commit to another person in an intimate relationship (and perhaps to raise children together) is as evident in homosexual relationships as it is in heterosexual relationships.

6.4: Relationships with Other Family Members

OBJECTIVE: Analyze the ways that family interactions influence adulthood experiences

Defining "family" is not an easy task. Each time I find a definition, I realize that it doesn't apply to my particular family group, or to the family that lives next door to me. It's not so much that we are unusual, but that family is a hard concept to pin down with a definition that includes all the people we consider family. We have biological relatives, adopted relatives, and step- and half-relatives. Some of us have close friends who function as family members. Then there is the situation of ex-family members, and who knows what will happen when surrogate mothers and sperm-donor fathers are considered! Personally, I like the solution suggested by gerontologist Rosemary Blieszner (2000), who writes that when it comes to researching family relationships, "It is not possible to identify family members via external observation. Rather, individuals must specify the members of their own families" (p. 92). Presumably, like beauty, family is in the eye of the beholder.

My guess is that your version of "family" may be complicated too. Unfortunately, research on family relationships in adulthood has not yet caught up to this complexity. Most attention has been directed to parent–child relationships, with less emphasis on sibling relationships or grandparent–grandchild links. There is essentially no information available on relationships between stepsiblings or in-laws (let alone former in-laws). In the future, I hope we will see explorations of a broader array of "family" connections and their effects on adult development.

▼ | **By the end of this module, you will be able to:**

6.4.1 Identify ways that families maintain intergenerational solidarity

6.4.2 Describe common parent interactions with adult children

6.4.3 Characterize grandparent–grandchild relationships

6.4.4 Explain how sibling relationships change over time

6.4.1: General Patterns of Family Interaction

OBJECTIVE: Identify ways that families maintain intergenerational solidarity

When my youngest child moved out of the house at age 18, I admit that I experienced a few moments of panic. Would he ever come back to see us? Why would he? He had a comfortable apartment, he was a good cook, he knew how to do his own laundry, and he had a good income. But Sunday rolled around, and there he was, sitting at the dining room table with my husband and me, his grandparents, his sister and her husband, and his 2-year-old nephew. And he has been there almost every Sunday since, for over 30 years, first bringing his girlfriend (who later became his wife), and then his children. For a number of years, he was a single dad raising two sons, and the three of them regularly graced our dinner table. Recently he has added a new wife to the group and her teenage son. And I know why. Because we are family, and once a week we touch base, catch up on the news, and recharge our batteries for the coming week.

During the 1970s and 1980s, social scientists grappled with the idea that **nuclear families** (parents and their children) in the United States were in danger of being isolated from their **extended families** (grandparents, aunts and uncles, cousins). The reason for their concern was that young families had become more mobile than ever before, moving across the country to seek out job opportunities that were not available in their hometowns. But closer examination showed that although the mobility was a fact of family life, the isolation was not. Families find ways to maintain **intergenerational solidarity**, or emotional cohesion between the generations, even when some members live far away.

Sociologists have theorized that the quality of family relationships can be evaluated on six dimensions of emotional cohesion (Bengtson & Schrader, 1982). This theory of intergenerational solidarity states that family relationships depend on:

- *Associational solidarity*—how often family members interact with each other and what types of activities they do together.
- *Affectional solidarity*—how positive the sentiments are that family members hold for each other and whether those sentiments are returned.
- *Consensual solidarity*—how well family members hold the same values, attitudes, and beliefs.
- *Functional solidarity*—how much family members do for each other in terms of services or assistance.
- *Normative solidarity*—how much family members feel a part of the family group and identify with each other.
- *Intergenerational family structure*—how many family members there are, how they are related, and how close they live to each other.

According to this theory, family members can be very close if they have frequent interactions, feel a great deal of affection toward each other, share basic attitudes and opinions, help each other when help is needed, agree with the basic beliefs of the family unit, and have the means to interact with each other (either living close together or having access to communication technology). To the extent that any of these factors is not present, the relationships will be less close.

WRITING PROMPT

Closer to Home

Evaluate your own family based on the six dimensions of emotional cohesion.

 The response entered here will appear in the performance dashboard and can be viewed by your instructor.

Submit

6.4.2: Parent–Child Relationships in Adulthood

OBJECTIVE: Describe common parent interactions with adult children

One big question in the study of parent–child relationships in adulthood is, "What happens to the attachment bond from childhood?" Does it end, leaving independent adult children ready to form new and different relationships with their parents? Or does it continue, with adjustments made for the adult status of the child? Bowlby (1969) claimed

that attachment diminished during adolescence and then disappeared, except in times of illness or extreme distress. This attachment is often transferred to romantic partners. One attachment theorist puts it this way: "If children are eventually to form their own households, their bonds of attachment to the parents must become attenuated and eventually end. Otherwise, independent living would be emotionally troubling. The relinquishing of attachment to parents appears to be of central importance among the individuation-achieving processes of late adolescence and early adulthood" (Weiss, 1986, p. 100).

Other theorists have suggested that attachment between parents and their children does not decline in adolescence, but changes slightly in form (Cicirelli, 1991). Instead of physical proximity being the key, communication becomes important. In adulthood, children and parents are capable of substituting symbols of each other (memories, photos, family heirlooms) for their physical presence and communicating through phone calls, text messages, social media, occasional visits, and other communications. I think my experiences and probably yours fit this explanation, and so do the data from recent studies.

Most adult children and their parents live near each other, have frequent contact, report feeling emotionally close, and share similar opinions. Studies of middle-aged adults have shown that most middle-aged parents have daily contact with their adult children and about 85% have at least weekly contact. This frequency has increased over the past 25 years, most likely due to the convenience and affordability of cell phones, text messages, e-mail, and other innovations (Fingerman et al., 2016).

Population researcher Ori Rubin (2015) surveyed over 1,200 adult children and their parents in the Netherlands and asked about how often they saw each other face-to-face and how often they were in touch via telecommunication. As the left panel in Figure 6.10 shows, the majority of adult children surveyed saw their parents face-to-face at least once a month, with the largest percentage seeing them weekly. The second panel in Figure 6.10 shows that the majority of adult children surveyed contacted their parents via some type of telecommunications at least once a week.

AFFECTION According to Bengtson's theory of intergenerational solidarity, affection is an important component in family relationships. Mutual expressions of affection between family members are often seen as a measure of how close the relationship is and how it is progressing. For example, young children often perceive their parents' affection as a finite resource, and when they observe their parents expressing affection to their siblings, they fear that there won't be enough left for themselves. This implicit belief is thought to fade away as the child becomes more cognitively mature and realizes that a parent's love is not a concrete, tangible commodity and that the old saying is

Figure 6.10 Percentage of Adult Children Seeing Parents or Telecommunicating Weekly

SOURCE: Rubin (2015).

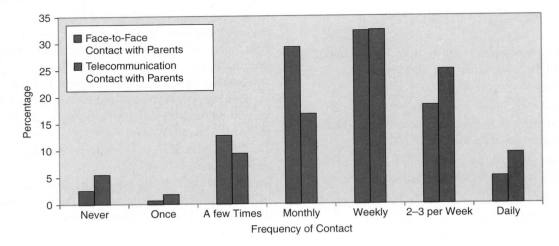

true, that "parents' hearts expand to hold all their children." However, a study by communication researchers Kory Floyd and Mark T. Morman (2005) shows that remnants of this belief still can be found in emerging adulthood:

Middle-aged fathers (average age 51) and their adult sons (average age 23) were asked how much affection the fathers expressed for their sons through either verbal statements (such as saying "I love you"), direct nonverbal gestures (such as hugging or kissing), or supportive behaviors (doing favors for them). The sons' responses depended on how many siblings they had—those who had no siblings reported receiving the most affection from their fathers, and those with many siblings reported receiving the least. In contrast, the fathers' reports of affection expressed toward their sons were not affected by the number of children in the family. Does this show that parental love is spread too thin when one has several children? Not really. What it more likely shows is that there can be real differences between children's perceptions of relationship quality and that of their parents, and that adult children who have to share a parent can believe they are being slighted when the parents' perception is quite different.

Another important component of intergenerational solidarity, according to Bengtson, is consensual solidarity, agreeing on values, attitudes, and beliefs. It is presumed that children will learn these lessons from their parents, but there is also evidence that parents' values, attitudes, and beliefs can be broadened by their adult children. A longitudinal study of older adults in the Netherlands demonstrated that the lifestyles and experiences the adult children introduce to their parents have an effect on the parents' attitudes in late adulthood. Sociologists Anne Rigt-Poortman and Theo van Tilburg (2005) surveyed 1,700 men and women who were between 70 and 100 years of age, asking them about their beliefs concerning gender equality and moral issues. They also asked questions about the unconventional life experiences of their own parents (whether their mothers had been

employed outside the home or either parent had previously been divorced) and their children (whether they had cohabited or divorced, whether their daughters worked or their sons did not work). Older people whose children had cohabited or divorced tended to be more progressive in their beliefs about gender role equality and their moral attitudes toward voluntary childlessness, abortion, and euthanasia than those whose adult children had not cohabited or divorced. Interestingly, the older adults were not influenced by how unconventional their own parents had been, or else they were no longer under the influence of childhood experiences that had occurred 70 or 80 years earlier.

The authors of this study suggested that parents whose adult children are demonstrating unconventional behavior, such as cohabiting or divorcing, face the decision to either change their attitudes or risk distancing themselves from their child. In a larger sense, the authors suggested, the influence young adults have on their parents in this respect is an important mechanism of social change whereby younger members of society, who are more apt to be influenced by cultural change, can pass their attitudes on to the older members of society, thus bringing greater progress to the overall group.

THE EFFECTS OF LATE-LIFE DIVORCE Although the overall divorce rate in the United States has remained stable or even dropped over the last 25 years, the divorce rate among couples 50 years of age and older has doubled. Many of these were remarriages, which are more apt to end in divorce than first marriages, but one-third were couples married 30 years or more and one in 10 were couples who had been married 40 years or more (Stepler, 2017a). Although few, if any, had young children living with them, most had adult children. What are the effects of having parents divorce when you are an adult? Communication researchers Jenna Abetz and Tiffany R. Wang (2017) interviewed 19 adults whose parents had divorced after the participants had moved out of the family home. The age range when they were interviewed was 23–59 years, and their parents had divorced when they were 18–37 years. This qualitative study brought out four problem areas.

Effects of Parent's Divorce During Adulthood

Many of the adult children never saw the signs of unhappiness in their parent's marriages—This was the most common problem area. They remembered happy childhoods and strong family connections.

> (Allison) I still don't have any answers as to like what exactly went wrong in their relationship aside from just interesting comments of, you know we dated for so long it was either get married or not. Yeah, almost like maybe they shouldn't have gotten married in the first place, which is kind of awkward to hear that. You know, I know it is a weird question, but was it ever a good marriage? And that question would have never been asked I think until now. I'm in my own marriage and kind of understanding what it takes for a marriage. And from their perspectives now that they're also removed by many years, was it ever a good marriage or was it always just something that they settled for? (Abetz & Wang, 2017, p. 201)

Taking on new roles, often long-term and not taken on willingly—Another concern of adult children whose parents divorce is centered on the new roles they take on, such as providing emotional or financial support for one parent or another. These new roles were often long-term and not taken on willingly. Participants reported feeling torn between a love for their parents and their own priorities.

> (Caroline) I wish Dad had married again . . . you have to take, like essentially you take responsibility for the parent who doesn't have anybody else, especially, you know, for me in my father's case; he's an only child, both his parents are deceased. He doesn't have a significant other. So when he was in the hospital last week and about to go in for surgery I knew that if something happened I am his advanced directive, which makes me responsible for his life basically if a decision has to be made, And that's a lot for anyone to handle. (p. 202)

Uncertainty about holidays and family events—The adult children in this study remembered the uncertainty they felt about holidays and family events after their parents divorced.

> (Matt) I think the biggest challenge is just trying to negotiate both sides and just trying to make sure that, you know, both parents feel like they have the attention and the relationship that they want, you know. Obviously when they were together that was a lot easier because you could, you know you'd go to visit, you'd visit both of them at the same time. Now it kind of doubles everything and just creates this negotiation that you have to do, you know like for anything, family events and that sort of thing, Christmases and everything like that. (p. 205)

Feeling of being caught in the middle, between two angry parents—The fourth type of reaction the authors of this study found was the feeling of being caught in the middle, between two angry parents.

> (Michelle) My mom is a very emotional person so she called and basically spilled all the information more than I needed to know at the time. And, like I said it made me very resentful towards him and in hindsight I was only hearing one side of the story. (p. 206)

Parents of young children who are going through a divorce are usually careful to keep the children away from their arguments and accusations and to keep their lives as stable as possible. It seems that this consideration should be extended to adult children. Even if they are living away from the family home and have families of their own, the way their divorcing parents behave toward them and the expectations their parents have of them can change their relationships and perceptions of their parents. It can also change their attitudes toward marriage and their own risk of marital problems and divorce (Murray & Kardatzke, 2009).

DEALING WITH ADULT CHILDREN IN CRISIS Unfortunately, not all children outgrow their childhood problems, and others acquire problems in adulthood. What effect does this have on older parents? Is there an age that parents can quit feeling responsible for their children's problems? Apparently not, at least not for most parents. A major cause of distress for middle-aged and older adults is the problems their adult children are having (Fingerman et al., 2017). Children's problems are a primary cause for depressive symptoms and worry in older adults, especially when those problems stem from the adult child's own behavior and lifestyle, such as substance abuse or incarceration (Birditt et al., 2010).

Developmental psychologist Karen L. Fingerman and her colleagues (2012) investigated the cumulative effects of multiple adult children on older parents for both positive and negative events. One general question was whether having a successful child caused an increase in well-being that matched the distress caused by a child with problems. The answer was that successful children did not have the same positive impact on their parents' lives as children with problems had in the negative direction. In other words, parents tend to react to negative events concerning their children more than to positive events. Another question concerned what cumulative effect children with problems and successful children had on their parents. The researchers found that just one child with problems had an effect on the parents' well-being, but that one successful child did not have the same effect—it takes many successful children to have an impact on parents' well-being. Fingerman and her colleagues concluded that the old adage is correct: *Parents are only as happy as their least happy child.*

6.4.3: Grandparent–Grandchild Relationships

OBJECTIVE: Characterize grandparent–grandchild relationships

Families have fewer children today than in generations past, and more older adults are living into late adulthood, which means that more of today's grandchildren and grandparents are enjoying a special relationship that extends into the grandchild's adult years (Antonucci et al., 2007). However, these relationships can differ a lot depending on the age of the grandchildren, the health of the grandparents, the distance between their residences, and many other factors. Still, we have some general information about these relationships.

We know that grandparents spend more time with younger grandchildren, but discuss more personal concerns with older grandchildren (Kemp, 2005). Grandparents report the same affection for their granddaughters as for their grandsons (Mansson & Booth-Butterfield, 2011). Married grandfathers have more interaction with their grandchildren than widowed grandfathers (Knudsen, 2012). About one of four grandparents name at least one adult grandchild in the innermost circle of their social convoy, most often a grandchild that they had an intense relationship with when they were a child (Geurts et al., 2012). In recent decades, grandfathers seem to have joined grandmothers in having nurturing relationships with their grandchildren. This can include being a surrogate parent, financial provider, playmate, advice giver, and family historian (Bates & Goodsell, 2013). Not only is this of benefit to the grandchildren, but it also benefits the grandfather's own mental health and well-being (Bates & Taylor, 2012).

In a study that included interviews with both grandparents and adult grandchildren, sociologist Candace Kemp

(2005) found that adult grandchildren and their grandparents view their relationships as a safety net—a potential source of support that provides security even though it may never be tapped. Both generations reported that they "just knew" that if they needed help, the other would be there for them. Actual help was common also, with grandparents providing college tuition and funds to help adult grandchildren buy homes and grandchildren helping with transportation and household chores. Adult grandchildren represent the future to their grandparents and give them a feeling of accomplishment; grandparents represent the past to their grandchildren, holding the keys to personal history and identity. It seems clear that adult grandchildren and their grandparents are able to build on their early years and develop unique relationships together in adulthood.

In a study several years ago, college students were asked to rank their grandparents according to the time they spent with them, the resources the grandparents shared with them, and the emotional closeness they felt to them. For all three categories, students ranked their mother's mothers the highest, followed by their mother's fathers, their father's mothers, and their father's fathers (DeKay, 2000). The results are shown in Figure 6.11. The same pattern has been found in many similar studies, and I don't think anyone would find it very surprising—in fact, I would have responded the same way about my grandparents at that age. However, psychologists W. Todd DeKay and Todd Shackelford (2000) explained these data using an evolutionary psychology perspective. They argue that the grandparents' rankings reflect the relative confidence each grandparent has, although not always conscious, that the grandchild is truly his or her biological descendant and as a result will carry their genes into a new generation.

Of course I can generate other reasons to explain why the mother's parents are perceived to invest more in the

Figure 6.11 How College Students Rate Their Grandparents

College students rate their maternal grandmothers highest on the time spent together, resources provided, and emotional closeness, followed by maternal grandfathers, paternal grandmothers, and last paternal grandfathers.

SOURCE: From DeKay (2000).

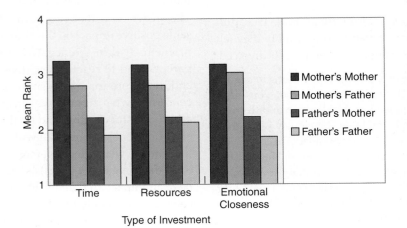

relationship with their grandchildren. Perhaps the young couple settled closer to the wife's parents than the husband's parents and it is due to proximity. Perhaps the mother, as kinkeeper, is more attuned to promoting the relationship between her children and her parents than her husband is with his parents. Perhaps the younger family is more similar to the maternal grandparents in traditions, social practices, and family customs because the wife usually promotes these things. Or perhaps we do base our emotional relationships on the probability that some grandchildren carry our genes and others may not.

CAREGIVING Increasing numbers of grandparents take over the residential care of their grandchildren when the parents are not able to, but many grandparents also serve as informal caregivers when their grandchildren live in single-parent families or families in which both parents work.

This is quite common in my neighborhood, and probably in yours, too. I often pick up my 10-year-old grandson at school, and I notice that the "parent pickup line" can easily be taken for the "grandparent pickup line." Many of the cars waiting for the bell to ring are driven by people my age. And on Lunch with Parents Day these same grandparents are there to have lunch with their grandchildren—most because the parents are at work some distance away and the grandparent is either retired or, in my case, has a more flexible schedule. This is considered *informal care* because the children don't live with us full time and we don't get paid (at least not in money).

Recently attention has turned to the role of grandparents in times of family crisis. Can grandparents "level the playing field" when grandchildren are at risk for social and emotional problems due to the divorce of their parents or subsequent remarriage? And, more timely, can grandparents help fill the gap that occurs when their unmarried daughters have children? In a study of over 900 grandchildren who were emerging adults (18 to 23 years of age), researchers found that those who had lived with a single parent or in stepparent homes had fewer depressive symptoms when they had a strong relationship with a grandparent (Ruiz & Silverstein, 2007). Another study of 324 emerging adults showed that the quality of their relationships with maternal grandmothers predicted their psychological adjustment following their parents' divorce (Henderson et al., 2009).

In a similar study, social work researcher Shalhevet Attar-Schwartz and her colleagues (Attar-Schwartz et al., 2009) questioned over 1,500 high school students in England and Wales, asking about the contact they had with their grandparents and their family structure. Information was also gathered about problems with school conduct and with peers. The kids in single-parent homes had the same level of involvement with their grandparents as kids in two-parent homes. However, when the problems of students in single-parent homes were compared to those of students in two-parent homes, the level of contact with the grandparents became important. Figure 6.12 shows that adolescents in single-parent homes with low levels of involvement with grandparents had more difficulties with school conduct and peers than those who had high levels of involvement with grandparents. According to this research, it is possible for grandparents to "level the playing field," at least for kids who are at risk for social problems as a result of living in single-parent homes.

Figure 6.12 School and Conduct Difficulties Among Teenagers, by Grandparental Involvement

Teenagers who live in single-parent homes have fewer difficulties and distress with school and peers if they have a close relationship with their grandparents. Those in two-parent homes showed few differences in difficulties based on grandparent involvement.

SOURCE: Attar-Schwartz et al. (2009).

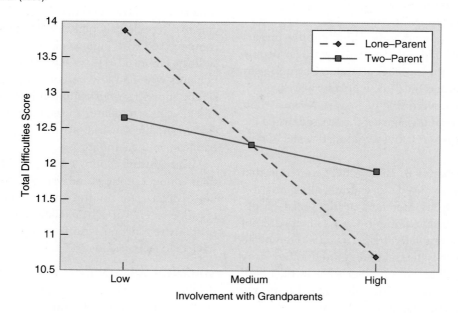

In the studies of at-risk grandchildren faring better when they had a close relationship with grandparents, it is important to reiterate that there was no difference between the grandparent–grandchild relationships for single-parent families and two-parent families. The difference was in the benefits of these relationships in times of trouble. Adolescents and emerging adults from single-parent homes who had close relationships with grandparents were more apt to have fewer social problems than kids from those single-parent homes who were not close to their grandparents.

THE GRANDMOTHER EFFECT   These last studies are good illustrations of a hypothesis offered by evolutionary psychologists and evolutionary anthropologists called the **grandmother effect** (Hawkes et al., 1997). This suggests that the presence of grandmothers (especially maternal grandmothers) has been a predictor of children's survival throughout recorded history. This hypothesis states that the trait of longevity (especially for women) has been favored in our species by natural selection because social groups that had more grandparents had an advantage in that the older members of the group helped with the birthing of the babies and the childcare (nest-tending tasks) and also provided knowledge and wisdom to the younger members of the group, making their survival more likely (Coall & Hertwig, 2011).

One current-day example of the grandmother effect comes from a longitudinal study in the Netherlands that followed three generations of families for 10 years (Kaptin et al., 2010). They found that parents who received childcare assistance from the children's grandparents were more apt to have more children in the next 10 years than parents who did not have this assistance. Because the Netherlands has such a low birthrate, these results were of particular interest in that country, but it also shows how older men and women, past reproductive age themselves, can have an effect on the birthrate of their group.

Another study showed how older people impart important knowledge and wisdom to the younger people in their cultural group. In 2004, a tsunami struck near Thailand and Burma, and the Moken people, who lived on islands near the coast, were able to survive because their elders knew how to read the signs of the sea and urged the group to flee to high ground, thus avoiding disaster (Greve & Bjorklund, 2009).

Anthropologist Sarah B. Hrdy (2011) contends that we mothers have never raised our children alone, that we have always had help by members of our social group, and I believe this is true. Although these helpers are not always kin, one type of related helper who is often available and willing to help is the children's grandmother. Hrdy described a grandmother as "a mother's ace in the hole." I know this describes my grandmother, and I hope my daughters-in-law will say that it describes me.

6.4.4: Relationships with Siblings

OBJECTIVE: Explain how sibling relationships change over time

Our relationships with siblings are the longest-lasting relationships we have. The great majority of adults have at least one living sibling. Descriptions of sibling relationships in everyday conversation range from exceptional closeness, to mutual apathy, to enduring rivalry. Although rivalry and apathy certainly both exist, moderate emotional closeness is the most common pattern. It is really quite unusual for a person to lose contact completely with a sibling in adulthood. Until the late 1990s, research on sibling relationships was limited to childhood and adolescence, but now there is a body of research investigating the importance of this relationship in middle and late adulthood (Suitor et al., 2016).

Adult siblings have better relationships if they feel they have been treated fairly by their parents, with no favoritism (Boll et al., 2005). Their memories of childhood fairness are more important in this regard than current fairness (Suitor et al., 2009). The strongest sibling relationships in adulthood are enjoyed by people who are single and those who have no children (Connidis, 2009). And, if you are a woman who is lucky enough to have a sister (I have three!), it will be no surprise to you that two sisters are the closest, followed by a brother-and-sister pair and then by two brothers. Once again, it is women—mothers, wives, sisters—who are usually the kinkeepers and who usually provide the family with nurturance and emotional support.

Sibling relationships are important in early adulthood in that they can help compensate for poor relationships with parents. Psychologist Avidan Milevsky (2005) surveyed over 200 men and women between the ages of 19 and 33, asking questions about their relationships with their siblings, their parents, and their peers. They were also given questions to measure their loneliness, depression, self-esteem, and life satisfaction. Those who had low support from their parents had significantly higher well-being scores if they were compensated with high levels of social support from their siblings. Figure 6.13 shows the well-being scores for the participants who had low parental support. Those with high sibling support scored significantly lower on the depression and loneliness measures and significantly higher on the self-esteem and life-satisfaction measures than participants who had low sibling support.

Young adult siblings also provide direct support to their younger brothers and sisters; in fact, they are the third line of defense for childrearing, after parents and grandparents (Derby & Ayala, 2013). They demonstrate a high degree of ability to function as surrogate parents, especially if they have help from friends and neighbors.

SIBLINGS AS ADULTS   Relationships with siblings decline in importance during the childrearing years. It is suggested that during this time, adults concentrate on their

Figure 6.13 Measures of Well-Being

Young adults with low levels of parental support score better on four measures of well-being.

SOURCE: Data from Milevsky (2005).

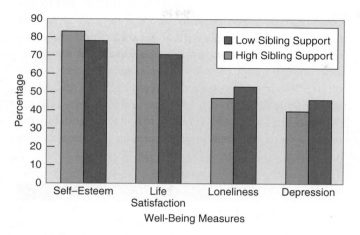

6.5: Friendships in Adulthood

OBJECTIVE: Evaluate the ways friendship circles affect adulthood

Developmental psychologist Dorothy Field (1999) defined **friendship** as "a voluntary social relationship carried out within a social context" (p. 325). She went on to stress the discretionary aspect of friendship; unlike other relationships, it depends not on proximity or blood ties or institutionalized norms, but on personal reasons that vary from individual to individual. As vague as the concept of friendship may be, it is still an important one, and although most of the developmental attention has been focused on friendships in childhood and adolescence, there have been a number of studies in the last decade or so that examine this topic in adulthood.

∨ | **By the end of this module, you will be able to:**

6.5.1 Explain how friendship networks change over time

6.5.2 Analyze the friendship functions of social media

6.5.1: Friendship Networks

OBJECTIVE: Explain how friendship networks change over time

Family networks stay stable in size over adulthood, but friendship networks are large in emerging adulthood and young adulthood as we seek out friends to explore our identities, establish ourselves in the work world, and establish a family of our own. However, once middle age arrives and we are focused on our partners and children, the number of people in our friendship networks starts declining, and that continues until the end of life. Not only do older adults have smaller friendship networks, but they also have less contact with their friends (Antonucci et al., 2009).

Social connection with friends brings us more than just a pleasant way to spend our time. Research in the last few decades has revealed that social connectedness is a leading factor in our health, well-being, and longevity (Carmichael et al., 2015). A number of studies have shown that having poor social connections was a bigger factor in premature death than tobacco use, obesity, and excessive alcohol use (Holt-Lunstad et al., 2010).

Psychologist Cheryl L. Carmichael and her colleagues (2015) located 129 middle-aged adults who had been part of a research study on social relationships when they were university undergraduates. These participants had been assessed again when they were in their 30s. Carmichael and her colleagues asked these participants, who were now in their 50s, to complete an online survey about their current social network. The questions involved the quantity of

children and their careers, leaving little time or energy to foster relationships with siblings. But even when these relationships are not foremost in adults' minds, they remain positive and supportive (Neyer, 2002).

In later adulthood, siblings become central to each other again, intensifying their bonds and offering each other support in their later years. Sociologist Deborah Gold (1996) interviewed a group of older adults about their relationships with their sisters and brothers over their adult years. The respondents were 65 years of age or older, had at least one living sibling, had been married at some point in their lives, had children, and were living independently in the community.

Gold asked about how various life events during adulthood might have contributed to the change in closeness between the sibling pairs. She found that events in early adulthood, especially marriage and the arrival of children, resulted in distance between siblings. In middle adulthood, events tended to bring siblings closer together, especially the deaths of their parents. Late adulthood further increased closeness. Retirement brought more free time to spend together and reunited some siblings whose jobs had required them to live far apart. Loss of spouse or illness brought siblings to help "fill in the blanks." Finally, in older adulthood, some siblings reported being the only surviving members of their family of origin and the only ones to share family memories.

To be fair, 18% of the respondents reported becoming more emotionally distant from their siblings with time. Some went through the typical distancing in early adulthood and never got back together; others had hoped life events would bring renewed closeness and were disappointed that they did not, especially when they had anticipated more help during bad times such as widowhood or illness.

friends they had (number) and the quality of those friendships (how close they were). Comparing the responses to those they had given in their 20s and in their 30s, the researchers found that both the quantity and quality of their social relationships predicted their social relationships in their 50s and also their psychological well-being. Those who had more friends and closer friendships in young adulthood were more apt to be less lonely and depressed in middle age.

Attachment theory has also been applied to friendships. Young adults who are identified as being insecurely attached (either preoccupied/anxious or dismissing/avoidant) reported that they felt less close to the members of their friendship group than those who had more secure attachment styles (preoccupied/anxious). Gallath and colleagues (2017) concluded that those with preoccupied/anxious attachment may perceive their friends as less close because they have a high desire for acceptance and excessive reassurance and that they actually pushed people away with their need for closeness. People with a dismissing/avoidant attachment style, who worry about trust and reliance, may strive not to depend on their friends lest they be disappointed. These findings on friendship ties show that attachment style not only extends into adulthood in terms of romantic relationships, but also friendships.

In later life, friendship networks are also important to health. Older people who have a good number of friends are better able to deal with age-related health problems and less likely to suffer from physical health problems and early death (Smith & Christakis, 2008). Having friends in later adulthood brings material aid, instrumental aid, and problem-solving help. It also provides emotional support, self-esteem, a sense of being important to others, and a decreased risk of mental health disorders. Physical health is also enhanced due to social contact. Studies show that receiving social support reduces blood pressure and lowers stress-related hormones (Cornwell & Shafer, 2016).

FRIENDSHIP FACTORS AND INFLUENCES Factors that influence friendship networks throughout adulthood are gender, race, and education. Women have larger friendship networks than men at all age levels, and women are more often named as friends by both other women and men. When asked which friends they receive support from, women typically name a number of people; men tend to name their wives. African American people have smaller friendship groups that contain more family members, but they have more contact with them than do white people. People in higher socioeconomic groups have larger numbers of overall friends, but the same number of close friends as people in lower socioeconomic groups. And men with professional jobs have friends from a wider geographic area than men who are skilled workers (Ajrouch et al., 2005).

Most of this research is based on the benefits one receives from their friendship network, but there are also physical, emotional, and social benefits one gets from giving support to friends. A few studies show that the most rewarding type of giving happens when it is freely chosen and when it is perceived to be effective (Inagaki & Orchek, 2017).

Researchers have found that friendships are not totally positive and worry-free. Although it is not a surprise that people would feel ambivalent about some family relationships, or even about one's spouse because those are generally constant members of one's social convoy, some people report that friends can cause mixed feelings, especially when they give unasked-for support and unsolicited advice. These feelings are not bad enough to end the friendship, but can be a source of stress in a relationship that should serve as protection from stress (Krause, 2007).

WRITING PROMPT

Your Own Network

How does each member of your social network provide support? What type of support do you provide for them?

 The response entered here will appear in the performance dashboard and can be viewed by your instructor.

Submit

6.5.2: Social Media Friends

OBJECTIVE: Analyze the friendship functions of social media

Another type of friendship is through social media, which allows users to interact with others from the comfort of their computers or smartphones. It gives the benefit of widening our social networks to include those we could seldom have face-to-face conversations with because of the distance, and also those we only want a brief word with every now and then (see 'Adult and Social Media').

I was fortunate that my father was interested in technology and was an early user of e-mail when he was in his 80s. He had complained that he had no male friends left—they had either died or moved away to be with relatives. He kept busy driving my mother and her women friends to water aerobics and to their Red Hat luncheons, and they even made him an honorary member, but he missed his buddies. With e-mail, he was able to connect with his brother, who lived 60 miles away and no longer drove. He also was in touch with a golfing friend who had moved across the country to live with his daughter and with his brother-in-law who was several states away taking care of his wife with dementia. Another benefit (to me) was that his hearing difficulties did not interfere with e-mail like they did with telephone conversations. He had lost the ability to hear high-pitched voices, and he had four daughters. So for the last years of his life our family felt blessed with social technology.

Adults and Social Media

Social Media Sites

Social media sites began around 2000 and became popular quickly with adolescents and young adults, but adults of all ages use it now. Figure 6.14 shows how social media use has increased for all ages of adults in the last decade (Pew Research Center, 2017).

Facebook

The most popular social media site as of this writing is Facebook. I admit to being a big fan of this 21st century way of relating to friends and family members. My husband and I come from large families and have many relatives, most of whom live hundreds of miles away. Facebook gives us a way to keep up with our siblings and also our 21 nieces and nephews (and their spouses and children). We also enjoy being "friends" with some of our former students as they start careers and families. If we look at adults in the United States who have Internet access, we find that over three-fourths of adults use Facebook. Figure 6.15 breaks this down by age and also shows the age breakdown for four other social media sites. For all of these modes of social communication, younger adults take the lead, followed by middle-aged adults and older adults (Greenwood et al., 2017).

Some younger adults report being "frazzled" by Facebook, especially college females who, compared to college males, report spending more time than intended on Facebook, losing sleep because of Facebook, feeling closer to Facebook friends than "real-life" friends, and generally feeling addicted (Thompson & Lougheed, 2012). More than half of all Facebook users report having voluntarily taken a

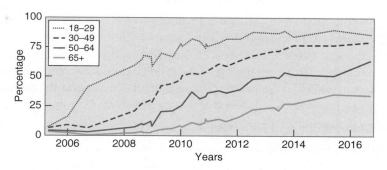

Figure 6.14 Social Media Use Has Increased in the Last Decade for Every Age Group in the United States

SOURCE: Pew Research Center (2017).

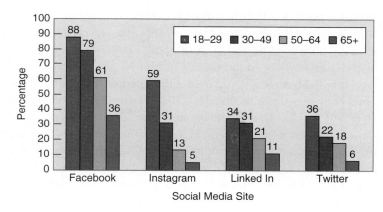

Figure 6.15 Younger Adults Use Every Type of Social Media More Than Older Adults

SOURCE: Greenwood et al. (2017).

break from using Facebook for several weeks or more (Rainie et al., 2013). However, researchers who reviewed 65 peer-reviewed articles pertaining to Facebook use found no relationship between time spent on Facebook or number of Facebook friends and depression (Frost & Rickwood, 2017).

Young Adults and Facebook

Many of my older friends comment that "kids today" are becoming socially isolated because they spend all their time on their phones and don't interact face-to-face anymore. Well, research proves that to be wrong. Several studies have found that most people who spend a lot of time using social media also spend a lot of time with face-to-face interactions (Anderson et al., 2012). Adults with anxious attachment styles (involving fear of rejection) report higher use of Facebook, and as a result of this social connectedness, report an increase in relationship satisfaction (Spradlin et al., 2019). This says to me that Facebook is not simply a way that shy and lonely people can have social interactions without face-to-face contact. People who are social enjoy face-to-face contact and social networking. People who are not social tend to do neither.

For the downside, a meta-analysis of data from over 100,000 adolescents and young adults show that the more time a young person spends on social media, the lower their grade point average, especially for college students and women (Liu et al., 2017). Psychologists Rachel L. Frost and Debra J. Rickwood (2017) reviewed 65 peer-reviewed articles on the effects of social media use and mental health outcomes. They found two disorders that were strongly related to social media use in a number of studies with high school and college students. One was alcohol-related behavior, which was correlated with both number of friends on Facebook and time spent on Facebook. Those who had the highest number of friends and who spent the most time on Facebook were more apt to reference alcohol use in their Facebook posts and also more apt to use alcohol, have alcohol-related problems, and engage in binge drinking. The other was body-image and disordered eating. Young people who use Facebook more had lower body satisfaction than nonusers, and this was true for men as well as women. They also were more apt to have disordered-eating attitudes, a drive for thinness, and posts that express body shame.

Middle-Aged Adults and Facebook

Middle-aged adults often use Facebook to feel close to their young adult children, and although that sounds intrusive, a recent study showed that most adult children did not consider it an invasion of their privacy and felt that it actually enhanced the closeness between the parent and adult child (Kanter et al., 2012). More skeptical researchers suggested that adult children accept their parents' friend requests because they can't easily decline due to the power differential between parent and child. Some even suggest that the increase in the number of young people using Twitter, Instagram, and other social media sites is due to the increase of parents (and grandparents) using Facebook (Wiederhold, 2012).

Older Adults and Facebook

Older adults use Facebook, but similar to the content of their social convoys, their "friends" lists contain more family members than actual friends. Just over a third of people 65 years of age and older use Facebook, but researchers hope that as this number increases, it will provide social contacts at a time when mobility might be limited and friends may be far away. It also could reduce loneliness, strengthen intergenerational ties, and make it easier for an older person to remain in his or her own home (Cornwell & Schafer, 2016).

SOCIAL MEDIA AROUND THE WORLD It came as a surprise to me to learn that a larger proportion of people who have Internet access in developing countries, such as Indonesia (90%), Malaysia (85%), and Nigeria (85%), are more likely to use social media than people in developed countries, such as the U.S. (71%), Japan (51%), and Germany (50%). This is shown in Figure 6.16. Foreign policy researcher Jacob Poushter (2016) suggests that the people in developing countries are hungry for social interaction and have limited opportunity for face-to-face communication due to poverty, lack of transportation, and distances between towns. There is an age gap in social media use in countries all over the world, developed or developing, with adults under age 35 using it significantly more than those over 35.

To end on a high note (because I am a big fan of social media), I'd like to share a study done by an international team of researchers. They were interested in whether online relationships would help reduce prejudice between groups previously in conflict. They chose 374 university students in Serbia, Cyprus, and Croatia, who had been in the ethnic majority (Serbs, Greek Cypriots, and Croats, respectively)

Figure 6.16 Social Networking Popular Among Global Internet Users
SOURCE: Poushter (2016).

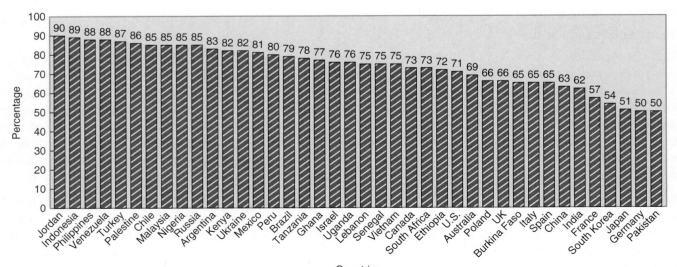

in their countries. They were questioned about their contact with people who were in the ethnic minorities in their countries (Albanians, Turkish Cypriots, and Serbs, respectively), both face-to-face or online. Then they were asked questions about anxiety they might feel in the presence of a large number of people from the ethnic minority, how much threat they perceived from the ethnic minority, and positive attitudes toward the ethnic minority. The results showed that online relationships contributed to more positive feelings toward the minority group in their countries, over and above the contribution made by face-to-face contacts.

This was true for the overall group and, separately, for the participants in each country. The authors agree that direct, face-to-face contact would be ideal for reaching agreements and achieving a deep level of understanding between the two groups who have a history of conflict, but when that is not possible, social networking sites provide an opportunity to communicate between opposing groups (Žeželj et al., 2017).

Many changes occur in all kinds of relationships over the adult years. We conclude with a table of changes that occur in major types of relationships over the adult years.

Review of Changes in Relationships over Adulthood

Characteristic	18–24 Years	25–39 Years	40–64 Years	65–74 Years	75+ Years
Intimate and Long-term Relationships	Intimate relationships take the form of dating or cohabitation. Partners are chosen based on strong feelings of lust and attraction and also suitability for short-term relationships. Early attachment styles may influence romantic relationships. Use of online dating sites is at a peak.	Long-term partners are often chosen based on physical attractiveness (by men) and resources and status (by women). Many cohabitation relationships become marriages. Negative interactions between spouses can result in unhappy marriages and divorce. Cohabitation after commitment often leads to happy marriages, especially if the culture has progressive ideas about women and religion. Highest percent identify as LGBT+.	Many couples in long-term marriages report still being intensely in love. Couples in unhappy long-term marriages have worse health and well-being than those who have divorced. Divorce is common, as is remarriage. Cohabitation is rare, but increasing.	Marriages are highest in satisfaction and psychological intimacy, lowest in conflict in the empty-nest years. Divorce rate is low, although many start new relationships after death of spouse.	Many are widowed, especially women, but most have adjusted by increasing the intensity of friendship group and family relationships. Lowest percent identify as LGBT+.
Social Networks	Social networks include mothers and friends from school. Other support comes through social media.	Social networks include parents and other family members, spouses, neighbors, colleagues from work, children, and social media.	Social networks narrow somewhat to include family, closer friends, and coworkers. Grandparenting begins for many.	Social networks no longer include parents and coworkers for most. Grandchildren are prominent.	Social networks are small but close and consist mostly of family members, often adult grandchildren who were close as children.

Summary: Social Relationships

6.1 Theories of Social Relationships

OBJECTIVE: Compare theories of social relationships

- Attachment theory was originally formulated to explain the relationship between infants and their parents. Subsequent hypotheses suggested that the attachments formed in infancy were relatively permanent and were reflected in other relationships later in life.

- Other theories of social relationships include the convoy model, which considers the group of significant people who travel with us in our lives at different points in time. Socioemotional theory states that as people grow older, they prefer to have a few close, emotional relationships instead of many more casual relationships. Another explanation for the importance of social relationships is provided by evolutionary psychology, stating that the tendency to bond together with similar people is a genetic mechanism passed down from our primitive ancestors because it contributed to their survival and reproductive success.

6.2 Establishing an Intimate Partnership

OBJECTIVE: **Determine how people choose intimate partners**

- Almost all adults experience relationships with intimate partners, and the formalization of intimate partnerships is found in all cultures. Most people of the world select their own partners. Some social scientists hypothesize that establishing an intimate partnership is a process that includes the lust system, the attraction system, and the attachment system, each involving a separate neurotransmitter system and pattern of brain activity.

- The relationship with an intimate partner is typically the most central relationship in adulthood. The process of partner selection has been explained traditionally by filter theory and exchange theory. More recently, evolutionary psychology suggests that people are attracted to others based on physical signs of good health and potential reproductive success.

6.3 Living in Intimate Partnerships

OBJECTIVE: **Evaluate the impact of intimate partnership on adulthood experiences**

- Attachment theory has also been used to explain success in creating romantic relationships. People who are classified as secure in their attachment in childhood will also have longer-lasting, happier romantic relationships than those who are in other, less secure categories.

- Longitudinal studies of couples that begin before marriage show early predictors of problem marriages, even during the engagement period. These include negative interactions, insults, lack of emotional support, and sarcasm, which result in unhappy relationships and ultimately divorce.

- Many couples cohabit before marriage, and they have higher divorce rates and lower levels of marital happiness than couples who marry without cohabiting. However, when couples commit to marry and then cohabit as an engaged couple, they have marriages as happy and long-lasting as couples who marry without cohabiting. The difference in happiness between married and cohabiting couples often depends on how the culture views women's roles and religion.

- About 3–4% of the population identifies themselves as gay, lesbian, bisexual, or transgender. Recently same-sex couples have been able to marry in the United States and other countries, and others have participated in commitment ceremonies to formalize their intimate partnership. Recent research on the relationships of same-sex couples shows that there are more similarities than differences when they are compared to heterosexual couples.

6.4 Relationships with Other Family Members

OBJECTIVE: **Analyze the ways that family interactions influence adulthood experiences**

- Interactions with adults and their parents occur at high and relatively constant levels throughout adulthood. Most parents and adult children have daily contact and 85% have at least weekly contact with each other. This increase is due to the convenience and affordability of communication technology, such as cell phones, texting, and e-mail.

- Late-life divorces are increasing, and a new issue for young and middle-aged adults is dealing with parental divorce. The problem has proved to be a serious one for many due to the realization that their memories of a happy family may have been faulty, the new roles they have to take on with their parents, the uncertainty about family traditions and holidays, and feeling caught in the middle between angry parents.

- The problems of one's children are always a cause for concern, even when the children are adults. Major causes of distress for older parents are children's divorces, financial problems, and drug or alcohol problems. Even one child with problems causes late-life distress.

- For the present generation, the grandparenting role is very broad and depends on many factors, such as the ages of the grandparent and grandchild, the distance between homes, and the relationship of the grandparents and the children's parents. Maternal grandparents are usually closer than paternal grandparents, especially if parents divorce. African American grandparents, especially grandmothers, have a more central role in the family than white grandparents.

- The relationship with maternal grandmothers is considered closest by their grandchildren, followed by maternal grandfathers, paternal grandmothers, and paternal grandfathers.

- Studies have shown that good relationships with grandparents can level the playing field for emerging adults who are at risk for social problems. Evolutionary psychology suggests a grandmother effect, pointing out that children with living grandmothers have been more apt to survive into adulthood throughout recorded history.

- In emerging adulthood and young adulthood, siblings may compensate for low parental support. Siblings often enjoy close relationships in adulthood, especially if they feel they have been treated fairly by their parents in childhood. Strongest sibling relationships are between sisters and those who are single or have no children. Sibling relationships are strongest in late adulthood.

6.5 Friendships in Adulthood

OBJECTIVE: Evaluate the ways friendship circles affect adulthood

- Friendships are important in emerging adulthood and young adulthood. Family relationships remain stable over the adult years, but the numbers of personal friends and acquaintances decline. Emerging adults and young adults count Facebook friends as part of their social networks. Middle-aged adults and older adults tend to use social media to interact with family members.

Social Relationships

Consider this chapter's discussion of the way friendships and other relationships change over time. What changes have you experienced in your own relationships over the past few years? What changes have you observed in relationships among family members? Write a short response that your classmates will read. Be sure to discuss specific examples.

 A minimum number of characters is required to post and earn points. After posting, your response can be viewed by your class and instructor, and you can participate in the class discussion.

Post

0 characters I 140 minimum

Chapter 7
Work and Retirement

A designer works for a fashion agency.

Learning Objectives

7.1 Analyze the relationship between adulthood and work

7.2 Describe sociocultural influences on career choice

7.3 Relate age to workplace experiences

7.4 Analyze the relationship between work and personal life

7.5 Evaluate retirement practices

A Word From the Author

Work World Then and Now

My husband has worked in the same job for over 40 years. It was the first job he took after graduate school, and he plans to retire from it in the next few years. So you can imagine the surprise when our daughter came home a few years ago to introduce us to her new boyfriend, Vinnie, who at 30 was on his third job since graduating from college. Once we got over the shock, we realized that in all other respects, he was a great guy. He was bright and hardworking.

He was happy to meet our large extended family and got thumbs-up ratings from all of them—young and old. He pitched in with the dishes on Sunday night, and he was a Red Sox fan. Best of all, he seemed to adore Heidi. As we got to know him, we realized that his career choice, Web designer, was very different from being a tenured professor. First, Vinnie didn't exactly work in an office. He worked at home and sometimes he worked at our house on his laptop when an emergency came up and he was visiting. Second, he didn't exactly have one job. He worked for an agency and had his own clients, too.

His coworkers changed frequently. Some lived in the same south Florida town Vinnie and Heidi live in and some worked online from distant places, like Boulder, Colorado. During their dating era, he changed jobs again and then while they were engaged, he started his own company. Now that they are married and have a new baby, he has taken on some work from his original employer to supplement the work he does for his own company. We have become very attached to our new son-in-law and see him as a good partner for our daughter and a good father to our new granddaughter, Amelia, but we have learned a lot.

Vinnie is not alone in his career path. Many of today's careers are not linear. The old idea of finding the right job and sticking with it doesn't always apply to today's young adults. It is safe to say that not one of our grandchildren will be like my husband, entering a job after graduation and staying there until retirement. Their work world is different and so are they.

This chapter is about work—its importance in our lives, how we choose careers, how careers are affected by age, how we balance career and personal life, and how we plan for and adjust to retirement.

7.1: The Importance of Work in Adulthood

OBJECTIVE: Analyze the relationship between adulthood and work

For most of us, our jobs occupy a hefty portion of our time, our thoughts, and our emotions. They determine in large part where we live, how well we live, and with whom we spend time—even after working hours. On another level, our jobs are incorporated into our identity and contribute to our self-esteem. The role of worker is not a static one; over the years, changes take place in the economy, technology, workforce composition, and social climate. Individuals change too; we go from intern to full-fledged professional as a result of attaining a degree. We go from full-time paid worker to full-time unpaid caregiver as the result of new parenthood. We go from work to retirement as a function of age. We go from retirement to part-time work when we find that the days are too long or the expenses of retirement are higher than we thought. These various work situations over the years of adulthood can be summed up in the term **career**—the patterns and sequences of occupations or related roles held by people across their working lives and into retirement.

This chapter includes a discussion of some of the major theories of career development, which reflect how careers have changed in the last century. It also covers how patterns of work are different for men and women, how the work experience changes with age, and the interaction of work and personal life. Finally, the chapter discusses retirement, which, it may surprise you to find out, is not simply the opposite of work.

∨ By the end of this module, you will be able to:

7.1.1 Describe theories of career development

7.1.2 Differentiate career patterns by binary gender

7.1.1: Theories of Career Development

OBJECTIVE: Describe theories of career development

Early theories of career development date back to the beginning of the 20th century when Frank Parsons (1909) first wrote about **person–environment fit**, stating that people will be more successful if they work in a field for which they are talented rather than taking a job for other reasons, such as following parents in the family business or filling a job that happens to be vacant at the right time. Later, David Super (1957) introduced the **life-span/life-space theory** of careers based on the concept that individuals develop careers in stages, and that career decisions are not isolated from other aspects of their lives. Along with a person's ability and talents, vocational counselors (not to mention individuals who are evaluating their own career paths) need to consider the relative importance of school, work, home, family, community, and leisure. Super created a number of career-development tests to assess individuals' career adjustment, interests, and values (Wang & Wanberg, 2017).

Vocational interests were the main focus of a theory by John Holland (1958). Holland divided vocational interests into six areas—social, investigative, realistic, enterprising, artistic, and conventional—sometimes abbreviated as SIREAC types (Figure 7.1).

Holland's theory is the basis of numerous tests given today by guidance counselors and vocational counselors. Most of these tests ask whether you like, dislike, or are indifferent to a long list of school subjects, activities, amusements, situations, types of people, and jobs. Your answers are converted into six scores, one for each type. The top three scores define your vocational interest type. For example, if you score highest on social (S), investigative (I), and artistic (A) factors, your vocational type would be identified as "SIA." This would help you (or your career planner) to consider a career that would be

Figure 7.1 Holland's Six Basic Types of Vocational Interests

SOURCE: Holland (1992).

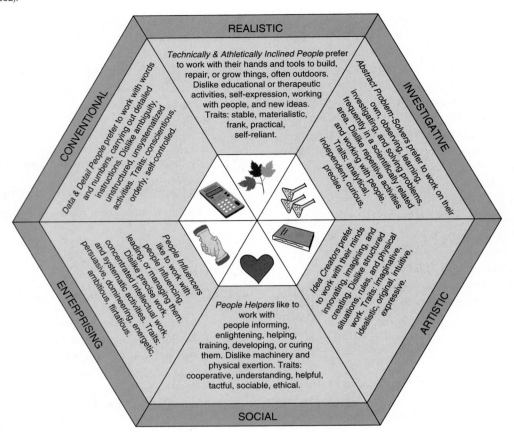

a good fit with your vocational interests (Holland, 1973, 1997). These tests are also available for free on the Internet by searching "career tests." One site recently reported that over 689,000 people had taken its test in the past 30 days, so Holland's theory is still helping people make wise career decisions.

The last theory I discuss here is Albert Bandura's (1991) **social-cognitive theory**, which is often applied to career development. Based on the concept of **self-efficacy**, or the belief in one's ability to succeed, this theory suggests that there is more to career success than selecting the type of job or career track that most closely matches your own abilities and interests (Lent et al., 1994). You also need to be proactive, believe in yourself, be self-regulated and self-motivated, and focus on your goals (Bindl et al., 2012).

The 1990s and 2000s brought big changes in the workplace, including globalization, downsizing, technological change, an increase in women entering (or returning to) the workplace, and organization restructuring. It became clear that employees could not depend on their employers to give them lifelong work or to look out for their best interests. There was more to career success than just selecting the right place to work. Now theories of career development

are *protean*, which means versatile and open to change, and *boundaryless*, which means, of course, without boundaries. People can develop careers that do not have to follow a specific pathway delineated by their employers; they can consider their own values, family responsibilities, sense of personal identity, and optimal level of job satisfaction. Careers are not subject to cultural or gender boundaries, and they do not have to progress, in terms of the worker getting higher and higher on the ladder of success or income (Briscoe & Hall, 2006).

7.1.2: Gender Differences in Career Patterns

OBJECTIVE: Differentiate career patterns by binary gender

The first big distinction in career patterns is between the work lives of men and women. Although women are now represented in all major fields of work, and men and women may perform their jobs equally well, gender is still a big factor in almost all aspects of careers. Knowing a person's gender predicts a lot about their career pattern.

How Are the Career Paths of Men and Women Different?

More men work full time than women—Figure 7.2 shows the difference in the percentage of men and women who hold full-time jobs. Why do more men work full-time than women? It's partly because of demographics; older people aren't as apt to work full time as younger people, and there are more women in older age groups than men. Another reason is a combination of biological and social factors. It is difficult for both parents of young children to work full time, and the mother is usually the spouse to quit her job or reduce her work schedule when a child is born or while children are young.

Men stay in full-time jobs longer than do women—Men usually start their work careers with full-time jobs and keep working full time until they retire. If their career is interrupted, it is usually due to being laid off and being unable to find another job. Women, on the other hand, are more apt to start working full time, leave the workforce when a child is born, go back to part-time work when the child is a few years old, perhaps stop again for a second child, and then go back to full-time work when the children are older. Women are also more apt to leave their own jobs when their spouses are transferred to another location, a situation that often leads to a period of unemployment before finding a new job.

Women are more apt to work in part-time jobs than men—This type of nonstandard work schedule is predominantly filled by women in the United States and worldwide. In the United States, 25% of women who work hold part-time jobs, compared to only 12% of men (U.S. Bureau of Labor Statistics, 2017c). While this type of work schedule may seem ideal for women who want to combine work and family, the downside is that most of these jobs are in the service sector and feature lower wages and fewer benefits.

One of the major impacts of men and women having different career paths is that women's career discontinuities result in lower salaries and lack of job advancement. Due to these (and other) factors, women earn less money than men even when they work full time. According to the U.S. Bureau of Labor Statistics (2017e), women's salaries average only 81% of men's salaries.

Having jobs with lower salaries, fewer benefits, and less chance for advancement, combined with moving from full- to part-time jobs to unpaid leaves of absence, has an obvious effect on women's career paths and financial security (and of course their family's financial security).

WRITING PROMPT

Gender Differences in Work

In your family, are there notable gender differences in work (i.e. who works full time, part time, or not at all)? What might be the cause of these differences? What might be an effective strategy to reduce such differences?

▶ The response entered here will appear in the performance dashboard and can be viewed by your instructor.

Submit

Figure 7.2 Percentage of Men and Women Over Age 16 in the United States that Hold Full-Time Jobs

As you can see, fewer women hold full-time jobs than men, but the difference is becoming smaller. Currently, about 65% of men and about 54% of women work full time.

SOURCE: U.S. Bureau of Labor Statistics (2017f).

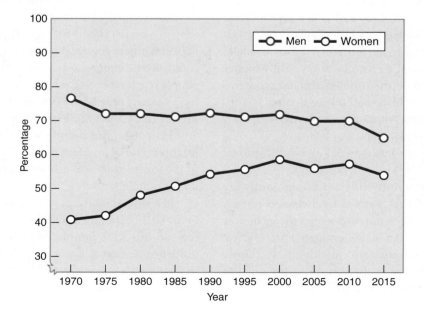

7.2: Selecting a Career

OBJECTIVE: Describe sociocultural influences on career choice

Selecting a career is not simply one big decision. As Super's theory suggests, careers develop over many years, and the path is not always linear. We may ask children, "What do you want to be when you grow up?" However, it is not that simple. Not many of us are working in the jobs we aspired to when we were children, or even the fields we thought of when we declared a major in college. Our careers depend on our interests and abilities, the education and training available (and affordable), the job market, the economy, and how welcoming certain professions are to people of our gender, race, and age. The following is a discussion of some of those twists, turns, and roadblocks on the career pathway.

> ⌄   **By the end of this module, you will be able to:**

7.2.1   Summarize the effects of gender on work experiences

7.2.2   Relate family to career choices

7.2.1: The Effects of Gender

OBJECTIVE: Summarize the effects of gender on work experiences

Gender is one of the major factors in career choice. Although there are few if any occupations that are not filled by both men and women, there is still a stereotype of "his and her" jobs, a social phenomenon known as **occupational gender segregation**. This doesn't mean that young men and women are routinely told in so many words that they should take certain jobs, but there is unspoken pressure to conform to what they see around them (Eagly & Wood, 2012). This is a particular problem for women, and it is a prime factor contributing to women's lower earnings (Bayard et al., 2003) and their lack of resources in the retirement years (Costello et al., 2003). The traditional men's jobs are typically higher in both status and income than the traditional women's jobs. These "his" jobs are also more likely to offer health-care benefits and pensions. Although women make up 47% of the labor force, they make up 60% of low-wage workers, defined as those who make less than $11 an hour (National Women's Law Center, 2017).

Many of the occupations filled predominantly by women are in helping fields, such as teachers and nurses. These require college degrees, but do not offer the income or chances for advancement that male-dominated professions, such as school administrators and doctors, have. Other women-dominated jobs are in the service sector, such as hairdressers and housekeepers (Figure 7.3).

Included in the male-dominated occupations are careers in the physical sciences, technology, engineering, and mathematics—known as the STEM areas. Twice as many men work in the physical sciences than women, three times as many men work in mathematics and computer sciences than women, and five times as many men work in engineering than women (U.S. Bureau of Labor Statistics, 2017d). Not only does this contribute to salary inequities for women, but it also means that our country (and the world) is not benefiting from the potential contributions of over half the population in these important fields. At a time that science and technology is being called on to solve problems such as global climate change, food resource scarcity, and our dependence on fossil fuel, we could use the full talents of both genders.

GENDER AND WORK INTERESTS   Despite laws against gender discrimination in the workplace, an increase in the number of women graduating from college, and research showing few gender-specific job abilities, occupational gender segregation remains a puzzle to vocational psychologists and others. Why are young men and women still choosing to go into "his and hers" jobs?

One answer is that, although there are not many differences in work-related skills and abilities, *there may be gender differences in work-related interests*. Vocational psychologist James Rounds and his colleagues (Su et al., 2009) conducted a meta-analysis of the results of vocational preference tests for over 500,000 emerging and young adults and found that women tend to be more interested in working with people and men tend to be more interested in working with things. Using the vocational interest categories that Holland devised (see Figure 7.1), Rounds and his colleagues found that the largest differences were that women scored higher on the social (S) factors and men scored higher on the realistic (R) factors. There were smaller but significant gender differences on the artistic (A) and conventional (C) factors in favor of women and the investigative (I) and enterprising (E) factors for men. While this could mean that there are innate gender differences in vocational interests, it could also be interpreted as showing that by the time young people reach emerging adulthood and start thinking about their careers, they have internalized the gender stereotypes presented by their families, teachers, and friends. Rounds and his colleagues point out that if this is true, parents, teachers, and counselors need to start addressing the topic in the lower grades of school before children's vocational interests stabilize.

In a similar study, psychologists Itamar Gati and Maya Perez (2014) examined data from over 37,000 young adults (age 18–20) who completed an in-depth Internet career-guidance session to see what gender differences appeared in their vocational interests. They also compared the results with a similar study done 20 years before (Gati et al., 1995).

Figure 7.3 Jobs Most Often Filled by Women

In these 13 jobs, women constitute 90% or more of the workers.

SOURCE: Data from U.S. Bureau of Labor Statistics (2017d).

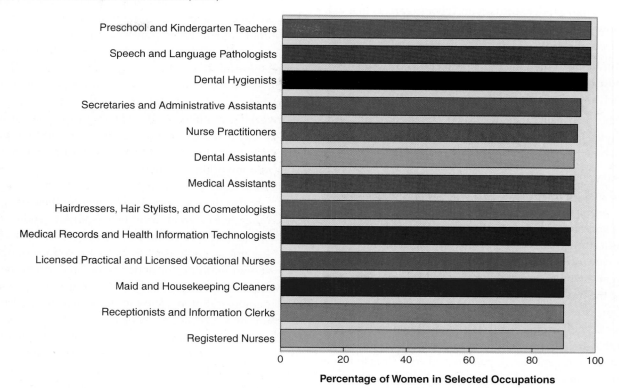

Percentage of Women in Selected Occupations

They found continued gender differences in one-third of the career aspects tested. Significantly more men still preferred STEM careers; significantly more women preferred conventional working hours, working with people, using artistic abilities, and jobs in the mental health and community service fields. More men still preferred jobs with high levels of income, but the gap was only half what it was in the previous study. Several gender differences had disappeared in the 20 years between studies. There were no longer significant differences in the number of men and women preferring careers that offered professional advancement and involved using negotiation and management skills, independence, and authoritativeness. The authors concluded that gender stereotypes still affect career preferences and career choice. While a number of men and women in these studies express preferences for careers that do not conform to gender stereotypes, there are still significant gender differences in many aspects of career preferences. These differences are more detrimental to women because, as mentioned before, the jobs they tend to prefer pay less, have fewer job benefits, and have less opportunity for advancement.

ANTICIPATING CAREER PATTERNS A second possibility for occupational gender segregation is that *men and women anticipate different career patterns*. One difference between men's and women's career decisions is that men

usually plan to work steadily until retirement, and women often plan to move in and out of the paid workforce as they have children. Women also choose jobs that have regular hours and fewer demands that would interfere with family life. For example, even though women are graduating from medical school and law school in record numbers, they are choosing specialties within those fields—anesthesiology, dermatology, real estate law, family law—that feature more regular work schedules but often lower salaries.

When people enter nontraditional occupations, it is women who are more likely than men to cross the gender segregation line. This reminds me of an extension of childhood gender roles when most toddler girls will play with both stereotypical female and male toys while toddler boys stick to stereotypical male toys (Ruble et al., 2006). A few studies have looked into women in nontraditional careers. For example, counseling psychologists Julia A. Ericksen and Donna E. Palladino Schultheiss (2009) reported that women in trades (such as painters, plumbers, and electricians) and construction jobs report having family members and mentors who encouraged them. Others felt they had a natural ability for this type of work and were independent enough not to be discouraged by other people's opinions. Not surprisingly, many of the women had a very strong sense of self; they were confident, self-assured, and comfortable with their career choices.

Men enter nontraditional occupations for a variety of reasons:

- Men who are young adults are more apt to express egalitarian gender attitudes and choose careers that will allow them time to spend with their children (Pedulla & Thébaud, 2015).
- Middle-aged men may have been laid off from jobs in industry and see growth in nontraditional-gender jobs such as health care.
- Other men realize that they may not be able to continue in physically strenuous jobs after middle age, so they switch to something less physically demanding (Semuels, 2017).

Interestingly, men who enter health care tend to gravitate toward less patient-centric jobs, such as home health-care aides, preferring more technical jobs, such as surgical technicians and radiology technicians (Dill et al., 2016).

As a strong believer in personal choice, it is difficult for me to view occupational gender segregation as a problem if men and women are making free and informed choices. Rather, the problem arises when these young people bow to social pressures to conform to gender stereotypes. It seems that some good suggestions have been offered by researchers in this area. Expose children to vocational possibilities at younger ages, encourage parents and educators to foster children's interests and talents regardless of gender, and make the workplace more family-friendly so that women (and men) don't have to choose between being a good parent and following their career dreams.

7.2.2: Family Influences

OBJECTIVE: Relate family to career choices

Families affect career choice in several ways. First, families can openly encourage their children to have high career aspirations, which includes support for higher education and vocational training. Middle-class parents are far more likely than working-class parents to encourage their children to attend college and to be engaged in their children's education. This is not just an ability difference in disguise. Even when you compare groups of high school students who are matched in terms of grades or test scores, it is still true that the students from middle-class families are more likely to aspire to further education and better-paying, higher-prestige jobs than their working-class peers (Tynkkynen et al., 2012).

Families can also affect the career choices of their children through the roles they model. This is especially true of mothers and daughters. Economics and business researcher Kathleen L. McGinn and her colleagues (McGinn et al., 2017) gathered survey data from adults age 18–60 from 24 countries that were part of the International Social Survey Programme to determine the effects of maternal employment on the gender attitudes and gender roles of

their children. Respondents answered questions about their family life, work life, roles, children, household management, partnerships, and income in the first wave, then again 10 years later. Results showed that women whose mothers had worked outside the home when they were children were more apt to be employed themselves than women whose mothers had not worked outside the home. Furthermore, these adult daughters of working mothers who were employed were more apt to have supervisory jobs, work more hours, and earn more money than the daughters of nonworking mothers. And what about the sons of working mothers? If they are fathers, they support their wives' careers by spending more time caring for the children than sons of nonworking mothers.

Aside from modeling positive roles in the workplace, mothers also have a more direct effect on their daughters when they hold stereotypical beliefs about gender differences in abilities. For example, mothers who believe that girls are not as good at math as boys produce daughters whose own math performance is lowered when they are reminded of their gender before doing math problems. This demonstration of *stereotype threat* was found for girls as young as 5 years of age, whereas girls whose mothers did not hold those beliefs were not affected by being reminded of their gender (Tomasetto et al., 2011). Although girls this age are far from entering careers, they seem to be old enough to be picking up attitudes from adults around them concerning what school subjects girls are good at and what subjects are best "left to the boys."

WRITING PROMPT

Your Family and Your Career

What kind of influence has your family had on your current career leanings?

▶ The response entered here will appear in the performance dashboard and can be viewed by your instructor.

Submit

7.3: Age Trends in the Workplace

OBJECTIVE: Relate age to workplace experiences

We hear a lot about the world population growing older, meaning that as more people reach older adulthood, the median age of people in your city or country (or the world) is increasing, too. Figure 7.4 shows a comparison of the U.S. population pyramids for 1950 and 2016. As you can see, the proportion of middle-aged and older people has grown in comparison to the younger groups.

Figure 7.4 Number of Men and Women in Each Age Group in 1950 and in 2016

SOURCE: CIA World Factbook. (2018).

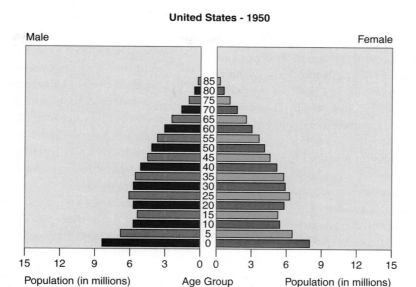

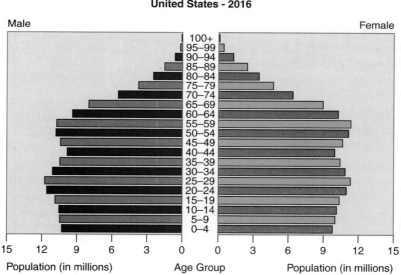

The labor force of a country is the number of people who are employed plus the number of people who are looking for work. In 1996, the median age of the U.S. labor force was 38; today, it is 42 and is expected to increase in the next few decades (U.S. Bureau of Labor Statistics, 2017b). This reflects the increase in the median age of our population. Other reasons for the increase in older adults in the workforce is that older people are generally healthier than in years past, jobs are less physically strenuous, and many older adults do not have enough resources to retire. Older people often have valuable skills that are not available in younger workers. The proportion of people over age 55 in the workforce has grown from 18% in 2008

(the year of the Great Recession) to 23% today (DeSilver, 2017). It has become a priority for researchers and employers to learn how to best manage this mature workforce. How do we make changes in the workplace to optimize the job performance, job training, and job satisfaction of workers of all ages?

⌄ **By the end of this module, you will be able to:**

7.3.1 Explain how age influences job performance

7.3.2 Describe age-related issues associated with the stages of career development

7.3.3 Characterize the job satisfaction curve

7.3.1: Job Performance

OBJECTIVE: Explain how age influences job performance

Normal aging involves gradual loss of some physical and mental abilities, beginning around the age of 30. Reaction time, sensory abilities, physical strength and dexterity, and cognitive flexibility all show significant declines over the course of adulthood, even for healthy people. Depending on the demands of one's job, it stands to reason that there may be some age-related decline in job performance. Surprisingly, research has shown minimal differences in the job performance between older workers and younger workers. Many studies have shown that **job expertise**, or the knowledge and skills a worker has accumulated after a good number of years on the job, may compensate for age-related changes in physical and cognitive abilities (Rudolph, 2016). This is known as **ability–expertise tradeoff**, and it explains how older, experienced workers can outperform younger, less-experienced workers in many jobs (Salthouse & Maurer, 1996).

An example of ability–expertise tradeoff is demonstrated in a classic study of typing ability among women who ranged in age from 19 to 72 (Salthouse, 1984). Two tasks were used: one that measured reaction time (ability) and one that measured typing speed (experience). Not surprisingly, reaction time decreased with age; older women took more time to react to visual stimuli. However, typing speed was the same regardless of age. How did this happen? Researchers explained that the older women relied on their increased job experience to compensate for their decreased general ability. As they typed one word, they read the next few words and were ready to type those words sooner than their younger colleagues, who processed the words one at a time.

Clearly, older workers in jobs that involve knowledge-based, crystallized abilities and highly practiced skills have less job-related decline and are able to swap expertise for some of the physical or cognitive slowdown they experience. Workers in jobs that require manual skills and fluid cognitive abilities may show more declines with age, but they are usually gradual, and there is a lot of variation in the abilities of older workers. Industrial and organizational psychologist Michael A. McDaniel and his colleagues (McDaniel et al., 2012) caution that decisions about hiring or retaining workers should not be based solely on chronological age. Often the workers themselves will leave jobs that are beyond their abilities or transfer to jobs with fewer demands, leaving older but capable workers on the job.

If you have a job, you probably know that core performance is not the whole story. There are many aspects of the job other than the major task for which you were hired. How does this whole package of abilities and attitudes change with age? Organizational behavior researchers Thomas W. H. Ng and Daniel C. Feldman (2008) conducted a meta-analysis of studies correlating the age of workers with job performance on a number of dimensions, including core task performance. Like other researchers, they found that age was not related to core task performance, but they also found that age is not related to on-the-job creativity either. Furthermore, older workers demonstrate more citizenship behaviors (compliance to norms, not complaining about trivial matters, helping fellow workers) and more on-the-job safety behaviors. Older workers also engage in fewer counterproductive work behaviors (workplace aggression, on-the-job substance abuse, tardiness, and voluntary absences from work).

These findings are particularly relevant today, considering that the average age of workers is steadily growing older throughout the world. For example, the largest segment of the U.S. workforce in 1980 was young adults 20–24 years of age; today, it is middle-aged adults 50–54 (U.S. Bureau of Labor Statistics, 2017a). This has brought about concern based on the stereotypes of older workers being less able to perform the jobs required and more difficult to get along with in the workplace. According to the studies cited earlier, these stereotypes are not supported by research and, in fact, for many aspects of job performance, workers get better with age.

7.3.2: Job Training and Retraining

OBJECTIVE: Describe age-related issues associated with the stages of career development

In Super's theory of career development he outlined 5 stages—growth, exploration, establishment, maintenance, and disengagement. His notion was that people may go back through some of these stages from time to time during their careers, a process he calls **career recycling**. As career paths become more flexible, this recycling process has become more common, especially for the stages of exploration and establishment. As things change in the workplace (businesses closing, downsizing, automation) and in workers' lives (young children starting school, older children completing college, job-related stress building up), individuals explore career options and often decide to retrain. For example, if you are in a college classroom at the moment, there is a good chance you are a **nontraditional student**, one who is over the age of 25 and probably engaged in career recycling. If you are not in this category, there is an excellent chance that the person seated next to you is.

Over 40% of college students today are 25 years of age or older (National Center for Education Statistics, 2017). Most of them have been in the workforce or have been working in the home raising their children and are now back for retraining to take the next step in their careers. Add to them the workers who are being retrained within their companies and the workers picking up new skill sets using Internet courses at home, and the total is a considerable proportion of adults of all ages who are engaged in job retraining. Research shows that younger workers have a slight edge when learning new job-related skills, but that some of that benefit could be explained by the related finding that older workers lack confidence in these learning situations. Older workers over age 55 are also slightly less willing to participate in training and career development (Ng & Feldman, 2012), possibly because they are reaching the end of their careers and don't feel they will reap the benefits of additional training. Still, it might be worthwhile for employers to help older employees gain the confidence to participate in training or skip the retraining for valuable older workers and reassign them to work they still do well.

7.3.3: Job Satisfaction

OBJECTIVE: Characterize the job satisfaction curve

The feelings we hold about our jobs are based on the work itself, the pay and promotion opportunities, and the feelings we have toward our coworkers and supervisors. Job satisfaction is important to the worker because it is closely related to life satisfaction, happiness, and positive affect; it is important to the organization for which we work because it predicts how well we will carry out the job requirements and how long we will stay in that particular job (Bowling et al., 2010). Although age changes in job satisfaction have been the topic of many research articles, there has not been a clear consensus about what these changes are. Most researchers agree that job satisfaction follows a "U-shaped curve," meaning that it is higher in the younger years and the older years and lower in the middle (Hochwarter et al., 2001).

Why should this set of feelings be higher in young adulthood, decline in middle age, reaching a low point around age 31, start going up again around 40, and continue to increase until retirement? One explanation is that the unhappy middle-aged workers leave the jobs they are not satisfied with and go to other jobs that are better fits. Another explanation is that younger workers start their careers with high expectations, but become disillusioned in middle age. As they leave middle age, they align their expectations with reality and feel more satisfied with their jobs. A final explanation is that younger workers are enthusiastic to be beginning their careers, but their enthusiasm declines as they deal with family and financial issues. But as they reach their 40s, they have usually been promoted into positions with better pay and work conditions (Heggestad & Andrews, 2012).

7.4: Work and Personal Life

OBJECTIVE: Analyze the relationship between work and personal life

Freud said that the defining features of life were work and love, and nowhere does this ring truer than in the intersection almost everyone experiences as we merge our jobs and personal lives. There is a bidirectional effect between work and the individual, work and committed relationships, and work and family. We may be more aware of the effects our personal lives have on our work, but our jobs also have profound effects on our personal lives. I start with work and the individual, then discuss work and various relationships—marriage, children, older family members who need care. And I even cover household labor, a frequent topic of discussion in many homes.

By the end of this module, you will be able to:

7.4.1 Identify work trends that lead to positive and negative outcomes for individuals

7.4.2 Explain how family-related cultural expectations and workplace options influence work experiences

7.4.1: Work and the Individual

OBJECTIVE: Identify work trends that lead to positive and negative outcomes for individuals

Our time on the job has effects on us as individuals, some good and some bad. One good effect is that people who have jobs featuring **cognitive complexity**, or higher levels of thinking and reasoning, are more apt to have better cognitive abilities in later life (Andel et al., 2016) and lower incidence of dementia (Potter et al., 2008). For example, one study of 70-year-olds showed that the more complex their pre-retirement occupations had been, the better their processing speed, general intelligence, and working memory abilities in retirement (Smart et al., 2014). On the negative side, **job strain**, which is the result of doing work that requires high levels of psychological demands from the worker but offers them little control, is related to lower levels of cognition at retirement and faster cognitive decline after retirement (Andel et al., 2015). Job strain has also been associated with higher incidence of heart disease (Backé et al., 2015), stroke (Huang et al., 2015), and type 2 diabetes (Huth et al., 2014).

One of the most-studied effects that work may have on an individual worker is **job burnout**, a combination of exhaustion, depersonalization, and reduced effectiveness on the job (Maslach et al., 2001). This is especially common among workers whose jobs involve expressing emotion or being empathetic, such as nurses and social workers. Burnout has commonalities with depression, but the symptoms of burnout are specific to the job environment, whereas depression is more pervasive. Job burnout has been related to anxiety disorders, musculoskeletal disorders (such as carpal tunnel syndrome, tendonitis, lower back problems), new cases of heart disease, and onset of type 2 diabetes (Ahola & Hakanen, 2014). Not surprisingly, job burnout is a good predictor of health-related absenteeism.

Not everyone in a difficult job responds to it with adverse reactions. For example, those who have strong social support from family and friends (Huynh et al., 2013), greater job satisfaction, better general health, and higher levels of life satisfaction will fare better when working in a stressful situation (Kozak et al., 2013). Several traits and coping styles relate to job stress and burnout: low levels of hardiness (being uninvolved in daily activities and resistant to change), external locus of control (attributing events to chance or powerful others instead of to one's own abilities and efforts), and avoidant coping style (dealing with stress in a passive and defensive way). Also, individuals who need to validate their own self-worth by achieving on the job are more apt to experience burnout (Blom, 2012).

In the last decade or so, industrial and organizational psychologists have been investigating the concept of **work engagement**, which is an active, positive approach to work characterized by vigor, dedication, and absorption (Schaufeli & Bakker, 2004). This is similar to job satisfaction, only more active and sustained, and seems like the opposite of job burnout. Workers who are engaged in their work are more productive and creative (Bakker, 2011). Work engagement comes from a combination of resources from the job (social support, feedback, skill variety, autonomy, and learning opportunities) and resources within the worker (self-efficacy, self-esteem, and optimism). Workers with high levels of work engagement are less likely to experience job burnout (Hakanen et al., 2018).

UNEMPLOYMENT **Unemployment** is the state of being without a paid job when you are willing to work. In 2017, 3.2% of the workforce in the United States over the age of 25 was unemployed. Unemployment is not distributed randomly through the population. Education is a significant

factor. People in the United States with a bachelor's degree have a lower rate of unemployment (2.1%) than those with only a high school diploma (4.2%). Race and ethnicity are factors, too; white adults have lower unemployment (2.8%) than Hispanic and Latino adults (3.9%) and black adults (5.8%) (U.S. Bureau of Labor Statistics, 2018a, 2018b, 2018c).

Unemployment figures depend on age, too, and one group of young people is gaining particular interest among labor economists around the world. Referred to as NEETs (neither employed nor being educated or trained), these 16- to 29-year-olds make up about 17% of that age bracket in the United States, which amounts to 10.3 million emerging and young adults (Figure 7.5). Although this number has declined slightly, it is still a subject of concern because without assistance, it is feared that these young people will not gain critical job skills, join the workforce, and make a living on their own. Some economists worry that countries with a large proportion of NEETs put them at risk for social unrest. In the United States, young people who fit this definition are mostly female (57%) and have a high school education or less (67%). They are more likely to be black or Hispanic and live in the southern or western states rather than the Northeast or Midwest. These areas also have high rates of adult unemployment, low levels of educational attainment, and a high degree of racial segregation (DeSilver, 2016).

To be fair, some of these young people, especially women, are raising their children or caring for other family members, but others either lack work-related skills or have skills that don't match the jobs available. Others lack social skills, such as the ability to work with others, or life skills, such as literacy and numeracy. This group of young adults who are not employed nor attending school or job training seems to be a widespread problem. In Europe, NEETs make up about 15% of that age bracket, or 13.4 million people.

Figure 7.5 Unemployment in the United States
A substantial proportion of young adults in the United States are neither employed nor in education or training (but the number is decreasing).

SOURCE: DeSilver (2016).

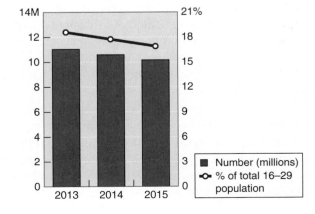

Programs are being implemented by the European Union to track young people who leave school or jobs and to offer alternative job training (Eurostat, 2017).

Although unemployment may occur for several reasons (relocation, recent graduation from college), most of the research on this topic concerns **job loss**—paid employment being taken away from an individual. Job loss can be the result of a business closing, jobs being outsourced overseas, or a slowdown in the market for some product or service. Job loss and the subsequent period of unemployment have strong impacts on workers' well-being, and this decrement can last past the time of reemployment (Daly & Delaney, 2013). Job loss also has a profound effect on the basic personality traits of individual workers. Psychologists Christopher J. Boyce and his colleagues examined data from the German Socio-Economic Panel Study to determine the effects of job loss on a representative sample of 6,769 German workers, about half men and half women (Boyce et al., 2015). The participants had been given personality tests at the beginning of the study and then again, 4 years later. Some had remained employed during the 4 years of the study (6,308) whereas others had lost their jobs during this time (461). Those who had experienced job loss, whether they regained their jobs or not, showed significant changes in their personalities that were not evident in those who remained employed for the duration of the study.

THE IMPACT OF JOB LOSS   Workers who lose their jobs are more apt to suffer from poor physical health and mental health problems such as anxiety, depression, and alcoholism (Nelson et al., 2001). The negative effects increase the longer the person has been unemployed. Surprisingly, women who have experienced job loss have higher rates of mental health problems and lower levels of life satisfaction than men in the same situation (McKee-Ryan et al., 2005). This could be because women are more apt to suffer from depression or it could reflect the fact that job loss represents a larger financial problem for women than for men.

Losing one's job is difficult for anyone, but there are some age differences:

- It is difficult for a young person just leaving school to be unemployed because it interferes with establishing a career and an identity as an adult (McKee-Ryan et al., 2005).

- It is difficult for older workers because of the problems they have finding new jobs and adjusting to new work conditions. A good number of older people take early retirement after losing their jobs because they have little hope of getting new ones.

- However, being laid off is worst for middle-aged adults. Usually they have reached a middle or high level in the company structure and have problems finding a job

with comparable pay and prestige, but they are also too young to retire with a pension or benefits.

Not surprisingly, it is not only the actual job loss that causes problems but also the threat of job loss.

Findings on Job Insecurity

Leon Grunberg, Sarah Yates Moore, and Edward Greenberg— Sociologist Leon Grunberg and his colleagues (Grunberg et al., 2001) found that workers who are exposed to layoffs among friends or coworkers experience significantly lower job security, higher levels of depression, and more symptoms of poor health than workers who have not been exposed to layoffs. This topic of **job insecurity**, or the anticipation of job loss by currently employed workers, has received a considerable amount of research attention in recent years due to the large numbers of mass layoffs of workers around the world.

Grand Cheng and Darius Chan—Psychologists Grand Cheng and Darius Chan (2008) performed a meta-analysis on 133 studies of job insecurity and reported that workers who felt higher levels of job insecurity reported lower levels of job satisfaction, commitment to the company, work performance, trust in the employer, and workplace involvement. They reported higher levels of health problems and higher levels of intentions to leave the job than workers who felt less job insecurity. The workers' ages and number of years on the job were significant mediators of the effects of job insecurity. The older the workers were and the longer they had been on the job, the more likely they were to report health problems. However, it was the younger workers and those who had been on the job less time who were more likely to be thinking about changing jobs, probably because they had less invested in the job, had fewer financial obligations, and had a better chance of finding a similar job somewhere else. The picture that emerges from these studies is that unemployment affects not only the workers who are forced off the job, but the remaining workers too. Their high levels of job insecurity result in low productivity and morale.

WRITING PROMPT

Job Loss and Stress

Think about someone you know who has suffered job loss. How did they deal with the related stress? What are some ways job loss–related stress might be reduced?

 The response entered here will appear in the performance dashboard and can be viewed by your instructor.

Submit

7.4.2: Work and Family Life

OBJECTIVE: Explain how family-related cultural expectations and workplace options influence work experiences

There is ample evidence that work has an influence on family life. However, it also seems that the family, in turn, has an effect on one's job. The effects that work and family have on each other have been called **spillover**, which refers to the extent that events in one domain influence the other. Spillover can be *work–family spillover*, in which events at work influence the worker's family life, or *family–work spillover*, in which family events affect the worker's job. According to this concept, if a worker receives a raise and commendation for excellence on the job, he or she can, as a result, be happier at home interacting with spouse and children. This would be an example of work–family spillover. If a worker has a child who has a slightly elevated temperature in the morning and he or she takes the child to daycare, instructing the staff to call if the condition worsens, it can lead to distraction and anxiety on the job, and this would be an example of family–work spillover.

For a good example of research on family–work spillover, economist Maurizio Mazzocco and his colleagues (Mazzocco, Ruiz, & Yamaguchi, 2014) examined the Panel Study of Income Dynamics and found that married men are more apt to have jobs than unmarried men and to work more hours on those jobs. The opposite is true of married women, who are less apt to be in the labor force and who work fewer hours than single women. To take things one step further, these researchers examined the data over time and found that this difference in work engagement does not appear suddenly when a couple ties the knot. As shown in Figure 7.6, women begin decreasing the hours they work about a year before the actual marriage begins

and men begin increasing the hours they work about 3–4 years before the marriage. This is an example of family-life factors (the anticipation of marriage) affecting work-life factors (being employed and the number of hours worked per year).

ADDING CHILDREN TO THE FAMILY Similar results of family–work spillover are found when children are added to the family. In the United States, approximately 61% of married couples with children under the age of 18 are considered "dual-career" families, meaning that both parents are employed (U.S. Census Bureau, 2017). In addition, a large number of single parents combine family and paid work. However, it is typical for men to remain in the labor force and for women to move into and out of employment due to family obligations. Figure 7.7 shows the percentage of fathers and mothers who are employed and who have children between 6–17 years and under 6 years of age (U.S. Bureau of Labor Statistics, 2017c). Higher percentages of fathers are employed than mothers in both age groups. The number of years women spend in the workplace during their careers depends on the number of children they have; the more children a woman has, the less time she spends in the workplace.

Why would men increase their time on the job when anticipating marriage and when adding children to the family? Why would women decrease theirs? To me, the explanation relates to Super's (1957) theory of career. One's job is not the sum total of one's career. When one marries (or plans to marry), the career of their spouse becomes a factor in the individual's own life. There are now household tasks to be performed and often the spouse who has the highest income works more hours to compensate for the time the other spouse loses from work while attending to those household tasks. If children arrive, the non-job-related tasks increase. According to economists, value from creating a

Figure 7.6 Work Engagement for Men and Women Before and After Marriage

Women tend to start working fewer hours 2 years before marriage; men start working more hours 4 years before marriage.

SOURCE: From Mazzocco et al. (2014).

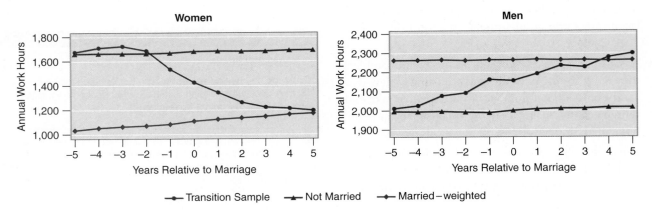

Figure 7.7 Percentage of Mothers and Fathers in the Labor Force and Age of Youngest Child

SOURCE: Data from U.S. Bureau of Labor Statistics (2017c).

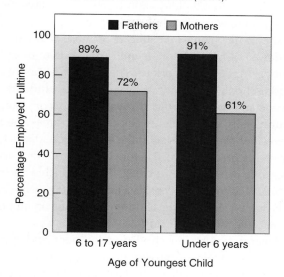

household and family is entered into the "quality of life" equation for the couple, along with the earned income. Recall how research has shown that men's contribution to housework stays level when they become fathers, but women's increases when a child is born. The result of fathers adding to their workdays and mothers adding to their housework is that parents working full time spend about equal numbers of hours taking care of their families, whether it is work in the home or work in paid jobs.

WORK–FAMILY SPILLOVER   For an example of work–family spillover, in which conditions at work affect the worker's home life, management researcher Remus Ilies and his colleagues (Ilies et al., 2017) questioned 129 employees of a large bank in northern China about their work life and home life. The unique part of this study was that the participants were sent the surveys electronically to their workplaces and to their homes, asking work-related questions to be answered in the workplace and home-related questions to be answered in the home. Surveys were sent to their offices at 9:00 A.M. and 4:30 P.M., and to their homes at 8:30 P.M., all on the same day. The office surveys pertained to moods at work (positive or negative), job satisfaction, and how immersed and energetic they felt about their daily work assignments. The home survey asked about moods at home (positive or negative), whether or not they had discussed their workday with their spouse, and how satisfied they felt with their work–family balance. The participants had also been given a test of intrinsic motivation, or how much they enjoyed their jobs. Results showed that the workers who were most immersed and energetic about their work assignments that day were more apt to share these feelings with their spouses, and that this sharing at home was related positively to family satisfaction and a

feeling of work–family balance for that day. Interestingly, these positive relationships were stronger for workers who reported that they generally enjoyed their jobs and found the work fun. For these workers, the positive feelings during their workdays spilled over at home when they shared their days with their spouses, and it further spilled over into family satisfaction and work–family balance, at least for that day.

As you can guess, dividing spillovers into those that start with work and those that start with the family doesn't really capture the reality of family life. For example, sometimes the spillover goes both ways—some event at work affects the family, which in turn affects the workplace. The remaining part of this section deals with those types of hybrid spillovers.

A longitudinal study followed working mothers from the time their children were born until they were in fifth grade, surveying them five times about the feelings they had toward their jobs and families. They found that women had more positive feelings about both job and family if they reported receiving more rewards at work, having more work commitment, and perceiving that their jobs benefitted their children. These researchers suggested that the answer to retaining women employees was not to reduce their job demands, but to find ways to facilitate working mothers' positive work–family spillover. One suggestion was to offer employment packages that not only include health care and vacation days, but on-site childcare and paid parental leave. Women need encouragement and support from employers and colleagues and financial rewards for their work (Zhou & Buehler, 2016).

For the 60–70% of mothers with dependent children who also have jobs outside the home, a major source of spillover is childcare. The increase of mothers in the workforce has been one of the biggest social changes over the last three generations. My grandmother was a stay-at-home mom, even when her children were adults and living in their own homes. My mother worked before she had children and then again after the children had left home. I have worked (or attended school) since my youngest started kindergarten. My daughter has worked since she was 16, taking part-time jobs as she attended high school and college. Now she is 37 and recently took 4 months of unpaid leave for the birth of her daughter, but now she is back at work full time with the baby in daycare. I would guess the same progression is true in the various generations of your family. Unfortunately, the childcare industry and the parent-related atmosphere of most organizations have not kept up with this social change, providing a major source of work–home spillover that affects both mothers and fathers.

PARENTAL LEAVE   One of the biggest problems is that the U.S. does not have a national **paid parental leave policy**, in which the employer and/or the state provide time off with pay to new parents. The Pew Research Center investigated 41 developed nations and found that the U.S. was the only one that has not mandated any paid leave when a woman gives birth or adopts a child (Livingston, 2016). Figure 7.8 shows the duration of paid maternity leave for those 41 countries, starting with Estonia, which provides 87 weeks of paid leave. Some countries provide this paid leave for mothers only and some include fathers, too. In most of these countries, paid parental leave is handled by a system similar to Social Security and is funded by payroll taxes from all workers. In the United States, California, New Jersey, and Rhode Island have state-mandated parental leave for partial salary, and some businesses provide paid parental leave without being required by law to do so. The U.S. does have the Family and Medical Leave Act (FMLA), which guarantees workers at large companies 12 weeks of job protection after the birth of a child (or other family caregiving event), but no pay. (This is how my daughter was able to return to her job 4 months after her daughter was born.) As a result, the median length of parental leave taken by new mothers in the United States is 11 weeks, and for fathers it is 1 week. Mothers with annual household incomes of $75,000 or more take off twice as many weeks (12) as those with annual household incomes under $30,000 (6) (Bialik, 2017).

The reality of spillover for parents is not limited to lack of parental leave. Children are objects of concern for 18 years (or more) and even when they are in school, the workday often begins before school starts and ends after school is dismissed, making early-morning care and after-school care a necessity. School holidays and teacher workdays do not correspond to workplace holidays, again requiring parents to make arrangements for childcare on those days. Summer vacation for schoolchildren is much longer than most U.S. employers give their workers. And even if a parent also attends school, like many of my university students, the holidays and breaks do not always coincide. For example, our university schedules a week of spring break the first full week of classes in March; the K–12 school district has their spring break the week before Easter. Since the earliest Easter ever recorded is March 22, it is impossible for these two breaks to coincide. There is a lot of anxiety on our campus Easter week when the children have time off and their parents have midterm exams!

Several experts on child development and human resource management have offered suggestions to organizations to make their workplace more family-friendly. These include using company communications for parents to network about work–family issues, assigning new parents a mentor who has older children and has successfully balanced home and work, making days off better align with school calendars, providing flexible work schedules, and providing onsite childcare for children of all ages (Dowling, 2017; Halpern, 2005).

Figure 7.8 Duration of Paid Maternity Leave

Of 41 developed countries, only the U.S. fails to provide paid parental leave to families.

SOURCE: Livingston (2016).

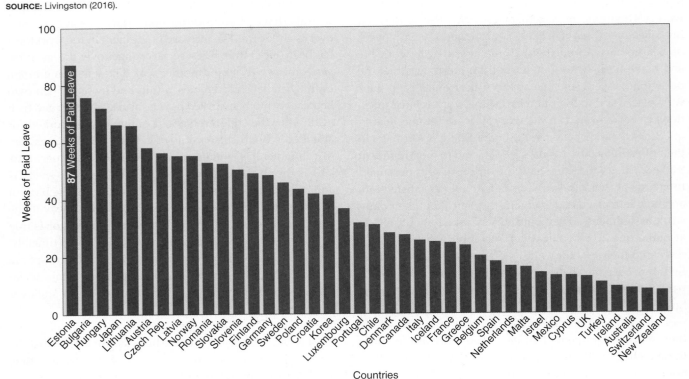

7.5: Retirement

OBJECTIVE: Evaluate retirement practices

The concept of **retirement**, or the career stage of leaving the workforce to pursue other interests such as part-time work, volunteer work, or leisure interests, is relatively new. My grandfather was the first person in his family to retire. He was the eldest son, and his father (as well as his grandfather) had been farmers who continued working until they died. Even if they had worked in salaried jobs, there was no Social Security until 1935 (and then it was called "old age survivors' insurance"). My grandfather worked for the city water department, and when he turned 65 in 1949, he was given a gold watch and a picture of himself shaking hands with the mayor. He began collecting Social Security, and several years later, so did my grandmother, who had never worked outside the home. Workers my grandfather's age were pioneers; they had no role models for retirement and may have felt a little sheepish about leaving the job while they were still able-bodied and had all their wits about them.

Today retirement is quite different. Many people spend 20 years or more in this stage, and many look forward to it. They spend these years doing a variety of things; they travel, take college classes, do volunteer work, and become political activists. Another difference today is that retirement is seldom an all-or-nothing state. People retire from one career after 20 years and then begin a second one or take a part-time job. Others start collecting a pension at age 62 and spend their days in leisure activities. It is really difficult to divide older adults into "retired" and "working" categories. Keeping all this in mind, I will jump in with both feet and write about when, how, and why people retire—and also where.

▼	**By the end of this module, you will be able to:**

7.5.1 Summarize financial and psychological issues in retirement preparation

7.5.2 Explain impacts on retirement age

7.5.3 Describe typical reasons for retirement

7.5.4 Analyze the effects of retirement

7.5.5 Describe alternatives to full retirement

7.5.6 Identify important factors leading to well-being after retirement

7.5.1: Preparation for Retirement

OBJECTIVE: Summarize financial and psychological issues in retirement preparation

Retirement is not something that happens to us suddenly or arbitrarily. In the United States most people decide when they will retire. Other countries have mandatory retirement at a certain age, and even some high-risk occupations in the United States require retirement, such as air traffic controllers at age 56 and airline pilots at age 65. Although young and middle-aged adults probably don't know when they will choose to retire, some of them are making preparations. They talk to financial advisors, put money aside in bank accounts or investments, and discuss retirement with their spouses and friends. Needless to say, this planning increases as they get older.

When work becomes less central to our lives, or leaves it entirely, we need something to fill our waking hours.

One big topic of concern in retirement planning is money. No job means no paycheck, so an important part of planning for retirement involves saving or investing. About half of workers in the United States have money in savings accounts for retirement. Some of the others have investments. But even if a person has no specific fund of money labeled "retirement," it does not mean that they are financially unprepared. According to economist Andrew Biggs (2016), almost everyone who has had a job for at least 10 years (or is married to someone who has had a job for 10 years) has been accumulating retirement benefits in his or her Social Security accounts and will continue to do so for as long as they have a job. A decreasing percentage (16%) of the workforce has pensions through their jobs.

That being said, psychologists remind us that there is more to retirement preparations than money. Adults of all ages need to think ahead about retirement and consider it as more than simply the absence of a job. Work occupies a large part of our adult lives, providing us with a role, status, social contacts, routines, and activity. When those aspects of work are removed, we need something to fill them up, and that works best if we plan ahead. People who make the transition to retirement more successfully and experience the greatest psychological well-being once retired are those who not only make financial plans ahead of time, but also plan for social interactions and leisure activities (Carse et al., 2017). The average age of retirement in the United States is coming down while life expectancy is going up; most of us will spend several decades in retirement, so the need for planning of all sorts becomes more important.

7.5.2: Timing of Retirement

OBJECTIVE: Explain impacts on retirement age

Just as planning varies, so does the actual timing of retirement. We tend to think of 66 as "retirement age" because that is the age at which people in the United States are able to start receiving full Social Security benefits. However, many people retire earlier, and many keep working past that age. Figure 7.9 shows the proportions of adults of various ages who are in the **labor force**, meaning they are either working or actively looking for jobs. These data extend back to 1990 and are projected to 2020. If you examine the figure, you will see that the proportion of adults in the labor force from age 25 to 54 has remained fairly stable, while those in older age groups have increased, with the sharpest increase for workers age 65–74 (U.S. Bureau of Labor Statistics, 2017a).

One reason for the increase in older workers is that each year the group of people reaching retirement age is healthier, on average, than the group before, so more of them are able to work if they choose to. Also, mandatory retirement was ended for most jobs in the United States in 1986, making it possible for older workers to continue in their jobs if they so desired. The number of physically demanding jobs declined from 20% in 1950 to 7.5% in the 1990s, making it easier for older adults to do the work required in many jobs. In addition, as of 2000, there is no longer a penalty for people age 66 and older who collect Social Security and continue to receive a paycheck. Finally, women make up larger parts of the older groups, and their workforce participation has increased steadily.

Figure 7.9 Percentage of Adults of Various Ages Who are in the Labor Force

The percentage of people in the U.S. workforce has remained about the same since 1990 for those 24–54 years of age, but increased for older workers.

SOURCE: Data from the U.S. Bureau of Labor Statistics (2017a).

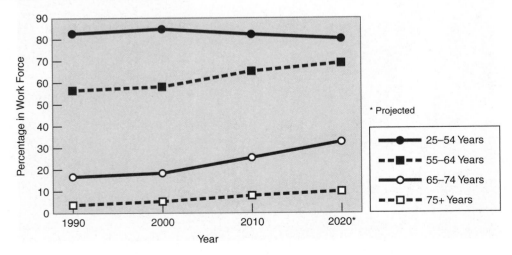

7.5.3: Reasons for Retirement

OBJECTIVE: Describe typical reasons for retirement

A good number of older workers do not have a chance to retire, but find themselves unemployed due to company layoffs, mergers, or bankruptcies and have difficulty finding another job at the same level and salary. A viable option for some of these individuals is to retire early. However, for most people, the decision of when to retire is more complex and depends on the interaction of a number of factors. Take a look at some of the factors affecting the decision to retire.

Factors Affecting the Decision to Retire

Finances—Economists and other social scientists have found that the biggest determinant in the decision to retire is finances. How much do they have saved and invested? What will their pensions be? How will retirement change their expenses? What will they gain from staying on the job? There is a need to balance the value of staying on the job with the value of retiring. The value of staying on the job is also known as **work-related value**. It is not only the worker's salary, but also the increase in pension and Social Security benefits to be received later if he or she continues working. For example, full Social Security benefits are currently available when workers reach 66 years of age; if they decide to retire between 62 and 66, they receive less than full benefits for the rest of their lives. If they retire between 66 and 70, they receive more than full benefits for the rest of their lives. Clearly, the longer a worker stays on the job, the higher the Social Security benefits will be. Some private pension plans work the same way. In addition, there are other values related to staying on the job, such as health insurance coverage for the worker and his or her family and other incentives the employer might offer for continued employment (Clark et al., 2004).

Workers weigh this package of value for staying on the job with the **retirement-related value**, or the value of retiring. In this package is personal wealth—how much is in savings, investments, home equity, and other assets. With the stock market downturn in 2008 and the dip in housing prices and sales, many people approaching retirement who were depending on returns from these investments decided to stay on the job, which helps explain the increase in the percentage of older men and women in the workforce. Retirement-related value also includes how much the worker would receive in Social Security and pension benefits, as well as what might be earned from other work, such as a part-time job or consulting work. The cost of health insurance coverage is also part of this package. Medicare, the national medical coverage for workers, is not available until a person reaches age 65, but some employers continue health insurance for retirees. Making these decisions is even more complex in many instances because the situation of a spouse must be added to the equation.

Health—Another important factor in the timing of retirement is health. Again, this is not a simple matter. Health problems can affect the decision to retire in two ways. Increased medical expenses and the need for health-care insurance can increase the chances that workers will stay on the job—and this involves not only the individual worker's health, but also that of his or her spouse and other family members (Carse et al., 2017). The second effect is that poor health can make working difficult and lead to a lower salary or a transfer to a lower-paying position, making retirement more attractive. This is especially common in physically demanding jobs. Alternatively, the poor health of a spouse or family member can lead to increased caregiving responsibilities and subsequent retirement. About 4% of people who try to combine caregiving and careers solve the problem by taking early retirement (Family Caregiver Alliance, 2016).

Family—Children can play a role in deciding when to retire. With parenthood coming later and retirement opportunities coming earlier, having children still in the home might be a reason to remain in the workforce. And even if the children are out of the home, parents may want to provide college tuition and other types of support. In addition, as discussed previously, an increasing number of grandparents are raising grandchildren, often without much financial help from the parents or the state. The consequence is that many grandparents delay retirement to support another generation of their families.

What about couples wanting to retire together? If partners are different ages, does the younger one retire early? Or does the older one delay retirement until the younger one is eligible? As romantic as this sounds, it is not necessarily what happens. In a survey study of over 2,000 heterosexual couples in their 60s who were both working, sociologists Maria Eismann and her colleagues (Eismann et al., 2017) found that slightly less than half of the participants preferred joint retirement, whereas slightly more than half did not prefer to retire at the same time. Those who wanted to retire at the same time were more strongly attached to each other and less strongly attached to their jobs.

Career Commitment—Some people find their jobs unpleasant and stressful, and they count the days until they can retire. Others could not imagine life without their jobs and plan to stay as long as possible. This factor is **career commitment**; those who are self-employed and highly committed to their careers retire later than those who work for others or are less committed. People with more education are more likely to retire later. Factors that determine earlier retirement are having physically demanding jobs, low levels of education, low standards for work, less identification with the organization, and more dissatisfaction with the job and with the supervisors (Wang & Wanberg, 2017).

Leisure-Time Interests—Another reason to retire is that life outside the workplace is calling. Workers who have hobbies, recreation interests, and active social lives are apt to retire earlier than those who do not. In addition, those who enjoy travel and doing home-improvement projects are more eager to retire.

7.5.4: Effects of Retirement

OBJECTIVE: Analyze the effects of retirement

Once a worker has retired, what happens? Does life change totally? Does health decline? The striking fact is that for most adults, retirement itself has remarkably few effects on lifestyle, health, activity, or attitudes. Retirement brings with it a few changes in terms of income, particularly where it comes from (see 'Changes in Income').

THE FEMINIZATION OF POVERTY   Like other social ills, poverty in old age is not equally distributed. According to the Shriver Center on Poverty Law (2016), older women

Changes in Income

Adults in the United States who are age 65 and older have a variety of income sources, the major one being Social Security, which makes up 49% of the average income for retirees. Figure 7.10 shows the proportion of income that comes from various sources (Federal Interagency Forum on Aging-Related Statistics, 2017). *Earnings* are from jobs they hold. *Pensions* are from private companies; state, local, or federal government; the military; or personal retirement accounts such as 401(k)s. *Asset income* is interest from savings, dividends from stock, and income from rental property.

However, the information in Figure 7.10 doesn't tell us how the incomes of retired adults compare to their pre-retirement incomes.

Figure 7.10 Proportion of Income that Comes from Various Sources

SOURCE: Data from Federal Interagency Forum on Aging-Related Statistics (2017).

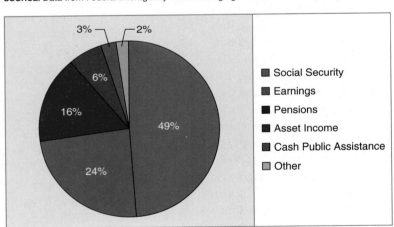

We know that income typically drops when retirement begins, but this may not have a negative effect on the retiree's lifestyle. Many own their homes free and clear and thus no longer have to make mortgage payments, their children are launched, they are eligible for Medicare and thus have potentially lower payments for health care, and they are entitled to many special senior-citizen benefits. When you include all these factors in the calculation, you find that many retirees have fewer expenses after they retire. In the United States, incomes for some older adults actually increase after retirement because the combination of Social Security and other government benefits is greater than the salaries they earned in their working years.

This upbeat report on the economic status of America's older population is possible primarily because of improvements in Social Security benefits in the United States over the past several decades. Indeed, the financial position of America's elderly has improved more than that of any other age group in recent years. As you can see in Figure 7.11, the percentage of people age 65 and over who were living in poverty in 1966 was almost 30%; in 2014, the most recent year for which we have data, the number was about 10% (Federal Interagency Forum on Age-Related Statistics, 2017).

Figure 7.11 Percentage of People Living in Poverty for Three Age Groups

A lower percentage of individuals in the United States 65 years of age and older live in poverty than those under 18.

SOURCE: Federal Interagency Forum on Age-Related Statistics (2016).

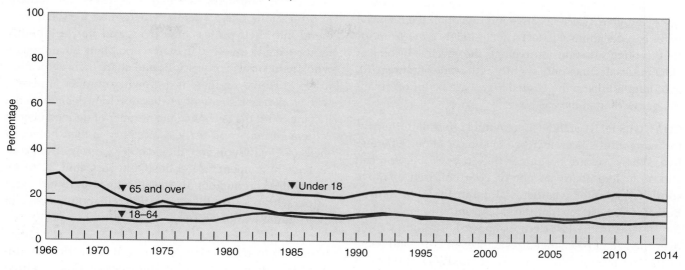

But just as the figures on the drop in income with retirement are misleadingly pessimistic, the figures on the rate of poverty for retired persons are misleadingly optimistic. Although the number living below the official poverty line (which was $16,460 a year in 2018 for a two-person household) has indeed dropped, there is still a large percentage in the category referred to as the "near poor," those whose incomes are between the poverty threshold and 25% above the poverty threshold (or $20,575 a year for a two-person household). In fact, this group is made up predominantly of older adults. And because these older adults are ineligible for many special programs designed to provide support for those whose incomes are below the poverty line, they are in many ways the worst off financially of any subset of the older population (U.S. Department of Health and Human Services, 2018).

are about twice as likely to live below the poverty line as older men, and black and Hispanic elders are considerably more likely to live in poverty than white elders. Combining these two factors, we find that the group most likely to be poor is African American women who are age 65 and older living alone.

This **feminization of poverty**, in which we find a larger proportion of women than men among the poor, especially among older adults, has many causes. An obvious one is that so many older women are widowed. In the United States, the Social Security rules are such that when a woman becomes a widow, she can be entitled to either her own Social Security benefits or 100% of her husband's Social Security benefits, whichever is higher (Social Security Administration, 2017). That may seem like a good deal, but in fact it results in a substantial drop in household income. When the husband was still alive, both spouses received Social Security support; after he dies, there is only one check, and the widow's total income will be somewhere between one-half and two-thirds of the previous household income, even though many of her expenses, such as housing and taxes, stay the same. This drops a great many women into poverty.

It is too simple to attribute older women's greater likelihood of poverty simply to widowhood or living alone. The

gendering of poverty in old age flows from a whole string of gender differences that women have experienced over their lifetimes and that come home to roost in their later years. Current cohorts of older women were much less likely to work throughout their adult years, less likely to be involved in private pension plans if they did work, and more likely to work at lower wages than their male peers, all of which affect their incomes at retirement. Add to this the reality of women moving into and out of the labor force to raise children or to care for elderly family members. The result is that women are less likely to receive pensions and, if they do, the amounts are lower than men receive.

Some consolation for younger women is that these figures represent a cohort of women whose roles did not necessarily include working outside the home or being involved in financial decisions. Hopefully, coming cohorts of women will reach retirement age with a more equitable distribution of personal income. It would be nice if we had a state-supported family-leave policy and other financial help for women who are the kinkeepers for so many, but the outlook is not optimistic. Women who choose to limit their income and career opportunities for family reasons, whether childcare or caregiving for adult family members, need to look ahead and make adjustments in their financial plans so that they will be compensated fairly in their later years. Perhaps the feminization of poverty will be ancient history when young adults of today reach retirement age.

Many of the statistics I've given you are quite discouraging and give a very negative impression of the financial status of older adults. But let us not lose sight of two important bits of information: On average, the effective income of older adults declines only slightly at the time of retirement, and older adults in the United States are better off financially now than in the past.

CHANGES IN RESIDENCE   Another effect of retirement for many adults is an increase in choices about where to live. When you are no longer tied to your job, you can choose to live nearer to one of your children or move south for sunnier weather. Although the U.S. Census Bureau (2016) states that the rate of moving is very low for all ages in the last decade, about 1.5 million people over the age of 65 changed residences in 2016, and some of the top reasons they gave were family (17%), health (13%), new or better homes (11%), less expensive homes (8%), and climate (2%).

WRITING PROMPT

Gender and Retirement

Do you know a woman who has delayed retirement for financial reasons? What are some of the factors that make it financially difficult for women to retire?

▶ The response entered here will appear in the performance dashboard and can be viewed by your instructor.

Submit

7.5.5: Alternatives to Full Retirement

OBJECTIVE: Describe alternatives to full retirement

Sociologist Sara E. Rix (2011) tells us that most older workers now go from full-time work to full-time retirement in stages that consist of various types of transitional employment. Retirement isn't always an all-or-nothing decision. Some older workers shift away from work in a number of different ways—if they do it at all. The following section tells about some of these alternatives to full retirement.

Transitioning to Retirement

Shunning Retirement—We all hear about middle-aged people who claim to enjoy work so much that they plan to keep working when they reach retirement age, even if they have comfortable pensions. If you are like me, you might be skeptical about these forecasts. Even so, about one third of people 65 and over are still in the labor force (U.S. Bureau of Labor Statistics, 2017a). Some of these "retirement shunners" are highly educated individuals in professions like academia, where their personal lives blend into their professional lives, and they are highly motivated and involved in their work. Many have spouses who are in similar professions and share their dedication to work. However, there is a growing number of people who work past retirement age because they depend on the income. With the decline in the number of defined benefit retirement plans and the loss of equity in their homes in the 2008 Great Recession, they require earnings from continued employment in later life (Quinn & Cahill, 2016). Of course this continuation in the labor force shuts out older adults with poor health, physically demanding jobs, and intermittent work histories.

Returning to the Workforce—According the the longitudinal Health and Retirement Study, about 15% of retired workers re-enter the labor force again (Cahill, et al., 2011). For example, my grandfather did just this. A few years after receiving his gold watch, he returned to work to start a plumbing business with my dad. My dad was just starting out in plumbing, and my grandfather was a master plumber. He worked with my dad for 8 years, helping him get the business up and running, and then retired again. There are many other reasons someone leaves retirement and returns to work—need for income, loneliness, need to feel useful, and restlessness, among others. A few even make another attempt at retirement and then go back to work for a third time!

Bridge Employment—Another nontraditional exit from the labor force is to leave one's job and engage in **bridge employment**, which can be a part-time job or a less stressful full-time job. This is done by about 60% of retired men, especially those who retire at early ages from jobs such as police work, the military, and other government jobs (Quinn & Cahill, 2016). Often the job is related to their careers—for instance, police officers who take jobs as security guards or as police officers in smaller towns. Others take their knowledge and expertise into the classroom and become teachers. Some enjoy the social interaction that comes with being supermarket baggers or discount store greeters.

The downside of these bridge jobs is that they typically pay less and have fewer benefits than full-time work. Research shows that workers who take bridge employment are younger, have higher levels of education, better financial conditions, and had lower levels of stress in their previous jobs (Wang & Wanberg, 2017).

A popular option for retirees is self-employment. A large number of self-employed workers start up their businesses after the age of 50, presumably as a bridge job or as a way to turn a hobby into an income-producing activity (Rix, 2011). My father-in-law, for example, retired from his job with the police force in a small New England town and started a lawn service in his neighborhood. He had always enjoyed doing yardwork, but with a large family to support, it was never a career option. Once he retired, he spent several days a week during spring and summer on "his lawns." When fall came he raked the leaves one last time and then headed for Florida until it was time to go back north for the spring fertilizer sale.

Phased Retirement—When an employer gives an older worker a reduced workload or a less strenuous job with the same company, it is known as **phased retirement**. These phased-retirement plans involve phased pensions, also, so that the workers receive a lower salary, but begin receiving partial pension payments. The benefits of this retirement plan for workers are obvious. They have their retirement cake and eat it too. They have a part-time salary, partial pension, and can still feel the pride and social support that come from having a job. They also have more free time and less workplace stress. The employers have top-level workers at reduced salaries who can be placed in whatever section of the company that needs the help, often serving as mentors or troubleshooters. And there is the overall benefit of keeping valued seniors in the workplace while still freeing up full-time jobs for younger workers.

Although phased retirement sounds like a win–win situation for both worker and company, only about 5% of U.S. industries provide it. These tend to be those who want to retain skilled workers (high-tech industries and utilities) or those that have labor shortages (education). The major reasons given for not providing phased retirement are problems with tax laws and age discrimination, although 90% of companies interviewed who do offer phased retirement reported that they were able to overcome those problems and were pleased with the results (U.S. Government Accountability Office, 2017). Economists suggest that older workers who would like phased retirement talk to their employers ahead of time, keep their skills up to date, and network with others who have succeeded in obtaining phased retirement (Hannon, 2017).

Volunteer Work—If you have visited a hospital, a school, or a museum lately, you have no doubt had contact with a retired person who donates his or her time to your community. About a quarter of adults over the age of 55 years

in the United States, the majority of them being retired, contribute their time to various community services (U.S. Bureau of Labor Statistics, 2016a, 2016b). Women are slightly more apt to volunteer than men. The types of volunteer work they do are religious-related programs (about 40%), social or community programs (16%), schools (13%), hospitals and health-care facilities (7%), and civic or political campaigns (6%). To give you an idea of the contribution these people make, the volunteer force of the National Senior Services Corps (which includes the Foster Grandparents Program, the Retired and Senior Volunteer Program, and the Senior Companion Program) consists of over 200,000 people 55 years of age and older. They tutor, counsel, care for, and mentor children; provide social support and instrumental support for the frail and elderly; and staff community projects such as blood drives and health-awareness seminars (National Senior Service Corps, 2017).

Volunteering in retirement is a two-way street. Numerous cross-sectional and longitudinal studies have shown that older adults who do volunteer work receive benefits in psychosocial areas, such as having less depression, more positive affect, higher perceived quality of life, and greater social networks. Physical health is also improved; volunteers report having increased physical activity, better fitness, and less decline in physical functioning than those who do not volunteer. And there are even cognitive benefits that come with volunteering in older adulthood, such as learning new skills, improving executive function, and improving verbal learning (Anderson et al., 2014).

7.5.6: Retirement and Well-Being

OBJECTIVE: Identify important factors leading to well-being after retirement

Researchers have studied the career stage of retirement for about a century now, with two major questions in mind: How does retirement affect the workers' overall well-being? and What can be done to enhance the retirement experience for older adults? For the first question, several studies have shown that about three-fourths of retired people report little change in their psychological well-being as a result of retirement. Of the remaining 25%, they reported either positive changes or an initial decrease in well-being followed by significant improvement. The best things that can be done to ensure a good adjustment to retirement is to engage in retirement planning, be married to someone who is also retired, and to ease into retirement with bridge employment (Wang & Wanberg, 2017). I have reviewed changes in careers over the years of adulthood in Table 7.1.

Table 7.1 Review of Changes in Careers over Adulthood

Characteristic	18–24 Years	25–39 Years	40–64 Years	65–74 Years	75+ Years
Vocational Interests	Vocational interests are affected by family support and parents' modelling work-related behavior. About 17% are neither employed nor in education or job training.	Vocational interests are acted on in selections of first jobs, college majors, or vocational training. More job changes are made than in previous generations.	Some workers retrain for new jobs due to layoffs in the 40s and early 50s. In late 50s and early 60s, they tend to take early retirement if laid off.	A growing number of workers continue their careers well past traditional retirement age. Some leave their major jobs and take bridge jobs that are less stressful or involve fewer hours. Others lend their skills and expertise as volunteer workers. Some workers this age retire and then return to work again, sometimes several times, depending on their health and expenses.	A growing number keep working into their late 70s and later because they are healthy and enjoy their work and/or they need the income.
Part-time vs. Full-time Jobs	Both men and women have part-time or entry-level jobs that may not be related to adult vocations.	Men tend to move into the full-time labor force and remain until retirement. Women move into and out of the full-time labor force as they have children and care for them.	The departure of children from home leads women to start new careers or take on new responsibilities in existing jobs.	Women retire at an earlier age than men. They are more apt to be widows and have lower retirement income and more chronic health conditions than men. They are more apt to live at or below the poverty line, especially black and Hispanic women.	This age group is predominantly widowed women. Many reap the results of a lifetime of gender inequality at this stage. Others with good financial resources and generous families do better.
Job Performance	Job performance is variable.	Job performance increases with experience.	Job performance remains high despite gradual declines in physical and cognitive abilities, probably due to expertise.	Job performance remains high for experts and those who maintain a high level of practice.	Most who are working do adequate jobs, but show a slowing down and lack of stamina compared to younger workers.
Job–Family Balance	The beginnings of job–family interactions.	Job–family intersection is difficult during this time as most couples combine careers, marriages, and children.	Job–family intersection is easier, but now can include caregiving for elderly parents or surrogate parenting of grandchildren.	Family responsibilities seldom interfere with work, although some older workers leave work to become caregivers for their spouses.	Too few are working to make an evaluation.
Retirement Planning	Little thought of retirement.	A few begin long-term financial planning.	Preparation for retirement begins in the 40s and early 50s, especially for men.	People this age are eligible for Social Security and Medicare, but the average senior depends on other sources for 51% of his or her income. Women have less retirement income than men their age from every source.	Many this age have retired once (or twice) already.

Summary: Work and Retirement

7.1 The Importance of Work in Adulthood

OBJECTIVE: Analyze the relationship between adulthood and work

- For most adults, career is a lifelong pattern of full-time and part-time work, time out for family responsibilities and retraining, and ultimately retirement pursuits.

It occupies a central part of our time, thoughts, personal identity, and self-esteem.

- Major theories in the field of career development and vocational interests are Parsons' theory of person–environment fit, Super's lifespan/life-space theory, Holland's theory of vocational interests, and Bandura's social-cognitive theory. Recent theories present career paths as being more open to change and self-determined.

- There are gender differences in the typical career paths of men and women. Women are less apt to work full time, more apt to move into and out of the labor force, and more apt to work part time than men. The result for women is lower income, less chance for advancement, fewer benefits during the work years, and less retirement income than men.

7.2 Selecting a Career

OBJECTIVE: Describe sociocultural influences on career choice

- Gender is a big factor in career selection. Both men and women tend to select careers that are stereotypically defined as gender-appropriate. Unfortunately, the "female" jobs usually pay less and have fewer benefits and chances of advancement than the "male" jobs. Although there are now laws against gender discrimination in the workplace, men and women show different work-related interests, with more women opting for work with people and more men opting for work with things. There are also gender differences in anticipated career patterns, with more women choosing careers that have regular hours and fewer demands that would interfere with family life and men choosing careers that are more demanding.

- Women are more likely than men to cross the gender segregation line, especially if they have the support of family and mentors and have a strong sense of self. When men take traditionally female jobs, their reasons depend on their ages. Young men who take traditionally female jobs are more egalitarian and family oriented. Middle-aged men may have been laid off from a stereotypically male job and see opportunities in stereotypically female jobs. They may also want to leave physically demanding jobs.

- Families affect career choice by supporting higher education and career aspirations of their children, which is done more by middle-class families than working-class families. They also model their own workplace roles.

7.3 Age Trends in the Workplace

OBJECTIVE: Relate age to workplace experiences

- Although physical, sensory, and cognitive declines accompany age, measures of actual job performance show no age-related declines. One explanation is that the expertise of older adults compensates for decline in abilities.

- A growing number of workers find their job skills obsolete or want to upgrade to a more complex job,

a process known as career recycling. A common place to do this is universities, where 40% of students are nontraditional students, which means they are over 25 years of age.

- Older workers express more satisfaction with their work lives than younger workers. Some explanations for this include attrition, cohort effects, and types of jobs each group typically has.

7.4 Work and Personal Life

OBJECTIVE: Analyze the relationship between work and personal life

- Job stress can have negative effects on the individual, including burnout, but not having a job can be even worse. Unemployment is a serious life crisis for most adults, and even more serious for middle-aged workers than for those of other ages. A large proportion of young adults, about 17%, have no jobs and are not enrolled in educational programs or job training. Even the possibility of job loss can cause stressful reactions.

- Studies show that men start increasing the number of hours that they work about 4 years before they get married and women tend to start decreasing the number of hours that they work about 1 year before they get married.

- Events at work can have an effect on family life, just like events at home can have an effect on work life. This spillover can be positive or negative. One significant incident of negative family–work spillover happens to many couples in the United States when a new child is born and the parents are not given paid parental leave as they are in other developed countries.

7.5 Retirement

OBJECTIVE: Evaluate retirement practices

- An increasing percentage of people in the United States over age 65 are remaining in the labor force. Some reasons are that they are healthier, there is no mandatory retirement for most workers, jobs have become less physically demanding, and they can't afford to retire. The timing of retirement is largely under the control of the worker, and it is important to look ahead and make plans for this stage of life, which can extend another few decades.

- There are many factors that influence the decision to retire. Among them are finances, health, family, career commitment, and leisure-time interests.

- For most people, retirement brings slightly lower incomes but also lower expenses. More women live in poverty after retirement than men, partly due to women's greater longevity, but also because of lower lifetime earnings, pensions, and savings.

- For some, retirement brings a change of residence. The main reasons are to be closer to family, health, new or better homes, less expensive homes, and climate.

- Nontraditional ways to leave the labor force include shunning retirement, returning to work after a period of retirement, bridge retirement, working part time, self-employment, and working as a volunteer. Phased retirement would be well accepted by workers, but companies worry about tax and discrimination complications. It is more common in Europe and Japan.

SHARED WRITING

Your Career Goals

Consider this chapter's discussion of career selection and how your career goals have fluctuated since childhood. What role did factors such as gender and family play in these changing career goals? How have these factors changed since your parents' generation (for better or worse)? Write a short response that your classmates will read. Be sure to discuss specific examples.

A minimum number of characters is required to post and earn points. After posting, your response can be viewed by your class and instructor, and you can participate in the class discussion.

Post   0 characters | 140 minimum

Chapter 8
Personality

Personality affects social interactions.

Learning Objectives

8.1 Apply the Five-Factor Model to concepts of personality

8.2 Analyze how personality impacts life experiences

8.3 Evaluate measures of personality change and stability

8.4 Interpret personality using theories of personality development

A Word From the Author

Growing Up Amidst a Variety of Human Behaviors

GROWING UP IN a large extended family is like having instant access to longitudinal information about a variety of human behaviors. One may not have observed all the "participants" through all the stages of their lives, but there are always older relatives to provide the missing "data." For example, as children, my sister Rose and I always enjoyed spending time with our grandmother's older sister, Aunt May. She was a retired teacher, had no children, and had never married, but her home was designed

for children's visits. She had a chess board, a Scrabble game, and a set of dominoes tucked under her sofa. There was a huge porch swing, an endless supply of home-baked cookies, and a workroom complete with a potter's wheel and kiln—the site of many "mud parties" she hosted for the kids in the family.

After one particularly fun-filled visit to her house, we commented to our mother that Aunt May was probably so patient and so much fun in her old age because she missed having children herself, but our mother laughed and said, "Oh no, Aunt May has always been good with children and a lot of fun. Age doesn't change a person's basic qualities. She was having 'mud and cookie' parties when I was your age and she was in her 40s. And your grandmother said May was like a second mother to her—always watching out for the younger kids in the family and making up games to amuse them."

Although our mother was not a research psychologist, she was voicing the basic concept of personality stability within an individual over the lifespan. I think most of us have our own theories about personality and age, some based on personal experience within our own families and some based on stereotypes. This chapter delves into the complex topic of personality stability and change in adulthood, sometimes supporting our personal theories and sometimes replacing them with others.

8.1: Personality Structures

OBJECTIVE: Apply the Five-Factor model to concepts of personality

Personality consists of a relatively enduring set of characteristics that define our individuality and affect our interactions with the environment and other people. The study of personality psychology encompasses a large range of interesting topics—traits, motivations, emotions, the self, coping strategies, and the like. In fact, before you took your first psychology course, this is probably what you thought the field was all about. It is one of the oldest specialties in psychology and has been a very active forum in the study of adult development. The main question is: What happens to personality as we go through adulthood and into old age? There appear to be only two possible answers to this question: Either personality is continuous or it changes. However, research over four decades has shown that the answer is not so simple. A better answer is: "It depends." It depends on which type of continuity or change is being studied, it depends on which personality factor we are interested in studying, and it depends on the age of the adults being studied, their life experiences and genetic makeup, and the way the data are gathered (Alea et al., 2004). So, if you like mental roller-coaster rides, hang on!

▼   **By the end of this module, you will be able to:**

8.1.1   Describe the Five-Factor Model of personality

8.1.2   Explain how differential continuity predicts personality stability

8.1.3   Relate mean-level change to personality

8.1.4   Explain how individual personality factors can change

8.1.5   Describe the relationship between variability and stability in a population

8.1.1: Personality Traits and Factors

OBJECTIVE: Describe the Five-Factor Model of personality

The early formulations of personality come from people such as Freud, Jung, and Erikson, developmental theorists whose ideas were based on the premise that many aspects of adult life, including personality, are dynamic and evolving throughout the life span in predictable ways. Many of these theories were based on specific changes at specific ages brought about by resolution of tension among competing forces in life.

About 30 years ago, a new generation of personality psychologists began arguing that it wasn't enough to have a popular theory that was enthusiastically endorsed; it was also important for a personality theory to be empirically tested and validated (McCrae & Costa, 1990). Therefore, it was necessary to define personality more precisely. One of the biggest problems was deciding just what the "enduring characteristics" were that should be studied empirically. What are the basic **personality traits**, or patterns of thoughts, feelings, and behaviors exhibited by our human species?

A good example of a personality trait is how a person typically behaves in social situations. Some people are retiring and some are outgoing. If you think of several people you know well and consider how they usually act around other people, you can probably arrange them along a continuum from most outgoing to most retiring. The continuum represents a personality trait, and the position each of your friends occupies along that dimension between outgoing and retiring illustrates how they rate on this trait. I use the term *typically* here so as not to confuse personality traits with **personality states**, which are more short-term characteristics of a person. If you go to a party after an argument with your best friend, your usual outgoing *trait* may be eclipsed by your withdrawn *state*, but your trait is still outgoing.

Personality traits were not new to psychology in 1990. To the contrary, there were too many of them: "Thousands of words, hundreds of published scales, and dozens of trait systems competed for the researcher's or reviewer's attention. How could one make any generalization about the influence of age on personality traits when there appear to be an unlimited number of traits?" (Costa & McCrae, 1997, p. 271).

The solution was to narrow down the great number of personality traits into a small number of **personality factors**, groups of traits that occur together in individuals. For example, if people who score high in modesty also score high in compliance (and those who score low in one also score low in the other), it stands to reason that tests that evaluate modesty and compliance are probably tapping into the same well. The basic question was: How many different wells (or factors) are there?

THE FIVE-FACTOR MODEL Personality psychologists Robert McCrae and Paul Costa (1987) started with two dimensions that had been long agreed upon, Neuroticism (N) and Extraversion (E). By using a procedure called *factor analysis*, they found evidence for three more factors: Openness (O), Agreeableness (A), and Conscientiousness (C). The result of this work was the **Five-Factor Model (FFM)** of personality (also known as the "Big Five Model"). Since that time, they have devised and revised a test instrument, the latest version of which is called the NEO Personality Inventory–3 (NEO-PI-3). This inventory has been translated into many languages and been administered with similar results to people representing a large number of backgrounds. Basically, researchers have found that no matter what the ages of the individuals tested or what their gender or cultural background, people's personality traits fell into patterns around these five factors, or personality structures.

The FFM is not the only factor analysis model of personality, and the NEO Personality Inventory is not the only test used to evaluate personality traits. There are also the Minnesota Multiphasic Personality Inventory (MMPI), the California Psychological Inventory (CPI; Gough, 1957/1987), the Sixteen Personality Factor Questionnaire (16PF; Cattell et al., 1970), and others. Currently, the FFM is the standard, and when other tests are used, their factors are often converted to the terminology of the NEO PI. But regardless of the test used, researchers had defined a limited set of personality factors and the traits that fell within them to begin scientific research on the question of what happens to personality over the course of adulthood.

PERSONALITY TYPES Some personality researchers have suggested that clusters of personality traits form personality types. Recently Martin Gerlach and his colleagues (2018) at Northwestern University examined data from over 1.5 million people from personality studies. They found evidence for several personality types.

Evidence of Personality Types

Role Model—This type of person is low in Neuroticism and high in Extraversion, Openness, and Conscientiousness.

Far more older than younger adults fit the profile of the "role model" type.

Self-Centered—This type of person is high in Extraversion but low in Agreeableness, Conscientiousness, and Openness. More younger than older adults fit the profile of the "self-centered" type.

8.1.2: Differential Continuity

OBJECTIVE: Explain how differential continuity predicts personality stability

Now that you know the history and methodology used to develop personality inventories, what does the study of personality factors tell us about personality continuity and change? One way of conceptualizing what happens to personality over adulthood is to investigate **differential continuity**, which refers to the stability of individuals' rank order within a group over time. In other words, do the most extraverted participants at Time 1 (for example, age 20) remain among the most extraverted participants at Time 2 (for example, age 50)? And do the lowest-ranked participants still score in the lowest ranks of Extraversion 30 years later? This type of question is usually answered by correlating the ranking order for the group of participants at Time 1 with their rankings at Time 2. If the correlation coefficient is positive and sufficiently high, it means the group generally stays in the same rank order, with those higher than others in a trait such as Extraversion remaining higher than others in Extraversion, and those lower than others in the trait remaining lower than others in that trait. More interesting, comparisons can be made between intervals in young adulthood (for example, age 20–30) and in older adulthood (for example, age 50–60), assessing whether this personality factor is more stable at one time of life than another.

Using this method, we know that personality trait rankings remain moderately stable throughout adulthood and that their stability increases with age (we get "stabler and stabler"). This is even true when the time period from childhood to early adulthood is included, which has long been thought to be a time of life-changing roles and identity decisions. Figure 8.1 shows the rank-order correlations from childhood to late adulthood, reflecting data from 152 studies of personality (Roberts & DelVecchio, 2000). As you can see, there is an increase in rank-order stability from age 6 to age 73. Other things we know about rank-order stability are that these patterns don't differ much from one personality factor to another, show no gender differences, and are very similar no matter what type of assessment method is used (Caspi et al., 2004).

Figure 8.1 Rank-Order Correlations from Childhood to Late Adulthood

Differential continuity is demonstrated in results from 152 studies showing that individuals' correlations from age to age in scores on various personality tests remain high from early childhood through late adulthood and increase in middle adulthood. People ranking high in some personality trait at one age tend to rank high in that trait on tests given to them at later ages, and the same is true for people who are in the middle or lower ranks.

SOURCE: Roberts and DelVecchio (2000).

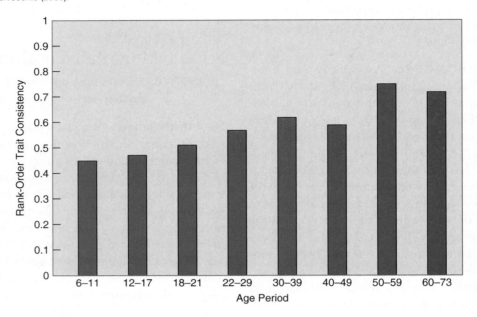

In summary, rankings of personality traits are surprisingly stable during childhood and throughout adulthood, increasing steadily until about age 50 and then leveling off. Even in the oldest groups, there is a correlation coefficient of around 0.70, which means that total stability has not been reached (as it would if the coefficient were 1.00), showing that there are still some changes taking place in rank order.

8.1.3: Mean-Level Change

OBJECTIVE: Relate mean-level change to personality

The concept of **mean-level change** refers to changes in a group's average scores over time. If your first-year college class were tested on some personality measure (for example, Conscientiousness) and then tested again in your senior year, would the averages of the group change significantly and, if so, why? Mean-level change is attributed to such factors as maturation (such as menopause for women at midlife) or cultural processes shared by a population (such as the normative changes of completing school, starting a career, and leaving the parental home).

Fifty personality researchers from around the globe, including McCrae and Costa, found that stereotypes of changes in personality during adulthood were relatively stable across 26 different countries (Chan et al., 2012). In Figure 8.2, you can see that both younger and older adults

are believed to be less neurotic than are adolescents. Extraversion is believed to decrease from adolescence to adulthood and decrease again from young adulthood into old age. Openness is believed to decrease even more dramatically from adolescence to young adulthood and from young adulthood to old age. Agreeableness is believed to increase from adolescence to young adulthood and increase again from young adulthood to old age, and Conscientiousness is believed to increase dramatically from adolescence to young adulthood and then decrease slightly from young adulthood to old age. Do these stereotypes of aging reflect real changes in personality across age?

McCrae and colleagues (2005) gave the NEO PI to adolescents, younger adults, and older adults in the United States. As can be seen from the dark bars in Figure 8.2, the responses of the participants were similar to the stereotypes. Neuroticism, Extraversion, and Openness decreased with age, whereas Agreeableness and Conscientiousness increased. In a cross-sectional study of participants from five different cultures, those over age 30 showed higher mean-level scores for Agreeableness and Conscientiousness, and those under age 30 showed higher scores for Extraversion, Openness, and Neuroticism (McCrae et al., 1999).

PATTERNS OF CHANGE In a meta-analysis of 92 studies, researchers found that personality factors not only changed with age, but also showed distinct patterns of change.

Figure 8.2 Stereotypes of Change in Personality

Results of a NEO PI given to adolescents, younger adults, and older adults in the United States.

SOURCE: McCrae et al. (2005).

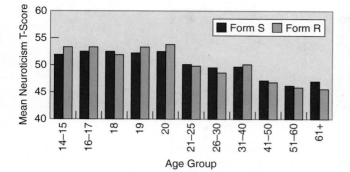

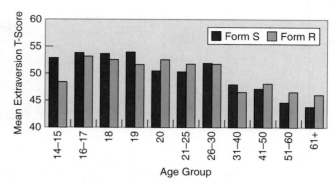

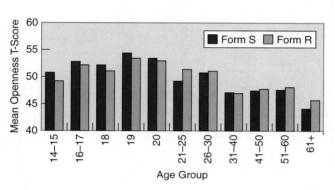

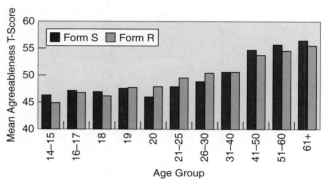

These patterns of change are shown in Figure 8.3. For example, Conscientiousness, Emotional Stability (the reverse of Neuroticism), and Social Dominance (one component of Extraversion) showed significant increases, especially in young adulthood. Participants increased in Openness and Social Vitality (a second component of Extraversion) in adolescence, but then decreased in old age. Agreeableness did not increase much from adolescence to middle age, but did increase between 50 and 60 years of age (Roberts et al., 2006).

Evidence for mean-level change in older adults is similar; personality trait scores from a group of 74- to 84-year-old participants were compared to an older group of participants 85–92 years of age, and researchers reported that the older group showed higher scores for Agreeableness. Furthermore, 14 years later, the "younger" group had shown an increase in these traits, which brought them up to the level of the original "older" group (Field & Millsap, 1991).

The message from these studies is that personality does change predictably with age and continues to change at least to the age of 92. We become more and more agreeable, more conscientious, more emotionally stable (or less neurotic), and more socially dominant. We become more open and socially vital in young adulthood, but then decline in old age. These patterns seem to be independent of gender and cultural influences.

8.1.4: Intra-Individual Variability

OBJECTIVE: Explain how individual personality factors can change

Another way to chart the progress of personality traits over adulthood is to look at **intra-individual variability**, or in other words, find out whether the personality traits of an individual remain stable over the years or change. This is done by giving personality tests to individuals at several points in time and then correlating each person's scores from Time 1 with the scores for Time 2, and so on. This is not the same as differential stability because you are correlating the actual scores, not the rank order. Personality researchers in Scotland conducted one study of this type (Harris et al., 2016). A Scottish mental survey that measured facets of dependability was conducted with 14-year-olds in 1947, and these researchers followed up on the participants when they were 77 years old. They found little stability in overall dependability across the lives of the participants, but they did find some stability in "stability of mood" and Conscientiousness. Another study of intra-individual variability correlated five-factor scores for men between the ages of 43 and 91, finding that most showed declines in Neuroticism and no changes in Extraversion with age. However, this was not true for all the participants, and many showed different patterns of individual variability even in very late adulthood

Figure 8.3 Patterns of Cumulative Change for Six Personality Traits

Each personality trait shows a different age-related pattern.

SOURCE: Roberts et al. (2006).

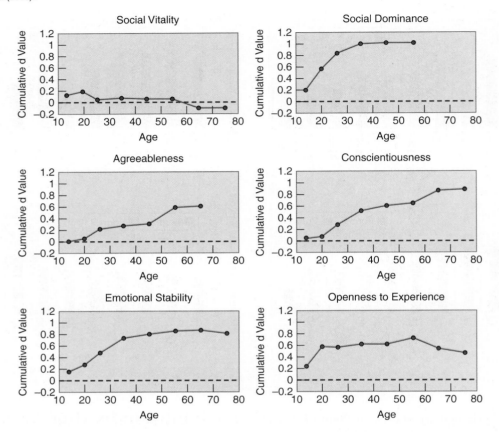

(Mroczek & Spiro, 2003). Recent studies have shown that scores on all five factors of personality show "unmistakable variability" in the rate and direction of change for individuals (Roberts & Mroczek, 2008).

Scientists with the Berlin Aging Study II (Mueller et al., 2016) followed over 1,200 people from age 65 to 88 because they wanted to know if personality changed during old age. Neuroticism and Conscientiousness both decreased with age during old age, Extraversion and Openness increased, and Agreeableness did not change. Interestingly, older adults who reported higher levels of Neuroticism also had higher levels of illness, lower grip strength, and slower cognitive speed, suggesting interesting links between personality and other areas of successful and unsuccessful aging.

MANIPULATING PERSONALITY Another important question addressed by researchers is: Can personality be changed intentionally? For example, psychologist Carol Dweck (2008) argued that personality is based on beliefs about the self and that it is possible to change some of those beliefs and, as a result, change personality. One set of beliefs that Dweck used in her research involved what people believe about their own intelligence. Those who believe

that their intelligence is malleable, that it can be improved, tend to be more open to learning, more willing to face challenges and persevere, and more resilient after failure—all traits that are important in school and in adult life. People who believe that their intelligence is fixed tend not to demonstrate those characteristics. In a number of experiments, people with fixed beliefs about their intelligence changed their way of thinking after receiving information about the brain and how new connections can be made when learning takes place. Once they believed that their intelligence was malleable, they began showing traits of openness, perseverance, and resilience similar to those who expressed malleable beliefs at the beginning of the study (Blackwell et al., 2007).

A similar study targeted African American college students who were entering historically white institutions. As Figure 8.4 shows, when the students were taught that their feelings of apprehension were normal but would not last long, and were given personal testimonies from second-year African American students telling them about their positive experiences, they reported better feelings of acceptance, took more challenging courses the following semester, were more apt to reach out to their professors for help, and made better grades than students in a control group (Walton & Cohen, 2007).

Figure 8.4 Changing Maladaptive Personality Traits Through Intervention

Not only do aspects of personality seem to change over time, but it is also possible to devise methods of changing maladaptive traits using interventions.

SOURCE: Walton and Cohen (2007).

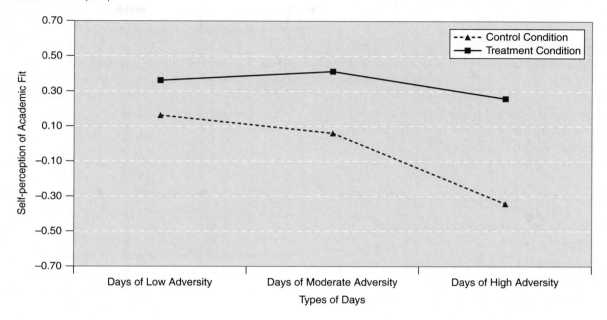

Certain major life events can also cause changes in personality. Researchers Jule Specht and colleagues (2011) conducted a four-year longitudinal study on personality in Germany. They looked at data from close to 15,000 in 2005 and again in 2009. People who got married during 4 four years of the study scored lower on Extraversion and Openness. People who became separated from their partner became more Agreeable, and men (but not women) became more Open. People who divorced became more Conscientious, as did people who had a baby or retired from a job. Some sex differences were observed. For example, women decreased in Conscientiousness when their spouse died, while men increased in Conscientiousness.

8.1.5: Continuity, Change, and Variability Coexist

OBJECTIVE: Describe the relationship between variability and stability in a population

How do human personality structures within a group show differential continuity, mean-level change, and intra-individual variability over time? Take exam scores, for example. I generally give three exams in my class on adolescent psychology. The class shows differential continuity because those who are the top students on the first exam are usually the top students on the second and third exams too, whereas those at the bottom of the grading scale tend to remain in that rank order. However, there is also considerable mean-level change. The average score for the first exam is always

significantly lower than the later exams. Some students don't take the subject matter seriously and are shocked to see questions about genetics, brain structures, and research findings. Others explain that they need to take one exam in a class before they know how to study for the next ones. Whatever the reason, almost everyone improves on the second exam, showing mean-level change for the class alongside differential continuity. And there is also intra-individual variability. Although most students follow the patterns described thus far, there are exceptions each semester. A student can start off strong with a top grade on the first exam, then get inundated with work as the semester goes on, floundering on the later exams as a result of trying to burn the candle at both ends. Another can start out strong, get frazzled at midterm, and then buckle down to pull up the grade on the final. The result is differential continuity, mean-level change, and intra-individual variability, all in the same class. And the same is true for personality traits across adulthood.

8.2: What Do Personality Traits Do?

OBJECTIVE: Analyze how personality impacts life experiences

While researchers have identified five major personality factors and a large number of traits associated with each factor—and they have explained the patterns of stability and change across adulthood—recently, work has been done on just what personality traits do other than define our uniqueness. Three areas have been identified that are shaped by personality: relationships, achievement, and health (Caspi et al., 2004).

> ## ▼ By the end of this module, you will be able to:

8.2.1 Describe ways personality can influence relationships

8.2.2 Determine the relationship between personality and achievement

8.2.3 Relate personality to health experiences

8.2.1: Personality and Relationships

OBJECTIVE: Describe ways personality can influence relationships

Personality traits are important in the development of intimate relationships in adulthood. Neuroticism and Agreeableness in particular are strong predictors of relationship outcome. The higher a person is in Neuroticism and the lower in Agreeableness, the more apt he or she is to be in conflicted, dissatisfying, and abusive relationships, and the more quickly the relationships will dissolve (Karney & Bradbury, 1995). In a longitudinal study that followed the relationships of adolescents into adulthood, researchers found that high levels of Neuroticism predicted that the individual would repeat the same negative experiences from relationship to relationship (Ehrensaft et al., 2004).

The influence of personality on intimate relationships happens in at least three ways.

Personality and Intimate Relationships

Choice of Relationship—First, personality helps determine with whom we choose to have a relationship, often someone with a similar personality. For example, a person who is high in Neuroticism would tend to seek a relationship with a person who shares that trait.

Behavior with Partners—Second, personality helps determine how we behave toward our partners and how we react to our partner's behavior. A person high in Neuroticism who is in a relationship with a similar person will express negative behavior toward the partner and will meet the partner's negative behavior with further escalation of negativity.

Influence on Partner's Behavior—Third, personality evokes certain behaviors from one's partners. For example, people high in Neuroticism and low in Agreeableness express behaviors that are known to be destructive to relationships—criticism, contempt, defensiveness, and stonewalling—behaviors that psychologist John Gottman (2011) has identified as very good predictors of future breakup or divorce.

8.2.2: Personality and Achievement

OBJECTIVE: Determine the relationship between personality and achievement

The personality traits that make up the factor of Conscientiousness are the most important predictors of a number of work-related markers of achievement, such as occupational attainment and job performance (Judge et al., 1999). The traits included in this factor include competence, order, dutifulness, and self-discipline. In fact, if you look around your classroom, you will probably see a lot of Conscientiousness being displayed because it also predicts academic achievement. These traits are integral to completing work effectively, paying attention, striving toward high standards, and inhibiting impulsive thoughts and behavior.

The traits involved in Conscientiousness could affect job achievement in several ways. First, people choose niches (jobs) that fit their personality traits. We feel comfortable doing things we are good at and get pleasure from. Second, people who display these behaviors are singled out by others to be given jobs and promotions. Third are selection processes; people who are not conscientious leave high-achievement jobs (or are asked to leave). And fourth is the obvious fact that people who are high in Conscientiousness actually do the job better (Caspi et al., 2004).

Researchers have shown that all five of the personality factors predict good job performance if the job is a good match for the personality (Judge et al., 1999). This finding should remind you of John Holland's theory of career selection.

These findings about personality traits and achievement depend on gender expectations and sociocultural contexts of the times. What is valid for today's adults may not have been the same for earlier cohorts of women. Psychologist Linda K. George and her colleagues (2011) examined longitudinal data on the Mills College women, born between 1935 and 1939 and found that women high in Conscientiousness during the college years were not more likely to be involved in careers than their classmates because they were adhering to their culturally defined roles of wife and mother. In fact, women high in Conscientiousness were more apt to report high commitment to their family roles all through their adult years. They had lower divorce rates, and their lack of career involvement did not handicap them financially in retirement because they had been conscientious about selecting a spouse who was a good provider. Clearly, the same personality trait that drives a young woman today to attend college and excel at her chosen career might have driven her great-grandmother to take cooking lessons and work hard to keep her marriage strong.

Another predictor of achievement is Openness. Martin Seligman and his colleagues (2018) have found evidence that people who are open to new experiences are more likely to be creative. More open people can see how information from disparate areas is connected and thus are more likely to succeed in creative and interdisciplinary fields.

8.2.3: Personality and Health

OBJECTIVE: Relate personality to health experiences

The most dramatic finding about personality is that it is closely related to health and longevity. People who have high levels of Conscientiousness (Hill et al., 2011) and low levels of Neuroticism (Danner et al., 2001) tend to live longer. Other studies show that people low in Agreeableness (having high levels of anger and hostility) are at higher risk for heart disease (Miller et al., 1996), and those who are high in Neuroticism report lower levels of mental and physical health (Löckenhoff et al., 2008).

This link between personality traits and health can take place in a number of ways. First, personality can directly affect the functioning of the body, as seems to be the case with the link between hostility and heart disease. The physiological reactions summoned by hostility act directly as pathogens to cause disease. Matina Luchetti and her colleagues (2014) found that conscientious people have less inflammation, which may be one of the reasons for the association between Conscientiousness and health. Second, personality can lead to behaviors that either promote or undermine health. People who are high in Agreeableness are more likely to have close relationships with supportive people, a factor known to be a buffer against stress-related diseases. People high in Neuroticism are more likely to smoke and indulge in other high-risk health behaviors (Graham et al., 2017), whereas those high in Conscientiousness are more likely to have regular checkups, watch their diets (Caspi et al., 2004), and follow their doctors' orders (Hill & Roberts, 2011). It is thus not surprising that people low in Conscientiousness are more likely to develop diabetes (Jokela et al., 2014). And fourth, personality may be linked with the type of coping behaviors a person chooses to use when confronted with stress (Scheier & Carver, 1993). For example, in a recent study,

the personality traits of Openness and Agreeableness were found to predict older adults' use of mindfulness-based stress-reduction techniques (Barkan et al., 2016).

RISKY BEHAVIOR AND CONSCIENTIOUSNESS In a meta-analysis of 194 studies, psychologist Brent Roberts and his colleagues (2005) correlated scores on Conscientiousness-related traits and nine different health behaviors, such as drug use, risky driving, and unsafe sex practices. Conscientiousness was significantly correlated with each of them, meaning that knowing a person's score on Conscientiousness would allow you to predict his or her likelihood of engaging in these health behaviors. The results are shown in Figure 8.5. As you can see, drug use, violence, risky driving, and excessive alcohol use show the largest correlations. The lower one's Conscientiousness score, the more likely one is to engage in those behaviors. Other behaviors shown in Figure 8.5 had smaller correlations but were still significantly predicted by Conscientiousness. As the authors stated,

> People who are not conscientious have quite a number of ways to experience premature mortality. They can die through car accidents, through acquisition of AIDS via risky sexual practices, through violent activities such as fights and suicides, and through drug overdoses. People can still suffer from an attenuated life span in middle age through not eating well, not exercising, and smoking tobacco, which all lead to heart disease and cancer. (p. 161)

A more recent study followed over 6,000 adults for 14 years and found that there was a 13% reduction in mortality over those 14 years for people high in Conscientiousness in part because that personality factor was associated with less heavy drinking, less smoking, and lower waist circumference (Turiano et al., 2015). An additional way personality traits can influence health was suggested by Roberts and his colleagues (2009). Using data from over 2,000 older adults, the researchers found that Conscientiousness contributes not only to one's own good health, but also to the good health of one's spouse. Men who had wives with high scores on Conscientiousness reported better health than those with low-scoring wives, and the same was true for women who had husbands with high scores in Conscientiousness. The reasons seem clear—within a long-term marriage, conscientious persons take care of their own health and also that of their spouse.

PERSONALITY AND CAREGIVING Personality traits also contribute to one's subjective health when in the role of an informal caregiver, a role many people will face during late middle age. In a study of over 500 informal caregivers, those who were high in Conscientiousness and Extraversion and low in Neuroticism reported better mental and physical health. In addition, Agreeableness was associated with better mental health, and Openness

Figure 8.5 Correlation between Conscientiousness and Health-Related Behavior

Conscientiousness is negatively correlated with a number of health-related behaviors. The higher the Conscientiousness score, the less likely a person will engage in drug use, violence, risky driving, excessive alcohol use, and other unhealthy behaviors.

SOURCE: Roberts et al. (2005).

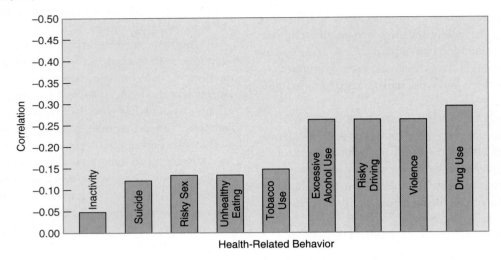

was associated with better physical health. However, the way these personality traits worked seemed to be that they affected the person's sense of self-efficacy—the belief that they can achieve their goals. And if those goals were caregiving for a family member, they did it better than those whose personality traits were at the other ends of the scales (Löckenhoff et al., 2011).

WRITING PROMPT

Personality Traits and Coping

Think of a difficult time in your life. Based on your own personality traits in terms of the Big Five, how might your personality factors have influenced the way that you coped with past difficulties?

> The response entered here will appear in the performance dashboard and can be viewed by your instructor.

[Submit]

8.3: Explanations of Continuity and Change

OBJECTIVE: Evaluate measures of personality change and stability

We know that there is evidence of both continuity and change in various personality traits, but what is less clear is why. What factors influence these features of personality? The explanations may sound familiar by now—genes and environment. There is also an explanation from evolutionary psychology that uses the interaction of both.

☑ By the end of this module, you will be able to:

8.3.1 Relate genetics to personality

8.3.2 Identify ways that interactions with the environment influence personality

8.3.3 Describe ways that evolution may have influenced the development of personality

8.3.4 Compare measures of personality by culture

8.3.1: Genetics

OBJECTIVE: Relate genetics to personality

To what extent do our genes determine our personalities? The short answer is "quite a lot." At least 20% of the variance in personality types is heritable. Furthermore, the five major factors are influenced by genetics to about the same extent, and there seem to be few gender differences.

Studies comparing the personality scores of monozygotic twins and dizygotic twins illustrate the extent of this genetic influence. Psychologist Rainer Riemann and his colleagues (1997) compiled personality data for nearly 1,000 pairs of adult twins in Germany and Poland to investigate the heritability of the Five-Factor Model of personality. Each participant completed a self-report questionnaire, and then the twins' scores were correlated with their cotwins' scores. As you can see in Figure 8.6, the identical-twin pairs, who shared the

Figure 8.6 Personality Scores of Monozygotic Twins and Dizygotic Twins

Monozygotic twins' scores for five personality factors show higher correlations than scores for dizygotic twins, suggesting that there is a genetic influence on personality traits.

SOURCE: Based on data from Riemann et al. (1997).

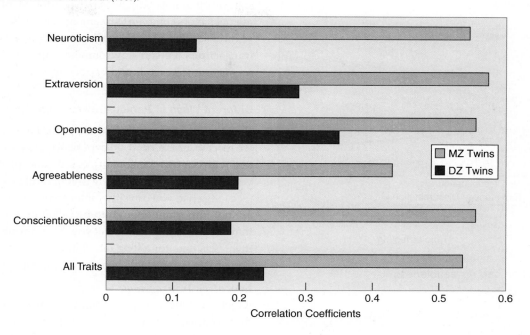

same genetic makeup, had significantly higher correlations than the fraternal-twin pairs, who shared only about 50% of their genes, suggesting that all five of these personality trait structures are moderately influenced by genetics.

In an interesting twist, Riemann and his colleagues (1997) also gave questionnaires to two friends of each twin and asked them to rate the twin's personality, providing an objective rating to compare with the self-reports. The two friends agreed with each other substantially (the correlation coefficient was 0.63), and the means of their scores agreed with the twins' self-reports moderately (the correlation coefficient was 0.55), all adding evidence to the heritability of personality traits.

8.3.2: Environmental Influences

OBJECTIVE: Identify ways that interactions with the environment influence personality

As important as genetic influences are on personality, the environment also has an effect, both directly and in combination with genetic factors. Although individuals' personality measures tend to remain stable in rank-order positions through adulthood, there is room for change, even in the later years, presumably due to environmental influences. Longitudinal studies of twins show that personality change is more influenced by genetics in childhood than in adulthood, meaning that environmental influences are more prominent in adulthood (Plomin & Nesselroade, 1997).

Changes in mean-level measures of personality are common and tend to occur mostly in young adulthood, a time that is very dense in role transitions (leaving home, starting careers, entering committed partnerships, becoming parents). For example, measures of social dominance, conscientiousness, and emotional stability all increase in mean level during young adulthood, leading some researchers to believe that "life experiences and life lessons centered in young adulthood are the most likely reasons for the patterns of development we see" (Roberts et al., 2006, p. 18). All cultures support these role transitions for young adults and have expectations for the content of these roles. This might explain why these traits develop universally at this time of life (Helson et al., 2002).

In addition, different cohorts show different mean levels of personality traits. For example, more recent cohorts show higher scores on measures of social dominance, conscientiousness, and emotional stability, perhaps showing the effects of changing social values and childrearing practices (Roberts et al., 2006).

When people experience discrimination, this can lead to negative effects on their personality (Figure 8.7). Researchers Angela Sutin and colleagues (2016) found that people who reported being discriminated against showed an increase in Neuroticism and a decrease in Agreeableness and Conscientiousness over the course of 4 years compared to those who did not report discrimination.

Discrimination and Personality

Figure 8.7 (a) Discrimination and Neuroticism

SOURCE: Sutin et al. (2016).

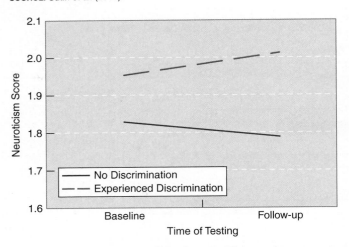

(b) Discrimination and Agreeableness

SOURCE: Sutin et al. (2016).

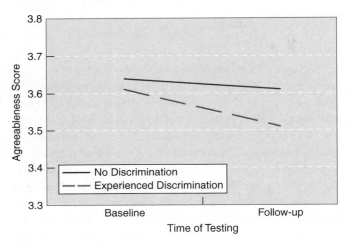

(c) Discrimination and Conscientiousness

SOURCE: Sutin et al. (2016).

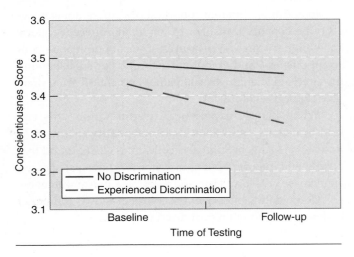

PERSON–ENVIRONMENT TRANSACTIONS We also have evidence that the environment works in combination with genetic factors to maintain differential stability. Psychologist Avshalom Caspi (1998; Caspi & Roberts, 1999) suggests that individuals' genetic endowment and environmental factors combine to maintain personality traits over the years of adulthood, a concept known as **person–environment transactions**. Person–environment transactions can be conscious or unconscious and happen in a variety of ways.

Different Ways of Person–Environment Transactions

Reactive Transactions—*Reactive transactions* take place when we react to, or interpret, an experience in a way that is consistent with our own personality or self-concept. If a friend calls you 2 days after your birthday to congratulate you and have a nice long chat, you can either interpret it as meaning that you are not important enough to be called on your birthday or that you are so important that your friend waited 2 days until there was time for a long talk. Either reaction would tend to perpetuate your established way of thinking about yourself.

Evocative Transactions—*Evocative transactions* are those in which we behave in a way that elicits reactions from others that confirm our own personality or self-concept. People who have low self-esteem often reject compliments or overtures of friendship and, as a result, end up even more convinced that they are not valued by others.

Proactive Transactions—*Proactive transactions* occur when we select roles and environments that best fit our personalities and self-concept. If you are not high on Extraversion, you will probably not make career decisions that put you into a job that involves working directly with people. Not only will you be happier in a more solitary work environment, but this choice will also serve to maintain your introverted traits.

Manipulative Transactions—*Manipulative transactions* are those strategies in which we attempt to change our current environments by causing change in the people around us. An example is an extraverted manager who is transferred into a quiet office and proceeds to motivate his coworkers to be more outgoing. To the extent that this maneuver is successful, the manager is creating an environment that serves to reinforce his or her own personality traits.

WRITING PROMPT

Person–Environment Transactions

Create a character, either based on someone you know or entirely fictional. What are some examples of the different types of person–environment transactions your character might experience?

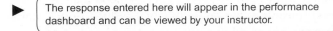

▶ The response entered here will appear in the performance dashboard and can be viewed by your instructor.

Submit

8.3.3: Evolutionary Psychology Explanations

OBJECTIVE: Describe ways that evolution may have influenced the development of personality

If personality structure has substantial genetic components and is similar in many cultures, it probably evolved over generations along with our other human traits. Evolutionary psychologist David Buss (1997) argued that personality traits are based on the most important features of the social groups our early ancestors lived in. It was important for our species to have indicators of who was good company (Extraversion), who was kind and supportive (Agreeableness), who put in sustained effort (Conscientiousness), who was emotionally undependable (Neuroticism), and who had good ideas (Openness). According to Buss, these differences (and the ability to perceive them in others) have been important to the survival of our species.

Buss also contended that personality traits have led to important individual differences linked to status, sexuality, and survival—all contributors to reproductive success (Buss, 2012). For example, scores on Extraversion measures are related to access to sexual partners (Eysenck, 1976), and Conscientiousness is related to work and status (Lund et al., 2007). The suggested mechanisms for this is **reactive heritability**, a process whereby individuals use the qualities they have inherited, such as strength or attractiveness, as a basis to determine strategies for survival and reproduction, such as developing a personality high in Extraversion (Lukaszewski & Rooney, 2010; Tooby & Cosmides, 1990).

8.3.4: Cultural Differences

OBJECTIVE: Compare measures of personality by culture

Recall that the Five-Factor Model was constructed by factor analysis of personality traits found in the U.S. population and then tested on people in other cultures with the goal of showing universality in underlying personality constructs, and it has been found to be stable across many cultures (McCrae et al., 2005). However, cultural and language differences have appeared (Cheung et al., 2008; De Raad et al., 2010; Hofer et al., 2014), causing researchers to take a different approach and construct alternative models of personality structures based on other cultures and other languages. These bottom-up, indigenous psychologies are being developed in areas of Latin America, Europe, and Asia and have covered constructs such as the selfless-self in Eastern religions (Verma, 1999) and the concepts of "face," harmony, reciprocity in relationships, predestined relationships, and mother–child attachments (Cheung et al., 2011). For example, the Chinese Personality Assessment Inventory was developed using these methods and consists of four personality factors: Social Potency/Expansiveness, Dependability, Accommodation, and Interpersonal Relatedness (Cheung et al., 2008).

Studies comparing the Chinese Personality Assessment Inventory with the NEO-Five-Factor Inventory have shown that the Chinese factor of Interpersonal Relatedness did not correspond to any of the NEO five factors, and that the NEO factor of Openness did not correspond with any of the Chinese factors. The Chinese Personality Assessment Inventory has since been translated into various languages—including Korean, Japanese, and

Dogs have evolved alongside humans for thousands of years. Which elements in a dog's personality help the species live among humans?

Vietnamese—and studies have shown that its personality constructs, especially Interpersonal Relatedness, are found in these collectivist cultures (Yang, 2006). The point of all this is that the Five-Factor Model was a great start, but now researchers are developing alternative models to learn more about what is universal about personality and what is particular to a given culture. With globalization, it is important for all of us—clinical psychologists, college professors, travelers, even good neighbors—to understand better "what makes others tick."

In this section I have covered research based on personality structures, mainly the Five-Factor Model that was defined by Costa and McCrae in the 1990s. Using the NEO Personality Inventory, researchers are able to assign scores to each factor, giving each participant in the study a numerical personality profile. These studies are usually done as self-reports and with very large groups of people. Once the scores are computed, the patterns can be analyzed to find out how personality changes over time, whether there are cultural differences, and the like. It is quick and relatively easy, and it is empirical. We have learned a lot about human personality from these studies—that is, personality of humans living in Western, individualistic cultures. And we are beginning to learn about personality in Eastern, collectivist cultures. However, these factor-analysis studies lack something in the depth and richness that we know reside within ourselves and the people we know well.

8.4: Theories of Personality Development

OBJECTIVE: Interpret personality using theories of personality development

Another approach to changes in personality across adulthood is to conduct research based on some of the early theories of personality development, most of which had their roots in Freudian psychoanalytic theory. Full explanations of these theories comprise a whole course in itself, so I only briefly describe them before going on to the current research findings. Although these researchers use different terminology and research methods, many of their findings fit well with the trait theory findings.

⌄ **By the end of this module, you will be able to:**

8.4.1 **Relate Erikson's stages of psychosocial development to personality changes over time**

8.4.2 **Outline Loevinger's stages of ego development**

8.4.3 **Differentiate between Vaillant's defense mechanisms**

8.4.4 **Analyze gender crossover for its influences**

8.4.5 **Summarize the approaches of positive psychology**

8.4.1: Psychosocial Development

OBJECTIVE: Relate Erikson's stages of psychosocial development to personality changes over time

One of the most influential theories of personality development is that of psychoanalyst Erik Erikson (1950, 1959, 1982), who proposed that psychosocial development continues over the entire lifespan and results from the interaction of our inner instincts and drives with outer cultural and social demands. For Erikson, a key concept is the gradual, stepwise emergence of a sense of identity. To develop a complete, stable personality, the person must move through and successfully resolve eight crises or dilemmas over the course of a lifetime. Each stage, or dilemma, emerges as the person is challenged by new relationships, tasks, or demands. As you can see in Table 8.1, each stage is defined by a pair of opposing possibilities.

Erikson also talked about the potential strengths to be gained from a healthy resolution of each dilemma, which are also listed in the table. A healthy resolution, according to Erikson, is finding a balance between the two possibilities.

ERIKSON AND ADULTHOOD   Four dilemmas describe adulthood, beginning with Stage V, *identity versus role confusion*, which is a central task of adolescence and those in their early 20s. In achieving **identity**, the young person must develop a specific ideology, a set of personal values and goals. In part, this is a shift from the here-and-now orientation of the child to a future orientation; teenagers must not only consider what or who they are but also what or who they will be. Erikson believed that the teenager or young adult must develop several linked identities: an occupational identity (What work will I do?), a gender or gender-role identity (How do I go about being a man or a woman?), and political and religious identities (What do I believe in?). If these identities are not developed, the young person suffers from a sense of confusion, a sense of not knowing what or who one is.

Stage VI, *intimacy versus isolation*, builds on the newly forged identity of adolescence. **Intimacy** is the ability to fuse your identity with somebody else's without fear that you're going to lose something yourself (Evans, 1969). Many young people, Erikson thought, make the mistake of thinking they will find their identity in a relationship, but in his view, it is only those who have already formed (or are well on the way to forming) a clear identity who can successfully enter the fusion of identities that he calls intimacy. For those whose identities are weak or unformed, relationships will remain

Table 8.1 Erikson's Stages of Psychosocial Development

Approximate Age (Years)	Stage	Potential Strength to Be Gained	Description
0–1	I. Basic trust versus mistrust	Hope	The infant must form a first, loving, trusting relationship with the caregiver or risk a persisting sense of mistrust.
2–3	II. Autonomy versus shame and doubt	Will	The child's energies are directed toward the development of key physical skills, including walking, grasping, and sphincter control. The child learns autonomy but may develop shame if not handled properly.
4–5	III. Initiative versus guilt	Purpose	The child continues to become more assertive and take more initiative, but may be too forceful and injure others or objects, which leads to guilt.
6–12	IV. Industry versus inferiority	Competence	The school-aged child must deal with the demands to learn new, complex skills or risk a sense of inferiority.
13–18	V. Identity versus role confusion	Fidelity	The teenager (or young adult) must achieve a sense of identity—both who he or she is and what he or she will be—in several areas, including occupation, gender role, politics, and religion. If not, the result is role confusion.
19–25	VI. Intimacy versus isolation	Love	The young adult must risk the immersion of self in a sense of "we," creating one or more truly intimate relationships, or suffer feelings of isolation.
25–65	VII. Generativity versus self-absorption and stagnation	Care	In early and middle adulthood, each must satisfy the need to be generative, to support the next generation, to turn outward from the self toward others. The alternative is stagnation.
65+	VIII. Ego integrity versus despair	Wisdom	If all previous stages have been dealt with reasonably well, the culmination is an acceptance of oneself as one is. If not, the result is despair.

SOURCE: Adapted from Erikson (1950, 1959, 1982).

shallow, and the young person will experience a sense of isolation or loneliness.

The next stage of personality development, Stage VII, is *generativity versus self-absorption and stagnation*. **Generativity** is concerned with establishing and guiding the next generation. It encompasses procreation, productivity, and creativity. The bearing and rearing of children is clearly a key element in Erikson's view of generativity, but it is not the only element. Serving as a mentor for younger colleagues, doing charitable work in society, and the like are also expressions of generativity. Adults who do not find some avenue for successful expression of generativity may become self-absorbed or experience a sense of stagnation. The strength that can emerge from this stage, according to Erikson, is care, which implies both taking care of and caring for or about others or society.

Erikson's final proposed stage, or Stage VIII, is *ego integrity versus despair*. **Ego integrity** is achieved when people look back over their lives and decide whether they find meaning and integration in their life review or meaninglessness and unproductivity. If they see that they have resolved well the conflicts that arose in each previous stage, they are able to reap the fruit of a well-lived life, which Erikson labels "wisdom."

EVALUATING ERIKSON'S STAGES Erikson was a good thinker. He had a combination of formal training in psychoanalysis and informal training in a variety of arenas—as an art student, in his work with Native American people, and in his studies of the lives of a diverse group of individuals such as Mahatma Ghandi, Martin Luther, and Adolf Hitler. His theory makes sense intuitively—it fits the way we think about our own lives and those of others. But how does it hold up under scientific scrutiny? A number of researchers have found ways to test Erikson's theory, with mixed results (See: Ways to Test Erickson's Theory).

In summary, empirical studies have shown that there is good evidence for Erikson's adult stages of psychosocial development. Although the ages do not always match Erikson's "optimal ages" for a stage, there is ample evidence that young adulthood is a time of emphasis on identity concerns. Midlife seems to be a time of forming generativity goals. Intimacy is important in young adulthood, as Erikson stated, but is also a concern at other ages. However, Erikson's theory held that stages are never "over," but are just replaced by new dilemmas, so it is not surprising that so important an aspect of life as intimacy is a concern throughout adulthood.

Ways to Test Erikson's Theory

Inventory of Psychosocial Development

Psychologist Susan Krauss Whitbourne and her colleagues devised a test instrument, the Inventory of Psychosocial Development (IPD), which provides numerical scores for Erikson's psychosocial stages (Walaskay et al., 1983–84). In a sequential study of men and women, they found that scores for Stage V (identity vs. role confusion) increased significantly when participants were between the ages of 20 and 31, but remained stable between the ages of 31 and 42. The mean scores for this group are depicted in Figure 8.8 by the black line marked Cohort 1.

This supports Erikson's views that adolescence and early adulthood is a time to question and explore alternative possibilities for adult identity. Eleven years later, the researchers repeated the testing on a new group of 20-year-olds, following them until they were 31. They found the same results, depicted in Figure 8.8 by the blue line labeled Cohort 2, showing that this was probably not an effect of just one particular cohort (Whitbourne et al., 1992).

Sexual Orientation

An important component of identity is sexual orientation. Psychologist Jerel P. Calzo and colleagues (2011) interviewed over 1,200 gay, lesbian, and bisexual adults between the ages of 18 and 84, asking, among other things, how old

Figure 8.8 Mean Scores for Erikson's Stage V

Mean scores for Erikson's Stage V (Identity) for two cohorts. Scores for both increase significantly between the ages of 20 and 31, but not at later ages.

SOURCE: Adapted from Whitbourne et al. (1992).

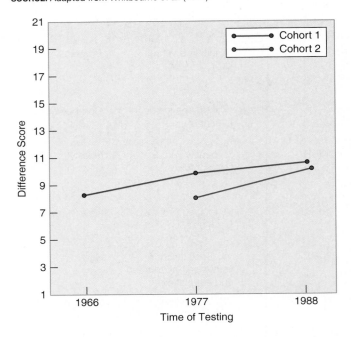

they were when they self-identified as gay, lesbian, or bisexual. The average age was 19.7 years, regardless of age cohort, showing that the formation of this type of identity also tends to occur around the same age as other types.

Late Development

Whitbourne and her colleagues (2009) followed two cohorts of men and women from the age of 20 to the age of 54, evaluating their progress in Erikson's stages of psychosocial development. They found slow increases in all stages, with cohort differences in ego integrity and gender differences in intimacy. Interestingly, individuals who were late in establishing their careers, entering into intimate relationships, or having children, and were at a disadvantage in psychosocial development in early adulthood, were able to catch up and show favorable outcomes by the time they reached middle age.

Generativity

Erikson's Stage VII (generativity versus stagnation) is the stage that has been studied the most. For example, psychologists Kennon Sheldon and Tim Kasser (2001) measured the personality development of a group of adults by asking them to list their current goals, or some of the things they are typically trying to do in their everyday lives that they may or may not be successful at. These goals were then coded according to which Eriksonian stage they best typified. Strivings that involved giving to others or making one's mark on the world were coded as Stage VII (generativity versus stagnation). Results showed that older people were more concerned with generativity than identity, supporting Erikson's belief that this is a major task in later years.

Intimacy Goals

Interestingly, Sheldon and Kasser (2001) also found that adults of all ages reported having intimacy goals, or in other words, listed personal goals that increased the quality of relationships. The researchers interpreted these findings as supporting Erikson's assumptions of lifelong development and the order in which the stages present themselves to individuals across the lifespan, but the lack of reduction of intimacy goals with age "raises the possibility that once mature psychosocial themes become salient within a person's life, they tend to remain important rather than fade away, to be replaced by new themes" (p. 495). Considering the importance that close connections with others have throughout life, it stands to reason that once an individual develops the ability to form intimate bonds, it will remain a priority in his or her list of goals.

The Loyola Generativity Scale

Another test instrument that measures generativity is the Loyola Generativity Scale (LGS), which consists of 20 statements that participants rate according to how well each applies to them personally (McAdams & de St. Aubin, 1992). These statements as shown in Table 8.2 reflect an overall orientation or attitude regarding generativity in one's life and social world.

Interestingly, male participants who were not fathers scored significantly lower on generativity than fathers and women in general. The researchers speculate that fatherhood may have a dramatic impact on men's generativity, increasing their concern for the next generation. (To be fair, one could also argue that experiencing an increase in generativity inspires men to become fathers.)

Generativity in Midlife

Psychologist Dan McAdams and his colleagues (1993, 1998) gave the LGS, along with several other generativity measures, to 152 men and women who made up a stratified random sample of citizens living in Evanston, Illinois. The participants represented three age groups of adults: young (22–27), midlife (37–42), and old (67–72). Results showed that adults in the midlife group, as predicted by Erikson's theory, scored higher on generativity than both the younger and the older groups (see Figure 8.9).

Longitudinal Studies

Christopher Einolf (2014) from DePaul University conducted a longitudinal study looking at generativity over a 10-year period using a subset of items from the Loyola Generativity Scale. He found that there was a great deal of rank-order stability in all age groups over the age of 30. In other words, people who were higher than others in generativity remained higher over the 10-year period, and people who were low in generativity relative to others remained lower. Average generativity levels increased for men in their middle to late 20s at the first test and middle to late 30s at the second test, but there was no age-related change for the women. Einolf found no effect of marriage or having children on generativity and thus was unable to replicate the findings of McAdams and de St. Aubin. More research on the effects of parenthood on generativity is clearly needed.

Recently Johanna Malone and her colleagues (2015) looked at longitudinal data from 159 men who had been followed for over 60 years. They found that higher levels of midlife psychosocial development in men predicted better cognitive abilities and lower levels of depression in old age.

Table 8.2 Loyola Generativity Scale

How well do each of the following statements apply to you? (Rate each item on a scale from 0 to 3, where 0 = never applies to me and 3 = applies to me very often. Items marked with * are reverse scored).

1. I try to pass along the knowledge I have gained through my experiences.
2. I do not feel that other people need me.*
3. I think I would like the work of a teacher.
4. I feel as though I have made a difference to many people.
5. I do not volunteer to work for a charity.*
6. I have made and created things that have had an impact on other people.
7. I try to be creative in most things that I do.
8. I think that I will be remembered for a long time after I die.
9. I believe that society cannot be responsible for providing food and shelter for all homeless people.*
10. Others would say that I have made unique contributions to society.
11. If I were unable to have children of my own, I would like to adopt children.
12. I have important skills that I try to teach others.
13. I feel that I have done nothing that will survive after I die.*
14. In general, my actions do not have a positive effect on other people.*
15. I feel as though I have done nothing of worth to contribute to others.*
16. I have made many commitments to many different kinds of people, groups, and activities in my life.
17. Other people say that I am a very productive person.
18. I have a responsibility to improve the neighborhood in which I live.
19. People come to me for advice.
20. I feel as though my contributions will exist after I die.

SOURCE: McAdams and de St. Aubin (1992).

Figure 8.9 Measures of Generativity

Adults in the midlife group (age 37 to 42) score higher on three measures of Erikson's Stage VII (Generativity) than either younger or older groups.

SOURCE: McAdams et al. (1998).

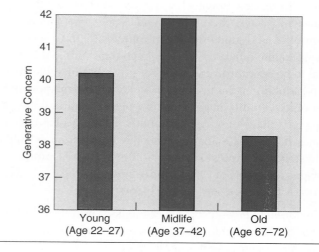

8.4.2: Ego Development

OBJECTIVE: Outline Loevinger's stages of ego development

A second theory with Freudian roots comes from psychologist Jane Loevinger (1976), who suggested a number of stagelike levels of ego development. Like Erikson, Loevinger believed that each level was built on the level that preceded it, but unlike Erikson's theory, a person must complete the developmental tasks in one stage before moving to the next. Although the early stage is typically completed in childhood, the stages have only very loose connections to ages. Thus, a wide range of stages of ego development would be represented among a group of adults of any given age. What Loevinger is describing, in essence, is a pathway along which she thinks we all must move. But the rate of movement and the final stage achieved differ widely from one person to the next, and that difference, according to Loevinger, is the basis of different personality types.

A number of stages have been presented over the 40 years or so this theory has been part of the field of developmental psychology. Some earlier stages are difficult to gather data on because they are most likely to be found in very young children. Later stages are also difficult because so few people have reached them.

Loevinger's Stages of Ego Development

Impulsive Stage—The earliest stage of ego development that can be measured is the *impulsive stage*. This occurs in small children when they become aware of themselves as separate entities from those around them. This separateness is verified when they experience impulses, but they don't have control over them at first, and their emotional range is narrow. They are egocentric and dependent in their interactions with others and preoccupied with bodily feelings. "In small children this stage is charming; when it persists into adolescence and adulthood, it is at best maladaptive and in some cases psychopathic" (Loevinger, 1997, p. 203).

Self-Protective Stage—During the next stage, the *self-protective stage*, the child becomes aware of his or her impulses and gains some control over them to secure at least an immediate advantage. In young children it is natural to be egocentric and self-protective, but in adolescence and adulthood, this becomes exploitation and manipulation of others. In this stage, there is a preoccupation with taking advantage of others and of others taking advantage of oneself, and this is often expressed in hostile humor. Unlike those in the impulsive stage, adults in the self-protective stage are capable of very adaptive behavior and can be very successful in terms of gaining money and power.

Conformist Stage—People in Loevinger's next stage, the *conformist stage*, are able to identify themselves with their reference group, whether it is family, peer group, or work group. They are very concerned with rules and deal with others using cooperation and loyalty. There is a preoccupation with appearances and outward behavior. They think in terms of stereotypes and are rather limited emotionally to standard clichés—they report being happy, sad, mad, glad, and so on.

Self-Aware Stage—The *self-aware stage* is characterized by awareness that there are allowable exceptions to the simple rules the conformists live by. People are aware that they don't always live up to the group's professed standards (and neither do other members of their group). They realize that they have an existence that is separate from their group, and this can be the basis of some loneliness and self-consciousness. It may not surprise you to know that this stage is the one most common in late adolescents and emerging adults.

Conscientious Stage—At the *conscientious stage*, people have formed their own ideals and standards instead of just seeking the approval of their group. They express their inner life using rich and varied words to describe their thoughts and emotions. Interpersonal relationships are intense. They have long-term goals and may even be overly conscientious. This stage may seem similar to Erikson's stage of identity versus role confusion, but Loevinger argues that it can occur well past adolescence and continue far into adulthood.

Individualistic Stage—The next stage is called the *individualistic stage*, and this is the time people take a broad view of life as a whole. They think in terms of psychological causes and are able to consider their own developmental processes. Their interpersonal relationships are mutual and they are preoccupied with a sense of individuality.

Autonomous and Integrated Stages—People in the *autonomous stage* begin to see the multifaceted nature of the world, not just the good and the bad. Life is complex, and most situations don't have simple answers or even one best answer. There is a lessening of the burden taken on at the conscientious stage and a respect for the autonomy of others, even one's own children. And there is the ability to see one's own life in the context of wider social concerns. (Another stage, the integrated stage, is very rare and is not included in most discussions. In this stage the ego is completely integrated.)

MEASURING EGO DEVELOPMENT Loevinger's theory deals with the integration of new perspectives on the self and others, and the stages, or levels, are measured by the Washington University Sentence Completion Test of Ego Development (Hy & Loevinger, 1996). In this test, participants are asked to complete 18 sentence stems, such as "My mother and I . . . ," "A man's job . . . ," and "Rules are . . ." Each response is scored according to guidelines, and then a total score is computed that corresponds to a particular stage or level of ego development.

The sentence-completion test is used to assess the ego development of adults across the lifespan. For example, young adults' ego development stage was found to be a reflection of problems experienced in childhood and adolescence. Most of those who had a history of externalizing disorders (attention problems or aggressive behavior) were below the conformist level at age 22, indicating that they had not reached a stage that involves respect for rules. Many of those who had a history of internalizing disorders (anxiety or depression) had not advanced beyond the conformist level at age 22, indicating that although they had respect for rules, they had not yet reached the self-aware level (Krettenauer et al., 2003).

Psychologists Jack Bauer and Dan McAdams (2004) interviewed middle-aged adults who had been through either a career change or a change in religion, asking questions about personal growth. They also computed their ego development stage according to the Washington University sentence-completion test described earlier. Participants who were at higher levels of ego development on the sentence-completion test were more apt to describe their career change and religion change in terms of *integrative themes* (having new perspectives on the self and others). These adults described their personal growth as increased self-awareness, better understanding of relationships, and a higher level of moral reasoning—all themes that reflect more complex thinking about one's life and meaningful relationships.

Janet Truluck and Bradley Courtenay (2002), researchers in adult education, gave older adults (55–85 years of age) the Washington University sentence-completion test to assess their ego development. There were no gender differences or age effects, but as shown in Figure 8.10,

Figure 8.10 Educational Attainment and Ego Development in Older Adults

In older adults (55–85 years of age), higher education is related to higher levels of ego development.

SOURCE: Based on data from Truluck and Courtenay (2002).

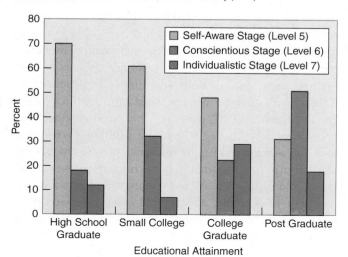

educational level was positively related to ego development. The proportion of people who scored in the self-aware stage was higher for those with only a high school education and declined for people with some college, for college graduates, and then for those with a postgraduate education. The proportion of those in the conscientious and individualistic stages generally increased with educational attainment. Although some researchers have found that educational level is related to ego development in earlier adulthood (Labouvie-Vief & Diehl, 1998), these findings of lifelong effects of education on ego development are interesting, especially considering that most of the older participants' education had been attained decades earlier.

8.4.3: Mature Adaptation

OBJECTIVE: Differentiate between Vaillant's defense mechanisms

A theory that seems to be a cross between Erikson's and Loevinger's theories is that of psychiatrist George Vaillant (1977, 1993). He begins by accepting Erikson's stages as the basic framework of development, but inserts an additional stage between Erikson's stages of intimacy and generativity at some time around the age of 30. Vaillant calls this stage *career consolidation*, the stage when young adults are intent on establishing their own competence, mastering a craft, or acquiring higher status or a positive reputation.

Like Loevinger, Vaillant describes a direction in which personality growth or development may occur, but he does not assume that everyone moves the same distance in this direction. In particular, Vaillant is interested in *mature adaptation*, potential progressive change in the ways adults adapt psychologically to the trials and tribulations they face. The major form of adaptation he discusses is the **defense mechanism**, Freud's term for a set of normal, unconscious strategies used for dealing with anxiety. Everyone has some anxiety, so everyone uses defense mechanisms of some kind. All of them involve some type of self-deception or distortion of reality. We forget things that make us uncomfortable or remember them in a way that is not so unpleasant; we give ourselves reasons for doing something we know we shouldn't do; we project our unacceptable feelings onto others rather than acknowledge them in ourselves. What Vaillant has added to Freud's concept is the notion that some defense mechanisms are more mature than others. In general, mature defenses involve less distortion of reality. They reflect more graceful, less uncomfortable ways of coping with difficulties. Vaillant's central thesis is that an adult's defense mechanisms must mature if he or she is to be able to cope effectively with the slings and arrows of normal life.

Vaillant arranged defense mechanisms into six levels, with the first level as the most mature. The six levels, along with examples of each, are shown in Table 8.3. Vaillant

Table 8.3 Vaillant's Six Levels of Defense Mechanisms

Level	Defense Mechanism	Example
I. High Adaptive Level	Altruism	Dealing with stress over health by participating in a race to raise funds for researching a disease.
II. Mental Inhibition Level	Repression	Dealing with stress over childlessness by expelling thoughts and wishes from conscious awareness.
III. Minor Image-Distorting Level	Omnipotence	Dealing with stress over military assignment by glorifying one's special training and high-tech equipment.
IV. Disavowal Level	Denial	Dealing with stress over marital problems by refusing to acknowledge that a hurtful incident, apparent to others, occurred.
V. Major Image-Distorting Level	Autistic Fantasy	Dealing with stress over potential layoffs by daydreaming about an ideal job instead of taking action to find a new one.
VI. Action Level	Help-Rejecting Complaining	Dealing with stress over money problems by complaining, but then rejecting offers of help and advice.

SOURCE: Adapted from APA (2000).

believed that people use defense mechanisms from several levels at any point in their lives and, at times of stress, may regress to lower levels. However, in the course of life maturation, adults add more and more adaptive defense mechanisms to their psychological toolboxes and use fewer and fewer of the less mature defense mechanisms. So instead of this being a stage theory with discreet steps of development, Vaillant (2002) considered his theory as more of a slope, with those who use more mature defense mechanisms having more integrated personalities and being more successful in their lives. Review each level in the table below. Then check your understanding by dragging and dropping each example to its correct position in the table.

Vaillant based many of his ideas on data from the Harvard Men's Study, a longitudinal study that began with 268 men of the 1922 graduating class of Harvard College and followed them throughout their lives (Heath, 1945). Although Vaillant was not born when the study began, he joined the research group in its 30th year and at age 85 as of this writing, he is still gathering data on the surviving participants. (Interestingly, his father, who died when Vaillant was 13, was an original participant in the study.)

ORIGINS OF VAILLANT'S WORK Vaillant's theory was based on data from numerous interviews, personality tests, and other measurements that were given to the men in the Harvard study over the years. When personality-factors research began to take center stage in the study of personality, he and his colleagues adapted the concept of the Five-Factor Model to fit the longitudinal study of Harvard men. By reviewing early interviews and test results, the researchers were able to assign scores for the five major personality factors to the men at age 22, some 45 years earlier. Then they gave the Five-Factor Personality Inventory (NEO PI) to the 163 surviving participants and compared the early scores with the later scores. The results showed low but significant intra-individual

stability for three factors—Neuroticism, Extraversion, and Openness—despite the cards stacked against the study, such as the very long interval between tests, the use of different tests, and Time 1 being at such a young age (Soldz & Vaillant, 1999).

In addition to looking at individual stability over a 45-year interval, Soldz and Vaillant (1999) also investigated other details of these men's lives to see if their early personality traits were related to actual events and outcomes over the life course. Some of the results were that Extraversion at the age of 22 predicted maximum income during one's working years; the higher a participant scored on this trait, the more money he made. Openness at age 22 predicted creative accomplishments during the men's lifetimes, and early Conscientiousness scores predicted good adult adjustment and low levels of depression, smoking, and alcohol abuse. (Recall earlier in this chapter that Conscientiousness is also related to good health.)

8.4.4: Gender Crossover

OBJECTIVE: Analyze gender crossover for its influences

Psychoanalyst Carl Jung (1933) believed that the second half of life was characterized by exploring and acknowledging the parts of oneself that had been hidden during the first half of life. Men allowed the softer, more nurturant parts of their personalities to emerge, whereas women became more independent and planful. Influenced by Jung's psychoanalytic thought about aging, anthropologist David Gutmann (1987) proposed that adult gender differences in personality begin in young adulthood when both men and women accentuate their own gender characteristics and suppress the other-gender characteristics to attract mates and reproduce. After the parenting years are over and these roles are not paramount in their lives, according to this theory, they are able to relax the suppression and allow some of the "other-gender" characteristics to emerge.

Gutmann referred to this relaxation of gender roles at midlife as **gender crossover**. He believed that aging does not represent a loss at this time but, rather, a gain in personal freedom and new roles within the "tribe." Gutmann also found support for his ideas in his experiences among the Mayan, Navajo, and Druze societies, showing that men move from active mastery, which involves making changes in external circumstances, to accommodative mastery, which is making changes in one's inner self, and that women move from accommodative to active mastery.

Psychologist Ravenna Helson and her colleagues (1997) reviewed data from three longitudinal studies of different cohorts of college students. They found support for Gutmann's theory in the responses of the women participants, most of whom expressed interest in marriage and family. The difference in cohorts was that the earlier cohorts (who were young adults in the 1930s and 1940s) were concerned about choosing between a career and a family, and the more recent ones (who were young adults in the 1980s) were concerned about combining both a career and a family. The males in the study seldom expressed those concerns.

Helson explored the reasons for change and ruled out the narrow interpretation of stereotypical gender traits as important for parenting; the dramatic increase in women's competence, independence, and self-confidence at midlife was evident whether the women were mothers or had remained childless. Furthermore, it depended on what opportunities were available for women at the time they were going through these age-related changes.

There seems to be evidence of men's and women's personalities blending in middle and late adulthood, but this does not constitute a true "crossover," in which women become more masculine than men and men become more feminine than women. What the research findings show is best described as an increased openness to the expression of previously unexpressed parts of the self. The cause for this blending does not strictly seem to be parenthood because it is not limited to those who have had children. The change seems to be stronger for women than for men. Helson suggests that we are viewing a complex biosocial phenomenon that involves hormones, social roles, historical changes, and economic climate.

WRITING PROMPT

Gender Crossover Today

What kind of meaning does the concept of "gender crossover" hold in a society where a percentage of people identify as nonbinary?

▶ The response entered here will appear in the performance dashboard and can be viewed by your instructor.

Submit

8.4.5: Positive Well-Being

OBJECTIVE: Summarize the approaches of positive psychology

Another approach that has its roots in psychoanalytic theory comes from psychologist Abraham Maslow (1968/1998), who traced his theoretical roots to Freud and offered some highly original insights. As a humanistic psychologist, Maslow's most central concern was with the development of motives or needs, which he divided into two main groups: deficiency motives and being motives. *Deficiency motives* involve instincts or drives to correct an imbalance or to maintain physical or emotional homeostasis, such as getting enough to eat, satisfying thirst, or obtaining enough love and respect from others. Deficiency motives are found in all animals. *Being motives*, in contrast, are distinctly human. Maslow argued that humans have unique desires to discover and understand, to give love to others, and to push for the optimum fulfillment of their inner potentials.

In general, Maslow believed that the satisfaction of deficiency motives prevents or cures illness, and re-creates homeostasis (inner balance). In contrast, the satisfaction of being motives produces positive health. The distinction is like the "difference between fending off threat or attack, and positive triumph and achievement" (Maslow, 1968/1998, p. 32). But being motives are quite fragile and do not typically emerge until well into adulthood, and then only under supportive circumstances. Maslow's well-known needs hierarchy (shown in Figure 8.11) reflects this aspect of his thinking. The lowest four levels all describe different deficiency motives, whereas only the highest level, the need for **self-actualization**, is a being motive. Furthermore, Maslow proposed that these five levels emerge sequentially in

---

Figure 8.11 Maslow's Hierarchy of Needs

Maslow's hierarchy of needs proposes that lower needs dominate the individual's motivations and that higher needs become prominent only late in life and when the lower needs are satisfied.

SOURCE: Maslow (1968/1998).

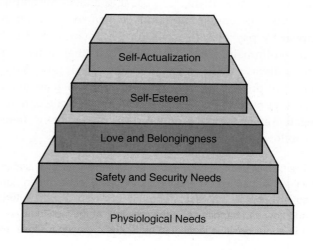

development and tend to dominate the system from the bottom up. That is, if you are starving, the physiological needs dominate. If you are being physically battered, the safety needs dominate. The need for self-actualization emerges only when all four types of deficiency needs are largely satisfied.

Instead of studying people with mental health problems, Maslow sought to understand the personalities and characteristics of those few adults who seemed to have risen to the top of the needs hierarchy and achieved significant levels of self-understanding and expression, people such as Eleanor Roosevelt, Albert Schweitzer, and Albert Einstein. Some of the key characteristics of self-actualized people, as Maslow saw them, are having an accurate perception of reality, being involved in deep personal relationships, being creative, and having a good-natured sense of humor. He described self-actualized individuals as having **peak experiences**—feelings of perfection and momentary separation from the self when one feels in unity with the universe.

ADAPTATIONS AND APPLICATIONS OF POSITIVE WELL-BEING Maslow and other humanistic psychologists such as Carl Rogers (1959) had their major influence in clinical psychology and self-help movements. In some of the later adaptations and applications of these ideas by others, the need for self-actualization has become more self-centered and less centered on the collective well-being of humankind than Maslow had envisioned. One reason is that Maslow's theory had little empirical testing; it was not stated very scientifically, and there were no means developed for assessing the dominance of the various motives he proposed. For some reason this theory did not attract the attention of research psychologists who might have picked up the ball and advanced it further down the field. However, there is something about Maslow's theory that is appealing to us; it fits our gut-level feeling of what life is all about. We can experience its truth in our lives almost every day. When we feel endangered by terrorist attacks, we are not too concerned about whether we will be graduating next year with two gold braids on our shoulders or just one.

There has been a renewed interest in humanistic psychology and new attempts to use it as a basis for empirical studies. Foremost among this movement has been the appeal by psychologists Martin Seligman and Mihaly Csikszentmihalyi (2000) for a new focus that turns away from a disease model of human behavior that is fixated on curing or preventing negative conditions such as mental illness, crime, failure, victimization, abuse, brain damage, negative effects of stress, and poverty. Instead, they offered the following focus on **positive psychology**:

> The field of positive psychology at the subjective level is about valued subjective experiences: well-being, contentment, and satisfaction (in the past); hope and optimism (for the future); and flow and happiness (in the present). At the individual level, it is about positive individual traits: the capacity for love and vocation, courage, interpersonal skill, aesthetic sensibility, perseverance, forgiveness, originality, future mindedness, spirituality, high talent, and wisdom. At the group level, it is about the civic virtues and the institutions that move individuals toward better citizenship: responsibility, nurturance, altruism, civility, moderation, tolerance, and work ethic. (p. 5)

SELF-DETERMINATION THEORY One result of this movement is a personality theory that has some components of Maslow's theory of self-actualization. This theory, formulated by psychologists Richard Ryan and Edward Deci (2000; Deci & Ryan, 2008b), is known as **self-determination theory**. It holds that personality is based on individuals' evolved inner resources for growth and integration. Ryan and Deci believe that the need for personal growth and personality development is an essential part of human nature. The extent to which we succeed in this endeavor is the basis of our personalities. They stress how important it is for individuals to experience what they call *eudaimonia*—a sense of integrity and well-being similar to Maslow's concept of self-actualization. They believe that too much emphasis is placed on *hedonia*—happiness that involves the presence of positive feelings and the absence of negative feelings (Deci & Ryan, 2008a). In contrast, they say that eudaimonia entails the basic needs for competence, autonomy, and relatedness. Ryan and Deci (2000) theorize that individuals cannot thrive without satisfying all three of these needs—and thus an environment that fosters competence and autonomy but not relatedness, for example, will result in a compromised sense of well-being.

Three Basic Needs of Self-Determination Theory

Competence—According to Ryan and Deci's theory, *Competence* is the feeling of effectiveness as one interacts with one's environment. It's not necessary to be the best, but in terms of the U.S. Army slogan, it's important to "be all that you can be." It's feeling challenged and seeing the results of your efforts. This can be difficult during late adulthood, but the authors caution that competence doesn't mean being better than before; sometimes it means modifying the environment, selecting which activities to perform, and redirecting extra resources to doing those activities well—a strategy they refer to as "having a choice over challenges."

Autonomy—The need for *autonomy* means that we need to feel that our actions are being done by our own volition. We are making decisions to act, and our actions reflect our true inner selves and not someone else's rules or guidelines. It means that a person is acting due to internal controls and not external ones. This is not always easy for independent adults, but it is much more difficult at other stages of life, such as childhood, adolescence, and the later years of adulthood when people are dependent on others to a greater degree. However, Ryan and LaGuardia (2000) believe that dependence does not rule out autonomy. In fact, they found that dependent patients in nursing homes that allow them to make many of their own decisions are both physically and psychologically healthier than patients in homes that allow less autonomy.

Relatedness—In self-determination theory, *Relatedness* refers to the feeling of being connected to, cared about, and belonging with significant others in one's life. It's the feeling that others are standing behind you with love and affection. Like the other basic needs, this one changes with age. In the later years, the quality of contact with friends and family members takes precedence over the quantity of contact. Kasser and Ryan (1999) found that the quality of relatedness and social support felt by nursing-home residents along with the sense of autonomy (and the support they felt for being autonomous) predicted positive outcomes, such as lower incidence of depression, higher satisfaction with life, and higher self-esteem.

Psychologist Christopher P. Niemiec and his colleagues (2009) applied the concepts of self-determination theory to recent college graduates to see if the types of goals and aspirations they had attained 2 years after graduation were related to their psychological well-being. They found that the graduates who expressed intrinsic goals (personal growth, close relationships, and community involvement) and had attained those goals 2 years after graduation showed better psychological well-being than those who had expressed extrinsic goals (money, fame, and image) and who had attained those goals. In fact, those who had attained extrinsic goals showed more indicators of psychological ill-being. The authors summed up their study with a quotation from Aristotle (around 350 BCE): "[Happiness] belongs more to those who have cultivated their character and mind to the uttermost, and kept acquisition of external goods within moderate limits, than it does to those who have managed to acquire more external goods than they can possibly use, and are lacking goods of the soul. . . . Any excessive amount of such things must either cause its possessor some injury, or, at any rate, bring him no benefit" (Aristotle, 1946, pp. 280–281).

Summary: Personality

8.1 Personality Structures

OBJECTIVE: Apply the Five-Factor Model to concepts of personality

- Early ideas about adult personality were based on grand theories of development that were popular and enthusiastically endorsed but not empirically tested and validated.

- One of the first methods of testing and validating ideas about personality was the trait structure approach, in which a small number of trait structures were identified through factor analysis. The most prominent of these models is Costa and McCrae's Five-Factor Model (FFM), which identifies Neuroticism, Extraversion, Openness to experience, Agreeableness, and Conscientiousness as the basic factors of human personality.

- Differential continuity has been found for the major five factors of personality through childhood and adulthood. People tend to keep their rank orders within groups regardless of gender. The level of stability increases with age through the 70s, but never becomes totally stable, showing that personality can change throughout life.

- What happens to personality traits as people get older? We become more agreeable and conscientious, less neurotic and open.

- Personality trait structures can be stable in some ways (differential continuity) and change in others (mean-level changes). The former is relative to others in your age group, the latter is your group in comparison to a different age group. You can be the most conscientious person in your age group throughout your life, but the average level of scores for that trait may increase as you (and your agemates) get older.

8.2 What Do Personality Traits Do?

OBJECTIVE: Analyze how personality impacts life experiences

- Personality traits are related to the development of intimate relationships, career success, and health in adulthood. People who are high in Agreeableness and low in Neuroticism have relationships that last longer and are more satisfying than those who are lower in these traits. Those who have high levels of Conscientiousness are more apt to do their jobs well and advance quickly in their careers than those who are lower in these traits. High levels of Conscientiousness and low levels of Neuroticism predict better health and longevity.

8.3 Explanations of Continuity and Change

OBJECTIVE: Evaluate measures of personality change and stability

- The five major personality structures have a significant genetic component, but there are mixed findings about the primary factors. The genetic influence is found to be greater in childhood than in adulthood, when environmental influences are stronger.

- People work together with their environments to keep their personalities stable by the way they interpret events, the way they act toward others that elicits responses compatible with their personalities, the way they select situations that fit and reinforce their personalities, and the way they make changes in surroundings that are incompatible with their personalities.

- Evolutionary psychologists argue that personality traits give us important survival cues about the people in our environment and, as a result, have been selected for throughout our evolutionary history. Furthermore, personality traits may develop to complement inherited physical characteristics to ensure survival and reproductive success.

- Researchers have been finding subtle cultural differences in personality traits and factors among Chinese, Korean, and Vietnamese groups and are developing alternative models and scales to measure personality traits in collectivist cultures.

8.4 Theories of Personality Development

OBJECTIVE: Interpret personality using theories of personality development

- Erikson's theory of psychosocial development states that personality development takes place in distinct stages over the lifespan. Each stage represents a conflict the individual must try to resolve. Each resolution attempt brings the potential for a new strength gained. Four stages take place in adulthood as individuals attempt to establish identities, form intimate partnerships, tend to the next generation, and find meaning at the end of their lives. Although Erikson's theory was not data based or scientifically tested before it was presented, recent research has shown that establishing an identity is a concern for most younger adults but not for most middle-aged adults and that this is true for intimacy also. Other studies have shown that middle-aged adults are more concerned with generativity goals than younger adults.

- Loevinger's theory of ego development parted with Erikson's theory on the concept of stages. She believed that adults make their way along the incline from one stage to the other, but don't have to complete the whole progression. Personality depends on which stage a person ultimately attains. The stages represent movement toward interdependence, values, attitudes toward rules, and evaluations of the self. Recent research has shown that Loevinger's test of ego development predicts how people will describe personal outcomes of life events, and that ego development increases with education.

- Vaillant's theory of mature adaptation is based on levels of defense mechanisms—normal, unconscious strategies we use for dealing with anxiety. He posed six levels, beginning with the most mature and proceeding on to those that involve more and more self-deception, suggesting that we use several levels, but the ones we use the most determine the maturity of our adaptations. Recent research has incorporated trait-theory tests with more traditional personality evaluations on a group of older Harvard men who have been studied longitudinally since they were undergraduates. Vaillant has found stability in rank for Neuroticism, Extraversion, and Openness over a 45-year period; some factors at the age of 22 predicted later outcomes in health and career.

- Gutmann's theory of gender crossover explains that young adults strive to display accentuated gender traits to attract mates and raise children. After the parenting years are over, they are able to express the hidden sides of their personalities by displaying the gender traits of the opposite sex. Studies show that there is a tendency for both men and women to incorporate characteristics of the other gender, but it's more of a blending than a true crossover, and it seems to be independent of being a parent.

- Maslow's theory of self-actualization consists of stages of a sort, in the form of a needs hierarchy, with the most-pressing biological needs coming first; once they are satisfied, the individual turns his or her attention to higher-level needs. The highest is self-actualization, which Maslow believed was seldom achieved. A recent reformulation of this theory is found in self-determination theory, which states our basic needs as being competence, autonomy, and relatedness. Research based on this idea has shown that fulfilling all three needs is necessary for high scores on a number of indicators of well-being, such as career success, good health, and life satisfaction.

SHARED WRITING

Human Personality Traits

Consider this chapter's discussion of personality traits. What are the basic personality traits or patterns of thoughts, feelings, and behaviors exhibited by humans? Why do you think these have become so fundamental to us as humans? How do they distinguish us from other animals? Write a short response that your classmates will read. Be sure to discuss specific examples.

  A minimum number of characters is required to post and earn points. After posting, your response can be viewed by your class and instructor, and you can participate in the class discussion.

Post

0 characters | 140 minimum

Chapter 9
The Quest for Meaning

The quest for meaning can take many forms.

Learning Objectives

9.1 Explain why we study the search for meaning

9.2 Analyze how interaction with meaning systems changes over time

9.3 Apply theories of spiritual development

9.4 Compare theories of meaning and personality

9.5 Analyze how individuals develop through transitions

9.6 Assess common metaphors used to make sense of the development of adult meaning systems

A Word from the Author

Seeking Spirituality

MY GRANDPARENTS lived next door throughout my childhood, and their search for meaning began and ended at the Presbyterian church. It was the center of their lives and the answer to all their questions. My grandfather began Sunday mornings teaching Sunday School to a group of teenage boys—most of whom were in the Boy Scout troop he led. Then he attended morning church service, where my grandmother played the organ. Wednesday nights were for Prayer Meeting. During the week, at least during their retirement years, they visited the sick and helped out in the food and clothing bank the church ran. Most of their friends and neighbors attended the same church. Ten percent of their income went to the church, and they did not drink alcohol, use tobacco, or dance. The Holy Bible (King James version) was part of their home decor, and it was well read. Before every meal around their table, we expressed appreciation for our food with a prayer beginning, "God is great, God is good. Let us thank Him for our food."

Today life is more complicated, and the search for meaning in our family has gone in new directions. I no longer attend church services, and only one of my three sisters does—and it is not the Presbyterian church of our childhood. We contribute to our community through civic donations and volunteer work, not through the church. Our talk about spiritual matters takes place in book clubs, at Sunday dinner, or at cocktail parties (where we drink alcohol and sometimes dance!). Around our dining room table are family members who seek meaning through yoga, psychotherapy, mindfulness, meditation, and science. Frequent guests include a friend who is a devout Catholic, a colleague who is Muslim, and a neighbor who believes that the answer to everything can be found in the teachings of Alcoholics Anonymous. Two young adult grandchildren are currently vocal atheists. Instead of a prayer, meals around our dinner table begin with "Bon appétit!"

Sometimes I think that my late grandparents would be horrified to see what kind of family I have created. But then I realize that we are all searching for the same thing. We are trying to find out why we are here, what is the best way to spend this lifetime, and how to prepare for what happens next (if anything does).

Spirituality is a common characteristic of our species. Burial sites that date back 30,000 years reveal bodies buried with food, pots, and weapons, seemingly provisions for the afterlife. Today, 80% of people in the United States say they believe in God and an additional 9% believe in some higher power or spiritual force. Almost half of Americans agree with the statement that "God or a higher power directly determines what happens in their lives all or most of the time" (Pew Research Center, 2018). This **quest for meaning**, also known as **spirituality**, is the self's search for ultimate knowledge of life through an individualized understanding of the sacred (Wink & Dillon, 2002). Whether through the practice of traditional religion or a personal quest to find self-enlightenment, the search for meaning is an integral part of the human experience. This chapter addresses that quest and how it unfolds over the adult years.

9.1: Why We Study the Quest for Meaning

OBJECTIVE: Explain why we study the search for meaning

While age-related changes in personality and the progression toward self-actualization are certainly aspects of inner growth in adulthood, there is another aspect to inner development—perhaps more speculative, but certainly no less vital to most of us—that touches on questions of meaning. As we move through adulthood, do we interpret our experiences differently? Do we attach different meanings to or understand our world in new ways? Do we become wiser, less worldly, or more spiritual?

Certainly, a link between advancing age and increasing wisdom has been part of the folk tradition in virtually every culture in the world, as evidenced by fairy tales, myths, and religious teachings (Campbell, 1949/1990). Adult development, according to these sources, brings an increased storehouse of worldly knowledge and experience. It also brings a different perspective on life, a different set of values, and a different worldview, a process often described as **self-transcendence**, or coming to know oneself as part of a larger whole that exists beyond the physical body and personal history. What I am interested in knowing is whether this process is part of—or potentially part of—the normal process of adult development.

By the end of this module, you will be able to:

9.1.1 Differentiate meaning from experience

9.1.2 Relate the quest for meaning to life as a human being

9.1.3 Describe ways that cultural traditions and psychological theorists have supported the concept of gerotranscendence

9.1.1: Meaning Matters

OBJECTIVE: Differentiate meaning from experience

Why talk about meaning? There are three major reasons that the discussion of meaning is interesting. First, different people attach different meanings to the same experience. Second, the quest for meaning is a basic human characteristic, and third, most cultures believe that spirituality and wisdom increase with age. I discuss all three of these reasons in the following sections.

It is the meaning we attach to experience that matters, rather than the experience itself.

Most fundamentally, psychologists have come to understand that individual experiences do not affect us in some uniform, automatic way; rather, it is the way we interpret an experience, the meaning we give it, that is really critical. There are certain basic assumptions individuals make about the world and their place in it, about themselves and their capacities that affect their interpretations of experiences. Such a system of meanings is sometimes referred to as an *internal working model* that determines how we experience the world. For example, according to attachment theory, we form internal working models of the attachment relationships we had with our parents, and these models influence the way we approach relationships with other people. If my internal model includes the assumption that "people are basically helpful and trustworthy," that assumption is clearly going to affect not only the experiences I will seek out, but also my interpretation of those experiences. The objective experiences each of us have are thus filtered through various internal working models before they convey meaning to us. I would argue that the ultimate consequence of any given experience is largely (if not wholly) determined by the meaning we attach and not the experience itself. To the extent that this is true, then, it is obviously important for us to try to understand the meaning systems that adults create.

WRITING PROMPT

A Meaningful Moment

Think of an event in your life that was particularly meaningful. How was the event itself different from the meaning you attached to it?

▶ The response entered here will appear in the performance dashboard and can be viewed by your instructor.

Submit

9.1.2: The Quest for Meaning is Human

OBJECTIVE: Relate the quest for meaning to life as a human being

The quest for meaning is a basic human characteristic.

A second reason for exploring this rather slippery area of adult development is that the quest for meaning is a central theme in the lives of most adults. This is echoed in the writings of many clinicians and theorists. Psychoanalyst Erich Fromm (1956) listed the need for meaning as one of the five central existential needs of human beings. Psychiatrist Viktor Frankl (1984) argued that the "will to meaning" is a basic human motive. Theologian and psychologist James Fowler has made a similar point: "One characteristic all human beings have in common is that we can't live without some sense that life is meaningful" (1981, p. 58). Thus, not only do we interpret our experiences and in this way "make meaning," but it may also be true that the need or motive to create meaningfulness is a vital one in our lives.

More recently, evolutionary psychologist Jesse Bering (2006) wrote that a sense of spirituality is an important component of our species' social cognitive system.

9.1.3: Cultures Support Gerotranscendence

OBJECTIVE: Describe ways that cultural traditions and psychological theorists have supported the concept of gerotranscendence

Most cultures support the tradition that spirituality and wisdom increase with age.

There has always been anecdotal evidence of **gerotranscendence**, the idea that meaning systems increase in quality as we age, beginning with myths and fairy tales about wise elders (Tornstam, 1996). Early theorists in psychology explained the development of meaning as a growth process. For example, psychoanalyst Carl Jung (1964) proposed that young adulthood was a time of turning outward, a time to establish relationships, start families, and concentrate on careers. But at midlife, when adults become aware of their own mortality, they turn inward and strive to expand their sense of self. In this way, the outward focus of the first half of life is balanced by the inward focus of the second half, completing the process of self-realization. Similarly, psychologist Klaus Riegel (1973) proposed that cognitive development extends to **postformal stages** that appear in midlife when adults are able to go beyond the linear and logical ways of thinking described in Piaget's formal operations stage. In this postformal stage, adults are able to view the world in a way that adds feelings and context to the logic and reason proposed by Piaget and use their cognitive abilities in a quest for meaning (Sinnott, 1994).

Regardless of whether changes in meaning systems over age are a function of normal development or the result of lifetime experience, it is generally agreed that the development of meaning systems in adulthood is a real phenomenon and worthy of scientific attention.

9.2: The Study of Age-Related Changes in Meaning Systems

OBJECTIVE: Analyze how interaction with meaning systems changes over time

We now come to a difficult question: how do we explore something so apparently fuzzy as changes in meaning systems? An obvious idea is to look at **religiosity**, the outward signs of spirituality, such as participation in religious services or being a member of a religious organization. Quantitative studies of such matters attempt to answer questions like: Do adults attend religious services more (or less) as they get older? Is there some kind of age-linked pattern?

Some theologians and psychologists believe that we need to dig deeper than observable behavior and use a measure of personal, individualized spirituality to answer questions about age-related changes in meaning systems. We all know of people who go through the motions of religiosity but cannot be described as spiritual. Some researchers use questionnaires asking about personal beliefs, and others use personal interviews, asking open-ended questions that give more depth but are more difficult to analyze. These studies of individualized spirituality are very fruitful because they have shown that personal beliefs about the quest for meaning are not necessarily related to religiosity.

Yet another approach is to use a qualitative method, such as reviewing case studies drawn from biographies or autobiographies, personal reports by well-known adults (politicians, saints, philosophers, mystics) about the steps and processes of their own inner development. Collections of such data have been analyzed, perhaps most impressively by William James (a distinguished early American psychologist) in his book *The Varieties of Religious Experience* (1902/1958) and by theologian and philosopher Evelyn Underhill in her book *Mysticism* (1911/1961). Of course, personal reports do not fit with our usual notion of "scientific evidence." The participants being studied are not representative of the general population, and the "data" may not be objectively gathered. Still, information from such sources makes a valuable contribution to theories of age-related changes in meaning systems. They tell us something about what may be possible or about the qualities, meaning systems, or capacities of a few extraordinary adults who appear to have explored the depths of the human spirit. Yet, even if we accept such descriptions as valid reports of inner processes, it is a very large leap to apply the described steps or processes to the experiences of ordinary folks. It is surely obvious (but nonetheless worth stating explicitly) that I bring my own meaning system to this discussion. I approach this subject with a strong hypothesis that there are "higher" levels of human potential than most of us have yet reached, whether they are expressed in Maslow's terms as self-actualization, in Loevinger's concept of the integrated personality, or in any other terms that express advanced progress in the quest for meaning. When I describe the various models of the development of meaning systems, I am inevitably filtering the theories and the evidence through this hypothesis.

I begin with some empirical research on the search for meaning in adulthood and then add some discussion of the development of moral thinking, which is a manifestation of spirituality. And finally, I discuss some qualitative work, namely some case studies of the quest for meaning by prominent writers and historical figures.

▽   **By the end of this module, you will be able to:**

9.2.1   Describe changes in spirituality over time in the United States

9.2.2   Relate spirituality to health

9.2.1: Changes in the Quest for Meaning

OBJECTIVE: Describe changes in spirituality over time in the United States

Let us begin with the empirical research on religion and spirituality. There has been a surge of research on these two topics in the last few decades. Out of curiosity, I checked the listings in the PsycINFO database for empirical journal articles with the keywords "religion" or "spirituality" since 1973. The number of articles has increased from zero in the first 10 years to over 7,000 in the most recent year. And one of the most-studied topics within this area has been age-related changes in religion and spirituality.

Overall attendance and membership in religious organizations have dropped in the United States over the last 50 years, but as you can see in Figure 9.1, attendance at religious services is higher for adults age 65 and older than for younger adults (Pew Research Center, 2014). Religious affiliation is also higher for older than younger adults in most other countries (Pew Research Center, 2018). The few longitudinal studies on this topic show a decline in religious participation in very late life, but this decline is related to declining health and functional ability (Benjamins et al., 2003). In general, the consensus seems to be that there is an increase in religiosity over the life course, with a short period of health-related dropoff at the end of life (Idler, 2006). In addition, data show that women attend religious services at higher rates than men for all ages and in all religions and countries studied (Miller & Stark, 2002). Religious participation is higher in the United States than in most European countries but lower than in most countries in Africa, the Middle East, South Asia, and Latin America (Pew Research Center, 2018).

When it comes to religious beliefs and private religious activities such as engaging in prayers, meditating, or reading sacred texts, cross-sectional studies show that older adults participate in private religious behavior more than younger people (Pew Research Center, 2018). And a longitudinal study that showed a dropoff in attendance at religious services in very late adulthood also showed stable or even increased levels of private religious practices for this age group at the same time (Idler et al., 2001).

Figure 9.1 Participation in Religious Activities in the United States

The conclusion from these studies is that there is an increase in religious beliefs and private religious activities over adulthood, with a period of stability at the end of life (Idler, 2006).

SOURCE: Pew Research Center (2014).

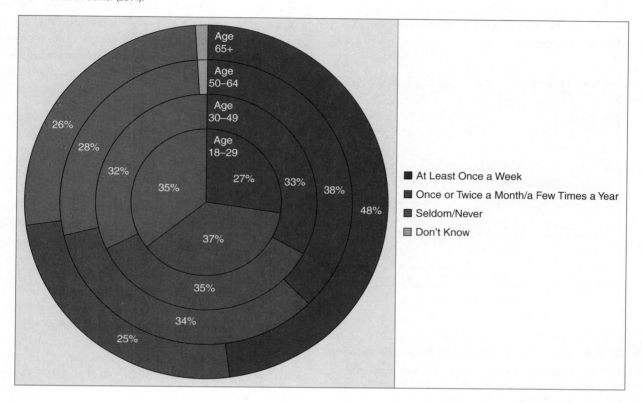

- At Least Once a Week
- Once or Twice a Month/a Few Times a Year
- Seldom/Never
- Don't Know

WRITING PROMPT

Spirituality over Time

Think about your own sense of spirituality. In what ways has it changed or remained the same since you were a child?

▶ The response entered here will appear in the performance dashboard and can be viewed by your instructor.

[Submit]

SPIRITUALITY BY GENDER AND COHORT In a longitudinal study that spanned 40 years, psychologist Paul Wink and sociologist Michele Dillon (2002) analyzed data from the Institute for Human Development longitudinal study to evaluate participants on their level of spirituality over the course of the study. The study included over 200 men and women, and most were interviewed four times between the ages of 31 and 78. In addition, the participants represented two cohorts, the younger born in 1927 and the older in 1920. The results are shown in Figure 9.2. As you can see, there was an increase in spirituality for women from middle to late-middle to older adulthood and an increase for men from late-middle to older adulthood.

When the younger and older cohorts were compared, Wink and Dillon (2002) found different patterns of spiritual development, as shown in Figure 9.3. The spirituality of the younger cohort increased significantly throughout their adult lives, whereas the spirituality of the older cohort, only increased in the last stage, between late-middle and older adulthood (although the older cohort was significantly more spiritual when they were young than the younger cohort). Wink and Dillon concluded that there is a tendency for men and women to increase in spirituality between the mid-50s and mid-70s. They become more involved with the quest for meaning as they become increasingly aware that their lives will end at some point in the future. The years from early to middle adulthood were more varied, depending on the gender and the cohort being studied. Women typically begin their quest for meaning in their 40s. In addition, people born less than a decade apart may show the same general increase in spirituality over adulthood, but they may show different patterns of spirituality. Wink and Dillon speculated that the younger cohort, who showed greater spirituality in their 30s, were living in the 60s when the "Age of Aquarius" was in its prime, and they were at an age that was more responsive to cultural changes than the older cohort, who were in their 40s at the time. So to answer the question of whether there is an increase in spirituality during adulthood, the answer is yes, but the timing depends on age, gender, and also the cultural conditions that prevail when adults are at certain critical ages.

Figure 9.2 Spirituality by Sex and Stage of Adulthood

Spirituality increases with age, but there are different patterns for men and women. Both men and women are stable in their spirituality until middle adulthood. Women begin an increase in middle adulthood, and this continues into late adulthood. In comparison, men don't begin an increase until late-middle adulthood.

SOURCE: Wink and Dillon (2002).

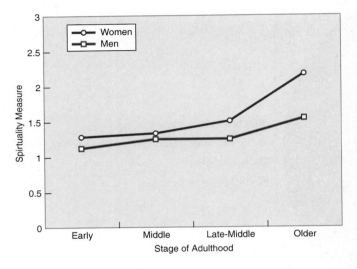

Figure 9.3 Spirituality by Cohort and Stage of Adulthood

The age-related increase in spirituality is different for two cohorts born 7 years apart. The older cohort (born in 1920) did not show an increase in spirituality until late-middle adulthood. In comparison, the younger cohort (born in 1927) showed an increase in spirituality throughout adulthood, from early adulthood until late adulthood.

SOURCE: Wink and Dillon (2002).

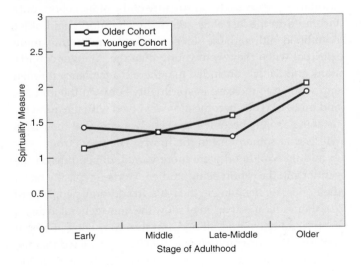

Psychologist Padmaprabha Dalby (2006) performed a meta-analysis on studies of changes in spirituality over the adult years and found an age-related increase in certain aspects of spirituality, such as integrity, humanistic concern, positive relationships with others, concern for the younger generations, relationship with a higher

power, self-transcendence, and acceptance of death. However, these increases seemed to be responses to the adversities of later adulthood, such as poor health, disability, one's own impending death, and the loss of loved ones, rather than related to age itself. This has been suggested as an alternative to the idea that an accumulation of general life experience brings forth self-transcendence, but as Dalby pointed out, there are no studies comparing people of the same ages who differ in health and other measures of adversity.

9.2.2: Religion, Spirituality, and Health

OBJECTIVE: Relate spirituality to health

In the past decade, a large number of studies in a variety of scientific fields, including psychology, epidemiology, and medicine, have explored the relationship religion and spirituality have with health. In general, consistent and robust findings have shown that people who attend religious services live longer than people who do not (Chida et al., 2009), and that this result is stronger for women than for men (Tartaro et al., 2005). Other studies have shown that religious involvement serves a protective role regarding mental health for European Americans, African Americans, and Asian Americans (Ai et al., 2013). Spirituality and religiosity are related to lower levels of anxiety and depression (Brown et al., 2013). A meta-analysis showed that attendance at religious services was associated with lower levels of cardiovascular deaths (Chida et al., 2009). Even when studies are controlled for healthy behaviors, socioeconomic factors, and health factors, religious practices and spirituality remain significant factors (Masters & Hooker, 2012).

In addition, meditation has been linked to both lower cortisol levels and lower blood pressure levels (Seeman et al., 2003). It has been demonstrated that people who possess the personality trait of hardiness and who are committed to finding meaning in their lives are more resilient to the effects of stress than those who have lower levels of this trait. These people have confidence that they will be able to cope with whatever situations life hands them and will find meaning in the process (Maddi, 2005).

What is it about religiosity and spirituality that affects health? A number of mechanisms have been suggested, including the fact that most religions promote healthy behavior, provide social support, teach coping skills, and promote positive emotions (McCullough et al., 2000). One reason that spirituality is linked with better health is that spirituality is associated with a reduction in loneliness (Gallegos & Segrin, 2018). Religiosity and spirituality can have a number of effects on our physical health (see 'Religious Participation and Stress').

Religious Participation and Stress

In one study of the effect of religious participation and spirituality on physiological stress reactions, psychologist Jessica Tartaro and her colleagues (2005) found that participants who scored high on a test of religiosity and spirituality showed lower levels of cortisol responses to lab-induced stress. The researchers gave the test to 60 undergraduate students who represented a variety of religious affiliations, including 22% who had their "own beliefs." Sample questions from this test are shown in Table 9.1.

Table 9.1 Sample Items from the Brief Multidimensional Measure of Religiousness/Spirituality (BMMRS)

I find strength and comfort in my religion	How often do you go to religious services?
many times a day.	More than once a week
every day.	Every week or more often
most days.	Every month or so
some days.	Once or twice a month
once in a while.	Once or twice a year
never or almost never.	Never
I am spiritually touched by the beauty of creation	**How often do you pray privately in places other than at church or synagogue?**
many times a day.	More than once a day
every day.	Once a day
most days.	A few times a week
some days.	Once a week
once in awhile.	A few times a month
never or almost never.	Once a month
	Never
I feel a deep sense of responsibility for reducing pain and suffering in the world.	**I think about how my life is part of a larger spiritual force**
Strongly agree	a great deal.
Agree	quite a bit.
Disagree	somewhat.
Strongly disagree	not at all.
I have forgiven those who hurt me.	**I try hard to carry my religious beliefs over into all my other dealings in life.**
Always or almost always	Strongly agree
Often	Agree
Seldom	Disagree
Never	Strongly disagree

SOURCE: Adapted from Underwood (2008).

Later the students' cortisol levels were measured before and after performing two computer tasks that had been shown to induce physiological indicators of stress reactivity. Cortisol is a hormone released as part of the stress response and is related to decreases in immune system response. Results are shown in Figure 9.4. For the question "To what extent do you consider yourself a religious person?" those who responded "not at all" showed significantly higher cortisol response levels than those who responded that they were "slightly," "moderately," or "very" religious. When responses to the specific religious or spiritual practices were examined, two areas were found to be associated with the cortisol response—forgiveness and frequency of prayer. The researchers concluded that religious practices and spiritual beliefs, especially forgiveness and prayer, may serve to protect individuals from the damaging effects of stress.

Figure 9.4 Religiosity and Stress Reactivity

Young adults who described themselves as "not being religious at all" had greater stress reactivity than those who describes themselves as being "slightly," "moderately," or "very" religious.

SOURCE: Tartaro et al. (2005).

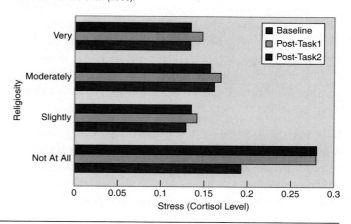

9.3: Theories of Spiritual Development

OBJECTIVE: Apply theories of spiritual development

For several reasons, it helps to begin an exploration of theories of spiritual development with a look at psychologist Lawrence Kohlberg's theory of the development of **moral reasoning**—reasoning about what is right and wrong. Although the questions Kohlberg addressed touch on only a corner of the subject, his basic theoretical model is the foundation of much of the current thinking about adults' evolving worldviews or meaning systems. Kohlberg's theory has been tested extensively with empirical research and is widely accepted by developmental psychologists, so it provides a relatively noncontroversial jumping-off point.

> ∨ **By the end of this module, you will be able to:**

9.3.1 Outline the stages of moral reasoning according to Kohlberg

9.3.2 Describe how faith changes over time according to Fowler

9.3.1: Development of Moral Reasoning

OBJECTIVE: Outline the stages of moral reasoning according to Kohlberg

Faced with a conflict between different values, on what basis do we decide what is morally right, fair, or just? Kohlberg argued, as an extension of Jean Piaget's theory of cognitive development, that we move through a sequence of stages in our moral reasoning, each stage growing out of, but superseding, the one that came before. In this view, each stage reflects a meaning system or model, an internally consistent and pervasive set of assumptions of right and wrong (Kohlberg, 1981, 1984).

Kohlberg made an important distinction between the decision one makes and the reason behind that decision. The issue is not whether a person thinks, for example, that stealing is wrong, but why he or she thinks it is wrong. Kohlberg searched for developmental changes in the reasoning about moral questions, just as Piaget searched for developmental changes in broader forms of logic.

THE MEASUREMENT PROCEDURE Kohlberg assessed a person's level or stage of moral reasoning by means of a moral judgment interview in which the participant is asked to respond to a series of hypothetical moral dilemmas. In each dilemma, two different principles are in conflict.

THE STAGES Based on many participants' responses to such dilemmas, Kohlberg concluded that there are three basic levels of moral reasoning, each of which can be divided further into two stages, resulting in six stages in all, summarized in Table 9.2.

The *preconventional level* is typical of most children under age 9 but is also found in some adolescents and in some adults, especially in criminal offenders. At both stages of this level, one sees rules as something outside oneself. In Stage 1, the *punishment-and-obedience orientation*, what is right is what is rewarded or what is not punished; in Stage 2, right is defined in terms of what brings pleasure or serves one's own needs. Stage 2 is sometimes described as the *naive hedonism orientation*, a phrase that captures some of the flavor of this stage.

At the *conventional level*, which is characteristic of most adolescents and most adults in Western culture, one internalizes the rules and expectations of one's family or peer group (at Stage 3) or of society (at Stage 4). Stage 3 is sometimes called the *good-boy or good-girl orientation*, whereas Stage 4 is sometimes labeled as the *social order–maintaining orientation*.

The *postconventional (or principled) level*, which is found in only a minority of adults, involves a search for the underlying reasons behind society's rules. At Stage 5, which Kohlberg calls the *social contract orientation*, laws and regulations are seen as important ways of ensuring fairness, but they are not perceived as immutable, nor do they necessarily perfectly reflect more fundamental moral principles. Because laws and contracts are usually in accord with such underlying principles, obeying society's laws is reasonable nearly all the time. But when the underlying principles or reasons are at variance with some specific social custom or rule, the Stage 5 adult argues on the basis of the fundamental principle, even if it means disobeying or disagreeing with a law. Civil rights protesters in the early 1960s, for example, typically supported their civil disobedience with Stage 5 reasoning. In addition, Stage 5 moral reasoning is related to concerns for the environment in college students, presumably because it is necessary to be able to consider the perspective of the other when dealing with competing interests and rights (Karpiak & Baril, 2008). Stage 6, known as the *individual principles of conscience orientation*, is simply a further extension of the same pattern, with the person searching for and then living in a way that is consistent with the deepest set of moral principles possible.

Kohlberg's theory of moral development was based on responses about moral dilemmas. In the now-famous Heinz dilemma, presented in this interactive, the participant must grapple with the question of whether a man named Heinz ought to steal a drug to save his dying wife if the only druggist who can provide it is demanding a higher price than he can pay. In this instance, the conflicting principles are the value of preserving life and the value

Table 9.2 Kohlberg's Stages of Moral Development

In Europe a woman was near death from a special kind of cancer. There was one drug that doctors thought might save her. It was a form of radium that a druggist in the same town had recently discovered. The drug was expensive to make, but the druggist was charging $2,000, or 10 times the cost of the drug, for a small (possibly lifesaving) dose. Heinz, the sick woman's husband, borrowed all the money he could, about $1,000, or half of what he needed. He told the druggist that his wife was dying and asked him to sell the drug cheaper or to let him pay later. The druggist replied, "No, I discovered the drug, and I'm going to make money from it." Heinz then became desperate and broke into the store to steal the drug for his wife.

Should Heinz have done that? Why or why not?

The following responses are examples of people operating in different stages of moral development:

Level 1: Preconventional morality

Stage 1: Punishment and obedience orientation

Yes, Heinz should take the drug. Why? Because if he lets his wife die, he could be responsible for it and get into trouble.

No, Heinz should not take the drug. Why? Because it is stealing. It doesn't belong to him and he can get arrested and punished.

Stage 2: Naive hedonism orientation

Yes, Heinz should take the drug. Why? Because he really isn't hurting the druggist, and he wants to help his wife. Maybe he can pay him later.

No, Heinz shouldn't take the drug. Why? The druggist is in business to make money. That's his job. He needs to make a profit.

Level 2: Conventional morality

Stage 3: Good-boy or good-girl orientation

Yes, Heinz should take the drug. Why? Because he is being a good husband and saving his wife's life. He would be wrong if he didn't save her.

No, Heinz should not take the drug. Why? Because he tried to buy it and he couldn't, so it's not his fault if his wife dies. He did his best.

Stage 4: Social order–maintaining orientation

Yes, Heinz should take the drug. Why? Because the druggist is wrong to be interested only in profits. But Heinz also must pay for the drug later and maybe confess that he took it. It's still wrong to steal.

No, Heinz should not take the drug. Why? Because even though it is natural to want to save your wife, you still need to obey the law. You can't just ignore it because of special circumstances.

Level 3: Postconventional (or principled) morality

Stage 5: Social contract orientation

Yes, Heinz should take the drug. Why? Although the law says he shouldn't, if you consider the whole picture, it would be reasonable for anyone in his situation to take the drug.

No, Heinz should not take the drug. Why? Although some good would come from him taking the drug, it still wouldn't justify violating the consensus of how people have agreed to live together. The ends don't justify the means.

Stage 6: Individual principles of conscience orientation

Yes, Heinz should take the drug. Why? When a person is faced with two conflicting principles, they need to judge which is higher and obey it. Human life is higher than possession.

No, Heinz should not take the drug. Why? Heinz needs to decide between his emotion and the law—both are "right" in a way, but he needs to decide what an ideally just person would do, and that would be not to steal the drug.

SOURCE: Based on Kohlberg (1976, 1984).

of respecting property and upholding the law, summarized in Table 9.2.

In his early work Kohlberg suggested that a fair number of college students reached Stage 6. In his later writings, however, he changed his mind and concluded that this universalistic stage is extremely uncommon (Colby & Kohlberg, 1987). The longitudinal data suggest that Stage 5 may be the typical "endpoint" of the developmental progression. Adults who reach Stage 6 (about 15% of those in their 30s in Kohlberg's samples) do indeed operate on some broad, general principles. What they lack, however, is "that which

is critical for our theoretical notion of Stage 6, namely, the organization of moral judgment around a clearly formulated moral principle of justice and respect for persons that provides a rationale for the primacy of this principle" (Kohlberg, 1984, p. 271). In other words, at Stage 5 one develops some broad principles that go beyond (or "behind") the social system; at Stage 6, the rare person develops a still broader and more general ethical system in which these basic principles are embedded. Among those Kohlberg listed as Stage 6 thinkers were Martin Luther King, Jr. and Mahatma Gandhi.

According to Kohlberg's theory, only a few individuals, such as Martin Luther King, Jr. (left) and Mahatma Gandhi (right), reach the highest level of moral reasoning.

Kohlberg and his colleagues also speculated about the existence of a still higher stage, Stage 7, a *unity orientation*, which they thought might emerge only toward the end of life, after an adult has spent some years living within a principled moral system. It is the confrontation of one's own death that can bring about this transition. As they ask the fundamental questions, "Why live?" and "How do I face death?" some people transcend the type of logical analysis that typifies all the earlier forms of moral reasoning and arrive at a still deeper or broader decentering. It is a sense of unity with being, with life, and/or with God (Kohlberg et al., 1983).

Another way to look at the shifts from preconventional to conventional to postconventional levels of reasoning is to see them as a process of **decentering**, a term Piaget used to describe cognitive development more generally as a movement outward from the self. At the preconventional level, the children's reference points are themselves—the consequences of their own actions, the rewards they may gain. At the conventional level, the reference point has moved outward away from the center of the self to the family or society. Finally, at the postconventional level, the adult searches for a still broader reference point, some set of underlying principles that lies behind or beyond social systems. Such a movement outward from the self is one of the constant themes in writings on the growth or development of meaning systems in adult life.

THE DATA Only longitudinal data can tell us whether Kohlberg's model is valid. If it is, not only should children and adults move from one step to the next in the order he proposes, but they should also not show regression to earlier stages. Kohlberg and his colleagues tested these hypotheses in three samples, all interviewed repeatedly, and each time

asked to discuss a series of moral dilemmas: (1) 84 boys from the Chicago area first interviewed when they were between ages 10 and 16 in 1956, and some of whom were reinterviewed up to five more times (the final interview was in 1976–1977, when they were in their 30s) (Colby et al., 1983); (2) a group of 23 boys and young men in Turkey (some from a rural village and some from large cities), followed over periods of up to 10 years into early adulthood (Nisan & Kohlberg, 1982); and (3) 64 male and female participants from kibbutzim (collective communities) in Israel, who were first tested as teenagers and then retested once or twice more over periods of up to 10 years (Snarey et al., 1985).

Figure 9.5 gives two kinds of information about the findings from these three studies. In the top half of the figure are total "moral maturity scores" derived from the interviews. These scores reflect each person's stage of moral reasoning and can range from 100 to 500. As you can see, in all three studies the average score went up steadily with age, although there are some interesting cultural differences in speed of movement through the stages. In the bottom half of the figure are the percent of answers to the moral dilemmas that reflected each stage of moral reasoning for the participants at each age. These data are for the Chicago sample only because it was studied over the longest period of time. As we would expect, the number of Stage 1 responses drops out quite early, whereas conventional morality (Stages 3 and 4) rises rapidly in the teenage years and remains high in adulthood. Only a very small percent of answers, even of respondents in their 30s, shows Stage 5 reasoning (postconventional reasoning), and none show Stage 6 reasoning.

Both analyses show the stages to be strongly sequential. The sequential pattern is supported by the fact that in none

Figure 9.5 Scores of Moral Reasoning Test and Percentage of Different Stages of Moral Development

The upper panel shows that scores of four diverse samples of boys on a moral reasoning test show a general increase from middle childhood through young adulthood. The lower panel shows the percent of responses given that reflect the different stages of moral development. It is clear that Stage 4 responses increase with age and that Stage 2 responses decrease.

SOURCES: Data from Colby et al. (1983); Nisan and Kohlberg (1982); Snarey et al. (1985).

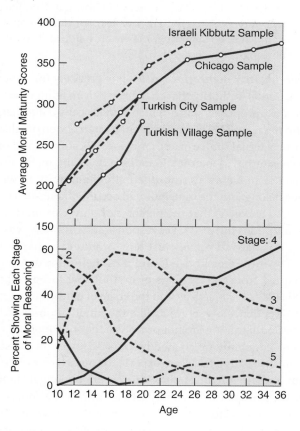

of these three studies was there a single participant who skipped a stage, and only about 5% showed regression. Each participant also showed a good deal of internal consistency at any one testing, using similar logic in analyzing each of several quite different moral problems. The same patterns were found in both shorter-term longitudinal studies (Walker, 1989) and in studies using a questionnaire method of measuring moral judgment rather than the more open-ended interview (Rest & Thoma, 1985).

Unfortunately, no equivalent longitudinal data exist for any adults past midlife. Cross-sectional results show no age differences in overall level of moral judgment between young, middle-aged, and older adults (Lonky et al., 1984; Pratt et al., 1983). Such findings might be taken to mean that the level of reasoning achieved in early adulthood remains relatively stable throughout adulthood. But the longitudinal data do not support such an assertion, at least not through the middle 30s. Among Kohlberg's sample were quite a few people who shifted from Stage 3 to Stage 4 while in their

20s and a few who moved to Stage 5 while in their 30s. At least some adults may thus continue to develop through Kohlberg's stages throughout adulthood. The only way to know this for sure would be to assess moral reasoning longitudinally over the full years of adult life.

EVALUATION AND COMMENT The body of evidence that has accumulated concerning the development of moral reasoning provides strong support for several aspects of Kohlberg's theory:

- There do appear to be stages that children and adults move through in developing concepts of fairness and morality.
- At least up to Stage 5, these stages appear to meet the tests of a hierarchical stage system. They occur in a fixed order, each emerging from and replacing the one that preceded it, and together forming a structural whole.
- The stage sequence appears to be universal. The specific content of moral decisions may differ from one culture to the next, but the overall form of logic seems to move through the same steps in every culture in which this has been studied—a list that includes 27 different countries, Western and non-Western, industrialized and nonindustrialized (Snarey, 1985).

The stages have relevance for real life as well as theory. For example, researchers in one study found that adults who reason at the principled level are more able than are those at the conventional level to deal positively and constructively with significant losses in their lives, such as the death of a family member or the breakup of a relationship (Lonky et al., 1984).

At the same time, a number of critics have pointed out that Kohlberg's theory is relatively narrow, focusing almost exclusively on the development of concepts of justice or fairness. Other aspects of moral/ethical reasoning, other facets of meaning systems, are omitted.

The most eloquent of the critics is psychologist Carol Gilligan (1982). She argued that Kohlberg was interested in concepts of justice and not concepts of care, so his theory and research largely ignore an ethical/moral system based on caring for others, on responsibility, on altruism or compassion. In particular, Gilligan proposed that women more often than men approach moral and ethical dilemmas from the point of view of responsibilities and caring, searching not for the "just" solution, but for the solution that best deals with the social relationships involved. She argues that men, in contrast, use a morality of justice more often than women.

Gilligan's argument that women are less likely to use a morality of justice and thus would score lower on Kohlberg's measures is not strongly supported by research findings. Studies comparing boys and girls on stage of moral reasoning using Kohlberg's revised scoring system have typically found no gender differences (Smetana et al., 1991), although several studies of adults do show the difference that Gilligan hypothesizes (Lyons, 1983). What is clear from the research to date is that girls and women can and do use moral reasoning based on principles of justice when they are presented with dilemmas in which that is a central issue.

9.3.2: Development of Faith

OBJECTIVE: Describe how faith changes over time according to Fowler

Faith is a set of assumptions or understandings about the nature of our connections with others and the world in which we live. Using this definition, it follows that each of us has a faith, whether or not we belong to a church or religious organization. Moral reasoning is a part of faith, but faith is broader.

Theologian and developmental psychologist James Fowler (1981) goes beyond questions of moral reasoning with his theory of faith development. At any point in our lives, he argues, each of us has a *master story*, which is "the answer you give to the questions of what life is about, or who's really in charge here, or how do I live to make my life a worthy, good one. It's a stance you take toward life" (1983, p. 60).

Like Kohlberg, Fowler is interested not in the specific content of one's faith, but in its structure or form. A Christian, a Hindu, a Jew, a Buddhist, a Muslim, and a Secular Humanist may all have faiths that are structurally similar but sharply different in content. And like Kohlberg, Fowler hypothesizes that each of us develops through a shared series of faith structures (or worldviews, broad internal working models, meaning systems, or whatever we choose to call them) over the course of childhood and adulthood. Like Piaget, Fowler believes that "the structural stage sequence is sequential, invariant, and hierarchical" (2001, p. 171). Two of the six stages Fowler proposed occur primarily in childhood and are not described here; the remaining four can be found among adults.

Stages of Faith

Synthetic-Conventional Faith—The first of the adult forms of faith, which Fowler calls *synthetic-conventional faith*, normally appears first in adolescence and then continues well into early adulthood. Like Kohlberg's level of conventional morality, conventional faith is rooted in the implicit assumption that authority is to be found outside oneself.

Many adults remain within this form of faith throughout their lives, defining themselves and interpreting their experiences within the meaning system of a group or a specific set of beliefs.

Let me give you an example from Fowler's own interviews. Mrs. H. is a 61-year-old southern woman who grew up on a tenant farm. At the time Fowler interviewed her, she had recently rededicated herself to the Baptist Church after many years away from church activity. At one point she said,

> I feel very sad and ashamed for the way I have wasted my life. I do know that God has forgiven me for every wrong that I've done, and that He loves me. I feel very close to God most of the time, now that I am active in the work of the church again. Of course there are times that I don't feel as close to Him as I'd like to, but I know that I am the one who moves away, not He. I've learned that we all have so much to be thankful for, if we only stop and count our blessings. (Fowler, 1981, p. 172)

Individuative-Reflective Faith—It is precisely this reliance on external authority that changes when an adult moves to the next proposed stage, which Fowler calls *individuative-reflective faith*. This move requires an interruption of reliance on an external source of authority—a relocation of authority from external to internal. In making this shift, many adults reject or move away from the faith community to which they belong. But the transition can occur without such rejections. The key is that the person not only reexamines old assumptions but also takes responsibility in a new way.

It is hard to convey just how profound a change this is. The metaphor I have found most helpful is one I have adapted from the writings of mythologist Joseph Campbell (1949/1990). It is as if in the stage of conventional faith we experience ourselves as like the moon, illuminated by reflected light. We are not ourselves the source of light (or knowledge) but are created by outside forces. In the stage of individuative faith, we experience ourselves as like the sun, radiating light of our own. We are no longer defined by the groups to which we belong; rather, we choose the groups, the relationships, based on our self-chosen beliefs or values. Thus, even if the specific beliefs we choose at this point are the same ones with which we have grown up, the underlying meaning system is changed.

Rebecca, a woman in her mid-30s, seems clearly to have made this transition:

> I know I have very defined boundaries and I protect them very carefully. I won't give up the slightest control. In any relationship I decide who gets in, how far, and when. What am I afraid of? I used to think I was afraid people would find out who I really was and then not like me. But I don't think that's it anymore. What I feel now is—"that's me. That's mine. It's what makes me. And I'm powerful. It's my negative side, maybe, but it's also my positive stuff—and there's a lot of that. What it is is me, it's my self—and if I let people in maybe they'll take it, maybe they'll use it—and I'll be gone." . . . This "self," if I had to represent it I think of two things: either a steel rod that runs through everything, a kind of solid fiber, or sort of like a ball at the center that is all together. (Kegan, 1982, pp. 240–241)

Conjunctive Faith—The next stage in Fowler's model, *conjunctive faith*, requires an opening outward from the self-preoccupation of the individuative reflective level. There is an openness here to paradox, a moving away from fixed truth toward a search for balance, not only of self and other, but also of mind and emotion, of rationality and ritual. The person who lives within this meaning system, which is not typically found before midlife, accepts that there are many truths, that others' beliefs, others' ideas, may be true for them—a point of view that not only brings far greater tolerance toward others but also very commonly brings the person to an interest in service or commitment to the welfare of others.

Here's one illustrative voice, that of Miss T., a 78-year-old woman who had been variously a Unitarian, a Quaker, and a follower of Krishnamurti and other Eastern teachers. When asked if there were beliefs and values everyone should hold, she said,

> If somebody asked me that and gave me just two minutes to answer it, I know what I'd say. It's a line from George Fox, the founder of Quakerism. It's old-fashioned English and it seems to me to have the entire program of anybody's life. It's a revolution, it's an enormous comfort, it's a peace maker. The line is: "There is that of God in every man." Now, you can start thinking about it. You can see that if you really did believe that, how it would change your relationships with people. It's far-reaching. It applies nationally and individually and class-wise; it reaches the whole. To anyone that I loved dearly I would say, "Put that in your little invisible locket and keep it forever." (Fowler, 1981, p. 194)

Other statements by Miss T. make it clear that the content of her faith at this point involves a kind of return to some of the elements of her earlier religious teachings, but she has reframed it, casting it in language that has meaning for her now and that focuses on finding fulfillment in service to others—all of which are significant elements of conjunctive faith.

Universalizing Faith—The final proposed stage in Fowler's system is *universalizing faith*. Like Kohlberg's Stage 6, reaching this stage is a relatively rare achievement, but Fowler argues that it is the next logical step. To some extent, it involves a step beyond individuality. In the stage of conjunctive faith, the person may be "open" and "integrated" but is still struggling with the paradox of searching for universality while attempting to preserve individuality. In the stage of universalizing faith, the person lives the principles, the imperatives, of absolute love and justice. Because such people live their lives based on such basic outward-oriented principles, they are heedless of their own self-preservation, much as Mother Theresa continued caring for the dying up until the end of her own life. They may even be seen by others as subversive to the structures of society or traditional religion because they do not begin with the assumption that society or religion is necessarily correct in its institutions or customs.

SOME BASIC POINTS ABOUT FOWLER'S STAGES
Some key points need emphasis.

- Like Kohlberg, Fowler assumes that these stages occur in a sequence, but that the sequence is only very roughly associated with age, especially in adulthood. Some adults remain within the same meaning system, the same faith structure, their entire lives; others make one or more transitions in their understanding of themselves and their relationships with others.

- Fowler contends that each stage has its "proper time" of ascendancy in a person's lifetime, a period at which that particular form of faith is most consistent with the demands of life. Most typically, the stage of conventional faith is in its ascendance in adolescence or early adulthood, and the stage of individuative-reflective faith in the years of the late 20s and 30s, whereas a transition to the stage of conjunctive faith, if it occurs at all, may occur around midlife. Finally, the stage of universalizing faith, if one can reach it, would be the optimal form of faith in old age, when issues of integrity and meaning become still more dominant.

- Fowler conceives of each stage as wider or more encompassing than the one that preceded it. And this greater breadth helps to foster both a greater capacity for a sense of sureness and serenity and a greater capacity for intimacy—with the self as well as with others.

RESEARCH FINDINGS   I am not aware of any longitudinal studies that have tested the sequential aspect of Fowler's theory. However, Fowler (1981) has reported some cross-sectional data that show the incidence of the stages of faith at each of several ages. He asked over 300 adolescents and adults open-ended questions about their faith and had raters assign a stage to each person based on these interviews. The results fit the theory relatively well, showing that conventional faith is most common in the teenage years, individuative-reflective faith among people in their 20s, and conjunctive faith emerging only in the 30s. Furthermore, only one person fit the category of universalizing faith, a man in his 60s.

Another study that offers consistent evidence comes from psychologist Gary Reker, who has developed a very similar model of the emergence of meaning systems over the years of adulthood. Reker (1991) argued that an adult can find meaning in life through any of a variety of sources, such as leisure activities, personal relationships, personal achievement, traditions and culture, altruism or service to others, or enduring values and ideals. Reker suggested that these various sources of meaning can be organized into four levels: *self-preoccupation*, in which meaning is found primarily through financial security or meeting basic needs; *individualism*, in which meaning is found in personal growth or achievement or through creative and leisure activities; *collectivism*, which includes meaning from traditions and culture and from societal causes; and *self-transcendence*, in which meaning is found through enduring values and ideals, religious activities, and altruism.

Reker's work does not provide a direct test of Fowler's model, but it is consistent with the basic idea that there may be systematic changes over the years of adulthood in the framework that adults use to define themselves and find meaning in their lives.

A PRELIMINARY ASSESSMENT Theories like Fowler's and research like Reker's supplement our thinking about adulthood in important ways, if only to help us focus on the importance of meaning systems and their possible sequential change with age. But it is still very early in our empirical exploration of this and related theories. The greatest immediate need is for good longitudinal data, perhaps initially covering the years that are thought to be transitional for many adults, but ultimately covering the entire adult age range.

WRITING PROMPT

Stages of Faith

How do Kohlberg's stages of moral development relate to Fowler's proposed stages of faith development?

 | The response entered here will appear in the performance dashboard and can be viewed by your instructor.

Submit

9.4: Integrating Meaning and Personality

OBJECTIVE: Compare theories of meaning and personality

There are some clear parallels between theories of moral and faith development and theories of personality development. In fact, the surface similarities are obvious, as you can see in Table 9.3.

Loevinger's conformist stage in her theory of ego development certainly sounds like both Kohlberg's conventional morality and Fowler's conventional faith. There seems to be agreement that in adolescence and early adulthood, people tend to be focused on adapting to the demands of the roles and relationships society imposes on them and assume that the source of authority is external.

Loevinger's conscientious and individualistic stages are a great deal like Maslow's layer of esteem needs, Kohlberg's social contract orientation, and Fowler's individuative-reflective faith. All four theorists agree that the next step involves a shift in the central source of meaning or self-definition from external to internal, accompanied by a preoccupation with the self and one's own abilities, skills, and potentials.

Loevinger's autonomous and integrated stages are similar to Fowler's conjunctive faith, possibly related to self-actualization needs as described by Maslow. All speak of a shift away from self-preoccupation toward a search for balance, a shift toward greater tolerance toward both self and others.

Finally, there seems to be agreement about a still higher stage that involves some form of self-transcendence: Kohlberg's unity orientation, Fowler's stage of universalizing faith, or Maslow's peak experiences.

Of course, we are not dealing with four independent visions here. Loevinger, Maslow, Kohlberg, and Fowler all knew of each other's work and were influenced by each other's ideas. This is particularly true in the case of Fowler

---

Table 9.3 Review of Stages of Personality, Morality, and Faith Development

This table compares four major theories of development. As you can see, all of these theories show an individual moving from concrete rules to a more abstract understanding of themselves and others.

General Stage	Loevinger's Stages of Ego Development	Maslow's Levels of Needs Hierarchy	Kohlberg's Stages of Moral Reasoning Development	Fowler's Stages of Faith Development
Conformist; Culture-bound Self	Conformist; Self-Aware Stages	Love and Belongingness Needs	Good-Boy or Good-Girl Orientation; Social Order Maintaining Orientation	Synthetic-Conventional Faith
Individuality	Conscientious; Individualistic Stages	Self-Esteem Needs	Social Contract Orientation	Individuative-Reflective Faith
Integration	Autonomous; Integrated Stages	Self-Actualization	Individual Principles of Conscience Orientation	Conjunctive Faith
Self-transcendence		Peak Experiences	Unity Orientation	Universalizing Faith

and Kohlberg because Fowler's theory is quite explicitly an extension of Kohlberg's model. So the fact that they all seem to agree does not mean that we have uncovered "truth" here. However, my confidence in the validity of the basic sequence these theorists describe is bolstered by three additional arguments.

Three Arguments for Validity

Argument 1—First, although they have influenced one another, there are still three quite distinct theoretical heritages involved. Kohlberg's and Fowler's work are rooted in Piaget's theory and in studies of normal children's thinking; Loevinger's work is rooted in Freud's theory and in clinical assessments of children and adults, including those with emotional disturbances; and Maslow's theory, although influenced by psychoanalytic thought, is based primarily on his own observations of a small number of highly unusual, self-actualized adults. The fact that one can arrive at such similar views of the sequence of emergence of meaning systems from such different roots makes the convergence more impressive.

Argument 2—Second, in the case of both Kohlberg's and Loevinger's models, we have reasonably strong supporting empirical evidence, especially concerning the first step in the commonly proposed adult sequence, of a move from conforming/conventional to individualistic stages. Transitions beyond that are simply much less well studied, in part because longitudinal studies have not yet followed adults past early midlife, perhaps in part because the later transitions are simply less common.

Argument 3—Finally, this basic model seems plausible to me because the sequence makes sense in terms of a still more encompassing developmental concept proposed by Robert Kegan.

∨　**By the end of this module, you will be able to:**

9.4.1 Explain the relationship between connection and independence according to Kegan

9.4.2 Outline the stages of mystical experience according to Underhill

9.4.1: A Synthesizing Model

OBJECTIVE: Explain the relationship between connection and independence according to Kegan

Psychologist Robert Kegan (1982) proposes that each of us has two enormously powerful and equal desires or motives built in. On the one hand, we deeply desire connection, the state of being joined or integrated with others. On the other

hand, we equally desire independence, the state of being differentiated from others. No accommodation between these two is really in balance, so whatever *evolutionary truce* (as Kegan calls each stage) we arrive at, it will lean further toward one than toward the other. Eventually, the unmet need becomes so strong that we are forced to change the system, to change our understanding. In the end, what this creates is a fundamental alternation, a moving back and forth of the pendulum, between perspectives or meaning systems centered on inclusion or union and perspectives centered on independence or separateness.

The child begins life in a symbiotic relationship with the parent, so the pendulum begins on the side of connection and union. By age 2 the child has pulled away and seeks independence, a separate identity. The conformist or conventional meaning system that we see in adolescence and early adulthood (if not later) is a move back toward connection with the group, while the transition to the individualistic meaning system is a return to separation and independence. The term *detribalization* fits nicely with Kegan's basic model (Levinson, 1978). In shifting the source of authority from external sources to one's own resources, there is at least initially a pushing-away of the tribe and all its rituals and rules.

If the model is correct, the step after this ought to be another return toward connection, which seems to me to be precisely what is proposed by most of the theorists I have described. As I see it, most of them talk about two substeps in this shift of the pendulum, with Fowler's conjunctive faith or Kohlberg's individual principles of conscience orientation being intermediate steps on the way toward the more complete position of union or community represented by Fowler's universalizing faith or Kohlberg's unity orientation.

Although my explanation here describes the process with the image of a pendulum moving back and forth, clearly Kegan is not proposing that movement is simply back and forth in a single groove. Instead, he sees the process as more like that of a spiral in which each shift to the other side of the polarity is at a more integrated level than the one before.

If such a basic alternation, such a spiral movement, really does form the underlying rhythm of development, why should we assume that it stops even at so lofty a point as Kohlberg's unity orientation? When I first understood this aspect of Kegan's theory, I had one of those startling "a-ha" experiences, for I realized that the stages of the mystical journey described in case studies by Underhill and by James could be linked seamlessly with the sequence Kegan was describing.

I am well aware that a discussion of such subjective mystical experiences here will seem to some to be going very far afield, perhaps totally outside the realm of psychology. But to me the risk is worth it, not only because in this way perhaps I can make a case for my own basic assumptions regarding the immense potential of the individual human spirit, but also because the pattern that emerges fits so remarkably well with the research evidence and the theories I have discussed thus far.

9.4.2: Stages of Mystical Experience

OBJECTIVE: Outline the stages of mystical experience according to Underhill

The stages I am describing here were suggested by theologian and philosopher Evelyn Underhill (1911/1961), based on her reading of autobiographies, biographies, and other writings of the lives of hundreds of people from many religious traditions, all of whom described some form of **mysticism**, or self-transcendent experience, in which they know that they are part of a larger whole and that they have an existence beyond their own physical body and personal history. The individuals Underhill studied did not describe all the steps or stages listed, but there was a remarkable degree of unanimity about the basic process, despite huge differences in historical period and religious background.

From Awakening to Unity

Step 1—Underhill calls this step *awakening*, and it seems to correspond to the usual endpoint in theories like Kohlberg's or Fowler's. It involves at least a brief self-transcendent experience, such as the peak experiences that Maslow describes. In Kegan's model, this step is clearly represented on the "union" end of the polarity; it is an awakening to the possibility of stepping outside one's own perspective and understanding the world from a point of deep connection.

Step 2—Underhill calls this step *purification*, and it is clearly a move back toward separateness. The person, having seen him- or herself from a broader perspective, also sees all his or her own imperfections, fruitless endeavors, and flaws. As St. Teresa of Ávila, one of the great mystics of the Christian tradition, put it, "In a room bathed in sunlight not a cobweb can remain hidden" (1562/1960, p. 181). To understand and eliminate the flaws—the cobwebs—the person must turn inward again. At this stage many people are strongly focused on self-discipline, including special spiritual disciplines such as regular prayer, meditation, and/or fasting.

Step 3—This step clearly moves us back toward union. Underhill calls this *illumination*. It involves a much deeper, more prolonged awareness of light, greater reality, or God and may in fact encompass some of what Kohlberg refers to as Stage 7.

Step 4—But even this illumination is not the end of the journey. Underhill finds two other steps described by many mystics that appear to lie beyond. The first of these, Stage 4, often called the *dark night of the soul*, involves a still further turn inward, back toward separateness. At Stage 3, illumination, the person still feels some personal satisfaction,

some personal pleasure or joy in having achieved illumination. According to mystics who have described these later stages, if one is to achieve ultimate union, even this personal pleasure must be abandoned. And the process of abandonment requires a turning back to the self, to awareness, and exploration, of all the remaining ways in which the separate self has survived. Only then can the person achieve the endpoint, Stage 5, which is *unity*—with God, with reality, with beauty, with the ultimate—however this may be described within a particular religious tradition.

I cannot say, of course, whether this sequence, this spiral of inner human progress, reflects the inevitable or ultimate path for us all. I can say only that the developmental analyses of stages of morality, or stages of faith or personality, that have been offered by many psychologists, for which we have at least some preliminary supporting evidence, appear to form a connected whole with the descriptions of stages of mystical illumination. For example, Jung (1917/1966) described similar stages in his journey to discover his own inner world through psychoanalysis. At the very least, we know that a pathway similar to this has been trod by a long series of remarkable individuals, whose descriptions of their inner journeys bear striking similarities. There may be many other paths or journeys. But the reflections of these remarkable few point the way toward the possibility of a far vaster potential of the human spirit than is apparent to most of us in our daily lives.

WRITING PROMPT

Connection and Independence

Think about your own drives for connection and independence. How do you balance these drives in your own life?

 The response entered here will appear in the performance dashboard and can be viewed by your instructor.

Submit

9.5: The Process of Transition

OBJECTIVE: Analyze how individuals develop through transitions

Coming down a bit from these lofty heights, but still assuming for the moment that there is some basic rhythm, some developmental sequence, in the forms of meaning we create, let me turn to a question that may be of special personal importance: What is the process by which transitions or transformations from one stage to the next take place? What triggers them? What are the common features of transitions? How are they traversed?

▼ **By the end of this module, you will be able to:**

9.5.1 Describe transition theory

9.5.2 Explain how stimuli may trigger transitions

9.5.3 Contextualize ways that people respond to triggers

9.5.1: Transition Theory

OBJECTIVE: Describe transition theory

Most developmental psychologists who propose stages of adult development have focused more on the stages than on the transition processes. But some common themes are repeated in the ways transitions are described.

A number of theorists have described transitions in parallel terms, with each shift from one level or stage to the next seen as a kind of death and rebirth—a death of the earlier sense of self, of the earlier faith, of the earlier equilibrium (James, 1902/1958; Kegan, 1980). The process typically involves first some glimpses or precursors or premonitions of another stage or view, which are then followed by a period (which may be brief or prolonged) in which the person struggles to deal with the two "selves" within. Sometimes the process is aborted and the person returns to the earlier equilibrium. Sometimes the person moves instead toward a new understanding, a new equilibrium.

The middle part of this process, when the old meaning system has been partially given up but a new equilibrium has not yet been reached, is often experienced as profoundly dislocating. Statements such as "I am beside myself" or "I was out of my mind" may be used (Kegan, 1980). The process of equilibration may be accompanied by an increase in physical or psychological symptoms of various kinds, including anxiety and depression.

Kegan perhaps best summarized the potential pain of the process: "Development is costly—for everyone, the developing person and those around him or her. Growth involves a separation from an old system of meaning. In practical terms this can involve both the agony of felt meaninglessness and the repudiation of commitments and investment. . . .

Developmental theory gives us a way of thinking about such pain that does not pathologize it" (1980, p. 439).

9.5.2: Triggering a Transition

OBJECTIVE: Explain how stimuli may trigger transitions

Transitions may emerge slowly or may occur rapidly; they may be the result of self-chosen activities such as therapy or exercise, the happenstances of ordinary life, or unexpected experiences. In Table 9.4, I have suggested some of the stimuli for such transitions, organized around what appear to be the three most frequent adult transitions: (1) from conformity to individuality, (2) from individuality to integration or conjunctive faith, and (3) from integration to self-transcendence. I offer this list quite tentatively. We clearly lack the longitudinal evidence that might allow us to say more fully what experiences may or may not stimulate a transition.

You can see in the table that I am suggesting that somewhat different experiences may be involved in each of these three transitions. Attending college or moving away from home into a quite different community seem to be particularly influential in promoting aspects of the transition to individuality. For example, in longitudinal studies, both Kohlberg (1973) and Rest and Thoma (1985) have found a correlation between the amount of college education completed and the level of moral reasoning. Principled reasoning was found only in those who had attended at least some college. This transition, then, seems to be precipitated by exposure to other assumptions, other faiths, other perspectives. Such a confrontation can produce disequilibrium, which may be dealt with by searching for a new, independent, self-chosen model.

I have also suggested that therapy may play some role in triggering or assisting with either of the first two transitions. In fact, helping a client to achieve full integration is the highest goal of many humanistically oriented therapies, such as those based on the work of Carl Rogers (1961/1995) or Fritz Perls (1973). But my hypothesis is that traditional

Table 9.4 Transitions from One Stage to Another: Some Possible Triggering Situations or Experiences That May Assist in Passing Through a Transition

Specific Transition	Intentional Activities That May Foster That Transition	Unintentional or Circumstantial Events That May Foster That Transition
From conformist to individualistic	Therapy; reading about other religions or faiths	Attending college; leaving home for other reasons, such as job or marriage; usual failures or reversals while "following the rules"; development of personal or professional skills
From individualistic to integrated	Therapy; introspection; short-term programs to heighten self-awareness (e.g., Gestalt workshops)	Illness or prolonged pain; death in the family or prolonged crisis; peak experiences
From integrated to self-transcendent	Meditation or prayer; various forms of yoga; self-discipline	Near-death experience; transcendent experiences such as peak or immediate mystical experiences

forms of therapy do little to assist the transition from integrated person to a level of self-transcendence. This transition, I think, requires or is assisted by a different form of active process, such as meditation, yoga, or systematic prayer.

Both painful experiences and transcendent ones can also be the occasion for a new transition. The death of a child or of a parent may reawaken our concern with ultimate questions of life and death. A failed marriage or discouragement at work may lead to questioning or to a loss of the sense of stability of one's present model. Peak experiences, too, by giving glimpses of something not readily comprehensible within a current view, may create a disequilibrium. Most adults who have had a near-death experience, for example, report that their lives are never again the same. Many change jobs or devote their lives to service in one way or another. Other forms of peak experiences or religious rebirth may have the same effect. In fact, the development of wisdom in old age is associated with exploring the meaning of difficult experiences in one's life (Weststrate & Gluck, 2017).

9.5.3: The Impact of Life Changes

OBJECTIVE: Contextualize ways that people respond to triggers

I have been consistently using the word *may* in the last few paragraphs to convey the fact that such life changes do not invariably result in significant reflection or decentering. In an argument reminiscent of the concept of scheduled and unscheduled changes, psychologists Patricia Gurin and Orville Brim (1984) have offered an interesting hypothesis to explain such differences in the impact of major life changes. In essence, they argued that widely shared, age-linked changes are not likely to trigger significant reassessments of the sense of self precisely because expected changes are interpreted differently than unexpected ones. Shared changes are most often attributed to causes outside oneself, for which one is not personally responsible. In contrast, unique or off-time life changes are more likely to lead to significant inner reappraisals precisely because it is difficult to attribute such experiences to outward causes. If everyone at your job has been laid off because the company has gone out of business during a recession, you need not reassess your own sense of self-worth. But if you are the only one fired during a time of expanding economy, it is much more difficult to maintain your sense of worth.

Some shared experiences, such as college, may commonly trigger reappraisals or restructuring of personality, moral judgment, or faith. But most age-graded experiences can be absorbed fairly readily into existing systems. It may then be the unique or mistimed experiences that are particularly significant for changes in meaning systems. This hypothesis remains to be tested but raises some intriguing issues.

9.6: Shapes of the Quest

OBJECTIVE: Assess common metaphors used to make sense of the development of adult meaning systems

It seems fair to say that most adults are engaged in some process of creating or searching for meaning in their lives. But this is not necessarily—perhaps not commonly—a conscious, deliberate process. The quest, however it happens, takes many shapes.

Our theories of the quest for meaning—the ways we try to make sense of the quest—are based in part on metaphors. We begin our search for understanding of adult development with a metaphor, and it colors all of what we choose to examine and all of what we see.

> ⌄ **By the end of this module, you will be able to:**
>
> **9.6.1** Discuss the strengths and limitations of the idea of life as journey
>
> **9.6.2** Examine the shortcomings of existing metaphors for meaning making

9.6.1: Life as Journey

OBJECTIVE: Discuss the strengths and limitations of the idea of life as journey

Some adults spend many years of adulthood in a conscious search for meaning, and their descriptions of the process are remarkably similar. But this may or may not mean that such a search, or even a nonconscious, or nonintentional, sequence of faiths, is a "natural" or essential part of adult development. A good number of equally spiritual adults, such as my grandparents, find meaning in their lives in quiet, conventional ways. They follow their childhood religions and find great richness in meaning as they delve deeper into the teachings and then teach it to young people themselves, never feeling the need to search alternative pathways. For some, the well-trodden path became that way for a reason.

It is important to realize that what many theorists have said is based on a single metaphor of development, the metaphor of "life as a journey." We imagine the adult walking up some hill or along some road, passing through steps or stages as he or she moves along. Implicit in this metaphor is the concept of a goal, an endpoint or *telos* (a Greek word from which our word *teleological* comes, meaning "having purpose or moving toward a goal"). This is a journey going somewhere. And if the purpose of the journey is thought of as personal growth, we must have some concept of an endpoint, of some highest level of personal growth.

Philosopher and television producer Sam Keen (1983) has suggested several ways other than "as journey" we might think of the process of development of adult meaning systems, two of which I find particularly appealing:

- "When we think of this eternal dimension of our being, the circle is more appropriate than the line. If life is a journey, then, it is not a pilgrimage but an odyssey in which one leaves and returns home again" (p. 31). Each step may be a circling back, a remembering of the "still point" within (to use poet T. S. Eliot's phrase). Progressively, we understand or know ourselves and our world differently with each movement of the circle, but there is no necessary endpoint.

- We can also think of the entire process as "musical themes that weave together to form a symphony; the themes that are central to each stage are anticipated in the previous stage and remain as resonant subthemes in subsequent stages" (p. 32). Another metaphor for this is that of life as a tapestry in which one weaves many colors. A person who creates many different meaning systems or faiths is weaving a tapestry with more colors, but it may be no more beautiful or pleasing than a tapestry woven intricately of fewer colors.

While the journey metaphor has dominated most of the current thinking, it is not the only way to think about the process. In fact, the linearity and teleology of the journey metaphor may well limit our thinking about changes in adult meaning systems.

9.6.2: Choosing a Metaphor

OBJECTIVE: Examine the shortcomings of existing metaphors for meaning making

If we are to understand the process of meaning making further, if we are to choose among several metaphors, what we need is a great deal more empirical information to answer questions like the following.

First, is there a longitudinal progression through Fowler's stages of faith or through equivalent sequences proposed by others, such as Loevinger's stages of ego development? A number of cross-sectional studies and several longitudinal studies suggest that some indicators of spiritual growth increase with age. But age alone does not cause much of anything except the number of candles on one's cake. We need to ask: Is it due to the collected wisdom that comes from experience, from some kind of biological change in the nervous system, from facing the adversities of late adulthood, or something else? There has been a very large increase in research in this area, and I am confident that answers to this question are forthcoming.

Second, what are the connections, if any, between movement through the several sequences described by the various theorists? If we measure a given person's moral reasoning, the stage of ego development in Loevinger's model, and the type of faith he or she holds, will that person be at the same stage in all three? And when a person shifts in one area, does the shift occur across the board? Alternatively, might integration occur only at the final steps, at the level of what Loevinger calls the "integrated person"? These questions have been explored for many years in children's stages of cognitive development and should be explored within the context of the quest for meaning in adulthood.

Third, assuming that longitudinal data confirm that there are stages of meaning making, we need to know what prompts a shift from one to the next. What supports a transition? What delays it? Finally, we need to know more about the possible connection between stages of faith (or models of meaning, or constructions of the self) and a sense of well-being, or greater physical health, or greater peace of mind. My own hypothesis is that one experiences greater happiness or satisfaction with one's life when it exists within a meaning system that lies at the "union" end of the dichotomy than when it is embedded in any of the more self-oriented stages.

Answers to some of these questions may be forthcoming in the next decades because researchers have begun to devise measuring scales for spirituality and to explore various components of the quest for meaning. The recent evidence of a connection between health and religious practices is a promising start to further investigations that include other forms of spirituality. And the work on genetic coding for spirituality (Anderson et al., 2017) brings its own intrigue to the mix.

Summary: The Quest for Meaning

One of the striking things about the information in this chapter is that it is possible to find such similar descriptions emerging from such different traditions. But the fact that there is a great deal of apparent unanimity in the theoretical (and personal) descriptions of the development of moral judgment, meaning systems, motive hierarchies, and spiritual evolution does not make this shared view true. For now, much of what I have said in this chapter remains tantalizing and intriguing speculation—but speculation that nonetheless points toward the potential for wisdom, compassion, even illumination within each adult.

9.1 Why We Study the Quest for Meaning

OBJECTIVE: Explain why we study the search for meaning

- The quest for meaning, or spirituality, is an integral part of the human experience, with signs of its existence found in archaeological sites, in all cultures today, and even as a genetic trait in humans.

- Psychology has long held that it is the meaning we attach to our experiences rather than the experiences themselves that defines reality for us. We filter experience through a set of basic assumptions we have each created, known as internal working models or meaning systems.

9.2 The Study of Age-Related Changes in Meaning Systems

OBJECTIVE: Analyze how interaction with meaning systems changes over time

- The idea of gerotranscendence, or the growth of meaning systems as we go through adulthood, is well known in literature, mythology, and psychological theories, although there is no agreement on what experiences in life cause the changes in meaning systems.

- Empirical study of religion and spirituality has increased dramatically in the last four decades, and most of the studies address the question of whether this trait changes as we age. Religious participation is greater in older adults than in younger adults, but there is a dropoff in late adulthood, possibly due to poor health. More women attend religious services and belong to religious organizations than men, and this gender difference is even greater for African Americans and Mexican Americans.

- Rates of private religious practices, such as prayer and reading sacred texts, also increase with age, but remain steady into late adulthood, when participation in religious services drops off. It is suggested that people in late adulthood retain their spiritual beliefs and private practices, even though they are no longer able to attend services.

- Two groups that were followed longitudinally show an increase in spirituality during the adult years, but women begin the increase earlier in adulthood than men. Those in a younger cohort showed a different pattern of increase than those in an older cohort, indicating that events we experience during our lifetimes also have an impact on changes in spirituality over time.

- It is as yet uncertain whether the experience of living for many years causes changes in spirituality, or whether the changes are due to the adversity older adults have to cope with. This will be an important topic of future research.

- People, especially women, who attend religious services live longer than those who do not. One reason is that spirituality is related to lower levels of cortisol response during stressful situations. Cortisol has been implicated in many of the negative physiological effects of stress reactions, such as lowered immune function. This finding has been replicated in a number of populations and for a number of measures of spirituality, especially forgiveness and frequency of prayer.

9.3 Theories of Spiritual Development

OBJECTIVE: Apply theories of spiritual development

- One theory of the development of meaning systems is Kohlberg's theory of the development of moral reasoning. Based on Piaget's theory of cognitive development, this theory consists of six stages of moral reasoning, evaluating the level of moral reasoning by the explanations people give for their responses to moral dilemmas. At the first level, preconventional, reasoning reflects the punishment and obedience orientation in which what is moral is simply behavior that is rewarded, and the naive hedonism orientation in which the moral choice is the one that brings pleasure. At the second level, conventional, moral decisions are explained by following rules of the family or society. The third level, postconventional, chooses moral responses based on a search for underlying reasons for rules and laws.

- Kohlberg's theory has been evaluated and refined over the years. For example, Carol Gilligan has pointed out that Kohlberg based his theory on interviews with boys, who use a system of justice, whereas girls may base their moral decisions on a system of caring.

- A second theory of spiritual development is Fowler's theory of faith development. Like Kohlberg, Fowler was interested in the individual search for meaning, not in specific beliefs. In Fowler's first stage, synthetic-conventional faith, meaning comes from an authority outside oneself. In the second stage, individuative-reflective faith, the individual takes responsibility for his or her own meaning system. In the third stage, conjunctive faith, an individual opens up to others' beliefs and welfare. Finally, there is universalizing faith, the full opening of a person to disregard personal concerns.

9.4 Integrating Meaning and Personality

OBJECTIVE: Compare theories of meaning and personality

- There are similarities among the theories that seek to explain the development of spirituality over the adult years. There are also similarities among the theories of spiritual development and the personality theories discussed in previous chapters. One theory that seems to encompass all of them is Kegan's synthesizing model, which proposes that we move between the need to be part of the group and the need to be individuals.

- Autobiographies, biographies, and case histories offer valuable information about individuals' search for meaning and thoughts about spiritualism. Underhill studied the accounts of many diverse individuals who described their quests for meaning, and she found commonalities in these quests that made up five possible stages. The first stage is awakening to a self-transcendence experience. This is followed by purification, in which the person is made aware of his or her faults and imperfections. The third stage is illumination, in which the person is made even more aware of the presence of a higher power. In the fourth stage, the person undergoes the dark night of the soul, turning inward for more critical self-examination. Stage 5 is unity, in which the individual feels one with the universe.

- This process described by Underhill has been described similarly by many people from different eras and fields of interest, for example, American psychologist William James in the early 20th century, Spanish nun St. Teresa of Ávila in the 16th century, and Swiss-born American psychoanalyst Carl Jung in the mid-20th century.

9.5 The Process of Transition

OBJECTIVE: Analyze how individuals develop through transitions

- The question of what factors lead to changes in meaning systems over adulthood is a relatively new topic of research. It is known that these changes may be triggered by unique life changes, by adversity, by peak experiences, and by intentionally pursuing self-knowledge and spiritual growth.

9.6 Shapes of the Quest

OBJECTIVE: Assess common metaphors used to make sense of the development of adult meaning systems

- Often, we try to make sense of the quest for meaning by using metaphors. Whatever metaphor we choose becomes the lens through which we see the development of adult meaning systems, possibly blinding us to alternative explanations.

- A great deal more empirical information is needed for us to make more sense of our many quests for meaning making.

SHARED WRITING

The Quest for Meaning

Consider this chapter's discussion of the quest for meaning. How is your own quest for meaning different from that of your parents' generation, and their parents' generation? What are the implications of these changes (for better or worse)? Write a short response that your classmates will read. Be sure to discuss specific examples.

 A minimum number of characters is required to post and earn points. After posting, your response can be viewed by your class and instructor, and you can participate in the class discussion.

Post   0 characters | 140 minimum

Chapter 10
Stress, Coping, and Resilience

Practicing yoga and spending time in nature are both great ways to reduce stress.

Learning Objectives

10.1 Determine the origins of stress

10.2 Relate stress to health outcomes

10.3 Evaluate coping techniques for stress

10.4 Analyze how resilience functions

A Word from the Author

Miguel's Journey

MIGUEL LEFT CUBA for Miami in an unusual way; he took a boat west to Mexico and then bought his way across the border into Texas. He was only 15. The other people in the group were eight pregnant women who were trying to have their babies in American hospitals—not so much for the medical care but so the babies would have U.S. citizenship. Despite being promised a safe journey across the border, Miguel and the women were left on the Mexican side of the shallow river to make their own ways across. Suddenly, gunshots rang out from somewhere. Miguel helped woman after woman cross the shallow

river and finally made it to safety himself before realizing he had been shot in the thigh. He ended up in the hospital with two of the women who had gone into labor during the river crossing.

This is an exciting story, and to the best of my knowledge it is true. I heard it from Miguel himself and saw the scar from the bullet wound in his thigh. He showed me photos of the two Mexican American teenagers, now living in Texas, whose mothers he had helped cross the river. They were named Miguel, after him, and he keeps in touch with their families. The amazing part of the story, to me, is that today he is so similar to my younger son, Derek. They are both American citizens, and they work together as civil engineers. They drive their trucks to work, go out in the field together, go home at night to their wives and children, and plan their vacations to Disney World or Las Vegas or the Bahamas. You would not notice any difference between Miguel and Derek except that Miguel has a touch of a Cuban accent (and a scar on his thigh). And yet my son grew up in a middle-class home and was riding a skateboard and playing Senior League baseball when he was 15. When I think about Miguel, I look around at the students in my classes, the people who work in my neighborhood grocery store, the woman who delivers my mail, and I wonder what their stories are. The more I get to know my fellow south Floridians, the more stories I hear like Miguel's. We have people who have come to our state on rafts made out of inner tubes and styrofoam coolers, people who have fled their country one step ahead of rebel troops, people who survived concentration camps and people who liberated concentration camps after World War II, people who have seen their relatives and neighbors killed, people who have survived earthquakes and hurricanes, and people who have been in prison for their political and religious beliefs. Adversity is not just in history books in our part of the country, and I'm sure the same is true of yours.

The main theme of this chapter is how people face the adversities of life, whether crossing a river to freedom, hiding in a classroom during a school shooting, or being caught in a traffic jam on the interstate with a crying baby buckled into the car seat behind you. How does stress affect us? What resources do we have to deal with it on a daily basis? And how do we cope with large-scale adversity and then get on with our lives? I begin with some of the leading theories and research on the effects of stress. Then I present some information on social support and other coping mechanisms. Finally, I turn to an examination of the most common response to stressful events, resilience.

10.1: Stress, Stressors, and Stress Reactions

OBJECTIVE: Determine the origins of stress

Stress is a set of physical, cognitive, and emotional responses that humans (and other organisms) display in reaction to demands from the environment. These environmental demands are known as **stressors**. The scientific study of stress (and stressors) is a very old field, going back to the early 1900s, and has been "claimed" by medical researchers and social scientists alike (Dougall & Baum, 2001). More than a century of research in many fields of enquiry have resulted in a large field of knowledge about stress and its antidote, **coping**.

  By the end of this module, you will be able to:

10.1.1 Compare theoretical explanations of stress

10.1.2 Differentiate types of stress

10.1.1: Stressors and Stress Reactions

OBJECTIVE: Compare theoretical explanations of stress

The best-known explanation of the stress response is that of medical researcher Hans Selye (1936), who first coined the term *stress* and then developed the concept of the **general adaptation syndrome**. According to Selye, there are three stages to general adaptation syndrome as shown in Figure 10.1. The body begins in homeostasis, which is an organism's state of stability and optimal functioning (see Seyle's General Adaptation Syndrome).

Selye postulated that the "return to rest" is never complete even after the stressor has stopped and the general adaptation syndrome is terminated. One almost gets back to one's former state, but not quite, leading some to suggest that the process of aging may thus simply be the accumulation of the effects of many years of stress.

Selye's theory was one of the earliest demonstrations of the link between psychological reactions and physical illnesses. He was careful not to claim that stress itself *caused* physical changes, but that our reaction to stress (which he called "distress") was the culprit, leaving the door open for others to suggest preventative measures, such as coping mechanisms and social support, which are discussed later in this chapter.

It has been almost a century since Selye's theory was published, and hundreds of studies have been done on the effects stress reactions have on the human immune system. Selye's idea of stress leading to a general suppression of the immune system has been refined to postulate two separate types of immune responses: a *natural immunity*, which is a quick defense against pathogens in general, and a *specific immunity*, which is slower and requires more energy because the body needs to identify specific pathogens and form matching lymphocytes to combat them. Ordinarily the two systems work in balance, but a stress reaction results in the natural immune system going quickly into overdrive and the specific immune system being suppressed to conserve energy. Stressful events of longer duration, such as bereavement, lead to a decline in the natural immune system over time and an increase in the specific immune system. And when stress is chronic—such as caregiving for a relative with dementia, being a refugee, or being unemployed for a long period of time—both immune systems eventually decline in function (Segerstrom & Miller, 2004).

THEORIES OF STRESS Evolutionary psychologists suggest that the reaction to acute stress (the fight-or-flight response) is an adaptive mechanism that enabled our primitive ancestors to summon optimal levels of energy

Selye's General Adaptation Syndrome

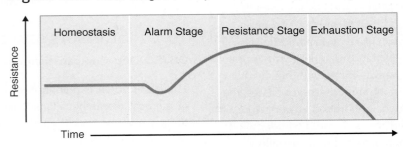

Figure 10.1 Three Stages of Selye's General Adaptation Syndrome

According to Selye, there are three stages to general adaptation syndrome. The body begins in homeostasis, which is an organism's state of stability and optimal functioning. When a stressor is detected, the first stage is the *alarm reaction*, in which the body quickly responds to a stressor by becoming alert and energized, preparing for "fight or flight." If the stressor continues for a longer time, the body goes into the second stage, *resistance*, in which it attempts to regain its normal state. During this stage, the thymus gland, which is involved in immune responses, decreases in size and function. Thus, in this phase, the person is able to control the initial alarm reaction to the stressor but does so at the expense of the immune function. If the stressor continues long enough (and many chronic stressors do continue over very long periods of time), the resistance phase cannot be sustained, and the person reaches the third stage, *exhaustion*, when some of the alarm-stage responses reappear. If the stressor is severe enough, according to Selye, exhaustion can be accompanied by physical illness or even death.

(increased adrenaline and increased blood supply to the heart and large muscles) while at the same time preparing the body for accelerated healing of wounds and prevention of infection from whatever antigens entered through them (natural immunity). Modern humans seldom need this set of responses because the types of stressors we encounter do not often have physical consequences, nor do they require us to defend ourselves physically. However, as with many other evolved mechanisms, the stress response reflects the demands of more primitive environments, resulting in a mismatch of physical responses to psychological events (Flinn et al., 2005).

Selye's theory took a **response-oriented viewpoint**, meaning that it was focused on the physiological reactions within the individual that resulted from exposure to stressors. Other researchers have focused on the stressors themselves. To do this, it is necessary to evaluate events in the environment to determine whether they are stressors and, if they are, the relative magnitude of the stress they cause. The earliest evaluation method came from psychiatrists Thomas Holmes and Richard Rahe (1967), who devised a checklist to rate the level of a person's stressors based on **life-change events**. This rating scale consists of 43 events with points assigned to each event depending on how much stress it causes. For example, death of a spouse is the most stressful at 100 points, being fired is 47 points, and getting a speeding ticket is 11 points. The researchers focused on life changes, not just negative events, and included some positive events, such as pregnancy (40 points), outstanding personal achievement (28 points), and vacation (13 points). Holmes and Rahe hypothesized that the more

points a person had accumulated in the recent past, the higher the stress level and the greater the chances of illness in the near future.

Holmes and Rahe approached the topic of stress from a **stimulus-oriented viewpoint**, meaning that their focus was on the stressors themselves, the stimuli that trigger the stress reactions, or more specifically, life events. Their rating scale, along with similar measures of life stressors, proved to be a fairly accurate predictor of physical illness and psychological symptoms. Most of the research today on stress reactions uses some form of a life-event rating scale. At the same time, serious questions have been raised about this definition of stress and this method of measurement. First of all, it is not so obvious that life changes all produce stress in the same way. Are positive life changes and negative life changes really equally stressful? And even among life changes that may be classed as negative, perhaps some subvarieties are more stress producing or more likely to lead to illness than others. And what about events that can be positive in one situation (pregnancy to a long-married couple who have been trying to conceive for years) and negative in another (pregnancy to an unprepared teenage girl)?

10.1.2: Types of Stress

OBJECTIVE: Differentiate types of stress

Several researchers have suggested subcategories of stressors or life-change events that may help answer some related questions. For example, sociologist Leonard Pearlin (1980) made a distinction between *short-term life events*, which are

Figure 10.2 Types of Stressors

U.S. adults from age 25 to 74 report that the largest proportion of their daily stressors arise from interpersonal tensions, followed by stressful events that happen to other people in their networks and events that happen at work or school.

SOURCE: Data from Almeida (2005).

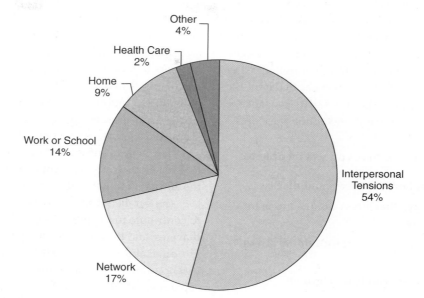

stressors that may cause immediate problems but have a definite beginning and end, and *chronic life strains*, which are continuous and ongoing. He explained that chronic life strains were the type of stressors that caused the most health problems and also eroded social relationships (ironically, the very interactions that help alleviate stress).

Another distinction is made between types of job-related stressors. *Work stress* is what a worker experiences on a job with high demands but a good amount of control and sense of personal accomplishment. *Work strain* results from situations in which a worker is faced with high demands but low control, no sense of personal accomplishment, and low reward (Nelson & Burke, 2002).

Lifespan developmental psychologist David Almeida (2005) distinguishes between *major life events*, such as divorce and death of a loved one, and *daily stressors*, the routine challenges of day-to-day living, such as work deadlines, malfunctioning computers, and arguments with children. Daily stressors also include more chronic challenges such as caring for an elderly parent or balancing the roles of a spouse, parent, and worker. Although he acknowledges that major life events may be associated with prolonged physiological reactions, he believes that daily stressors, which occur far more frequently, also have serious effects on one's well-being. Almeida contends that the daily stressors not only have direct and immediate effects on emotional and physical functioning, but also accumulate over time to create persistent problems that may result in more serious stress reactions.

Daily stressors are difficult to measure because they are small issues that are not easily recalled over time, so Almeida used a diary method to follow the daily stressors

of about 1,500 adults, part of a nationally representative sample of people in the United States participating in the National Study of Daily Experiences (NSDE). Instead of requiring participants to keep their own diaries (and perhaps fail to fill them out on a regular basis), he had telephone interviewers call each person in the study each evening during an 8-day period. And instead of using a checklist, the interviewers asked semistructured questions that allowed the participants to tell about their daily stressors and their subjective appraisals of the events (Almeida, 2005).

Almeida and his colleagues found that adults in the United States typically experienced at least one stressor on 40% of the days studied and more than one on 10% of the days. The most common stressors were interpersonal arguments and tensions, which accounted for half of the reported stressful events. The types of stressors are shown in Figure 10.2, along with the frequency with which they were reported. Interestingly, the subjective appraisal of the severity of stressful events overall was "average," whereas the objective appraisals, given by expert coders, were "low." In other words, we tend to perceive our own stressful events as more severe than they are perceived by a noninvolved rater (Almeida & Horn, 2004).

10.2: Effects of Stress

OBJECTIVE: Relate stress to health outcomes

If you recall Selye's theory, stressors cause physiological stress reactions that lead to lowered immune function and ultimately may cause physical disease and mental health disorders. Early studies showed a significant relationship between self-rated life-change events and a number of health problems, but the effects were very small and it was difficult to know which came first, the stressors or the health problems. Also, there is the problem of stress causing an increase in unhealthy behaviors, such as tobacco and alcohol use and overeating, and certain common factors, such as poverty, causing both a high number of stressors and poor health. Recent researchers have controlled many of these confounds to concentrate on the areas that have the most promise for unwrapping the stress/disease package and finding effective treatment and prevention measures.

▼ **By the end of this module, you will be able to:**

10.2.1 Describe links between stress and disease

10.2.2 Summarize ways that stress can lead to mental health disorders

10.2.3 Identify factors that impact individual stress outcomes

10.2.4 Explain how stress can lead to growth

10.2.1: Physical Disease

OBJECTIVE: Describe links between stress and disease

Stressors have been found to be related to **mortality risk—** the chance that an individual will die within a certain period of time. Health psychology researcher Jessica J. Chiang and her colleagues (Chiang et al., 2018), examined data from the Midlife Development in the United States (MIDUS) study. Over 1,300 middle-aged adults had been called by researchers for eight consecutive nights and asked about stressful events they encountered that day. The stressors they were

asked about included having an argument, avoiding an argument, and experiencing a work-related stressor, a home-related stressor, or discrimination. They were also asked about their positive and negative emotional reactions to the stressors. During the next 20 years, 310 of the participants died. Researchers compared the data of the deceased participants with those of the surviving participants and found a positive relationship between the total number of stressors reported by participants during that 8-day period and their risk of dying in the next 20 years. They also found a positive relationship between the increase in negative emotions in response to stressors and the risk of dying in the next 20 years. They concluded that participants who reported high numbers of daily stressful events and negative reactions to those events were more apt to have died the 20 years following the initial study.

The number of stressors a person reports has been found to contribute to the progression of heart disease, the risk of diabetes, and the onset of some cancers. For example, a longitudinal study of over 10,000 women in Finland showed that accumulation of stressful life events, such as divorce or separation, death of a husband, personal illness or injury, job loss, or death of a close friend or relative, was associated with an increased risk of breast cancer. Women were surveyed in the initial stage of the study and asked to report stressful life events they had experienced in the last 5 years. Fifteen years later, 180 incidents of breast cancer had been reported for women in the study (doctors are required to report all cancer diagnoses to the Finnish Cancer Registry). Grouping the women by how many stressful life events they reported (none, one, two, or three or more), researchers found a linear relationship, as shown in Figure 10.3, between the number of stressful events and the incidence of breast cancer in the subsequent 15 years (Lillberg et al., 2003).

Figure 10.3 Relationship Between Breast Cancer and the Number of Stressful Events

Women who reported one, two, or three or more major life events in the previous 5 years were significantly more likely to be diagnosed with breast cancer during the next 15 years than those who reported no major life events. The more events reported, the greater incidence of breast cancer.

SOURCE: Adapted from Lillberg, Verkasalo, Kaprio, et al. (2003).

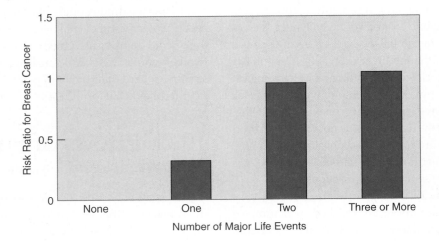

The greater the number of stressful events they reported, the greater the women's chance of having breast cancer, and because the surveys had been done years before the cancer appeared and not after the fact, this is very strong support that stressors are related to subsequent physical illness.

STRESS AND DISEASE   Other studies have shown a link between stress and heart disease. Researchers followed almost 13,000 men for 15 years and demonstrated that work-related stress (such as being fired or laid off, not being able to work because of a disability, failure of a business) was related to an increased risk of death from heart disease. Men were given physical examinations and surveys annually for 6 years. Nine years after the study was completed, death records were examined along with causes of death. When the men were grouped according to the number of job stressors they had reported during the study, researchers found a linear relationship between the number of stressful events and the incidence of death due to heart disease in the 9 years since the study ended. The greater the number of stressful events, the higher the risk of death from heart disease (Matthews & Gump, 2002).

Another group of researchers examined the relationship between stressful life events and subsequent risk for heart disease and diabetes. The 149 male participants filled out the Holmes and Rahe questionnaire (described earlier in this chapter), reporting the life-change events they had experienced in the previous 5 years. Then they were tested for various markers of risk for cardiovascular disease and diabetes (high blood pressure, high HDL cholesterol, obesity, high levels of glucose in the blood). Men who were at the highest risk for cardiovascular disease and diabetes had significantly higher scores on their life-change events questionnaires than those at low risk (Fabre et al., 2013). These studies, and many more, provide support that life stressors and a variety of physical illnesses are strongly related.

10.2.2: Mental Health Disorders

OBJECTIVE: Summarize ways that stress can lead to mental health disorders

Stressful life events are associated with the onset of various mental disorders, such as depression and anxiety, and this relationship has been demonstrated in a number of studies, though the effect is relatively small, showing that many factors other than exposure to stressors are at work. However, one's reaction to those stressors seems to have a more substantial effect on which of us will develop a mental health disorder and which will not. For example, you probably know someone who has broken up with their girlfriend or boyfriend, spent a few sad days moping around in their pajamas, and then was back to their usual demeanor, perhaps even telling you that it was a learning experience never to date someone so self-centered or so much older than they are.

And you probably know another person who had a similar breakup but was incapacitated the rest of the semester. The difference is how they reacted to the stressful event.

In the diary study described earlier, in which 1,500 adults of all ages were called every evening for 8 consecutive days to report on the stressors in their day, they were also asked to report on their overall moods (Almeida, 2005). Ten years after the study was completed, over half of the original participants were contacted again to find out about their current emotional health. Participants who had reported high levels of negativity on days they had no stressors were more apt to have symptoms of mood disorders 10 years later than those with lower levels of negativity on days with no stressors (Charles et al., 2013). It seems that these participants' long-term reactivity to earlier stressors was a predictor of subsequent mood disorders; those who had long-lasting negative reactions to stressors that occurred days before were those who were most apt to report symptoms of depression, anxiety, or bipolar disorder.

One type of mental health disorder linked directly to stressful events is **posttraumatic stress disorder (PTSD)**, the psychological response to trauma, such as military combat, rape, terrorist attacks, natural disasters, or automobile accidents. This disorder was first identified by the American Psychiatric Association (APA) in 1980, although it has been described throughout history as battle fatigue, shell shock, nervous breakdown, and other nonscientific terms. Symptoms of PTSD include reexperiencing the event in intrusive thoughts and dreams, numbing of general responses, avoiding stimuli associated with the event, and increased arousal of physiological stress mechanisms. **Acute stress disorder** is the term used for reactions to trauma that are similar to PTSD, but diminish within a month. About half of PTSD cases begin with acute stress disorder (American Psychiatric Association, 2013).

Lifetime risk for PTSD in the United States is about 9%; it is much lower in Europe and most Asian, African, and Latin American countries, which are around 1%. Not surprisingly, PTSD occurs at higher rates among people who are in jobs that entail more trauma exposure, such as veterans, police, firefighters, and emergency medical personnel. It is estimated that 33–50% of those who have survived rape, military combat and captivity, or persecution from ethnic or political genocide develop PTSD. Women are more apt to develop PTSD. U.S. Latinos, African Americans, and American Indians have higher rates of PTSD than the U.S. non-Latino white population; U.S. Asian Americans have the lowest rates. Older adults are less likely to develop PTSD, but they may develop long-lasting symptoms that do not fit the full definition of PTSD but still are considered mental health disorders due to trauma. One of the best predictors that a person will develop PTSD is having a history of trauma, especially physical violence (American Psychiatric Association, 2013).

TREATING PTSD Recommended treatment for PTSD includes cognitive-behavioral therapy and prolonged exposure therapy, in which the therapist guides the patient back through memories of the traumatic event and helps him or her to engage with reminders of the event rather than avoiding them (American Psychological Association, 2017). Other techniques, such as mindfulness training and equine assisted therapy, may also help reduce PTSD symptoms (Earles et al., 2015). In a World Health Organization survey of PTSD patients from 28 countries, researchers found that about a third of all cases were in full remission within 1 year, many in 6 months (Kessler et al., 2017). The remission rates for specific traumas are shown in Figure 10.4.

Researchers often accompany first responders after traumatic incidents—such as the terrorist bombing at the Ariana Grande concert in Manchester, England, the aftermaths of Hurricane Harvey in Texas and Hurricane Maria in Puerto Rico, the Las Vegas massacre, and the Parkland school shooting—ready to gather data on the victims, the bystanders, and the rescue workers. Around the world, researchers have tagged along with rescuers in war zones, at the sites of genocide and mass rape, in areas where famine has occurred, and in refugee camps. Although it may seem cold-hearted to be using victims as research participants during these difficult times, a lot of the knowledge conveyed in this chapter is the result of such projects.

For example, because of this research, we know that about one-third of people will show symptoms of PTSD within a week of a traumatic event, and about 10% will continue showing those symptoms a year later (Gorman, 2005). We also know that the most valuable help mental health providers can give to people exposed to trauma is to promote feelings of safety, calmness, self-efficacy, community connectedness, and hope. Survivors need their practical needs attended to first, such as medical care, information about family members, food, clothing, and shelter. The time

for therapy comes later, if at all. For most survivors, symptoms of PTSD are short-lived and resilience is the norm (Watson et al., 2011).

Mental health problems due to stress can be passed down in families, as has been demonstrated by studies of Holocaust survivors and their adult children, who, although they did not experience the Holocaust themselves, are more apt to develop depression and anxiety disorders than other adults their ages (Yehuda et al., 2008). They are also more apt to develop PTSD if exposed to trauma in their own lives (Yehuda et al., 2001). Psychologist Yael Danieli and her colleagues (Danieli et al., 2017) were interested in finding out which adult children of Holocaust survivors were at risk for mental health problems. They conducted clinical interviews with almost 200 adult children of Holocaust survivors, asking them about their parents' posttraumatic adaptation, their own relationship with and feelings about their parents, and their own mental health in the last 12 months. Those who expressed the highest level of *reparative adaptational impacts* regarding their parents, that is, feeling that their job as children was to undo the past and heal their parents, were most likely to develop psychological disorders. Some 46% of adult children who expressed the need to repair the past for their parents reported that they had suffered from mood disorders or anxiety disorders in the past 12 months (the average in the United States is about 15%). In contrast, only 8% of adult children who did not express this need to undo the past and heal their parents had experienced mood disorders or anxiety disorders. This study emphasizes that the most important factor in the mental health problems of adult children of Holocaust survivors is the adult children's perceptions of the impact the Holocaust had on their parents and what their role is to remedy it. (One bright note in this study is that over half of the adult children who had high levels of reparative adaptational impact had reported no symptoms of anxiety or depression in the past 12 months.)

Figure 10.4 Remission Rates for Specific Traumas

Speed of recovery for PTSD patients in 29 countries by trauma type. (Recovery is defined as length of time until all symptoms are in remission.)

SOURCE: Kessler et al. (2017).

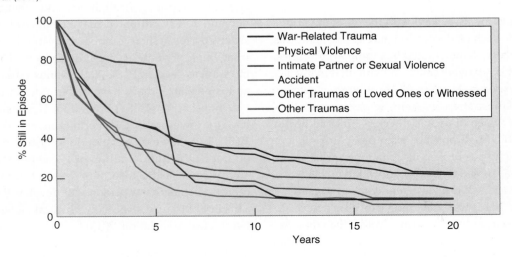

10.2.3: Individual Differences in Stress-Related Disorders

OBJECTIVE: Identify factors that impact individual stress outcomes

Everyone is exposed to stressors on a daily basis, and everyone meets these stressors with stress reactions, but not everyone suffers from physical disease and mental disorders as a result. In fact, the majority of people handle stress very well. Of course, the type of stress and the amount of stress can make a difference, but researchers have found that factors such as gender, age, racial discrimination, and environment–gene interactions affect an individual's susceptibility to stress-related health problems.

GENDER When it comes to daily stressors, women report more days with at least one stressor than do men. Women and men also report different sources of stress. Men are more apt than women to report daily stressors related to work or school, whereas women are more apt than men to report experiencing daily stressors as a result of things that happened to people in their social or family networks. Men are more apt to report stressors that threaten them financially; women are more apt to report stressors that threaten the ways others feel about them (Almeida, 2005).

Some researchers argue that Selye's theory of fight or flight applies only to men, and that women have a totally different reaction to stressors. Social psychologist Shelley Taylor (2002) argued that males and females have evolved different survival and reproductive behaviors, and that women may have developed a response to stress that differs from the one typically seen in studies of men. Instead of fight or flight, Taylor suggested that women have a genetic response to stress that involves "tend and befriend." Instead of being based on either fleeing the dangerous situation or defeating an aggressor, as is the case with men, this response in women is aimed at tending to one's immature offspring and seeking support from others, especially other women. These researchers believe that female responses to stress are based on the attachment–caregiving process and may be regulated, in part, by sex hormones (Taylor et al., 2006). The effects of age-related decline in these hormones needs to be examined (Almeida et al., 2011).

This research fits well with other findings on gender differences in social behavior. Women tend to have larger social networks, have deeper and more emotional friendships, and are more apt to respond to emotional events by seeking out friends and talking. They tend to be the kinkeepers and caregivers in families. It has been well demonstrated that men and women do not react with the same intensity to stress. Why not differences in the role of stressors in their lives?

There are also gender differences in PTSD. Men are exposed to more trauma than women during their lifetimes, but women are more likely to experience PTSD as a result of trauma. Figure 10.5 shows the number of traumatic events men and women report and the incidence of PTSD for both genders. However, this does not tell the whole story. Some events are more apt to lead to PTSD for one gender than another. For example, women are much more likely to experience rape than men (9% vs. 1%), but men are more likely to suffer from PTSD as a result (65% vs. 46%). Men have a higher rate of experiencing physical assault than women (11% vs. 6%), but women's rates of developing PTSD as a result are higher than men's (21% vs. 2%). Clearly the likelihood of developing PTSD as the result of a traumatic experience depends on more factors than just the objective severity of the event (Yehuda, 2002).

AGE In general, the number of daily stressors reported decreases with age. The highest number of stressors is reported by young adults, and the lowest is reported by older adults (Almeida et al., 2011). There are several reasons for this. First, younger people have more complex lives than older people, thus more potential sources of stressors. Older people have more experience with stressful events and, presumably, have developed some expertise in avoiding or coping with situations that might become stressors. Although

---

Figure 10.5 Lifetime Prevalence of PTSD

Men experience more trauma in their lifetimes, but women are more likely to develop PTSD.

SOURCE: Data from Yehuda (2002).

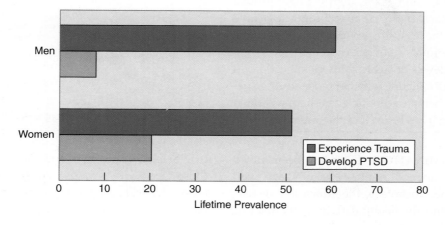

Lifetime Prevalence

older people often have more chronic health problems and experience more loss in their lives, they often compare their own situation with that of others their age and consider themselves to be doing well. A large number of older adults consider themselves to be in excellent or very good health, but at the same time report a number of chronic health conditions. The question of how people of different ages react to stressors is not easily answered (see 'Stressors and Age').

Stressors and Age

In Almeida's diary study, participants ranged in age from 25 to 74. Approximately half were men and half were women. As seen in Figure 10.6, the proportion of days that people reported experiencing any stressors declined after middle adulthood, and women reported more days with stressors than men at all ages (Almeida & Horn, 2004).

Some research shows that older people have a lifetime of experience with daily stressors and have learned how to cope with them better than younger people. Other research shows that stress from major life events builds up over time and that older people are apt to be more vulnerable than younger people because they have had more years to experience major life events (Brown & Frahm, 2016). For example, one study of Holocaust survivors shows higher rates of depression 60 years later (Trappler et al., 2007), whereas a study of another group of Holocaust survivors shows resilient coping in old age (Sagi-Schwartz et al., 2013). It seems that there is more to the experience of a traumatic event than just being there. Individuals interpret events differently and face them with different resources. Then over the years, they find different ways to go on with their lives. They have different levels of support from friends and family.

One study, using a longitudinal design, gives us a little more information about age and the effects of experiencing a major life event. Developmental psychologist Stacey Scott and her colleagues (2013) surveyed over 2,200 people throughout the United States, including 104 who were residents of New York City. The participants, who ranged in age from 18 to 101, were questioned 2 months after the terrorist attack on September 11, 2001, and then five more times in the following 3 years. In each interview they were asked about their posttraumatic stress symptoms and their fear of future attacks. Figure 10.7 shows how the participants in various age groups reported posttraumatic stress symptoms. There was a significant difference in the amount of stress reported at almost each testing point, with older groups reporting more stress than younger groups 2 months after the attack. By 1 year after the attack, people over age 75 reported the least stress while other age groups reported similar amounts of stress. At 36 months, all the groups showed low levels of stress, with the oldest group reporting the lowest. Predicting whether older adults experience more stress when a traumatic event happens often depends on how long it has been since the traumatic event.

Figure 10.6 Daily Stressors for Men and Women over the Adult Years

Daily stressors decline beginning in middle age, and women report more daily stressors than men at all ages.

SOURCE: Adapted from Almeida and Horn (2004).

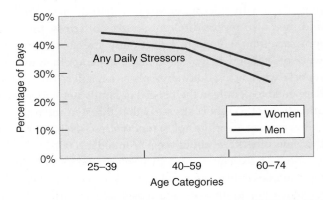

Figure 10.7 Rates of PTSD After 9/11 by Age Group

Older adults report more posttraumatic stress symptoms than younger groups 6 months after the September 11, 2001, terrorist attacks on the World Trade Center and Pentagon, but all age groups show a lessening of symptoms a year after the attack.

SOURCE: Scott, Poulin, and Silver (2013).

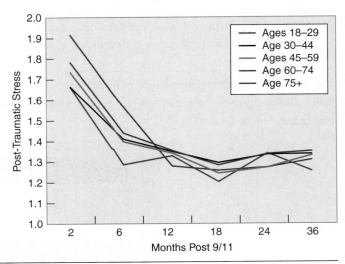

PERCEIVED DISCRIMINATION It has long been known that women and members of minority groups face overt discrimination in the workplace, the education system, the justice system, and the health care industry, leading to worse life outcomes and more stress than men and those in majority groups, which in turn lead to low levels of physical and psychological health (Paradies, 2006). However, a second factor, **perceived discrimination,**

occurs when an individual realizes or believes themselves to be the target of discrimination. This type of subtle, subjective discrimination has been linked to both psychological and physical health through two pathways, increased stress and unhealthy behaviors (Pascoe & Smart Richman, 2009).

Psychologist Michael T. Schmitt and his colleagues evaluated the data from 43 cross-sectional studies and 54 longitudinal studies and determined that perceived discrimination was negatively correlated with psychological well-being (Schmitt et al., 2014). Furthermore, because the longitudinal studies showed the same negative correlation, the researchers could hypothesize that the perceived discrimination had a causal effect on psychological well-being. The strongest effects of perceived discrimination on well-being were found for sexual orientation, mental illness, physical disabilities, HIV+ status, and weight. Race and gender had weaker effects. Children experienced stronger effects of perceived discrimination than adults, and disadvantaged people experienced stronger effects of perceived discrimination than advantaged people.

Studies have been done of various groups with results that show perceived discrimination has a negative effect on well-being. For example, in a study of 110 African American college women, a relationship was found between perceived racism and changes in blood pressure following a public-speaking task. The higher the women's reports of perceived racism, the more their systolic blood pressure was elevated as a result of giving a short talk before an audience (Clark, 2006). Some researchers have studied discrimination against older people and found that those who reported being discriminated against showed lower levels of recall and gait speed (Shankar & Hinds, 2017). Other researchers studied Asian American adults and found that higher rates of perceived discrimination were associated with greater depressive symptoms (Chau et al., 2018). Health-related effects of perceived discrimination have been demonstrated in groups of U.S. citizens of Irish, Jewish, Polish, and Italian descent. Those who perceive chronic discrimination against their groups were two to six times more likely to show high-risk markers for cardiovascular disease than people in those same groups who do not perceive discrimination (Hunte & Williams, 2009). Sexual and gender minority individuals were given diaries to record their daily episodes of perceived discrimination and their nicotine, alcohol, and drug use. Their experience of perceived discrimination was positively associated with their nicotine, alcohol, and drug use, suggesting that perceived discrimination may trigger negative health behaviors (Livingston et al., 2017).

It seems that perceived discrimination is almost a universal response by individuals who believe that their membership in a group is causing them to be treated unfairly. This subjective feeling may lead to a variety of physical and psychological health problems, independent of any

detrimental treatment they actually experience as a member of that group.

ENVIRONMENT–GENE INTERACTIONS In the last decade, researchers have become aware that the differences in genetic expression between two people are due more to the environment they lived in than their gender and ancestry (Slavich & Cole, 2013). In other words, the expression of our genes can be influenced by the external social conditions we experience, especially how we subjectively perceive those conditions. This emerging field of research is known as **human social genomics**, the study of changes in gene expression due to subjective perceptions of the social environment.

One of the first studies to show the effect of social environment on gene expression was conducted by biopsychologist Steve W. Cole and his colleagues (Cole et al., 2007), using a group of socially isolated individuals and a control group who were more socially integrated. Earlier research had shown that people who are socially isolated have more incidences of illness and die at earlier ages than those who are more socially integrated in their communities. The researchers discovered immune response genes that differentiated the groups. When the genomes of the participants were examined, it was found that the altered genes were those involved in regulating inflammation, a key symptom of many of the diseases socially isolated individuals develop. Figure 10.8 shows the activity of the pro-inflammatory genes for the socially integrated group is significantly lower than the socially isolated group.

Figure 10.8 Inflammation and Social Isolation

Participants who were socially integrated showed more activity in anti-inflammatory genes and less activity in pro-inflammatory genes. The isolated group showed less activity in anti-inflammatory gene activity and more in pro-inflammatory activity. This suggests that social experiences can alter genes.

SOURCE: Cole et al. (2007).

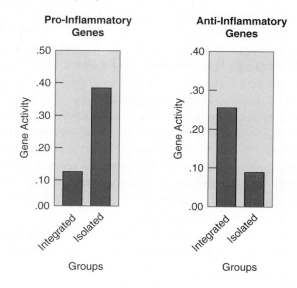

In contrast, the anti-inflammatory gene activity is significantly lower for the socially integrated group. The researchers suggest that the social experiences of older people can alter their genes, and these altered genes can lead to physical illness by producing pro-inflammatory or anti-inflammatory elements.

Similar genetic changes have been found in groups experiencing other types of stress, such as ongoing interpersonal difficulties (Murphy et al., 2013), low socioeconomic status (Chen et al., 2011), and posttraumatic stress disorder (Knight et al., 2016). This is also an explanation of how discrimination might affect health, as discussed in the previous section. These studies show the inaccuracy of our long-standing beliefs that one's biological makeup is set at conception (or at birth) and is not affected by the social environment. Individual differences in adulthood have been shaped by our perceptions of the social environment, and those differences have altered the way our genes are expressed on an individual basis.

10.2.4: Stress-Related Growth

OBJECTIVE: Explain how stress can lead to growth

Popular folk wisdom holds that the Chinese word for "crisis" is made up of two characters—one meaning "danger" and one meaning "opportunity." Other cultures have equivalent words of wisdom to express the idea that "what doesn't kill us makes us stronger." The same idea is what has motivated a wave of research examining **stress-related growth**—the positive changes that follow the experience of stressful life events. Indeed, this idea is not a new one. Many theories of development, such as Erikson's, discussed in chapter 8 on personality, include the concept that crisis, or stress, can make useful changes in the individual and that personal growth may result from facing difficult life events.

Some studies examining the negative effects of stress also found some positive effects. One early study of middle-aged adults whose parents had recently died showed that although the participants reported typical symptoms of emotional distress, many also reported that they had experienced personal growth as a result of the loss, in that they finally felt they were complete adults with increased self-confidence and a sense of maturity. They also reported that they had learned to value personal relationships more (Scharlach & Fredrickson, 1993). Similar results were noted in studies of divorce (Helson & Roberts, 1994) and widowhood (Lieberman, 1996). Studies of the aftermath of the terrorist attacks on September 11, 2001, revealed positive and prosocial reactions to the tragedy, including reports of interpersonal closeness and an increase in blood donations, charitable giving, and volunteerism (Morgan et al., 2011).

More recently, a study of stress-related growth in veterans of the Korean War and World War II involved surveys of over 1,000 men who served during that time and whose average age at the time of the survey was 65.5 years. Researchers found that those who had been exposed to combat were more apt to believe that there had been positive aspects of their service. Furthermore, those combat veterans who reported more positive aspects to their service were more apt to report positive well-being in later life. Researchers concluded that combat veterans who focus on the positive aspects of their military experience have better chances for optimal aging (Lee et al., 2017).

Stress-related growth has also been studied in breast cancer survivors (Connerty & Knott, 2013), Palestinian adults living in Gaza (Kira et al., 2012), Israeli ex-prisoners of war (Dekel et al., 2012), and low-income mothers who survived Hurricane Katrina (Lowe et al., 2013), among other groups. The findings generally agree that, depending on the stressful event itself, the personal beliefs of the individual, and the support available, people in dire circumstances are able to later report personal growth, increased wisdom, growth in relationships with others, a new appreciation for life, a new sense of maturity, a stronger religious belief, or a greater sense of self-efficacy and self-confidence.

10.3: Coping with Stress

OBJECTIVE: Evaluate coping techniques for stress

There has been a shift recently in psychology from the "illness" model of stress, which catalogues symptoms, probabilities, and groups more prone to stress-related disorders, to a "wellness" approach, which involves prevention, preparation, and early intervention immediately after trauma occurs (Friedman, 2005). These priorities emphasize the importance of **resistance resources**, the personal and social resources that may buffer a person from the impact of stress. Central among these are individual coping responses, a sense of personal control, and the availability of social support.

By the end of this module, you will be able to:

10.3.1 Compare coping behaviors

10.3.2 Relate social support to stress outcomes

10.3.1: Types of Coping Behaviors

OBJECTIVE: Compare coping behaviors

At the top of the list of protections against the effects of stressors in our lives are **coping behaviors**, an all-purpose term that refers to anything you might think, feel, and do to reduce the effects of stressful events. Suppose that you received a rejection letter from a graduate program you had been working hard to get into. Or suppose that your apartment was damaged by a fire and most of your belongings were lost. How would you cope with these stressors? There are a number of behaviors you might employ, and some of them are found in Table 10.1, which lists styles of coping and examples of each from the Brief COPE Inventory (Carver, 1997).

These are not the only ways of coping. Many theorists and investigators have made their own lists and organized them into useful subcategories. One way of doing this is to divide coping mechanisms into four categories: problem focused, emotion focused, meaning focused, and social coping (Folkman & Moskowitz, 2004).

Other Subcategories of Ways of Coping

Problem-Focused Coping—**Problem-focused coping** directly addresses the problem causing distress. If you were not accepted into your first-choice graduate school, calling the school for more information would be an example of problem-focused coping. You might inquire about whether you could reapply for midyear acceptance or ask if it would be helpful to retake your admission exams. For the problem of having a fire in your apartment, calling the insurance company would be an example of a problem-focused coping

strategy, as would taking an inventory of the things that were damaged and making plans about how to replace them.

In a study of the aftermath of the Washington, DC, sniper attacks in 2002, psychologists Ari Zivotofsky and Meni Koslowsky (2005) surveyed 144 residents of the area to find out about their coping strategies in response to 3 weeks of random shootings that left 10 residents dead and four injured. Specifically, they asked people about changes in their usual routines, which would be considered problem-focused coping. Figure 10.9 shows the activities that male and female respondents said they had restricted to cope with the stress of the situation. The first seven activities were mentioned significantly more often by women than men; the last activity, socializing with friends, showed no gender differences—possibly because it provided social support, which in itself is a buffer against stress.

Emotion-Focused Coping—The second category of coping mechanisms is **emotion-focused coping**, which includes ways that people try to decrease the negative emotions associated with the stressful situation. Dealing with the rejection from graduate school by going out and running for an hour is a good example. Using alcohol or drugs to cope with the stress is also emotion focused, but is not a good example because it can lead to even more stress in your life. Distancing oneself from the problem emotionally can be helpful in some cases and maladaptive in others.

The use of drugs and alcohol as a coping mechanism may not be an effective one, but for college students, substance abuse of all kinds is related to stress levels. Interestingly, this relationship differs by gender and by race. In a large study of over 1,500 students at a large midwestern university in the United States, general college-life

Table 10.1 Styles of Coping and Examples from the Brief COPE Inventory

Style of Coping	Example
Self-distraction	"I've been turning to work or other activities to take my mind off things."
Active coping	"I've been concentrating my efforts on doing something about the situation I'm in."
Denial	"I've been saying to myself, 'This isn't real.'"
Substance use	"I've been using alcohol or other drugs to make myself feel better."
Use of emotional support	"I've been getting comfort and understanding from someone."
Use of instrumental support	"I've been getting help and advice from other people."
Behavioral disengagement	"I've been giving up trying to deal with it."
Venting	"I've been saying things to let my unpleasant feelings escape."
Positive reframing	"I've been looking for something good in what is happening."
Planning	"I've been trying to come up with a strategy about what to do."
Humor	"I've been making jokes about it."
Acceptance	"I've been learning to live with it."
Religion	"I've been praying or meditating."
Self-blame	"I've been criticizing myself."

SOURCE: Adapted from Carver (1997).

Figure 10.9 How Men and Women Restricted Various Activities as a Result of DC Sniper Attacks

Men and women in Washington, DC, used problem-focused coping with the DC sniper attacks by restricting their usual activities in many areas. Women reduced activities significantly more than men for all types of activities except socializing with friends (a source of social support).

SOURCE: Data from Zivotofsky and Kosiowsky (2005).

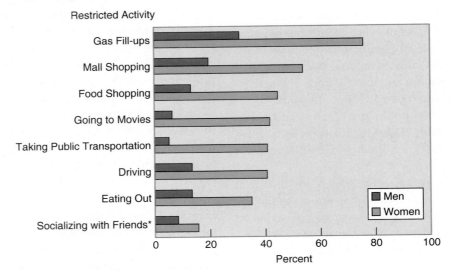

*No Significant Gender Difference

stress (such as problems with professors, grades, or relationships) was associated with increased alcohol use for all groups except black men. Traumatic stress (such as being victimized or witnessing violence) was related to alcohol problems for white students only and with binge drinking for white female students only. Although this was only one university, and the sample was not a representative one, the authors suggested that university counselors consider the larger finding that substance-abuse problems can be symptoms of underlying stress (Broman, 2005).

In the study described earlier that was done in the aftermath of the DC sniper, a number of emotion-focused coping strategies were reported in addition to the problem-focused strategies shown earlier in Figure 10.9. These included taking medication, disconnecting, watching the news, blaming the government, and blaming the terrorists. Unlike the problem-focused strategies discussed earlier, there were no gender differences in these ways of coping (Zivotofsky & Koslowsky, 2005).

Meaning-Focused Coping—**Meaning-focused coping** includes ways that people find to manage the meaning of a stressful situation. Telling yourself that you would probably be happier at a different graduate school that doesn't have such a rigorous program, is closer to home, or is where your best friend is going is an example of decreasing the stress by reframing the stressful situation of being rejected. Dealing with the fire in your apartment, you could tell yourself that the loss was only material things and it's good no one was hurt, or you could tell yourself that everything happens for a reason—both would be meaning focused ways

to cope. Such coping is especially useful in chronic stress situations like caregiving, where people often report that they are simply following religious teachings or fulfilling their marriage vows.

Social-Focused Coping—The fourth category of coping strategies, **social-focused coping**, involves seeking help from others, both instrumental and emotional support. If you call your best friend to share your bad news about your graduate school rejection, and he or she offers kind words of support, you are engaging in social coping. And if you ask your parents to help you replace the belongings you lost in the fire (and they do), that's more of the same. In the study discussed earlier of mechanisms people used to cope with the stress of a sniper at large, one of the more-reported ways of coping was to call or be in touch with relatives or friends. And although women reported using this form of social coping more than men, the numbers were high for both—92% of the women and 68% of the men (Zivotofsky & Koslowsky, 2005). This was also seen after the terrorist attacks on September 11, 2001, when the number of phone calls and Internet messages reached a record high all over the world. When we are stressed, whether as individuals or as a nation, we seek comfort in contacting those in our support networks.

EVALUATING THE EFFECTIVENESS OF COPING Which coping mechanisms are the best in a given situation? Sometimes it depends on whether you feel that you are in control of the problem or not. If you feel in control, then problem-focused coping is usually the most effective. An example would be a student who has an exam coming up and feels stressed. Problem-focused coping would include reviewing notes or meeting with a study group. But in a situation that offers little feeling of control, such as dealing with chronic illness, emotion-focused coping gives greater stress relief. Some examples would be distancing and finding other activities to keep one's mind occupied.

Two abilities are important in dealing with the stressors one encounters in life. First is the ability to use a variety of coping skills, depending on the situation, known as *coping flexibility*. The other is the ability to match the appropriate coping skill with the situation at hand, known as *goodness of fit* (Folkman & Moskowitz, 2004).

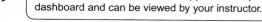

WRITING PROMPT

Coping with Stress

Think about a particularly stressful event in your own life. How did you cope with this stress?

▶ | The response entered here will appear in the performance dashboard and can be viewed by your instructor.

Submit

10.3.2: Social Support

OBJECTIVE: Relate social support to stress outcomes

Social support (sometimes known as *social relatedness*), refers to the actual affect, affirmation, and aid received from others and also the perception that one is cared for and that social support is available if needed. Numerous studies have established that social support provides major protection for both physical and mental health (Uchino et al., 2012). The lack of social support is *loneliness*, and adults who are lonelier have a higher risk of disease, death, and depression than adults with stronger social support (Holt-Lunstad et al., 2010). Similar patterns have been found in other countries, including Sweden (Rosengren et al., 1993), China (Williams et al., 2017), and South Korea (Choi et al., 2018), showing that the link between social support and well-being is not restricted to the United States or even to Western cultures.

THE BUFFERING EFFECT OF SOCIAL SUPPORT The beneficial effect of social support is even clearer when a person is under high stress. That is, the negative effect of stress on health and happiness is smaller for those who have adequate social support than for those whose social support is weak. This pattern of results is usually described as the **buffering effect** of social support, meaning that it won't keep stressors from entering one's life, but it will provide some protection against the harm they do. It may not be a

coincidence that many of the top-rated life changes on the Holmes and Rahe list involve losses in one's social support system, such as divorce, separation, death of a loved one, and loss of a job.

In a study of veterans who had been exposed to warzone stress 10 years earlier (during the Gulf War of 1990–1991), the amount of encouragement and assistance they perceived from other unit members, unit leaders, and the military in general was related to the amount of depression they reported since their return from the war. For both men and women, the less social support they perceived receiving, the higher level of depression they reported. These findings indicate that social support in a high-stress situation may serve as a buffer against later stress reactions such as depression and that social support is an important buffer against negative mental health consequences of stress and trauma (Vogt et al., 2005).

Psychologist Adam W. Fingerhut (2018) investigated the role of social support for gay men when faced with minority stress, which he defined as discrimination based on one's sexual orientation. He asked 89 gay men to provide baseline information about their social support from friends and family, their feelings of connectedness to the gay community, and their mental health. The participants were asked to keep a diary for 14 days, recording their experiences with minority stress and their daily affect, or emotional state. The 89 participants recorded over 1,000 episodes of minority stress over the 14 days of the study. Daily minority stress was associated with negative affect; that is, on days participants experienced more minority stress, they reported more negative affect. As shown in Figure 10.10, those with stronger support from friends (red line) had less negative affect overall than those with less support from friends (blue line). Furthermore, when faced with higher

Figure 10.10 Social Support and Minority Stress

Gay men with higher levels of social support display lower and more stable affect when faced with daily minority stress.

SOURCE: Fingerhut (2018).

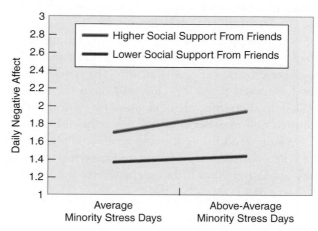

levels of minority stress, participants with stronger support from friends did not increase their negative affect as much as those who had less support from friends. Moods for participants with higher levels of social support from friends were fairly stable regardless of the daily discrimination they faced for being gay. This protection was not present for support from family or feelings of connectedness to the gay community.

SOME NEGATIVE EFFECTS OF SOCIAL NETWORKS
Lest I give the impression that there is nothing but sweetness and light in the world of social relationships, let me quickly add that there are also associated costs. Network systems are generally reciprocal. Not only do you receive support, but you give it as well. At some points in the life course, such as the early parenting years, the giving side of the equation seems to be more heavily weighted than the receiving side, a situation that may increase stress.

Everyday social interactions can also be a significant source of hassles. Most of us have at least some regular interactions with people we do not like or who irritate us to distraction. When these negative social interactions involve anger, dislike, criticism, or undermining, especially when the negative feelings come from people who are central to our social convoy, they have a substantial negative effect on one's overall feeling of well-being. Studies of African American and black Caribbean families show that while positive family support is associated with low rates of depression, negative family interactions are associated with higher rates of depression (Taylor et al., 2015). Researchers have found that the success of homeless people in a program to provide homes and health care is related to a decrease in former social support networks, usually shedding burdensome and abusive relationships (Golembiewski et al., 2017).

Social support can operate in a negative way even if it is well intentioned—for example, when the support given is not what is needed, or the offer of support is perceived as criticism, or intrusion, or an insult to our independence. When this occurs, instead of buffering, the misdirected social support can result in our losing the desire to cope, reducing our efforts to cope, or making our coping efforts less effective (DeLongis & Holtzman, 2005).

Social support at a time of chronic strain, such as financial problems or long-term caregiving, can also have negative effects, especially in the late years of adulthood. Support providers may not have the resources to sustain their support over the long periods of time required and may begin to feel resentful and frustrated as a result. In addition, the care receivers may not have the wherewithal to reciprocate and may feel as though they are losing what little independence they have left (Krause, 2006).

10.4: Resilience

OBJECTIVE: Analyze how resilience functions

I have covered various stressors and stress reactions, ways that people can cope with stress once it sets in, and how people may gain personal growth from their stressful experiences, but as you can tell from the statistics, not everyone who is exposed to stress, even traumatic stress, suffers its effects. Recently, in an effort to emphasize the positive outcomes in psychology, researchers have been investigating **resilience**, the maintenance of healthy functioning following exposure to potential trauma.

Resilience is not the same as recovery and is quite different from chronic and delayed posttraumatic stress reactions and recovery. Figure 10.11 shows the trajectories of resilience compared to these three other outcomes. As you can see, chronic stress symptoms, which 10–30% of people exposed to trauma experience, are severe reactions immediately after the traumatic event and remain severe 2 years afterward. Delayed-stress reactions, which account for 5–10% of reactions, begin moderate but have increased to severe 2 years after the trauma. Recovery, reported by 15–35%, begins with moderate-to-severe reactions but has become mild 2 years after trauma. Resilience is a reaction that may involve slightly increased disruption at the time of

Figure 10.11 Stress Reactions Over Time by Severity of Event

Of four outcomes people can have after exposure to trauma, the most prevalent is resilience. Others, such as chronic stress reaction, delayed stress reaction, and recovery, are not as typical as resilience.

SOURCE: Bonanno (2005).

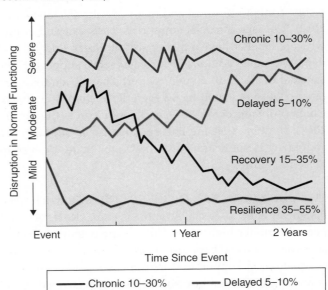

the trauma, but never leaves the mild range. According to psychologist George Bonanno (2005), resilience is the most common response to traumatic stress, found in 35–55% of people who are exposed to a traumatic event.

By the end of this module, you will be able to:

10.4.1 Relate trauma reactions to resilience

10.4.2 Identify personality traits associated with resilience

10.4.3 Explain how positive psychology is used to build resilience in military veterans

10.4.1: Reactions to Trauma

OBJECTIVE: Relate trauma reactions to resilience

In studies of a variety of traumatic events, resilience is the most common long-term outcome, not recovery or PTSD. Studies that investigate the responses of widows or widowers after the death of their spouses show that reactions of resilience are near 50% (Mancini et al., 2009). Contrary to popular belief, there is no evidence that these individuals will later suffer from "delayed grief," or that they were only superficially attached to their spouses. In a longitudinal study of older married couples, those who became widowed in the course of the study were followed for 18 months after the deaths of their spouses, and almost half the survivors showed only low levels of depression and had relatively few sustained symptoms of grief. When the marital histories of these resilient widowed individuals were examined, there were no signs of marital problems or of cold, distant personalities. They did have high scores on acceptance of death, belief in a just world, and having a strong support network. And they did have moments of intense sadness and yearning for their spouses, but these grief symptoms did not interfere with their ability to continue with their lives, including their ability to feel positive emotions (Bonanno et al., 2002).

Studies of the aftermath of the September 11 terrorist attacks show that about 13% of those who had direct exposure to the World Trade Center attack had PTSD 2 years later, along with about 4% of those who lived in the vicinity. Rescue workers reported 12%, whereas Pentagon staff and people who were evacuated from the World Trade Center after the attack reported about 15% PTSD prevalence (Neria et al., 2011). For military personnel serving in Iraq and Afghanistan (or both), it is estimated that most have personally experienced traumatic events and that around 10% will eventually develop PTSD or related disorders (Hoge et al., 2004).

Although these rates are disturbing, they support the findings that resilience is the most common response

to trauma of many kinds. Intervention is important for those who will sustain or eventually develop extreme levels of chronic stress, but the current practice of giving all exposed individuals psychological treatment may actually undermine their natural resilience processes and impede their recovery (Mayou et al., 2000). Some researchers are proposing that first-response personnel develop a screening device that would quickly identify people at high risk of PTSD (such as those who have experienced prior trauma and have low social support), and not interfere with anyone who is responding with genuine resilience (Mancini & Bonanno, 2009).

10.4.2: Personality Traits and Resilience

OBJECTIVE: Identify personality traits associated with resilience

We know a little about people who are prone to PTSD, but what about the people who are prone to resilience? A few factors have been identified, such as perceived control, self-identity, and optimism.

Predicting Resilience

Perceived Control—When faced with traumatic circumstances, such as childhood sexual abuse or poverty, individuals with high levels of **perceived control**, who believe that they are able to influence circumstances and attain their goals, are less apt to suffer physical and mental health problems as a result of stress exposure than those who do not have that personality trait.

Those who have high levels of perceived control, also known as *mastery*, likely appraise these events as being less stressful and they are better able to use adaptive coping mechanisms. In a study examining how perceived control affected the health of adults who had experienced trauma during their lives, psychologist Ari J. Elliot and his colleagues (2018) examined data from about 5,000 middle-aged adults who were participants in the Midlife in the United States Study (MIDUS). These participants had been asked to report whether certain traumatic events had happened to them, such as parental alcohol or substance abuse, death of a parent, divorce of parents, physical or sexual abuse, emotional abuse, or childhood life-threatening illness. They had also been given a test of perceived control (and various health measures). In the years since the data were gathered, 551 of the participants had died. Elliot and his colleagues divided the participants into three groups, based on their perceived control scores— low, average, and high. They then plotted the death rate of the participants based on the lifetime trauma they had

Figure 10.12 Relative Hazards Associated with Lifetime Trauma at Varying Levels of Mastery

The more traumatic events participants reported at middle age predicted risk of early death for those who had a low sense of perceived control (blue line).

SOURCE: Elliot et al. (2018).

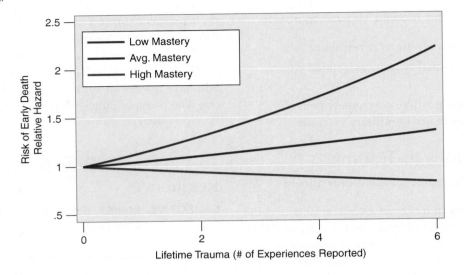

reported. Figure 10.12 shows these findings. The low perceived-control group (solid line) had increasingly greater chances of death the more traumatic experiences they had reported in their lifetimes.

Self-Identity—Another personality trait that seems to promote resilience is **self-identity**, or a strong sense of self. When trauma occurs, whether a natural disaster or a criminal assault, it often results in having one's world "turned upside down." The familiar becomes strange, routines are disrupted, and usual sources of comfort are not available. In a number of studies, individuals with a strong sense of self appear to experience less stress at these times than people who have lower levels of self-identity. They feel a continuity of the self and are better able to cope with the changes around them (Mancini & Bonanno, 2009).

Optimism—People who score high on measures of **optimism**, which is a positive outlook on life, are more apt to have better physical and mental health (Carver & Scheier, 2014) and have fewer stress symptoms after trauma (Frazier et al., 2011). This was demonstrated by psychologist Marianne Skogbrott Birkeland and her team of researchers (Birkeland et al., 2017), who studied survivors of the 2011 terrorist bombing in Oslo, Norway, in which a car bomb exploded in the city center, killing eight people and injuring 209. Ten months after the bombing, the researchers surveyed 259 people who were working that day in the buildings nearest the bombing, assessing their optimism, stress symptoms, and their exposure to the violence. They found that optimism seems to protect individuals from developing high levels of stress symptoms following the attack, whether they were in high- or low-exposure situations. The researchers suggest that optimists believe that they can actively cope with trauma and they tend to exaggerate the positive aspects of a situation. After a trauma, optimists may encode information differently than nonoptimists, giving them less-distressing memories of a traumatic incident.

Polystrengths—Researchers have recently studied **polystrengths**, or clusters of personality traits that may provide protection and resilience in the face of adversity. Psychologist Sherry Hamby and her colleagues (Hamby et al., 2018), surveyed over 2,500 individuals from emerging adulthood to middle age living in a rural, low-income community who were often exposed to high levels of interpersonal victimization and financial strain. In fact, almost 99% of the participants reported some recent adversity, such as witnessing an assault, being socially excluded by peers, being assaulted by a nonrelated peer, not being able to pay family bills, unemployment, and death of a family member. Although those with the highest level of adversity had lower levels of well-being and mental health, more than half the sample reported high levels of well-being and posttraumatic growth. For example, "I am satisfied with my life" was selected by 77% of the participants; "I have a lot to be proud of" (88%); "I discovered I am stronger than I thought I was" (84%); "I changed my priorities about what is important in life" (69%). For the group of people in this study, the protective factors that produced the most resilience were emotional regulation, emotional awareness, a sense of purpose, optimism, and psychological endurance.

10.4.3: Resilience in Military Deployment

OBJECTIVE: Explain how positive psychology is used to build resilience in military veterans

The National Center for Veterans Affairs (2016) reports that around 15% of U.S. veterans have experienced PTSD within the last 12 months. The average for the civilian population during this time period is 3.5%. Most of the traumatic incidents are from combat situations, and the prevalence depends on the duties the soldier is assigned, the politics surrounding the war, where the war is fought, and the enemy faced. Other PTSD is the result of military sexual assault and harassment. Among veterans who use VA health care, 23% of women report sexual assault while in the military. Fifty-five percent of women and 38% of men who are veterans report sexual harassment.

One of the problems in treating veterans with PTSD is that many are unwilling to report the symptoms. Each veteran returning from deployment is surveyed about various health symptoms using the Post-Deployment Health Assessment (PDHA) and is told that the responses will be included on their official service records. Fearing stigma and discrimination, many veterans are unwilling to admit mental health symptoms and are afraid that their answers will affect future deployment. One solution for this that is being tested is using a virtual therapist who asks questions about various health symptoms and responds with appropriate, reassuring answers (Lucas et al., 2017). This virtual therapist appears on a video screen in a digital representation of a human interviewer who can portray humanlike facial expressions and natural conversation. This system "reads" 66 facial points on the veteran's face and analyzes speech patterns. Most importantly, the veteran is assured that his or her responses will not be recorded.

Tests of this virtual therapist (named "Ellie" in this study) compared veterans' responses to questions about PTSD symptoms with the usual PDHA (which would be included in their official service record), a computer-administered version of the PDHA (which would remain anonymous), and PDHA questions about PTSD symptoms administered by the virtual therapist, Ellie. Figure 10.13 shows the results. Ellie was able to elicit more positive answers about PTSD symptoms than both the official PDHA and the anonymous PDHA for this group of returning veterans. The researchers suggest that virtual therapists, such as Ellie, are able to provide a good combination of privacy and rapport—both necessary for optimal reporting of information that might bring stigmatization and discrimination to the individuals who are being questioned.

Proponents of positive psychology, working with the U.S. Army, have proposed a way to identify individual soldiers who are susceptible to PTSD and provide special interventions as part of their training procedure (Cornum et al., 2011; Vie et al., 2016). Treating mental fitness similarly to physical fitness, these researchers devised the General Assessment Tool (GAT) that compares each soldier with the Army norms for emotional, social, family, and spiritual fitness (Peterson et al., 2011). Over 40,000 soldiers have been trained to teach the resilience skills and hundreds of thousands of soldiers have participated in the training (Positive Psychology Center, 2018).

Figure 10.13 PTSD Symptom Reporting

Returning soldiers who are asked about PTSD symptoms by a virtual therapist report more symptoms than when asked on standard or anonymous surveys.

SOURCE: Lucas et al. (2017).

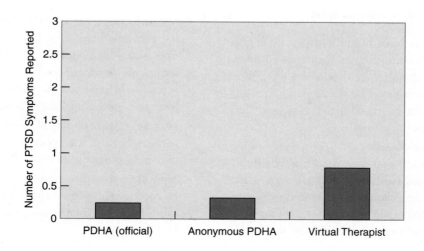

Summary: Stress, Coping, and Resilience

Our lives are full of stressors, and they tend to increase as we move through adulthood and take on more and more roles. In the best of all possible worlds there would be no hostile drivers on the road, no natural disasters, no terrorist attacks, and no demanding bosses. But here in reality, those things exist. The secret to a happy and productive life seems to be three-pronged: managing our reactions to stressors before they affect our health, strengthening effective coping skills, and building up resilience. This seems to be one area in which we gain expertise with age, and it might be wise to take some cues from the elders in our lives and how they handle stressors.

10.1 Stress, Stressors, and Stress Reactions

OBJECTIVE: Determine the origins of stress

- The best-known theory of stress response is Selye's general adaptation syndrome, in which we meet stressors with alarm reactions, followed by resistance and exhaustion if the stressor is still present. This sequence of events has an effect on the body's immune system and can lead to an increase in natural immunity at the expense of specific immunity, resulting in a lowered defense against specific diseases.

- Types of stressors have been studied, and scoring systems have been proposed to rate the number and intensity of stressors in a person's life. Early studies showed that there was a relationship between the number and intensity of stressors and some health outcomes.

- The most common types of stressors are interpersonal tensions, followed by things that happen to other people in one's family or social network and things that happen at work or at school.

10.2 Effects of Stress

OBJECTIVE: Relate stress to health outcomes

- Longitudinal studies have linked stress with higher overall mortality risk and higher incidence of breast cancer, cardiovascular disease, and diabetes. Stress, especially long-lasting negative reactions to stressors, has also been shown to be linked to depression, anxiety, and bipolar disorder.

- Posttraumatic stress disorder (PTSD), a long-lasting, extreme reaction to acute stress, is a mental health disorder strongly related to stress. Similar reactions that last a month or less are known as acute stress disorder. PTSD is treated with cognitive-behavioral therapy and prolonged exposure therapy. Worldwide surveys of individuals with PTSD show that about one-third were in full remission within 1 year, many within 6 months.

- Men and women may have different sources of stress and different reactions. Evolutionary psychologists suggest that the response systems of men developed differently from those of women due to the types of threats each gender was exposed to in our primitive ancestors' time. Men respond with "fight or flight," women with "tend and befriend." Men are exposed to more trauma, but women are more likely to develop PTSD.

- Daily stressors decline over the adult years, and older people react less to them. Older people may be more affected by trauma initially, but they recover more quickly.

- Overt discrimination can lead to increased stress and decreased life for women and minority groups, but some researchers have suggested that perceived discrimination can also be linked to psychological and physical health. The strongest effects seem to be for people who perceive discrimination due to their sexual orientation, mental illness, physical disabilities, HIV+ status, and weight. Similar effects are seen for racial and gender discrimination, including U.S. citizens of Irish, Jewish, Polish, and Italian descent and those who perceive sexual and gender discrimination.

- Stress, such as social isolation, can change our biological makeup by altering specific genes that affect our immune responses.

- Along with the negative effects of stress, there is evidence that some people experience personal growth, increased wisdom, new appreciation for life, and a stronger religious belief.

10.3 Coping with Stress

OBJECTIVE: Evaluate coping techniques for stress

- The measures we take to reduce stress are known as coping. Problem-focused coping directly addresses the source of the stress. Emotion-focused coping is an attempt to reduce the emotional reactions. Meaning-focused coping is used to help us make sense of the situation, and social-focused coping is seeking help from others close to you.

- All categories of coping skills are useful if implemented at the right time. It is important to have a wide repertoire of coping skills and to know when to use which one.

- New ideas in coping research involve proactive coping, or coping with something before it happens, and religious coping, which is using one's religious or spiritual beliefs to cope.

- Social support is an important antidote for stress because it serves as a buffer to provide some protection against the negative effects of stress. Social networks can also be a source of stress, if the interactions are difficult or the support offered is not welcome or what is needed.

10.4 Resilience

OBJECTIVE: Analyze how resilience functions

- The most common reaction to stress is resilience, maintaining healthy functioning. Even with extreme trauma such as the September 11 terrorist attacks, most of the people involved did not suffer disruption of their normal functioning.

- Resilience has been misdiagnosed as "delayed PTSD" in trauma victims and "denial" in bereaved spouses. The popular idea that it is necessary for a person to experience debilitating stress reactions to trauma or the death of a loved one is not supported by research. Engaging these people in "grief work" may undermine their resilience.

- One feature of resilient people is the personality trait of perceived control. Other features are a strong sense of self-identity and optimism. A group of polystrengths have been identified that are associated with resilience in the face of extreme victimization and poverty—emotional regulation, emotional awareness, a sense of purpose, optimism, and psychological endurance.

- The 12-month prevalence for PTSD rates is higher among veterans (15%) than civilians (3.5%). Most is the result of combat situations, but 23% of women report sexual assault while in the military and 55% report sexual harassment; 38% of men report sexual harassment.

- Veterans are reluctant to report adverse effects of military service. A group of researchers have attacked this problem by creating a virtual therapist who asks questions about symptoms of PTSD, combining privacy and rapport, and encouraging returning soldiers to be more open about the effects of their service than the standard survey (that becomes part of their official record) or anonymous surveys (that do not become part of their official records).

- Psychology researchers and military leaders have devised a way to assess the mental fitness of soldiers with the intent of fostering resilience and preventing PTSD. The attributes being evaluated are emotional, social, family, and spiritual fitness.

SHARED WRITING

Coping with Stress

Consider someone you know who is good at coping with stress and someone who struggles to cope with stress. How do their strategies differ? What are the positive and negative implications of these strategies? Write a short response that your classmates will read. Be sure to discuss specific examples.

 A minimum number of characters is required to post and earn points. After posting, your response can be viewed by your class and instructor, and you can participate in the class discussion.

Post   0 characters I 140 minimum

Chapter 11
Death and Bereavement

Meditation is one of many ways to cope with the grief of loss.

Learning Objectives

11.1 Analyze how death changes social systems

11.2 Evaluate the ways individuals adapt to death

11.3 Analyze practices associated with bereavement

A Word from the Author

Dying, A Journey in Itself

DAVID TASMA was a young man with inoperable cancer. He was dying in an English hospital, alone with no family. His native language was Polish, and he did not fully understand the conversations that surrounded him. He was Jewish and did not feel comforted by the Anglican priests who visited the ward. Although his medical care was skilled and efficient, he faced death feeling frustrated and distressed. His only consolation was a young woman—a social worker who visited him and patiently listened as he struggled to speak about his childhood, his family, and his thoughts about death. For 2 months she sat with him daily as he went through the physical and mental process of dying. His greatest fear, he told her, was that he would leave this earth without making a mark on it. He was young and had no children. He had never written a book or built a house or planted a field of corn. Perhaps they fell in love; we don't know. When he died, he left her all that he had, about 500 pounds, and the seed of an idea: that dying involves much more than physical pain; there is also the social pain of leaving loved ones, the mental pain of trying to know the unknowable, the spiritual pain of finding meaning in the life-and-death process, and the emotional pain of fear, disappointment, frustration, and regret. The medical community had nothing to offer the dying.

The young social worker was Cicely Saunders, founder of the modern hospice movement. The event recounted took place in 1948, and as a tribute to David Tasma, Saunders dedicated her life to finding ways for society to minister to its members at the end of their lives. She was one of the few women to become a medical doctor in England in the 1950s, and the first medical doctor of either gender to specialize in the treatment of dying patients. Ten years later, she opened St. Christopher's Hospice in London in memory of her friend, showing that he had indeed made his mark on the world—inspiring over 8,000 hospice centers in more than 100 countries. These centers all give the same message—one that defined Saunders's long career: "You matter because you are you, and you matter to the last moment of your life." Dame Cicely died at the age of 82 at the hospice she had founded (Field, 2005).

This chapter is about death—how we think about it at different ages, how we cope with the death of loved ones, and how we face the reality of our own. This has long been a central topic in psychoanalytic theory and clinical psychology, but recently it has become a topic of interest for researchers in many other fields. I begin by discussing how we think about death, then explore the process of death, and finally consider how we cope with the death of a loved one. This is a difficult topic, but a universal one—one that must be included in a course on adulthood and aging.

11.1: Understanding Death

OBJECTIVE: Analyze how death changes social systems

Death has a significant impact on individuals, families, and the community. The meaning of death changes with age and goes well beyond the simple understanding of inevitability and universality. Most broadly, death has important social meaning. The death of any one person changes the roles and relationships of everyone else in a family. When an elder dies, everyone else in that particular lineage moves up one step in the generational system. Beyond the family, death also affects other roles; for instance, it makes opportunities for younger adults to take on significant tasks. Retirement serves some of the same functions because the older adult "steps aside" for the younger, but death brings many permanent changes in social systems.

> ▼ **By the end of this module, you will be able to:**

11.1.1 Compare interpretations of the meaning of death

11.1.2 Identify factors related to death anxiety

11.1.3 Describe ways that people signal death acceptance

11.1.1: Meanings of Death

OBJECTIVE: Compare interpretations of the meaning of death

Four meanings that death may have for adults have been identified. Typically, all four meanings of death are present in any person's meaning system.

Interpretations of Death

Death as an organizer of time—Death defines the endpoint of one's life, so the concept of "time until death" may be an important one for a person trying to organize his or her life. In fact, sociologist Bernice Neugarten suggests that one of the key changes in thinking in middle age is a switch in the way one marks one's own lifetime, from time since birth to time until death. Her interviews with middle-aged adults frequently yielded statements like the following: "Before I was 35, the future just stretched forth. There would be time to do and see and carry out all the plans I had. . . . Now I keep thinking, will I have time enough to finish off some of the things I want to do?" (1970, p. 78).

Death as punishment—Children are quite likely to think of death as punishment for being bad. But this view and its reverse (that long life is the reward for being good) are still common in adults. Such a view is strengthened by religious teachings that emphasize a link between sin and death.

Death as transition—Death involves a transition—from life to some sort of life after death, or from life to nothingness. In a Pew Research Center survey, 75% of people in the United States said that they believed in an afterlife, meaning that they would exist afterz death with some sort of consciousness (Sandstrom & Alper, 2014), and 27% believed in reincarnation, meaning that they had lived before and will live again in another body after death (Harris Poll, 2005).

Death as loss—Perhaps most pervasively, death is seen by most of us as a loss—loss of the ability to complete projects or carry out plans; loss of one's body; loss of experiencing, of taste, smell, and touch; loss of relationships with people. Unlike beliefs in an afterlife, in this domain there are age differences. In particular, the specific losses that adults associate with death appear to change as they move through the adult years. Young adults are more concerned about loss of opportunity to experience things and about the loss of family relationships; older adults may be more concerned with the loss of time to complete some inner work (Kalish, 1985).

11.1.2: Death Anxiety

OBJECTIVE: Identify factors related to death anxiety

The most studied aspect of attitudes toward death is **death anxiety**, or fear of death. This fear is strongly linked to the view of death as a loss. If we fear death, it is, in part, because we fear the loss of experience, sensation, and relationships. Fear of death may also include fear of the pain or suffering or indignity often involved in the process of death, fear that one will not be able to cope well with such pain or suffering, fear of whatever punishment may come after death, and a fundamental fear of loss of the self. Adults' attitudes toward death, and their approaches to it, are influenced by many of the same qualities that affect the way they approach other life changes or dilemmas (see 'Elements in Fear of Death'). In some sense, all adult life is a process of moving toward death.

Elements in Fear of Death

Age

Researchers have quite consistently found that middle-aged adults show the greatest fear of death, and older adults the least with young adults falling somewhere in between (De Raedt et al., 2013). These results are consistent with the idea that one of the central tasks of midlife is to come to terms with the inevitability of death. The greater awareness of body changes and aging that is part of this period, coupled perhaps with the death of one's parents, breaks down the defenses we have all erected against the knowledge of and fear of death. In particular, the death of one's parents may be especially shocking and disturbing, not only because of the specific loss to be mourned but also because you must face the realization that you are now the oldest generation in the family lineage and thus "next in line" for death. So in midlife we become more aware of the fear, more preoccupied with death and its imminence. In these years, many adults grope toward new ways of thinking about death, eventually accepting it in a different way, so that the fear recedes in old age. This does not mean that older adults are unconcerned with death. On the contrary, they are more likely to talk about it and think about it than younger adults. Even though death is highly salient to older adults, it is apparently not as frightening as it was in midlife.

Religiosity

Religiosity, the degree of one's religious or spiritual belief, is another element in the fear of death. Presumably, there would be a negative correlation, the more religiosity one expresses, the less fear of death one should have. However, research findings show that there is no direct relationship between religiosity and fear of death. For example, in a study of older adults (70–80 years of age), those who were low in religiosity and those who were high in religiosity feared death less than participants who were moderate in their religious and spiritual beliefs. It was an inverted U-shaped function. The researchers suggest that those who are high in religiosity are not anxious about death because they believe that there is an afterlife and they have earned a place there. Those low in religiosity are not anxious about death because they don't believe there is an afterlife and aren't worried about missing out on any rewards. It's just those in the middle, the moderately religious, who are anxious about death because they believe there may be an afterlife and they may not have earned a place in it (Wink & Scott, 2005).

Intrinsic religiosity is practiced by people who live their lives according to their religious beliefs and seek meaning in life through their religion. In addition, intrinsic religiosity had a strong positive relationship with anticipation of a better existence after death (Ardelt & Koenig, 2006).

In later years, however, intrinsic religiosity has a purpose because this is a time when actively participating in religious activities becomes difficult and the need is more for finding answers to fundamental questions of life, such as *Where did we come from? Where are we going?* and *Why are we here?* (McFadden, 2000).

Extrinsic religiosity is practiced by people who use religion for social purposes and as an arena for doing good deeds; In a study of older adults, extrinsic religiosity was positively related to death anxiety—those who scored higher on measures of extrinsic religiosity had higher fears of death. Researchers suggest that extrinsic religiosity might be useful for middle-aged adults whose focus is social support and opportunities for generative activities, such as volunteer work within the religious community.

Gender

Death anxiety is also linked with gender. A number of studies from various cultures show that women have higher levels of death anxiety than men. This gender difference was found for a group of Episcopal parishioners in New York (Harding et al., 2005); young adults in Egypt, Kuwait, and Syria (Abdel-Khalek, 2004); and college students in western Canada (Chow, 2017). However, it has been suggested that this may be an artifact of the higher rates of anxiety disorders of all kinds for women. However, a study of over 400 college students showed that females report higher levels of death anxiety than males, even when controlling for depression and other possible confounds (Eshbaugh & Henninger, 2013).

Personality Traits

Certain personality traits seem to be factors in people's attitudes toward death. Self-esteem has been related to death anxiety, with high levels of self-esteem seeming to serve as a buffer against the fear of death (Reyes et al., 2017). Another study investigated the link between death anxiety and a **sense of purpose in life**, the extent to which individuals feel they have discovered satisfying personal goals and believe that their lives have been worthwhile. Psychologists Monika Ardelt and Cynthia Koenig (2006) studied a group of adults who were 61 years of age and older (some healthy and some hospice patients). Those who had a higher sense of purpose in life had lower death anxiety. This was especially interesting

because general religiosity, for this sample, was not related to death anxiety. Related to this is the finding that regrets are linked to death anxiety. People who feel a great deal of regret, both for things they have done (or not done) in the past and things they may not do in the future, have higher levels of death anxiety (Tomer & Eliason, 2005).

Such findings suggest that adults who have successfully completed the major tasks of adult life, adequately fulfilled the demands of the roles they occupied, and developed inwardly are able to face death with greater equanimity. In contrast, adults who have not been able to resolve the various tasks and dilemmas of adulthood face their late adult years more fearfully, more anxiously, and with what Erikson (1982) describes as despair. Fear of death may be merely one facet of such despair.

11.1.3: Accepting the Reality of One's Eventual Death

OBJECTIVE: Describe ways that people signal death acceptance

Coming to grips with one's eventual death is known as **finitude**. It is a process that occurs over time and at many levels (Johnson, 2009). At a practical level, for example, you can make out a will or obtain life insurance. Such preparations become more common with increasing age, especially in late middle age and thereafter. For example, older people are more apt to have life insurance than younger people. They are also more likely to prepare for death by making a will; according to a recent Gallup Poll, only 41% of all adults in the United States have done so, but among adults who are 65 years of age or older, 68% have done so (Jones, 2016).

At a somewhat deeper level, adults may start making preparations for death through some process of **reminiscence**, or reviewing their memories. This is often done by writing a memoir or autobiography or seeking out old friends and relatives to talk with about the past. A study of reminiscence activities with patients who have mild Alzheimer's disease showed that this activity helped them realize they have lived a full life and are better able to accept death more calmly (El Haj & Antoine, 2016). Researchers suggest using photos of old cars as a stimulus for eliciting memories (Anderson & Weber, 2015) or accounts of professional baseball games of the past (Wingbermuehle et al., 2014). Other researchers have found good results with a virtual partner asking questions and providing attention and guidance (Lancioni et al., 2015).

One type of planning for eventual death that has become increasingly popular recently is the **living will**, a document that takes effect if you are no longer able to express your wishes about end-of-life decisions. These documents (which may differ from state to state) give people the opportunity to decide, while they are still healthy, which specific treatments they would accept or refuse if they had a terminal illness or permanent disability and were not able to communicate their wishes. Living wills can be prepared with the assistance of an attorney or by using forms available on the Internet. For adults of all ages in the United States, about 35% have a living will, but for adults age 65 and over, 54% do (Lipka, 2014).

Living wills help alleviate the fear that dying will be a long and painful process. A person writing one can take responsibility for his or her own end-of-life decisions and not burden family members. And they help avoid situations in which various family members hold different strong beliefs about end-of-life decisions.

Another way people accept the reality of their eventual death is to become an **organ transplant donor**, agreeing that at the time of death, their usable organs and other tissue can be transplanted to people who have been approved to receive them. The technology of organ transplantation has advanced faster than the concept of being a donor has been accepted by the public. At the moment thousands of patients are waiting for donated organs, but only 45% of people in the United States are registered organ donors (Wen, 2014). The process of becoming an organ donor varies by area, but in many states it can be done quickly when you renew your driver's license. Facebook allows members to display their organ donor status on their timelines under Life Events–Health and Fitness.

Who chooses to be an organ transplant donor? Review of studies on organ donations finds that religiosity is negatively related to the willingness to be an organ donor, probably because some religions promote the integrity of the body as necessary for eternal life. Individuals with spiritual beliefs

that involve universalism and benevolence are more apt to be donors, as are those with high levels of self-esteem, prosocial attitudes, and self-efficacy (Falomir-Pichastor et al., 2011).

11.2: The Process of Death

OBJECTIVE: Evaluate the ways individuals adapt to death

Death and mourning have always been part of the human experience, but the thoughts people have about death and the way mourning is expressed differ from culture to culture and era to era. Fifty years ago, no textbook about adult development or gerontology would have included a chapter like this one. Science and medicine have long been fixated on life and lifesaving treatment. Death was viewed as a failure of science; dying people were isolated in hospital wards, and every attempt was made to "cure" them. The idea of welcoming death or even accepting it was not discussed. This mindset was changed largely through the writings of physician Elisabeth Kübler-Ross (1969), whose book *On Death and Dying* was acclaimed for having "brought death out of the darkness."

By the end of this module, you will be able to:

11.2.1   Outline the stages of reactions to death

11.2.2   Explain why farewells are important in the dying process

11.2.3   Relate diagnosis pessimism to death

11.2.4   Compare experiences of dying in different settings

11.2.5   Analyze values and options in choosing the time of death

11.2.1: Stages of Reactions to Death

OBJECTIVE: Outline the stages of reactions to death

Kübler-Ross's (1974) book was based on her work with terminally ill adults and children and is probably best known for describing five stages of dying: denial, anger, bargaining, depression, and acceptance (Table 11.1). Although she later wrote that these stages are not experienced by all people and do not necessarily occur in this order, her terminology

Table 11.1 Reactions to Death

Stages	Description
Denial	When confronted with a terminal diagnosis, the first reaction most patients report is some form of "No, not me!" "It must be a mistake," "The lab reports must have been mixed up," "I don't feel that sick, so it can't be true," "I'll get another doctor's opinion." All these are forms of denial. Kübler-Ross argued that denial is a valuable, constructive first defense. It gives the patient a period of time in which to marshal other strategies of coping with the shock.
Anger	The classic second reaction, so Kübler-Ross argued, is "Why me?" The patient resents those who are healthy and becomes angry at whatever fate put him or her in this position. This may be reflected in angry outbursts at nurses, family members, doctors—anyone within reach.
Bargaining	At some point, Kübler-Ross saw anger being replaced by a new kind of defense. The patient now tries to "make a deal" with doctors, with nurses, with God. "If I do what I'm told and don't yell at everyone, then I'll be able to live till Christmas." She described one woman with terminal cancer who wanted to live long enough to attend the wedding of her oldest son.
Depression	Bargaining only works for so long, however, and as disease processes continue and the signs of the body's decline become more obvious, patients typically become depressed. This is a kind of mourning—for the loss of relationships as well as of one's own life.
Acceptance	The final step, according to this theory, is a quiet understanding, a readiness for death. The patient is no longer depressed but may be quiet, even serene. In a widely quoted passage, newspaperman Stewart Alsop (1973), who was dying of leukemia, described his own acceptance: "A dying man needs to die as a sleepy man needs to sleep, and there comes a time when it is wrong, as well as useless, to resist" (p. 299).

is still used to describe the reactions to impending death of both the person who is dying and those who are bereaved. I describe these stages because they are often used to describe the constellation of reactions to impending death.

Since the publication of Kübler-Ross's *On Death and Dying* in 1969, the way we treat the process of dying has changed in many ways. Patients with terminal conditions are considered to be whole people with wishes and needs, not just failures of medical science. The vast majority do not want to die in a hospital ward, but prefer to be at home in their familiar surroundings. Most reach a point when they choose not to continue with heroic measures that might give them a few more days or weeks of life at the expense of their comfort and dignity. But refusing medical treatment does not mean that they don't need professional care (Balk, 2016). There is still a need for pain management, spiritual counseling, and accurate information about their condition and the time they have left. From loved ones there is a need for social support, listening, forgiving, and even laughter.

Perhaps more important than her stage theory, Kübler-Ross identified three key issues: (1) the dying are still alive and have unfinished needs they may want to address, (2) we need to listen actively to the dying and identify with their needs to provide effectively for them, and (3) we need to learn from the dying to know ourselves better and our potential for living (Corr, 1993).

11.2.2: The Importance of Farewells

OBJECTIVE: Explain why farewells are important in the dying process

One aspect of the process of dying that is not reflected in Kübler-Ross's stages or in most research on dying, but that is clearly a significant feature for the dying person and his or her family, is the process of saying farewell (Seale et al.,

2015). A study in Australia by sociologists Allan Kellehear and Terry Lewin (1988–1989) gave us a first exploration of such goodbyes. They interviewed 90 terminally ill cancer patients, all of whom had been told they were within a year of death, and a smaller group of 10 patients, who were in hospice care and thought to be within 3 months of death. Most had known they had cancer for over a year before the interview but had only recently been given a specific short-term prognosis. Subjects were asked whether they had already said some goodbyes or intended future farewells to family or friends and, if so, when and under what circumstances. The minority (19 of the 100) said they did not plan any farewells at all. The rest had either already begun to say goodbye (22 of the 100) or had planned their farewells for the final days of their lives—deathbed goodbyes, if you will.

The early farewells had often been in the form of a letter or a gift, such as giving money to a child or grandchild or passing on personal treasures to a member of the family who might especially cherish them. One woman made dolls that she gave to friends, relatives, and hospital staff. Another knit baby clothes to give to each of her daughters for babies they planned to have someday.

More commonly, both planned and completed farewells were in the form of conversations. One subject asked her brother to come for a visit so that she could see and talk to him one last time; others arranged with friends for one last get-together, saying goodbye quite explicitly on these occasions. Those who anticipated saying farewell only in the last hours of their conscious life imagined these occasions to be times when loving words would be spoken or a goodbye look would be exchanged.

All such farewells, whether spoken or not, can be thought of as forms of gifts. By saying goodbye to someone, the dying person signals that that person matters enough to warrant a farewell. Saying goodbye also serves to make the death real, to force the imminent death out of the realm of denial into acceptance by others as well as by the dying person. Finally, farewells may make the dying easier, especially if they are completed before the final moments of life. They may make it easier for the dying person to disengage and to reach a point of acceptance.

WRITING PROMPT

Refusal to Accept Death Diagnosis

Some people remain in the early stages of death acceptance. How can this be harmful to the terminally ill person?

 The response entered here will appear in the performance dashboard and can be viewed by your instructor.

Submit

11.2.3: Individual Adaptations to Dying

OBJECTIVE: Relate diagnosis pessimism to death

The process of dying varies hugely from one person to the next, not only in the emotions expressed (or not expressed), but also in the physical process. Some experience a long, slow decline; others die instantly, with no "stages" or phases at all. Some experience great pain; others little or none. Similarly, the way each person handles the process also varies. Some fight hard against dying; others appear to accept it early in the process and struggle no further. Some remain calm; others fall into deep depression. The question that researchers have begun to ask is whether such variations in the emotional response to impending or probable death have any effect at all on the physical process of dying.

In an early study, psychiatrist Steven Greer and his colleagues (Greer, 1991; Pettingale et al., 1985) followed a group of 62 women diagnosed with early stages of breast cancer. Three months after the original diagnosis, each woman was interviewed at some length, and her reaction to the diagnosis and to her treatment was classed in one of five groups:

1. *Positive avoidance (denial).* Patient rejects the diagnosis and the evidence presented to her.

2. *Fighting spirit.* Patient shows optimism and actively searches for more information about her diagnosis. Expresses the desire to fight the disease in any way possible.

3. *Stoic acceptance (fatalism).* Patient acknowledges the diagnosis, but does not seek further information and continues with her normal life.

4. *Helplessness/hopelessness.* Patient is overwhelmed by the diagnosis and considers themselves gravely ill and without hope.

5. *Anxious preoccupation.* Patient responds to the diagnosis with extreme anxiety and interprets additional information pessimistically. She interprets all body sensations as possible recurrence.

Greer checked on the survival rates of these five groups 15 years later. Only 35% of those whose initial reaction had been either positive avoidance (denial) or fighting spirit had died of cancer, compared to 76% of those whose initial reaction had been stoic acceptance, anxious preoccupation, or helplessness/hopelessness. Because the five groups had not differed initially in the stage of their disease or in treatment, these results support the hypothesis that psychological response contributes to disease progress, just as coping strategies more generally affect the likelihood of disease in the first place.

COPING STYLES In a more recent study, researchers gave coping-strategy tests to patients after having a heart attack. The test gave patients scores for task-oriented coping, emotion-oriented coping, and avoidant coping. Over the next 5 years, patients were followed and those who had high scores on task-oriented coping were less apt to have died or had another heart attack than those who had low scores. Task-oriented coping involves purposeful attempts to solve the problem at hand, change the situation, or think about the situation in a more productive way. Neither emotion-oriented coping nor avoidant coping showed any effect (Messerli-Bürgy et al., 2015).

Another study of coping styles involved almost 300 patients who had experienced heart attacks and were admitted to the hospital. After they were stabilized, they were given a test that evaluated their optimism, asking them whether they agree or disagree with statements such as "In uncertain times, I usually expect the best." A year after their heart attacks, those with higher optimism scores had better physical and mental health than those with lower scores. Furthermore, those higher in optimism were more apt to have quit smoking and modified their diets to include more fruits and vegetables.

These results show individual differences in the ways we react to the diagnosis of a potentially fatal disease. The way we cope with this news can affect how we comply with the treatment and medical advice and may also affect the course of the disease. The good news is that there are ways we can change our coping strategies and personality traits to those that promote better health outcomes (Magidson et al., 2014; Meevissen et al., 2011; Renner et al., 2014).

11.2.4: Choosing Where to Die

OBJECTIVE: Compare experiences of dying in different settings

In the United States and other industrialized countries today, the majority of adults report that they would prefer to die in their homes, but the fact is that the great majority die in hospitals and nursing homes (Balk, 2016). For example, patients' preferences for place of terminal care and place of death were gathered for 96 end-stage cancer patients in Denmark. More than three-fourths of them (84%) wished to be cared for at home, and 71% wished to die at home. Of those who expressed these wishes, only half were cared for and died at home. What made the difference? Two major factors were having a spouse or partner at home and being in contact with a palliative care team (Brogaard et al., 2012).

In a large study that surveyed family members of individuals who had died of chronic disease, physician Joan Teno and her colleagues (2004) asked about the details of the deaths. The sample, which consisted of over 1,500 families, was selected to be representative of the 1.97 million deaths from chronic illnesses that occurred that year in the United States. Respondents were asked about their deceased family members' last place of care; the results showed that one-third died at home, and two-thirds died in an institution, either a hospital or a nursing home. However, the critical difference in quality of care was not whether they died at home or not, but whether they received home-care nursing services, or **hospice care**, which is care focused on pain relief, emotional support, and spiritual comfort for the dying person and his or her family. When asked about the quality of care the deceased family member had received at the end of

life, the responses indicated that there was little difference between dying at home with nursing services, dying in a nursing home, and dying in a hospital—fewer than half of the respondents reported that their family members who had spent their last days in these situations received "excellent" care. In contrast, over 70% of the respondents whose family members had died at home with hospice care evaluated this care as "excellent." Unfortunately, the number of people whose family members died at home with hospice care represented only about 16% of the total survey respondents.

Figure 11.1 shows some of the problem areas survey respondents reported in this study, divided by whether their loved ones died at home with home-care nursing services, at home with hospice care, in a nursing home, or in a hospital. As you can see, the biggest concern was lack of emotional support for the patient, which was reported by twice as many respondents whose family members had their final care at home with home nursing care (70%) than at home with hospice care (35%). The same ratio is shown for lack of emotional support for the family, with families of those dying at home with home health nursing reporting this problem twice as often (45%) as those at home with hospice care (21%).

Teno and colleagues (2004) concluded that although the study only tapped the respondents' perceptions of their family members' care and, at that, only after some time had

---

Figure 11.1 Problem Areas Reported by Family Members After Death of a Loved One

Family members of a deceased loved one report fewer problem areas with hospice care in the home than other end-of-life care situations.

SOURCE: Data from Teno et al. (2004).

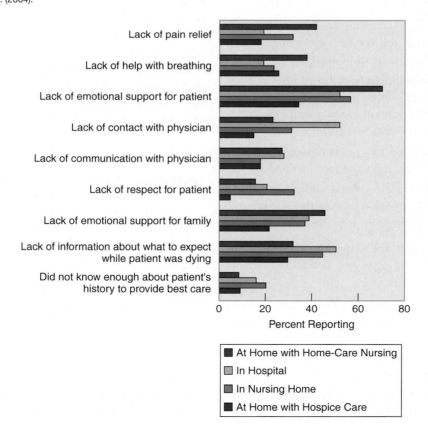

passed, it is still appropriate to be alarmed about the problems associated with end-of-life care in the United States. The authors were especially concerned about the problems reported with nursing homes, which are more apt to be the last places of care for the very old. We will have more and more elderly people requiring end-of-life care in the years to come, at a time when nursing homes are receiving less and less federal support. In addition, hospitals are unable to keep terminally ill patients, so are increasingly transferring them to nursing homes.

HOSPICE CARE   What exactly does hospice care consist of today, and why is it so successful in providing "excellent" services to dying people and their families?

The hospice movement was given a good deal of impetus by Kübler-Ross's writings because she emphasized the importance of a **good death**, meaning a death with dignity, with maximum consciousness and minimum pain, and with the patient and the patient's family having full information and control over the process. Hospice care began in England in the 1960s. It started in the 1970s in the United States as a grassroots movement to give terminal cancer patients an alternative to continued aggressive treatment. By 1982, the idea had gained so much support that Congress was persuaded to add hospice care to the list of benefits paid for by Medicare. Today there are more than 4,000 hospice programs in the United States, serving over a million terminally ill patients and their families each year (National Hospice and Palliative Care Organization, 2017).

The philosophy that underlies the **hospice approach** has several aspects:

- Control over the care and the care-receiving setting should belong to the patient and family.
- Medical care provided should be *palliative*, not curative, meaning that pain should be alleviated and comfort maximized, but a minimum of invasive or life-prolonging measures should be undertaken.
- Death should be viewed as a normal, inevitable part of life, not to be avoided but to be faced and accepted.
- A multidisciplinary team is involved, which can include a physician, nurses, social workers, therapists, and chaplains or other spiritual leaders (Torpy et al., 2012).

In real terms, this philosophy translates into a constellation of services available to the dying person and his or her family and friends. These services are:

- An interdisciplinary team of physicians, nurses, social workers, counselors, home health aides, clergy, therapists, and trained volunteers who care for the patient based on their areas of expertise to relieve symptoms and provide support to the patient and his or her family.
- Pain and symptom control that helps the patient be comfortable yet in control of his or her life.

- Spiritual care for the patient and his or her family, based on their individual beliefs, to help the patient find meaning, say goodbye, or perform religious rituals.
- Home care for those who are able to stay in their own homes, but also inpatient care in hospitals or nursing homes when needed.
- Respite care for family caregivers.
- Family conferences to enable family members to learn about the patient's condition and to share feelings, talk about expectations, learn about dying, and ask questions.
- Bereavement care from counselors and clergy to help family members through the grieving process with visits, phone calls, and support groups.
- Coordinated care provided by the interdisciplinary team to communicate with the physicians, home-care agency, and community professionals such as pharmacists, clergy, and funeral directors.

Over 44% of deaths in the United States currently take place under the care of a hospice program. The most common condition patients seek hospice care for is terminal cancer (28%). Although hospice is designed to provide care during the last 6 months of a person's life, the average length of care is just over 2 months, primarily because of the difficulty of predicting the course of many terminal illnesses (National Hospice and Palliative Care Association, 2017). The reason families don't use hospice services is because of the increasing number of patients dying of heart disease and Alzheimer's disease (which are not as predictable), the psychological blocks patients and family have against accepting death as imminent, and the difficulty some physicians (and family members) have in ceasing aggressive treatment. The result is that although hospice care is a positive move toward allowing people to have a "good death," it is still used by a small number of people and for a short period of time.

11.2.5: Choosing When to Die
OBJECTIVE: Analyze values and options in choosing the time of death

Another way of looking at the advances of modern medicine is that instead of extending life, it prolongs death. Today about 90% of the people who die each year do so after experiencing prolonged illnesses and steady decline. Many believe that there is a fundamental right to die a good death and to choose when, how, and where it will occur.

In 1976, California passed the first law in the United States concerning living wills, documents which allow individuals to legally express the wish that if they are in a condition with no hope of recovery, no heroic measures should be taken to extend their lives. Living wills are now valid in all 50 states of the United States and in many other countries.

In 1990 the U.S. Supreme Court ruled that Americans have the right to refuse medical treatment, even if refusing it will result in death.

In 1997 voters in Oregon passed the Death with Dignity Act, which allows for **physician-assisted suicide**, meaning that under certain circumstances, physicians are allowed to assist patients to obtain medication that will end their lives. Among other requirements, the patient must request the medication voluntarily, be terminally ill, and be mentally competent, and these points must be confirmed by a second physician. There is a waiting period of 15 days, and the prescription must be registered with the state. Despite the warnings by opponents of this law, not many terminally ill patients have requested physician-assisted deaths. The first year this option was available, 24 people received prescriptions, and 16 used them to end their lives. In 2017, 218 people received prescriptions, and 143 used them to end their lives (Oregon Health Authority, 2018a). Figure 11.2 shows the number of patients in Oregon who sought and received prescriptions to end their lives and the number who used the medication to end their lives since the program began.

Oregon keeps careful records of requests and prescriptions for physician-assisted suicides. In 2017, 218 prescriptions were written by 92 different doctors, and the median age of the patient was 74 years. The large majority were white (94%), had at least a bachelor's degree (49%), had cancer (77%), died at home (90%), and were in hospice care (91%). Almost all (99%) had some form of health insurance, meaning that they were not choosing this outcome because of the inability to pay for further treatment of their diseases. The most frequent reasons given for the decisions to end their lives were first, decreasing ability to participate in activities that made life enjoyable for them, followed by loss of autonomy and loss of dignity (Oregon Health Authority, 2018b). As of this writing, the states of Washington, Montana, Vermont, and California also have physician-assisted suicide provisions, as do the countries of Canada, Belgium, Luxembourg, the Netherlands, and Switzerland.

ATTITUDES TOWARD ASSISTED SUICIDE The Harris Poll found that the majority of adults (72%) in the United States support physician-assisted suicide, and these respondents represented a variety of age groups, education levels, and political affiliations. However, some religious groups still strongly oppose this practice because they feel there is a purpose to one's final days (Thompson, 2014).

Physician and bioethicist Ezekial Emanuel and his colleagues (2000) surveyed almost 1,000 terminally ill patients about their attitudes toward physician-assisted suicide. Although a majority (60%) of the patients supported it hypothetically, only about 10% seriously considered it for themselves. Those who were more likely to consider physician-assisted suicide had depressive symptoms, had substantial caregiving needs, and were in pain. Those who were less likely to consider it felt appreciated, were 65 years of age or older, and were African American. Interestingly, about 4 months later, the surviving patients were interviewed again, and about half of each group had changed their minds. Those who now favored physician-assisted suicide were more likely to have developed depressive symptoms or breathing difficulties.

This is an interesting study for several reasons. It is the first study that actually interviewed terminally ill patients about physician-assisted suicide, making a distinction between the hypothetical construct and the actual application to oneself. It is also interesting because it showed that the key indicators in this decision were more social than medical. It followed up on the patients and showed that the wish to be assisted in suicide was not consistent over time for about half of the patients. These findings show the importance of evaluating patients for depression, unrelieved pain and breathing difficulties, and the feeling that they are a burden or unappreciated when considering physician-assisted suicide. And it also reinforces the idea of having a waiting period between requesting the medication and receiving it.

Figure 11.2 Prescriptions Received under Oregon's Death with Dignity Act versus Prescriptions Used to End One's Life

Since 1998, more terminally ill patients in Oregon are requesting prescriptions to end their lives, but a smaller percentage actually use them.

SOURCE: Oregon Health Authority (2018a).

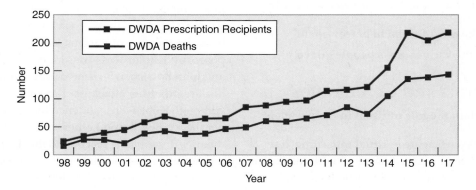

Certainly the advances we have made in medicine and health care have given us a whole host of blessings. It is very unusual for a woman to die in childbirth or a toddler not to live to adulthood. Many of us reach middle age with all our siblings and our parents still in our lives. Our children often have four grandparents and probably a few great-grandparents, too. But there is a downside, and that is our diminished opportunity to die a "good death," as described this way:

> Humans have faced all manner of challenges over time. As things go, the challenge of having the opportunity to grow old and die slowly is not such a bad thing. However, it is a challenge. Society has simply never been in this position before. We have to work on language, categories, framing, meanings, rituals, habits, social organization, service delivery, financing, and community commitment. Much remains to be learned and done. The burgeoning numbers of persons living into old age and coming to the end of life makes the need for that learning and implementing all the more urgent. (Wilkinson & Lynn, 2001, p. 457)

WRITING PROMPT

The Right to Die

Does your state have provisions for legal physician-assisted suicide? Do you think physician-assisted suicide should be legal? Why or why not?

> The response entered here will appear in the performance dashboard and can be viewed by your instructor.

Submit

11.3: Rituals and Grieving

OBJECTIVE: Analyze practices associated with bereavement

Whether a death is sudden or prolonged, anticipated or unexpected, it leaves survivors who must somehow come to terms with the loss and eventually pick up the pieces of their lives. The form these rituals take depends on where one lives, their culture, their religious practices, and the personal preferences of the deceased and the family.

   By the end of this module, you will be able to:

11.3.1   Explain the role of ritual in bereavement

11.3.2   Describe the various ways people grieve

11.3.1: Funerals and Ceremonies

OBJECTIVE: Explain the role of ritual in bereavement

All human cultures participate in **ritual mourning,** a set of symbolic rites and ceremonies associated with death. Far from being empty gestures, these rituals have clear and

important functions. As sociologists Victor Marshall and Judith Levy put it, "Rituals provide a . . . means through which societies simultaneously seek to control the disruptiveness of death and to make it meaningful. . . . The funeral exists as a formal means to accomplish the work of completing a biography, managing grief, and building new social relationships after the death" (1990, pp. 246, 253).

One way rituals accomplish these goals is by giving the bereaved a specific role to play. The content of the role differs markedly from one culture to the next, but the clarity of the role in most cases provides a shape to the days or weeks immediately following the death of a loved person. In the United States these rituals prescribe what one should wear, who should be notified, who should be fed, what demeanor one should show, and far more. Depending on one's religious background, one may need to arrange to sit shiva, or gather friends and family for a wake, or arrange a memorial service. One may be expected to respond stoically or to wail and tear one's hair. Whatever the social rules, there is a role to be filled that provides shape to the first numbing hours and days following the death of someone important to us.

Rituals can also give some meaning to death by emphasizing the meaning of the life of the person who has died. It is not accidental that most death rituals include testimonials, photographs, biographies, and witnessing. By telling the story of the person's life, by describing that life's value and meaning, the death can be accepted more readily. And of course, ceremonies can also provide meaning by placing the death in a larger philosophical or religious context.

The United States, which is known as a nation of immigrants, has a very diverse collection of funeral and mourning rituals. There are many subgroups, and Table 11.2 shows the practices of some of the major ones. As you can see below, there are very large differences in the ways people express their loss and pay tribute to their loved ones.

11.3.2: The Process of Grieving

OBJECTIVE: Describe the various ways people grieve

When the funeral or memorial service is over, what do you do then? How does a person handle the grief of this kind of loss, whether it be of a spouse, a parent, a child, a friend, or a lover? The topic of grief was dominated for many years by stage theories of various kinds, such as the ones proposed by Kübler-Ross (described earlier in the chapter) and John Bowlby, who is no doubt familiar to you from the discussion of his attachment theory in an earlier chapter. Although Kübler-Ross softened the stagelike progression in her theory, Bowlby and others did not. These neo-Freudian theories describe the reaction to the death of a loved one as a series of stages and state that everyone must go through all the stages in a fixed order. At any given moment in

Table 11.2 Funeral Rituals and Practices among U.S. Cultural Groups

Cultural Group	Predominant Religious Beliefs	Mourning Traditions	Funeral Traditions
African American (in the South)	Protestant; believe that all will be reunited in heaven and that events in life are in accordance with God's plan	Open and emotional grief by men and women. Many wear black to signify mourning.	Viewing of the body at home; large gathering of family and community members; funeral in church with support for mourners from church "nurses." Burial in cemetery, often with favorite belongings of the deceased in the casket, such as CDs, sports uniforms, trophies, and photos.
African American (immigrants from Western Africa and Caribbean West Indies)	Mostly Catholic mixed with African folk-medicine beliefs, some Protestant	Long period of mourning and elaborate ceremonies, including prayers, drumming, and singing. Photographs are taken of the deceased. Children are included in all parts of mourning to instill respect for ancestors.	Traditional, formal funeral ceremonies conducted by males in native dialects passed down from elders. Paid for by the community and extended family. No embalming or cremation. Usually burial, but cremation sometimes allowed if remains are returned to homeland.
U.S. Latinos (Cuban, Puerto Rican, and Dominican descent)	Catholic; believe that death is entry to heaven and that there is a continued relationship between the living and the dead	Women express grief openly; men control emotions and remain "strong."	Open-casket wake for two days as family gathers with food, prayers, candles. Funeral is traditional mass, and burial is in a Catholic cemetery.
U.S. immigrants from Muslim countries (Caribbean islands, Asian and African countries)	Islam; believe that the purpose of life is to prepare for eternity; at death the soul is exposed to Allah for judgment	Crying is acceptable, but no extreme emotional displays, such as wailing.	Burial must take place within 24 hours. Imam directs funeral. No viewing of remains, no embalming, no cremation. Deceased is buried facing Mecca. Women are not allowed to visit cemeteries.
Asian immigrants from China	Mixture of Taoism, ancestor worship, veneration of local deities, Buddhism	The more mourners and the more emotion expressed, the more the person was loved. After the funeral, the family observes a 100-day period of mourning during which they wear a piece of colored cloth signifying their relationship to the deceased.	Determined by the age of the deceased. Children and young adults without children do not have full funeral rites. Wake takes place in the home with traditional rules about what colors different family members must wear and where people must sit. Guests donate money to help pay the expenses. Coffin goes from home to cemetery, which is on a hill. The higher the gravesite, the more prestige. The eldest son brings back earth from the grave to be used at home in a shrine to the deceased family member.
Asian immigrants from Thailand, Vietnam, Myanmar, and Cambodia	Buddhism; believe that death is an opportunity for improvement in the next life	Deep mourning, sometimes with somatic (bodily) symptoms.	Wake with open casket in home for 1–3 days. Family wears white clothing or headbands. Funeral includes altar with flowers, fruit, incense, water, and candles. Ceremony begins with 1 hour of chanting by priests. Mourners place pinch of ashes in a bowl and say personal prayer for the deceased. Private cremation witnessed by a priest.
Indian	Hindu; believe that birth and death are part of a cycle; good actions in life (karma) lead to final liberation of the soul	Mourning is done to let the soul know that it should depart and to let the family say goodbye.	Body is bathed and dressed in new clothes, then cremated before the next sunrise to ensure the soul's transition to the next world. Family conducts rituals for 10 days, and on the 11th, the soul leaves the earth. No burial, no embalming. Children participate in all parts of the ceremony. Remains are sent to India or scattered over a river in the United States along with flowers.
Native American (Navajo and related tribes)	Navajo tradition mixed with Catholic and Protestant; believe that the soul is present in the products the person created (pottery, blankets)	Mourners sprinkle dirt on the casket before burial.	Deceased is wrapped in Navajo blankets and placed in the casket. Broken pots or frayed blankets are included to help the release of the soul from these products. Also in the casket are an extra set of clothing, food, water, and personal items. Services are in English and Navajo. Burial is facing east to west. No footprints are left in the dirt around the grave to confuse spirit guide.

(Continued)

Table 11.2 *(Continued)*

Cultural Group	Predominant Religious Beliefs	Mourning Traditions	Funeral Traditions
European Americans, Christian faith	Believe in afterlife, that friends and family will be reunited in heaven	Mourners wear black clothing or black armbands. Some put dark wreath on the door of the deceased person's home.	Gathering in a funeral home or church in the days before the funeral to console each other and pay final respects to the deceased. Sometimes the casket is open so mourners can view the body. Funeral is at church or funeral home. The clergy conducts a service with prayers and songs. Friends and family members eulogize the deceased. Catholics celebrate mass. Burial takes place after service with a short graveside ceremony. Mourners gather at the home of the deceased or close relative to have a meal and continue consolation. Cremation is more common for Protestants than Catholics.
European Americans, Jewish faith	Believe that one's good works live on in the hearts and minds of others; no specific teachings on the afterlife; funeral is celebration of the life of the deceased	Family "sits shiva" for a week in the home and mourns by sitting on low stools, covering mirrors, not attending to clothing or appearance, and wearing a black ribbon or torn clothes. Friends bring food to the house and attend to the needs of the family.	Funeral and burial take place soon after death. Deceased is buried in plain shroud and simple casket to symbolize that all were created equal by God. Earth from Israel may be sprinkled on casket during burial. Family says traditional prayers for 1 year, after which a headstone can be put on the grave.

SOURCES: Adapted from Hazell (1997); Lobar (2006); Santillanes (1997); Techner (1997).

the process, the bereaved person is either in one stage or another, never in two at once. According to these theories, one cannot skip stages or return to a stage once one has left it. The result of this "grief work" is that at the end of the stages, the bereaved have adjusted to the loss and regained their normal lives.

Bowlby's (1982) theory has four stages—numbness, yearning, disorganization, and despair—followed by a time of reorganization, while Kübler-Ross's (1974) has five (denial, anger, bargaining, depression, and acceptance). Research does not support the claim that these stages are experienced in the stated order or even experienced by all bereaved individuals. For example, one critic wrote:

> We are discovering that just as there are multitudinous ways of living, there are numerous ways of dying and grieving. . . . The hard data do not support the existence of any procrustean stages or schedules that characterize terminal illness or mourning. This does not mean that, for example, Kübler-Ross's "stages of dying" and Bowlby's "phases of mourning" cannot provide us with implications and insights into the dynamics and process of dying and grief, but they are very far from being inexorable hoops through which most terminally ill individuals and mourners inevitably pass. We should beware of promulgating a coercive orthodoxy of how to die or mourn. (Feifel, 1990, p. 540)

Some argue that it would be better to think in terms of themes or aspects rather than stages, such as themes of numbness, yearning, anger, disorganization, and despair. In the first few days or weeks after the death of a loved one, the dominant theme is likely to be numbness, with yearning coming later but perhaps not replacing numbness totally. Exhaustion may be a later theme, although yearning could also occur at that time. Like Kübler-Ross's stages of death acceptance, Bowlby's stages of mourning are perhaps best viewed as descriptors of human emotions that many people experience in bereavement, but not in totality and not in this specific order.

However, for many decades Bowlby's theory was the basis for professional understanding of grief by psychologists, counselors, health-care professionals, and clergy. In fact, as I discussed in the chapter on stress and resilience, the dominant belief was that failure to experience trauma and the proper stages of grief was a sign that normal, healthy grieving had not taken place and that some pathology was present, such as repression or denial (Rando, 1993). In these cases, clinical intervention was recommended to help the person work through hidden, unresolved grief feelings (Jacobs, 1993). The obvious alternative was that the loved one must not have been truly "loved." More recently, researchers have found that many bereaved people do not follow any particular set of stages. In fact, the most common reaction to grief is *resilience*, the maintenance of healthy functioning after a potentially traumatic event.

POSITIVE GRIEF In an early study of participants who had recently experienced the death of their spouses, almost half failed to show even mild symptoms of depression following the loss (Zisook et al., 1997). Similar studies showed that positive emotions, including genuine smiling and laughter, are not only present when the bereaved discuss their recent losses, but seem to promote well-being (Bonanno & Kaltman,1999; Bonanno & Keltner, 1997).

In a longitudinal study, gay men who had been caregivers for their partners with AIDS were interviewed shortly after their partners' deaths. The bereaved partners' appraisals of the experience were more positive than negative; many said that they had experienced feelings of personal strength and self-growth, and that their relationships had become stronger. Twelve months later, the individuals who had been the most positive in their appraisals of the caregiving experience were more likely to show high levels of psychological well-being (Moskowitz et al., 2003). These studies and others with similar findings show that the experiences of actual bereaved people do not follow traditional theory; the typical reaction to the death of a spouse or partner was not all-encompassing negative thoughts and feelings occurring in predictable stages. Furthermore, the participants who did not follow the theory were not maladjusted or in need of clinical intervention. To the contrary, those who showed the most positive thoughts and affect were the best adjusted a year later. One problem remained—how genuine was their grief? Did they truly have a close and loving relationship with the deceased person, or did the lack of negative grief simply indicate that there wasn't much to mourn? Asking a person about a relationship with a recently deceased partner may not bring forth an honest answer.

To investigate this possibility, psychologist George Bonanno and his colleagues (2002) conducted a longitudinal study that covered the time before bereavement. They recruited 1,500 older married couples and interviewed them over the course of several years about their relationships, attachment styles, coping mechanisms, and personal adjustment. During this time 205 participants experienced the death of their spouse. Using the preloss data, researchers were able to evaluate the quality of the marriage before the death occurred along with the adjustment of the widowed spouse for 18 months afterward. The researchers were able to distinguish five patterns of adjustment and the preloss factors that predicted each pattern (see 'Adjusting to the Death of a Loved One').

Adjusting to the Death of a Loved One

The results are illustrated in the Figure 11.3. The most common pattern of adjustment following the death of a spouse was resilience (46%), followed by chronic grief (16%), common grief (11%), depressed-improved (10%), and chronic depression (8%). When the quality of the marriage was compared to the grief response, there were no differences between the top three groups (resilience, chronic grief, common grief). The one group that showed significantly low quality-of-marriage scores was the depressed-improved group, which, as you can see in the figure, had high levels of depression before the death of their spouse and improved after the spouse died. This suggests strongly that the popular view that the relative absence of grief shown by bereaved individuals is due to poor relationships before their loss is only appropriate for about 10% of cases.

Bonanno and his colleagues (2005) conducted a similar study with a population of bereaved spouses, bereaved parents, and bereaved gay men and found similar levels of resilience. They also found no association between the reaction to bereavement and the quality of relationship or the caregiver burden before death. However, there was an association between reaction to bereavement and personal adjustment, with participants who were rated more positively and better adjusted by close friends being more apt to react to the loss of a loved one with resilience.

Figure 11.3 Five Patterns of Grief

Bereaved spouses studied before loss, at the time of loss, and 18 months after loss show five distinct patterns of grief, the most common being resilience.

SOURCE: Bonanno et al. (2002).

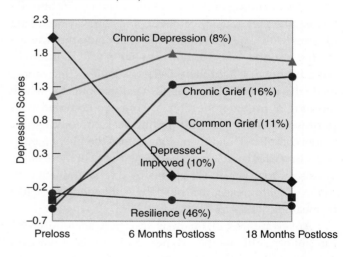

In summary, recent research has shown that the stage theories of bereavement, such as those proposed by Bowlby and Kübler-Ross, are helpful in defining possible reactions people may have to the death of a loved one, but do not describe the common path that grief takes for the majority of bereaved individuals. Grief is highly personal and individualized. It is also complex. No doubt bereaved individuals run the gamut of reactions described by theorists, but most are not overwhelmed by their grief or unable to function in their usual roles. They have moments of yearning and despair, but they also have moments of positive feelings—of appreciation to those who offer support, words of comfort for others who share their loss, fond memories of their loved one, and even some funny stories and jokes. Grief is not an altered state of consciousness to be feared. The death of a loved one is painful, and a departed loved one will never be forgotten, but for most people, death becomes part of life, and life goes on.

HELPING THE WIDOWED How do you help someone who has become widowed cope? It depends. For those who are deeply distressed or depressed, you could suggest a support group or counseling. Don't tell them to cheer up or push them to get back into "life as usual." But if they seem to be coping well and not showing high levels of grief, consider that it might be a normal, healthy reaction, and don't be shocked if they host a dinner party for a small group of friends 2 months after the funeral. Or if a widower begins to date before the traditional year of mourning is over, don't automatically think that his marriage must not have been a good one. When people are coping well, don't suggest that they need to "let it all out" or "take time to grieve." As usual, the best way to be helpful to a person dealing with such a loss is to be highly attentive to the signals you are receiving, rather than to impose your own ideas of what is normal or expected.

Finally, let us not lose sight of the fact that loss can also lead to growth. Indeed, many of the widows report that they changed as a result of their husband's death, and that the change was in the direction of greater independence and greater skill. Like all crises and all major life changes, bereavement can be an opportunity as well as, or instead of, a disabling experience. How we respond is likely to depend very heavily on the patterns we have established from early childhood: our temperament or personality, our internal working models of attachment and self, our intellectual skills, and the social networks we have created.

Summary: Death and Bereavement

Our understanding of death and its meaning, our attitude toward the inevitability of death, and the way we come to terms with that inevitability affect not only the way we die but also the way we choose to live our lives throughout adulthood. David Steindl-Rast, a Benedictine monk, made this point: "Death . . . is an event that puts the whole meaning of life into question. We may be occupied with purposeful activities, with getting tasks accomplished, works completed, and then along comes the phenomenon of death—whether it is our final death or one of those many deaths through which we go day by day. And death confronts us with the fact that purpose is not enough. We live by meaning" (1977, p. 22).

An awareness of death is thus not something we can put off until one day we hear a diagnosis of our own impending demise. It can, instead, help to define and give meaning to daily life. My grandmother's funeral was ended with the invitation: "Let us go forth and celebrate life!" It is a good ending for any discussion of death.

11.1 Understanding Death

OBJECTIVE: Analyze how death changes social systems

- Death is an inevitable fact of life, and the way we think about it, how we cope with the deaths of loved ones, and how we come to terms with the reality of our own

ultimate deaths are topics of interest for those concerned with adult development.

- Death has various meanings. To some it is an organizer of time, to others it is punishment (and long life is a reward). Most believe that death is a transition either to an afterlife or to a new life through reincarnation. The most pervasive meaning of death is loss—of opportunity, of relationships, of time.

- Death anxiety has been studied extensively. We know that it occurs most strongly in middle-aged adults and people of midlevel religiosity. Middle age is a time when the effects of aging become noticeable. Older adults think more about death, but have less fear. Those who are midlevel in religious beliefs seem to fear death more because presumably they believe there may be an afterlife but have not prepared for it. Women express more death anxiety than men, but that might reflect higher rates of anxiety in general. Those who feel a sense of purpose in life and few regrets are less likely to fear death.

- People accept the reality of their own eventual death by purchasing life insurance, making wills, collecting memories, and reminiscing about their lives. In recent years, as medical technology has become able to extend life, many people have come to fear the dying process more than they fear death itself. They also have concerns about leaving family members to make the difficult decisions about such matters. A good number of adults have drawn living wills that express the limits they want in end-of-life care. Another way people accept the eventuality of their own death is by becoming an organ transplant donor.

11.2 The Process of Death

OBJECTIVE: **Evaluate the ways individuals adapt to death**

- Physician Elisabeth Kübler-Ross was the first to write about the personal acceptance of death some 40 years ago. Before that time, the focus was on extending life, not accepting death. She described five stages of death reactions, and although not everyone goes through these stages, and they do not always occur in the same sequence, her descriptions are accurate, and her terminology is used in every field that deals with death. The stages are denial, anger, bargaining, depression, and acceptance.

- Kübler-Ross identified three key issues about the dying process: Those who are dying are still alive and have unfinished needs, we need to listen to them to be able to provide the care they need, and we need to learn from the dying how to live ourselves.

- Dying people can accept the reality of their death by giving farewell messages to their loved ones. These can be conversations, letters, or gifts.

- Psychological responses to disease seem to have an effect on the course of the illness. Those who react to a diagnosis of a potentially terminal disease with positive avoidance (denial), with a fighting spirit are more apt to survive than those who show anxiety, depression, or fatalism.

- Most people express the wish to die at home in familiar surroundings, but the majority die in hospitals and nursing homes. An alternative for those who have predictable terminal conditions, such as cancer, is hospice care. A hospice provides a team of professionals and volunteers who focus on pain relief, emotional support, and spiritual comfort for the patient and family, usually in their own home. The goal of hospice is not to cure the patient but to provide a good death. Families of people who have died in hospice care report significantly fewer concerns about their care than those whose family members died in hospitals, nursing homes, or at home with home nursing care.

- A good number of people believe that they have the right to control when they die, and several countries, along with the states of Oregon, Washington, Montana, California, and Vermont, have enacted laws that allow physicians, under certain conditions, to assist dying patients in ending their lives. In 2017 this option was used by 92 people in Oregon to end their lives; they tended to be younger, more educated, and more apt to have cancer than other people who died in that state in 2017.

11.3 Rituals and Grieving

OBJECTIVE: **Analyze practices associated with bereavement**

- A defining characteristic of our species is that we have ritual ways of dealing with the death of a member of our community. The earliest evidence of human habitations usually consists of ancient graves with decorative objects placed around the remains. Each culture has its own traditions, and in the United States, a nation of immigrants from many cultures, there are many ways of expressing loss and grief. The only common bond is that we feel loss and grief when someone dies who has touched our lives, either directly or as a public figure.

- There are also many ways of feeling personal grief. There is no set of stages or processes that everyone experiences, and the way one feels grief does not reflect one's bond with the deceased.

- The most common reaction to the death of a loved one is resilience. Most people are able to function in a healthy way despite their genuine feelings of loss and sorrow. These feelings are accompanied by fond memories, concern for others, appreciation of social support, and even laughter. The pattern of bereavement is not related to the quality of the relationship before death in most cases. It is related to the quality of the bereaved person's overall adjustment.

- The death of a loved one can lead to gains, and bereavement can lead to personal growth.

SHARED WRITING

Choosing When to Die

Consider this chapter's discussion of "choosing when to die." How much control should a person have over when they die? How much control should family members have? Write a short response that your classmates will read. Be sure to give concrete reasons in your discussion.

 A minimum number of characters is required to post and earn points. After posting, your response can be viewed by your class and instructor, and you can participate in the class discussion.

Post   0 characters | 140 minimum

Chapter 12
The Successful Journey

Successful aging journeys can take many forms.

 ## Learning Objectives

12.1 Summarize major themes in adult development

12.2 Evaluate measures of life success

12.3 Analyze adulthood according to models of growth and development

12.4 Determine the elements of successful aging

A Word From the Author

Ah, This is the Life!

HANK WAKES UP every morning and makes himself a glass of fresh-squeezed orange juice, commenting to the world in general, "Ah, this is the life!" He is just short of his 80th birthday and has not had an easy life. He has scars on his chin and upper lip from having an incoming shell blow up in his face as he and his regiment of Marines stormed Peleliu Island in World War II. He has scars on his chest from coronary-bypass surgery and discolored places on his arms and legs due to the blood thinner he takes to ward off more heart trouble. He has a pacemaker and defibrillator implanted in his chest and needs surgery to have his batteries changed from time to time. He tells his great-grandsons that Grandma B. has a remote control device in her handbag, and if he gets "out of line," she will turn it on and make him behave. They think this is the funniest thing they have ever heard.

Hank and his wife raised five kids and supported them by always working at least two jobs. He married after the war and lived in his in-laws' house while he and his father built a house next door for the new family. Two years after they moved in, his father-in-law lost his eyesight (and his job), and the in-laws moved in with the new family, who now had three sons—a 2-year-old and a new pair of twins. Within 3 years of leaving the Marines, he was 26 and the head of a household of seven people.

When I first met Hank, he was a 60-year-old police officer—a job he did not like, but that had good pay and medical insurance, plus a chance for overtime. On Saturday nights he would turn on the TV a little before 8:00 and wait for the lottery drawing. He would pat the phone on the table next to him and say, "If I win, the first thing I will do is call the chief and put in my two-weeks' notice." Then he would talk about what he would do with the winnings—buy a mansion on the hill for his wife, take a cruise around the world, send all his grandchildren to college, buy a vacation home on the beach in Florida.

Well, Hank never won the lottery, but he did leave his job when he retired a few years later, and he did buy a new house for his wife, smaller and newer than the family homestead. He started a lawn service and gave the college-aged grandkids jobs in the summer to help with their tuition. He bought a condo in Florida. He took a cruise to the Bahamas. He lives on a budget, watches his diet carefully, follows his doctor's orders strictly, and gets plenty of exercise on the small golf course near his condo. He and his wife go to concerts at the community center on Friday nights and out for pizza on Wednesdays (coupon night). He attends church and plays cards with the neighbors. He has a new cell phone with unlimited long-distance calls, so he talks to all his children and grandchildren every Sunday evening, wherever they are.

By most yardsticks, Hank's journey of adulthood has been a good one. He served his country, took care of his family, parented successful children, nurtured grandchildren, sustained a happy marriage for over 60 years, and is loved and respected by everyone who knows him. But by his own yardstick, he is the luckiest guy in the world. Hank happens to be my father-in-law, but over the years I have met many men and women like him. Despite the headlines in the papers and the lead stories on the nightly news, the vast majority of people in this country and in developed countries all over the world are satisfied with their lives and view themselves as successful adults. This chapter is about the journeys of people like Hank and the millions of other adults of every age who greet the world each morning saying, "Ah, this is the life!"

I plan to start this chapter with a summary of the major themes of development that describe the typical person's experience on the journey of adulthood. Our lives are not neatly sliced up in separate topics. As you have no doubt sensed, the topics merge into each other. I'd like to present whole lives in this chapter and how we evaluate our progress on the journey of adulthood.

12.1: Themes of Adult Development

OBJECTIVE: **Summarize major themes in adult development**

In this last chapter, we include a mega-table (Table 12.1) showing a chronological review that spans from emerging adulthood (18–24 years) to late adulthood (75 years and over).

As always, these ages are approximate. Also note that the table describes the typical sequence of events for an adult who follows the culturally defined order of role transitions at the appropriate ages. I'll have more to say about individual pathways later in this chapter. For now, though, it is important to think about the typical or average. The normative pattern is to marry and have one's first child in the 20s. The children then typically leave home by the time one is about 50. Most people make major career changes in their mid-60s when they retire, change to part-time work, or become volunteer workers. Each row of the table represents a highly condensed version of one facet of the change that we might see over the lifetime of a person who follows such a modal pattern.

Of the seven horizontal rows in the table, four seem to describe genuinely maturational or developmental sequences. Clearly, the physical and mental changes described in the first two rows are strongly related to highly predictable and widely shared physical processes. Although the rate of change is affected by lifestyle and habits, the sequences appear to be maturational. More tentatively, I have argued that the sequences of change in personality and in systems of meaning may also be developmental in the sense I have used that term throughout the text. These are not strongly age-linked changes, but there is at least some evidence that they are sequential and not merely a function of particular or culture-specific changes in roles or life experiences. The remaining three rows, covering roles, tasks, and relationships, seem to describe sequences that are common insofar as they are shared by many adults in a given cohort and a given culture. If the timing or the sequence of these roles or tasks changes in any particular culture, however, the pattern described in the table will change as well.

Table 12.1 Review of Changes in Eight Different Domains of Adult Functioning

Characteristics	Emerging Adulthood (18–24 Years)	Early Adulthood (25–39 Years)	Middle Adulthood (40–64 Years)	Older Adulthood (65–74 Years)	Late Adulthood (75+ Years)
Physical change	Peak functioning in most body systems and physical abilities; optimal biological reproductive years; health habits established now will create pattern of later well-being. Bone mass is still increasing. Obesity is present for some, and many do not follow diet and exercise recommendations.	High levels of functioning continue. Slight declines in sensory functioning appear. Weight and girth increase; Obesity is present for about one-third. Bone mass begins slight decline.	Noticeable signs of physical decline in some areas (e.g., near vision, stamina, muscle, and cardiovascular functioning). Climacteric ends reproduction for women suddenly around 50, and diminishes it gradually for men. Weight and girth increase; about one-third are obese. Wrinkled skin and hair loss become apparent for many. Bone mass shows sharp decline for women.	Physical decline more noticeable, but rate of decline is still relatively slow: reaction time slows. Weight decreases for many as bone and muscle mass decrease; about one-third experience osteoarthritis. More decline in sensory systems; dark adaptation becomes a problem. Taste and smell deficits become noticeable for many.	Acceleration in decline of physical abilities and sensory functioning. About one-half have developed cataracts. Increased degeneration of muscles.
Cognitive change	Peak period of cognitive skill on most measures, fastest reaction time. Most depend on parents for important decisions. Driving safety is low, and electronics use is high and skilled.	Most memory abilities show slight but gradual declines except crystallized abilities, semantic and procedural memory. Decision making increases. Driving safety increases. Electronic use is integral part of lives.	Small declines continue for all except crystallized abilities (which peak), semantic and procedural memory. Decision making increases due to experience. Driving safety is good. Electronic use is variable.	More slow decline for memory systems except crystallized abilities and procedural memory. Decision making remains good. Driving begins to decline, but may be helped with training. Electronic use can be valuable to help with day-to-day tasks.	All systems have gradual decline, including crystallized abilities, but not procedural memory. Decision making can be affected by cognitive loss and health disorders (and prescription drugs). Cognitive decline may be minimized by physical exercise. Driving safety declines sharply. Electronic use continues to be helpful if started at earlier age.
Family and gender roles	Family roles are mixture of childhood and adult roles, and young people move in and out of them. Gender roles are egalitarian for most.	Major family roles are acquired (e.g., spouse, parent). Advances in these areas dominate life. Clear separation of gender roles.	Launch children; postparental phase; for many, added role of caregiver for elderly family members. Grandparent role begins for most.	Grandparent role continues in importance; significantly less dominance of gender roles.	Participation in family roles declines as activities are restricted. Role of care receiver begins for some.
Relationships	Family relationships are similar to childhood; peers are important socially. Romantic relationships consist of short-term dating for most.	Emphasis on forming new friendships, cohabitation, and marriage. Continued relationship with parents, siblings, and often grandparents. When children arrive, the focus turns toward parenting and away from other relationships.	Increased marital satisfaction as focus turns from parenting to other relationships. Adult children remain important. Increased importance of relationships with siblings and friends.	High marital satisfaction for those who have spouses; friendships and sibling relationships may become more intimate. Interactions with adult children frequent but not central to well-being. Relationships with grandchildren is important.	Majority are widowed; small network of close friends and siblings remain important.

Table 12.1 (*Continued*)

Characteristics	Emerging Adulthood (18–24 Years)	Early Adulthood (25–39 Years)	Middle Adulthood (40–64 Years)	Older Adulthood (65–74 Years)	Late Adulthood (75+ Years)
Work roles	Vocational interests present for most. Jobs are part time or entry level and not related to vocational interests. Job performance is variable. Little thought of retirement plans. Residential moves are for college or military service.	Emphasis on choosing career, changing jobs, and establishing oneself in a career.	Peak years of career success and income for most, also work satisfaction. Slight physical and cognitive decline is compensated for by increases in job expertise.	Most leave their full-time jobs and take less stressful or part-time jobs, do volunteer work, or retire entirely.	Work roles unimportant for most. Some continue to volunteer.
Personality and meaning	Establish identity in areas of occupation, gender role, and political and religious beliefs. Begin to see the self as separate from the group. Accentuate own gender characteristics and repress opposite-gender characteristics.	Establish intimacy in relationships. Increased individuality (self-confidence, independence, autonomy). Form own ideas and standards. Gender differences remain high.	Establish generativity within family or workplace. Some sign of a softening of the individuality of the earlier period; fewer immature defenses; possibly autonomous level. Increase in spirituality for some, especially women. Gender differences begin to soften as children leave home.	Task of ego integrity; perhaps more interiority; a few may reach integrated level. Increase in spirituality for most.	Continuation of previous pattern. Increase in spirituality for most, even if outward signs decrease.
Major tasks	Establish self as an adult by completing education or job training, become independent from parents financially, make own decisions, become an autonomous member of community.	Renegotiate relationship with parents; form intimate partnerships; begin family, begin career, create individual identity, strive for success in both personal and professional life.	Guide children into adulthood; cope with death of parents; strengthen marriage; redefine life goals; achieve individuality; care for aging family members.	Find alternative to lifelong jobs; cope with health problems of self and spouse; redefine life goals and sense of self.	Come to terms with one's own life, possibly through reviewing memories or writing a memoir. Cope with the deaths of loved ones and the eventuality of own death. Value remaining family members and friends, and other remaining joys in life.

A second way to look at the table is to read down the columns rather than across the rows. This gives some sense of the various patterns that may occur simultaneously.

▼ **By the end of this module, you will be able to:**

12.1.1   Identify major influences on emerging adults

12.1.2   Characterize adulthood from age 25 to 39

12.1.3   Contextualize issues in middle adulthood

12.1.4   Explain how role changes impact older adulthood

12.1.5   Describe adulthood after age 75

12.1.1: Emerging Adulthood (Ages 18–24)

OBJECTIVE: Identify major influences on emerging adults

Although we have always had adults in this age group, of course, they have become a distinct group, sufficiently different from the 25- to 39-year-old group to merit their own category—*emerging adults*. Developmental psychologists attribute this phenomenon to the increased time it takes adolescents to become full-fledged adults. No longer do young people graduate from high school and move directly into adult roles in the workforce, the military, or as stay-at-home mothers as they did several generations ago. Slowly this transition has increased until what we consider "full adulthood", doesn't occur until the mid-20s for most. Developmental psychologist Jeffrey Arnett (1994, 2000, 2007) began to write about this group in the 1990s, coining the term "emerging adults" a few years later. Researchers who worked with young people this age held their first conference in 2003, and since then, the stage of emerging adulthood has been included in journals, textbooks, classroom curricula, and the popular press. According to Arnett (2004), there are five major tasks of this period.

What is involved in the stage of emerging adulthood?

Identity Exploration—This entails looking at the possibilities for their lives in a variety of areas, especially love and work. Determining what kind of adult life they will have, what they will believe in, and what they will value. In what way will they be like their parents, and in what way will they be different? This is similar to the psychosocial stages of *identity versus role confusion* and *intimacy versus isolation* theorized by Erik Erikson (1950, 1959).

Positive Instability—This type of instability involves young people finding their way by trial and error—starting in one direction and then changing course if that is not a good way for them. This happens in choosing majors in college, deciding where to live, determining who will be their long-term partner, and other parts of their life plan.

Focusing on the Self—At no other time of life is a person more self-focused than during emerging adulthood. They are between the age that they are subject to their parents' rules and the age that they are constrained by marriage, family, and workplace rules. The result is wide-open options on everything from what to have for breakfast to whether to drop out of college or not. And the decision is largely up to the emerging adult him- or herself.

Feeling In-Between—If adulthood means being responsible for yourself, making your own decisions, and being financially independent, most emerging adults feel like they have one foot in childhood and one in adulthood. These aspects of adulthood come gradually, and it is not surprising that the in-between, ambiguous feeling is part of this time of life.

Imagining Possibilities—In adolescence, a young person's environment is determined largely by parents, but during emerging adulthood, many possibilities become evident. Those who grew up in difficult circumstances can make changes so their lives will be better. This can be a time of seeking new friends and new role models. And for those who grew up in more positive environments, there are still possibilities to imagine and changes that can be made before the responsibilities of young adulthood take place.

The years of emerging adulthood feature peak physical condition. All systems are at their best, and top athletes will never perform better. Neuronal development is finally complete. Death and disease rates are both low. All cognitive processes are at peak except crystallized intelligence, which depends on education and experience. Yet with all this good health and top thinking skills, there are the harbingers of later problems. A significant proportion of emerging adults are overweight and obese; they do not eat healthy or exercise at the recommended level for continued good health. They smoke, and they subject their hearing apparatus to loud noises at sports events and concerts. Those of us who are past this age are of two minds—first, we want to lecture about valuing good health and youth, and second, we remember our own emerging adulthood years with great pleasure and remember our own reactions to advice from our elders.

Emerging adults move into young adulthood at different rates of development. They also enter some areas (such as starting a career) and not others (such as finding a partner or starting a family). But the social clock is ticking.

12.1.2: Young Adulthood (Ages 25–39)

OBJECTIVE: Characterize adulthood from age 25 to 39

Anyone who has been this age has probably been told by older people to enjoy it, that it is "the prime of life." This can be a frightening thought for the typical young adult, who is struggling to balance school, work, and family obligations. The truth is that although young adulthood may be a time of top performances in physical and cognitive abilities, it is also the period of adult life with the most changes. Consider that during these years, most young adults:

- Move into more major roles than at any other time in their lives: a work role, marriage, and parenthood.

- Have jobs that are the most physically demanding, least interesting, least challenging, and lowest paying than at any other time in their careers.

- Form romantic partnerships and select long-term partners for marriage or cohabitation relationships.

- Become parents of one or more children, participating in marathon childcare during the early years.

Fortunately, young adults have a number of valuable assets to help them deal with these high levels of demand. Most obviously, like emerging adulthood, these are years in which body and mind are at top performance. Neurological speed is at maximum, so physical and mental reaction time is swift; new information is learned easily and recalled easily; the immune system is highly efficient, so one recovers quickly from disease or injury; and the cardiovascular system is

Close friendships are particularly important during young adulthood.

similarly at its best, so sports can be played with speed and endurance.

Young adults deal with the changes by creating a network of friendships and other close relationships—part of what Erik Erikson talks about as the stage of *intimacy versus isolation*. Friendships are not only numerous but also particularly important in these years; those who have small friendship networks report more loneliness and depressive symptoms than socially isolated people at other stages of adulthood.

DEPENDENCE AND INDIVIDUATION Perhaps because the role demands are so powerful, the young adult's sense of him- or herself, the meaning system with which he or she interprets all these experiences, seems to be dominated by rules, by conformity, by a sense that authority is external to the self. We think of these years as a time when the young person is becoming independent, but in becoming independent of their parents, most young adults are not becoming individualized in their search for meaning. Most are still locked into a conformist view, seeing things in black-and-white terms, looking to outside authority to tell them the rules. The years of young adulthood are a time of maximal *tribalization*. We define ourselves by our tribe and our place in the tribe.

The years of emerging adulthood are typically spent on periods of dependence and searching (for the right career, the right major in school, the right girlfriend or boyfriend), but young adulthood is spent in overdrive. Once the course of the journey of adulthood is set, young adults usually waste no time settling into their myriad roles and working at being successful spouses, workers, and parents.

At the same time, the conventional worldview they entered adulthood with slowly begins to give way to a more individualistic outlook. This change comes over time and seems to happen for several reasons. Among other things, we discover that following the rules doesn't always lead to reward, a realization that causes us to question the system itself. Neither marriage nor having children, for example, leads to unmitigated bliss, as evidenced by the well-replicated drop in marital satisfaction after the birth of the first child and during the period when the children are young. For those who married in their early or middle 20s, this drop in satisfaction occurs in their late 20s and 30s, contributing to a kind of disillusionment with the entire role system. A second reason for the change in perspective, I think, is that this is the time in which we develop highly individualized skills. In conforming to the external role demand that we find work and pursuing it, we also discover our own talents and capacities, a discovery that helps to turn our focus inward. We become more aware of our own individuality, more aware of the parts of ourselves that existing roles do not allow us to express.

But although the individualization process begins in our 30s, it is nonetheless true that this period of young adulthood, like the period from 18 to 25, is dominated by the social clock. In our 30s we may begin to chafe at the strictures of the roles in which we find ourselves; we may be less and less likely to define ourselves solely or largely in terms of the roles we occupy, but the role demands are still extremely powerful in this period. This fact tends to make the lives of those in young adulthood more like one another than will be true at any later point. To be sure, some adults do not follow the normative pattern, and their lives are less predictable. But the vast majority of adults do enter into the broad river of family and work roles in their mid-20s and are moved along with the common flow as their children grow older and their work status progresses. One of the key changes as we move into middle adult life is that the power of these roles declines; the social clock begins to be less audible, less compelling.

12.1.3: Middle Adulthood (Ages 40–64)

OBJECTIVE: Contextualize issues in middle adulthood

Although the change is usually gradual rather than abrupt, the period of middle adulthood is really quite distinctly different from the years that come before.

BIOLOGICAL AND SOCIAL CLOCKS Most obviously, the biological clock begins to be audible because it is during these years that the first signs of physical aging become apparent—the changes in the eyes that mean most adults require glasses for reading; loss of elasticity in the skin that makes wrinkles more noticeable; the diminished reproductive capacity, most noticeable for women but present for men as well; the heightened risk for major diseases, such as heart disease or cancer; the slight but measurable slowing in reaction time or physical stamina; perhaps some slowing in the speed of bringing names or other specific information out of long-term memory.

The early stages of this physical aging process normally don't involve much functional loss. Mental skills may be a trifle slower but not enough slower that you can't do your job well or learn something new, such as using social media. In fact, the expertise gained from experience compensates for the physical and cognitive slowing. Achieving and maintaining fitness may take more work, but it's still quite possible. If you've been out of shape, you can even improve significantly by running faster or doing more pushups than you could when you were 30. But as you move through these middle years toward older adulthood, the signs of

aging become more and more apparent and less and less easy to overcome.

At the same time, the social clock becomes much less significant. If you had your children in your 20s, then by your late 40s or early 50s they are likely to be on their way to independence. And in your work life you are likely to have reached the highest level that you will achieve. You know the role well, and the drive to achieve may peak and then decline. You may find satisfaction in the achievement of young colleagues you have mentored rather than in your own accomplishments.

If young adulthood is a time of *tribalization*, the middle years bring *detribalization*, perhaps part of a deeper shift in personality or meaning systems toward a more individualistic view. The greater openness to self that emerges at this time includes an openness to unexpressed parts of the self, parts that are likely to be outside the prescribed roles. The change is thus both external and internal.

If you think about the relationship of these two clocks over the years of adulthood, you might visualize them as something like the pattern in Figure 12.1. The specific point of crossover of these two chronologies is obviously going to differ from one adult to another, but it is most likely to occur sometime in this middle-adulthood period.

Figure 12.1 Relative Potency or Importance of Biological and Social Clocks

One way to think about the different phases or stages of adulthood is in terms of the relative potency or importance of the biological and social clocks. Except for the issue of childbearing for women, the biological clock is relatively unimportant until sometime in midlife, after which it becomes increasingly important. The social clock follows an opposite pattern.

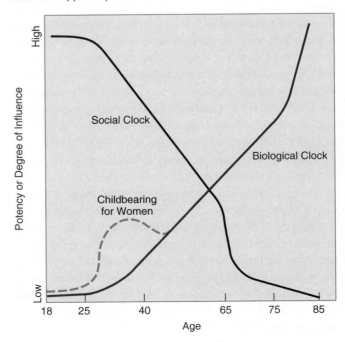

WORK AND MARRIAGE   One of the ironies is that the decline in the centrality of work and relationship roles in midlife is often accompanied by greater satisfaction with both work and relationships. You'll recall that both marital and work satisfaction rise in the years of middle adulthood. As always, there are undoubtedly many reasons for the rise, including the fact that the actual work one is doing in these years is likely to be less physically demanding, more interesting, and more rewarded than was true in young adulthood, and that once the children are older and require less hands-on parenting, one of the major strains on a marriage declines. But the improvement in satisfaction with both work and relationships may also be a reflection of the inner shift of perspective I have been talking about. Adults who experience the world from a more individualist or conscientious perspective take responsibility for their own actions, so they may find ways to make their work and relationships more pleasant. Or they may choose to change jobs or partners.

This sense of choice is a key aspect of this age period. There are certainly still roles to be filled; one does not stop being a parent just because the children have been launched; one still has work roles to fill, relationships with one's own parents, with friends, with the community. But adults in middle life have more choices about how they will fill these roles, both because the roles of this age have more leeway and because we now perceive roles differently, as being less compellingly prescriptive.

Is this picture too rosy? For those who have not been there yet, midlife sounds like the best of all worlds. And as someone who is there already, I tend to agree. In midlife we have more choices; our work and marital satisfaction is likely to rise, and there is a likelihood of some inner growth or transformation as well. To be sure, there is also the growing awareness of physical aging, but for most of us such an awareness is not dominant. We still feel fit and capable. It sounds as if these years, when both the biological and the social clocks are ticking away quietly in the background, are the best of all worlds.

But isn't this also the time when the infamous midlife crisis is supposed to hit? In this more negative view, large numbers of middle-aged adults are seen as anxious, unsure, dissatisfied with earlier life choices, unhappy with their biological decline, and frantically searching for solutions, whether it is a job change, a new spouse, or a facelift. Can these two views be reconciled?

THE MYTH OF THE MIDLIFE CRISIS   An interesting part of our popular culture involves the **midlife crisis**, portrayed as a time when the responsible middle-aged person makes a 180-degree turn on the road of life and suddenly becomes irresponsible. Movies, novels, and TV shows have entertained us with stories of staid bankers who suddenly trade in their gray sedans for red sports cars and start coloring their hair. Often these crises involve leaving one's long-term

spouse and becoming involved with a younger person who has a more carefree lifestyle. We may even know of middle-aged people who have had a "breakdown" of some kind and made drastic lifestyle changes as a result. But is this something that happens to a great number of people in middle age? Is it something of a typical developmental stage in adulthood? Is the midlife crisis predictable?

The early accounts of midlife crises come from psychoanalyst Elliott Jacques (1965), who based his ideas on clinical samples, and journalist Gail Sheehy (1976), who based her ideas on in-depth interviews with 40 people. Because these books were focused on problems and negative-biased information, the concept of midlife being a time of stress and crisis has not been substantiated by research on more representative groups. More recent research in peer-reviewed journals, including the following, has used nonclinical participants and less biased questioning. These show a little different picture of midlife development (see 'Studying Midlife').

In summary, the midlife crisis (along with its cousin, the empty-nest syndrome) is, to some extent, an aspect of individual personality rather than a characteristic of this particular age period. And, as sociologist Glen Elder, Jr. (1979) would remind us, it can also be a product of the cultural and historical events we experienced at earlier stages of our lives.

12.1.4: Older Adulthood (Ages 65–74)

OBJECTIVE: Explain how role changes impact older adulthood

In many ways people in this group are more like middle-aged adults than like those in late adulthood. So why make a division at age 65? From a physical point of view there is nothing notable about age 65 that would suggest that some new stage or phase has begun. Certainly, some adults in this age range experience significant disease or chronic disability. But the norm is rather that small—albeit noticeable—physical changes or declines continue to accumulate at roughly the same rate as was true in one's middle years. Hearing loss is now more likely to become a problem, as is arthritis; one is likely to have an increased sense of being a bit slower. But for most adults (in developed countries at least) the rate of physical or mental change does not appear to accelerate in these years. What makes this 10-year period unique is the rapid drop in role demands that accompanies retirement, a drop that once again changes the balance between the social clock and the biological clock.

There is certainly little evidence that this change is marked by any kind of crisis. Research on retirement shows no increase in illness, depression, or other distress that can be linked causally to the retirement itself. For those who must retire because of ill health, the picture is rather

Studying Midlife

Wethington Study

For example, a survey of over 700 adults between 28 and 78 years of age showed that 26% of the respondents (both male and female in equal numbers) claimed they had experienced a midlife crisis (Wethington, 2000). When questioned more closely, the events they described were not crises, nor had they occurred at midlife. Instead, the term *midlife crisis* seems to have come to mean coping successfully with some threatening situation in one's adult life and making personal changes as a result. People reported that these events had taken place at almost any age during adulthood, though they considered them "midlife crises." Figure 12.2 shows that midlife crises are reported by adults of all ages and by women more than men.

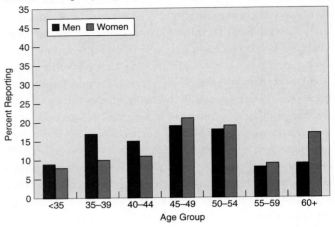

Figure 12.2 Occurrence of "Midlife" Crises by Age

SOURCE: Wethington (2000).

Depression Age

Another explanation of the midlife crisis is that it depends on what sort of "crisis" is being measured. In a review of data for a random sample of 500,000 people living in the United States and in Europe, researchers found that the typical person's happiness is at the lowest in middle age (Blanchflower & Oswald, 2008). This was true for both American and European participants, for men and women, and for a number of different measures of "happiness." For example, asking participants about depression showed the same distribution. The largest proportion of people responding that anxiety or depression were major health problems was at age 44 years, and the proportion declined steadily for those younger and older.

Predicting Happiness

However, longitudinal evidence shows that there is a difference between whether an adult is reporting their current life satisfaction or predicting their future life satisfaction. Psychologist Margie Lachman and her colleagues (2015) found that current life satisfaction increases with age while predicted life satisfaction decreases with age. Figure 12.3 illustrates their findings that in early adulthood, the future looks brighter than the present, and no wonder. Young adults are working hard toward that future—in their studies, their job training, their early relationships. However, in middle age, when they have achieved those goals, the present looks better and the future predictions for life satisfaction have declined. By older adulthood, the present is best and the future is not so rosy.

Longitudinal Studies

Other longitudinal evidence offers little support for the expectation of widespread midlife crises. For instance, in an analysis of the participants in the Berkeley and Oakland longitudinal studies, researchers found no indication of a widespread upheaval in midlife. Those who experience a genuine upheaval at this period of life, and perhaps 5% of the population do, are likely to be people who have experienced upheavals at other times as well (Haan, 1981). In George Vaillant's life-long study of Harvard men, he noted that difficulties such as divorce, depression, and job loss happen at all ages throughout adulthood, but when they occur in midlife, we say, "Ah-ha! The midlife crisis . . .!" (1995, p. 80). In contrast, Vaillant found in his study that the Harvard men considered the period from 35 to 49 years to be the happiest time of their lives and 21 to 35 years as the unhappiest.

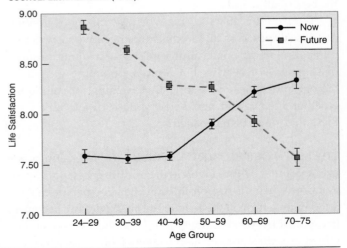

Figure 12.3 Report of Current and Future Life Satisfaction

SOURCE: Lachman et al. (2015).

different; for this subgroup retirement is linked with further declines in health and perhaps depression. But for the majority, every indication is that mental health is as good—or perhaps better—in this age group than at younger ages. Figure 12.4 shows that high satisfaction with retirement decreases with age.

What does mark this change is the loss of the work role, which is of course accompanied by a continuing decline in the centrality of other roles. Spousal roles continue, of course, for those whose spouse is still living; there is still some parental role, although that too is less demanding and less clearly defined; the roles of friend and of brother or sister to one's aging siblings may actually become more central. But even more than was true in middle life, these roles are flexible and full of choices.

12.1.5: Late Adulthood (Age 75 and Older)

OBJECTIVE: Describe adulthood after age 75

The fastest-growing segment of the U.S. population is the group in late adulthood. As life expectancy increases, more and more of us are living well past what we once considered "old age." And as health has improved, it is often not until these years that the processes of physical and mental aging begin to accelerate. It is at this point that the functional reserve of many physical systems is likely to fall below the level required for everyday activities, creating a new level of dependence or disability.

I do not want to make too big a deal of the age of 75. The demarcation point between the period of older adulthood and late adulthood is more a function of health than of age. Some adults may be frail at 60; others may still be robust and active at 85. But if you look at the norms, as I have been doing in this chapter, it appears that age 75 is roughly where the shift begins to take place, at least in today's cohorts in the United States and other developed countries.

Our knowledge of late adulthood is growing. Only in recent years have there been large numbers of adults in this group; only quite recently has the Census Bureau begun to divide some of its statistics for older adults into decades rather than merely lumping everyone over age 65 into a single category. But we do have some information that points to a qualitative change that takes place at roughly this time.

Longitudinal studies of cognitive abilities show that the acceleration in the decline in total mental ability scores starts at about 70 or 75. There is decline before that, but the rate of decline increases in late adulthood. And as one moves into the 80s and beyond, the incidence of physical and mental frailty rises rapidly. Psychologist Edwin Shneidman (1989), writing about the decade of one's 70s, puts it this way: "Consider that when one is a septuagenarian, one's parents are gone, children are grown, mandatory work is done; health is not too bad, and responsibilities are relatively light, with time, at long last, for focus on the self. These can be sunset years, golden years, an Indian Summer, a period of relatively mild weather for both soma and psyche in the late autumn or early winter of life, a decade of greater independence and increased opportunities for further self-development" (p. 684). But what is it that adults in this period of early old age choose to do with their lives? Do they remain active and involved, or do they begin to withdraw, to turn inward toward self-development or reminiscence? If there is controversy about this age period, it has centered on some variant of this question. The issue is usually framed in the terms of disengagement in old age.

DISENGAGEMENT   Over 50 years ago, the term **disengagement** was proposed by gerontologists Elaine Cumming

---

Figure 12.4 Satisfaction with Retirement Over Time

The proportion of retirees who report being "very satisfied" with retirement decreases with age, probably due to health problems and other losses.
SOURCE: Banerjee (2016).

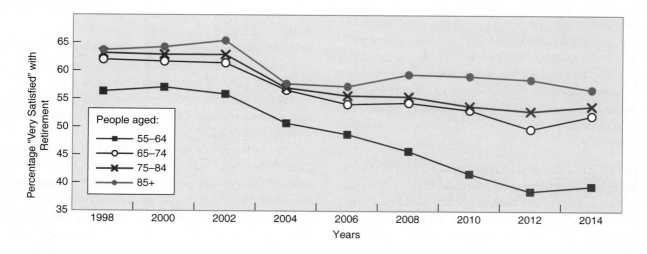

and William Henry (1961) to describe what they saw as a key psychological process in old age. This process was seen as having three features or aspects:

1. Adults' social "life space" shrinks with age, a change especially noticeable in the period from age 75 on when we interact with fewer and fewer others and fill fewer and fewer roles as we move through late adulthood.

2. In the roles and relationships that remain, the aging person becomes more individualized, less governed by rules and norms.

3. The aging person anticipates this set of changes and actively embraces them, disengaging more and more from roles and relationships (Cumming, 1975).

Few would disagree with the first two of these points. In late adulthood, most people do show a decline in the number of social activities they engage in, they occupy fewer roles, and their roles have fewer clear prescriptions. Adults of this age participate in fewer clubs or organizations, go to religious services less often, and have a smaller network of friends.

But the third of Cumming and Henry's points about disengagement is in considerable dispute. They argued that disengagement is not only natural but also optimally healthy in late adulthood, so that those who show the most disengagement are going to be the happiest and healthiest. And this is simply not supported by the research. There is no indication that those who show the greatest decline in social activity (who "disengage" the most) are happier or healthier. On the contrary, the common finding is that the least disengaged adults (or the most engaged adults) report greater satisfaction with themselves and their lives, are healthiest, and have the highest morale.

The picture is not totally one-sided. On the other side of the ledger is a significant body of work pointing to the conclusion that solitude is quite a comfortable state for many older adults. Note, for example, that among all age groups, loneliness is least common among the elderly. Indeed, some older adults clearly find considerable satisfaction in an independent, socially isolated (highly disengaged) life pattern. Clearly it is possible to choose and to find contentment in a largely disengaged lifestyle in these older years. But does this mean that disengagement is necessary for mental health? On the contrary, most of the evidence says exactly the opposite. For most older adults, social involvement is both a sign of, and probably a cause of, higher levels of satisfaction. Those who do not have satisfactory contact with others, particularly with friends, are typically less satisfied with their lives.

RESERVE CAPACITY AND ADAPTING TO LIMITATIONS
Psychologists Paul Baltes and Margaret Baltes (1990) suggested that one of the key features of late adulthood is that the person operates much closer to the edge of reserve capacity than is the case for younger or middle-aged adults.

Table 12.2 Process of Late Adulthood and Examples

Process	Example
Select	Marathon runner limits self to 10K runs
Optimize	Invests in knee brace for problem knee
Compensate	Celebrates finishing the race, not coming in first

To cope with this fact, and with the fact of various physical declines, one must use a process that they call **selective optimization with compensation** (Table 12.2). Older adults *select* the range of activities or arenas in which they will operate, concentrating energy and time on needs or demands that are truly central. They *optimize* their reserves by learning new strategies and keeping old skills well practiced. And when needed, they *compensate* for losses.

The very fact that such selection, optimization, and compensation are necessary in later adulthood is a crucial point. Reserve capacities are reduced, but it is also crucial to realize that many adults in this age group can and do compensate and adjust their lives to their changing circumstances.

LIFE REVIEW   Recall that the stage Erikson proposes for late adulthood is *ego integrity versus despair*. One of Erikson's notions was that to achieve wisdom, which is the potential strength to be gained at this stage, older adults must think back over their lives and try to come to terms with the person they once were and the one they are now.

Over 50 years ago, Robert Butler (1963), a professor of geriatric medicine, expanded on Erikson's idea. In one article, which has become one of the classics in the study of aging, Butler proposed that in old age, all of us go through a process he called **life review**, in which there is a "progressive return to consciousness of past experience, and particularly, the resurgence of unresolved conflicts" (p. 53). Butler argued that in this final stage of life, as preparation for our now clearly impending deaths, we engage in *reminiscence*, which is an analytic and evaluative review of our earlier life. According to Butler, such a review is a necessary part of achieving ego integrity, and the wisdom that results from it, at the end of life.

This is an attractive hypothesis, and Butler's ideas have inspired hundreds of scientific studies of reminiscence and life review, yielding a number of practical applications. The usefulness of reminiscence for older adults can be grouped into seven functions (Westerhof & Bohlmeijer, 2014), as shown in Table 12.3.

This idea of life review is found in many activities. Clinical psychologists use life review to establish rapport with older patients and to support their mental health. Community groups have classes to instruct adults of all ages in writing memoirs. Veterans talk to schoolchildren about their service, older craft workers keep their traditions

Table 12.3 Functions of Reminiscence for Older Adults

Self-identity	Reflecting on the life course to arrive at a clear sense of self.
Problem solving	Remembering past problem-solving techniques for use in the present.
Teaching	Sharing personal experiences and life lessons with others.
Conversation	Connecting or reconnecting with others through shared memories.
Maintaining intimacy with the past	Using reminiscence to keep alive memories of absent loved ones.
Intellectual stimulation	Reliving interesting events when our own lives are limited by physical or mental limitations.
Preparation for death	Using the past to become more accepting of our mortality.

SOURCE: Based on Westerhof and Bohlmeijer (2014).

alive by teaching younger people, Holocaust survivors talk to high school kids about their experiences, and grandparents make photo albums of their lives to share with their grandchildren. Museums around the country welcome letters, collections, and photos from older adults who had firsthand experiences to share.

Is life review solely an activity of the elderly? Probably not. We know that people of all ages talk about their memories and enjoy looking over photos and other memorabilia of times past. Do all older adults engage in life review? Does storytelling count or does it have to involve self-reflection? Is it necessary for older adults to engage in reminiscence to achieve some form of ego integrity in late life? These are interesting questions and good topics for future research.

On the whole, I think there is good reason to doubt the validity of Butler's hypothesis that life review is a necessary part of late adulthood. At the same time, it is clear that some kind of preparation for death is an inevitable, or even central, part of life in these last years. Although death certainly comes to adults of all ages, most younger adults can continue to push the idea of death away: that's something for later. But in the years past age 75, the imminence of death is inescapable and must be faced by each of us. Life review may be one of the ways this is done.

12.2: Variations in Successful Development

OBJECTIVE: Evaluate measures of life success

The study of adult development is based on the means of large groups of people. It gives us information on the *typical* person's life changes and the *average* type of behavior. It is important information and very useful to professionals and to

the layperson who wants to learn some general truths about the development of adults in general. But for the individual reflecting on his or her own life, it is less useful. Few of us fit the average; few of us are on the typical journey of adulthood.

Personally, I have not practiced what I preach as typical adult development. I married early and had three children before I was 25. I spent my young adulthood as a stay-at-home mom, tending to the children and volunteering at the neighborhood library. Once they were all in school, I enrolled at the local community college, and by the time the kids were in middle school, I was writing magazine articles on parenting and teaching part time at the university where I had received my master's degree in developmental psychology. This is certainly not the typical career path (and not the typical career). I was *off-time*—younger than the parents of my children's friends and older than my fellow students.

I became a divorced mother when my youngest was still at home, and then within one wonderful year I remarried and became a grandmother for the first time. What a combination of new roles! Fortunately, my new husband, a professor of child development, saw instant grandfatherhood as a bonus. At 50, I enrolled in a PhD program and 3 years later marched down the aisle to Elgar's *Pomp and Circumstance* at the University of Georgia to be hooded in red and black, with four generations of relatives applauding.

Since that time I have taught a variety of developmental psychology courses at a satellite campus of our local state university. For several summers I taught a group of advanced high school students from all over our state who wanted to come live in the dorms for 2 weeks and take a highly condensed college course. And I have switched roles a bit and become a student in our university's lifelong learning program, attending lectures in a variety of subjects from oceanography to neuroscience to Renaissance art. Most people my age are retired, but since I started my career so late in life, I want to keep going. On the other hand, I realize that the young professors I interact with are no longer my peer group, but the age of my children (and sometimes my grandchildren).

My own version of the journey of adulthood has been interesting, but it was not easy. I am tempted to add the warning: *Do not try this yourselves!* But few of us have master plans for our lives. Most of us make one small decision at a time, and sometimes we are a bit surprised when we look back and see what the big picture looks like.

No doubt your own journey of adulthood has aspects that do not fit the typical. Knowing all about the means and the norms of adult development still leaves some questions. To fully understand the process of adult development and change, we also have to understand the ways in which individuals' lives are likely to differ, the variations in their reactions to the stresses and challenges they will encounter, and the eventual satisfaction or inner growth they may achieve.

12.2.1 Identify major influences on quality of life

12.2.2 Determine factors relevant to life satisfaction

12.2.1: Individual Differences in Quality of Life

OBJECTIVE: Identify major influences on quality of life

What factors are responsible for one person's high level of life satisfaction on the journey of adulthood and another person's lower level?

Six Major Factors Responsible for Satisfaction of Life

Education and Income—Education and income go hand-in-hand in determining which individuals will more likely experience successful aging and which will not (Olshansky et al., 2012). Education level determines what jobs a person is eligible for and, as a result, their income trajectory. Education and income comprise ones' socioeconomic status (SES), and this determines in large part the worker's partner, family stability, neighborhood safety, social network, and quality of health care, all of which determine physical and mental health (Jürges et al., 2013). In recent years in the United States, the gap between people in high socioeconomic groups and low socioeconomic groups has increased, especially for black men and women. Even though the proportion of people in the United States with less than 12 years of education is declining, their lifestyles and experiences give them lower chances of successful aging than those with higher levels of education and income (Antonucci et al., 2016).

Cohort—As each age group reaches older adulthood, they are healthier and have more education and income than the cohort before. Since successful aging depends on these factors, today's older adults have a higher quality of life than their parents did at the same age. Disability rates are getting lower, people are having longer lifespans, and, more importantly, longer healthy lifespans. Today's elders who are 85 years old and older are functioning independently at rates significantly higher than previous cohorts, probably due to higher educational attainment (Antonucci et al., 2016). However, I must mention that this increase in successful aging with each succeeding cohort is in jeopardy because of high rates of physical illness among young people today (e.g., diabetes and hypertension) and mental illness (e.g., depression and anxiety), though efforts are being made to change this before they reach older adulthood themselves (Blazer & Hybels, 2014).

Work Satisfaction—The quality of life in older adulthood is influenced by our career experiences. Work satisfaction depends on the type of job one has; jobs that offer autonomy and flexibility bring more satisfaction than those that don't offer a sense of identity and are monotonous. This is important not just for the hours one spends at work, but because of job spillover, work satisfaction spreads into general life satisfaction, coloring one's self-perception, partnership, and family life, and in extreme cases, leading to job burnout and depressive symptoms (Hakanan & Schaufeli, 2012). Women who work outside the home experience job frustration over receiving lower wages than their male counterparts, and women who have children have work-related stress because, at least in the United States, there are no family care provisions to help when they need to care for young children, aging parents, or ill spouses (Sherman et al., 2013). That being said, work in later life seems to contribute to physical, mental, and social health, probably because it keeps people engaged in those areas (Börsch-Supan & Schuth, 2014). For example, older adults in countries that have the least generous retirement practices end up retiring later, but they score higher on cognitive tests than those who encourage earlier retirement (Rohwedder & Willis, 2010). This benefit is not confined to paid work, but is also present in older adults who do volunteer work (Moen & Flood, 2013). The future will undoubtedly bring a more age-diverse workforce, and although we can't deny an age-related decline in some cognitive abilities, they seem to be offset by the expertise and strong work ethic that older adults bring to the workplace (Antonucci et al., 2016).

Family—The old adage about children being a comfort to their parents in old age does not seem to apply to today's older adults. First, there are more older adults who do not have children and second, those who do have children, they have fewer than in generations before. However, this has not resulted in a lower quality of life for these people as they grow older. Middle-aged adults who are childless often form *fictive families*, which consist of close friends and relatives, many of whom do have children. One of my friends, who is approaching 60, has no children of her own but is proud godmother of five. They visit her frequently, and one of them lived with her while he attended college in her city. She helped one buy a car and she bought a cello for another that showed musical talent. She has pictures to show and stories to tell about each. They have enriched her life, and she has enriched theirs. When these kinds of relationships are formed during young and middle adulthood, they are apt to continue into the later years and, like my friend's godchildren, be a source of subjective well-being (Dykstra & Hagestad, 2007).

The exception to this rosy picture is the case of divorced fathers (or fathers who never married their children's mothers), many of whom provide little support (financial or emotional) to their children as they grow up. As these fathers approach older adulthood, they have often lost contact with their children and receive little support (financially or emotionally) from them. This is especially true if the father remarries and raises more children or stepchildren (Sherman et al., 2013).

Country of Residence—Each year, a team of researchers from Columbia University compiles a list of the top places to live for older adults, based on social and economic elements that contribute to the well-being of an aging population (Chen et al., 2018). The elements are:

- Productivity and engagement—how well older adults are connected both inside and outside the workforce
- Well-being—the state of being physically and mentally healthy
- Equity—the difference in economic security and well-being between the "haves" and "have-nots"
- Cohesion—social connectedness between generations
- Security—retirement support and assured physical safety

The top five countries in the most recent list are Norway, Sweden, United States, Netherlands, and Japan. The United States is the best country for productivity and engagement, but halfway down the list for equity.

Social Comparisons—It seems to be part of our human character to compare ourselves to others, especially on aspects of ourselves that aren't easily measured, such as quality of life. This may be one of the reasons that older adults consider themselves to be enjoying a high level of well-being and good health, even though their health is not as good as it was in earlier adulthood and their activities and social circles are limited. The trick seems to be comparing oneself with others in the same age group. "Compared to others my age, I'm doing great!" This was demonstrated in several studies of older adults that showed they were more apt to compare themselves to others who are less advantaged than they are (Clark, 2013).

In summary, quality of life in adulthood is determined largely by health, income, education, and the people we choose to compare ourselves with. Another contributing factor is having a sense of control, meaning, or purpose in one's life. It is probably more informative to list the factors that don't matter much: age, race and ethnicity, and living in a country with a healthy economy. And factors that matter somewhat (but are probably part of health, income, and education) are gender, marital status, activities, and religious participation. I look forward to a comprehensive study that will take all these factors into account and give us a model showing the proximal and distal effects of quality of life in adulthood.

12.2.2: Other Measures of Life Success

OBJECTIVE: Determine factors relevant to life satisfaction

The quality of life that individuals report is one of the best measures of success in the adult years. But there are other ways of defining successful adulthood that rely on professional assessments of psychological health or on objective measures of life success. Two approaches, both involving analyses of rich longitudinal data, are particularly interesting.

In 1928, pioneer developmental psychologists began a study with newborns in Berkeley, California, and followed these participants and their families until they were 36 years of age, collecting data on their health, cognitive development, social situation, family life, personality, behavior, and parents' childrearing practices and personalities. In adulthood, they were interviewed about their education, marital status, employment, residence, offspring, and relationship with parents (Eichorn, 1973). Researchers working with the Berkeley Growth Study data developed a measure of ideal adult adjustment that they call *psychological health*. In this research, psychotherapists and theorists agreed that the pattern of qualities of an optimally healthy person includes the capacity for work and satisfying relationships, a sense of moral purpose, and a realistic perception of self and society. According to this view, adults who are psychologically healthy show a great deal of warmth, compassion, dependability and responsibility, insight, productivity, candor, and calmness. They value their independence and autonomy as well as their intellectual skill and behave in a sympathetic and considerate manner, consistent with their personal standards and ethics (Peskin & Livson, 1981).

A second longitudinal study that has been used to identify the factors that lead to success in life was the Grant Study, which was most recently directed by psychiatrist George Vaillant (1977). This study began in 1939 and included male Harvard students. The study continued to collect data on these participants until the end of their lives, some 70 years later. Vaillant was interested in finding a set of objective criteria reflecting *psychosocial adjustment* and then determining what factors in the men's childhood or adult lives predict good or poor psychosocial adjustment.

STUDY RESULTS   Despite their quite different strategies for measuring successful aging, the findings from the Berkeley and Grant studies are reasonably consistent and lead to some intriguing suggestions about the ingredients of a healthy or successful adult life. Both studies show that the most successful and well-adjusted middle-aged adults had grown up in warm, supportive, intellectually stimulating families (Vaillant & Vaillant, 1990). In the Berkeley study, researchers found that those who were higher in psychological health at age 30 or 40 had grown up with parents who were rated as more open-minded and more intellectually competent, with good marital relationships. Their mothers had been warmer, more giving and nondefensive, more pleasant and poised (Peskin & Livson, 1981). Similarly, the men who were rated as having the best adjustment at midlife had come from warmer families and had had better relationships with both their fathers and mothers in childhood than had the least well-adjusted men (Vaillant, 1974).

Both studies also show that well-adjusted or successful middle-aged adults began adulthood with more personal resources, including better-rated psychological and physical health at college age, a practical, well-organized approach in college, and greater intellectual competence. Both of these sets of findings are pretty much what we might expect. To put it most directly, those who age well are those who start out well. To be sure, none of the correlations is terribly large, so even among the midlife participants there were some who began with two strikes against them but nonetheless looked healthy and successful at age 45 or 50 and some who started out with many advantages but did not turn out well. But in general, the findings point to a kind of consistency up until midlife.

Yet when the researchers looked at their participants again at retirement age, a very different picture appeared. Among these 173 men, no measure of early family environment remained a significant predictor of psychosocial adjustment at 63, nor did any measure of early-adult intellectual competence. Those who turned out to be "successful" 63-year-olds had been rated as slightly more personally integrated when they were in college, and they had had slightly better relationships with their siblings. But other than that, there were simply no childhood or early-adulthood characteristics that differentiated those who had turned out well and those who had turned out less well.

What does predict health and adjustment at age 63 among these men is health and adjustment at midlife. The least successful 63-year-olds were those who had used mood-altering drugs at midlife (primarily prescribed drugs intended to deal with depression or anxiety), abused alcohol or smoked heavily, and used mostly immature defense mechanisms in their 30s and 40s.

STUDY CONSIDERATIONS These findings come from only a single study, one that only included men, and only very well-educated professional men at that. So we shouldn't make too many huge theoretical leaps from this empirical platform. Still, the pattern of results suggests one (or both) of two possibilities:

1. It may be that each era in adult life simply calls for different skills and qualities, so that what predicts success or healthy adjustment at one age is simply not the same as what predicts it at another age. As one example, college-aged intellectual competence may be a better predictor of psychosocial health at midlife simply because at midlife adults are still in the midst of their most productive working years, when intellectual skill is more central. By retirement age, this may not be so critical an ingredient.

2. Alternatively, we might think of a successful adult life not as something preordained by one's childhood or early-adult qualities, but as something created from the resources and opportunities available over the

Many long-term studies show that the best predictor of successful aging is good health and adjustment in middle age.

How might advantages, resources, and opportunities over a lifetime differ for a trans woman of color than for the men of the Grant study? How might these impact her life satisfaction as she grows older?

course of the decades. Those who start out with certain familial and personal advantages have a greater chance of encountering still further advantages, but it is what one does with the experiences—stressful as well as constructive—that determines the long-term success or psychosocial health one achieves. The choices we make in early adulthood help to shape the people we become in midlife; our midlife qualities in turn help to shape the kind of older people we become—a process I might describe as cumulative continuity. Early-childhood environment or personal qualities such as personality or intellectual competence are not unimportant, but by age 65 their influence is indirect rather than direct.

It seems likely that both of these options are at least partially true, but it is the second possibility that I find especially compelling. It helps to make sense of a series of other facts and findings.

CHILDLESS MEN IN OLDER ADULTHOOD One relevant fragment comes from yet another longitudinal study in which George Vaillant has been involved, in this case of a group of 343 Boston men, all white, and nearly all from lower-class or working-class families. As teenagers, these men had been part of a nondelinquent comparison group in a major study of delinquency originated by criminologists Sheldon Glueck and Eleanor Glueck (1950, 1968). They had been interviewed at length when they were in early adolescence and were then reinterviewed by the Gluecks when they were age 25 and 31 and by Vaillant and his colleagues

when they were in their late 40s. In one analysis by the Vaillant group (Snarey et al., 1987), the researchers looked at the outcomes for those men who had not had children at the normative time to see how they had handled their childlessness.

Of the group of childless men, those independently rated at age 47 as clearly generative in Erikson's terms were likely to have responded by finding someone else's child to parent, such as by adopting a child, joining an organization like Big Brothers/Big Sisters, or becoming an active uncle. Those childless men who were rated low in generativity at 47 were much less likely to have adopted a child; if they had chosen a substitute it was more likely a pet. Among the childless men, the generative and the nongenerative had not differed at the beginning of adult life in either social class or level of industry, so the eventual differences in psychosocial maturity do not seem to be the result of differences that existed at age 20. Rather, they seem to be a result of the way the men responded to or coped with an unexpected or nonnormative event in early adult life, namely childlessness.

The central point is that there are many pathways through adulthood. The pathway each of us follows is affected by the departure point, but it is the choices we make as we go along, and our ability to learn from the experiences that confront us, that shape the people we become 50 or 60 years later. If we are going to understand the journey of adulthood, we need a model that will allow us to make some order of the diversity of lifetimes that results from such choices and such learning or lack of it.

Your Own Quality of Life

How is your quality of life these days? Using yourself or someone you know as an example, tell what factors are influencing your (or their) current quality of life.

> The response entered here will appear in the performance dashboard and can be viewed by your instructor.

Submit

12.3: A Model of Adult Growth and Development

OBJECTIVE: Analyze adulthood according to models of growth and development

I am sure it is clear to you already that the model I have sketched in this chapter, complex as it is, is nonetheless too simplistic. It is doubtless also too culture specific, although I have tried to state the elements of the model broadly enough to encompass patterns across cultures. It may also be quite wrong in a number of respects.

Despite these obvious limitations, however, the model may give you some sense of the rules or laws that seem to govern the richness and variety of adult life. In the midst of a bewildering array of adult patterns there does appear to be order, but the order is not so much in fixed, age-related sequences of events as in process. To understand adult development, it is useful to uncover the ways in which all the pathways, all the gullies, are alike. But it is equally important to understand the factors and processes that affect the choices adults will have and the way they will respond to those choices as individuals.

With that in mind, let me offer a set of four propositions.

By the end of this module, you will be able to:

12.3.1 Explain the concept of a sequential process of adulthood

12.3.2 Identify the elements that impact a life trajectory

12.3.3 Compare the roles of stability and instability on a life trajectory

12.3.4 Differentiate the impacts of positive and negative variables on adult development

12.3.1: Proposition 1

OBJECTIVE: Explain the concept of a sequential process of adulthood

There are shared, basic sequential physical and psychological developments occurring during adulthood, roughly (but not precisely) age linked.

What are some sequential features common to adulthood in your culture?

Whatever other processes may influence adult life, it is clear that the entire journey occurs along a road with certain common features. The body and the mind change in predictable ways with age. These changes, in turn, affect the way adults define themselves and the way they experience the world around them. I place the sequence of changes in self-definition or meaning system in the same category. The difference is that unlike physical and mental changes, the process of ego development or spiritual change is not an inevitable accompaniment of aging, but a possibility or potentiality.

Within the general confines of these basic processes and sequences of development, however, there are many individual pathways—many possible sequences of roles and relationships, many different levels of growth or life satisfaction or "success."

12.3.2: Proposition 2

OBJECTIVE: Identify the elements that impact a life trajectory

Each adult's development occurs primarily within a specific pathway or trajectory, strongly influenced by the starting conditions of education, family background, ethnicity, intelligence, and personality.

I can best depict this individuality by borrowing biologist Conrad Waddington's (1957) image of the epigenetic landscape, a variation of which is shown in Figure 12.5. Waddington introduced this idea in a discussion of the strongly "canalized" development of embryos, but the same concept can serve for a discussion of adult development. The original Waddington image was of a mountain with a series of gullies running down it. He demonstrated how a marble placed at the top had an almost infinite number of possibilities for its final destination at the bottom of the mountain, due to the many possible intersections of gullies and ravines. However, because some of the gullies are deeper than others, some outcomes have a greater probability than others. In my version of this metaphor, the bottom of the mountain represents late adulthood, and the top of the mountain represents young adulthood. In our adult years, each of us must somehow make our way down the mountain. Because we are all going down the same mountain (following the same basic path of physical, mental, and spiritual development), all journeys will have some features in common. But this metaphor also allows for wide variations in the specific events and outcomes of the journey.

Figure 12.5 Journey of Adulthood and the Quality of Outcome

One way to illustrate the journey of adulthood is with the image of a mountain landscape. One begins the journey at the top and follows along in the ravines and gullies toward the bottom. There are many options and alternative paths, and the landscape changes as cultural and social changes occur.

SOURCE: Adapted from Waddington (1957).

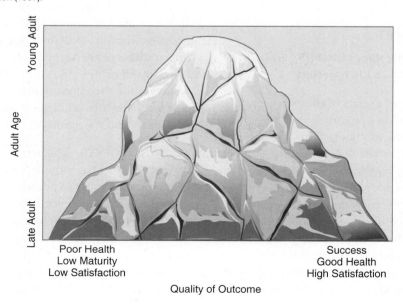

Imagine a marble placed in one of the gullies at the top of the mountain. The pathway it follows to the bottom of the mountain will be heavily influenced by the gully in which it starts. If I also assume that the main pathways are deeper than the side tracks, then shifting from the track in which one starts is less probable than continuing along the same track. Nonetheless, the presence of choice points or junctions makes it possible for marbles starting in the same gully to end up in widely varying places at the bottom of the mountain. From any given starting point, some pathways and some outcomes are much more likely than others. But many possible pathways diverge from any one gully. In addition, the landscape is constantly shifting in response to environmental changes, such as cultural or historical influences and changes in health.

This model or metaphor certainly fits with the general findings from Vaillant's long-term study of the Grant study men. The gully one starts in certainly does have an effect on where you are likely to be on the mountain at midlife. But the eventual endpoint is much more strongly linked to where you were at midlife than where you started out. One might depict this idea using the mountain-and-gully model by showing the main gullies becoming deeper and deeper (harder to get out of) as you trace them down the mountain.

The model also fits with another finding I mentioned earlier in this chapter that there is an increase in the variability of scores on various measures of health, mental skills, personality, and attitudes with increasing age. In early adulthood, the various alternative gullies are more like each other (closer together) than is true 40 or 60 years later.

Still another feature implicit in Figure 12.5 as I have drawn it is significant enough to state as a separate proposition.

12.3.3: Proposition 3

OBJECTIVE: Compare the roles of stability and instability on a life trajectory

Each pathway is made up of a series of alternating episodes of stable life structure and disequilibrium.

In the mountain-and-gully metaphor, the stable life structures are reflected in the long, straight stretches between junction points; the junctions represent the disequilibria. I conceive of each stable life structure as the balance one achieves among the collection of role demands one is then facing, given the skills and temperamental qualities at one's command. This balance is normally reflected in a stable, externally observable life pattern: getting up at a particular time every day to get the kids off to school, going off to your job, doing the grocery shopping on Saturday,

having dinner with your mother every Sunday, going out to dinner with your spouse every Valentine's Day. It is also reflected in the quality and specific features of relationships and in the meaning system through which we filter all these experiences. These patterns are not totally fixed, of course. We all make small adjustments regularly, as demands or opportunities change. But there do appear to be times in each adult's life when a temporary balance is achieved.

THE RELATIONSHIP OF STABLE PERIODS AND AGE
These alternating periods of stability and disequilibrium or transition appear to be related to age. I have suggested a rough age linkage in Figure 12.5 by showing more choice points at some levels of the mountain than at others. It seems to me that the content of the stable structures at each approximate age, and the issues dealt with during each transition, are somewhat predictable. After all, we are going down/along the same mountain. There is a set of tasks or issues that confront most adults in a particular sequence as they age, as I outlined in Table 12.1. In early adulthood this includes separating from one's family of origin, creating a stable central partnership, bearing and beginning to rear children, and establishing satisfying work.

In middle adulthood the tasks include launching one's children into independence, caring for aging parents, redefining parental and spousal roles, exploring one's own inner nature, and coming to terms with the aging of one's body and with the death of one's parents. An adult who follows the modal "social clock" will thus be likely to encounter transitions at certain ages and to deal with shared issues at each transition. But I am not persuaded that there is only one order, or only one set of ages, at which these tasks are or can be confronted. In this respect the mountain-and-gully model is misleading because it does not convey the variability in the timing of major choice points, such as what happens when an adult does not marry, does not have children until his or her 30s or 40s, becomes physically disabled or widowed or ill in the early adult years, or the like. But whatever the variations in timing, it still appears to me to be valid to describe adult life as alternating between periods of stability and transition.

TURNING POINTS The periods of disequilibrium, which we might think of as turning points in individual lives, may be triggered by any one or more of a whole series of events. There is no way to depict these in the mountain-and-gully model, so I have to turn to a more common kind of two-dimensional diagram, the (very complicated!) flowchart or path diagram as shown in Figure 12.6.

Let's discuss the major sources of disequilibrium listed on the left-hand side of Figure 12.6.

Figure 12.6 Sources of Disequilibrium

I know this is complicated, but take a crack at it anyway. This is a model of disequilibrium and its resolution. I am suggesting that such a process occurs repeatedly during adulthood, with the effects of these transitions accumulating over time. Each such transition affects the pathway (the gully) along which the adult then moves.

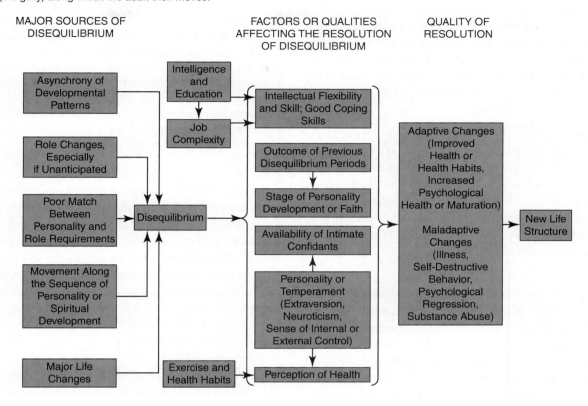

Major Sources of Disequilibrium

Asynchrony of Developmental Patterns—**Asynchrony of developmental patterns** occur in the several different dimensions of adult change or growth. When physical development, mental development, or role patterns are out of sync, there is tension or disequilibrium in the system. Being significantly off-time in any one dimension of adulthood automatically creates asynchrony and is thus associated with higher rates of stress. Having a first child in your late 30s is not only a role change but also an asynchronous role change, which should increase the likelihood of a major disequilibrium, just as will the failure to have children at all, as among the childless men in the Glueck-Vaillant study of working-class men mentioned earlier. The general rule, as I have indicated, is that on-time role changes seldom trigger major crises or self-reexamination precisely because they are shared with one's peers. You can easily explain both the change and the strain it may cause as originating "outside" yourself. Nonnormative changes, by contrast, are difficult to explain away except with reference to your own choices or failures or successes.

These more individual experiences, then, are far more likely than the normative ones to bring about reassessment or redefinition of the self, of values, and of systems of meaning.

Role Transitions—**Role transitions** include becoming a spouse or a parent, the departure of the last child from home, retirement, and changes in jobs.

Poor Match Between Personality and Role Requirements—This is, in some sense, another kind of asynchrony. For example, research shows that adults who looked psychologically healthy at age 50 but had shown signs of distress or disturbance at 40 were likely to have had qualities as teenagers that didn't match the then-prevalent gender roles. The less social and more intellectual young women in this group tried to fit into a mold of full-time homemaking and found it distressing; the more creative and emotional men tried to fit into the mold of the gray-flannel-suit society and were disturbed at age 40. Both groups went through a process in their 40s of freeing themselves of the constraints of those early, ill-fitting roles and emerged at 50 looking very much put together (Livson, 1981).

Personality or Spiritual Development—**Personality or spiritual development** can trigger disequilibrium, such as any movement along the dimensions described by Erikson or by Fowler's stages of faith. Such inner changes typically occur in response to the disequilibrium-causing agents I have just described. But once begun, a transition, say from conformist to conscientious ego structure, or from individuative to conjunctive faith, carries its own disequilibrium. Any new stable life structure that emerges at the end of the disequilibrium period must be built on the new sense of self, or faith, that has evolved.

Major Life Changes—**Major life changes** are particularly losses in relationships, such as the death of a close family member or friend or the loss of a friendship or love relationship. Although unanticipated or off-time changes may be the most difficult in most instances, anticipated changes that involve such relationship losses, such as the death of your parents when you are in your 40s or 50s, still call for significant reassessment and reorganization.

Whether a person will experience a disequilibrium period as a crisis or merely as a rather transitory phase seems to depend on at least two things: the number of different sources of disequilibrium and the individual's own personality and coping skills. When there is a pileup of disequilibrium-producing events within a narrow span of years—such as changes in roles, major relationship losses, and asynchronous physical changes—anyone is likely to experience a major transition. But the tendency to respond to this pileup as a crisis may also reflect relatively high levels of neuroticism, low levels of extraversion, or the lack of effective coping skills.

In the model I am proposing here, it is our response to these disequilibrium periods that determines our pathway down the mountain, which leads me to the fourth basic proposition.

12.3.4: Proposition 4

OBJECTIVE: Differentiate the impacts of positive and negative variables on adult development

The outcome of periods of disequilibrium may be either positive (psychological growth, maturity, improved health), neutral, or negative (regression or immaturity, ill health).

What kind of outcome occurs at any choice point—which channel one follows—is determined or affected by a wide range of variables. Intellectual flexibility or skill seems to be an especially critical ingredient in leading to the "higher" stages of maturity and growth that Vaillant and Loevinger describe. Our adult intellectual flexibility, in turn,

is influenced by the complexity of the environments in which we live, particularly complexity on the job (either a job outside the home or even housework). Sociologist Janet Giele (1982) put it well:

> It is the degree of social complexity on the job or in other aspects of everyday life that appears critical. Those who must learn a great deal and adapt to many different roles seem to be the most concerned with trying to evolve an abstract self, conscience, or life structure that can integrate all these discrete events. By contrast, those with a simple job, limited by meager education and narrow contacts, are less apt to experience aging as a process that enhances autonomy or elaborates one's mental powers. (p. 8)

And, of course, job complexity is itself partially determined by the level of education we have attained. Well-educated adults are more likely to find complex jobs and are thus more likely to maintain or increase their intellectual flexibility. Linkages such as these help create the pattern of predictability between early adulthood and midlife, but because none of these relationships is anywhere near a perfect correlation, there is a good deal of room for shifts from one gully to another. Some blue-collar jobs, for example, are quite complex, whereas some white-collar jobs are not, and such variations may tend to push people out of the groove in which they started.

Underlying temperamental tendencies are another key ingredient. Adults who are high in what Costa and McCrae call *Neuroticism* appear to be more likely to respond to disequilibrium by increases in substance abuse, illness, depression, or regressive patterns of defense. Adults with less neurotic or more extraverted temperaments, in contrast, respond to disequilibrium by reaching out to others and by searching for constructive solutions.

The availability of close supportive confidants is also a significant factor, clearly not independent of temperament. Adults who lack close friends or the supportive intimacy of a good marriage are more likely to have serious physical ailments in midlife or to have significant emotional disturbances, to drink or use drugs, and to use more immature forms of defense. Friendless or lonely adults more often come from unloving and unsupportive families, but a poor early environment can be overcome more readily if the adult manages to form at least one close, intimate relationship. Vaillant described several men in the Grant study who had grown up in unloving or highly stressful families and were withdrawn or even fairly neurotic as college students, but nonetheless went on to become successful and emotionally mature adults. One of the common ingredients in the lives of these men, especially compared to those with similar backgrounds who had poorer outcomes, was the presence of a "healing" relationship with a spouse. Similarly, sociologist

David Quinton and his colleagues (1993) looked at the adult lives of several groups of young people in England, some of whom had had teenage histories of delinquency. They found that a continuation of problem behavior (such as criminality) was far less likely when the person had a nondeviant, supportive partner than when the problem teen later joined up with a nonsupportive or problem partner. Thus, early maladaptive behavior can be redirected, or "healed," through an appropriately supportive partner relationship. Health may also make some difference in the way an adult responds to a period of disequilibrium. Poor health reduces options; it also reduces your level of energy, which affects the range of coping strategies open to you or the eventual life structures you can create.

CUMULATIVE EFFECTS OF TRANSITIONS   As a final point, I would argue that the effects of these several disequilibrium periods are cumulative, a process that sociologist Gunhild Hagestad and psychologist Bernice Neugarten (1985) described as the "transition domino effect." The cumulative effect of earlier stages or transitions is a key element in Erikson's theory of development. Unresolved conflicts and dilemmas remain as unfinished business—excess emotional baggage that makes each succeeding stage more difficult to resolve successfully. Vaillant and others who have studied adults from childhood through midlife have found some support for this notion. Harvard men in the Grant study who could reasonably be described as having failed to develop trust in their early childhood did have many more difficulties in the first few decades of adulthood. They were more pessimistic, self-doubting, passive, and dependent as adults and showed many more maladaptive or unsuccessful outcomes compared to those with more trusting childhoods.

Other forms of cumulative effect operate as well. One major off-time experience early in life, for example, may trigger a whole series of subsequent off-time or stressful experiences. The most obvious example is the impact of adolescent parenthood, which often leads to early school departure, which in turn affects the complexity of the job one is likely to find, which affects intellectual flexibility, and so on through the years.

ADAPTIVE OR MALADAPTIVE OUTCOMES VERSUS HAPPINESS   It is important to emphasize that the range of possible outcomes I have labeled adaptive and maladaptive changes are not identical to happiness and unhappiness. Maladaptive changes such as illness, substance abuse, suicide attempts, or depression are obviously correlated with unhappiness. But such adaptive changes as improved health habits, increased social activity, or movement along the sequence of stages of ego or spiritual development are not uniformly associated with increases in happiness. For example, McCrae and Costa (1983) did not find that adults at the conscientious or higher levels of ego development reported any higher life satisfaction than did adults at the conformist stage. Thus, profound changes can result from a disequilibrium period without being reflected in alterations of overall happiness or life satisfaction. Instead, a change in the ego-development stage may alter the criteria of happiness one applies to one's life. As McCrae and Costa say:

> We suggest that the quality and quantity of happiness do not vary with levels of maturity, but that the circumstances that occasion happiness or unhappiness, the criteria of satisfaction or dissatisfaction with life, may vary with ego level. The needs and concerns, aspirations and irritations of more mature individuals will doubtless be different—more subtle, more individualistic, less egocentric. The less psychologically mature person may evaluate his or her life in terms of money, status, and sex; the more mature, in terms of achievement, altruism, and love. (p. 247)

Maturing does not automatically make an adult happy, as demonstrated by (among other things) the lack of correlation between age and happiness. Maturing and other adaptive changes alter the agenda and thus alter the life structures we create and the way we evaluate those life structures.

WRITING PROMPT

Choosing Paths

Give an example of a deep main pathway you have been on and a choice point you reached to change paths. How would you describe the effort involved in moving from a deep gully to an alternative pathway?

 The response entered here will appear in the performance dashboard and can be viewed by your instructor.

Submit

12.4: Successful Aging

OBJECTIVE: Determine the elements of successful aging

A generation ago, college students taking a course in adulthood and aging would have a far different text book than this one. Chances are it would catalog various categories of physical health that decline with age and numerous abilities that are lost when individuals reach certain milestones. As you have undoubtedly noticed, things have changed, and I hope you are taking away a different picture of adulthood development and aging that has a more positive message. If so, you can thank proponents of a school of thought called "successful aging."

First, Paul Baltes and his colleagues (1980) were the forerunners of successful aging with their *lifespan developmental psychology approach*, in which they told us that there are interesting things going on after adolescence that are worth studying; it is not just overall loss and decline. There are interesting changes that can be measured, and they are not all deterioration; there are gains in many areas. Development takes place in the context of our lives. Many types of decline can be modified, prevented, or delayed. We can compensate for many types of losses, and these changes are topics of study in many disciplines besides psychology. Second, Urie Bronfenbrenner (1979) told us with his *ecological systems approach* that we can't learn much just studying the individuals' developmental process. We have to consider the ecology surrounding them. Adult development does not take place in a vacuum, but is influenced by family, social group, workplace, neighborhood, racial-ethnic group, and even the political system that operates in one's country.

In 1998, gerontologist John W. Rowe and psychologist Robert L. Kahn published the results of the MacArthur Foundation Study in a popular book titled *Successful Aging*. Instead of following the downhill path older people take from age 60 on, they concentrated on the many older adults that remain physically and mentally strong throughout their lives. They found that although genetics provide the blueprint for our early development, they become less and less important as we grow older and the environment takes center stage. The good news is that many aspects of the environment are under our own control, such as what we eat, how often we exercise, and how we spend our leisure time. This book gave adults of all ages a better view of what aging is for many people and what it may be for them if they made modifications in their lifestyles and attitudes.

Following the concept of successful aging, researchers concentrated on five strategies to help adults of all ages improve their quality of life in the present and help ensure their successful aging in older and late adulthood (Depp et al., 2014).

▼   **By the end of this module, you will be able to:**

12.4.1   **Relate physical and mental exercise to successful aging**

12.4.2   **Explain the role of social engagement on successful aging**

12.4.3   **Summarize data on the role of diet on successful aging**

12.4.4   **Describe the benefits of meditation and yoga**

12.4.1: Physical and Mental Exercise

OBJECTIVE: **Relate physical and mental exercise to successful aging**

The American College of Sports Medicine has recommended at least 150 minutes of moderate physical exercise a week, or 30 minutes five times a week (Chodzko-Zajko et al., 2009). Adults of all ages who manage to do this have lower levels of cardiovascular disease, diabetes, and osteoarthritis. Adults who are physically active have lower levels of cognitive decline, depression, and anxiety. Table 12.4 highlights some recommendations for adult exercise.

Exercising the mind, too, has its benefits. A review of 21 studies have shown that cognitive training in a controlled setting may improve specific mental functions, such as memory performance, processing speed, executive function, attention, and fluid intelligence, although it is not clear whether these improvements will generalize to memory

---

Table 12.4 Exercise Recommendations for All Adults

Adults should move more and sit less throughout the day. Some physical activity is better than none. Adults who sit less and do any amount of moderate-to-vigorous physical activity gain some health benefits.

For substantial health benefits, adults should do at least 150 minutes (2 hours and 30 minutes) to 300 minutes (5 hours) a week of moderate-intensity, or 75 minutes (1 hour and 15 minutes) to 150 minutes (2 hours and 30 minutes) a week of vigorous-intensity aerobic physical activity, or an equivalent combination of moderate- and vigorous-intensity aerobic activity. Preferably, aerobic activity should be spread throughout the week.

Additional health benefits are gained by engaging in physical activity beyond the equivalent of 300 minutes (5 hours) of moderate-intensity physical activity a week.

Adults should also do muscle-strengthening activities of moderate or greater intensity and that involve all major muscle groups on 2 or more days a week, as these activities provide additional health benefits.

Recommendations for Older Adults or Adults with Chronic Health Conditions

As part of their weekly physical activity, older adults should do multicomponent physical activity that includes balance training as well as aerobic and muscle-strengthening activities.

Older adults should determine their level of effort for physical activity relative to their level of fitness.

Older adults with chronic conditions should understand whether and how their conditions affect their ability to do regular physical activity safely.

When older adults cannot do 150 minutes of moderate-intensity aerobic activity a week because of chronic conditions, they should be as physically active as their abilities and conditions allow.

SOURCE: U.S. Department of Health and Human Services (2018).

tasks of everyday living (Reijnders et al., 2013). Casual gaming, which involves commercially produced apps of "brain games," are used by 200 million people in the world. These apps have been advertised as products that improve cognitive abilities in older adults and prevent dementia. Numerous studies of these casual games have shown there is no evidence that playing these games improves cognitive abilities and, more importantly, no mental exercise has been shown to prevent or cure dementias such as Alzheimer's disease (Willis & Belleville, 2016). A better idea is to join a bridge club or chess club where you will get a mental workout along with social engagement.

12.4.2: Social Engagement

OBJECTIVE: Explain the role of social engagement on successful aging

People of any age who have regular social contact with family and friends enjoy better health and well-being than those who are more isolated, but it is especially true in later adulthood (Cherry et al., 2013). Various studies have shown the physical and mental health benefits of number of friends, number of hours spent outside the home, and number of types of relationships, such as family, friends, neighbors, social club members, and golf buddies. Figure 12.7 shows that the greater the number of social roles an older adult has, the better their score on cognitive tests (Ellwardt et al., 2015). Interventions aimed at improving social skills and increasing chances for social contact have been successful in adults of all ages (Masi et al., 2011).

WRITING PROMPT

Social Networks and Your Life

Describe one aspect of your social network, either currently or in the past. How has it helped improve your quality of life?

▶ The response entered here will appear in the performance dashboard and can be viewed by your instructor.

Submit

12.4.3: Diet and Nutrition

OBJECTIVE: Summarize data on the role of diet on successful aging

Caloric restriction is related to greater longevity in laboratory animals and also, in early clinical trials, humans. Many studies of the effectiveness of supplements, such as ginkgo biloba and vitamin D have not shown that they provide any benefits to memory or other cognitive processes. However, following the Mediterranean diet has been found to lower the risk for cognitive decline and to reduce rates of cardiovascular disease and depression (Scarmeas et al., 2009). This diet is a plant-based diet that replaces saturated fats (butter) with polyunsaturated fats (olive oil), replaces salt with herbs and spices, limits red meat to once or twice a month, and includes fish and/or poultry at least twice a week.

Figure 12.7 Social Roles and Cognition

The more social roles, the better the cognition, at least for older adults.

SOURCE: Ellwardt et al. (2015).

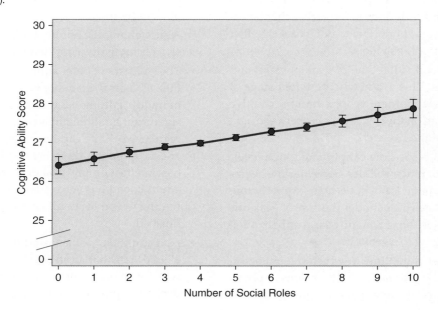

12.4.4: Complementary and Alternative Medicine

OBJECTIVE: **Describe the benefits of meditation and yoga**

The practice of yoga is very old, but the research exploring its effectiveness is fairly recent. In one study of women age 45–80 who practiced yoga, those who did it regularly reported more positive attitudes, mental mastery, and feelings of vitality than those who practices it less regularly (Moliver et al., 2013). In another study, older men and women who had sleep problems participated in yoga classes twice a week for 12 weeks. At the end of that time, they reported significant improvements in sleep quality and general well-being, with lower levels of fatigue, depression, anxiety, and stress (Halpern et al., 2014).

Another practice that has become popular is meditation. Older adults who had meditated for more than 10 years performed better on tests of cognitive skills than those who did not meditate at all (Prakash et al., 2012).

Perhaps the most remarkable thing about this journey is that, with all its potential pitfalls and dilemmas, most adults pass through it with reasonable happiness and satisfaction, acquiring a modicum of wisdom on the way to pass along to those who travel behind them. May your journey be successful!

Practicing yoga is just one of many practices that may increase overall well-being.

Summary: The Successful Journey

12.1 Themes of Adult Development

OBJECTIVE: **Summarize major themes in adult development**

- To understand adult development, it is important to divide it into topics, as is done in the earlier chapters of this book. But it is also important to put it back together again and view people as wholes.

- Emerging adulthood is the time of peak physical and cognitive abilities. This is a newly identified stage of adulthood defined by identity exploration, positive instability, focusing on the self, feeling in-between, and imagining possibilities.

- Young adulthood is the time of continued high levels of physical and cognitive abilities. Some decline begins as early as age 30, but it is not noticeable except for top-performing athletes. This period is the time of peak role transitions, relationship formation, and tribalization (a sense of belonging to a group).

- Middle adulthood is the time in which the biological clock begins to tick noticeably. The first signs of physical aging appear and the first signs of cognitive decline, though it is slight. Reproductive ability declines for both men and women, and then ends for women. The social clock becomes less loud. There is more flexibility in family roles and careers. There is time to question the rules and actions of the tribe and to become more of an individual.

- Although middle adulthood is known as a time of crisis, this myth does not stand up to empirical research.

- The hallmark of older adulthood is retirement. There is little biological difference between this group and those in middle adulthood, but the social differences can be significant if retirement is considered. The end of one's regular work life can have major financial and social effects, although there is no evidence that retirement has an effect on physical or mental health. Most older adults spend this stage adapting to a new lifestyle and finding new roles to fill now that the role of worker is finished.

- Late adulthood is the fastest-growing age group in the United States and in all developed countries. As a result, we know more about this age than ever before. The slow decline in physical and cognitive abilities that began back in early adulthood speeds up in late adulthood. This is accompanied by a decrease in social activities and social networks. However, most people this age enjoy fewer but closer relationships. The hypothesis that those who disengage from the world are mentally healthier has not held up to close examination.

- Late adulthood is a time for reviewing one's life and perhaps coming to grips with one's eventual death. Some adults in this time of life write memoirs or mend fences with former friends and family members.

12.2 Variations in Successful Development

OBJECTIVE: Evaluate measures of life success

- Although this book emphasizes the typical pathways through adulthood, there are many variations that can lead to success and well-being.
- Quality of life for adulthood in the United States depends highly on socioeconomic status and health. These two factors explain many of the more distal predictors, such as race and gender. Another factor is age, with older adults reporting greater quality of life than middle-aged or young adults. Those who are happily married, participate in physical and social activities, feel they have control over their lives, and base their comparisons on others their age also report higher quality of life.

12.3 A Model of Adult Growth and Development

OBJECTIVE: Analyze adulthood according to models of growth and development

- Despite the variability in adult development, most of us have similarities in our journeys of adulthood, and these journeys are strongly influenced by our education, family background, intelligence, and personality.

- The developmental pathways we travel along are made up of alternating stable times and times of disequilibrium. The periods of disequilibrium can result in positive change, negative change, or neutral outcomes.

12.4 Successful Aging

OBJECTIVE: Determine the elements of successful aging

- Most adults pass through adulthood with reasonable happiness and satisfaction, picking up some wisdom along the way and passing it along to those who come behind them.

SHARED WRITING

Success in Life

Consider this chapter's discussion of "success in life." How do you measure success in life and why does this matter? How do your measurements of success compare to those of your parents' generation? Write a short response that your classmates will read. Be sure to give concrete reasons in your discussion.

► A minimum number of characters is required to post and earn points. After posting, your response can be viewed by your class and instructor, and you can participate in the class discussion.

Post   0 characters | 140 minimum

Glossary

ability–expertise tradeoff   observation that as general ability declines with age, job expertise increases.

accommodate   ability of the lens of the eye to change shape to focus on near or far objects, or small print.

acute conditions   short-term health disorders.

acute stress disorder   reactions to trauma that are similar to PTSD, but diminish within a month.

adaptive nature of cognition   how cognitive abilities adapt to life changes across a lifetime.

addictive disorders   disorders typified by intense desire for and compulsion to use a substance or complete an action, such as gambling, when any related triggers are present.

ADLs (activities of daily living)   basic self-care activities.

adult development   changes that take place within individuals as they progress from emerging adulthood to the end of life.

ageism   discrimination against those who are in a later (or earlier) period of adulthood.

age-related macular degeneration   visual disorder of the retina, causing central vision loss.

aging in place   the ability of older people to remain in their own homes their whole lives.

Alzheimer's disease   progressive, incurable deterioration of key areas of the brain.

antibodies   proteins that react to foreign organisms such as viruses and other infectious agents.

antioxidants   substances that protect against oxidative damage from free radicals.

anxiety disorders   category of mental health disorders that involves feelings of fear, threat, and dread when no obvious danger is present.

atherosclerosis   process by which fat-laden deposits called plaques form in the artery walls.

attachment   strong affectional bond an infant forms with his or her caregivers.

attachment behaviors   outward expressions of attachment.

attachment orientation   patterns of expectations, needs, and emotions one exhibits in interpersonal relationships that extend beyond the early attachment figures.

attachment theory   Bowlby's theory that infants form strong affectional bonds with their caregivers that provide basic security and understanding of the world and serve as a foundation for later relationships.

attrition   dropout rate of participants during a study.

atypical   not typical; unique to the individual.

average lifespan   the number that comes from adding up the ages at which everyone in a certain population dies and then dividing by the number of people in that population.

B cells   cells of the immune system produced in the bone marrow that manufacture antibodies.

balance   ability to adapt one's body position to change.

behavioral genetics   study of the contributions genes make to individual behavior.

bioecological model   model of development proposed by Bronfenbrenner that points out that we must consider the developing person within the context of multiple environments.

biological age   measure of an individual's physical condition.

biological clock   patterns of change over adulthood in health and physical functioning.

body mass index (BMI)   number derived from a person's weight and height; a standard indicator of body composition.

bone mass density (BMD)   measurement of bone density used to diagnose osteoporosis.

bridge employment   part-time job or less stressful full-time job usually taken after retirement.

buffering effect   pattern of results that cushion the outcomes of a distressing situation.

caloric restriction (CR)   diet in which calories are severely reduced, but containing essential nutrients; found to slow down aging in animal studies.

cancer   disease in which abnormal cells undergo rapidly accelerated, uncontrolled division and later move into adjacent normal tissues.

cardiovascular disease   disorder of the heart and blood vessels that occurs more frequently with age.

career   patterns and sequences of occupations or related roles held by people across their working lives and into retirement.

career commitment   factor that plays a role in how long an individual remains in his or her job.

career recycling   in vocational psychology, the notion that people may go back and revisit earlier stages of career development.

caregiving orientation   system that is activated in adults when they interact with infants and young children, causing them to respond to the appearance and behavior of younger members of the species (and often other species) by providing security, comfort, and protection.

cataracts   visual disorder characterized by gradual clouding of the lens of the eye.

change   slow and gradual movement in a predictable direction.

chronic conditions   long-term health disorders.

chronic traumatic encephalopathy (CTE)   type of dementia that has increased prevalence for individuals who have suffered traumatic brain injury (TBI).

chronological age   number of years that have passed since birth.

climacteric   time of life for men and women that involves the reduction of sex hormone production resulting in the loss of reproductive ability.

cochlea   small shell-shaped structure in the inner ear containing auditory receptor cells.

cognitive complexity   higher levels of thinking and reasoning.

cohabitation   living together in an intimate partnership without marriage.

cohort   group of people who share a common historical experience at the same stage of life.

commonalities   aspects that are typical of adult life.

communal qualities personal characteristics that nurture and bring people together, such as being expressive and affectionate; stereotypical female qualities.

community dwelling living in one's own home either with a spouse or alone.

comparison of means statistical analysis that allows researchers to determine whether the difference in measurements taken on two groups are large enough to be considered statistically significant.

complementary and alternative medicine providers healthcare providers whose treatments are not supported by scientific data.

contextual perspective approach to cognition that considers the context within which thought processes take place.

continuous property of development that is slow and gradual, taking us in a predictable direction.

convoy ever-changing network of social relationships that surrounds each of us throughout our lives.

coping behaviors thoughts, feelings, and actions that serve to reduce the effects of stressful events.

coping ways to reduce the effects of stress reactions.

correlational analysis statistical analysis that tells us the extent to which two sets of scores on the same individuals vary together.

cross-sectional study in the study of development, research method in which data is gathered at one time from groups of participants who represent different age groups.

crystallized intelligence learned abilities based on education and experience, measured by vocabulary and by verbal comprehension.

cultures large social environment in which development takes place.

cyclic GMP substance released by the brain during sexual arousal.

dark adaptation ability of the pupil of the eye to adjust to changes in the amount of available light.

death anxiety fear of death.

decentering cognitive movement outward from the self.

declarative memory knowledge that is available to conscious awareness and can be assessed by recall or recognition tests.

defense mechanism in Vaillant's theory of mature adaptation, the set of normal, unconscious strategies used for dealing with anxiety.

dementia category of various types of brain damage and disease that involve significant impairment of memory, judgment, social functioning, and control of emotions.

descriptive research type of data gathering that defines the current state of participants on some measure of interest.

developmental-origins hypothesis explanation that events during the fetal period, infancy, and the early years of childhood are significant factors in subsequent adult health.

developmental psychology field of study that deals with changes that take place in behavior, thoughts, and emotions of individuals as they go from conception to the end of life.

dexterity skill and grace in physical movement, especially in the use of the hands.

DHEA (dehydroepiandrosterone) hormone involved in the production of sex hormones for both males and females.

diabetes disease in which the body is not able to metabolize insulin.

differential continuity stability of individuals' rank order within a group over time.

digit-span task test in which the participant hears a list of digits and is asked to recall them in exact order.

discrimination prejudicial treatment.

disengagement early hypothesis that held that late adulthood is a time when people withdraw from activities and relationships in preparation for the end of life.

distal causes factors that were present in the distant past.

divided attention attending to more than one task at a time.

DNA methylation chemical process by which genes are modified in epigenetic inheritance.

economic exchange theory explanation of gender roles stating that men and women form intimate partnerships based on an exchange of goods and services.

egalitarian roles roles based on equality between genders.

ego integrity in Erikson's theory of psychosocial development, the tendency older adults develop to review their life for meaning and integration.

elder abuse an intentional act by a caregiver or other trusted person that causes harm to an older adult.

emerging adulthood period of transition from adolescence to young adulthood (approximately 18–25 years of age).

emotion-focused coping stress-reducing technique that directly addresses the emotions causing stress.

empirical research scientific studies of observable events that are measured and evaluated statistically.

epigenetic inheritance process in which the genes one receives at conception are modified by subsequent environmental events that occur during the prenatal period and throughout the lifespan.

episodic memory in information processing, the segment of the long-term store that contains information about sequences of events.

erectile dysfunction (ED) the inability for a man to have an erection adequate for satisfactory sexual performance.

estrogen female sex hormone.

evolutionary psychology field of psychology that explains human behavior in terms of genetic patterns that were useful in our primitive ancestors for survival and reproduction success.

exchange theory theory that we select mates by evaluating the assets we have to offer in a relationship and the assets the potential mates have to offer, and try to make the best deal.

executive function in cognition, the process involved in regulating attention and coordinating new and old information.

experimental design empirical study that has a high level of experimental control.

extended families grandparents, aunts and uncles, cousins, and other relatives beyond the nuclear family of parents and children.

external changes changes that are visible and apparent to those we encounter.

faith a set of assumptions or understandings about the nature of our connections with others and the world in which we live.

feminization of poverty term used to describe the trend that an increasingly larger proportion of people living in poverty are women.

filter theory theory that we select mates by using finer and finer filtering mechanisms.

finitude process of coming to grips with one's eventual death.

Five-factor model inventory of five basic personality factors first demonstrated by Costa and McCrae.

fluid intelligence basic adaptive abilities, measured by tests of digit span, response speed, and abstract reasoning.

Flynn effect term for the increase shown in IQ scores over the last century, due mainly to changes of modern life.

free radicals   molecules or atoms that possess an unpaired electron; by-products of cell metabolism.

friendship   voluntary interpersonal relationship carried out within a social context.

functional age   measure of how well an individual is functioning in various aspects of adulthood.

g   general intellectual capacity, which influences the way we approach many different tasks.

gender crossover   relaxation of gender roles that is hypothesized to occur in men and women when the parenting years are over.

gender ideology   attitudes and beliefs about the roles and equality of men and women.

gender roles   actual behaviors and attitudes of men and women in a given culture during a given historical era.

gender schema theory   theory that states children are taught to view the world and themselves through gender-polarized lenses that make artificial or exaggerated distinctions between what is masculine and what is feminine.

gender stereotypes   sets of shared beliefs or generalizations about how men and women in a society ought to behave.

general adaptation syndrome   in Selye's theory, three stages of symptoms that occur in response to stress: alarm reaction, resistance, and exhaustion.

generativity   in Erikson's theory of psychosocial development, the tendency middle-aged adults develop to help establish and guide the next generation.

genotype   individual's complement of genes.

gerotranscendence   idea that meaning systems increase in quality as we age.

GH   synthetic version of human growth hormone that is prescribed for a limited number of conditions but widely used as an antiaging drug.

glaucoma   visual disorder characterized by a buildup of pressure inside the eye that can lead to blindness if not treated.

good death   death with dignity, with maximum consciousness and minimum pain.

grandmother effect   suggestion that the presence of grandmothers (especially maternal grandmothers) has ensured children's survival through recorded history.

Hayflick limit   maximum number of times cells are programmed to divide for a species.

hormone replacement therapy (HRT)   therapy in which women take estrogen and progestin at menopause to replace hormones once produced by the ovaries; relieves menopause symptoms.

hospice approach   philosophy that underlies hospice care. Specifically that death is an inevitable part of life, that the dying person and the family should be involved in as much of the care as possible and have control over the setting, and that no life-prolonging measures should be taken.

hospice care   end-of-life care focused on pain relief, emotional support, and spiritual comfort for dying patients and their families.

hostility   negative cognitive set against others.

human social genomics   study of changes in gene expression that result from subjective perceptions of the environment.

IADLs (instrumental activities of daily living)   complex everyday tasks.

identity   in Erikson's theory of psychosocial development, the set of personal values and goals a young adult develops pertaining to gender, occupation, and religious beliefs.

individual differences   aspects that are unique to the individual, not part of the whole group.

insomnia   inability to have normal sleep patterns.

instrumental qualities   personal characteristics that have an active impact, such as being competitive, adventurous, and physically strong; stereotypical male qualities.

intelligence   visible indicator of the efficiency of various cognitive processes that work together behind the scenes to process information.

interactionist view   idea that genetics influence how one interacts with the environment and the environment one chooses.

intergenerational effects   prenatal experiences that affect the female fetus in adulthood and also her subsequent offspring.

intergenerational solidarity   extent to which family members of different generations are close to each other.

internal changes   changes to ourselves that are not immediately apparent to the casual observer.

internal working model   in Bowlby's attachment theory, the set of beliefs and assumptions a person has about the nature of all relationships based on specific experiences in childhood.

intimacy   in Erikson's theory of psychosocial development, the ability young adults develop that allows them to enter into intimate relationships without losing their own sense of self.

intra-individual variability   stability or instability of personality traits within an individual over time.

IQ (intelligence quotient)   score on an intelligence test that reflects general intellectual capacity.

job burnout   job-related condition that is a combination of exhaustion, depersonalization, and reduced effectiveness.

job expertise   high level of skill that results from years of experience at a certain job.

job insecurity   anticipation of job loss by currently employed workers.

job loss   having paid employment taken away from an individual.

job strain   the result of doing work that requires high levels of psychological demands from the worker but offers him or her little control.

labor force   those who are officially working at paid jobs.

lens   transparent structure in the eye that focuses light rays on receptors in the retina.

libido   sexual desire.

life review   an analytic and evaluative review of our earlier life.

life-change events   in Holmes and Rahe's theory, events that alter the status quo of an individual's life; when accumulated can lead to stress reactions.

life-span developmental psychology approach   idea that development is lifelong, multidimensional, plastic, contextual, and has multiple causes.

life-span/life-space theory   concept that individuals develop careers in stages, and that career decisions are not isolated from other aspects of their lives.

living will   legal document that states a person's end-of-life decisions.

lonely   the perception of social isolation.

longitudinal study   research method in which data is gathered over a period of time from the same group of people as they age.

long-term memory   component of memory where information can be stored for many years or even forever.

major depressive disorder   disorder typified by a long-term, pervasive sense of helplessness and hopelessness.

mate selection   process of choosing a long-term partner for an intimate relationship.

maximum lifespan   the longest an individual from a species can live; for humans it is about 120 years.

meaning-focused coping   stress-reducing technique that refers to anything you might think, feel, and do to give a positive meaning to a stressful situation.

mean-level change   changes in a group's average scores over time.

medication adherence   ability of patients to follow their physicians' instructions about taking their prescribed medication in the right dosages, at the right time, and for the right length of time.

memory   ability to retain or store information and retrieve it when needed.

menopause   cessation of women's menstrual periods, occurring 12 months after the final menstrual period; climacteric.

meta-analysis   analysis of data from a large number of studies that deal with the same research question, yielding more powerful results.

midlife crisis   popular myth that portrays middle age as a time of unstable and unpredictable behavior.

mild cognitive impairment (MCI)   condition in which patients show some cognitive symptoms, but not all those necessary for a diagnosis of Alzheimer's disease.

moral reasoning   analyzing what is right and wrong, judging the rightness or wrongness of an act.

morbidity rate   illness rate.

mortality rate   probability of dying in any one year.

mysticism   self-transcendent experience.

name-retrieval failures   failure to come up with a name, known or celebrity, as in "the name of that actor who used to be on *Star Trek* and now does hotel commercials."

neurofibrillary tangles   webs of degenerating neurons found in the brains of Alzheimer's patients..

neurogenesis   growth of new neurons.

neurons   cells in the brain and nervous system.

nondeclarative (implicit) memory   memory system responsible for learning and retaining new skills.

nonnormative life events   aspects that influence one's life that are unique to the individual.

nontraditional student   in college, a student who is older than age 25.

normative age-graded influences   common effects of age that are experienced by most adults.

normative history-graded influences   effects connected to historical events and conditions that are experienced by everyone within a culture at that time.

nuclear families   parents and their children.

nursing home   a place for people to live when they don't need to be in a hospital but can't be taken care of at home.

obesity   condition in which one's weight-to-height ratio increases to a point that has an adverse effect on health; usually measured in terms of body mass index.

occupational gender segregation   separation of jobs into stereotypical male and female categories.

olfactory membrane   specialized part of the nasal membrane that contains olfactory receptor cells.

optimism   positive outlook on life.

organ transplant donor   individual who agrees to the transplantation, at the time of death, of his or her usable organs and other tissue to approved recipients.

osteoarthritis   condition caused by loss of cartilage that protects the bones at the joints; can involve pain, swelling, and loss of motion.

osteoporosis   severe loss of bone mass.

paid parental leave policy   program in which the employer and/or the state provide time off with pay to new parents.

parental investment theory   in evolutionary psychology, the explanation that men and women evolved different behaviors and interests because the women have more invested in each child than the men.

peak experiences   in Maslow's theory of positive well-being, the feeling of perfection and momentary separation from the self when one feels in unity with the universe.

perceived control   belief that one can influence his or her circumstances and attain his or her goals.

perceived discrimination   realization or belief that one is the target of discrimination.

personal interview   research method in which the experimenter meets with the participant and gathers data directly, often through open-ended and follow-up questions.

personality   enduring set of characteristics that define our individuality and affect our interactions with the environment and other people.

personality factors   groups of personality traits that occur together in most individuals.

personality states   short-term patterns of thoughts, feelings, and behaviors.

personality traits   stable patterns of thoughts, feelings, and behaviors.

person–environment fit   idea that people will be more successful if they work in a field for which they are talented rather than taking a job for other reasons.

person–environment transactions   combinations of genetic endowment and environmental factors that maintain the stability of personality traits over time.

phased retirement   situation in which an older person continues to work for an employer part time as a transition to retirement.

phobias   anxiety disorders that involve fears and avoidance out of proportion to the danger presented.

physician-assisted suicide   situation in which physicians are legally allowed to assist patients, under certain circumstances, to obtain medication that will end their lives.

plaques   fat-laden deposits formed in the coronary artery walls as a result of inflammation.

plasticity   in neurons, the ability to form new connections or grow new extensions.

polystrength   clusters or personality traits that may provide protection and resilience in the face of adversity.

positive psychology   emphasis of psychology research to turn away from negative outcomes, such as mental illness and crime, and toward positive outcomes, such as well-being, optimism, and spiritual growth.

positivity bias   tendency for older adults to remember emotionally positive stimuli over emotionally negative stimuli.

postformal stages   adult stage of cognitive development that involves thinking beyond the linear and logical ways.

posttraumatic stress disorder (PTSD) psychological response to a traumatic experience. Symptoms include reexperiencing the event in intrusive thoughts and dreams, numbing of general responses, avoiding stimuli associated with the event, and increased arousal of the physiological stress mechanisms.

presbyopia visual condition caused by loss of elasticity in the lens, resulting in the inability to focus sharply on nearby objects.

prevalence proportion of people experiencing a certain disorder at a given time.

primary aging physical changes that are gradual, shared, and largely inevitable as people grow older.

problem-focused coping stress-reducing techniques that directly address the problem causing stress.

progesterone female sex hormone.

prospective memory ability to remember to do something later on or at a specific time in the future.

proximal causes factors present in the immediate environment.

psychological age measure of an individual's ability to deal effectively with the environment.

psychometrics field of psychology that studies the measurement of human abilities.

pupil opening in the eye that changes in diameter in response to available light.

qualitative research research without numerical data, such as case studies, interviews, participant observations, direct observations, and exploring documents, artifacts, and archival records.

quantitative research research with numerical data.

quest for meaning search for ultimate knowledge of life through an individualized understanding of the sacred.

reactive heritability process whereby individuals use the qualities they have inherited as a basis to determine strategies for survival and reproduction.

reliability extent to which a test instrument gives the same results repeatedly under the same conditions.

religiosity outward expression of spiritual beliefs.

reminiscence review of one's personal memories.

replicative senescence state in which older cells stop dividing.

resilience ability to maintain healthy functioning following exposure to potential trauma.

resistance resources personal and social resources that may buffer a person from the impact of stress.

response-oriented viewpoint explanations of stress that focus on the physiological reactions within an individual.

retina structure at the back of the eye that contains receptor cells.

retirement career stage in which an older worker leaves the full-time workforce to pursue other interests, such as part-time work, volunteer work, or leisure interests.

retirement-related value in retirement decisions, the amount of personal wealth one has, plus Social Security and pension benefits, salary from part-time jobs, and health insurance benefits available if one retires; can be weighed against work-related value.

ritual mourning set of symbolic rites and ceremonies associated with death and bereavement.

role transitions changes in roles due to changes in the individual or in his or her life circumstances.

secondary aging physical changes that are sudden, not shared, and often caused by disease, poor health habits, and environmental events as people grow older.

selective optimization with compensation process described by Baltes and Baltes in which older people cope with limitations by selecting their activities, optimizing their strategies, and compensating for their losses.

self-actualization in Maslow's theory, the drive to become everything that one is capable of being. It is reached when more basic needs are met.

self-determination theory explanation of personality based on individuals' evolved inner resources for growth and integration.

self-efficacy the belief in one's ability to succeed.

self-identity strong sense of self.

self-transcendence knowing the self as part of a larger whole that exists beyond the physical body and personal history.

semantic memory in information processing, the segment of the long-term store that contains factual information.

senile plaques small, circular deposits of a dense protein, beta-amyloid.

sense of purpose in life discovery of satisfying personal goals and the belief that one's life has been worthwhile.

sensorineural hearing loss inability to discriminate between loud and soft sounds caused by damage to receptors in the inner ear.

sequential study series of several longitudinal studies begun at different points in time.

short-term memory memory component involved in holding information for several seconds and then either discarding or processing it.

sleep apnea pause in breathing during sleep due to constriction of the airway.

social age measure of the number and type of roles an individual has taken on at a specific point in his or her life.

social anxiety feeling fear and anxiety about social situations, such as meeting new people or performing before an audience.

social clock patterns of change over adulthood in social roles; time schedule of the normal sequence of adult life experiences.

social relationships dynamic, recurrent patterns of interactions with other individuals.

social role theory explanation of gender roles based on children viewing the gender divisions around them and then modeling their behavior on those divisions.

social roles expected behaviors and attitudes that come with one's position in society.

social support positive affect, affirmation, and aid received from others at stressful times.

social timing pattern of when we occupy certain roles, how long we occupy them, and the order in which we move from one to another.

social-cognitive theory theory that suggests that career success involves being proactive, believing in yourself, being self-regulated and self-motivated, and focusing on your goals.

social-focused coping coping that involves seeking both instrumental and emotional support from others.

sociobiographical history level of professional prestige, social position, and income that one experiences throughout one's life.

socioeconomic level combined rating of income level and educational attainment.

socioemotional selectivity theory according to Carstensen, the explanation that people emphasize more meaningful, emotionally satisfying social relationships as they become older because they are more aware of the end of life than younger people.

spillover the extent that events in one domain influence another.

spirituality   an individual's personal quest for meaning; an inner process often distinguished from religiosity, which involves outward signs of a quest for meaning.

stability   having little or no change for significant periods of time.

stages   parts of the lifespan when there seems to be no progress for some time, followed by an abrupt change.

stamina   ability to sustain moderate or strenuous activity.

standardized tests   established instruments that measure a specific trait or behavior.

stem cells   immature undifferentiated cells that can multiply easily and mature into many different kinds of cells.

stereotype threat   anxiety that arises when members of a group are put in positions that might confirm widely held, negative stereotypes about themselves; this anxiety often results in confirmation of that stereotype.

stimulus-oriented viewpoint   explanations of stress that are focused on the stressors themselves, the stimuli or life events, that trigger the stress reactions.

stress   set of physical, cognitive, and emotional responses that humans (and other organisms) display in reaction to stressors or demands from the environment.

stressors   environmental demands that lead to stress reactions.

stress-related growth   positive changes that follow the experience of stressful life events.

substance-related disorders   disorders typified by intense desire for and compulsion to use a substance when any related triggers are present.

survey questionnaire   written form that participants can fill out on their own consisting of structured and focused questions.

T cells   cells of the immune system produced in the thymus gland that reject and consume harmful or foreign cells.

taste buds   receptor cells for taste found on the tongue, mouth, and throat.

telomeres   lengths of repeating DNA that chromosomes have at their tips.

testosterone   major male sex hormone.

transition to adulthood   period during which young people take on the social roles of early adulthood.

traumatic brain injury (TBI)   head injury severe enough to result in loss of consciousness; increases risk of dementia, especially chronic traumatic encephalopathy (CTE).

twin studies   studies that compare similarities of monozygotic twin pairs with dizygotic twin pairs on some behavior or trait of interest; results can give information on the extent of genetic contribution to that behavior or trait.

type A behavior pattern   state of being achievement-striving, competitive, and involved in one's job to excess.

typical   common to most people.

unemployment   state of being without a paid job when you are willing to work.

useful field of view (UFOV)   area of the visual field that can be processed in one glance.

validity   extent to which a test instrument measures what it claims to measure.

visual acuity   ability to perceive detail in a visual pattern.

visual search   the process of searching your environment in an attempt to locate a particular item.

vocational interests   in vocational psychology, personal attitudes, competencies, and values a person has relating to his or her career; basis of Holland's theory of career selection.

word-finding failures   feeling many middle-aged and older adults get when they know the word they want to use but just can't locate it at the moment; often referred to as the *tip-of-the-tongue phenomenon.*

work engagement   approach to work that is active, positive, and characterized by vigor, dedication, and absorption.

working memory   the part of short-term memory that performs cognitive operations on information.

work-related value   in retirement decisions, the amount of salary, pension, and Social Security benefits a worker will receive later if he or she continues working; can be weighed against retirement-related value.

References

CHAPTER 1

Baltes, P. B., & Mayer, K. U. (Eds.). (1999). *The Berlin aging study: Aging from 70 to 100*. Cambridge, England: Cambridge University Press.

Baltes, P. B., Reese, H. W., & Lipsitt, L. P. (1980). Life-span developmental psychology. *Annual Review of Psychology, 31*, 65–110.

Baltes, P. B. (1987). Theoretical propositions of life-span developmental psychology: *On the dynamics between growth and decline. Developmental Psychology 23*, 611–626.

Bronfenbrenner, U. (1979). *The ecology of human development*. Cambridge, MA: Harvard University Press.

Bronfenbrenner, U., & Morris, P. A. (2006). The bioecological model of human development. In W. Damon & R. M. Lerner (Eds.), *Handbook of child psychology: Vol. 1. Theoretical models of human development* (6th ed., pp. 793–828). New York: John Wiley.

Carlson, J. F., Geisinger, K. F., & Jonson, J. L. (Eds.). (2017). *Mental Measurements Yearbook* (20th ed.). Lincoln: University of Nebraska Press.

Elder, G. H., Jr. (1979). Historical change in life patterns and personality. In P. B. Baltes & O. G. Brim, Jr. (Eds.), *Lifespan development and behavior* (Vol. 2, pp. 117–159). New York: Academic Press.

Greenberg, G., Halpern, C. T., Hood, K. E., et al. (2010). Developmental systems, nature-nurture, and the role of genes in behavior and development: On the legacy of Gilbert Gottlieb. In G. Greenberg, C. T. Halpern, K. E. Hood, et al. (Eds.), *Handbook of developmental systems, behavior and genetics*. Malden, MA: Wiley Blackwell.

Hequembourg, A., & Brallier, S. (2005). Gendered stories of parental caregiving among siblings. *Journal of Aging Studies, 19*, 53–71.

Kremen, W. S., & Lyons, M. J. (2011). Behavior genetics of aging. In K. W. Schaie & S. L. Willis (Eds.), *Handbook of the psychology of aging* (7th ed., pp. 93–107). San Diego, CA: Academic Press.

Lerner, R. M. (2006). Developmental science, developmental systems, and contemporary theories of human development. In W. Damon & R. M. Lerner (Gen. Eds.), *Handbook of Child Psychology* (6th ed.), R. M. Lerner (Vol. Ed.), Vol. 1, *Theoretical models of human development* (pp. 1–17). New York: Wiley.

McGowan, P. O., Sasaki, A., D'Alessio, A. C., et al. (2009). Epigenetic regulators of the glucocorticoid receptor in human brain associates with childhood abuse. *Nature Neuroscience, 12*, 342–348.

Neugarten, B. (1976). Adaptation and the life cycle. *Counseling Psychologist, 6*, 16–20.

North, M. S., & Fiske, S. T. (2015). Modern attitudes toward older adults in the aging world: A cross-cultural meta-analysis. *Psychological Bulletin, 141*, 993–1021.

Plomin, R., DeFries, J. C., Kropnik, V. S., et al. (2012). *Behavioral genetics* (6th ed.). New York: Worth.

Radloff, L. S. (1977). The CES-D Scale: A self-report depression scale for research in the general population. *Applied Psychological Measurement, 1*, 385–401.

Riley, K. P., Snowdon, D. A., Desrosiers, M. F., et al. (2005). Early life linguistic ability, late life cognitive function, and neuropathology: Findings from the Nun Study. *Neurobiology of Aging, 26*, 341–347.

Salkind, N. J. (2011). *Exploring research* (8th ed.). Upper Saddle River, NJ: Pearson.

Sameroff, A. J. (Ed.) (2009). *The transactional model of development: How children and contexts shape each other*. Washington, DC: American Psychological Association.

Seubert, J., Laukka, E. J., Rizzuto, D., et al. (2017). Prevalence and correlates of olfactory dysfunction in old age: A population-based study. *Journals of Gerontology: Medical Sciences, 72*, 1072–1079.

Snowdon, D. (2001). *Aging with grace: What the Nun Study teaches us about leading longer, healthier, more meaningful lives*. New York: Bantam Books.

Spotts, E. L., Neiderhiser, J. M., Towers, H., et al. (2004). Genetic and environmental influences on marital relationships. *Journal of Family Psychology, 18*, 107–119.

Vaillant, G. E. (2002). *Aging well: Surprising guideposts to a happier life from the landmark Harvard study*. Boston, MA: Little Brown.

Vargas Lascano, D. I., Galambos, N. L., Krahn, H. J., et al. (2015). Growth in perceived control across 25 years from the late teens to midlife: The role of personal and parents' education. *Developmental Psychology, 51*, 124–135.

Whitbourne, S. K., Zuschlag, M. K., Elliot, L. B., et al. (1992). Psychosocial development in adulthood: A 22-year sequential study. *Journal of Personality and Social Psychology, 63*, 260–271.

CHAPTER 2

Almeida, O. P., Waterreus, A., Spry, N., et al. (2004). One-year follow-up study of the association between chemical castration, sex hormones, beta-amyloid, memory, and depression in men. *Psychoneuroendocrinology, 29*, 1071–1081.

American Academy of Ophthamology. (2018). *What are cataracts?* Retrieved March 19, 2019, from https://www.aao.org/eye-health/diseases/what-are-cataracts

American Academy of Orthopaedic Surgeons. (2016a). *OrthoInfo: Total hip replacement.* Retrieved September 13, 2017, from http://orthoinfo.aaos.org/topic.cfm?topic=a00377

American Academy of Orthopaedic Surgeons. (2016b). *OrthoInfo: Total knee replacement.* Retrieved September 13, 2017, from http://orthoinfo.aaos.org/topic.cfm?topic=a00389

American Academy of Sleep Medicine. (2016). *Hidden health crisis costing America billions.* Retrieved September 22, 2017, from https://aasm.org/resources/pdf/sleep-apnea-economic-crisis.pdf

American Cancer Society. (2015). *Menopausal hormone therapy and cancer risk.* Retrieved November 10, 2016, from https://www.cancer.org/cancer/cancer-causes/medical-treatments/menopausal-hormone-replacement-therapy-and-cancer-risk.html

American Hair Loss Association. (2010). *Hair loss fact sheet.* Retrieved May 8, 2012, from http://www.americanhairloss.org

American Nutrition Association (2011). *USDA defines food deserts.* Retrieved October 18,2012 from http://americannutritionassociation.org/newsletter/usda-defines-food-deserts

American Society of Plastic Surgeons. (2016). *Plastic surgery statistics report – 2015.* Retrieved October 20, 2016, from https://d2wirczt3b6wjm.cloudfront.net/News/Statistics/2015/plastic-surgery-statistics-full-report-2015.pdf

Apple, D. M., Solano-Fonseca, R., & Kokovay, E. (2017). Neurogenesis in the aging brain. *Biochemical Pharmacology, 141*, 77–85.

Beers, M. H. (2004). *Merck manual of health and aging*. Whitehouse Station, NJ: Merck Research Labs.

Bengtson, V. L., & Settersten, R. A., Jr. (2016). Theories of aging: Developments within and across disciplinary boundaries. In V. L. Bengtson & R. A. Settersten, Jr. (Eds.), *Handbook of theories of aging* (3rd ed., pp. 1–7). New York: Springer.

Birzniece, V., Nelson, A. E., & Ho, K. K. (2011). Growth hormone and physical performance. *Trends in Endocrinology and Metabolism, 22,* 171–178.

Buman, M. P., Hekler, E. B., Bliwise, D. L., et al. (2011). Moderators and mediators of exercise-induced objective sleep improvements in midlife and older adults with sleep complaints. *Health Psychology, 30,* 579–587.

Buring, J., & Lee I.-M. (2012). *Women's Health Study: Going strong for 18 years!* Retrieved October 12, 2012, from http://whs.bwh.harvard.edu/methods/html

Carskadon, M. A. (2009). Sleep, adolescence, and learning. *Frontiers of Neuroscience, 3,* 470–471.

Catoni, C., Peters, A., Schaefer, H. M. (2008). Life history trade-offs are influenced by the diversity, availability and interactions of dietary antioxidants. *Animal Behaviour, 76,* 1107–1119.

Centers for Disease Control and Prevention. (2015a). *Check for safety: A home fall prevention checklist for older adults.* Retrieved September 22, 2017, from https://www.cdc.gov/steadi/pdf/check_for_safety_brochure-a.pdf

Centers for Disease Control and Prevention. (2015b). *Common eye disorders.* Retrieve October 20, 2016, from https://www.cdc.gov/visionhealth/basics/ced/index.html

Centers for Disease Control and Prevention. (2015c). *Osteoarthritis.* Retrieved September 13, 2017, from https://www.cdc.gov/arthritis/basics/osteoarthritis.htm

Centers for Disease Control and Prevention. (2016a). *Defining adult overweight and obesity.* Retrieved October 20, 2016, from https://www.cdc.gov/obesity/adult/defining.html

Centers for Disease Control and Prevention. (2016b). *Health, United States, 2015 – Poverty.* Retrieved October 27, 2016, from http://www.cdc.gov/nchs/hus/poverty.htm

Centers for Disease Control and Prevention. (2016c). *High blood pressure facts.* Retrieved September 4, 2017, from https://www.cdc.gov/dhdsp/data_statistics/fact_sheets/fs_bloodpressure.htm

Centers for Disease Control and Prevention. (2016d). *1 in 3 adults don't get enough sleep.* Retrieved September 22, 2017, from https://www.cdc.gov/media/releases/2016/p0215-enough-sleep.html

Cherkas, L. F., Hunkin, J. L., Kato, B. S., et al. (2008). The association between physical activity in leisure time and leukocyte telomere length. *Archives of Internal Medicine, 168,* 154–158.

Colman, R. J., Anderson, R. M., Johnson, S. C., et al. (2009). Caloric restriction delays disease onset and mortality in rhesus monkeys. *Science, 325,* 201–204.

Cudmore, V., Henn, P., O'Tuathaigh, C. M. P., et al. (2017). Age-related hearing loss and communication breakdown in the clinical setting. *Journal of the American Medical Association Otolaryngology – Head and Neck Surgery, 143,* 274–285.

Dalal, P. K., & Agarwal, M. (2015). Postmenopausal syndrome. *Indian Journal of Psychology, 57,* S222–S232.

DeLamater, J. (2012). Sexual expression in later life: A review and synthesis. *Journal of Sex Research, 49,* 125–141.

DeLamater, J., & Moorman, S. M. (2007). Sexual behavior in later life. *Journal of Aging and Health, 19,* 921–945.

Douglass, R., & Heckman, G. (2010). Drug-related taste disturbance: A contributing factor in geriatric syndromes. *Canadian Family Physician, 56,* 1142–1147.

Epel, E. S., Blackburn, E. H., Lin, J., et al. (2004). Accelerated telomere shortening in response to life stress. *Proceedings of the National Academy of Sciences U.S.A., 101,* 17312–17315.

Epelbaum, E. (2008). Neuroendocrinology and aging. *Journal of Neuroendocrinology, 20,* 808–811.

Fabbri, E., An, Y., Gonzalez-Freire, M., et al. (2016). Bioavailable testosterone linearly declines over a wide age spectrum in men and women from the Baltimore Longitudinal Study of Aging. *Journals of Gerontology: Biological Sciences and Medical Sciences, 71,* 1202–1209.

Florido, R., Tchkonia, T., & Kirkland, J. L. (2011). Aging and adipose tissue. In E. J. Masoro & S. N. Austad (Eds.), *Handbook of the biology of aging* (7th ed., pp. 119–139). San Diego, CA: Academic Press.

Fontana, L., Colman, R. J., Holloszy, J. O., et al. (2011). Calorie restriction in nonhuman and human primates. In E. J. Masoro & S. N. Austad (Eds.), *Handbook of the biology of aging* (7th ed., pp. 447–462). San Diego, CA: Academic Press.

Fraser, J., Maticka-Tyndale, E., & Smylie, L. (2004). Sexuality of Canadian women at midlife. *Canadian Journal of Human Sexuality, 13,* 171–187.

Fryar, C. D., Gu, Q., Ogden, C. L., et al. (2016). *Anthropometric reference data for children and adults: United States, 2011–2014.* Retrieved September 22, 2017, from https://www.cdc.gov/nchs/data/series/sr_03/sr03_039.pdf

Fukunaga, A., Uematsu, H., & Sugimoto, K. (2005). Influence of aging on taste perception and oral somatic sensation. *Journals of Gerontology: Biological and Medical Sciences, 60,* 109–113.

Garnick, M. B. (2015). Testosterone replacement therapy faces FDA scrutiny. *Journal of the American Medical Association, 313,* 563–564.

Glaucoma Research Foundation. (2016). *Glaucoma facts and stats.* Retrieved October 21, 2016, from http://www.glaucoma.org/glaucoma/glaucoma-facts-and-stats.php

Gredilla, R. (2011). DNA damage and base excision repair in mitochondria and their role in aging. *Journal of Aging Research, 2011,* 1–9.

Grundfast, K. M., & Liu, S. W. (2017). What otolaryngologists need to know about hearing aids. *Journal of the American Medical Association Otolaryngology – Head and Neck Surgery, 143,* 109–110.

Halter, J. B. (2011). Aging and insulin secretion. In E. J. Masoro & S. N. Austad (Eds.), *Handbook of the biology of aging* (pp. 373–384). San Diego, CA: Academic Press.

Harmon, D. (1956). Aging: A theory based on free radical and radiation chemistry. *Journal of Gerontology, 11,* 298–300.

Harris, J. D., Gerrie, B. J., Varner, K. E., et al. (2015). Radiographic prevalence of dysplasia, cam, and pincer deformities in elite ballet. *American Journal of Sports Medicine, 44,* 20–27.

Harrison, E. D., Strong, R., Sharp, Z. D., et al. (2009). Rapamycin fed late in life extends lifespan in genetically heterogeneous mice. *Nature, 460,* 392–395.

Hayflick, L. (1977). The cellular basis for biological aging. In C. E. Finch & L. Hayflick (Eds.), *Handbook of the biology of aging* (pp. 159–186). New York: Van Nostrand Reinhold.

Hayflick, L. (1994). *How and why we age.* New York: Ballantine Books.

Hearing Loss Association of America. (2017). *Hearing loss facts and statistics.* Retrieved August 25, 2017, from http://www.hearingloss.org/sites/default/files/docs/HearingLoss_Facts_Statistics.pdf

Hoffman, H. J., Dobie, R. A., Losonsky, K. G., et al. (2017). Declining prevalence of hearing loss in U.S. adults aged 20 to 69 years. *Journal of the American Medical Association Otolaryngology – Head and Neck Surgery, 143,* 274–285.

Hornsby, A. K., Redhead, Y. T., Rees, D. J., et al. (2016). Short-term calorie restriction enhances adult hippocampal neurogenesis and remote fear memory in a Ghsr-dependent manner. *Psychoneuroendocrinology, 63,* 198–207.

Hornsby, P. J. (2001). Cell proliferation in mammalian aging. In E. J. Masoro & S. N. Austad (Eds.), *Handbook of the biology of aging* (pp. 207–245). San Diego, CA: Academic Press. https://www.cdc.gov/bloodpressure/facts.htm

Jacob, J. A. (2016). Can nonhormonal treatment dial down the heat during menopause? *Journal of the American Medical Association, 315,* 14–16.

Jaspers, L., Feys, F., & Bramer, W. M. (2016). Efficacy and safety of flibanserin for the treatment of hypoactive sexual desire disorder in women: A systematic review and meta-analysis. *Journal of the American Medical Association – Internal Medicine, 176,* 453–462.

Kapahi, P., & Kockel, L. (2011). TOR: A conserved nutrient-sensing pathway that determines life-span across species. In E. J. Masoro & S. N. Austad (Eds.), *Handbook of the biology of aging* (7th ed., pp. 203–214). San Diego, CA: Academic Press.

Kennedy, B. K. (2016). Advances in biological theories of aging. In V. L. Bengtson & R. A. Settersten (Eds.), *Handbook of theories of aging* (3rd ed., pp. 107–111). New York: Springer.

Kretzschmar, K., & Clevers, H. (2016). Organoids: Modeling development and the stem cell niche in dish. *Developmental Cell, 38,* 590–600.

Kritchevsky, S. B. (2016). Nutrition and healthy aging. *Journals of Gerontology: Medical Science, 71,* 1303–1305.

Kusy, K., Krol-Zielinska, M., Domaszewska, K., et al. (2012). Gas exchange threshold in male speed–power versus endurance athletes ages 20–90 years. *Medicine & Science in Sports & Exercise, 44,* 2415–2422.

Laumann, E. O., Das, A., & Waite, L. J. (2008). Sexual dysfunction among older adults: Prevalence and risk factors from a nationally representative sample of men and women 57–85 years of age. *Journal of Sexual Medicine, 5,* 2300–2311.

Lillis, J., Levin, M. E., & Hayes, S. C. (2011). Exploring the relationship between body mass index and health-related quality of life: A pilot study of the impact of weight self-stigma and experiential avoidance. *Journal of Health Psychology, 16,* 722–727.

Liu, H., Bravata, D. M., Olkin, I., et al. (2007). Systematic review: The effects of growth hormone in the healthy elderly. *Annals of Internal Medicine, 146,* 104–115.

Lockley, S. W., & Foster, R. G. (2012). *Sleep: A very short introduction.* New York: Oxford University Press.

Looker, A. C., & Frenk, S. M. (2015). *Percentage of adults aged 65 and over with osteoporosis or low bone mass at the femur neck or lumbar spine.* Retrieved October 24, 2016, from https://www.cdc.gov/nchs/data/hestat/osteoporsis/osteoporosis2005_2010.htm

Mahieu, L., & Gastmans, C. (2012). Sexuality in institutionalized elderly persons: A systematic review of argument-based ethics literature. *International Psychogeriatrics, 24,* 346–357.

Martires, K. J., Fu, P., Polster, A. M., et al. (2009). Factors that affect skin aging: A cohort-based survey on twins. *Archives of Dermatology, 145,* 1375–1379.

Masoro, E. J. (2011). Terminal weight loss, frailty, and mortality. In E. J. Masoro & S. N. Austad (Eds.), *Handbook of the biology of aging* (7th ed., pp. 321–331). San Diego, CA: Academic Press.

McCay, C. M., Crowell, M. F., & Maynard, L. A. (1935). The effect of retarded growth upon the length of life span and upon the ultimate body size. *Journal of Nutrition, 10,* 63–79.

McClearn, G. E., Vogler, G. P., & Hofer, S. M. (2001). Environment-gene and gene-gene interactions. In E. J. Masoro & S. N. Austad (Eds.), *Handbook of the biology of aging* (pp. 423–444). San Diego, CA: Academic Press.

Medina, J. J. (1996). *The clock of ages: Why we age, how we age, winding back the clock.* Cambridge, UK: Cambridge University Press.

Miller, R. A., Harrison, D. E., Astle, C. M., et al. (2011). Rapamycin, but not resveratrol or simvastatin, extends lifespan of genetically heterogeneous mice. *Journals of Gerontology: Biological and Medical Sciences, 66,* 191–201.

Mustelin, L., Silventoinen, K., Pietilainen, K., et al. (2009). Physical activity reduces the influence of genetic effects on BMI and waist circumference: A study in young adult twins. *International Journal of Obesity, 33,* 29–36.

Nair, K. S., Rizza, R. A., O'Brien, P., et al. (2006). DHEA in elderly women and DHEA and testosterone in elderly men. *New England Journal of Medicine, 355,* 1647–1659.

National Eye Institute. (2015). *Facts about age-related macular degeneration.* Retrieved October 21, 2016, from https://nei.nih.gov/health/maculardegen/armd_facts

National Institute of Diabetes and Digestive and Kidney Disorders. (2017). *Erectile dysfunction.* Retrieved September 22, 2017, from https://www.niddk.nih.gov/health-information/urologic-diseases/erectile-dysfunction/definition-facts

National Institute on Aging (2013). *Aging and your eyes.* Retrieved August 18, 2013, from http://www.nia.nih.gov/health/publication/aging-and-your-eyes#.UnvA1BYlc1k

National Institutes of Health. (2008). *Research for a new age: Normal aging.* Retrieved October 29, 2012, from http://www.healthandage.com/html/min/nih/content/booklets/research_new_age/page3.htm\#start

National Osteoporosis Foundation. (2016). *What is osteoporosis and what causes it?* Retrieved October 24, 2016, from https://www.nof.org/patients/what-is-osteoporosis/

Oertelt-Prigione, S., Parol, R., Krohn, S., et al. (2010). Analysis of sex and gender-specific research reveals a common increase in publications and marked differences between disciplines. *BMC Medicine, 8,* 70–80.

Ogden, C. L., Carroll, M. D., Fryar, C. D., et al. (2015). *Prevalence of obesity among adults in 2011–2014.* Retrieved September 22, 2017, from https://www.cdc.gov/nchs/products/databriefs/db219.htm

Olshansky, S. J., Antonucci, T., Berkman, L., et al. (2012). Differences in life expectancy due to race and educational differences are widening, and in many cases may not catch up. *Health Affairs, 31,* 1803–1813.

Ortega-Alonso, A., Sipilä, S., Kujala, U. M., et al. (2009). Genetic influences on change in BMI from middle to old age: A 29-year follow-up study of twin sisters. *Behavior Genetics, 39,* 154–164.

Owen, D. (2015). *Beyond taste buds: The science of delicious.* Retrieved November 10, 2017, from http://ngm.nationalgeographic.com/2015/12/food-science-of-taste-text

Park J. H., Glass, Z., Sayed, K., et al. (2013). Calorie restriction alleviates the age-related decrease in in neural progenitor cell division in the aging brain. *European Journal of Neuroscience, 37,* 1987–1993.

Passarino, G., De Rango, F., & Montesanto, A. (2016). Human longevity: Genetics or lifestyle? It takes two to tango. *Immunity and Ageing, 12,* 12–22.

Polivy J., Herman, C. P., & Coelho, J. S. (2008). Caloric restriction in the presence of attractive food cues: External cues, eating, and weight. *Physiology and Behavior, 94,* 729–733.

Porter, R. S. (2009). *Home health handbook.* Hoboken, NJ: Wiley.

Punnoose, A. R. (2012). Insomnia. *Journal of the American Medical Association, 307,* 2653.

Reed, N. S., Betz, J., Kendig, N., et al. (2017). Personal sound amplification products vs a conventional hearing aid for speech understanding in noise. *Journal of the American Medical Association, 318,* 89–90.

Reider, B. (2016). Tips on point. *American Journal of Sports Medicine, 44,* 17–19.

Robinson, J. K., & Bigby, M. (2011). Prevention of melanoma with regular sunscreen use. *Journal of the American Medical Association, 306,* 302–303.

Rosenbloom, C., & Bahns, M. (2006). What can we learn about diet and physical activity from master athletes? *Nutrition Today, 40,* 267–272.

Rosenfeld, I. (2005). *Breakthrough health.* Emmaus, PA: Rodale Press.

Ruby, M. B., Dunn, E. W., Perrino, A., et al. (2011). The invisible benefits of exercise. *Health Psychology, 30,* 67–74.

Seib, D., & Martin-Villalba, A. (2015). Neurogenesis in the normal ageing hippocampus: A mini-review. *Gerontology, 61,* 327–325.

Shifren, J. L., & Hanfling, S. (2010). *Sexuality in midlife and beyond: Harvard Medical School Special Health Report.* Boston, MA: Harvard University Press.

Thomas, H. N., Hess, R., & Thurston, R. C. (2015). Correlates of sexual activity and satisfaction in midlife and older women. *Annals of Family Medicine, 13*(4), 336–342.

Tomic, D., Gallicchio, L., Whiteman, M. K., et al. (2006). Factors associated with determinants of sexual functioning in midlife women. *Maturitas, 53*, 144–157.

U.S. Department of Labor. (2012). *Occupational noise exposure regulations*. Retrieved May 4, 2012, from http://www.osha.gov/pls/oshaweb/owadisp. show_document?p_table=standards&p_id=9735

Valente, M., & Amlani, A. M. (2017). Cost as a barrier for hearing aid adoption. *Journal of the American Medical Association Otolaryngology – Head and Neck Surgery, 143*, 647–648.

Valleda, S. A., Plambeck, K. E., Middeldorp, J., et al. (2014). Young blood reverses age-related impairments in cognitive function and synaptic plasticity in mice. *National Medicine, 20*, 659–663.

Vickers, A. J., Cronin, A. M., Maschino, A. C., et al. (2012). Acupuncture for chronic pain: Individual patient data meta-analysis. *Archives of Internal Medicine, 172*, 1–10.

Vigdorchik, J. M., Nepple, J. J., Eftekhary, M., et al. (2016). What is the association of elite sporting activities with the development of hip osteoarthritis? *American Journal of Sports Medicine, 45*, 961–964.

Woloshin, S., & Schwartz, L. M. (2016). U.S. Food and Drug Administration approval of filbanserin: Even the score does not add up. *Journal of the American Medical Association – Internal Medicine, 176*, 439–442.

World Health Organization. (2015). *Visual impairment and blindness*. Retrieved October 21, 2016, from http://www.who.int/mediacentre/factsheets/fs282/en/

World Health Organization. (2016). *Causes of blindness and visual impairment*. Retrieved October 20, 2016, from http://www.who.int/blindness/causes/en/

CHAPTER 3

Allman, J., Rosin, A., Kumar, R., et al. (1998). Parenting and survival in anthropoid primates: Caretakers live longer. *Proceedings of the National Academy of Sciences, 95*, 6866–6869.

Alzheimer's Association. (2017). *Alzheimer's disease facts and figures*. Retrieved September 29, 2017, from http://www.alz.org/facts/overview.asp

American Cancer Society (2019). *Stay healthy: Risk factors for cancer*. Retrieved June 12, 2019 from https://www.cancer.org/healthy.html

American Psychiatric Association (1980). *Diagnostic and statistical manual of mental disorders* (3rd ed.). Washington, DC: Author.

American Psychiatric Association. (2013). *Diagnostic and statistical manual of mental disorders* (5th ed.). Arlington, VA: Author.

American Psychological Association. (2016). *Beyond worry: How psychologists help with anxiety disorders*. Retrieved October 6, 2017, from http://www.apa.org/helpcenter/anxiety.aspx

American Psychological Association. (2017). *Data on behavioral health in the United States*. Retrieved October 6, 2017, from http://www.apa.org/helpcenter/data-behavioral-health.aspx

Angel, J. L., Mudrazija, S., & Benson, R. (2016). Racial and ethnic inequalities in health. In L. K. George & K. F. Ferraro (Eds.), *Handbook of aging and the social sciences* (8th ed., pp. 123–141). San Diego, CA: Academic Press.

Anxiety and Depression Society of America. (2016). *Preventing anxiety and depression*. Retrieved October 12, 2017, from https://adaa.org/tips-manage-anxiety-and-stress

Ault-Brutus, A. A. (2012). Changes in racial-ethnic disparities in use and adequacy of mental health care in the United States, 1900–2003. *Psychiatric Services, 63*, 531–540.

Austad, S. N. (2011). Sex differences in longevity and aging. In E. J. Masoro & S. N. Austad (Eds.), *Handbook of the biology of aging* (7th ed., pp. 479–495). San Diego, CA: Academic Press.

Barker, D. J., Winter, P. D., Osmond, C., et al. (1989). Weight in infancy and death from ischaemic heart disease. *Lancet, 2*, 577–580.

Baun, M. M., & Johnson, R. A. (2010). Human/animal interaction and successful aging. In A. H. Fine (Ed.), *Handbook on animal-assisted therapy: Theoretical foundations and guidelines for practice* (3rd ed., pp. 283–300). San Diego, CA: Academic Press.

Bengtsson, T., & Lindström, M. (2003). Airborne infectious diseases during infancy and mortality in later life in southern Sweden, 1766–1894. *International Journal of Epidemiology, 32*, 286–294.

Berdasco, M., & Esteller, M. (2010). Aberrant epigenetic landscape in cancer: How cellular identity goes awry. *Developmental Cell, 19*, 698–711.

Blackwell, D. L., Lucas, J. W., & Clarke, T. C. (2014). *Summary health statistics for U.S. adults: National Health Interview Survey, 2012*. Retrieved October 3, 2017, from https://www.cdc.gov/nchs/data/series/sr_10/sr10_260.pdf

Bokenberger, K., Pedersen, N. L., Gatz, M., et al. (2014). The type A behavior pattern and cardiovascular disease as predictors of dementia. *Health Psychology, 32*, 1593–1601.

Bosman, J. (2017). Inside a killer drug epidemic: A look at America's opioid crisis. *New York Times*. Retrieved October 13, 2017, from https://www.nytimes.com/2017/01/06/us/opioid-crisis-epidemic.html

Breslau, J., Lane, M., Sampson, N., et al. (2008). Mental disorders and subsequent educational attainment in a US national sample. *Journal of Psychiatric Research, 42*(9), 708–716.

Brown, T. H., Richardson, L. J., Hargrove, T. W., et al. (2016). Using multiple-hierarchy stratification and life course approaches to understand health inequalities: The intersecting consequences of race, gender, SES, and age. *Journal of Health and Social Behavior, 57*, 200–222.

Calder, N., & Aitken, R. (2008). An exploratory study of the influences that comprise the sun protection of young adults. *International Journal of Consumer Studies, 32*, 579–587.

Centers for Disease Control and Prevention. (2011). *Breast cancer rates by race and ethnicity*. Retrieved January 20, 2013, from http://www.cdc.gov/cancer/breast/statistics/race.htm

Centers for Disease Control and Prevention (2012). *Health, United States, 2011. With special feature on socioeconomic status and health*. Retrieved January 29, 2013 from https://www.cdc.gov/nchs/data/hus/hus11.pdf

Centers for Disease Control and Prevention. (2017). *Health, United States: 2015, with special features on racial and ethnic disparities*. Retrieved December 1, 2017, from http://www.cdc.gov/nchs/data/hus/hus15.pdf

Centers for Disease Control and Prevention (2017a). *10 leading causes of death by age group, United States – 2016*. Retrieved July 1, 2018 from https://www.cdc.gov/injury/images/lc-charts/leading_causes_of_death_age_group_2016_1056w814h.gif

Centers for Disease Control and Prevention (2017b). *Health, United States, 2016*. Retrieved June 14, 2018 from https://www.cdc.gov/nchs/data/hus/2016/021.pdf

Centers for Disease Control and Prevention (2017c). *Women and heart disease fact sheet*. Retrieved September 29, 2017 from https://www.cdc.gov/dhdsp/data_statistics/fact_sheets/fs_women_heart.htm

Centers for Disease Control and Prevention. (2018). *Vital statistics rapid release: Provisional drug overdose death counts*. Retrieved July 1, 2018, from https://www.cdc.gov/nchs/nvss/vsrr/drug-overdose-data.htm

Chetty, R., Stepner, M., Abraham, S., et al. (2016). The association between income and life expectancy in the United States, 2001–2014. *Journal of the American Medical Association, 315*, 1750–1766.

Chida, Y., & Hamer, M. (2008). Chronic psychosocial factors and acute physiological responses to laboratory-induced stress in healthy populations: A quantitative review of 30 years of investigations. *Psychological Bulletin, 134*, 829–885.

Coren, S. (2010). Foreword. In A. H. Fine (Ed.), *Handbook on animal-assisted therapy* (3rd ed., pp. xv–xviii). San Diego, CA: Academic Press.

Couzin, J. (2005). To what extent are genetic variation and personal health linked? *Science, 309,* 81.

Cuthbertson, A. (2017). *AI Robot Companion Wants to Keep Old People Company.* Newsweek. January 11, 2017, https://www.newsweek.com/ai-ageing-companion-alexa-old-people-elliq-artificial-intelligence-541481

Dowell, D., Arias, E., Kochanek, K., et al. (2017). Contribution of opioid-involved poisoning to the change in life expectancy in the United States 2000–2015. *Journal of the American Medical Association, 318,* 1065–1067.

Ellis, M. J., Ding, L., Shen, D., et al. (2012). Whole genome analysis informs breast cancer response to aromatase inhibition. *Nature, 486,* 353–360.

Erikson, W., Lee, C., & von Schrader, S. (2016). *2015 disability status report: United States.* Retrieved October 13, 2017, from http://www.disabilitystatistics.org/StatusReports/2015-PDF/2015-StatusReport_US.pdf

Finch C. E., & Crimmins, E. M. (2004). Inflammatory exposure and historical changes in human life-spans. *Science, 305,* 1736–1739.

Freedman, V. A. (2011). Disability, functioning, and aging. In R. H. Binstock & L. K. George (Eds.), *Handbook of aging and the social sciences* (7th ed., pp. 57–71). San Diego, CA: Academic Press.

Friedman, M., & Rosenman, R. H. (1959). Association of a specific overt behavior pattern with increases in blood cholesterol, blood clotting time, incidence of arcus senilis and clinical coronary artery disease. *Journal of the American Medical Association, 169,* 1286–1296.

Gluckman, P. D., & Hanson, M. A. (2004). Living with the past: Evolution, development, and pattern of disease. *Science, 305,* 1733–1739.

Goel, M. S., McCarthy, E. P., Phillips, R. S., et al. (2004). Obesity among U.S. immigrant subgroups by duration of residence. *Journal of the American Medical Association, 292,* 2860–2867.

Halter, J. B. (2011). Aging and insulin secretion. In E. J. Masoro & S. N. Austad (Eds.), *Handbook of the biology of aging* (pp. 373–384). San Diego, CA: Academic Press.

He, W., & Muenchrath, M. N. (2011). *90+ in the United States: 2006–2008.* U.S. Census Bureau. Retrieved February 12, 2013, from www.census.gov/prod/2011pubs/acs-17.pdf

Herd, P., Robert, S. A., & House, J. S. (2011). Health disparities among older adults: Life course influences and policy solutions. In R. H. Binstock & L. K. George (Eds.), *Handbook of aging and the social sciences* (7th ed., pp. 121–134). San Diego, CA: Academic Press.

Herman, W. H., & Rothberg, A. E. (2015). Prevalence of diabetes in the United States: A glimmer of hope? *Journal of the American Medical Association, 314,* 1005–1007.

Heron, M., Hoyert, D. L., Murphy, S. L., et al. (2009). Deaths: Final data for 2006. *National Vital Statistics Reports, 57,* 1–134.

Hevey, D., McGee, H. M., & Horgan, J. H. (2012). Comparative optimism among patients with coronary heart disease (CHD) is associated with fewer adverse clinical events 12 months later. *Journal of Behavioral Medicine, 37,* 300–307.

Holden, C. (2005). Sex and the suffering brain. *Science, 308,* 1574–1577.

Hope, C. W., McGurk, D., Thomas, J. L., et al. (2008). Mild traumatic brain injury in U.S. soldiers returning home from Iraq. *New England Journal of Medicine, 358,* 453–463.

Hoyert, D. L., & Xu, J. (2012, October 10). Deaths: Preliminary data for 2011. *National Vital Statistics Reports, 61(6).* Retrieved November 17, 2012, from http://www.cdc.gov/nchs/data/nvsr/nvsr61/nvsr61_06.pdf

Indian Health Services. (2016). *Indian Health Services: Disparities.* Retrieved December 21, 2016, from https://www.ihs.gov/newsroom/factsheets/disparities/

Jackson, J. S., Knight, K. M., & Rafferty, J. A. (2010). Rave and unhealthy behaviors: Chronic stress, the HPA axis, and physical and mental health over the life course. *American Journal of Public Health, 100,* 933–939.

Jonsson, T., Atwal, J. K., Steinberg, S., et al. (2012). A mutation in APP protects against Alzheimer's disease and age-related cognitive decline. *Nature, 488,* 96–99.

Kelly, S. (2016). New surgical robots may get a boost in operating rooms. *Scientific American.* Retrieved July 24, 2018, from https://www.scientificamerican.com/article/new-surgical-robots-may-get-a-boost-in-operating-rooms/?print=true

Kessler, R. C., Berglund, P., Demler, O., et al. (2005). Lifetime prevalence and age-of-onset distributions of *DSM-IV* disorders in the National Comorbidity Survey Replication. *Archives of General Psychiatry, 62,* 593–602.

Kraus, L. (2015). *Disability statistics annual report – 2015.* Retrieved November 8, 2016, from http://www.disabilitycompendium.org/docs/default-source/2015-compendium/annualreport_2015_final.pdf

Kugelmass, H. (2016). "Sorry, I'm not accepting new patients": An audit study of access to mental health care. *Journal of Health and Social Behavior, 57,* 168–183.

Kuh, D., & Ben-Shlomo, Y. (2016). Early life origins of adult health and aging. In L. K. George & K. F. Ferraro (Eds.), *Handbook of aging and the social sciences* (8th ed., pp. 101–122). San Diego, CA: Academic Press.

Lamond, A. J., Depp, C. A., Allison, M., et al. (2008). Measurement and predictors of resilience among community-dwelling older women. *Journal of Psychiatric Research, 43,* 148–154.

Legato, M. J. (2016). Consideration of sex differences in medicine to improve health care and patients outcomes. *Journal of the American Medical Association, 316,* 1865–1866.

Lemogne, C., Consoli, S. M., Geoffroy-Perez, B., et al. (2013). Personality and the risk of cancer: A 16-year follow-up study of the GAZEL cohort. *Psychosomatic Medicine, 75,* 262–271.

Lemogne, C., Schuster, J.-P., Levenstein, S., et al. (2015) Hostility and the risk of peptic ulcer in the GAZEL cohort. *Health Psychology, 34,* 181–185.

Linden, W., Phillips, M. J., & Leclerc, J. (2007). Psychological treatment of cardiac patients: A meta-analysis. *European Heart Journal, 28,* 2972–2954.

Looker, A. C., Isfahani, N. S., Fan, B., et al (2017). *FRAX-based estimates of 10-year probability of hip and major osteoporotic fracture among adults aged 40 and over:* United States, 2013 and 2014. Retrieved June 11, 2019 from https://www.cdc.gov/nchs/data/nshsr/nshsr103.pdf

Lyles, C. R., Karter, A. J., Young, B. A., et al. (2011). Correlates of patient-reported racial/ethnic health care discrimination in the Diabetes Study of North Carolina (DISTANCE). *Journal of Healthcare for the Poor and Underserved, 22,* 211–225.

Maciosek, M. V., Coffield, A. B., Flottemesch, T. J., et al. (2010). Greater use of preventive services in U.S. health care could save lives at little or no cost. *Health Affairs, 29,* 1656–1660.

Markides, K. S., & Coreil, J. (1986). The health of Hispanics in the southwestern United States: An epidemiologic paradox. *Public Health Reports, 101,* 253–265.

Mastorci, F., Vicentini, M., Viltart, O., et al. (2009). Long-term effects of prenatal stress: Changes in adult cardiovascular regulation and sensitivity to stress. *Neuroscience and Biobehavioral Reviews, 33,* 191–203.

Mez, J., Daneshvar, D. H., Kiernan, P. T., et al. (2017). Clinico-pathological evaluation of chronic trauma encephalopathy in players of American football. *Journal of the American Medical Association, 318,* 360–370.

Miller, B. A., Chu, K. C., Hankey, B. F., et al. (2007). Cancer incidence and mortality patterns among specific Asian and Pacific Islander populations in the U.S. *Cancer Causes and Control, 19,* 227–256.

Miller, G. E., Cohen, S., Janicki-Deverts, D., et al. (2016). Viral challenge reveals further evidence of skin-deep resilience in African Americans from disadvantaged backgrounds. *Health Psychology, 25,* 1225–1234.

Muoio, D. (2015). Japan is running out of people to take care of the elderly, so it's making robots instead. *Business Insider.* Retrieved October 1, 2017, from http://www.businessinsider.com/japan-developing-carebots-for-elderly-care-2015-11

National Center of Addiction and Substance Abuse. (2016). *Who develops addiction?* Retrieved October 13, 2017, from https://www.centeronaddiction.org/addiction/addiction-risk-factors

National Institute of Mental Health. (2016). *Depression: Treatment and therapies.* Retrieved October 7, 2017, from https://www.nimh.nih.gov/health/topics/depression/index.shtml#part_145399

National Institute of Mental Health. (2017). *Anxiety disorders: Treatment.* Retrieved October 6, 2017, from https://www.nimh.nih.gov/health/topics/anxiety-disorders/index.shtml

National Institute on Aging. (2011). *NIH commissioned census report describes oldest Americans.* Retrieved November 17, 2012, from http://www.nia.nih.gov/newsroom/2011/11/nih-commissioned-census-bureau-report-describes-oldest-americans

National Institute on Drug Abuse. (2016). *Fentanyl.* Retrieved October 12, 2017, from https://www.drugabuse.gov/publications/drugfacts/fentanyl

National Jewish Health Centers. (2018). *Cystic fibrosis: Life expectancy.* Retrieved July 25, 2018, from https://www.nationaljewish.org/conditions/cystic-fibrosis-cf/life-expectancy

Office of Disease Prevention and Health Promotion. (2016) *Healthy People 2020: Physical activity.* Retrieved December 15, 2016, from https://www.healthypeople.gov/2020/topics-objectives/topic/physical-activity#5072

Omalu, B., Hammers, J. L., Bailes, J., et al. (2011). Chronic traumatic encephalopathy in an Iraqi war veteran with posttraumatic stress disorder who committed suicide. *Neurosurgical Focus, 31,* E3.

Pressman, S. D., Gallagher, M. W., & Lopez, S. J. (2013). Is the emotion–health connection a "first world problem"? *Psychological Science, 24,* 544–549.

Purnell, J. Q., Selzer, F., & Wahed, A. S. (2016). Type 2 diabetes remission rates after laparoscopic gastric bypass and gastric banding: Results of the longitudinal assessment of bariatric surgery study. *Diabetes Care, 39,* 1101–1107.

Reed, D., & Yano, K. (1997). Cardiovascular disease among elderly Asian Americans. In L. G. Martin & B. J. Soldo (Eds.), *Racial and ethnic differences in the health of older Americans* (pp. 270–284). Washington, DC: National Academy Press.

Ritchie & Roser (2018). Our world in data: *Causes of death.* Retrieved July 23, 2018 from https://ourworldindata.org/causes-of-death

Roberts, A. H. (1969). *Brain damage in boxers: A study of the prevalence of traumatic encephalopathy among ex-professional boxers.* London: Pittman.

Ruthig, J. C., & Allery, A. (2008). Native American elders' health congruence: The role of gender and corresponding functional well-being, hospital admissions, and social engagement. *Journal of Health Psychology, 13,* 1072–1091.

Seligman, M. E. P. (1991). *Learned optimism.* New York: Knopf.

Shippee, T. P., Schafer, M. H., & Ferraro, K. F. (2012). Beyond the barriers: Racial discrimination and the use of complementary and alternative medicine among Black Americans. *Social Science and Medicine, 74,* 1155–1162.

Siegel, R. L., Miller, K. D., & Jenal, A. (2016). Cancer statistics: 2016. *CA: A Cancer Journal for Clinicians, 66,* 7–30.

Simon, S. (2017). *Cancer facts and figures: Death rate down 25% since 1991.* Retrieved January 5, 2017, from http://www.cancer.org/cancer/news/news/cancer-facts-and-figures-death-rate-down-25-since-1991

Smith, B. J., Lightfoot, S. A., Lerner, M. R., et al. (2009). Induction of cardiovascular pathology in a novel model of low-grade chronic inflammation. *Cardiovascular Pathology, 18,* 1–10.

Smith, T. W., & Gallo, L. C. (2001). Personality traits as risk factors for physical illness. In A. Baum, T. A. Revenson, & J. E. Singer (Eds.), *Handbook of health psychology* (pp. 139–173). Mahwah, NJ: Erlbaum.

Stöppler, M. C. (2015). *Women's health.* Retrieved December 15, 2016, from http://www.medicinenet.com/womens_health/page4.htm

Storandt, M. (2008). Cognitive deficits in the early stages of Alzheimer's disease. *Current Directions in Psychological Science, 17,* 198–202.

Substance Abuse and Mental Health Services Administration. (2016). *Treatment for substance abuse disorders.* Retrieved October 13, 2017, from https://www.samhsa.gov/treatment/substance-use-disorders

Thoits, P. A. (2010). Stress and health: Major findings and policy implications. *Journal of Health and Social Behavior, 51,* S41–S53.

U. S. Department of Health and Human Services. (2016). *Lesbian, gay, bisexual, and transgender health.* Retrieved December 23, 2016, from https://www.healthypeople.gov/2020/topics-objectives/topic/lesbian-gay-bisexual-and-transgender-health

Unson, C., Trella, P., Chowdhury, S., et al. (2008). Strategies for living long and healthy lives: Perspectives of older African/Caribbean-American women. *Journal of Applied Communication Research, 36,* 459–478.

Wang, P. S., Berglund, P., Olfson, M., et al. (2005). Failure and delay in initial treatment contact after first onset of mental disorder in the National Comorbidity Survey Replication. *Archives of General Psychiatry, 62,* 603–613.

Wang, P. S., Lane, M., Olfson, M., et al. (2005). Twelve-month use of mental health services in the United States. *Archives of General Psychiatry, 62,* 629–640.

Williams, G. C. (1957). Pleiotropy, natural selection, and the evolution of senescence. *Evolution, 11,* 398–411.

World Health Organization. (2012). *Ten leading causes of deaths in 2008: High-income and low- and middle-income countries.* Retrieved November 17, 2012, from http://gamapserver.who.int/gho/interactive_charts/mbd/cod_2008/graph.html

World Health Organization. (2016a). *Global report on diabetes.* Retrieved November 17, 2016, from http://apps.who.int/iris/bitstream/10665/204871/1/9789241565257_eng.pdf

World Health Organization. (2016b). *Mental health: Gender and women's mental health.* Retrieved December 15, 2016, from http://www.who.int/mental_health/prevention/genderwomen/en/

World Health Organization. (2017a). *Depression and other common mental disorders: Global health estimates.* Retrieved October 6, 2017, from http://apps.who.int/iris/bitstream/10665/254610/1/WHO-MSD-MER-2017.2-eng.pdf?ua=1

World Health Organization. (2017b). *Mental disorders: Fact sheet.* Retrieved October 6, 2017, from http://www.who.int/mediacentre/factsheets/fs396/en/

World Health Organization. (2009). *Global Health Risks.* Retrieved July 23, 2018, from https://www.who.int/healthinfo/global_burden_disease/GlobalHealthRisks_report_full.pdf

Yamanski, K., Uchida, K., & Katsuma, R. (2009). An intervention study of the effects of the coping strategy of "finding positive meaning" on positive affect and health. *International Journal of Psychology, 44,* 249–259.

Yu, J. W., Adams, S. H., Burns, J., et al. (2008). Use of mental health counseling as adolescents become young adults. *Journal of Adolescent Health, 43,* 268–276.

Ziol-Guest, K. M., Duncan, G. J., & Kalil, A. (2009). Early childhood poverty and adult body mass index. *American Journal of Public Health, 99,* 527–532.

CHAPTER 4

Ackerman, P. L. (2008). Knowledge and cognitive aging. In F. I. M. Craik & T. A. Salthouse (Eds.), *The handbook of aging and cognition* (3rd ed., pp. 443–489). New York: Psychology Press.

Adams, C., Smith, M. C., Pasupathi, M., et al. (2002). Social context effects on story recall in older and younger women: Does the listener make a difference? *Journals of Gerontology: Psychological and Social Sciences, 57,* 28–40.

Anderson, M. (2015). *For vast majority of seniors who own one, a smartphone equals "freedom."* Pew Research Center. Retrieved April 11, 2019, from https://www.pewresearch.org/fact-tank/2015/04/29/seniors-smartphones/

Ardila, A., Ostrosky-Solis, F., Rosselli, M., et al. (2000). Age related decline during normal aging: The complex effect of education. *Archives of Clinical Neuropsychology, 15,* 495–513.

Atchley, P., & Dressel, J. (2004). Conversation limits the functional field of view. *Human Factors: The Journal of the Human Factors and Ergonomics Society, 46,* 664–673.

Bäckman, L., & Nilsson, L. G. (1996). Semantic memory functions across the adult life span. *European Psychologist, 1,* 27–33.

Bäckman, L., Small, B. J., & Wahlin, Å. (2001). Aging and memory: Cognitive and biological perspectives. In J. E. Birren & K. W. Schaie (Eds.), *Handbook of the psychology of aging* (5th ed., pp. 349–377). San Diego, CA: Academic Press.

Bäckman, L., Small, B. J., Wahlin, Å., et al. (2000). Cognitive functioning in very old age. In F. I. M. Craik & T. A. Salthouse (Eds.), *The handbook of aging and cognition* (pp. 499–558). Hillsdale, NJ: Erlbaum.

Baddeley, A. D. (1986). *Working memory.* Oxford, UK: Oxford University Press.

Bailey, H., Dunlosky, J., & Hertzog, C. (2009). Does differential strategy use account for age-related deficits in working memory performance? *Psychology and Aging, 24,* 82–92.

Baldwin, C. L., & Ash, I. K. (2011). Impact of sensory acuity on auditory working memory span in young and older adults. *Psychology and Aging, 26,* 85–91.

Baltes, P. B., & Lindenberger, U. (1997). Emergence of a powerful connection between sensory and cognitive function across the adult life span: A new window to the study of cognitive aging? *Psychology and Aging, 12,* 12–21.

Baltes, P. B., & Staudinger, U. M. (1993). The search for a psychology of wisdom. *Current Directions in Psychological Science, 2,* 75–80.

Ben-David, B. M., Erel, H., Goy, H., et al. (2015). "Older is always better": Age-related differences in vocabulary scores across 16 years. *Psychology and Aging, 30,* 856–862.

Berg, C. A., & Sternberg, R. J. (2003). Multiple perspectives on the development of adult intelligence. In J. Demick & C. Andreoletti (Eds.), *Handbook of adult development* (pp. 103–119). New York: Kluwer.

Bielak, A. A. M., Gerstorf, D., Kiely, K. M., et al. (2011). Depressive symptoms predict decline in perceptual speed in older adulthood. *Psychology and Aging, 26,* 576–583.

Birkhill, W. R., & Schaie, K. W. (1975). The effects of differential reinforcement of cautiousness in intellectual performance among the elderly. *Journals of Gerontology: Psychological and Social Sciences, 30,* 578–583.

Bissig, D., & Lustig, C. (2007). Who benefits from psychological training? *Psychological Science, 18,* 720–726.

Blair, C. (2006). How similar are fluid cognition and general intelligence?: A developmental neuroscience perspective on fluid cognition as an aspect of human cognitive ability. *Behavioral and Brain Sciences, 29,* 109–125.

Blanchard-Fields, F. (2007). Everyday problem solving and emotion: An adult developmental perspective. *Current Directions in Psychological Science, 16,* 26–31.

Blanchard-Fields, F., Mienaltowski, A., & Seay, R. B. (2007). Age differences in everyday problem-solving effectiveness: Older adults select more effective strategies for interpersonal problems. *Journals of Gerontology: Psychological and Social Sciences, 62,* 61–64.

Borella, E., Carbone, E., Pastore, M., et al. (2017). Working memory training for healthy older adults: The role of individual characteristics in explaining short- and long-term gains. *Frontiers in Human Neurosciences, 11,* 178–191.

Brébion, G., Smith, M. J., & Ehrlich, M. F. (1997). Working memory and aging: Deficit or strategy differences? *Aging, Neuropsychology, and Cognition, 4,* 58–73.

Brehmer, Y., Li, S.-C., Müller, V., et al. (2007). Memory plasticity across the life span: Uncovering children's latent potential. *Developmental Psychology, 43,* 465–478.

Brennan, A. A., Bruderer, A. J., Liu-Ambrose, T., et al. (2017). Lifespan changes in attention revisited: Everyday visual search. *Canadian Journal of Experimental Psychology/Revue canadienne de psychologie expérimentale, 71,* 160–171.

Burack, O. R., & Lachman, M. E. (1996). The effects of list-making on recall in young and elderly adults. *Journals of Gerontology: Psychological and Social Sciences, 51,* 226–233.

Burke, D. M., & Shafto, M. A. (2008). Language and aging. In F. I. M. Craik & T. A. Salthouse (Eds.), *The handbook of aging and cognition* (3rd ed., pp. 373–443). New York: Psychology Press.

Cansino, S., Estrada Manilla, E, Hernández Ramos, J. G., et al. (2013). The rate of source memory decline across the adult lifespan. *Developmental Psychology, 49,* 973–985.

Cappell, K. S., Gmeindl, L., & Reuter-Lorenz, P. A. (2010). Age differences in DLPFC recruitment during verbal working memory depend on memory load. *Cortex, 46,* 462–473.

Carstensen, L. L., & Mikels, J. A. (2005). At the intersection of emotion and cognition: Aging and the positivity effect. *Current Directions in Psychological Science, 14,* 117–121.

Carstensen, L. L., Isaacowitz, D. M., & Charles, S. T. (1999). Taking time seriously: A theory of socioemotional selectivity. *American Psychologist, 54,* 165–181.

Carstensen, L. L., Mickels, J. A., & Mather, M. (2006). Aging and the intersection of cognition, motivation, and emotion. In R. H. Binstock & L. K. George (Eds.), *Handbook of aging and the social sciences* (6th ed., pp. 343–362). San Diego, CA: Academic Press.

Cattell, R. B. (1963). Theory of fluid and crystallized intelligence: A critical experiment. *Journal of Educational Psychology, 54,* 1–22.

Cepeda, N. J., Kramer, A. F., & Gonzalez de Sather, J. C. M. (2001). Changes in executive control across the life-span: Examination of task switching performance. *Developmental Psychology, 37,* 715–730.

Charles, S. T., Mather, M., & Carstensen, L. L. (2003). Aging and emotional memory: The forgettable nature of negative images for older adults. *Journal of Experimental Psychology: General, 132,* 310–324.

Charness, N. (1981). Visual short-term memory and aging in chess players. *Journals of Gerontology: Psychological and Social Sciences, 36,* 615–619.

Checchi, K. D., Huybrechts, K. F., Avorn, J., et al. (2014). Electronic medication packaging devices and medication adherence: a systematic review. *Journal of the American Medical Association, 312,* 1237–1247.

Chu, C.-H., Chen, A.-G., Hung, T.-M., et al. (2015). Exercise and fitness modulate cognitive function in older adults. *Psychology and Aging, 30,* 843–848.

Clarkson-Smith, L., & Hartley, A. A. (1990). The game of bridge as an exercise in working memory and reasoning. *Journals of Gerontology: Psychological and Social Sciences, 45,* 233–238.

Colcombe, S., & Kramer, A. F. (2003). Fitness effects on the cognitive function of older adults: A meta-analytic study. *Psychological Science, 14,* 125–130.

Colcombe, S., Erickson, K. I., Raz, N., et al. (2003). Aerobic fitness reduces brain tissue loss in aging humans. *Journals of Gerontology: Biological and Medical Sciences, 58,* 176–180.

Compton, D. M., Bachman, L. D., Brand, D., et al. (2000). Age-associated changes in cognitive function in highly educated adults: Emerging myths and realities. *International Journal of Geriatric Psychiatry, 15*, 75–85.

Craik, F. I. M. (2000). Age related changes in human memory. In D. Park & N. Schwarz (Eds.), *Cognitive aging: A primer* (pp. 75–92). Philadelphia, PA: Taylor & Francis.

Craik, F. I. M., & Byrd, M. (1982). Aging and cognitive deficits: The role of attentional resources. In F. I. M. Craik & S. Trehub (Eds.), *Aging and cognitive processes* (pp. 191–211). New York: Plenum Press.

Cullum, S., Huppert, F. A., McGee, M., et al. (2000). Decline across different domains of cognitive function in normal ageing: Results of a longitudinal population-based study using CAMCOG. *International Journal of Geriatric Psychiatry, 15*, 853–862.

Deary, I. J., Batty, G. D., Pattie, A., et al. (2008). More intelligent, more dependable children live longer: A 55-year longitudinal study of a representative sample of the Scottish nation. *Psychological Science, 19*, 874–880.

Desrichard, O., & Köpetz, C. (2005). A threat in the elder: The impact of task instructions, self-efficacy and performance expectations on memory performance in the elderly. *European Journal of Social Psychology, 35*, 537–552.

Dixon, R. A. (2000). Concepts and mechanisms of gains in cognitive aging. In D. Park & N. Schwarz (Eds.), *Cognitive aging: A primer* (pp. 23–42). Philadelphia, PA: Taylor & Francis.

Dixon, R. A., de Frias, C. M., & Maitland, S. B. (2001). Memory in midlife. In M. E. Lachman (Ed.), *Handbook of midlife development* (pp. 248–278). New York: Wiley.

Dykiert, D., Der, G., Starr, J. M., et al. (2012). Sex differences in reaction time mean and intraindividual variability across the life span. *Developmental Psychology, 48*, 1262–1276.

Earles, J. L., Kersten, A. W., Curtayne, E. S., et al. (2008). That's the man who did it, or was it a woman?: Actor similarity and binding errors in event memory. *Psychonomic Bulletin Review, 15*, 1185–1189.

Earles, J. L., Kersten, A. W., Vernon, L. L., et al. (2016). Memory for positive, negative and neutral events in younger and older adults: Does emotion influence binding in event memory? *Cognition and Emotion, 30*, 378–388.

Einstein, G. O., & McDaniel, M. A. (2005). Prospective memory: Multiple retrieval processes. *Current Directions in Psychological Science, 14*, 286–290.

Emery, C. F., Finkel, D., & Pedersen, N. L. (2012). Pulmonary function as a cause of cognitive aging. *Psychological Science, 23*, 1024–1032.

Fahlander, K., Wahlin, Å., Fastborn, J., et al. (2000). The relationship between signs of cardiovascular deficiency and cognitive performance in old age: A population-based study. *Journals of Gerontology: Psychological and Social Sciences, 55*, 259–265.

Flynn, J. R. (1987). Massive IQ gains in 14 nations: What IQ tests really measure. *Psychological Bulletin, 101*, 171–191.

Fung, H. H., & Carstensen, L. L. (2003). Sending memorable messages to the old: Age differences in preferences and memory for advertisements. *Journal of Personality and Social Psychology, 85*, 163–178.

Getzmann, S., Golob, E. J., & Wascher, E. (2016). Focused and divided attention in a simulated cocktail-party situation: ERP evidence from younger and older adults. *Neurobiology of Aging, 41*, 138–149.

Gottfredson, L. S., & Deary, I. J. (2004). Intelligence predicts health and longevity, but why? *Current Directions in Psychological Science, 13*, 1–4.

Gow, A. J., Johnson, W., Pattie, A., et al. (2011). Stability and change in intelligence from age 11 to ages 70, 79, and 87: The Lothian Birth Cohorts of 1921 and 1936. *Psychology and Aging, 26*, 232–240.

Gregoire, J., & Van der Linden, M. (1997). Effects of age on forward and backward digit span. *Aging, Neuropsychology, and Cognition, 4*, 140–149.

Gross, A. L., & Rebok, G. W. (2011). Memory training and strategy use in older adults: Results from the ACTIVE Study. *Psychology and Aging, 26*, 503–517.

Gruber-Baldini, A. L., Schaie, K. W., & Willis, S. L. (1995). Similarity in married couples: A longitudinal study of mental abilities and flexible-rigidity. *Journal of Personality and Social Psychology: Personality Processes and Individual Differences, 69*, 191–203.

Guye, S., & von Bastian, C. C. (2017). Working memory training in older adults: evidence for the absence of transfer. *Psychology and Aging, 32*, 732–746.

Håkansson, K., Ledreux, A., Daffner, K., et al. (2017). BDNF responses in healthy older persons to 35 minutes of physical exercise cognitive training, and mindfulness: Associations with working memory function. *Journal of Alzheimer's Disease, 55*, 645–657.

Hale, S., Rose, N. S., Myerson, J., et al. (2011). The structure of working memory abilities across the adult life span. *Psychology and Aging, 26*, 92–110.

Hargis, M. B., & Castel, A. D. (2017). Younger and older adults' associative memory for social information: The role of information importance. *Psychology and Aging, 32*, 325–330.

Henry, J. D., MacLeod, M. S., Phillips, L. H., et al. (2004). A meta-analytic review of prospective memory and aging. *Psychology and Aging, 19*, 27–39.

Henry, J. D., Rendell, P. G., Phillips, L. H., et al. (2012). Prospective memory reminders: A laboratory investigation of initiation source and age effects. *Quarterly Journal of Experimental Psychology, 65*, 1274–1287.

Hershey, D. A., & Wilson, J. A. (1997). Age differences in performance awareness on a complex financial decision-making task. *Experimental Aging Research, 23*, 257–273.

Hess, T. M. (2005). Memory and aging in context. *Psychological Bulletin, 131*, 383–406.

Hess, T. M., Auman, C., Colcombe, S. J., et al. (2003). The impact of stereotype threat on age differences in memory performance. *Journals of Gerontology: Psychological and Social Sciences, 58*, 3–11.

Hess, T. M., Hinson, J. T., & Statham, J. A. (2004). Implicit and explicit stereotype activation effects on memory: Do age and awareness moderate the impact of priming? *Psychology and Aging, 19*, 495–505.

Hogeboom, D. L., McDermott, R. J., Perrin, K. M., et al. (2010). Internet use and social networking among middle aged and older adults. *Educational Gerontology, 36*, 93–111.

Horn, J. L., & Cattell, R. B. (1966). Refinement and test of the theory of fluid and crystallized intelligence. *Journal of Educational Psychology, 57*, 253–270.

Horn, J. L., & Hofer, S. M. (1992). Major abilities and development in the adult period. In R. J. Sternberg & C. A. Berg (Eds.), *Intellectual development* (pp. 44–99). Cambridge, UK: Cambridge University Press.

Hoyer, W. J., & Verhaeghen, P. (2006). Memory and aging. In J. E. Birren & K. W. Schaie (Eds.), *Handbook of the psychology of aging* (6th ed., pp. 209–232). San Diego, CA: Academic Press.

Hultsch, D. F., Hertzog, C., Dixon, R. A., et al. (1998). *Memory change in the aged*. Cambridge, UK: Cambridge University Press.

Insurance Institute for Highway Safety. (2018). *Teenagers: Driving carries extra risk for them*. Retrieved April 11, 2019, from https://www.iihs.org/iihs/topics/t/teenagers/fatalityfacts/teenagers

James, W. (1890). The perception of reality. *Principles of Psychology, 2*, 283–324.

Jennings, J. M., Webster, L. M., Kleykamp, B. A., et al. (2005). Recollection training and transfer effects in older adults: Successful use of a repetition-lag procedure. *Aging, Neuropsychology, and Cognition, 12*, 278–298.

Jensen, A. R. (1998). *The g factor: The science of mental ability*. Westport, CT: Praeger.

Johnson, M. M. S. (1993). Thinking about strategies during, before, and after making a decision. *Psychology and Aging, 8*, 231–141.

Jones, L. B., Rothbart, M. K., & Posner, M. I. (2003). Development of executive attention in preschool children. *Developmental Science, 6,* 498–504.

Kersten, A. W., Earles, J. L., Curtayne, E. S., et al. (2008). Adult age differences in binding actors and actions in memory for events. *Memory and Cognition, 36,* 119–131.

Kim, S., Healey, M. K., Goldstein, D., et al. (2008). Age differences in choice satisfaction: A positivity effect in decision making. *Psychology and Aging, 23,* 33–38.

Kinderman, S. S., & Brown, G. G. (1997). Depression and memory in the elderly: A meta-analysis. *Journal of Clinical and Experimental Neuropsychology, 19,* 625–642.

Kliegel, M., Mackinlay, R., & Jäger, T. (2008). Complex prospective memory: Development across the lifespan and the role of task interruption. *Developmental Psychology, 44,* 612–617.

Kliegl, R., Smith, J., & Baltes, P. B. (1990). On the locus and process of magnification of age differences during mnemonic training. *Developmental Psychology, 26,* 894–904.

Kramer, A. F., & Willis, S. L. (2002). Enhancing the cognitive vitality of older adults. *Current Directions in Psychological Science, 11,* 173–177.

Kretzschmar, F., Pleimling, D., Hosemann, J., et al. (2013). Subjective impressions do not mirror online reading effort: Concurrent EEG-eyetracking evidence from the reading of books and digital media. *PLoS ONE, 8,* e56178.

Lane, C. J., & Zelinski, E. M. (2003). Longitudinal hierarchical linear models of the Memory Functioning Questionnaire. *Psychology and Aging, 18,* 38–53.

Laursen, P. (1997). The impact of aging on cognitive function. *Acta Neurologica Scandinavica Supplementum, 96,* 7–86.

Levy, B. R., & Leifheit-Limson, E. (2009). The stereotype-matching effect: Greater influence on functioning when age stereotypes correspond to outcomes. *Psychology and Aging, 24,* 230–233.

Li, S. C., Lindenberger, U., Hommel, B., et al. (2004). Transformations in the couplings among intellectual abilities and constituent cognitive processes across the life span. *Psychological Science, 15,* 155–163.

Lin, F. R. (2011). Hearing loss and cognition among older adults in the United States. *Journals of Gerontology: Biological Sciences and Medical Sciences, 66,* 1131–1136.

Lin, F. R., Ferrucci, L., Metter, E. J., et al. (2011). Hearing loss and cognition in the Baltimore Longitudinal Study of Aging. *Neuropsychology, 25,* 761–770.

Lindenberger, U., & Baltes, P. B. (1994). Sensory functioning and intelligence in old age: A strong connection. *Psychology and Aging, 9,* 339–355.

Lindenberger, U., & Baltes, P. B. (1997). Intellectual functioning in old and very old age: Cross-sectional results from the Berlin Aging Study. *Psychology and Aging, 12,* 410–432.

Loprinzi, P. D. (2016). Epidemiological investigation of muscle-strengthening activities and conitive function among older adults. *Chronic Illness, 12,* 157–162.

Loprinzi, P. D., Edwards, M. K., Crush, E., et al. (2018). Dose–response association between physical activity and cognitive function in a national sample of older adults. *American Journal of Health Promotion, 32,* 554–560.

Maillot, P., Perrot, A., & Hartley, A. (2012). Effects of interactive physical-activity video-game training on physical and cognitive function in older adults. *Psychology and Aging, 27,* 589–600.

Manly, J. J., Jacobs, D. M., Sano, M., et al. (1999). Effect of literacy on neuropsychological test performance in nondemented, education-matched elders. *Journal of the International Neuropsychological Society, 5,* 191–202.

Masunaga, H., & Horn, J. (2001). Expertise and age-related changes in the components of intelligence. *Psychology and Aging, 16,* 293–311.

Mather, M., & Carstensen, L. L. (2003). Aging and attentional biases for emotional faces. *Psychological Science, 14,* 409–415.

Maylor, E. A. (1990). Age and prospective memory. *Quarterly Journal of Experimental Psychology, 42A,* 471–493.

Mazerolle, M., Régner, I., Morisset, P., et al. (2012). Stereotype threat strengthens automatic recall and undermines controlled processes in older adults. *Psychological Science, 23,* 723–727.

McCarthy, J. (2018). *Older Americans' use of Facebook up from 2011.* Retrieved April 11, 2019, from https://news.gallup.com/poll/233456/older-americans-facebook-2011.aspx?utm_source=alert&utm_medium=email&utm_content=morelink&utm_campaign=syndication

McClearn, G. E., Johansson, B., Berg, S., et al. (1997). Substantial genetic influence on cognitive abilities in twins 80 or more years old. *Science, 276,* 1560–1563.

McGue, M., Bouchard, T. J., Iacono, W. G., et al. (1993). Behavioral genetics of cognitive ability: A life-span perspective. In R. Plomin & G. E. McClearn (Eds.), *Nature, nurture, and psychology* (pp. 59–76). Washington, DC: American Psychological Association.

Melby-Lervåg, M., Redick, T. S., & Hulme, C. (2016). Working memory training does not improve performance on measures of intelligence of other measures of "far transfer": Evidence from a meta-analytic review. *Perspectives on Psychological Sciences, 11,* 512–534.

Meyer, B. J. F., Russo, C., & Talbot, A. (1995). Diverse comprehension and problem solving: Decisions about the treatment of breast cancer by women across the life span. *Psychology and Aging, 10,* 84–103.

Mikels, J. S., Larkin, G. R., Reuter-Lorenz, P. A., et al. (2005). Divergent trajectories in the aging mind: Changes in working memory for affective versus visual information with age. *Psychology and Aging, 20,* 542–553.

Miyake, A., & Friedman, N. P. (2012). The nature and organization of individual differences in executive functions: Four general conclusions. *Current Directions in Psychological Sciences, 21,* 8–14.

National Highway Traffic Safety Administration. (2015). *Motor vehicle traffic crashes as a leading cause of death in the United States, 2010 and 2011.* Retrieved April 11, 2019, from https://www.pewresearch.org/fact-tank/2015/04/29/seniors-smartphones/ https://crashstats.nhtsa.dot.gov/Api/Public/ViewPublication/812203

Nisbett, R. E., Aronson, J., Blair, C., et al. (2012). Intelligence: New findings and theoretical directions. *American Psychologist, 67,* 130–156.

Old, S. R., & Naveh-Benjamin, M. (2012). Age differences in memory for names: The effect of prelearned semantic associations. *Psychology and Aging, 27,* 462–473.

Ornstein. P. A., & Light, L. L. (2010). Memory development across the life span. In R. M. Lerner (Series Ed.) & W. F. Overton (Vol. Ed.), *Handbook of life-span development: Vol. 1. Biology, cognition, and methods across the life span* (pp. 295–305). Hoboken, NJ: Wiley.

Parisi, J. M., Gross, A. L., Marsiske, M., et al. (2017). Control beliefs and cognition over a 10-year period: Findings from the ACTIVE Trial. *Psychology and Aging, 32,* 69–75.

Park, D. C., & McDonough, I. (2013). The dynamic aging mind: Revelations from functional neuroimaging research. *Perspectives in Psychological Science, 8,* 62–67.

Park, D. C., Lautenschlager, G., Hedden, T., et al. (2002). Models of visuospatial and verbal memory across the adult life span. *Psychology and Aging, 17,* 299–320.

Plomin, R., DeFries, J. C., McClearn, G. E., et al. (2008). *Behavioral genetics* (5th ed.). New York: Worth.

Pollatsek, A., Romoser, M. R. E., & Fisher, D. L. (2012). Identifying and remediating failures of selective attention in older drivers. *Current Directions in Psychological Science, 21,* 3–7.

Ponds, R. W. H. M., van Boxtel, M. P. J., & Jolles, J. (2000). Age-related changes in subjective cognitive functioning. *Educational Gerontology, 26,* 67–81.

Reuter-Lorenz, P. A. (2013). Aging and cognitive neuroimaging: A fertile union. *Perspectives on Psychological Science, 8,* 68–71.

Rodrigue, K. M., Kennedy, K. M., & Raz, N. (2005). Aging and longitudinal change in perceptual-motor skill acquisition in healthy adults. *Journals of Gerontology: Psychological and Social Sciences, 60,* 174–181.

Roenker, D. L., Cissell, G. M., Ball, K. K., et al. (2003). Speed-of-processing and driving simulator training result in improved driving performance. *Human Factors: The Journal of the Human Factors and Ergonomics Society, 45,* 218–233.

Rogers, R. L., Meyer, J. S., & Mortel, K. F. (1990). After reaching retirement age physical activity sustains cerebral perfusion and cognition. *Journal of the American Geriatric Society, 38,* 123–128.

Rönnlund, M., Nyberg, L., Bäckman, L., et al. (2005). Stability, growth, and decline in adult life span development of declarative memory: Cross-sectional and longitudinal data from a population-based study. *Psychology and Aging, 20,* 3–18.

Sabaté, E. (2003). *Adherence to long-term therapies: Evidence for action.* Geneva, Switzerland: World Health Organization.

Salthouse, T. A. (1991). *Theoretical perspectives on cognitive aging.* Hillsdale, NJ: Erlbaum.

Salthouse, T. A. (1996). The processing-speed theory of adult age differences in cognition. *Psychological Review, 103,* 401–428.

Salthouse, T. A. (2004). What and when of cognitive aging. *Current Directions in Psychological Science, 13,* 140–144.

Salthouse, T. A. (2016). Aging cognition unconfounded by prior test experience. *Journals of Gerontology: Psychological Sciences & Social Sciences, 71,* 49–58.

Salthouse, T. A., Babcock, R. L., Skovronek, E., et al. (1990). Age and experience effects in spatial visualization. *Developmental Psychology, 26,* 128–136.

Samrani, G., Bäckman, L., & Persson, J. (2017). Age-differences in the temporal properties of proactive interference in working memory. *Psychology and Aging, 32,* 722–731.

Sanfey, A. C., & Hastie, R. (2000). Judgment and decision making across the adult life span: A tutorial review of psychological research. In D. Park & N. Schwarz (Eds.), *Cognitive aging: A primer* (pp. 253–273). Philadelphia, PA: Taylor & Francis.

Schacter, D. L. (1997). False recognition and the brain. *Current Directions in Psychological Science, 6,* 65–70.

Schaie, K. W. (1983). What can we learn from the longitudinal study of adult development? In K. W. Schaiae (Ed.), *Longitudinal studies of adult psychological development* (pp. 1–19). New York: Guilford Press.

Schaie, K. W. (1994). The course of adult intellectual development. *American Psychologist, 49,* 304–313.

Schaie, K. W. (1996). Intellectual development in adulthood. In J. E. Birren & K. W. Schaie (Eds.), *Handbook of the psychology of aging* (4th ed., pp. 265–286). San Diego, CA: Academic Press.

Schaie, K. W. (2006). Intelligence. In R. Schulz (Ed.), *Encyclopedia of aging* (4th ed., pp. 600–602). New York: Springer.

Schaie, K. W. (2013). *Developmental influences on adult intelligence: The Seattle Longitudinal Study* (2nd ed.). New York: Oxford University Press.

Schaie, K. W., & Willis, S. L. (1986). Can decline in adult intellectual functioning be reversed? *Developmental Psychology, 22,* 223–232.

Schaie, K. W., & Zanjani, F. (2006). Intellectual development across adulthood. In C. Hoare (Ed.), *Oxford handbook of adult development and learning* (pp. 99–122). New York: Oxford University Press.

Schneider-Graces, N. J., Gordon, B. A., Brumback-Peltz, C. R., et al. (2010). Span, CRUNCH, and beyond: Working memory capacity and the aging brain. *Journal of Cognitive Neuroscience, 22,* 655–669.

Schooler, C., Caplan, L., & Oates, G. (1998). Aging and work: An overview. In K. W. Schaie & C. Schooler (Eds.), *Impact of work on older adults* (pp. 1–10). New York: Springer.

Schryer, E., & Ross, M. (2012). Evaluating the valence of remembered events: The importance of age and self-relevance. *Psychology and Aging, 27,* 237–242.

Shafto, M. A., Burke, D. M., Stamatakis, E. A., et al. (2007). On the tip-of-the-tongue: Neural correlates of increased word-finding failures in normal aging. *Journal of Cognitive Neuroscience, 19,* 2060–2070.

Sims, R. V., McGwin, G., Jr., Allman, R. M., et al. (2000). Exploratory study of incident vehicle crashes among older drivers. *Journals of Gerontology: Biological and Medical Sciences, 55,* 22–27.

Sinnott, J. D. (1996). The development of complex reasoning: Postformal thought. In F. Blanchard-Fields & T. Hess (Eds.), *Perspectives on cognitive change in adulthood and aging* (pp. 358–383). New York: McGraw-Hill.

Smith R. E., & Hunt, R. R. (2014) Prospective memory in young and older adults: The effects of task importance and ongoing task load. *Aging, Neuropsychology, and Cognition, 21,* 411–431.

Smith, A., & Anderson, M. (2018). *Social media use in 2018: A majority of Americans use Facebook and YouTube, but young adults are especially heavy users of Snapchat and Instagram.* Retrieved June 11, 2019 from https://www.pewinternet.org/2018/03/01/social-media-use-in-2018/

Smith, C. D., Walton, A., Loveland, A. D., et al. (2005). Memories that last in old age: Motor skill learning and memory preservation. *Neurobiology of Aging, 26,* 883–890.

Smith, J., & Baltes, P. B. (1999). Trends and profiles of psychological functioning in very old age. In P. B. Baltes & K. U. Mayer (Eds.), *The Berlin Aging Study: Aging from 70 to 100* (pp. 197–226). Cambridge, UK: Cambridge University Press.

Spearman, C. (1904). General intelligence, objectively determined and measured. *American Journal of Psychology, 15,* 201–203.

Tulving, E. (1985). How many memory systems are there? *American Psychologist, 40,* 385–398.

Tulving, E. (2005). Episodic memory and autonoesis: Uniquely human? In H. S. Terrace & J. Metcalfe (Eds.), *The missing link in cognition: Origins of self-reflective consciousness* (pp. 3–56). New York: Oxford University Press.

U.S. Census Bureau. (2012a). *College enrollment by sex, age, race, and Hispanic origin.* Retrieved April 29, 2013, from http://www.census.gov/compendia/statab/2012/tables/12s0281.pdf

Uttl, B., & Van Alstine, C. L. (2003). Rising verbal intelligence scores: Implications for research and clinical practice. *Psychology and Aging, 18,* 616–621.

Verhaegen, C., Collette, F., & Majerus, S. (2014). The impact of aging and hearing status on verbal short-term memory. *Aging, Neuropsychology, and Cognition, 21,* 464–482.

Waldstein, S. R., & Katzel, L. I. (2006). Interactive relations of central versus total obesity and blood pressure in cognitive function. *International Journal of Obesity (London), 30,* 201–207.

Weatherbee, S. R., & Allaire, J. C. (2008). Everyday cognition and mortality: Performance differences and predictive utility of the Everyday Cognition Battery. *Psychology and Aging, 23,* 216–221.

Wechsler, D. (1939). *The measurement of adult intelligence.* Baltimore, MD: Williams & Wilkins.

Willis, S. L., & Schaie, K. W. (1994). Cognitive training in the normal elderly. In F. Forette, Y. Christen, & F. Boller (Eds.), *Plasticité cérébrale et stimulation cognitive* (pp. 91–113). Paris: Foundational National de Gérontologie.

Willis, S. L., Tennstedt, S. L., Marsiske, M., et al. (2006). Long-term effects of cognitive training on everyday functional outcomes in older adults. *Journal of the American Medical Association, 296,* 2805–2814.

Wilson, R. S., Bennett, D. A., Beckett, L. A., et al. (1999). Cognitive activity in older persons from a geographically defined population. *Journals of Gerontology: Psychological and Social Sciences, 54,* 155–160.

Wingfield, A., Tun, P. A., & McCoy, S. L. (2005). Hearing loss in older adulthood: What it is and how it interacts with cognitive performance. *Current Directions in Psychological Science, 14,* 144–148.

Worthy, D. A., Gorlik, M. A., Pacheco, J. L., et al. (2011). With age comes wisdom: Decision making in younger and older adults. *Psychological Science, 22,* 1375–1380.

Yesavage, J., Lapp, D., & Sheikh, J. A. (1989). Mnemonics as modified for use by the elderly. In L. W. Poon, D. Rubin, & B. Wilson (Eds.), *Everyday cognition in adulthood and late life* (pp. 509–544). Cambridge, MA: Cambridge University Press.

Yi, Y., & Friedman, D. (2014). Age-related differences in working memory: ERPs reveal age-related delays in selection- and inhibition-related processes. *Aging, Neuropsychology, and Cognition, 21*, 483–513.

Zhu, W., Wadley, V. G., Howard, V. J., et al. (2016). Objectively measured physical activity and cognitive function in older adults. *Medicine and Science in Sports and Exercise, 49*, 47–53.

Zogg, J. B., Woods, S. P., Sauceda, J. A., et al. (2012). The role of prospective memory in medication adherence: A review of an emerging literature. *Journal of Behavioral Medicine, 35*, 47–62.

CHAPTER 5

American Psychological Association. (2017a). *Mental and physical health effects of family caregiving.* Retrieved June 30, 2017, from http://www.apa.org/pi/about/publications/caregivers/faq/health-effects.aspx

American Psychological Association. (2017b). *Positive aspects of caregiving.* Retrieved June 30, 2017, from http://www.apa.org/pi/about/publications/caregivers/faq/positive-aspects.aspx

Amirkhanyan, A. A., & Wolf, D. A. (2003). Caregiver stress and noncaregiver stress: Exploring the pathways of psychiatric morbidity. *The Gerontologist, 43*, 817–827.

Anesensel, C. S., Harig, F., & Wight, R. G. (2016). Aging, neighborhoods, and the built environment. In L. K. George & K. F. Ferraro (Eds.), *Handbook of aging and the social sciences* (8th ed., pp. 315–335). San Diego, CA: Academic Press.

Antonucci, T. C., Berkman, L., Börsch-Supan, A., et al. (2016). Society and the individual at the dawn of the twenty-first century. In K. W. Schaie & S. L. Willis (Eds.), *Handbook of the psychology of aging* (8th ed., pp. 41–62). San Diego, CA: Academic Press.

Arnett, J. J. (2000). Emerging adulthood. *American Psychologist, 55*, 469–480.

Arnett, J. J. (2007). Emerging adulthood: What is it, and what is it good for? *Child Development Perspectives, 1*, 68–73.

Azaola, M. C. (2012). Becoming a migrant: Aspirations of youths during their transition to adulthood in rural Mexico. *Journal of Youth Studies, 15*, 875–889.

Bayer, A.-H., & Harper, L. (2000). *Fixing to stay: National survey of housing and home modification issues.* Retrieved July 25, 2017, from https://assets.aarp.org/rgcenter/il/home_mod.pdf

Becker, G. (1981). *A treatise on the family.* Cambridge, MA: Harvard University Press.

Belsky, J., & Kelly, J. (1994). *The transition to parenthood: How a first child changes marriage. Why some couples grow together and others apart.* New York: Dell.

Belsky, J., Spanier, G. B., & Rovine, M. (1983). Stability and change in marriage across the transition to parenthood. *Journal of Marriage and the Family, 45*, 567–577.

Bem, S. L. (1981). Gender schema theory: A cognitive account of sex typing. *Psychological Review, 88*, 354–364.

Bem, S. L. (1993). *The lenses of gender: Transforming the debate on sexual inequality.* New Haven, CT: Yale University Press.

Boivin, J., Bunting, L., Collins, J. A., et al. (2007). International estimates of infertility prevalence and treatment-seeking: Potential need and demand for infertility medical care. *Human Reproduction, 22*, 1506–1512.

Bureau of Labor Statistics. (2016). *American Time Use Survey.* Retrieved December 17, 2018, from https://www.bls.gov/tus/tables/a6_1115.htm

Bureau of Labor Statistics. (2017). *Economic news release: Employment status of parents by age of youngest child and family type, 2015–2016.* Retrieved June 14, 2017, from https://www.bls.gov/news.release/famee.t04.htm

Canário, C., & Figueiredo, B. (2016). Partner relationship from early pregnancy to 30 months postpartum: Gender and parity effects. *Couple and Family Psychology: Research and Practice, 5*, 226–239.

Centers for Disease Control and Prevention (CDC). (2016). *Infertility.* Retrieved July 11, 2017, from https://www.cdc.gov/nchs/fastats/infertility.htm

Centers for Disease Control and Prevention (CDC). (2017a). *ART success rates.* Retrieved July 11, 2017, from https://www.cdc.gov/art/artdata/index.html

Centers for Disease Control and Prevention (CDC). (2017b). *Births and natality.* Retrieved June 5, 2017, from https://www.cdc.gov/nchs/fastats/births.htm

Centers for Disease Control and Prevention. (2017c). *Unmarried childbearing.* Retrieved June 5, 2017, from https://www.cdc.gov/nchs/fastats/unmarried-childbearing.htm

Chang, E., Wilbur, K. H., & Silverstein, M. (2010). The effects of childlessness on the care and psychological well-being of older adults with disabilities. *Aging and Mental Health, 14*, 712–719.

Cheng, S.-T., Mak, E. P. M., Lau, R. W. I., et al. (2015). Voices of Alzheimer caregivers on positive aspects of caregiving. *The Gerontologist, 56*, 451–460.

Copen, C. E., Daniels, K., & Mosher, W. D. (2013). *First premarital cohabitation in the United States 2006–2010 National Survey of Family Growth* (National Health Statistics Report No. 64). Retrieved May 30, 2017, from https://www.cdc.gov/nchs/data/nhsr/nhsr064.pdf

Cowan, C. P., & Cowan, P. A. (1995). Interventions to ease the transition to parenthood: Why they are needed and what they can do. *Family Relations, 44*, 412–423.

Craig, J., & Foster, H. (2013). Desistance in the transition to adulthood: The roles of marriage, military, and gender. *Deviant Behavior, 34*, 208–223.

Cumming, E., & Henry, W. E. (1961). *Growing old.* New York: Basic Books.

Deaux, K., & Lewis, L. L. (1984). Structure of gender stereotypes: Interrelationships among components and gender labels. *Journal of Personality and Social Psychology, 46*, 991–1004.

Doty, P., Nadash, P., & Racco, N. (2015). Long-term care financing: Lessons from France. *Milbank Quarterly, 93*, 359–391.

Douglass, C. B. (2007). From duty to desire: Emerging adulthood in Europe and its consequences. *Child Development Perspectives, 1*, 101–108.

Eagly, A. H. (1987). *Sex differences in social behavior: A social role interpretation.* Hillsdale, NJ: Erlbaum.

Eagly, A. H. (1995). The science and politics of comparing men and women. *American Psychologist, 50*, 145–158.

Elder, G. H., Jr. (1995). The life course paradigm: Social change and individual development. In P. Moen, G. H. Elder, Jr., & K. Luscher (Eds.), *Examining lives in context: Perspectives on the ecology of human development* (pp. 101–139). Washington, DC: American Psychological Association.

Elder, G. H., Jr. (2001). Life course: Sociological aspects. In N. J. Smelser & P. B. Baltes (Eds.), *International encyclopedia of the social and behavioral sciences* (Vol. 13, pp. 8817–8821). Oxford, UK: Elsevier.

Facio, A., Resett, S., Micocci, F., et al. (2007). Emerging adulthood in Argentina: An age of diversity and possibilities. *Child Development Perspectives, 1*, 115–118.

Family Caregiver Alliance. (2016). *Caregiver statistics: Demographics.* Retrieved June 24, 2017, from https://www.caregiver.org/caregiver-statistics-demographics

Ferraro, K. F. (2001). Aging and role transitions. In R. H. Binstock & L. K. George (Eds.), *Handbook of aging and the social sciences* (5th ed., pp. 313–330). San Diego, CA: Academic Press.

Fleeson, W. (2004). The quality of American life at the end of the century. In O. G. Brim, C. D. Ryff, & R. C. Kessler (Eds.), *How healthy are we?: A national study of well-being at midlife* (pp. 252–272). Chicago: University of Chicago Press.

Fredman, L., Bertrand, R. M., Martire, L. M., et al. (2006). Leisure-time exercise and overall physical activity in older women caregivers and non-caregivers from the Caregiver-SOF Study. *Preventive Medicine, 43*, 226–229.

Fry, R. (2014). *New census data show more Americans are tying the knot, but mostly it is the college-educated.* Pew Research Center. Retrieved May 30, 2017, from http://www.pewresearch.org/fact-tank/2014/02/06/new-census-data-show-more-americans-are-tying-the-knot-but-mostly-its-the-college-educated/

Fry, R. (2016). *For the first time in modern era, living with parents edges out other living arrangements for 18 to 34 year olds.* Pew Research Center. Retrieved May 25, 2017, from http://www.pewsocialtrends.org/2016/05/24/2-living-with-mom-andor-dad-more-common-for-sons-than-daughters/st_2016-05-24_young-adults-living-06/

Galambos, N. L., & Martinez, M. L. (2007). Poised for emerging adulthood in Latin America: A pleasure for the privileged. *Child Development Perspectives, 1*, 109–114.

Galst, J. P. (2017). The elusive connection between stress and infertility: A research review with clinical implications. *Journal of Psychotherapy Integration, 28*, 1–13.

Geary, D. C. (2005). Evolution of paternal investment. In D. M. Buss (Ed.), *The handbook of evolutionary psychology* (pp. 483–505). New York: Wiley.

Goldberg, A. E., & Perry-Jenkins, M. (2007). The division of labor and perceptions of parental roles: Lesbian couples across the transition to parenthood. *Journal of Social and Personal Relationships, 24*, 297–318.

Goldberg, A. E., Smith, J. Z., & Perry-Jenkins, M. (2012). The division of labor in lesbian, gay, and heterosexual new adoptive parents. *Journal of Marriage and Family, 74*, 812–828.

Gottman, J. M., Gottman, J. S., & Shapiro, A. F. (2010). A new couples approach to interventions for the transition to parenthood. In M. S. Schulz, M. K. Pruett, P. Kerig, et al. (Eds.), *Strengthening couple relationships for optimal child development: Lessons from research and intervention* (pp. 165–179). Washington, DC: American Psychological Association.

Gutmann, D. (1987). *Reclaimed powers: Toward a new psychology of men and women in later life.* New York: Basic Books.

Hagestad, G. O., & Neugarten, B. L. (1985). Age and the life course. In R. H. Binstock & E. Shana (Eds.), *Handbook of aging and the social sciences* (2nd ed., pp. 35–61). New York: Van Nostrand Reinhold.

Haines, E. L., Deaux, K., & Lofaro, N. (2016). The times they are a-changing . . . or are they not?: A comparison of gender stereotypes, 1983–2014. *Psychology of Women, 40*, 353–363.

Hareven, T. K. (2001). Historical perspectives on aging and family relations. In R. H. Binstock & L. K. George (Eds.), *Handbook of aging and the social sciences* (5th ed., pp. 141–159). San Diego, CA: Academic Press.

Heckhausen, J. (2001). Adaptation and resilience in midlife. In M. E. Lachman (Ed.), *Handbook of midlife development* (pp. 345–394). New York: Wiley.

Jung, C. G. (1971). *Psychological types* (Collected works of C. G. Jung, Volume 6). Princeton, NJ: Princeton University Press

Kreider, R. M., & Ellis, R. (2011). *Number, timing, and duration of marriages and divorces: 2009.* Retrieved March 27, 2013, from http://www.census.gov/prod/2011pubs/p70-125.pdf

Krogstad, J. M. (2015). *Pew Research Center: Five facts about American grandparents.* Retrieved June 23, 2017, from http://www.pewresearch.org/fact-tank/2015/09/13/5-facts-about-american-grandparents/

Lachs, M. S., & Pillemer, K. A. (2015). Elder abuse. *New England Journal of Medicine, 373*, 1947–1956.

Lampkin, C. L. (2012). *AARP: Insights and spending habits of modern grandparents.* Retrieved March 22, 2013, from http://www.aarp.org/content/dam/aarp/research/surveys_statistics/general/2012/Insights-and-Spending-Habits-of-Modern-Grandparents-AARP.pdf

Lemaster, P., Delaney, R., & Strough, J. (2017). Crossover, degendering, or . . . ?: A multidimensional approach to life-span gender development. *Sex Roles, 76*, 669–681.

Lemasters, E. E. (1957). Parenthood as a crisis. *Marriage and Family Living, 19*, 352–355.

Leopold, T. (2012). The legacy of leaving home: Long-term effects of coresidence on parent–child relationships. *Journal of Marriage and Family, 74*, 399–412.

Livingston, G. (2015). *Childlessness falls, family size grows among highly educated women.* Pew Research Center. Retrieved July 5, 2017, from http://www.pewsocialtrends.org/2015/05/07/childlessness-falls-family-size-grows-among-highly-educated-women/

Luhmann, M., & Hawkley, L. C. (2016). Age differences in loneliness from late adolescence to oldest old age. *Developmental Psychology, 16*, 943–959.

Luscombe, B. (2014). *Why aren't you married?* Pew Research Center. Retrieved July 5, 2017, from http://time.com/3422624/report-millennials-marriage/

Manago, A. M. (2012). The new emerging adult in Chiapas, Mexico: Perceptions of traditional values change among first-generation Maya university students. *Journal of Adolescent Research, 27*, 663–713.

Martin, J. A., Hamilton, B. E., Ventura, S. J., et al. (2012). *Births: Final data for 2010. National Vital Statistics Report.* Centers for Disease Control and Prevention. Retrieved March 18, 2013, from http://www.cdc.gov/nchs/data/nvsr/nvsr61/nvsr61_01.pdf\#table01

McAdams, D. P. (2001). Generativity in midlife. In M. E. Lachman (Ed.), *Handbook of midlife development* (pp. 395–443). New York: Wiley.

McGinn, K. L., Ruiz Castro, M., & Long Lingo, E. (2019). Learning from mum: Cross-national evidence linking maternal employment and adult children's outcomes. *Work, Employment and Society, 33*, 374–400.

National Alliance of Caregiving. (2015). *Caregiving in the U.S. 2015.* Retrieved June 24, 2017, from http://www.prweb.com/releases/2015/06/prweb12765231.htm

National Center on Elder Abuse. (2016). *Research, statistics, data.* Retrieved July 21, 2017, from https://ncea.acl.gov/whatwedo/research/statistics.html

Nelson, L. J., & Chen, X. (2007). Emerging adulthood in China: The role of social and cultural factors. *Child Development Perspectives, 1*, 86–91.

Neugarten, B. L. (1996). *The meanings of age: Selected papers of Bernice L. Neugarten.* Chicago: University of Chicago Press.

Neugarten, B. L., Moore, J. W., & Lowe, J. C. (1965). Age norms, age constraints, and adult socialization. *American Journal of Sociology, 70*, 710–717.

Newcomer, R. J., Kang, T., & Doty, P. (2012) Allowing spouses to be paid personal care providers: Spouse availability and effects on Medicaid-funded service use and expenditures. *The Gerontologist, 52*, 517–530.

Nitsche, N., & Grunow, D. (2015). Housework over the course of a relationship: Gender ideology, resources, and the division of housework from a growth curve perspective. *Advances in Life Course Research, 28*, 80–94.

Organisation for Economic Cooperation and Development. (2016). *Mean age of women at first birth, 1970, 1995, and 2014.* Retrieved June 13, 2017, from https://www.oecd.org/els/soc/SF_2_3_Age_mothers_childbirth.pdf

Phelan, K. (2005). Generativity and psychological well-being in middle-age adults. *Dissertation Abstracts International: Section B: The Sciences and Engineering, 65*, 4323.

Roberto, K. A. (2016). Abusive relationships in late life. In L. K. George & K. F. Ferraro (Eds.), *Handbook of aging and the social sciences* (8th ed., pp. 337–353). San Diego, CA: Academic Press.

Rosenberger, N. (2007). Rethinking emerging adulthood in Japan: Perspectives from long-term single women. *Child Development Perspectives*, 1, 92–95.

Rossi, A. S. (2004). The menopause transition and aging processes. In O. G. Brim, C. D. Ryff, & R. C. Kessler (Eds.), *How healthy are we?: A national study of well-being at midlife* (pp. 153–201). University of Chicago Press.

Roth, D. L., Perkins, M., Wadley, V. G., et al. (2009). Family caregiving and emotional strain: Associations with quality of life in a large national sample of middle-aged and older adults. *Quality of Life Research*, 18, 679–688.

Sayer, L. C. (2006). Economic aspects of divorce and relationship dissolution. In M. A. Fine & J. H. Harvey (Eds.), *Handbook of divorce and relationship dissolution* (pp. 385–406). Mahwah, NJ: Erlbaum.

Schmidt, D. P. (2017). *The truth about sex differences*. Retrieved December 27, 2017, from https://www.psychologytoday.com/articles/201711/the-truth-about-sex-differences

Schulenberg, J. E., Sameroff, A. J., & Cicchetti, D. (2004). The transition to adulthood as a critical juncture in the course of psychopathology and mental health. *Development and Psychopathology*, 16, 799–806.

Shanahan, M. J. (2000). Pathways to adulthood in changing societies: Variability and mechanisms in life course perspective. *Annual Review of Sociology*, 26, 667–692.

Silverstein, M., & Marenco, A. (2001). How Americans enact the grandparent role over the life course. *Journal of Family Issues*, 22, 493–522.

Stepler, R. (2016). *Smaller share of women ages 65 and older are living alone*. Retrieved February 25, 2017, from http://www.pewsocialtrends.org/files/2016/02/ST_2016-02-18_older-adult-FINAL.pdf

Stringer, H. (2017). Psychologists who treat the trauma of infertility. *APA Monitor on Psychology*, 48, 70–72.

Trivers, R. L. (1972). Parental investment and sexual selection. In B. Campbell (Ed.), *Sexual selection and the descent of man: 1871–1971* (pp. 136–179). Chicago: Aldine.

Tynkkynen, L., Tolvanen, A., & Salmela-Aro, K. (2012). Trajectories of educational expectations from adolescence to young adulthood in Finland. *Developmental Psychology*, 48, 1674–1685.

U.S. Census Bureau. (2016). *Current population survey, chart 7: Grandchildren under age 18 living in the home of their grandparents: 1970 to 2014*. Retrieved June 23, 2017, from https://www.census.gov/newsroom/press-releases/2014/cb14-194.html

U.S. Department of Health and Human Services. (2017). *A profile of older Americans: 2016*. Retrieved July 25, 2017 from https://www.giaging.org/documents/A_Profile_of_Older_Americans__2016.pdf

Van Alstine Makomenaw, M. (2012). Welcome to a new world: Experiences of American Indian tribal college and university transfer students at predominantly white institutions. *International Journal of Qualitative Studies in Education*, 25, 855–866.

Vespa, J. (2017). *United States Census Bureau: The changing economics and demographics of young adulthood, 1975–2016*. Retrieved May 25, 2017, from https://www.census.gov/content/dam/Census/library/publications/2017/demo/p20-579.pdf

Vespa, J., Lewis, J. M., & Kreider, R. M. (2013). *America's families and living arrangements, 2013*. Retrieved June 26, 2017, from https://www.census.gov/prod/2013pubs/p20-570.pdf

Weaver, S. E., & Coleman, M. (2005). A mothering but not a mother role: A grounded theory study of the nonresidential stepmother role. *Journal of Social and Personal Relationships*, 22, 477–497.

Williams, J. E., & Best, D. L. (1990). *Measuring sex stereotypes: A multination study* (Rev. ed.). Newbury Park, CA: Sage.

Wiltz, T. (2016). *Why more grandparents are raising children: Pew Charitable Trust*. Retrieved June 23, 2017, from http://www.pewtrusts.org/en/research-and-analysis/blogs/stateline/2016/11/02/why-more-grandparents-are-raising-children

Wolff, J. L., Mulcahy, J., Huang, J., et al. (2018). Family caregiver of older adults, 1999–2015: Trends in characteristics, circumstances, and role-related appraisal. *The Gerontologist*, 58, 1021–1032.

Zhang, Z., & Hayward, M. D. (2001). Childlessness and the psychological well-being of older persons. *Journals of Gerontology: Psychological and Social Sciences*, 56, 311–320.

CHAPTER 6

Abetz, J., & Wang, T. R. (2017). "Were they ever really happy the way that I remember?": Exploring sources of uncertainty for adult children of divorce. *Journal of Divorce and Remarriage*, 58, 194–211.

Ainsworth, M. D. S., Blehar, M., Waters, E., et al. (1978). *Patterns of attachment*. Hillsdale, NJ: Erlbaum.

Ajrouch, K. J., Blandon, A. Y., & Antonucci, T. C. (2005). Social networks among men and women: The effects of age and socioeconomic status. *Journals of Gerontology: Psychological and Social Sciences*, 60, 311–317.

Alterovitz, S. S.-R., & Mendelsohn, G. A. (2011). Partner preferences across the life span: Online dating by older adults. *Psychology of Popular Media Culture*, 1, 89–95.

Anderson, B., Fagan, P., Woodnutt, T., et al. (2012). Facebook psychology: Popular questions answered by research. *Psychology of Popular Media Culture*, 1, 23–37.

Anderson, R. (2016). *The ugly truth about online dating*. Retrieved November 17, 2017, from https://www.psychologytoday.com/blog/the-mating-game/201609/the-ugly-truth-about-online-dating

Antonucci, T. C. (1986). Social support networks: A hierarchical mapping technique. *Generations*, 3, 10–12.

Antonucci, T. C. (1990). Social supports and social relationships. In R. H. Binstock & L. K. George (Eds.), *Handbook of aging and the social sciences* (3rd ed., pp. 205–226). San Diego, CA: Academic Press.

Antonucci, T. C., Akiyama, H., & Takahashi, K. (2004). Attachment and close relationships across the life span. *Attachment and Human Development*, 6, 353–370.

Antonucci, T. C., Birditt, K. S., & Akiyama, H. (2009). Convoys of social relations: An interdisciplinary approach. In V. Bengston, M. Silverstein, N. Putney, et al. (Eds.), *Handbook of theories of aging* (pp. 247–260.). New York: Springer.

Antonucci, T., Jackson, J. S., & Biggs, S. (2007). *Intergenerational relations: Theory, research, and policy*. Malden, MA: Blackwell.

Aron, A., Fisher, H., Mashek, D., et al. (2005). Reward, motivation, and emotion systems associated with early-stage intense romantic love. *Journal of Neurophysiology*, 93, 327–337.

Attar-Schwartz, S., Tan, J.-P., Buchanan, A., et al. (2009). Grandparent and adolescent adjustment in two-parent biological, lone-parent, and step-families. *Journal of Family Psychology*, 23, 67–75.

Balsam, K. F., Rothblum, E. D., & Beauchaine, T. P. (2005). Victimization over the life span: A comparison of lesbian, gay, bisexual, and heterosexual siblings. *Journal of Consulting and Clinical Psychology*, 73, 477–487.

Bartholomew, K. (1990). Avoidance of intimacy: An attachment perspective. *Journal of Social and Personal Relationships*, 7, 147–178.

Bartholomew, K., & Horowitz, L. M. (1991). Attachment styles among young adults: A test of a four-category model. *Journal of Personality and Social Psychology*, 61, 226–244.

Bates, J. S., & Goodsell, T. L. (2013). Male kin relationships: Grandfathers, grandsons, and generativity. *Marriage and Family Review*, 49, 28–50.

Bates, J. S., & Taylor, A. C. (2012). Grandfather involvement and aging men's mental health. *American Journal of Men's Health*, 6, 229–239.

Baumeister, R. F., & Leary, M. R. (1995). The need to belong: Desire for interpersonal attachments as a fundamental human motivation. *Psychological Bulletin, 117*, 497–529.

Bengtson, V. L., & Schrader, S. S. (1982). Parent–child relations. In D. Mangen & W. Peterson (Eds.), *Research instruments in social gerontology* (pp. 114–128). Minneapolis: University of Minnesota Press.

Birditt, K. S., Fingerman, K. L., & Zarit, S. (2010). Adult children's problems and successes: Implications for intergenerational ambivalence. *Journals of Gerontology: Psychological and Social Sciences, 65*, 146–153.

Blieszner, R. (2000). Close relationships in old age. In C. Hendrick & S. S. Hendrick (Eds.), *Close relationships: A sourcebook* (pp. 85–95). Thousand Oaks, CA: Sage.

Boll, T., Ferring, D., & Filipp, S. H. (2005). Effects of parental differential treatment on relationship quality with siblings and parents: Justice evaluations as mediators. *Social Justice Research, 18*, 155–182.

Bourassa, K. J., Sbarra, D. A., & Whisman, M. A. (2015). Women in very low quality marriages gain life satisfaction following divorce. *Journal of Family Psychology, 29*, 490–499.

Bowlby, J. (1969). *Attachment and loss: Vol. 1. Attachment*. New York: Basic Books.

Bowlby, J. (1973). *Attachment and loss: Vol. 2. Separation: Anxiety and anger*. New York: Basic Books.

Brown, A. (2017). *5 key findings about LGBT Americans*. Retrieved November 18, 2017, from http://www.pewresearch.org/fact-tank/2017/06/13/5-key-findings-about-lgbt-americans/

Buss, D. M. (2009). How can evolutionary psychology successfully explain personality and individual differences? *Perspectives on Psychological Science, 4*, 359–366.

Buss, D. M., & Kenrick, D. T. (1998). Evolutionary social psychology. In D. T. Gilbert, S. T. Fisk, & G. Lindzey (Eds.), *The handbook of social psychology* (4th ed., Vol. 2, pp. 982–1026). New York: McGraw-Hill.

Campbell, L., & Ellis, B. J. (2005). Commitment, love, and mate retention. In D. M. Buss (Ed.), *The handbook of evolutionary psychology* (pp. 419–442). New York: Wiley.

Caporeal, L. R. (1997). The evolution of truly social cognition: The core configuration model. *Personality and Social Psychology Review, 1*, 276–298.

Carmalt, J. H., Cawley, J., Joyner, K., et al. (2008). Body weight and matching with a physically attractive romantic partner. *Journal of Marriage and Family, 70*, 1287–1296.

Carmichael, C. L., Reis, H. T., & Duberstein, P. R. (2015). In your 20s it's quantity: The prognostic value of social activity across 30 years of adulthood. *Psychology and Aging, 30*, 95–105.

Carstensen, L. L. (1995). Evidence for a life span theory of socioemotional selectivity. *Current Directions in Psychological Science, 4*, 151–156.

Carstensen, L. L., Mickels, J. A., & Mather, M. (2006). Aging and the intersection of cognition, motivation, and emotion. In R. H. Binstock & L. K. George (Eds.), *Handbook of aging and the social sciences* (6th ed., pp. 343–362). San Diego, CA: Academic Press.

Cate, R. M., & Lloyd, S. A. (1992). *Courtship*. Newbury Park, CA: Sage.

Cate, R. M., Levin, L. A., & Richmond, L. S. (2002). Premarital relationship stability: A review of recent research. *Journal of Social and Personal Relationships, 19*, 261–284.

Chopik, W. J., Edelstein, R. S., & Grimm, K. J. (2017). Longitudinal changes in attachment orientation over a 59-year period. *Journal of Personality and Social Psychology, 116*, 598–611.

Cicirelli, V. G. (1991). Attachment theory in old age: Protection of the attached figure. In K. Pillemer & K. McCartney (Eds.), *Parent–child relations throughout life* (pp. 2–42). Hillsdale, NJ: Erlbaum.

Clausell, E., & Roisman, G. I. (2009). Outness: Big Five personality traits and same-sex relationship quality. *Journal of Social and Personality Relationships, 26*, 211–226.

Clements, M. L., Stanley, S. M., & Markman, H. J. (2004). Before they say "I do": Discriminating among marital outcomes over 13 years. *Journal of Marriage and Family, 66*, 613–626.

Coall, D. A., & Hertwig, R. (2011). Grandparental investment: A relic of the past or a resource for the future? *Current Directions in Psychological Science, 20*, 93–98.

Connidis, I. A. (2009). *Family ties and aging* (2nd ed.). Los Angeles, CA: Sage.

Cornwell, B., & Schafer, M. H. (2016). Social networks in later life. In L. K. George & K. F. Ferraro (Eds.), *Handbook of aging and the social sciences* (8th ed., pp. 181–201). San Diego, CA: Academic Press.

D'Angelo, J. D., & Toma, C. L. (2017). There are plenty of fish in the sea: The effects of choice overload and reversibility on online daters' satisfaction with selected partners. *Media Psychology, 20*, 1–27.

de Waal, F. (1996). *Good natured: The origins of right and wrong in humans and other animals*. Cambridge, MA: Harvard University Press.

DeKay, W. T. (2000). Evolutionary psychology. In W. C. Nichols, N. A. Pace-Nichols, D. S. Becvar, et al. (Eds.), *Handbook of family development and intervention* (pp. 23–40). New York: Wiley.

DeKay, W. T., & Shackelford, T. K. (2000). Toward an evolutionary approach to social cognition. *Evolution and Cognition, 6*, 185–195.

Derby, R. W., & Ayala, J. (2013). Am I my brother's keeper?: Adult siblings raising younger siblings. *Journal of Human Behavior in the Social Environment, 23*, 193–210.

Fales, M. R., Frederick, D. A., Garcia, J. R., et al. (2016). Mating markets and bargaining hands: Mate preferences for attractiveness and resources in two national U.S. studies. *Personality and Individual Differences, 88*, 78–87.

Feeney, J., & Noller, P. (1996). *Adult attachment*. Thousand Oaks, CA: Sage.

Field, D. (1999). Continuity and change in friendships in advanced old age: Findings from the Berkeley older generation study. *International Journal of Aging and Human Development, 48*, 325–346.

Filmore, J. M., Baretto, D., & Ysasi, N. S. (2016). Counseling gay and lesbian couples. In I. Marini M. A. Stebnicki (Eds.), *The professional counselor's desk reference* (2nd ed., pp. 403–408). New York: Springer.

Fingerman, K. L., Cheng, Y.-P., Birditt, K., et al. (2012). Only as happy as the least happy child: Multiple grown children's problems and successes and middle-aged parents' well-being. *Journals of Gerontology: Psychological and Social Sciences, 67*, 184–193.

Fingerman, K. L., Kim, K., Birditt, K. S., et al. (2016). The ties that bind: Midlife parents' daily experiences with grown children. *Journal of Marriage and Family, 78*, 431–450.

Fisher, H. E., Xu, X., Aron, A., et al. (2016). Intense, passionate, romantic love: A natural addiction?: How the fields that investigate romance and substance abuse can inform each other. *Frontiers in Psychology, 7*, 687.

Fisher, H. L. (2000). Lust, attraction, attachment: Biology and evolution of the three primary emotion systems for mating, reproduction, and parenting. *Journal of Sex Education and Therapy, 25*, 96–104.

Fisher, H. L. (2004). *Why we love: The nature and chemistry of romantic love*. New York: Henry Holt.

Floyd, K., & Morman, M. T. (2005). Fathers' and sons' reports of fathers' affectionate communication: Implications of a naïve theory of affection. *Journal of Social and Personal Relationships, 22*, 99–109.

Fraley, R. C., Roisman, G. I., Booth-LaForce, C., et al. (2013). Interpersonal and genetic origins of adult attachment styles: A longitudinal study from infancy to early adulthood. *Journal of Personality and Social Psychology, 104*, 817–838.

Frost, R. L., & Rickwood, D. J. (2017). A systematic review of the mental health outcomes associated with Facebook use. *Computers in Human Behavior, 76*, 576–600.

Gallath, O., Karantzas, G. C., & Selcuk, E. (2017). A net of friends: Investigating friendship by integrating attachment theory and social network analysis. *Personality and Social Psychology Bulletin, 43,* 1546–1565.

Garanzini, S., Yee, A., Gottman, J., et al. (2017). Results of Gottman method couples therapy with gay and lesbian couples. *Journal of Marital and Family Therapy, 43,* 674–684.

Gates, G. J (2016). *In U.S., more adults identifying as LGBT: Gallup Poll.* Retrieved November 18, 2017, from http://news.gallup.com/poll/201731/lgbt-identification-rises.aspx

Geurts, T., van Tilburg, T. G., & Rigt-Poortman, A. (2012). The grandparent–grandchild relationship in childhood and into adulthood: A matter of continuation? *Personal Relationships, 19,* 267–278.

Gold, D. T. (1996). Continuities and discontinuities in sibling relationships across the life span. In V. L. Bengtson (Ed.), *Adulthood and aging: Research on continuities and discontinuities (pp. 228–243).* New York: Springer.

Gottman, J. M. (2011). *The science of trust: Emotional attunement for couples.* New York: Norton.

Gottman, J. M., & Notarius, C. I. (2000). Marital research in the 20th century and a research agenda for the 21st century. *Family Process, 41,* 159–197.

Greenwood, S., Perrin, A., & Duggan. M. (2017). *Social media update 2016.* Retrieved October 27, 2017, from http://www.pewinternet.org/2016/11/11/social-media-update-2016/

Greve, W., & Bjorklund, D. F. (2009). The Nestor effect: Extending evolutionary psychology to a lifespan perspective. *Developmental Review, 29,* 163–179.

Harman, J. J. (2011). How similar or different are homosexual and heterosexual relationships? In G. W. Lewandowski, Jr., T. J. Loving, B. Le, et al. (Eds.), *The science of relationships (pp. 60–66).* Dubuque, IA: Kendall Hunt.

Hatfield, E. (1988). Passionate and compassionate love. In R. J. Sternberg & M. L. Barnes (Eds.), *The psychology of love* (pp. 191–217). New Haven, CT: Yale University Press.

Hawkes, K., O'Connell, J. F., & Blurton Jones, N. G. (1997). Hazda women's time allocation, offspring provisioning, and the evolution of long post-menopausal lifespans. *Current Anthropology, 38,* 551–577.

Hawkins, D. N., & Booth, A. (2005). Unhappily ever after: Effects of long-term, low quality marriages on well-being. *Social Forces, 84,* 451–471.

Hazan, C., & Shaver, P. (1987). Romantic love conceptualized as an attachment process. *Journal of Personality and Social Psychology, 52,* 511–524.

Hazan, C., & Shaver, P. (1990). Love and work: An attachment theoretical perspective. *Journal of Personality and Social Psychology, 59,* 270–280.

Henderson, C. E., Hayslip, B., Jr., Sanders, L. M., et al. (2009). Grandmother–grandchild relationship quality predicts psychological adjustment among youth from divorced families. *Journal of Family Issues, 30,* 1245–1264.

Hewitt, B., & de Vaus, D. (2009). Change in the association between premarital cohabitation and separation: Australia 1954–2000. *Journal of Marriage and Family, 71,* 353–361.

Holt-Lunstad, J., Smith, T. B., & Layton, J. B. (2010). Social relationships and mortality risk: A meta-analytic review. *PLoS Medicine, 7,* e1000316.

Hrdy, S. B. (2011). *Mothers and others: The evolutionary origins of mutual understanding.* Cambridge, MA: Belknap.

Inagaki T. K., & Orchek, E. (2017). On the benefits of giving social support: When, why, and how support providers gain by caring for others. *Current Directions in Psychological Science, 26,* 109–115.

Jankowiak, W. R., & Fischer, E. F. (1992). A cross-cultural perspective on romantic love. *Ethnology, 31,* 149.

Jones, E. (1981). *The life and work of Sigmund Freud.* New York: Basic Books.

Kahn, R. L., & Antonucci, T. C. (1980). Convoys over the life course: Attachment, roles, and social support. In P. B. Baltes & O. Brim (Eds.), *Life-span development and behavior* (Vol. 3, pp. 253–268). New York: Academic Press.

Kanter, M., Afifi, T., & Robbins, S. (2012). The impact of parents "friending" their young adult child on Facebook on perceptions of parental privacy invasions and parent–child relationship quality. *Journal of Communications, 62,* 900–917.

Kaptin, R., Thomese, F., van Tilburg, T. G., et al. (2010). Support for the cooperative breeding hypothesis in a contemporary Dutch population. *Human Nature, 21,* 393–405.

Kemp, C. L. (2005). Dimensions of grandparent–adult grandchild relationships: From family ties to intergenerational friendships. *Canadian Journal on Aging, 24,* 161–178.

Kline, G. H., Stanley, S. M., Markman, H. J., et al. (2004). Timing is everything: Pre-engagement cohabitation and increased risk for poor marital outcomes. *Journal of Family Psychology, 18,* 311–318.

Knudsen, K. (2012). European grandparents' solicitude: Why older men can be relatively good grandparents. *Acta Sociologica, 55,* 231–250.

Krause, N. (2007). Longitudinal study of social support and meaning in life. *Psychology and Aging, 22,* 456–465.

Kryla-Lighthall, N., & Mather, M. (2009). The role of cognitive control in older adults' emotional well-being. In V. Berngtson, D. Gans, N. Putney, et al. (Eds.), *Handbook of theories of aging* (pp. 323–344). New York: Springer.

Kurdek, L. A. (2004). Are gay and lesbian cohabiting couples really different from heterosexual married couples? *Journal of Marriage and Family, 66,* 880–900.

Lee, K. S., & Ono, H. (2012). Marriage, cohabitation, and happiness: A cross-national analysis of 27 countries. *Journal of Marriage and Family, 74,* 953–972.

Liu, D., Kirschner, P. A., & Karpinski, A. C. (2017). A meta-analysis of academic performance and social network site use among adolescents and young adults. *Computers in Human Behavior, 77,* 148–157.

Loew, B., Rhoades, G., Markman, H., et al. (2012). Internet delivery of PREP-based education for at-risk couples. *Journal of Couple and Relationship Therapy, 11,* 291–309.

Loving, T. J. (2011). Should I live with my partner before we get married? In G. W. Lewandowski, Jr., T. J. Loving, B. Le, et al. (Eds.), *The science of relationships* (pp. 80–83). Dubuque, IA: Kendall Hunt.

Magdol, L., Moffitt, T. E., Caspi, A., et al. (1998). Developmental antecedents of partner abuse: A prospective-longitudinal study. *Journal of Abnormal Psychology, 107,* 375–389.

Mansson, D. H., & Booth-Butterfield, M. (2011). Grandparents' expressions of affection for their grandchildren: Examining grandchildren's relational attitudes and behaviors. *Southern Communication Journal, 76,* 424–442.

Markman, H. J., & Rhoades, G. K. (2012). Relationship education research: Current status and future directions. *Journal of Marriage and Family Therapy, 38,* 169–200.

Markman, H. J., Rhoades, G. K., Stanley, S. M., et al. (2010a). A randomized clinical trial of the effectiveness of premarital intervention: Moderators of divorce outcomes. *Journal of Family Psychology, 27,* 165–172.

Markman, H. J., Stanley, S. M., & Blumberg, S. L. (2010b). *Fighting for your marriage* (3rd ed.). San Francisco, CA: Jossey-Bass.

Masci, D., Brown, A., & Kiley, J. (2017). *Five facts about same-sex marriage.* Pew Research Center. Retrieved November 20, 2017, from http://www.pewresearch.org/fact-tank/2017/06/26/same-sex-marriage/

McClain, L., & Brown, S. L. (2017). The roles of fathers' involvement and coparenting in relationship quality among cohabiting and married parents. *Sex Roles, 76,* 334–354.

McGee, E., & Shevlin, M. (2009). Effect of humor on interpersonal attraction and mate selection. *Journal of Psychology: Interdisciplinary and Applied, 143*, 67–77.

Meuwly, N., & Schoebi, D. (2017). Social psychological and related theories on long-term committed romantic relationships. *Evolutionary Behavioral Sciences, 11*, 106–120.

Michelson, K. D., Kessler, R. C., & Shaver, P. R. (1997). Adult attachment in a nationally representative sample. *Journal of Personality and Social Psychology, 73*, 1092–1106.

Mikulincer, M., & Orbach, I. (1995). Attachment styles and repressive defensiveness: The accessibility and architecture of affective memories. *Journal of Personality and Social Psychology, 5*, 917–925.

Mikulincer, M., & Shaver, P. R. (2009). An attachment and behavioral systems perspective on social support. *Journal of Social and Personal Relationships, 26*, 7–19.

Milevsky, A. (2005). Compensatory patterns of sibling support in emerging adulthood: Variations in loneliness, self-esteem, depression, and life satisfaction. *Journal of Social and Personal Relationships, 22*, 743–755.

Murray, C. E., & Kardatzke, K. N. (2009). Addressing the needs of adult children of divorce in premarital counseling: Research-based guidelines for practice. *The Family Journal, 17*, 126–133.

Neyer, F. J. (2002). Twin relationships in old age: A developmental perspective. *Journal of Social and Personality Relationships, 20*, 31–53.

O'Leary, K. D., Acevedo, B. P., Aron, A., et al. (2012). Is long-term love more than a rare phenomenon? If so, what are its correlates? *Social Psychological and Personality Science, 3*, 241–249.

Pew Research Center. (2017). *Social media fact sheet.* Retrieved October 27, 2017, from http://www.pewinternet.org/fact-sheet/social-media/

Poushter, J. (2016). *Social networking very popular among adult internet users in emerging and developing nations.* Retrieved October 30, 2017, from http://www.pewglobal.org/2016/02/22/social-networking-very-popular-among-adult-internet-users-in-emerging-and-developing-nations/

Rainie, L., Smith, A., & Duggan, M. (2013). *Coming and going on Facebook.* Pew Research Center Report. Retrieved April 22, 2013, from http://pewinternet.org/Reports/2013/Coming-and-going-on-facebook/Key-Findings.aspx

Rhoades, G. K., Stanley, S. M., & Markman, H. J. (2009). The pre-engagement cohabitation effect: A replication and extension of previous findings. *Journal of Family Psychology, 30*, 233–258.

Rigt-Poortman, A., & van Tilburg, T. G. (2005). Past experiences and older adults' attitudes: A life course perspective. *Ageing and Society, 25*, 19–30.

Rubin, O. (2015). Contact between parents and adult children: the role of time constraints, commuting and automobility. *Journal of Transport Geography, 49*, 76–84.

Ruiz, S. A., & Silverstein, M. (2007). Relationships with grandparents and the emotional well-being of late adolescent and young adult grandchildren. *Journal of Social Issues, 63*, 793–808.

Salmon, C. (2017). Long-term romantic relationships: Adaptationist approaches. *Evolutionary Behavioral Sciences, 11*, 121–130.

Sander, J., Schupp, J., & Richter, D. (2017). Getting together: Social contact frequency across the life span. *Developmental Psychology, 53*, 1571–1588.

Shackelford, T. K., Schmitt, D. P., & Buss, D. M. (2005). Universal dimensions of human mate preferences. *Personality and Individual Differences, 39*, 447–458.

Simpson, J. A., Collins, W. A., & Salvatore, J. E. (2011). Impact of early interpersonal experience on adult romantic relationship functioning: Recent findings from the Minnesota Longitudinal Study of Risk and Adaptation. *Current Directions in Psychological Science, 20*, 355–359.

Smith, A., & Anderson, M. (2016). *Five facts about online dating.* Pew Research Center. Retrieved November 17, 2017, from http://www.pewresearch.org/fact-tank/2016/02/29/5-facts-about-online-dating/

Smith, K. P., & Christakis, N. A. (2008). Social networks and health. *Annual Review of Sociology, 34*, 405–429.

Spradlin, A., Cuttler, C., Bunce, J. P., et al. (2019). #Connected: Facebook may facilitate face-to-face relationships for introverts. *Psychology of Popular Media Culture, 8*, 34–40.

Stanley, S. M., Rhoades, G. K., Amato, P. R., et al. (2010). The timing of cohabitation and engagement: Impact on first and second marriages. *Journal of Marriage and Family, 72*, 906–918.

Stepler, R. (2017a). *Led by Baby Boomers, divorce rates climb for America's 50+ population.* Retrieved November 25, 2017, from http://www.pewresearch.org/fact-tank/2017/03/09/led-by-baby-boomers-divorce-rates-climb-for-americas-50-population/

Stepler, R. (2017b). *Number of U.S. adults cohabiting with a partner continues to rise, especially among those 50 and older.* Pew Research Center. Retrieved May 24, 2019, from http://www.pewresearch.org/fact-tank/2017/04/06/number-of-u-s-adults-cohabiting-with-a-partner-continues-to-rise-especially-among-those-50-and-older/

Sternberg, R. J. (1986). A triangular theory of love. *Psychological Review, 93*, 119–135.

Suitor, J. J., Gilligan, M., & Pillemer, K. (2016). Stability, change, and complexity in later-life families. In L. K. George & K. F. Ferraro (Eds.), *Handbook of aging and the social sciences* (8th ed., pp. 205–226). San Diego, CA: Academic Press.

Suitor, J. J., Sechrist, J., Plikuhn, M., et al. (2009). The role of perceived maternal favoritism in sibling relations in midlife. *Journal of Marriage and Family, 71*, 1026–1038.

Tennov, D. (1979). *Love and limerance.* New York: Stein & Day.

Thompson, S. H., & Lougheed, E. (2012). Frazzled by Facebook?: An exploratory study of gender differences in social networking communication among undergraduate men and women. *College Student Journal, 46*, 88–98.

Tighe, L. A., Birditt, K. S., & Antonucci, T. C. (2016). Intergenerational ambivalence in adolescence and early adulthood: Implications for depressive symptoms over time. *Developmental psychology, 52*, 824.

U.S. Department of Health and Human Services. (2017). *Lesbian, gay, bisexual, and transgender health.* Retrieved November 20, 2017, from https://www.healthypeople.gov/2020/topics-objectives/topic/lesbian-gay-bisexual-and-transgender-health

van IJzendoorn, M. (1995). Adult attachment representations, parental responsiveness, and infant attachment: A meta-analysis on the predictive validity of the Adult Attachment Interview. *Psychological Bulletin, 117*, 387–403.

Waters, E., Merrick, S. K., Albersheim, L. J., et al. (1995, March). *Attachment security from infancy to early adulthood: A 20-year longitudinal study.* Poster presented at the biennial meeting of the Society for Research in Child Development, Indianapolis, IN.

Weiss, R. S. (1982). Attachment in adult life. In C. M. Parkes & J. Stevenson-Hinde (Eds.), *The place of attachment in human behavior* (pp. 171–184). New York: Basic Books.

Weiss, R. S. (1986). Continuities and transformation in social relationships from childhood to adulthood. In W. W. Hartup & Z. Rubin (Eds.), *On relationships and development* (pp. 95–110). Hillsdale, NJ: Erlbaum.

Wiederhold, B. K. (2012). As parents invade Facebook, teens tweet more. *Cyberpsychology, Behavior, and Social -Networking, 15*, 385.

Woods, L. N., & Emery, R. E. (2002). The cohabitation effect on divorce: Causation or selection? *Journal of Divorce and Remarriage, 37*, 101–122.

Wright, M. R., & Brown, S. L. (2017). Psychological well-being among older adults: The role of partnership status. *Journal of Marriage and Family, 79*, 833–849.

Žeželj, I. L., Ioannou, M., Franc, R., et al. (2017). The role of inter-ethnic online friendships in prejudice reduction in post-conflict societies: Evidence from Serbia, Croatia, and Cyprus. *Computers in Human Behavior*, 76, 386–395.

Zhang, Y. (2017). Premarital cohabitation and marital dissolution in postreform China. *Journal of Marriage and Family*, 79, 1435–1449.

CHAPTER 7

Ahola, K., & Hakanen, J. J. (2014). Burnout and health. In M. P. Leiter, A. B. Bakker, & C. Maslach (Eds.), *Burnout at work: A psychological perspective* (pp. 10–31). New York: Psychology Press.

Andel, R., Finkel, D., & Pedersen, N. L. (2016). Effect of preretirement work complexity and postretirement leisure activity on cognitive aging. *Journals of Gerontology: Psychological Sciences and Social Sciences*, 71, 849–856.

Andel, R., Infurna, F. J., Hahn Rickenbach, E. A., et al. (2015). Job strain and trajectories of change in episodic memory before and after retirement: Results from the health and retirement Study. *Journal of Epidemiology and Community Health*, 69, 442–446.

Anderson, N. D., Damianakis, T., Kröger, E., et al. (2014). The benefits associated with volunteering among seniors: A critical review and recommendations for future research. *Psychological Bulletin*, 140, 1505.

Backé, E.-M., Seidler, A., Latza, U., et al. (2015). The role of psychological stress at work for the development of cardiovascular disease: A systematic review. *International Archives of Occupational and Environmental Health*, 85, 67–79.

Bakker, A. B. (2011). An evidence-based model of work engagement. *Current Directions in Psychological Science*, 20, 265–269.

Bandura, A. (1991). Social cognitive theory of self-regulation. *Organizational Behavior and Human Decision Processes*, 50, 248–287.

Bayard, K., Hellerstein, J., Neumark, D., et al. (2003). New evidence on sex segregation and sex differences in wages from matched employee–employer data. *Journal of Labor Economics*, 21, 887–922.

Bialik, K. (2017). *Six facts about U.S. mothers*. Retrieved January 25, 2018, from http://www.pewresearch.org/fact-tank/2017/05/11/6-facts-about-u-s-mothers/

Biggs, A. (2016). How many Americans are saving for retirement? How many should be? *Forbes*. Retrieved January 27, 2018, from https://www.forbes.com/sites/andrewbiggs/2016/09/20/how-many-americans-are-saving-for-retirement-how-many-should-be/#2e16cc816705

Bindl, U. K., Parker, S. K., Toterdell, P., et al. (2012). Fuel of the self-starter: How mood relates to proactive goal regulation. *Journal of Applied Psychology*, 97, 134–150.

Blom, V. (2012). Contingent self-esteem, stressors, and burnout in working women and men. *Work: Journal of Prevention, Assessment and Rehabilitation*, 43, 123–131.

Bowling, N. A., Eschleman, K. J., & Wang, Q. (2010). A meta-analytic examination of the relationship between job satisfaction and subjective well-being. *Journal of Occupational and Organisational Psychology*, 83, 915–934.

Boyce, C. J., Wood, A. M., & Daly, M., et al. (2015). Personality change following unemployment. *Journal of Applied Psychology*, 100, 991–1011.

Briscoe, J. P., & Hall, D. T. (2006). The interplay of boundaryless and protean careers: Combination and implications. *Journal of Vocational Behavior*, 69, 4–18.

Cahill, K. E., Giandrea, M. D., & Quinn, J. F., (June, 2011). Monthly Labor Review: *Bureau of Labor Statistics*.

Carse, T., Griffin, B., & Lyons, M. (2017). The dark side of engagement for older workers. *Journal of Personnel Psychology*, 16, 161–171.

Cheng, G. H.-L., & Chan, D. K.-S. (2008). Who suffers more from job insecurity?: A meta-analytic review. *Applied Psychology: An International Review*, 57, 272–303.

Clark, R. L., Burkhauser, R. V., Moon, M., et al. (2004). *The economics of an aging society*. Malden, MA: Blackwell.

Costello, C. B., Wight, V. R., & Stone, A. J. (2003). *The American woman 2003–2004*. New York: Palgrave Macmillan.

Daly, M., & Delaney, L. (2013). The scarring effect of unemployment throughout adulthood on psychological distress at age 50: Estimates controlling for early adulthood distress and childhood psychological factors. *Social Science and Medicine*, 80, 19–23.

DeSilver, D. (2016). *Millions of young people in U.S. and EU are neither working or learning*. Retrieved January 11, 2018, from http://www.pewresearch.org/fact-tank/2016/01/28/us-eu-neet-population/

DeSilver, D. (2017). *5 ways the workforce has changed, a decade since the Great Recession*. Retrieved January 3, 2016, from http://www.pewresearch.org/fact-tank/2017/11/30/5-ways-the-u-s-workforce-has-changed-a-decade-since-the-great-recession-began/

Dill, J. S., Price-Glynn, K., & Rakovski, C. (2016). Does the "glass escalator" compensate for the devaluation of care work occupations? *Gender and Society*, 30, 334–360.

Dowling, D. W. (2017). The best ways your organization can support working parents. *Harvard Business Review*. Retrieved January 26, 2018, from https://hbr.org/2017/01/the-best-ways-your-organization-can-support-working-parents

Eagly, A. H., & Wood, W. (2012). Social role theory. In P. A. M. Van Lange, A. W. Kruglanski, & E. T. Higgins (Eds.), *Handbook of theories of social psychology* (Vol. 2, pp. 458–476). Los Angeles, CA: Sage.

Eismann, M., Henkens K., & Kalmijn, M. (2017). Spousal preferences for joint retirement: Evidence from a multi-actor survey among older dual-earner couples. *Psychology and Aging*, 32, 689–697.

Ericksen, J. A., & Schultheiss, D. E. P. (2009). Women pursuing careers in trades and construction. *Journal of Career Development*, 36, 68–89.

Eurostat. (2017). *Share of young people neither in employment nor in education and training, by age*. Retrieved January 11, 2017, from http://ec.europa.eu/eurostat/statistics-explained/index.php/File:Share_of_young_people_neither_in_employment_nor_in_education_and_training,_by_age,_EU-28,_2006–16.PNG

Family Caregiver Alliance. (2016). *Caregiver statistics: Work and caregiving*. Retrieved February 1, 2018, from https://www.caregiver.org/caregiver-statistics-work-and-caregiving

Federal Interagency Forum on Aging-Related Statistics. (2017). *Older Americans: Key indicators of well-being*. Retrieved February 5, 2018, from https://agingstats.gov/docs/LatestReport/Older-Americans-2016-Key-Indicators-of-WellBeing.pdf

Gati, I, Osipow, S. H., & Givon, M. (1995). Gender differences in career decision making: The content and structure of preferences. *Journal of Counseling Psychology*, 42, 204–216.

Gati, I., & Perez, M. (2014). Gender differences in career preferences from 1990 to 2010: Gaps reduced but not eliminated. *Journal of Counseling Psychology*, 61, 63.

Grunberg, L., Moore, S. Y., & Greenberg, E. (2001). Differences in psychological and physical health among layoff survivors: The effect of layoff contact. *Journal of Occupational Health Psychology*, 6, 15–25.

Hakanen, J. J., Peeters, M. C. W., & Schaufeli, W. B. (2018). Different types of employee well-being across time ad relationships with job crafting. *Journal of Occupational Health Psychology*, 23, 289–301.

Halpern, D. F. (2005). Psychology at the intersection of work and family: Recommendations for employers, working families, and policymakers. *American Psychologist*, 60, 397–409.

Hannon, K. (2017). *Hoping for a phased retirement?: Don't count on it*. Retrieved February 6, 2018, from https://www.forbes.com/sites/nextavenue/2017/08/04/hoping-for-a-phased-retirement-dont-count-on-it/#4767273a1d61

Heggestad, E. D., & Andrews, A. M. (2012). Aging, personality, and work attitudes. In W. C. Borman & J. W. Hedge (Eds.), *The Oxford handbook of work and aging* (pp. 256–279). New York: Oxford University Press.

Hochwarter, W. A., Ferris, G. R., Perrewe, P. L., et al. (2001). A note on the nonlinearity of the age-job-satisfaction relationship. *Journal of Applied Social Psychology*, 31, 1223–1237.

Holland, J. L. (1958). A personality inventory employing occupational titles. *Journal of Applied Psychology*, 42, 336–342.

Holland, J. L. (1973). Making vocational choices: A theory of careers. Englewood Cliffs, NJ: Prentice Hall.

Holland, J. L. (1992). Making vocational choice: A theory of personalities and work environments (2nd ed.). Odessa, FL: Psychological Assessment Resources.

Holland, J. L. (1997). *Making vocational choice: A theory of personalities and work environments* (3rd ed.). Odessa, FL: Psychological Assessment Resources.

Huang, Y., Xu, S., Hua, J., et al. (2015). Association between job strain and risk of incidence stroke: A meta-analysis. *Neurology*, 85, 1648–1654.

Huth, C., Thorand, B., Baumert, J., et al. (2014). Job strain as a risk factor for the onset of Type-2 diabetes mellitus: Findings from the MONICA/KORA Augsburg cohort study. *Psychosomatic Medicine*, 76, 562–568.

Huynh, J. Y., Xanthopoulou, D., & Winefield, A. H. (2013). Social support moderates the impact of demands on burnout and organizational connectedness: A two-wave study of volunteer firefighters. *Journal of Occupational Health Psychology*, 18, 9–15.

Ilies, R., Liu, X.-Y., Liu, Y., et al. (2017). Why do employees have better family lives when they are engaged in work? *Journal of Applied Psychology*. 102, 956–970.

Kozak, A., Kersten, M., Schillmöller, Z., et al. (2013). Psychosocial work-related predictors and consequences of personal burnout among staff working with people with intellectual disabilities. *Research in Developmental Disabilities*, 34, 102–115.

Lent, R. W., Brown, S. D., & Hackett, G. (1994). Toward a unifying social cognitive theory of career and academic interest, choices, and performance. *Journal of Vocational Behavior*, 45, 79–122.

Livingston, G. (2016). *Among 41 nations, U. S. is the outlier when it comes to paid parental leave*. Retrieved January 15, 2018, from http://www.pewresearch.org/fact-tank/2016/09/26/u-s-lacks-mandated-paid-parental-leave/

Maslach, C., Schaufeli, W. B., & Leiter, M. P. (2001). Job burnout. *Annual Review of Psychology*, 52, 397–422.

Mazzocco, M., Ruiz, C., & Yamaguchi, S. (2014). Labor supply and household dynamics. *American Economic Review: Papers and Proceedings*, 104, 354–359.

McDaniel, M. A., Pesta, B. J., & Banks, G. C. (2012). Job performance and the aging worker. In W. C. Borman & J. W. Hedge (Eds.), *The Oxford handbook of work and aging* (pp. 280–297). New York: Oxford University Press.

McGinn, K. L., Ruiz Castro, M., & Lingo, E. L. (2018). Learning from mum: Cross-national evidence linking maternal employment and adult children's outcomes. *Work, Employment and Society*, 3, 374–400.

McKee-Ryan, F. M., Song, A., Wanberg, C. R., et al. (2005). Psychological and physical well-being during unemployment: A meta-analytic study. *Journal of Applied Psychology*, 90, 53–76.

National Center for Education Statistics. (2017). *Digest of education statistics*. Retrieved January 10, 2018, from https://nces.ed.gov/programs/digest/d16/tables/dt16_303.40.asp?current=yes

National Senior Service Corps. (2017). *Senior Corps fact sheet*. Retrieved February 6, 2018, from https://www.nationalservice.gov/newsroom/marketing/fact-sheets/senior-corps

National Women's Law Center. (2017). *Low-wage jobs are women's jobs: The overrepresentation of women in low-wage work*. Retrieved December 5, 2017, from https://nwlc.org/resources/low-wage-jobs-are-womens-jobs-the-overrepresentation-of-women-in-low-wage-work/

Nelson, D. L., Quick, J. C., & Simmons, B. L. (2001). Preventive management of work stress: Current themes and future challenges. In A. Baum, T. A. Revenson, & J. E. Singer (Eds.), *Handbook of health psychology* (pp. 349–363). Mahwah, NJ: Erlbaum.

Ng, T. W. H., & Feldman, D. C. (2008). The relationship of age to ten dimensions of job performance. *Journal of Applied Psychology*, 93, 392–423.

Ng, T. W. H., & Feldman, D. C. (2012). Evaluating six common stereotypes about older workers with meta-analytical data. *Personnel Psychology*, 65, 821–858.

Parsons, E. (1909). *Choosing a vocation*. Boston: Houghton Mifflin

Pedulla, D. S., & Thébaud, S. (2015). Can we finish the revolution?: Gender, work-family ideals, and institutional constraint. *American Sociological Review*, 80, 116–139.

Potter, G. G., Helms M. J., & Plassman, B. L. (2008). Associations of job demands and intelligence with cognitive performance among men in late life. *Neurology*, 70, 1803–1808.

Quinn, J. F., & Cahill, K. E. (2016). The new world of retirement income security in America. *American Psychologist*, 71, 121–333.

Rix, S. E. (2011). Employment and aging. In R. H. Binstock & L. K. George (Eds.), *Handbook of aging and the social sciences* (7th ed., pp. 193–206). San Diego, CA: Academic Press.

Ruble, D. N., Martin, C. L., & Berenbaum, S. A. (2006). Gender development. In N. Eisenberg (Vol. Ed.) and W. Damon & R. M. Lerner (Gen. Eds.), *Handbook of child psychology: Vol. 3. Social, emotional, and personality development* (6th ed., pp. 858–932). Hoboken, NJ: Wiley.

Rudolph, C. W. (2016). Lifespan developmental perspectives on working: A literature review of motivational theories. *Work, Aging, and Retirement*, 2, 130–158.

Salthouse, T. A. (1984). Effects of age and skill in typing. *Journal of Experimental Psychology: General*, 113, 345–371.

Salthouse, T. A. (1996). The processing-speed theory of adult age differences in cognition. *Psychological Review*, 103, 401–428.

Schaufeli, W. B., & Bakker, A. B. (2004). Job demands, job resources and their relationship with burnout and engagement: A multisample study. *Journal of Organizational Behavior*, 25, 293–315.

Semuels, A. (2017). The girls are leaving their brothers behind. *The Atlantic*. Retrieved March 6, 2019, from https://www.theatlantic.com/business/archive/2017/11/gender-education-gap/546677/

Shriver Center on Poverty Law. (2016). *Older women and poverty*. Retrieved February 5, 2018, from http://www.ncdsv.org/SSNCPL_Woman-View-Older-Women-and-Poverty_3-30-2016.pdf

Smart, E. L., Gow, A. J., & Deary, I. J. (2014). Occupational complexity and lifetime cognitive abilities. *Neurology*, 83, 2285–2291.

Social Security Administration. (2017). *Survivor planner: How much would your benefit be?* Retrieved February 6, 2017, from https://www.ssa.gov/planners/survivors/ifyou5.html

Su, R., Rounds, J., & Armstrong, P. I. (2009). Men and things, women and people: A meta-analysis of sex differences in interests. *Psychological Bulletin*, 135, 859–884.

Super, D. E. (1957). *The psychology of careers*. New York: Harper & Row.

Tomasetto, C., Alparone, F. R., & Cadinu, M. (2011). Girls' math performance under stereotype threat: The moderating role of mothers' gender stereotypes. *Developmental Psychology*, 47, 943–949.

Tynkkynen, L., Tolvanen, A., & Salmela-Aro, K. (2012). Trajectories of educational expectations from adolescence to young adulthood in Finland. *Developmental Psychology*, 48, 1674–1685.

U.S. Bureau of Labor Statistics. (2016a). Volunteers by selected characteristics – 2015. Retrieved February 6, 2018 from https://www.bls.gov/news.release/volun.t01.htm

U.S. Bureau of Labor Statistics. (2016b). Volunteers by type of main organization for which volunteer activities were performed and selected characteristics – 2015. Retrieved February 6, 2018, from https://www.bls.gov/news.release/volun.t04.htm

U. S. Bureau of Labor Statistics. (2017a). *Civilian labor force participation rate by age, sex, race, and ethnicity.* Retrieved January 29, 2018, from https://www.bls.gov/emp/ep_table_303.htm

U.S. Bureau of Labor Statistics. (2017b). Employment projections: Medium age of the labor force, by sex, race, and ethnicity. Retrieved December 31, 2017, from https://www.bls.gov/emp/ep_table_306.htm

U. S. Bureau of Labor Statistics. (2017c). *Employment status of the population by sex, marital status, and presence and age of own children under 18.* Retrieved January 24, 2018, from https://www.bls.gov/news.release/famee.t05.htm

U. S. Bureau of Labor Statistics. (2017d). *Labor force statistics from the Current Population Survey.* Retrieved December 13, 2017, from https://www.bls.gov/cps/cpsaat11.htm

U.S. Bureau of Labor Statistics. (2017e). Number of jobs, labor market experience, and earnings growth among American's at 50: Results from a longitudinal study. Retrieved December 5, 2017, from https://www.bls.gov/news.release/pdf/nlsoy.pdf

U.S. Bureau of Labor Statistics. (2017f). Women in the labor force: A data book. Retrieved December 5, 2017, from https://www.bls.gov/opub/reports/womens-databook/2016/home.htm

U. S. Bureau of Labor Statistics. (2018a). *Employment status of the civilian population 25 years and over by educational attainment.* Retrieved January 11, 2018, from

U. S. Bureau of Labor Statistics. (2018b). *Labor force statistics from the current population survey.* Retrieved January 11, 2018, from https://www.bls.gov/web/empsit/cpseea10.htm

U. S. Bureau of Labor Statistics. (2018c). Labor force statistics from the Current Population Survey, Table E-16. Retrieved January 11, 2018, from https://www.bls.gov/web/empsit/cpsee_e16.htm

U.S. Census Bureau. (2016). *Americans moving at historically low rates, Census Bureau reports.* Retrieved February 6, 2017, from https://www.census.gov/newsroom/press-releases/2016/cb16-189.html

U.S. Census Bureau. (2017). *Married couple family groups by labor force status of both spouses: 2017.* Retrieved January 26, 2018, from http://www2.census.gov/programs-surveys/cps/techdocs/cpsmar17.pdf

U.S. Department of Health and Human Services. (2018). *U. S. federal poverty guidelines used to determine financial eligibility for certain federal programs.* Retrieved February 8, 2018, from https://aspe.hhs.gov/poverty-guidelines

U.S. Government Accountability Office. (2017). *Phased retirement programs, although uncommon, provide flexibility for workers and employers.* Retrieved February 6, 2018, from https://www.gao.gov/products/GAO-17-536

Wang, M., & Wanberg, C. R. (2017). 10 years of applied psychology research on individual careers: From career management to retirement. *Journal of Applied Psychology, 102,* 536–563.

Wang, M., & Wanberg, C. R. (2017). 100 years of applied psychology research on individual careers: From career management to retirement. *Journal of Applied Psychology, 102,* 546–563.

Zhou, N., & Buehler, C. (2016) Family, employment, and individual resource-based antecedents of maternal work–family enrichment from infancy through middle childhood. *Journal of Occupational Health Psychology, 21,* 309–321.

CHAPTER 8

Alea, N., Diehl, M., & Bluck, S. (2004). Personality and emotion in late life. In *Encyclopedia of applied psychology* (pp. 1–10). San Diego, CA: Elsevier.

American Psychiatric Association. (2000). *Diagnostic and statistical manual of mental disorders* (4th ed.). Washington, DC: Author.

Aristotle. (1946). *The politics of Aristotle* (E. Barker, Trans.). London: Oxford University Press.

Barkan, T., Hoerger, M., Gallegos, A. M., et al. (2016). Personality predicts utilization of mindfulness-based stress reduction during and post-intervention in a community sample of older adults. *Journal of Alternative and Complementary Medicine, 22,* 390–395.

Bauer, J. J., & McAdams, D. P. (2004). Personal growth in adults' stories of life transitions. *Journal of Personality, 72,* 573–602.

Blackwell, L., Trzesniewski, K., & Dweck, C. S. (2007). Implicit theories of intelligence predict achievement across an adolescent transition: A longitudinal study and an intervention. *Child Development, 78,* 246–263.

Buss, D. M. (1997). Evolutionary foundations of personality. In R. Hogan, J. Johnson, & S. Briggs (Eds.), *Handbook of personality psychology* (pp. 317–344). San Diego, CA: Academic Press.

Buss, D. M. (2012). *Evolutionary psychology: The new science of the mind* (4th ed.). Boston: Allyn & Bacon.

Calzo, J. P., Antonucci, T. C., Mays, V. M., et al. (2011). Retrospective recall of sexual orientation identity development among gay, lesbian, and bisexual adults. *Developmental Psychology, 47,* 1658–1673.

Caspi, A. (1998). Personality development across the life course. In W. Damon (Series Ed.) & N. Eisenberg (Vol. Ed.), *Handbook of child psychology: Vol. 3. Social, emotional, and personality development* (pp. 311–388). New York: Wiley.

Caspi, A., & Roberts, B. W. (1999). Personality continuity and change across the life course. In L. A. Pervin & O. P. John (Eds.), *Handbook of personality psychology: Theory and research* (pp. 300–326). New York: Guilford Press.

Caspi, A., Roberts, B. W., & Shiner, R. L. (2004). Personality development: Stability and change. *Annual Review of Psychology, 56,* 453–484.

Cattell, R. B., Eber, H. W., & Tatsuoka, M. M. (1970). *Handbook for the Sixteen Personality Factor Questionnaire.* Champaign, IL: Institute for Personality and Ability Testing.

Chan, W., McCrae, R. R., De Fruyt, F., et al. (2012). Stereotypes of age differences in personality traits: Universal and accurate? *Journal of Personality and Social Psychology, 103,* 1050.

Cheung, F. M., Cheung, S. F., Zhang, J. X., et al. (2008). Convergent validity of the Chinese Personality Assessment Inventory and the Minnesota Multiphasic Personality Inventory-2: Preliminary findings with a normative sample. *Journal of Personality Assessment, 82,* 92–103.

Cheung, F. M., van de Vijver, F. J. R., & Leong, F. T. L. (2011). Toward a new approach to the study of personality in culture. *American Psychologist, 66,* 593–603.

Costa, P. T., Jr., & McCrae, R. R. (1997). Longitudinal stability of adult personality. In R. Hogan, J. Johnson, & S. Briggs (Eds.), *Handbook of personality psychology* (pp. 269–290). San Diego, CA: Academic Press.

Danner, D. D., Snowdon, D. A., & Friesen, W. V. (2001). Positive emotions in early life and longevity: Findings from the Nun Study. *Journal of Personality and Social Psychology, 80,* 804–813.

De Raad, B., Barelds, D. P. H., Levert, E., et al. (2010). Only three factors of personality description are fully replicable across languages: A comparison of 14 trait taxonomies. *Journal of Personality and Social Psychology, 98,* 160–173.

Deci, E. L., & Ryan, R. M. (2008a). Hedonia, eudaimonia, and well being: An introduction. *Journal of Happiness Studies, 9,* 1–11.

Deci, E. L., & Ryan, R. M. (2008b). Self-determination theory: A macrotheory of human motivation, development, and health. *Canadian Psychology, 49,* 182–185.

Dweck, C. S. (2008). Can personality be changed?: The role of beliefs in personality and change. *Current Directions in Psychological Science, 17,* 391–394.

Ehrensaft, M., Moffitt, T. E., & Caspi, A. (2004). Clinically abusive relationships in an unselected birth cohort: Men's and women's participation and developmental antecedents. *Journal of Abnormal Psychology, 113,* 258–270.

Einolf, C. J. (2014). Stability and change in generative concern: Evidence from a longitudinal survey. *Journal of Research in Personality, 51,* 54–61.

Erikson, E. H. (1950). *Childhood and society*. New York: Norton.

Erikson, E. H. (1959). *Identity and the life cycle*. New York: Norton.

Erikson, E. H. (1982). *The life cycle completed*. New York: Norton.

Evans, R. I. (1969). *Dialogue with Erik Erikson*. New York: Dutton.

Eysenck, H. J. (1976). *Sex and personality*. Austin, Texas: University of Texas Press.

Field, D., & Millsap, R. E. (1991). Personality in advanced old age: Continuity or change? *Journals of Gerontology: Psychological and Social Sciences, 46*, 299–308.

George, L. G., Helson, R., & John, O. P. (2011). The "CEO" of women's work lives: How the Big Five Conscientiousness, Extraversion, and Openness predict 50 years of work experiences in a changing sociocultural context. *Journal of Personality and Social Psychology, 101*, 812–830.

Gerlach, M., Farb, B., Revelle, W., et al. (2018). A robust data-driven approach identifies four personality types across four large data sets. *Nature Human Behaviour, 2*, 735.

Gottman, J. M. (2011). *The science of trust: Emotional attunement for couples*. New York: Norton.

Gough, H. G. (1957/1987). *Manual for the California Psychological Inventory*. Palo Alto, CA: Consulting Psychologists Press.

Graham, E. K., Rutsohn, J. P., Turiano, N. A., et al. (2017). Personality predicts mortality risk: An integrative data analysis of 15 international longitudinal studies. *Journal of Research in Personality, 70*, 174–186.

Gutmann, D. (1987). *Reclaimed powers: Toward a new psychology of men and women in later life*. New York: Basic Books.

Harris, M. A., Brett, C. E., Starr, J. M., et al. (2016). Personality and other lifelong influences on older-age health and wellbeing: Preliminary findings in two Scottish samples. *European Journal of Personality, 30*, 438–455.

Heath, C. W. (1945). *What people are*. Cambridge, MA: Harvard University Press.

Helson, R., & Kwan, V. S. Y. (2000). Personality development in adulthood: The broad picture and processes in one longitudinal sample. In S. Hampson (Ed.), *Advances in personality psychology* (Vol. 1, pp. 77–106). London: Routledge.

Helson, R., Kwan, V. S. Y., John, O. P., et al. (2002). The growing evidence for personality change in adulthood: Findings from research with personality inventories. *Journal of Research in Personality, 36*, 287–306.

Helson, R., Pals, J., & Solomon, M. (1997). Is there adult development distinctive to women? In R. Hogan, J. Johnson, & S. Briggs (Eds.), *Handbook of personality psychology* (pp. 291–314). San Diego, CA: Academic Press.

Hill, P. L., & Roberts, B. W. (2011). The role of adherence in the relationship between conscientiousness and perceived health. *Health Psychology, 30*, 797–804.

Hill, P. L., Turiano, N. A., Hurd, M. D., et al. (2011). Conscientiousness and longevity: An examination of possible mediators. *Health Psychology, 30*, 536–541.

Hofer, J., Busch, H., Au, A., et al. (2014). For the benefit of others: Generativity and meaning in life in the elderly in four cultures. *Psychology and Aging, 29*, 764.

Hy, L. X., & Loevinger, J. (1996). *Measuring ego development*. Mahwah, NJ: Erlbaum

Jokela, M., Elovainio, M., Nyberg, S. T., et al. (2014). Personality and risk of diabetes in adults: Pooled analysis of 5 cohort studies. *Health Psychology, 33*, 1618.

Judge, T. A., Higgins, C. A., Thoreson, C. J., et al. (1999). The Big Five personality traits, general mental ability, and career success across the life span. *Personnel Psychology, 52*, 621–652.

Jung, C. G. (1933). *Modern man in search of a soul*. New York: Harcourt, Brace, & World.

Karney, B. R., & Bradbury, T. N. (1995). The longitudinal course of marital quality and stability: A review of theory, method, and research. *Psychological Bulletin, 118*, 3–34.

Kasser, V. M., & Ryan, R. M. (1999). The relation of psychological needs for autonomy and relatedness to health, vitality, well-being, and mortality in a nursing home. *Journal of Applied Social Psychology, 29*, 935–954.

Krettenauer, T., Ullrich, M., Hofmann, V., et al. (2003). Behavioral problems in childhood and adolescence as predictors of ego-level attainment in early adulthood. *Merrill-Palmer Quarterly, 49*, 125–153.

Labouvie-Vief, G., & Diehl, M. (1998). The role of ego development in the adult self. In P. M. Westenberg, A. Blasi, & L. D. Cohn (Eds.), *Personality development: Theoretical, empirical, and clinical investigations of Loevinger's conception of ego development* (pp. 219–235). London: Erlbaum.

Löckenhoff, C. E., Duberstein, P. R., Friedman, B., et al. (2011). Five-factor personality traits and subjective health among caregivers: The role of caregiver strain and self-efficacy. *Psychology and Aging, 26*, 592–604.

Löckenhoff, C. E., Sutin, A. R., Ferrucci, L., et al. (2008). Personality traits and subjective health in the later years: The association between NEO-PI-R and SF-36 in advanced age is influenced by health status. *Journal of Research in Personality, 42*, 1334–1346.

Loevinger, J. (1976). *Ego development*. San Francisco: Jossey-Bass.

Loevinger, J. (1997). Stages of personality development. In R. Hogan, J. Johnson, & S. Briggs (Eds.), *Handbook of personality psychology* (pp. 199–208). San Diego, CA: Academic Press.

Luchetti, M., Barkley, J. M., Stephan, Y., et al. (2014). Five-factor model personality traits and inflammatory markers: New data and a meta-analysis. *Psychoneuroendocrinology, 50*, 181–193.

Lukaszewski, A. W., & Rooney, J. R. (2010). *The origins of extraversion: Joint effects of facultative calibration and genetic polymorphism*. Paper presented at the annual meeting of Human Behavior and Evolution Society, Eugene, OR.

Lund, O. C. H., Tamnes, C. K., Moestue, C., et al. (2007). Tactics of hierarchy negotiation. *Journal of Research in Personality, 41*, 25–44.

Maslow, A. H. (1968/1998). *Toward a psychology of being* (3rd ed.). New York: Wiley.

McAdams, D. P., & de St. Aubin, E. (1992). A theory of generativity and its assessment through self-report, behavioral acts, and narrative themes in autobiography. *Journal of Personality and Social Psychology, 62*, 1003–1015.

McAdams, D. P., de St. Aubin, E., & Logan, R. L. (1993). Generativity among young, midlife, and older adults. *Psychology and Aging, 8*, 221–230.

McAdams, D. P., Hart, H. M., & Maruna, S. (1998). The anatomy of generativity. In D. P. McAdams & E. de St. Aubin (Eds.), *Generativity and adult development: How and why we care for the next generation* (pp. 7–43). Washington, DC: American Psychological Association.

McCrae, R. E. & Costa, P. T. (1987). Validation of the five-factor model of personality across instruments and observers. *Journal of Personality and Social Psychology, 52*, 81–90.

McCrae, R. R., & Costa, P. T., Jr. (1990). *Personality in adulthood*. New York: Guilford Press.

McCrae, R. R., Costa, P. T., Jr., Pedroso de Lima, M., et al. (1999). Age differences in personality across the adult life span: Parallels in five cultures. *Developmental Psychology, 35*, 466–477.

McCrae, R. R., Terracciano, A., & 78 members of the Personality Profiles of Cultures Project. (2005). Universal features of personality traits from the observer's perspective: Data from 50 cultures. *Journal of Personality and Social Psychology, 88*, 547–561.

Miller, T. Q., Smith, T. W., Turner, C. W., et al. (1996). A meta-analytic review of research on hostility and physical health. *Psychological Bulletin, 119*, 322–348.

Mroczek, D. K., & Spiro, A. (2003). Personality structure, process, variance between and within: Integration by means of a developmental framework. *Journals of Gerontology: Psychological and Social Sciences, 58*, 305–306.

Mueller, S., Wagner, J., Drewelies, J., et al. (2016). Personality development in old age relates to physical health and cognitive performance: Evidence from the Berlin Aging Study II. *Journal of Research in Personality, 65,* 94–108.

Niemiec, C. P., Ryan, R. M., & Deci, E. L. (2009). The path taken: Consequences of attaining intrinsic and extrinsic aspirations in post-college life. *Journal of Research in Personality, 73,* 291–308.

Plomin, R., & Nesselroade, J. R. (1997). Behavioral genetics and personality change. *Journal of Personality, 58,* 191–220.

Riemann, R., Angleitner, A., & Strelau, J. (1997). Genetic and environmental influences on personality: A study of twins reared together using the self- and peer-report NEO-FFI scales. *Journal of Personality, 65,* 449–475.

Roberts B. W., & DelVecchio, W. F. (2000). The rank-order consistency of personality traits from childhood to old age: A quantitative review of longitudinal studies. *Psychological Bulletin, 126,* 3–25.

Roberts, B. W., & Mroczek, D. (2008). Personality trait change in adulthood. *Current Directions in Psychological Science, 17,* 31–35.

Roberts, B. W., Smith, J., Jackson, J. J., et al. (2009). Compensatory conscientiousness and health in older couples. *Psychological Science, 5,* 553–559.

Roberts, B. W., Walton, K. E., & Bogg, T. (2005). Conscientiousness and health across the life course. *Review of General Psychology, 9,* 156–168.

Roberts, B. W., Walton, K. E., & Viechtbauer, W. (2006). Patterns of mean-level change in personality traits across the life course: A meta-analysis of longitudinal studies. *Psychological Bulletin, 132,* 1–25.

Rogers, C. (1959). A theory of therapy, personality and interpersonal relationships as developed in the client-centered framework. In S. Koch (Ed.), *Psychology: A study of a science: Vol. 3. Formulations of the person and the social context.* New York: McGraw-Hill.

Ryan, R. M., & Deci, E. L. (2000). Self-determination theory and facilitation of intrinsic motivation, social development, and well-being. *American Psychologist, 55,* 68–78.

Ryan, R. M., & La Guardia, J. G. (2000). What is being optimized?: Self-determination theory and basic psychological needs. In S. H. Qualls & N. Abeles (Eds.), *Psychology and the aging revolution: How we adapt to longer life* (pp. 145–172). Washington, DC: American Psychological Association.

Scheier, M. F., & Carver, C. S. (1993). On the power of positive thinking. *Current Directions in Psychological Science, 2,* 26–30.

Seligman, M. E. P., & Csikszentmihalyi, M. (2000). Positive psychology: An introduction. *American Psychologist, 55,* 5–14.

Sheldon, K. M., & Kasser, T. (2001). Getting older, getting better?: Personal strivings and psychological maturity across the life span. *Developmental Psychology, 37,* 491–501.

Soldz, S., & Vaillant, G. E. (1999). The big five personality traits and the life course: A 45-year longitudinal study. *Journal of Research in Personality, 33,* 208–232.

Specht, J., Egloff, B., & Schmukle, S. C. (2011). Stability and change of personality across the life course: The impact of age and major life events on mean-level and rank-order stability of the Big Five. *Journal of Personality and Social Psychology, 101,* 862.

Sutin, A. R., Stephan, Y., & Terracciano, A. (2016). Perceived discrimination and personality development in adulthood. *Developmental Psychology, 52,* 155.

Tooby, J., & Cosmides, L. (1990). On the universality of human nature and the uniqueness of the individual: The role of genetics and adaptation. *Journal of Personality, 58,* 17–68.

Truluck, J. E., & Courtenay, B. C. (2002). Ego development and the influence of gender, age, and educational levels among older adults. *Educational Gerontology, 28,* 325–336.

Turiano, N. A., Chapman, B. P., Gruenewald, T. L., et al. (2015). Personality and the leading behavioral contributors of mortality. *Health Psychology, 34,* 51.

Vaillant, G. E. (1977). *Adaptation to life: How the best and brightest come of age.* Boston: Little, Brown.

Vaillant, G. E. (1993). *Wisdom of the ego.* Cambridge, MA: Harvard University Press.

Vaillant, G. E. (2002). *Aging well: Surprising guideposts to a happier life from the landmark Harvard study.* Boston: Little, Brown.

Verma, J. (1999). Hinduism, Islam, and Buddhism: The source of Asian values. In K. Leung, U. Kim, S. Yamaguchi, et al. (Eds.), *Progress in Asian social psychologies* (pp. 23–36). Singapore: Wiley.

Walaskay, M., Whitbourne, S. K., & Nehrke, M. F. (1983–84). Construction and validation of an ego-integrity status interview. *International Journal of Aging and Human Development, 18,* 61–72.

Walton, G. M., & Cohen, G. L. (2007). A question of belonging: Race, fit, and achievement. *Journal of Personality and Social Psychology, 92,* 82–96.

Whitbourne, S. K., Sneed, J. R., & Sayer, A. (2009). Psychosocial development from college through midlife: A 34-year sequential study. *Developmental Psychology, 45,* 1328–1340.

Whitbourne, S. K., Zuschlag, M. K., Elliot, L. B., et al. (1992). Psychosocial development in adulthood: A 22-year sequential study. *Journal of Personality and Social Psychology, 63,* 260–271.

Yang, K.-S. (2006). Indigenous personality research: The Chinese case. In U. Kim, K.-S. Yang, & K.-K. Hwang (Eds.), *Indigenous and cultural psychology: Understanding people in context* (pp. 285–314). New York: Springer.

CHAPTER 9

Ai, A. L., Huang, B., Biorck, J., et al. (2013). Religious attendance and major depression among Asian Americans from a national database: The mediation of social support. *Psychology of Religion and Spirituality, 5,* 78–89.

Anderson, M., Miller, L., Wickramaratne, P., et al. (2017). Genetic correlates of spirituality/religion and depression: A study in offspring and grandchildren at high and low familial risk for depression. *Spirituality in Clinical Practice, 4,* 43–63.

Benjamins, M. R., Musick, M. A., Gold, D. T., et al. (2003). Age-related declines in activity level: The relationship between chronic illness and religious activities. *Journals of Gerontology: Psychological and Social Sciences, 58,* 377–385.

Bering, J. M. (2006). The folk psychology of souls. *Behavioral and Brain Sciences, 29,* 453–498.

Brown, D. R., Carney, J. S., Parrish, M. S., et al. (2013). Assessing spirituality: The relationship between spirituality and mental health. *Journal of Spirituality and Mental Health, 15,* 107–122.

Campbell, J. (1949/1990). *Hero with a thousand faces.* Princeton, NJ: Princeton University Press.

Chida, Y., Steptoe, A., & Powell, L. H. (2009). Religiosity/spirituality and mortality. *Psychotherapy and Psychosomatics, 78,* 81–90.

Colby, A., & Kohlberg, L. (1987). *The measurement of moral judgment: Vol. 1. Theoretical foundations and research validation.* Cambridge, MA: Cambridge University Press.

Colby, A., Kohlberg, L., Gibbs, J., et al. (1983). A longitudinal study of moral judgment. *Monographs of the Society for Research in Child Development, 48*(1–2, Serial No. 200).

Dalby, P. (2006). Is there a process of spiritual change or development associated with ageing?: A critical review of research. *Aging and Mental Health, 10,* 4–12.

Fowler, J. (1981). *Stages of faith.* New York: Harper & Row.

Fowler, J. (1983). Stages of faith: PT conversation with James Fowler. *Psychology Today, 17,* 55–62.

Fowler, J. W. (2001). *Weaving the new creation: Stages of faith and the public church.* Eugene, OR: Wipf and Stock.

Frankl, V. E. (1984). *Man's search for meaning* (3rd ed.). New York: Simon & Schuster.

Fromm, E. (1956). *The art of loving.* New York: Harper & Row.

Gallegos, M. L., & Segrin, C. (2018). Exploring the mediating role of loneliness in the relationship between spirituality and health: Implications for the Latino health paradox. *Psychology of Religion and Spirituality.* [Advance online publication]

Gilligan, C. (1982). *In a different voice: Psychological theory and women's development.* Cambridge, MA: Harvard University Press.

Gurin, P., & Brim, O. G., Jr. (1984). Change in self in adulthood: The example of a sense of control. In P. B. Baltes & O. G. Brim, Jr. (Eds.), *Life-span development and behavior* (pp. 282–334). Orlando, FL: Academic Press.

Idler, E. L. (2006). Religion and aging. In R. H. Binstock & L. K. George (Eds.), *Handbook of aging and the social sciences* (pp. 277–300). San Diego, CA: Academic Press.

Idler, E. L., Kasl, S. V., & Hays, J. C. (2001). Patterns of religious practice and belief in the last years of life. *Journals of Gerontology: Psychological and Social Sciences, 56,* 326–334.

James, W. (1902/1958). *The varieties of religious experience.* New York: Mentor.

Jung, C. G. (1917/1966). *Two essays on analytical psychology.* London: Routledge.

Jung, C. G. (1964). *Man and his symbols.* New York: Laurel.

Karpiak, C. P., & Baril, G. L. (2008). Moral reasoning and concern for the environment. *Journal of Environmental Psychology, 28,* 203–208.

Keen, S. (1983). *The passionate life: Stages of loving.* New York: Harper & Row.

Kegan, R. (1980). There the dance is: Religious dimensions of developmental theory. In J. W. Fowler & A. Vergote (Eds.), *Toward moral and religious maturity* (pp. 403–440). Morristown, NJ: Silver Burdette.

Kegan, R. (1982). *The evolving self.* Cambridge, MA: Harvard University Press.

Kohlberg, L. (1973). Continuities in childhood and adult moral development revisited. In P. B. Baltes & K. W. Schaie (Eds.), *Life-span developmental psychology: Personality and socialization* (pp. 180–204). New York: Academic Press.

Kohlberg, L. (1981). *Essays on moral development: Vol. 1. The philosophy of moral development.* New York: Harper & Row.

Kohlberg, L. (1984). *Essays on moral development: Vol. 2. The psychology of moral development.* San Francisco, CA: Harper & Row.

Kohlberg, L., Levine, C., & Hewer, A. (1983). *Moral stages: A current formulation and a response to critics.* New York: Karger.

Levinson, D. J. (1978). *The seasons of a man's life.* New York: Knopf.

Lonky, E., Kaus, C. R., & Roodin, P. A. (1984). Life experience and mode of coping: Relation to moral judgment in adulthood. *Developmental Psychology, 20,* 1159–1167.

Lyons, N. P. (1983). Two perspectives: On self, relationships, and morality. *Harvard Educational Review, 53,* 125–145.

Maddi, S. R. (2005). On hardiness and other pathways to resilience. *American Psychologist, 60,* 261–262.

Masters, K. S., & Hooker, S. A. (2012). Religiousness/spirituality, cardiovascular disease, and cancer: Cultural integration for health research and intervention. *Journal of Consulting and Clinical Psychology, 81,* 206–216.

McCullough, M. E., Hoyt, W. T., Larson, D. B., et al. (2000). Religious involvement and mortality: A meta-analytic review. *Health Psychology, 19,* 211–222.

Miller, A. S., & Stark, R. (2002). Gender and religiousness: Can socialization explanations be saved? *American Journal of Sociology, 197,* 1399–1423.

Nisan, M., & Kohlberg, L. (1982). Universality and variation in moral judgment: A longitudinal and cross-sectional study in Turkey. *Child Development, 53,* 865–876.

Perls, F. (1973). *The Gestalt approach and eye witness to therapy.* Palo Alto, CA: Science and Behavior Books.

Pew Research Center. (2014). *Attendance at religious services by age group.* Retrieved from http://www.pewforum.org/religious-landscape-study/compare/attendance-at-religious-services/by/age-distribution/

Pew Research Center. (2018). *When Americans say they believe in God, what do they mean?* Retrieved June 11, 2019 from http://www.pewforum.org/2018/04/25/when-americans-say-they-believe-in-god-what-do-they-mean/

Pratt, M. W., Golding, G., & Hunter, W. J. (1983). Aging as ripening: Character and consistency of moral judgment in young, mature, and older adults. *Human Development, 36,* 277–288.

Reker, G. T. (1991). *Contextual and thematic analyses of sources of provisional meaning: A life-span perspective.* Paper presented at the biennial meeting of the International Society for the Study of Behavioral Development, Minneapolis, MN.

Rest, J. R., & Thoma, S. J. (1985). Relation of moral judgment development to formal education. *Developmental Psychology, 21,* 709–714.

Riegel, K. (1973). Dialectic operations: The final period of cognitive development. *Human Development, 16,* 346–370.

Rogers, C. (1961/1995). *On becoming a person: A therapist's view of psychotherapy.* New York: Houghton Mifflin.

Seeman, T. E., Dubin, L., & Seeman, M. (2003). Religiosity/spirituality and health: A critical review of the evidence for biological pathways. *American Psychologist, 58,* 53–63.

Sinnott, J. D. (1994). Development and yearning: Cognitive aspects of spiritual development. *Journal of Adult Development, 1,* 91–99.

Smetana, J. G., Killen, M., & Turiel, E. (1991). Children's reasoning about interpersonal and moral conflicts. *Child Development, 62,* 629–644.

Snarey, J. R. (1985). Cross-cultural universality of social-moral development: A critical review of the Kohlbergian research. *Psychological Bulletin, 97,* 202–232.

Snarey, J. R., Reimer, J., & Kohlberg, L. (1985). Development of social-moral reasoning among kibbutz adolescents: A longitudinal cross-sectional study. *Developmental Psychology, 21,* 3–17.

Tartaro, J., Luecken, L. J., & Gunn, H. E. (2005). Exploring heart and soul: Effects of religiosity/spirituality and gender on blood pressure and cortisol stress response. *Journal of Health Psychology, 10,* 753–766.

Teresa of Ávila, St. (1562/1960). *Interior castle.* Garden City, NJ: Image Books.

Tornstam, L. (1996). Gerotranscendence—A theory about maturing into old age. *Journal of Aging and Identity, 1,* 37–50.

Underhill, E. (1911/1961). *Mysticism.* New York: Dutton.

Underwood, L. (2008). Measuring "spirituality". *Journal of Nervous and Mental Disease, 196,* 715–716.

Walker, L. J. (1989). A longitudinal study of moral reasoning. *Child Development, 60,* 157–160.

Weststrate, N. M., & Glück, J. (2017). Hard-earned wisdom: Exploratory processing of difficult life experience is positively associated with wisdom. *Developmental Psychology, 53,* 800–814.

Wink, P., & Dillon, M. (2002). Spiritual development across the adult life course: Findings from a longitudinal study. *Journal of Adult Development, 9,* 79–94.

CHAPTER 10

Almeida, D. M. (2005). Resilience and vulnerability to daily stressors assessed via diary methods. *Current Directions in Psychological Science, 14,* 64–68.

Almeida, D. M., & Horn, M. C. (2004). Is daily life more stressful during middle adulthood? In O. G. Brim, C. D. Ryff, & R. C. Kessler (Eds.), *How healthy are we?: A national study of well-being at midlife* (pp. 425–451). Chicago: University of Chicago Press.

Almeida, D. M., Piazza, J. R., Stawski, R. S., & Klein, L. C. (2011). The speedometer of life: Stress, health and aging. In K. W. Schaie & S. L. Willis (Eds.), The handbooks of aging consisting of three Vols. Handbook of the psychology of aging (pp. 191–206). San Diego, CA, US: Elsevier Academic Press.

American Psychiatric Association. (2013). *Diagnostic and statistical manual of mental disorders* (5th ed.). Arlington, VA: Author.

American Psychological Association (2017). *Clinical practice guidelines or the treatment of posttraumatic stress disorder in adults.* Retrieved February 20, 2018 from https://www.apa.org/ptsd-guideline/ptsd.pdf

Birkeland, M. S., Blix, I., Solberg, Ø., et al. (2017). Does optimism act as a buffer against posttraumatic stress over time?: A longitudinal study of the protective role of optimism after the 2011 Oslo bombing. *Psychological Trauma: Theory, Research, Practice, and Policy, 9,* 207–213.

Bonanno, G. A. (2005). Resilience in the face of potential trauma. *Current Directions in Psychological Science, 14,* 135–138.

Bonanno, G. A., Wortman, C. B., Lehman, D. R., et al. (2002). Resilience to loss and chronic grief: A prospective study from pre-loss to 18 months post-loss. *Journal of Personality and Social Psychology, 83,* 1150–1164.

Broman, C. L. (2005). Stress, race, and substance abuse in college. *College Student Journal, 38,* 340–352.

Brown, L. M., & Frahm, K. A. (2016). The impact of disasters: Implications for the well-being of older adults. In L. K George & K. F. Ferraro (Eds.), *Handbook of aging and the social sciences* (8th ed., pp. 357–374). London: Academic Press.

Carver, C. S. (1997). You want to measure coping but your protocol's too long: Consider the Brief COPE. *International Journal of Behavioral Medicine, 4,* 92–100.

Carver, C. S., & Scheier, M. F. (2014). Dispositional optimism. *Trends in Cognitive Sciences, 18,* 293–299.

Charles, S. T., Piazza, J. R., Mogle, J., et al. (2013). The wear and tear of daily stressors on mental health. *Psychological Science, 24,* 733–741.

Chau, V., Bowie, J. V., & Juon, H.-S. (2018). The association of perceived discrimination and depressive symptoms among Chinese, Korean, and Vietnamese Americans. *Cultural Diversity and Ethnic Minority Psychology, 24,* 389–399.

Chen, E., Miller, G. E., Kobor, M. S., et al. (2011). Maternal warmth buffers the effects of low early-life socioeconomic status on pro-inflammatory signaling in adulthood. *Molecular Psychiatry, 16,* 729–737.

Chiang, J. J., Turiano, N. A., Mroczek, D. K., et al. (2018). Affective reactivity to daily stress and 20-year mortality risk in adults with chronic illness: Findings from the National Study of Daily Experiences. *Health Psychology, 37,* 170–178.

Choi, E., Kwon, Y., Lee, M. et al. (2018). Social relatedness and physical health are more strongly related in older than younger adults: Findings from the Korean Adult Longitudinal Study. *Frontiers in Psychology, 9,* January 19.

Clark, R. (2006). Perceived racism and vascular reactivity in black college women: Moderating effects of seeking social support. *Health Psychology, 25,* 20–25.

Cole, S. W., Hawkley, L. C., Arevalo, J. M., et al. (2007). Social regulation of gene expression in human leukocytes. *Genome Biology, 8,* R189.

Connerty, T. J., & Knott, V. (2013). Promoting positive change in the face of adversity: Experiences of cancer and posttraumatic growth. *European Journal of Cancer Care, 22,* 334–344.

Cornum, R., Matthews, M. D., & Seligman, M. E. P. (2011). Comprehensive soldier fitness. *American Psychologist, 66,* 4–9.

Danieli, Y., Norris, F. H., & Engdahl, B. (2017). A question of who, not if: Psychological disorders in Holocaust survivors' children. *Psychological Trauma: Theory, Research, Practice, and Policy, 9,* 96–106.

Dekel, S., Ein-Dor, T., & Solomon, Z. (2012). Posttraumatic growth and posttraumatic stress: A longitudinal study. *Psychological Trauma: Theory, Research, Practice, and Policy, 4,* 94–101.

DeLongis, A., & Holtzman, S. (2005). Coping in context: The role of stress, social support, and personality in coping. *Journal of Personality, 73,* 1633–1656.

Dougall, A. L., & Baum, A. (2001). Stress, health and illness. In A. Baum, T. A. Revenson, & J. E. Singer (Eds.), *Handbook of health psychology* (pp. 321–337). Mahwah, NJ: Erlbaum.

Earles, J. L., Vernon, L. L., & Yetz, J. P. (2015). Equine-assisted therapy for anxiety and post-traumatic stress symptoms. Journal of Traumatic Stress, 28, 149–152.

Elliot, A. J., Turiano, N. A., Infurna, F. J., et al. (2018). Lifetime trauma, perceived control, and all-cause mortality: Results from the Midlife in the United States study. *Health Psychology, 28,* 262–270.

Fabre, B., Grosman, H., Mazza, O., et al. (2013). Relationship between cortisol, life events, and metabolic syndrome in men. *Stress: The International Journal of the Biology of Stress, 16,* 16–23.

Fingerhut, A. W. (2018). The role of social support and gay identity in the stress processes of a sample of Caucasian gay men. *Psychology of Sexual Orientation and Gender Diversity, 5,* 294–302.

Flinn, M. V., Ward, C. V., & Noone, R. J. (2005). Hormones and the human family. In D. M. Buss (Ed.), *The handbook of evolutionary psychology* (pp. 552–580). New York: Wiley.

Folkman, S., & Moskowitz, J. T. (2004). Coping: Pitfalls and promises. *Annual Review of Psychology, 55,* 745–774.

Frazier, P. A., Gavian, M., Hirai, R., et al. (2011). Prospective predictors of posttraumatic stress disorder symptoms: Direct and mediated relations. *Psychological Trauma: Theory, Research, Practice, and Policy, 3,* 27.

Friedman, M. J. (2005). Introduction: Every crisis is an opportunity. *CNS Spectrum, 10,* 96–98.

Golembiewski, E., Watson, D. P., Robison, L., et al. (2017). Social network decay as potential recovery from homelessness: A mixed methods study in Housing First program. *Social Science (Basel), 6,* 96.

Gorman, J. M. (2005). In the wake of trauma. *CNS Spectrums, 10,* 81–85.

Hamby, S., Grych, J., & Banyard, V. (2018). Resilience portfolios and poly-strengths: Identifying protective factors associated with thriving after adversity. *Psychology of Violence, 8,* 172–183.

Helson, R., & Roberts, B. W. (1994). Ego development and personality change in adulthood. *Journal of Personality and Social Psychology, 66,* 911–920.

Hoge, C. W., Castro, C. A., Messer, S. C., et al. (2004). Combat duty in Iraq and Afghanistan, mental health problems, and barriers to care. *New England Journal of Medicine, 351,* 13–22.

Holmes, T. H., & Rahe, R. H. (1967). The Social Readjustment Rating Scale. *Journal of Psychosomatic Research, 11,* 213–218.

Holt-Lunstad, J., Smith, T. B., & Layton, J. B. (2010). Social relationships and mortality risk: A meta-analytic review. *PLoS Medicine, 7(7),* e1000316.

Hunte, H. E. R., & Williams, D. R. (2009). The association between perceived discrimination and obesity in a population-based multi-racial and multi-ethnic adult sample. *American Journal of Public Health, 99,* 1285–1292.

Kessler, R. C., Aguilar-Gaxiola, S., Alonso, J., et al. (2017). Trauma and OTSD in the WHO World Mental Health Surveys, *European Journal of Psychotraumatology, 8,* 1353–1383.

Kira, I., Abou-Median, S., Ashby, J., et al. (2012). Post-traumatic Growth Inventory: Psychometric properties of the Arabic version in Palestinian adults. *International Journal of Educational and Psychological Assessment, 11,* 120–137.

Knight, J. M., Rizzo, J. D., Logan, B. R., et al. (2016). Low socioeconomic status, adverse gene expression profiles, and clinical outcomes in hematopoietic stem cell transplant recipients. *Clinical Cancer Research, 22,* 69–78.

Krause, N. (2006). Social relationships in late life. In R. H. Binstock & L. K. George (Eds.), *Handbook of aging and the social sciences* (pp. 181–200). San Diego, CA: Academic Press.

Lee, H., Aldwin, C., Choun, S. et al. (2017). Does combat exposure affect well-being in later life?: The VA Normative Aging Study. *Psychological Trauma: Research, Practice, and Policy, 9*, 672–676.

Lieberman, M. (1996). *Doors close, doors open: Widows, grieving and growing.* New York: Putnam.

Lillberg, K., Verkasalo, P. K., Kaprio, J., et al. (2003). Stressful life events and risk of breast cancer in 10,808 women: A cohort study. *American Journal of Epidemiology, 157*, 415–423.

Livingston, N. A., Flentje, A., Heck, N. C., et al. (2017). Ecological momentary assessment of daily discrimination experiences and nicotine, alcohol, and drug use among sexual and gender minority individuals. *Journal of Counseling and Clinical Psychology, 85*, 1131–1143.

Lowe, S. R., Manove, E. E., & Rhodes, J. E. (2013). Post-traumatic stress and posttraumatic growth among low-income mothers who survived Hurricane Katrina. *Journal of Consulting and Clinical Psychology, 81*, 877–889.

Lucas, G. M., Rizzo, A., Gratch, J., et al. (2017). Reporting mental health symptoms: Breaking down barriers to care with virtual human interviewers. *Frontiers in Robotics and AI, 4*, 51.

Mancini, A. D., & Bonanno, G. A. (2009). Predictors and parameters of resilience to loss: Toward an individual differences model. *Journal of Personality, 77*, 1805–1832.

Mancini, A. D., Robinaugh, D., Shear, K., et al. (2009). Does attachment avoidance help people cope with loss?: The moderating effect of relationship quality. *Journal of Clinical Psychology, 65*, 1127–1136.

Matthews, K. A., & Gump, B. B. (2002). Chronic work stress and marital dissolution increase risk of posttrial mortality in men from the Multiple Risk Factor Intervention trial. *Archives of Internal Medicine, 162*, 309–315.

Mayou, R. A., Ehlers, A., & Hobbs, M. (2000). Psychological debriefing for road traffic accident victims. *British Journal of Psychiatry, 176*, 589–593.

Morgan, G. S., Wisneski, D. C., & Skitka, L. J. (2011). The expulsion from Disneyland: The social psychology impact of 9/11. *American Psychologist, 66*, 447–454.

Murphy, M. L. M., Slavich, G. M., Rohleder, N., et al. (2013). Targeted rejection triggers differential pro- and anti-inflammatory gene expression in adolescents as a function of social status. *Clinical Psychological Science, 1*, 30–40.

National Center for Veterans Affairs. (2016). *PTSD.* Retrieved March 7, 2018, from https://www.ptsd.va.gov/public/PTSD-overview/basics/how-common-is-ptsd.asp

Nelson, D. L., & Burke, R. J. (2002). *Gender, work stress, and health.* Washington, DC: American Psychological Association.

Neria, Y., DiGrande, L., & Adams, B. (2011). Posttraumatic stress disorder following the September 11, 2001, terrorist attacks: A review of the literature among highly exposed populations. *American Psychologist, 66*, 429–446.

Paradies, Y. C. (2006). Defining, conceptualizing, and characterizing racism in health research. *Critical Public Health, 16*, 143–157.

Pascoe. E., & Smart Richman, L. (2009). Perceived discrimination and health: A met-analytic review. *Psychological Bulletin, 135*, 531–554.

Pearlin, L. I. (1980). Life strains and psychological distress among adults. In N. J. Smelser & E. H. Erikson (Eds.), *Themes of work and love in adulthood* (pp. 174–192). Cambridge, MA: Harvard University Press.

Peterson, C., Park, N., & Castro, C. A. (2011). Assessment for the U. S. Army Comprehensive Soldier Fitness Program. *American Psychologist, 66*, 10–18.

Positive Psychology Center. (2018). *University of Pennsylvania Resilience Training for the Army.* Retrieved March 87, 2018, from https://ppc.sas.upenn.edu/services/resilience-training-army

Rosengren, A., Orth-Gomér, K., Wedel, H., et al. (1993). Stressful life events, social support, and mortality in men born in 1933. *British Medical Journal, 307*, 1102–1105.

Sagi-Schwartz, A., Bakermans-Kranenburg, M. J., Linn, S., et al. (2013). Against all odds: Genocidal trauma is associated with longer life-expectancy of the survivors. *PLOS ONE, 8*, e69179.

Scharlach, A. E., & Fredrickson, K. I. (1993). Reactions to the death of a parent during midlife. *Omega, 27*, 307–319.

Schmitt, M. T., Branscombe, N. R., Postmes, T., et al. (2014). The consequences of perceived discrimination for psychological well-being: A meta-analytic review. *Psychological Bulletin, 140*, 921–948.

Scott, S. B., Poulin, M. J., & Silver, R. C. (2013). A lifespan perspective on terrorism: Age differences in trajectories of response to 9/11. *Developmental Psychology, 49*, 986–998.

Segerstrom, S. C., & Miller, G. E. (2004). Psychological stress and the human immune system: A meta-analytic study of 30 years of inquiry. *Psychological Bulletin, 130*, 601–630.

Selye, H. (1936). A syndrome produced by diverse nocuous agents. *Nature, 138*, 32.

Shankar, A., & Hinds, P. (2017). Perceived discrimination: Associations with physical and cognitive function in older adults. *Health Psychology, 36*, 1126–1134.

Slavich, G. M., & Cole, S. W. (2013). The emerging field of human social genomics. *Clinical Psychological Science, 1*, 331–348.

Taylor, R. J., Chae, D. H., Lincoln, K. D., et al. (2015). Extended family and friendship support networks are both protective and risk factors for major depressive disorder and depressive symptoms among African-American and black Caribbeans. *Journal of Nervous and Mental Diseases, 203*, 132–140.

Taylor, S. E. (2002). *The tending instinct: How nurturing is essential to who we are and how we live.* New York: Holt.

Taylor, S. E., Gonzaga, G. C., Klein, L. C., et al. (2006). Relation of oxytocin to psychological stress responses and hypothalamic-pituitary-adrenocortical axis activity in older women. *Psychosomatic medicine, 68*, 238–245.

Trappler, B., Cohen, C. I., & Tulloo, R. (2007). Impact of early lifetime trauma in later life: Depression among Holocaust survivors 60 years after the liberation of Auschwitz. *American Journal of Geriatric Psychology, 15*, 79–83.

Uchino, B. N., Bowen, K., Carlisle, M., et al. (2012). Psychological pathways linking social support to health outcomes: A visit with the "ghosts" of research past, present, and future. *Social Science and Medicine, 74*, 949–957.

Vie, L. L., Scheier, L. M., Lester, P. B., et al. (2016). Initial validation of the U.S Army Global Assessment Tool. *Military Psychology, 28*, 468–487.

Vogt, D. S., Pless, A. P., King, L. A., et al. (2005). Deployment stressors, gender, and mental health outcomes among Gulf War I veterans. *Journal of Traumatic Stress, 18*, 115–127.

Watson. P. J., Brymer, M. J., & Bonanno, G. A. (2011). Postdisaster psychological intervention since 9/11. *American Psychologist, 66*, 482–494.

Williams, L., Zhang, R., & Packard, K. C. (2017). Factors affecting the physical and mental health of older adult in China: The importance of marital status, child proximity, and gender. *SSM Popular Health, 3*, 20–36.

Yehuda, R. (2002). Current concepts: Post-traumatic stress disorder. *New England Journal of Medicine, 346*, 108–114.

Yehuda, R., Bell, A., Bierer, L. M., & Schmeidler, J. (2008). Maternal, not paternal, PTSD is related to increased risk for PTSD in offspring of Holocaust survivors. *Journal of Psychiatric Research, 42*, 1104–1111.

Yehuda, R., Halligan, S. L., & Bierer, L. M. (2001). Relationship of parental trauma exposure and PTSD to PTSD, depressive and anxiety disorders in offspring. *Journal of Psychiatric Research, 35*, 261–270.

Zivotofsky, A. Z., & Koslowsky, M. (2005). Short communication: Gender differences in coping with the major external stress of the Washington, DC, sniper. *Stress and Health, 21*, 27–31.

CHAPTER 11

Abdel-Khalek, A. M. (2004). The Arabic Scale of Death Anxiety (ASDA): Its development, validation, and results in three Arab countries. *Death Studies, 28*, 435–457.

Alsop, S. (1973). *Stay of execution.* New York: Lippincott.

Anderson, K. A., & Weber, K. V. (2015). Auto therapy: Using automobiles as vehicles for reminiscence with older adults. *Journal of Gerontological Social Work, 58*, 469–483.

Ardelt, M., & Koenig, C. S. (2006). The role of religion for hospice patients and relatively healthy older adults. *Research on Aging, 28*, 184–215.

Balk, D. E. (2016). The psychology of death and dying in later life. In K. W. Schaie & S. L. Willis (Eds.), *Handbook of the psychology of aging* (8th ed., pp. 475–489). San Diego, CA: Academic Press.

Bonanno, G. A., & Kaltman, S. (1999). Toward an integrative perspective on bereavement. *Psychological Bulletin, 125*, 760–776.

Bonanno, G. A., & Keltner, D. (1997). Facial expressions of emotion and the course of conjugal bereavement. *Journal of Abnormal Psychology, 106*, 126–137.

Bonanno, G. A., Moskowitz, J. T., Papa, A., et al. (2005). Resilience to loss in bereaved spouses, bereaved parents, and bereaved gay men. *Journal of Personality and Social Psychology, 88*, 827–843.

Bonanno, G. A., Wortman, C. B., Lehman, D. R., et al. (2002). Resilience to loss and chronic grief: A prospective study from pre-loss to 18 months post-loss. *Journal of Personality and Social Psychology, 83*, 1150–1164.

Bowlby, J. (1982). Attachment and loss: Retrospect and prospect. *American Journal of Orthopsychiatry, 52*, 664–678.

Brogaard, T., Neergaard, M. A., & Sokolowski, T. (2012). Congruence between preferred and actual place of care and death among Danish cancer patients. *Palliative Medicine, 27*, 155–164.

Chow, H. P. H. (2017). A time to be born and a time to die: Exploring the determinants of death anxiety among university students in a western Canadian city. *Death Studies, 41*, 345–352.

Corr, C. A. (1993). Coping with dying: Lessons we should and should not learn from the work of Elisabeth Kubler-Ross. *Death Studies, 17*, 69–83.

De Raedt, R., Koster, E. H. W., & Ryckewaert, R. (2013). Aging and attentional bias for death-related and general threat-related information: Less avoidance in older as compared with middle-aged adults. *Journals of Gerontology: Psychological and Social Sciences, 68*, 41–48.

El Haj, M., & & Antoine, P. (2016). Death preparation and boredom reduction as functions of reminiscence in Alzheimer's disease. *Journal of Alzheimer's Disease, 54*, 515–523.

Emanuel, E. J., Fairclough, D. L., & Emanuel, L. L. (2000). Attitudes and desires related to euthanasia and physician-assisted suicide among terminally ill patients and their caregivers. *Journal of the American Medical Association, 284*, 2460–2468.

Erikson, E. H. (1982). *The life cycle completed.* New York: Norton.

Eshbaugh, E., & Henninger, W. (2013). Potential mediators of the relationship between gender and death anxiety. *Individual Differences Research, 11*, 22–30.

Falomir-Pichastor, J. M., Berent, J. A., & Pereira, A. (2011). Social psychological factors of post-mortem organ donation: A theoretical review of determinants and promotion strategies. *Health Psychology Review, 7*, 202–247.

Feifel, H. (1990). Psychology and death: Meaningful rediscovery. *American Psychologist, 45*, 537–543.

Field, B. (2005). *Science hero: Dame Cicely Saunders.* Retrieved May 16, 2006, from http://myhero.com/myhero.asp?hero=Cicely_Saunders>06

Greer, S. (1991). Psychological response to cancer and survival. *Psychological Medicine, 21*, 43–49.

Harding, S. R., Flannelly, K. J., Weaver, A. J., et al. (2005). The influence of religion on death anxiety and death acceptance. *Mental Health, Religion, & Culture, 8*, 253–261.

Harris Poll. (2005). *The religions and other beliefs of Americans 2005.* Retrieved May 16, 2006, from http://www.harrisinteractive.com/harris_poll/index.asp?PID=618

Hazell, L. V. (1997). Cross-cultural funeral rites. *Director, 69*, 53–55.

Jacobs, S. (1993). *Pathologic grief: Maladaption to loss.* Washington, DC: American Psychiatric Press.

Johnson, M. L. (2009). Spirituality, finitude, and theories of the life span. In V. L. Bengtson, M. Silverstein, N. M. Putney, et al. (Eds.), *Handbook of theories of aging* (pp. 659–673). New York: Springer.

Jones, J. M. (2016). *Majority in U.S. do not have a will.* Retrieved March 18, 2018, from http://news.gallup.com/poll/191651/majority-not.aspx

Kalish, R. A. (1985). The social context of death and dying. In R. H. Binstock & E. Shanas (Eds.), *Handbook of aging and the social sciences* (pp. 149–170). New York: Van Nostrand Reinhold.

Kellehear, A., & Lewin, T. (1988–1989). Farewells by the dying: A sociological study. *Omega: Journal of Death and Dying, 19*, 275–292.

Kübler-Ross, E. (1974). *Questions and answers on death and dying.* New York: Macmillan.

Lancioni, G. E., Singh, N. N., & O'Reilly, M. F. (2015). Patients with moderate Alzheimer's disease engage in verbal reminiscence with the support of a computer-aided program: A pilot study. *Frontiers in Aging Neuroscience, 7*, 109.

Lipka, M. (2014). *5 facts about Americans' views on life-and-death issues.* Retrieved March 18, 2018, from http://www.pewresearch.org/fact-tank/2014/01/07/5-facts-about-americans-views-on-life-and-death-issues/

Lobar, S. L. (2006). Cross-cultural beliefs, ceremonies, and rituals surrounding death of a loved one. *Pediatric Nursing, 32*, 44–50.

Magidson, J. F., Roberts, B. W., Collado-Rodriguez, A., et al. (2014). Theory-driven intervention for changing personality: Expectancy value theory, behavioral activation, and conscientiousness. *Developmental Psychology, 50*, 1442–1450.

Marshall, V. W., & Levy, J. A. (1990). Aging and dying. In R. H. Binstock & L. K. George (Eds.), *Handbook of aging and the social sciences* (pp. 245–260). San Diego, CA: Academic Press.

McFadden, S. H. (2000). Religion and meaning in late life. In G. T. Reker & K. Chamberlain (Eds.), *Exploring existential meaning: Optimizing human development across the life span* (pp. 171–183). Thousand Oaks, CA: Sage.

Meevissen, Y. M., Peters, M. L., & Alberts, H. J. (2011). Become more optimistic by imagining a best possible self: Effects of a two-week intervention. *Journal of Behavior Therapy and Experimental Psychiatry, 42*, 371–378.

Messerli-Bürgy, N., Molloy, G., Poole, L, et al. (2015). Psychological coping and recurrent major adverse cardiac events following acute coronary syndrome. *British Journal of Psychiatry, 207*, 256–261.

Moskowitz, J. T., Folkman, S., & Acree, M. (2003). Do positive psychological states shed light on recovery from bereavement? Findings from a 3-year longitudinal study. *Death Studies, 27*, 471–500.

National Hospice and Palliative Care Association. (2017). *Facts and figures: Hospice care in America.* Retrieved March 18, 2018, from https://www.nhpco.org/sites/default/files/public/Statistics_Research/2016_Facts_Figures.pdf

Neugarten, B. L. (1970). Dynamics of transition of middle age to old age. *Journal of Geriatric Psychiatry, 4*, 71–87.

Oregon Health Authority. (2018a). *Death with Dignity Act.* Retrieved March 18, 2018. from http://www.oregon.gov/oha/PH/PROVIDERPARTNERRESOURCES/EVALUATIONRESEARCH/DEATHWITHDIGNITYACT/Pages/index.aspx

Oregon Health Authority. (2018b). *Oregon Death with Dignity Act: 2017 data summary.* Retrieved March 18, 2018, from http://www.oregon.gov/oha/PH/PROVIDERPARTNERRESOURCES/EVALUATIONRESEARCH/DEATHWITHDIGNITYACT/Documents/year20.pdf

Pettingale, K. W., Morris, T., Greer, S., et al. (1985). Mental attitudes to cancer: An additional prognostic factor. *Lancet, 1,* 750.

Rando, T. A. (1993). *Treatment of complicated mourning.* Champaign, IL: Research Press.

Renner, F., Schwartz, P., & Peters, M. L. (2014). Effects of a best-possible-self imagery exercise on mood and dysfunctional attitudes. *Psychiatry Research, 215,* 105–110.

Reyes, M. E. S., Amistoso, M. N. G., Babaran, C. A. C., et al. (2017). Death anxiety and self-esteem of Filipino youths and older adults. *North American Journal of Psychology, 19,* 435–350.

Sandstrom, A., & Alper, B. A. (2014). *If the U.S. had 100 people: Charting Americans' religious beliefs and practices.* Retrieved March 18, 2018, from http://www.pewresearch.org/fact-tank/2016/12/01/if-the-u-s-had-100-people-charting-americans-religious-beliefs-and-practices/

Santillanes, G. (1997). Releasing the spirit: A lesson in Native American funeral rituals. *Director, 69,* 32–34.

Seale, C., Raus, K., Bruinsma, S., et al. (2015). The language of sedation in end-of-life care: The ethical reasoning of care providers in three countries. *Health, 19,* 339–354.

Steindl-Rast, B. D. (1977). Learning to die. *Parabola, 2,* 22–31.

Techner, D. (1997). The Jewish funeral—A celebration of life. *Director, 69,* 18–20.

Teno, J. M., Clarridge, B. R., Casey, V., et al. (2004). Family perspectives on end-of-life care at the last place of care. *Journal of the American Medical Association, 291,* 88–93.

Thompson, D. (2014). *Most Americans agree with right to die movement.* Retrieved March 18, 2018, from https://theharrispoll.com/by-dennis-thompson-healthday-reporter/

Tomer, A., & Eliason, G. (2005). Life regrets and death attitudes in college students. *Omega: Journal of Death and Dying, 51,* 173–195.

Torpy, J. M., Burke, A., & Golub, R. M. (2012). Elements of hospice care. *Journal of the American Medical Association, 308,* 200.

Wen, T. (2014, November 10). Why don't more people want to donate their organs? *The Atlantic.* Retrieved March 18, 2018 from https://www.theatlantic.com/health/archive/2014/11/why-dont-people-want-to-donate-their-organs/382297/

Wilkinson, A. M., & Lynn, J. (2001). The end of life. In R. H. Binstock & L. K. George (Eds.), *Handbook of aging and the social sciences* (pp. 444–461). San Diego, CA: Academic Press.

Wingbermuehle, C., Bryer, D., Berg-Weger, M., et al. (2014). Baseball reminiscence league: A model for supporting persons with dementia. *Journal of the American Medical Directors Association, 15,* 85–89.

Wink, P., & Scott, J. (2005). Does religiousness buffer against the fear of death and dying in late adulthood?: Findings from a longitudinal study. *Journals of Gerontology: Psychological and Social Sciences, 60,* 207–214.

Zisook, S., Paulus, M., Shuchter, S. R., et al. (1997). The many faces of depression following spousal bereavement. *Journal of Affective Disorders, 45,* 85–94.

CHAPTER 12

Antonucci, T. C., Berkman, L., Börsch-Supan, A., et al. (2016). Society and the individual and the dawn of the Twenty-first Century. In K. W. Schaie & S. L. Willis (Eds.), *Handbook of the psychology of aging* (8th ed., pp. 41–62). San Diego, CA: Academic Press.

Arnett, J. J. (1994). Are college students adults?: Their conceptions of the transition to adulthood. *Journal of Adult Development, 1,* 213–224.

Arnett, J. J. (2000). Emerging adulthood. *American Psychologist, 55,* 469–480.

Arnett, J. J. (2004). *Emerging adulthood: The winding road from late teens through the twenties.* Oxford, UK: Oxford University Press.

Arnett, J. J. (2007). Emerging adulthood: What is it, and what is it good for? *Child Development Perspectives, 1,* 68–73.

Baltes, P. B., & Baltes, M. M. (1990). Psychological perspectives on successful aging: The model of selective optimization with compensation. In P. B. Baltes & M. M. Baltes (Eds.), *Successful aging: Perspective from the behavioral sciences* (pp. 1–34). Cambridge, UK: Cambridge University Press.

Baltes, P. B., Reese, H. W., & Lipsitt, L. P. (1980). Life-span developmental psychology. *Annual Review of Psychology, 31,* 65–110.

Banerjee, S. (2016, April). Trends in retirement satisfaction in the United States: Fewer having a great time. *EBRI Notes, 27,* 4–12.

Blanchflower, D. G., & Oswald, A. J. (2008). Is well-being U-shaped over the life cycle? *Social Science and Medicine, 66,* 1733–1749.

Blazer, D. G., & Hybels, C. F. (2014). Depression in later life: Epidemiology, assessments impact, and treatment. In I. H. Gotlib & C. L. Hammen (Eds.), *Handbook of depression* (3rd ed., pp. 492–509). New York: Guilford Press.

Börsch-Supan, A., & Schuth, M. (2013). Early retirement, mental health and social networks. In D. A. Wise (Ed.), *Discoveries in the economics of aging* (pp. 225–255). Chicago, IL: University of Chicago Press.

Bronfenbrenner, U. (1979). *The ecology of human development.* Cambridge, MA: Harvard University Press.

Butler, R. N. (1963). The life review: An interpretation of reminiscence in the aged. *Psychiatry, 26,* 65–76.

Chen, C., Goldman, D. P., Zissimopoulos, J., et al. (2018). Multidimensional comparison of countries' adaptation to societal aging. *Proceedings of the National Academy of Sciences U.S.A., 115,* 9169–9174.

Cherry, K. E., Walker, E. J., Brown, J. S., et al. (2013). Social engagement and heath in younger, older, and oldest-old adults in the Louisiana Healthy Aging Study (LHAS). *Applied Gerontology 32,* 51–75.

Chodzko-Zajko, W. J., Proctor, D. N., Fiatarone Singh, M. A., et al. (2009). Exercise and physical activity for older adults. *Medical Science Sports Exercise, 41,* 1510–1530.

Clark, A. E. (2013) Social comparisons, health and well-being. *Revue d'Épidémiologie et de Santé Publique, 61,* S184–S188.

Cumming, E. (1975). Engagement with an old theory. *International Journal of Aging and Human Development, 6,* 187–191.

Cumming, E., & Henry, W. E. (1961). *Growing old.* New York: Basic Books.

Depp, C. A., Harmell, A. L., & Jeste, D. (2014). Strategies for successful aging: A research update. *Current Psychiatry Reports, 16,* 476.

Dykstra, P. A., & Hagestad, G. O. (2007). Roads less taken: Developing a nuanced view of older adults without children. *Journal of Family Issues, 28,* 1275–1310.

Eichorn, D. H. (1973). The Berkeley longitudinal studies: Continuities and correlates of behaviour. *Canadian Journal of Behavioural Science/Revue canadienne des sciences du comportement, 5,* 297–320.

Elder, G. H., Jr. (1979). Historical change in life patterns and personality. In P. B. Baltes & O. G. Brim, Jr. (Eds.), *Lifespan development and behavior* (Vol. 2, pp. 117–159). New York: Academic Press.

Ellwardt, L., Van Tilburg, T. G., & Aartsen, M. J. (2015). The mix matters: Complex personal networks relate to higher cognitive functioning in old age. *Social Science and Medicine, 125,* 107–115.

Erikson, E. H. (1950). *Childhood and society.* New York: Norton.

Erikson, E. H. (1959). *Identity and the life cycle.* New York: Norton.

Giele, J. Z. (1982). Women in adulthood: Unanswered questions. In J. Z. Giele (Ed.), *Women in the middle years* (pp. 1–36). New York: Wiley.

Glueck, S., & Glueck, E. (1950). *Unraveling juvenile delinquency.* New York: Commonwealth Fund.

Glueck, S., & Glueck, E. (1968). *Delinquents and nondelinquents in perspective*. Cambridge, MA: Harvard University Press.

Haan, N. (1981). Common dimensions of personality development: Early adolescence to middle life. In D. H. Eichorn, J. A. Clausen, N. Haan, et al. (Eds.), *Present and past in middle life* (pp. 117–153). New York: Academic Press.

Hagestad, G. O., & Neugarten, B. L. (1985). Age and the life course. In R. H. Binstock & E. Shana (Eds.), *Handbook of aging and the social sciences* (2nd ed., pp. 35–61). New York: Van Nostrand Reinhold.

Hakanen, J., & Schaufeli, W. (2012). Do burnout and work engagement predict depressive symptoms and life satisfaction?: A three-wave seven-year prospective study. *Journal of Affective Disorders, 141,* 415–424.

Halpern, J., Cohen, M., Kennedy, G., et al. (2014). Yoga for improving sleep quality and quality of life for older adults. *Alternative Therapies in Health and Medicine, 20,* 37–46.

Jacques, E. (1965). Death and the mid-life crisis. *International Journal of Psychoanalysis, 46,* 502–514.

Jürges, H., Kruk, E., & Reinhold, S. (2013). The effect of compulsory schooling on health—evidence from biomarkers. *Journal of population economics, 26,* 645–672.

Lachman, M. E., Teshale, S., & Agrigoroaei, S. (2015). Midlife as a pivotal period in the life course: Balancing growth and decline at the crossroads of youth and old age. *International Journal of Behavioral Development, 39,* 20–31.

Livson, F. B. (1981). Paths to psychological health in the middle years: Sex differences. In D. H. Eichorn, J. A. Clausen, N. Haan, et al. (Eds.), *Present and past in middle life* (pp. 195–221). New York: Academic Press.

Masi, C. M., Chen, H. Y., Hawkley, L. C., et al. (2011). A meta-analysis of interventions to reduce loneliness. *Personality and Social Psychology Review, 15,* 219–266.

McCrae, R. R., & Costa, P. T., Jr. (1983). Psychological maturity and subjective well-being: Toward a new synthesis. *Developmental Psychology, 19,* 243–248.

Moen, P., & Flood, S. (2013). Limited engagements?: Women's and men's work/volunteer time in the encore life course stage. *Social Problems, 60,* 206–233.

Moliver, N., Mika, E., Chartrand, M., et al. (2013). Yoga experience as a predictor of psychological wellness in women over 45 years. *International Journal of Yoga, 6,* 11–19.

Olshansky, S. J., Beard, J., & Börsch-Supan, A. (2012). The longevity dividend: Health as an investment. *Global Population Ageing: Peril or Promise?,* p. 57.

Peskin, H., & Livson, N. (1981). Uses of the past in adult psychological health. In D. H. Eichorn, J. A. Clausen, N. Haan, et al. (Eds.), *Present and past in middle life* (pp. 158–194). New York: Academic Press.

Prakash, R., Rastogi, P., Dubey, I., et al. (2012). Long-term concentrative meditation and cognitive performance among older adults. *Aging Neuropsychology, and Cognition, 19,* 479–494.

Quinton, D., Pickles, A., Maughan, B., et al. (1993). Partners, peers, and pathways: Assortive pairing and continuities in conduct disorder. *Development and Psychopathology, 5,* 763–783.

Reijnders, J., van Heugten, C., & van Boxtel, M. (2013). Cognitive interventions in healthy older adults and people with mild cognitive impairment: A systematic review. *Ageing Research Review, 12,* 263–275.

Rocketto, L. (2011). *ACSM releases new exercise guidelines.* Retrieved June 11, 2019 from https://greatist.com/fitness/acsm-releases-new-exercise-guidelines

Rohwedder, S., & Willis, R. J. (2010). Mental retirement. *Journal of Economic Perspectives, 24,* 119–138.

Rowe, J. W., & Kahn, R. L. (1998). *Successful aging.* New York: Pantheon Books.

Scarmeas, N., Stern, Y., Mayeux, R., et al. (2009). Mediterranean diet and mild cognitive impairment. *Archives of Neurology, 66,* 216–225.

Sheehy, G. (1976). *Passages.* New York: Dutton.

Sherman, C. W., Webster, N. J., & Antonucci, T. C. (2013). Dementia caregiving in the context of late-life remarriage: Support networks, relationship quality, and well-being. *Journal of Marriage and Family, 75,* 1149–1163.

Shneidman, E. S. (1989). The Indian summer of life: A preliminary study of septuagenarians. *American Psychologist, 44,* 684–694.

Snarey, J. R., Son, L., Kuehne, V. S., et al. (1987). The role of parenting in men's psychosocial development: A longitudinal study of early adulthood infertility and midlife generativity. *Developmental Psychology, 23,* 593–603.

Vaillant, G. E. (1974). Natural history of male psychological health, II: Some antecedents of healthy adult adjustment. *Archives of General Psychiatry, 31,* 15–22.

Vaillant, G. E. (1977). *Adaptation to life: How the best and brightest come of age.* Boston, MA: Little, Brown.

Vaillant, G. E. (1995). *Adaptation to life.* Cambridge, MA: Harvard University Press.

Vaillant, G. E., & Vaillant, C. O. (1990). Natural history of male psychological health, XII: A 45-year study of predictors of successful aging at 65. *American Journal of Psychiatry, 147,* 31–37.

Waddington, C. H. (1957). *The strategy of the genes.* London: Allen & Son.

Westerhof, G. J., & Bohlmeijer, E. T. (2014). Celebrating 50 years of research and applications in reminiscence and life review: State of the art and new directions. *Journal of Aging Studies, 29,* 107–114.

Wethington, E. (2000). Expecting stress: Americans and their "midlife crisis." *Motivation and Emotion, 24,* 85–103.

Willis, S. L., & Belleville, S. (2016). Cognitive training in later adulthood. In K. W. Schaie & S. L. Willis (Eds.), *Handbook of the psychology of aging* (8th ed., pp. 219–243). San Diego, CA: Academic Press.

Credits

Image Credits

About the Author xv: Lindsey Smith: Lindsey Smith.

Chapter 1 001: Getty Images: AdShooter/E+/Getty Images; **004: Barbara Bjorklund:** Barbara Bjorklund.

Chapter 2 022: Getty Images: JGI/Jamie Grill/Getty Images; **030: Shutterstock:** medejaja/Shutterstock.

Chapter 3 050: Shutterstock: wavebreakmedia/Shutterstock; **053: Shutterstock:** Photodiem/Shutterstock; **055: Shutterstock:** Diamond_Images/Shutterstock; **064: Shutterstock:** Africa Studio/Shutterstock.

Chapter 4 077: Shutterstock: Shutterstock.

Chapter 5 103: Shutterstock: Blend Images/Shutterstock; **110: Shutterstock:** wavebreakmedia/Shutterstock; **115: Shutterstock:** Shutterstock.

Chapter 6 127: Shutterstock: Shutterstock.

Chapter 7 156: 123RF: bialasiewicz/123RF; **171: 123RF:** ginasanders/123RF.

Chapter 8 181: Shutterstock: XiXinXing/Shutterstock; **193: Shutterstock:** NORRIE3699/Shutterstock; **201: John Wiley & Sons, Inc.:** Maslow, A. H. (1968/1998). Toward a psychology of being (3rd ed.). New York: Wiley.

Chapter 9 205: Shutterstock: StockImageFactory.com/Shutterstock; **214: 123RF:** bbourdages/123RF; **214: Shutterstock:** SNEHIT/Shutterstock.

Chapter 10 226: Shutterstock: Syda Productions/Shutterstock.

Chapter 11 246: Shutterstock: Fotoluminate LLC/Shutterstock; **248: Shutterstock:** Jostein Hauge/Shutterstock; **248: Shutterstock:** imtmphoto/Shutterstock; **249: Shutterstock:** Jaggat Rashidi/Shutterstock; **249: Shutterstock:** Budimir Jevtic/Shutterstock.

Chapter 12 262: Shutterstock: Shutterstock; **267: 123RF:** nyul/123RF; **276: Shutterstock:** Diego Cervo/Shutterstock; **277: Shutterstock:** wavebreakmedia/Shutterstock; **286: Shutterstock:** sirtravelalot/Shutterstock.

Text Credits

Chapter 1 010: American Psychological Association (US): From Baltes, P. B. (1987) "Theoretical propositions of life-span developmental psychology: On the dynamics between growth and decline" Developmental Psychology, 23, 611–626; **011: Elsevier:** Bronfenbrenner, U. (1994). Ecological models of human development. In International Encyclopedia of Education (Vol. 3, 2nd ed.). Oxford: Elsevier; **012: Oxford University Press:** Seubert, J., Laukka, E. J., Rizzuto, D., et al. (2017). Prevalence and correlates of olfactory dysfunction in old age: A population-based study. Journals of Gerontology: Medical Sciences, 72, 1072–1079; **013: Oxford University Press:** Seubert, J., Laukka, E. J., Rizzuto, D., et al. (2017). Prevalence and correlates of olfactory dysfunction in old age: A population-based study. Journals of Gerontology: Medical Sciences, 72, 1072–1079; **014: American Psychological Association (US):** Vargas Lascano, D. I., Galambos, N. L., Krahn, H. J., & Lachman, M. E. (2015). Growth in perceived control across 25 years from the late teens to midlife: The role of personal and parents' education. Developmental Psychology, 51(1), 124–135; **014: American Psychological Association (US):** Vargas Lascano, D. I., Galambos, N. L., Krahn, H. J., & Lachman, M. E. (2015). Growth in perceived control across 25 years from the late teens to midlife: The role of personal and parents' education. Developmental Psychology, 51(1), 124–135; **015: American Psychological Association (US):** From Whitbourne, S. K., Zuschlag, M. K. Elliot, L. B., et al. (1992) "Psychosocial development in adulthood: a 22-year sequential study" Journal of Personality and Social Psychology, 63, 260–271; **016: American Psychological Association (US):** From Whitbourne, S. K., Zuschlag, M. K. Elliot, L. B., et al. (1992) "Psychosocial development in adulthood: a 22-year sequential study" Journal of Personality and Social Psychology, 63, 260–271; **018: American Psychological Association (US):** From Spotts, E. L., Neiderhiser, J. M., Towers, H., et al. (2004) Genetic and environmental influences on marital relationships. Journal of Family Psychology, 18, 107–119; **019: Pearson Education, Inc.:** SALKIND, NEIL, J., EXPLORING RESEARCH, 8th Ed., (c) 2012. Reprinted and Electronically reproduced by permission of Pearson Education Inc., Upper Saddle River, New Jersey; **020: Bantam Books:** David Snowdon, Aging with Grace: What the Nun Study Teaches Us about Leading Longer, Healthier, and More Meaningful Lives (Bantam Books, 2001), 24.

Chapter 2 Page. 023: Springer: Vern L. Bengtson, Richard Settersten, Jr., Handbook of Theories of Aging, Third Edition (Springer, 2016); **023: Springer:** Vern L. Bengtson, Richard Settersten, Jr., Handbook of Theories of Aging, Third Edition (Springer, 2016); **023: Springer:** Kennedy, B. K. (2016). Advances in biological theories of aging. In V. L. Bengtson & R. A. Settersten (Eds.), Handbook of Theories of Aging, 3rd ed. (107–111). New York: Springer; **027: National Center for Health Statistics:** Fryar, C. D., Gu, Q., Ogden, C. L., et al. (2016). Anthropometric reference data for children and adults: United States, 2011–2014. National Center for Health Statistics. Retrieved on September 22, 2017, from https://www.cdc.gov/nchs/data/series/sr_03/sr03_039.pdf; **028: U.S. Centers for Disease Control and Prevention:** U.S. Centers for Disease Control and Prevention (2016). Defining adult overweight and obesity. Retrieved October 20, 2016 from https://www.cdc.gov/obesity/adult/defining.html; **029: U.S. Centers for Disease Control and Prevention:** Ogden, C. L., Carroll, M. D., Fryar, C. D., et al. (2015). Prevalence of obesity among adults in 2011–2014. Retrieved on September 22, 2017 from https://www.cdc.gov/nchs/

products/databriefs/db219.htm; **030: American Society of Plastic Surgeons:** American Society of Plastic Surgeons (2016). Plastic surgery statistics report – 2015. Retrieved October 20, 2016 from https://d2wirczt3b6wjm.cloudfront.net/News/Statistics/2015/plastic-surgery-statistics-full-report-2015.pdf; **032: National Eye Institute:** National Eye Institute (2015). Facts about age-related macular degeneration. Retrieved October 21, 2016 from https://nei.nih.gov/health/maculardegen/armd_facts; **033: American Medical Association:** Hoffman, H. J., Dobie, R. A., Losonsky, K. G., et al. (2017). Declining prevalence of hearing loss in U.S. adults aged 20 to 69 years. Journal of the American Medical Association Otolaryngology – Head Neck Surgery, 2017; 143(3): 274–285; **034: U.S. Department of Labor:** US Department of Labor, 2012. Permissible noise exposure levels. (Table G-18); **037: U.S. Centers for Disease Control and Prevention:** Data from U.S. Centers for Disease Control and Prevention, 2016; **044: American Medical Association:** Woloshin, S., & Schwartz, L. M. (2016). U.S. Food and Drug Administration approval of filbanserin: Even the score does not add up. Journal of the American Medical Association – Internal Medicine, 176, 439–442; **044: American Medical Association:** Jaspers, L., Feys, F., & Bramer, W. M. (2016). Efficacy and safety of flibanserin for the treatment of hypoactive sexual desire disorder in women: A systematic review and meta-analysis. Journal of the American Medical Association – Internal Medicine, 176, 453–462; **047: U.S. Department of Agriculture:** USDA Economic Research Service.

Chapter 3 051: Institute for Health Metrics and Evaluation: Ritchie & Roser (2018). Our world in data: Causes of death. Retrieved on July 23, 2018 from https://ourworldindata.org/causes-of-death; **052: U.S. Centers for Disease Control and Prevention:** U.S. Centers for Disease Control and Prevention (2016) Health, United States: 2015, with special features on racial and ethnic disparities. Retrieved December 1, 2017, from http://www.cdc.gov/nchs/data/hus/hus15.pdf; **052: National Center for Health Statistics:** Data from U.S. Centers for Disease Control and Prevention (2017). 10 leading causes of death by age group, United States – 2016. Retrieved on July 1, 2018 from https://www.cdc.gov/injury/images/lc-charts/leading_causes_of_death_age_group_2016_1056w814h.gif; **053: Cornell University:** Erickson, W., Lee, C., & von Schrader, S. (2016). 2015 Disability Status Report: United States. Ithaca, NY: Cornell University Yang Tan Institute on Employment and Disability (YTI). http://www.disabilitystatistics.org/StatusReports/2015-PDF/2015-StatusReport_US.pdf; **055: U.S. Centers for Disease Control and Prevention:** U.S. Centers for Disease Control and Prevention (2012f); **056: Wiley-Blackwell:** Siegel, R. L., Miller, K. D., & Jenal, A. (2016). Cancer statistics: 2016. CA: A Cancer Journal for Clinicians, 66, 7–30; **057: U.S. Centers for Disease Control and Prevention:** U.S. Centers for Disease Control and Prevention (2016); **057: U.S. Center for Disease Control and Prevention:** U.S. Center for Disease Control and Prevention (2015); **059: Alzheimer's Association:** Alzheimer's Association (2017); **060: National Institute of Mental Health:** National Institute of Mental Health (2017). Anxiety disorders: Treatment. Retrieved on October 6, 2017 from https://www.nimh.nih.gov/health/topics/anxiety-disorders/index.shtml; **061: National Institute of Mental Health:** National Institute of Mental Health (2016). Depression: Treatment and therapies. Retrieved on October 6, 2017 from https://www.nimh.nih.gov/health/topics/depression/index.shtml#part_145399; **062: American Psychiatric Publishing:** American Psychiatric Association (2013). Diagnostic and statistical manual of mental disorders, 5th ed. Washington, DC: APA; **062: U.S. Centers for Disease Control and Prevention:** U.S. Centers for Disease Control and Prevention (2018). Vital statistics rapid release: Provisional drug overdose death counts. Retrieved July 1, 2018 from https://www.cdc.gov/nchs/nvss/vsrr/drug-overdose-data.htm; **063: National Center of Addiction and Substance Abuse:** National Center of Addiction and Substance Abuse (2016); **067: U.S. Centers for Disease Control and Prevention:** U.S. Centers for Disease Control and Prevention (2016) Health, United States: 2015, with special features on racial and ethnic disparities. Retrieved December 1, 2017, from http://www.cdc.gov/nchs/data/hus/hus15.pdf; **068: American Medical Association:** Chetty, R., Stepner, M., Abraham, S., et al. (2016) The association between income and life expectancy in the United States, 2001–2014. Journal of the American Medical Association, 315, 1750–1766; **068: U.S. Centers for Disease Control and Prevention:** U.S. Centers for Disease Control and Prevention (2012b). Health United States 2012: With special feature on socioeconomic status and health. Retrieved on June 1, 2018 from https://www.cdc.gov/nchs/data/hus/hus12.pdf; **069: U.S. Centers for Disease Control and Prevention:** U.S. Centers for Disease Control and Prevention (2012b). Health United States 2012: With special feature on socioeconomic status and health. Retrieved on June 1, 2018 from https://www.cdc.gov/nchs/data/hus/hus12.pdf; **071: SAGE Publishing:** Kugelmass, H. (2016). "Sorry, I'm not accepting new patients": An audit study of access to mental health care. Journal of Health and Social Behavior, 57, 168–183.

Chapter 4 078: Elsevier Inc: Getzmann, S., Golob, E. J., & Wascher, E. (2016). Neurobioogy of Aging, 41, 138–149; **080: American Psychological Association:** Park, D. C., Lautenschlager, G., Hedden, T., et al. (2002). Models of visuospatial and verbal memory across the adult life span, Psychology and Aging, 17, 299–320; **082: American Psychological Association:** Rönnlund, M., Nyberg, L., Bäckman, L., et al. (2005). Stability, growth, and decline in adult life span development of declarative memory: Cross-sectional and longitudinal data from a population-based study. Psychology and Aging, 20, 3–18; **083: Sage Publications, Inc:** Maylor, E. A. (1990). Age and prospective memory. Quarterly Journal of Experimental Psychology, 42A, 471–493; **085: American Psychological Association:** Hess, T. M. (2005). Memory and aging in context. Psychological Bulletin, 131, 383–406; **086: Sage Publications, Inc:** Mazerolle, M., Régner, I., Morisset, P., et al. (2012). Stereotype threat strengthens automatic recall and undermines controlled processes in older adults. Psychological Science, 23, 723–727; **086: The Williams & Wilkins Company:** Wechsler, D. (1939). The measurement of adult intelligence. Baltimore, MD: Williams & Wilkins; **087: American Psychological Association:** Data from Schaie (1983), The Course of Adult Intellectual Development, American Psychologist. Vol. 49. No. 4. 304–313; **088: Academic Press:** Schaie, K. W. (1996). Intellectual development in adulthood. In J. E. Birren & K. W. Schaie (Eds.), Handbook of the psychology of aging (4th ed., 265–286). San Diego, CA: Academic Press; **088: Springer:** Berg, C. A., & Sternberg, R. J. (2003). Multiple perspectives on the development of adult intelligence. In J. Demick & C. Andreoletti (Eds.), Handbook of adult development (103–119). New York: Kluwer; **089: Sage Publications, Inc:** Salthouse, T. A. (2004). What and when of cognitive aging. Current Directions in Psychological Science, 13, 140–144; **092: Oxford University Press:** Blanchard-Fields, F., Mienaltowski, A., & Seay, R. B. (2007). Age differences in everyday problem-solving effectiveness: Older adults select more effective strategies for interpersonal problems. Journals of Gerontology: Psychological and Social Sciences, 62, 61–64; **092: Association for Psychological Science:** Blanchard-Fields, F. (2007). Everyday problem solving and emotion: An adult developmental perspective. Current Directions in Psychological Science, 16, 26–31; **092: American Psychological Association:** Fung, H. H., & Carstensen, L. L. (2003). Sending memorable messages to the old: Age differences in preferences and memory for advertisements. Journal of Personality and Social Psychology, 85, 163–178; **093: American Psychological Association:** Charles, S. T., Mather, M., & Carstensen, L. L. (2003). Aging and emotional memory: The forgettable nature of negative images for older adults. Journal of Experimental Psychology: General, 132, 310–324; **093: Association for Psychological Science:** Carstensen, L. L., & Mikels, J. A. (2005). At the intersection of emotion and cognition: Aging and the positivity effect. Current Directions in Psychological Science, 14, 117–121; **095: American Association for the Advancement of Science:** McClearn, G. E., Johansson, B., Berg, S., et al. (1997). Substantial genetic influence on cognitive abilities in twins 80 or more years old. Science, 276, 1560–1563.

Chapter 5   108: Pew Research Center: Fry, R. (2016). For the first time in modern era, living with parents edges out other living arrangements for 18 to 34 year olds. Pew Research Center. Retrieved May 25, 2017, from http://www.pewsocialtrends.org/2016/05/24/2-living-with-mom-andor-dad-more-common-for-sons-than-daughters/st_2016-05-24_young-adults-living-06/; **109: Pew Research Center:** Fry, R. (2016). For the first time in modern era, living with parents edges out other living arrangements for 18 to 34 year olds. Pew Research Center. Retrieved May 25, 2017, from http://www.pewsocialtrends.org/2016/05/24/2-living-with-mom-andor-dad-more-common-for-sons-than-daughters/st_2016-05-24_young-adults-living-06/; **110: Pew Research Center:** Fry, R. (2014). New census data show more Americans are tying the knot, but mostly it is the college-educated. Pew Research Center. Retrieved on May 30, 2017 from http://www.pewresearch.org/fact-tank/2014/02/06/new-census-data-show-more-americans-are-tying-the-knot-but-mostly-its-the-college-educated/; **110: Center for Disease Control and Prevention:** Copen, C. E., Daniels, K., & Mosher, W. D. (2013). First premarital cohabitation in the United States 2006–2010 National Survey of Family Growth. National Health Statistics Report No. 64. Retrieved on May 30, 2017; **110: Center for Disease Control and Prevention:** Copen, C. E., Daniels, K., & Mosher, W. D. (2013). First premarital cohabitation in the United States 2006–2010 National Survey of Family Growth. National Health Statistics Report No. 64. Retrieved on May 30, 2017. https://pdfs.semanticscholar.org/8316/28e0207591f277d6798f532f394b594bff37.pdf?_ga=2.148754039.1566108503.1543888747-436323648.1543888747; **111: Center for Disease Control and Prevention:** Daugherty, J., & Copen, C. (2016). National Health Statistics Report: Trends in attitudes about marriage, childbearing, and sexual behavior: United States, 2002, 2006–2010, and 2011–2014. Retrieved on June 15, 2016, from https://www.cdc.gov/nchs/data/nhsr/nhsr092.pdf; **112: Organisation for Economic Co-operation and Development:** Organisation for Economic Cooperation and Development (2016). Mean age of women at first birth, 1970, 1995, and 2014. Retrieved on June 13, 2017 from https://www.oecd.org/els/soc/SF_2_3_Age_mothers_childbirth.pdf; **113: Elsevier:** Nitsche, N. & Grunow, D. (2015). Housework over the course of a relationship: Gender ideology, resources, and the division of housework from a growth curve perspective. Advances in Life Course Research, 28, 80–94; **113: U.S. Bureau of Labor Statistics:** U.S. Bureau of Labor Statistics (2016); **117: Pew Research Center:** Jens Manuel Krogstad, "5 facts about American grandparents" Pew Research Center September 13, 2015. http://www.pewresearch.org/fact-tank/2015/09/13/5-facts-about-american-grandparents/; **119: Oxford University Press:** Cheng, Sheung-Tak, et al. "Voices of Alzheimer Caregivers on Positive Aspects of Caregiving." The Gerontologist, vol. 56, no. 3, 2015, 451–460, doi:10.1093/geront/gnu118; **120: Pew Research Center:** Stepler, R. (2016). Smaller share of women ages 65 and older are living alone. Retrieved on February 25, 2017 from http://www.pewresearch.org/wp-content/uploads/sites/3/2016/02/ST_2016-02-18_older-adult-FINAL.pdf; **122: Family Caregiver Alliance:** Caregiver Statistics: Demographics, Family Caregiver Alliance. https://www.caregiver.org/caregiver-statistics-demographics; **123: Pew Research Center:** Livingston, G. (2015). Childlessness falls, family size grows among highly educated women. Pew Research Center. Retrieved on July 5, 2017 from http://www.pewsocialtrends.org/2015/05/07/childlessness-falls-family-size-grows-among-highly-educated-women/.

Chapter 6   128: Sage: Rodney M. Cate, Lauren A. Levin, Lucinda S. Richmond, "Premarital relationship stability: A review of recent research." Journal of Social and Personal Relationships, 19(2), 261–284. 2002. https://journals.sagepub.com/doi/abs/10.1177/0265407502192005; **129: Taylor and Francis:** Toni Antonucci, Hiroko Akiyama & Keiko Takahashi, "Attachment and close relationships across the life span," Attachment & Human Development, pages 353–370, volume 6, 2004. https://www.tandfonline.com/doi/abs/10.1080/1461673042000303136; **130: Urban Institute:** Gregory Acs, Amrita Maitreyi, Alana L. Conner, Hazel Rose Markus, Nisha G. Patel, Sarah Lyons-Padilla, and Jennifer L. Eberhardt, Measuring Mobility from Poverty, April 2018; **131: American Psychological Association (United States):** A Word about Social Relationships Sander, J., Schupp, J., & Richter, D. (2017). Getting together: Social contact frequency across the life span. Developmental Psychology, 53, 1571–1588; **132: Frontiers:** Fisher, H. E., Xu, X., Aron, A., et al. (2016) Intense, passionate, romantic love: A natural addiction? How the fields that investigate romance and substance abuse can inform each other. Frontiers in Psychology, 7, 687; **133: Elsevier:** Fales, M. R., Frederick, D. A., Garcia, J. R., et al. (2016). Mating markets and bargaining hands: Mate preferences for attractiveness and resources in two national U.S. studies. Personality and Individual Differences, 88, 78–87; **134: Pew Research Center:** Aaron Smith, Monica Anderson (2016). Five facts about online dating. Pew Research Center. Retrieved on November 17, 2017 from http://www.pewresearch.org/fact-tank/2016/02/29/5-facts-about-online-dating/; **136: American Psychological Association:** Chopik, W. J. (2017). Longitudinal Changes in Attachment Orientation over a 59-year Period. Journal of Personality and Social Psychology.

doi:10.31234/osf.io/3xhe4; **136: American Psychological Association:** Chopik, W. J. (2017). Longitudinal Changes in Attachment Orientation over a 59-year Period. Journal of Personality and Social Psychology. doi:10.31234/osf.io/3xhe4; **138: Sage:** K. Daniel O'Leary, Bianca P. Acevedo, Arthur Aron, Leonie Huddy, and Debra Mashek, "Is Long-Term Love More Than A Rare Phenomenon? If So, What Are Its Correlates?," Social Psychological and Personality Science, pages 240–249, Sage Publications 2012; **139: Pew Research Center:** Renee Stepler, "Number of U.S. adults cohabiting with a partner continues to rise, especially among those 50 and older: Pew Research Center April 6, 2017 http://www.pewresearch.org/fact-tank/2017/04/06/number-of-u-s-adults-cohabiting-with-a-partner-continues-to-rise-especially-among-those-50-and-older/; **139: Wiley:** Lee, K. S., & Ono, H. (2012). Marriage, cohabitation and happiness: A cross-national analysis of 27 countries. Journal of Marriage and Family, 74, 953–972; **141: Gallup:** Gates, G. J. (2016). In U.S., more adults identifying as LGBT: Gallup Poll. Retrieved on November 18, 2017 from http://news.gallup.com/poll/201731/lgbt-identification-rises.aspx; **143: Lawrence Erlbaum Associates, Incorporated:** W. W. Hartup, Z. Rubin, Relationships and Development (Lawrence Erlbaum Associates, Incorporated, 1986), 100; **145: Taylor & Francis:** Abetz, J., & Wang, T. R. (2017). "Were they ever really happy the way that I remember?": Exploring sources of uncertainty for adult children of divorce. Journal of Divorce and Remarriage, 58, 194–211; **145: Taylor & Francis:** Abetz, J., & Wang, T. R. (2017). "Were they ever really happy the way that I remember?": Exploring sources of uncertainty for adult children of divorce. Journal of Divorce and Remarriage, 58, 194–211; **145: Taylor & Francis:** Abetz, J., & Wang, T. R. (2017). "Were they ever really happy the way that I remember?": Exploring sources of uncertainty for adult children of divorce. Journal of Divorce and Remarriage, 58, 194–211; **145: Taylor & Francis:** Abetz, J., & Wang, T. R. (2017). "Were they ever really happy the way that I remember?": Exploring sources of uncertainty for adult children of divorce. Journal of Divorce and Remarriage, 58, 194–211; **146: MIT Press:** DeKay, W. T., & Shackelford, T. K. (2000). Toward an evolutionary approach to social cognition. Evolution and Cognition, 6, 185–195; **147: American Psychological Association (United States):** Shalhevet Attar-Schwartz, Jo-Pei Tan, Ann Buchanan, et al., "Grandparenting and Adolescent Adjustment in Two-Parent Biological, Lone-Parent, and Step-Families," Journal of Family Psychology 2009, 23(1), 67–75; **149: SAGE:** Milevsky, A. (2005). Compensatory patterns of sibling support in emerging adulthood: Variations in loneliness, self-esteem, depression, and life satisfaction. Journal of Social and Personal Relationships, 22, 743–755; **151: Pew Research Center:** Pew Research Center (2017). Social media fact sheet, Pew Research Center. Retrieved on October 27, 2017 from http://www.pewinternet.org/fact-sheet/social-media/; **151: Pew Research Center:** Greenwood, S., Perrin, A., & Duggan. M. (2017). Social media update 2016. Retrieved on October 27, 2017 from http://www.pewinternet.org/2016/11/11/social-media-update-2016/; **152: Pew Research Center:** Jacob Poushter, "Smartphone Ownership and Internet Usage Continues to Climb in Emerging Economies," Pew Research Center, FEBRUARY 22, 2016. http://www.pewresearch.org/wp-content/uploads/sites/2/2016/02/pew_research_center_global_technology_report_final_february_22__2016.pdf.

Chapter 7 158: Psychological Assessment Resources: Holland, J. L. (1992) Making vocational choice: A theory of personalities and work environments, 2/e. Copyright © 1992 by Psychological Assessment Resources. Reprinted by permission; **159: United States Department of Labor:** U.S. Bureau of Labor Statistics (2017a). Women in the labor force: A data book. Retrieved on December 5, 2017 from https://www.bls.gov/opub/reports/womens-databook/2016/home.htm; **161: United States Department of Labor:** U.S. Bureau of Labor Statistics (2017c). Labor force statistics from the Current Population Survey. Retrieved on Dec. 13, 2017 from https://www.bls.gov/cps/cpsaat11.htm; **163: Central Intelligence Agency:** CIA World Factbook (2018). Retrieved on January 4, 2019 from https://www.cia.gov/library/publications/the-world-factbook/geos/us.html; **166: Pew Research Center:** DeSilver, D. (2016). Millions of young people in U.S. and EU are neither working or learning. Retrieved on January 11, 2018 from http://www.pewresearch.org/fact-tank/2016/01/28/us-eu-neet-population/; **168: American Economic Association:** Mazzocco, M., Ruiz, C., & Yamaguchi, S. (2014). Labor supply and household dynamics. American Economic Review: Papers and Proceedings, 104, 354–359; **169: United States Department of Labor:** U.S. Bureau of Labor Statistics (2017). Employment status of the population by sex, marital status, and presence and age of own children under 18. Retrieved on January 24, 2018 from https://www.bls.gov/news.release/famee.t05.htm; **170: Pew Research Center:** Livingston, G. (2016). Among 41 nations, U.S. is the outlier when it comes to paid parental leave. Retrieved on January 15th, 2018 from http://www.pewresearch.org/fact-tank/2016/09/26/u-s-lacks-mandated-paid-parental-leave/; **172: United States Department of Labor:** U.S. Bureau of Labor Statistics (2017). Employment status of the population by sex, marital status, and presence and age of own children under 18. Retrieved on January 24, 2018 from https://www.bls.gov/news.release/famee.t05.htm; **174: Federal Interagency Forum on Aging-Related Statistics:** Federal Interagency Forum on Aging-Related Statistics (2017). Older Americans: Key indicators of well-being. Retrieved on February 5, 2018 from https://agingstats.gov/docs/LatestReport/Older-Americans-2016-Key-Indicators-of-WellBeing.pdf; **175: Federal Interagency Forum on Aging-Related Statistics:** Federal Interagency Forum on Aging-Related Statistics (2017). Older Americans: Key indicators of well-being. Retrieved on February 5, 2018 from https://agingstats.gov/docs/LatestReport/Older-Americans-2016-Key-Indicators-of-WellBeing.pdf.

Chapter 8 182: Elsevier: Costa, P. T., Jr., & McCrae, R. R. (1997). Longitudinal stability of adult personality. In R. Hogan, J. Johnson, & S. Briggs (Eds.), Handbook of personality psychology (269–290). San Diego, CA: Academic Press; **184: American Psychological Association:** Roberts B. W., & DelVecchio, W. F. (2000). The rank-order consistency of personality traits from childhood to old age: A quantitative review of longitudinal studies. Psychological Bulletin, 126, 3–25; **185: American Psychological Association:** McCrae, R. R., Terracciano, A., & 78 members of the Personality Profiles of Cultures Project. (2005). Universal features of personality traits from the observer's perspective: Data from 50 cultures. Journal of Personality and Social Psychology, 88, 547–561; **186: American Psychological Association:** Roberts, B. W., Walton, K. E., & Viechtbauer, W. (2006). Patterns of mean-level change in personality traits across the life course: A meta-analysis of longitudinal studies. Psychological Bulletin, 132, 1–25; **187: American Psychological Association:** Walton, G. M., & Cohen, G. L. (2007). A question of belonging: Race, fit, and achievement. Journal of Personality and Social Psychology, 92, 82–96; **189: American Psychological Association:** Roberts, B. W., Walton, K. E., & Bogg, T. (2005). Conscientiousness and health across the life course. Review of General Psychology, 9, 156–168; **190: American Psychological Association:** Roberts, B. W., Walton, K. E., & Bogg, T. (2005). Conscientiousness and health across the life course. Review of General Psychology, 9, 156–168; **191: American Psychological Association:** Riemann, R., Angleitner, A., & Strelau, J. (1997). Genetic and environmental influences on personality: A study of twins reared together using the self- and peer-report NEO-FFI scales. Journal of Personality, 65, 449–475; **191: American Psychological Association:** Roberts, B. W., Walton, K. E., & Viechtbauer, W. (2006). Patterns of mean-level change in personality traits across the life course: A meta-analysis of longitudinal studies. Psychological Bulletin, 132, 1–25; **195: Pearson Education:** Adapted from Erikson (1950, 1959, 1982); **195: W. W. Norton & Company, Inc.:** Erikson, E. H. (1950). Childhood and society. New York: Norton; **195: W. W. Norton & Company, Inc.:** Erikson, E. H. (1959). Identity and the life cycle. New York: Norton. (Reissued 1980); **195: W. W. Norton & Company, Inc.:** Erikson, E. H. (1982). The life cycle completed. New York: Norton; **196: American Psychological Association:** Whitbourne, S. K., Zuschlag, M. K., Elliot, L. B., et al. (1992). Psychosocial development in adulthood: A 22-year sequential study. Journal of Personality and Social Psychology, 63, 260–271; **197: American Psychological Association:** McAdams, D. P., & de St. Aubin, E. (1992). A theory of generativity and its assessment through self-report, behavioral acts, and narrative themes in autobiography. Journal of Personality and Social Psychology, 62, 1003–1015; **197: American Psychological Association:** McAdams, D. P., Hart, H. M., & Maruna, S. (1998). The anatomy of generativity. In D. P. McAdams & E. de St. Aubin (Eds.), Generativity and adult development: How and why we care for the next generation (7–43). Washington, DC: American Psychological Association; **198: Elsevier:** Loevinger, J. (1997). Stages of personality development. In R. Hogan, J. Johnson, & S. Briggs (Eds.), Handbook of personality psychology (199–208). San Diego, CA: Academic Press; **200: American Psychiatric Association:** American Psychiatric Association. (2000). Diagnostic and statistical manual of mental disorders (4th ed.). Washington, DC: American Psychiatric Association; **201: John Wiley & Sons, Inc.:** Maslow, A. H. (1968/1998). Toward a psychology of being (3rd ed.). New York: Wiley; **202: American Psychological Association:** Seligman, M. E. P., & Csikszentmihalyi, M. (2000). Positive psychology: An introduction. American Psychologist, 55, 5–14; **202: U.S. Army:** Slogan for U.S. Army; **203: Oxford University Press:** Aristotle. (1946). The politics of Aristotle (E. Barker, Trans.). London, England: Oxford University Press. (Original work written around 350 BCE.).

Chapter 9 **206: Pew Research Center:** Pew Research Center, 2018; **207: Harper Collins:** Fowler (1981) Stages of Faith, pages 171–172. HarperCollins Publishers, 1981; **209: Pew Research Center:** Pew Research Center, 2014; **210: Springer**

Nature Switzerland AG: Wink & Dillon (2002) Spiritual development across the adult life course: Findings from a longitudinal study Journal of Adult Development, 9, © 2002. Reprinted with kind permission from Springer Science+Business Media; **210: Springer Nature Switzerland AG:** Wink & Dillon (2002) Spiritual development across the adult life course: Findings from a longitudinal study Journal of Adult Development, 9, © 2002. Reprinted with kind permission from Springer Science+Business Media; **211: Journal of Health Psychology:** Data from Tartaro, J., Leucken, L. J. & Gunn, H. E. (2005) Exploring heart and soul: Effects of religiousity/spirituality and gender on blood pressure and cortisol stress response. Journal of Health Psychology, 10, pg 760 fig. 2; **213: Harper Collins:** Kohlberg, L. (1984). Essays on moral development: Vol. 2. The psychology of moral development. San Francisco, CA: Harper & Row; **216: Sussex Publishers, LLC:** Fowler, J. (1983). Stages of faith: PT conversation with James Fowler. Psychology Today, 17, 55–62; **216: Harper Collins:** Fowler (1981) Stages of Faith, pages 171–172. Harper Collins Publishers, 1981; **216: Harvard University Press:** R. Kegan (1982) The Evolving Self. Cambridge, MA: Harvard University Press; **217: Harper Collins:** Fowler (1981) Stages of Faith, pages 171–172. Harper Collins Publishers, 1981; **220: Knopf Doubleday Publishing Group:** Teresa of Ávila, St. (1562/1960). Interior castle. Garden City, NJ: Image Books; **221: Harvard University Press:** R. Kegan (1980) There the dance is: Religious dimensions of development theory. In J. Fowler & A. Vergote. Toward Moral & Religious Maturity (pp 403–440) 1980 Silver Burdette. (c) 1980 Reprinted by permission of the author; **223: Harper Collins:** Sam Keen, The Passionate Life. (New York: HarperCollins Publishers) Copyright (c) 1983. Reprinted by permission of the author; **223: Harper Collins:** Sam Keen, The Passionate Life. (New York: HarperCollins Publishers) Copyright (c) 1983. Reprinted by permission of the author.

Chapter 10 **229: Association for Psychological Science:** Data from Almeida, D. M. (2005). Resilience and vulnerability to daily stressors assessed via diary methods. Current Directions in Psychological Sciences, 14, 64–68; **230: Johns Hopkins Bloomberg School of Public Health:** Lillberg, K., Verkasalo, P. K., Kaprio, J., et al. (2003). Stressful life events and risk of breast cancer in 10,808 women: A cohort study. American Journal of Epidemiology, 157, 415–423; **232: Taylor & Francis:** Kessler, R. C., Aguilar-Gaxiola, S., Alonso, J., et al. (2017) Trauma and OTSD in the WHO World Mental Health Surveys, European Journal of Psychotraumatology, 8, 1353–1383; **233: Massachusetts Medical Society:** Yehuda, R., (2002). Current concepts: Post-traumatic stress disorder. New England Journal of Medicine, 346, 108–114; **234: University of Chicago Press:** Almeida, D. M., & Horn, M. C. (2004). Is daily life more stressful during middle adulthood? In O. G. Brim, C. D. Ryff, & R. C. Kessler (Eds.), How healthy are we? A national study of well-being at midlife (425–451). Chicago: University of Chicago Press; **234: Developmental psychology:** Scott, S. B., Poulin, M. J., & Silver, R. C. (2013). A lifespam perspective on terrorism: Age differences in trajectories of response to 9/11. Developmental Psychology, 49, 986–998; **237: Springer Nature:** Carver, C. S. (1997). You want to measure coping by your protocol's too long: Consider the brief COPE. International Journal of Behavioral Medicine, 4, 92–100; **240: Sage Publications:** Bonanno, G. A. (2005). Resilience in the face of potential trauma. Current Directions in Psychological Sciences, 14, 135–138; **242: American Psychological Association:** Elliot, A. J., Turiano, N. A., Infurna, F. J., et al. (2018). Lifetime trauma, perceived control, and al-cause mortality: Results from the Midlife in the United States Study. Health Psychology, 262–270; **243: Frontiers in Robotics and AI:** Lucas, G. M., Rizzo, A., Gratch, J., et al., (2017). Reporting mental health symptoms: Breaking down barriers to care with virtual human interviewers. Frontiers in Robotics and AI, 4, 51.

Chapter 11 247: Elsevier: Neugarten, B. L. (1970). Dynamics of transition of middle age to old age. Journal of Geriatric Psychiatry, 4, 71–87; **251: Taylor and Francis:** Corr, C. A. (1993). Coping with dying: Lessons we should and should not learn from the work of Elisabeth Kubler-Ross. Death Studies, 17, 69–83; **251: Wolters Kluwer:** Alsop, S. (1973). Stay ofexecution. New York: Lippincott; **253: American medical association:** Data from Teno, J. M., Clarridge, B. R., Casey, V., et al. (2004). Family perspectives on end-of-life care at the last place of care. Journal of the American Medical Association, 291, 88–93. American Medical Association, 2004; **255: Death with Dignity:** Oregon Health Authority (2018). Oregon Death With Dignity Act: 2017 data summary, Retrieved on March 18, 2018 from http://www.oregon .gov/oha/PH/PROVIDERPARTNERRESOURCES/ EVALUATIONRESEARCH/DEATHWITHDIGNITYACT/ Documents/year20.pdf; **256: Elsevier:** Wilkinson, A. M. & Lynn, J. (2001). The end of life. In R. H. Binstock & L. K. George (Eds.), Handbook of aging and the social sciences (441–461). San Diego, CA: Academic Press; **256: Elsevier:** Victor W. Marshall and Judith A. Levy (1990) Aging and dying. In Handbook of Aging and the Social Sciences, 3rd Edition (invited but reviewed). Robert Binstock and Linda George (Eds.). San Francisco: Academic Press, 245–260; **258: American Psychological Association:** Feifel, H. (1990). Psychology and death: Meaningful rediscovery. American Psychologist, 45, 537–543; **259: American Psychological Association:** Bonanno, G. A., Wortman, C. B., Lehman, D. R., et al. (2002). Resilience to loss and chronic grief: A prospective study from pre-loss to 18 months post-loss. Journal of Personality and Social Psychology, 83, 1150–1164; **260: Parabola Magazine:** Steindl-Rast, 1977, 22 Steindl-Rast, B. D. (1977). Learning to die. Parabola, 2, 22–31.

Chapter 12 270: Plenum Publishing Corporation: Wethington, E. (2000). Expecting stress: Americans and the "midlife crisis." Motivation and Emotion, 24, 85–103; **Elsevier:** Blanchflower, D. G., & Oswald, A. J. (2008). Is well-being U-shaped over the life cycle?. Social science & medicine, 66(8), 1733–1749; **270: SAGE Publications:** Lachman, M. E., Teshale, S., & Agrigoroaei, S. (2015). Midlife as a pivotal period in the life course: Balancing growth and decline at the crossroads of youth and old age. International journal of behavioral development, 39(1), 20–31; **271: American Psychological Association:** Shneidman, E. S. (1989). The Indian summer of life: A preliminary study of septuagenarians. American Psychologist, 44, 684–694. American Psychological Association; **272: SAGE Publications:** Cumming, E. (1975). Engagement with an old theory. International Journal of Aging and Human Development, 6, 187–191; **272: Oxford University Press:** Butler, R. N. (1993). The importance of basic research in gerontology. Age and Ageing, 22, S53–S55; **282: John Wiley & Sons, Inc:** Giele, J. Z. (1982). Women in adulthood: Unanswered questions. In J. Z. Giele (Ed.), Women in the middle years (1–36). New York: Wiley; **283: Elsevier:** McCrae & Costa, 1983, Joint factors in self-reports and ratings: Neuroticism, Extraversion, and Openness to Experience. Personality and Individual Differences, 4, 245–255; **284: ACSM:** American College of Sports Medicine, 2011. https://greatist .com/fitness/acsm-releases-new-exercise-guidelines; **285: Elsevier:** Ellwardt, L., Van Tilburg, T. G., Aartsen, M. J. (2015). The mix matters: Complex personal networks relate to higher cognitive functioning in old age. Social Science and Medicine, 125, 107–115.

Author Index

A

Aartsen, M. J., 285
Abdel-Khalek, A. M., 249
Abetz, J., 144, 145
Abou-Median, S., 236
Acevedo, B. P., 138
Ackerman, P. L.
Acree, M., 259
Adams, B., 241
Adams, S. H., 63
Afifi, T., 152
Agarwal, M., 39
Agrigoroaei, S., 270
Aguilar-Gaxiola, S., 232
Ahola, K., 166
Ai, A. L., 210
Ainsworth, M. D. S., 128
Aitken, R., 72
Ajrouch, K. J., 150
Akiyama, H., 129, 149
Albersheim, L. J., 129
Alberts, H. J., 252
Aldwin, C., 236
Alea, N., 182
Allaire, J. C., 89
Allery, A, 72
Allison, M., 72
Allman, J., 66
Allman, R. M., 99
Almeida, D. M., 229, 233
Almeida, O. P., 38, 229, 234
Alonso, J., 232
Alparone, F. R., 162
Alper, B. A., 247
Alsop, S., 251
Alterovitz, S. S.-R., 134
Alzheimer's Association, 58, 59
Amato, P. R., 139
American Academy of Ophthamology, 32
American Academy of Orthopaedic Surgeons, 36
American Academy of Sleep Medicine, 42

American Cancer Society, 39, 56, 57
American Hair Loss Association, 30
American Nutrition Association, 46
American Psychiatric Association, 60, 200, 231
American Psychological Association, 60, 118, 119, 232
American Society of Plastic Surgeons, 29–31
Amirkhanyan, A. A., 118
Amistoso, M. N. G., 249
Amlani, A. M., 34
An, Y., 38
Andel, R., 165, 166
Anderson, B., 151
Anderson, K. A., 250
Anderson, M., 98, 134, 223
Anderson, R., 134, 135
Anderson, R. M., 25
Andrews, A. M., 165
Anesensel, C. S., 121
Angel, J. L., 69, 70
Antoine, P., 250
Antonucci, T., 46, 146
Antonucci, T. C., 118, 123, 129, 130, 150, 196, 274, 275
Anxiety and Depression Society of America, 60
Apple, D. M., 25, 38
Ardelt, M., 248
Ardila, A.,96
Arevalo, J. M., 235
Arias, E., 62
Aristotle, 203
Armstrong, P. I., 160
Arnett, J. J., 107, 226, 266
Aron, A., 132, 138
Aronson, J., 86
Ash, I. K., 94
Ashby, J., 236
Astle, C. M., 25

Atchley, P., 100
Attar-Schwartz, S., 147
Atwal, J. K., 65
Au, A., 193
Ault-Brutus, A. A., 70
Auman, C., 85
Austad, S. N., 66
Avorn, J., 97
Ayala, J., 148
Azaola, M. C., 109

B

Babaran, C. A. C., 249
Babcock, R. L., 95
Bachman, L. D., 95
Bäckman, L., 80, 81, 82, 83, 94, 95
Baddeley, A. D., 80
Bahns, M., 46
Bailes, J., 59
Bailey, H., 81
Bakermans-Kranenburg, M. J., 234
Bakker, A. B., 166
Baldwin, C. L., 94
Balk, D. E., 251, 253
Ball, K. K., 100
Balsam, K. F., 142
Baltes, M. M., 272
Baltes, P. B., 10, 13, 82, 84, 94, 95, 101, 272, 284
Bandura, A., 158
Banerjee, S., 271
Banks, G. C., 164
Banyard, V., 242
Barelds, D. P. H., 193
Baretto, D., 141
Baril, G. L., 212
Barkan, T., 189
Barker, D. J., 73
Bartholomew, K., 135
Bates, J. S., 146
Batty, G. D., 89
Bauer, J. J., 199

Baum, A., 227
Baumeister, R. F., 131
Baumert, J., 166
Baun, M. M., 64
Bayard, K., 160
Bayer, A.-H., 121
Beard, J., 274
Beauchaine, T. P., 142
Becker, G., 112
Beckett, L. A, 96
Beers, M. H., 37, 38
Bell, A., 232
Belleville, S., 285
Belsky, J., 114
Bem, S. L., 106
Ben-David, B. M., 83
Bengtson, V. L., 23, 143
Bengtsson, T., 73
Benjamins, M. R., 208
Bennett, D. A., 96
Ben-Shlomo, Y., 73
Benson, R., 69, 70
Berdasco, M., 56
Berenbaum, S. A., 161
Berent, J. A., 250
Berg, C. A., 80, 88
Berg, S., 94, 95
Berglund, P., 60, 61, 63, 66, 69, 70
Berg-Weger, M., 250
Bering, J. M., 207
Berkman, L., 46, 118, 123, 274
Bertrand, R. M., 118
Best, D. L., 106
Betz, J., 34
Bialik, K., 170
Bielak, A. A. M., 94
Bierer, L. M., 232
Bigby, M., 45
Biggs, A., 172
Biggs, S., 146
Bindl, U. K., 158
Biorck, J., 210
Birditt, K. S., 130, 143, 145, 149
Birkeland, M. S., 242
Birkhill, W. R., 90
Birzniece, V., 40
Bissig, D., 84
Bjorklund, D. F., 148
Blackburn, E. H., 24
Blackwell, D. L., 53, 66

Blackwell, L., 186
Blair, C., 86, 88
Blanchard-Fields, F., 92
Blanchflower, D. G., 270
Blandon, A. Y., 150
Blazer, D. G., 274
Blehar, M., 128
Blieszner, R., 142
Bliwise, D. L., 42
Blix, I., 242
Blom, V., 166
Bluck, S., 182
Blumberg, S. L., 137
Blurton Jones, N. G., 148
Bohlmeijer, E. T., 272, 273
Boivin, J., 124
Bokenberger, K., 72
Boll, T., 148
Bonanno, G. A., 232, 240, 241, 242, 258, 259
Booth, A., 138
Booth-Butterfield, M., 146
Booth-LaForce, C., 136
Borella, E., 84
Börsch-Supan, A., 118, 123, 274
Bosman, J., 62
Bouchard, T. J., 94
Bourassa, K. J., 138
Bowen, K., 239
Bowie, J. V., 235
Bowlby, J., 128, 130, 143, 258
Bowling, N. A., 165
Boyce, C. J., 167
Brallier, S., 19
Bramer, W. M., 44
Brand, D., 95
Branscombe, N. R., 235
Bravata, D. M., 40
Brébion, G., 81
Brehmer, Y., 84
Brennan, A. A., 79
Breslau, J., 63
Brett, C. E., 185
Brim, O. G., Jr., 222
Briscoe, J. P., 158
Brogaard, T., 253
Broman, C. L., 2368
Bronfenbrenner, U., 10, 11, 20, 284
Brown, A., 140, 141

Brown, D. R., 210
Brown, G. G., 94
Brown, J. S., 285
Brown, L. M., 234
Brown, S. D., 158
Brown, S. L., 140
Brown, T. H., 67, 234
Bruderer, A. J., 79
Bruinsma, S., 251
Brumback-Peltz, C. R., 81
Bryer, D., 250
Brymer, M. J., 232
Buchanan, A., 147
Buehler, C., 169
Buman, M. P., 42
Bunce, J. P., 151
Bunting, L., 124
Burack, O. R., 84
Bureau of Labor Statistics, 112, 113
Buring, J., 39
Burke, A., 254
Burke, D. M., 82, 83
Burke, R. J., 229
Burkhauser, R. V., 173
Busch, H., 193
Buss, D. M., 133, 134, 193
Butler, R. N., 272
Byrd, M., 81

C

Cadinu, M., 162
Cahill, K. E., 176
Calder, N., 72
Calzo, J. P., 196
Campbell, J., 206
Campbell, L., 132, 135
Canário, C., 115
Cansino, S., 82
Caplan, L., 96
Caporeal, L. R., 130
Cappell, K. S., 81
Carbone, E., 84
Carlisle, M., 239
Carlson, J. F., 15
Carmalt, J. H., 133
Carmichael, C. L., 149
Carney, J. S., 210
Carroll, M. D., 27, 29
Carse, T., 172, 173

Carskadon, M. A., 41
Carstensen, L. L., 82, 92, 93, 130
Carver, C. S., 189, 237, 242
Casey, V., 253
Caspi, A., 139, 183, 188, 189, 192
Castel, A. D., 98
Castro, C. A., 241, 243
Cate, R. M., 128, 132
Catoni, C., 38
Cattell, R. B., 88, 183
Cawley, J., 133
Centers for Disease Control and Prevention, 27, 32, 35–37, 41, 46, 52, 55, 57, 66, 67, 69, 74, 111, 124
Cepeda, N. J., 83
Chae, D. H., 240
Chan, D. K.-S., 167
Chan, W., 184
Chang, E., 124
Chapman, B. P., 189
Charles, S. T., 92, 93, 231
Charness, N., 96
Chartrand, M., 286
Chau, V., 235
Checchi, K. D., 97
Chen, A.-G., 90
Chen, C., 275
Chen, E., 236
Chen, H. Y., 285
Chen, X., 107
Cheng, G. H.-L., 167
Cheng, S.-T., 119
Cheng, Y.-P., 145
Cherkas, L. F., 24
Cherry, K. E., 285
Cheung, F. M., 193
Cheung, S. F., 193
Chiang, J. J., 230
Chida, Y., 72, 210
Chodzko-Zajko, W. J., 284
Choi, E., 239
Chopik, W. J., 136
Choun, S., 236
Chow, H. P. H., 249
Chowdhury, S., 72
Christakis, N. A., 150
Chu, C.-H., 90
Chu, K. C., 69
Cicchetti, D., 107

Cicirelli, V. G., 143
Cissell, G. M., 100
Clark, A. E., 275
Clark, R., 235
Clark, R. L., 173
Clarke, T. C., 53, 66
Clarkson-Smith, L., 96
Clarridge, B. R., 253
Clausell, E., 141
Clements, M. L., 137
Clevers, H., 25
Coall, D. A., 148
Coelho, J. S., 25
Coffield, A. B., 63
Cohen, C. I., 234
Cohen, G. L., 186, 187
Cohen, M., 286
Cohen, S., 72
Colby, A., 213
Colcombe, S., 90, 96
Colcombe, S. J., 85
Cole, S. W., 235
Coleman, M., 125
Collado-Rodriguez, A., 252
Collette, F., 80
Collins, J. A., 124
Collins, W. A., 135, 136
Colman, R. J., 25
Compton, D. M., 95
Connerty, T. J., 236
Connidis, I. A., 148
Consoli, S. M., 72
Copen, C. E., 110
Coreil, J., 69
Coren, S., 64
Cornum, R., 243
Cornwell, B., 150, 152
Corr, C. A., 251
Cosmides, L., 193
Costa, P. T., Jr., 182, 283
Costello, C. B., 160
Courtenay, B. C., 199
Couzin, J., 65
Cowan, C. P., 114
Cowan, P. A., 114
Craig, J., 107
Craik, F. I. M., 81, 83
Crimmins, E. M., 73
Cronin, A. M., 36
Crowell, M. F., 25

Crush, E., 96
Csikszentmihalyi, M., 202
Cudmore, V., 33
Cullum, S., 95
Cumming, E., 104, 271, 272
Curtayne, E. S., 82
Cuthbertson, A., 64
Cuttler, C., 151

D
Daffner, K., 84
Dalal, P. K., 39
Dalby, P., 210
Daly, M., 167
Daneshvar, D. H., 59
D'Angelo, J. D., 134
Danieli, Y., 232
Daniels, K., 110
Danner, D. D., 189
Das, A., 44
de Frias, C. M., 83
De Fruyt, F., 184
De Raad, B., 193
De Raedt, R., 248
De Rango, F., 25
de Vaus, D., 139
de Waal, F., 131
Deary, I. J., 89, 90, 165
Deaux, K., 106
Deci, E. L., 202
DeFries, J. C., 8, 94
DeKay, W. T., 146
Dekel, S., 236
DeLamater, J., 42, 44, 45
Delaney, L., 167
Delaney, R., 116
DeLongis, A., 240
Demler, O., 60, 61, 69, 70
Depp, C. A., 72, 284
Der, G., 89
Derby, R. W., 148
DeSilver, D., 163, 166
Desrichard, O., 85
Desrosiers, M. F., 20
Diehl, M., 182
DiGrande, L., 241
Dill, J. S., 162
Dillon, M., 206, 209, 210
Ding, L., 56
Dixon, R. A., 81, 83, 101

Dobie, R. A., 33
Domaszewska, K., 40
Doty, P., 122
Dougall, A. L., 227
Douglass, C. B., 107
Douglass, R., 35
Dowell, D., 62
Dowling, D. W., 170
Dressel, J., 100
Duberstein, P. R., 149
Dubey, I., 286
Dubin, L., 210
Duggan, M., 151
Duggan. M., 151
Duncan, G. J., 73
Dunlosky, J., 81
Dweck, C. S., 186
Dykiert, D., 89
Dykstra, P. A., 274

E
Eagly, A. H., 106, 160
Earles, J. L., 82, 232
Eber, H. W., 183
Edelstein, R. S., 136
Edwards, M. K., 96
Žeželj, I. L., 153
Eftekhary, M., 36
Egloff, B., 187
Ehlers, A., 241
Ehrensaft, M., 188
Ehrlich, M. F., 81
Eichorn, D. H., 275
Ein-Dor, T., 236
Einolf, C. J., 197
Einstein, G. O., 83
Eismann, M., 173
El Haj, M., 250
Elder, G. H., Jr., 7, 106, 107, 269
Eliason, G., 249
Elliot, A. J., 241, 242
Elliot, L. B., 15, 16, 196
Ellis, M. J., 56
Ellis, R., 124
Ellwardt, L., 285
Elovainio, M., 189
Emanuel, E. J., 255
Emanuel, L. L., 255
Emery, C. F., 94
Emery, R. E., 139

Engdahl, B., 232
Epel, E. S., 24
Epelbaum, E., 39
Erel, H., 83
Ericksen, J. A., 161
Erickson, K. I., 96
Erikson, E. H., 194, 195, 249, 266
Erikson, W., 53
Eschleman, K. J., 165
Eshbaugh, E., 249
Esteller, M., 56
Estrada Manilla, E., 82
Eurostat, 167
Evans, R. I., 194
Eysenck, H. J., 193

F
Fabbri, E., 38
Fabre, B., 231
Facio, A., 107
Fagan, P., 151
Fahlander, K., 94
Fairclough, D. L., 255
Fales, M. R., 133
Falomir-Pichastor, J. M., 250
Family Caregiver Alliance, 122, 173
Fan, B., 35
Farb, B., 183
Fastborn, J., 94
Federal Interagency Forum on Aging-Related Statistics, 174
Feeney, J., 135
Feifel, H., 258
Feldman, D. C., 164, 165
Ferraro, K. F., 71, 104
Ferring, D., 148
Ferris, G. R., 165
Ferrucci, L., 94
Feys, F., 44
Fiatarone Singh, M. A., 284
Field, B., 247
Field, D., 149, 185
Figueiredo, B., 115
Filipp, S. H., 148
Filmore, J. M., 141
Finch C. E., 73
Fingerhut, A. W., 239
Fingerman, K. L., 143, 145

Finkel, D., 94, 165
Fischer, E. F., 132
Fisher, D. L., 100
Fisher, H., 132
Fisher, H. L., 132
Fiske, S. T., 17
Flannelly, K. J., 249
Fleeson, W., 115
Flentje, A., 235
Flinn, M. V., 228
Flood, S., 274
Florido, R., 27
Flottemesch, T. J., 63
Floyd, K., 144
Flynn, J. R., 88
Folkman, S., 237, 239, 259
Fontana, L., 25
Foster, H., 107
Foster, R. G, 41, 42
Fowler, J., 216
Frahm, K. A., 234
Fraley, R. C., 136
Franc, R., 153
Frankl, V. E., 207
Fraser, J., 42
Frazier, P. A., 242
Frederick, D. A., 133
Fredman, L., 118
Fredrickson, K. I., 236
Freedman, V. A., 54
Frenk, S. M., 35
Friedman, D., 81
Friedman, M., 72
Friedman, M. J., 236
Friedman, N. P., 81
Friesen, W. V., 189
Fromm, E., 207
Frost, R. L., 151
Fry, R., 109, 110
Fryar, C. D., 27, 29
Fu, P., 45
Fukunaga, A., 34
Fung, H. H., 82, 92

G
Galambos, N. L., 13, 14, 107
Gallagher, M. W., 72
Gallath, O., 150
Gallegos, A. M., 189
Gallegos, M. L., 210

Gallicchio, L., 43
Gallo, L. C., 72
Galst, J. P., 124
Garanzini, S., 141
Garcia, J. R., 133
Garnick, M. B., 39
Gastmans, C., 44
Gates, G. J, 141
Gati, I., 160
Gatz, M., 72
Gavian, M., 242
Geary, D. C., 106
Geisinger, K. F., 15
George, L. G., 188
Gerlach, M., 183
Gerrie, B. J., 36
Gerstorf, D., 94
Getzmann, S., 78
Geurts, T., 146
Giandrea, M. D., 176
Gibbs, J., 214, 215
Giele, J. Z., 282
Gilligan, C., 215
Gilligan, M., 148
Givon, M., 160
Glass, Z., 38, 78
Glaucoma Research
    Foundation, 32
Glück, J., 222
Gluckman, P. D., 73
Glueck, E., 277
Glueck, S., 277
Gmeindl, L., 81
Goel, M. S., 69
Gold, D. T., 149, 208
Goldberg, A. E., 114
Golding, G., 215
Goldman, D. P., 275
Goldstein, D., 93
Golembiewski, E., 240
Golob, E. J., 78
Golub, R. M., 254
Gonzaga, G. C., 233
Gonzalez de Sather, J. C. M., 83
Gonzalez-Freire, M., 38
Goodsell, T. L., 146
Gordon, B. A., 81
Gorlik, M. A., 101
Gorman, J. M., 232
Gottfredson, L. S., 89, 90

Gottman, J., 141
Gottman, J. M., 114, 137, 188
Gottman, J. S., 114
Gough, H. G., 183
Gow, A. J., 88, 165
Goy, H., 83
Graham, E. K., 189
Gratch, J., 243
Gredilla, R., 24
Greenberg, E., 167
Greenberg, G., 9
Greenwood, S., 151
Greer, S., 252
Gregoire, J., 80
Greve, W., 148
Griffin, B., 172, 173
Grimm, K. J., 136
Grosman, H., 231
Gross, A. L., 84, 86, 90
Gruber-Baldini, A. L., 96
Gruenewald, T. L., 189
Grunberg, L., 167
Grundfast, K. M., 34
Grunow, D., 112–114
Grych, J., 242
Gu, Q., 27
Gunn, H. E., 210, 211
Gurin, P., 222
Gutmann, D., 116, 200
Guye, S., 84

H

Haan, N., 270
Hackett, G., 158
Hagestad, G. O., 109, 274, 283
Hahn Rickenbach, E. A., 166
Haines, E. L., 106
Hakanan, J., 274
Hakanen, J. J., 166
Håkansson, K., 84
Hale, S., 80, 81
Hall, D. T, 158
Halligan, S. L., 232
Halpern, C. T., 9
Halpern, D. F., 170
Halpern, J., 286
Halter, J. B., 38, 57
Hamby, S., 242
Hamer, M, 72, 210
Hamilton, B. E., 112

Hammers, J. L., 59
Hanfling, S., 42–44
Hankey, B. F., 69
Hannon, K., 177
Hanson, M. A, 73
Harding, S. R., 249
Hareven, T. K., 116
Hargis, M. B., 98
Hargrove, T. W., 67, 234
Harig, F., 121
Harman, J. J., 141
Harmell, A. L., 284
Harmon, D., 24
Harper, L., 121
Harris, J. D., 36
Harris, M. A., 185
Harris Poll, 247
Harrison, D. E., 25
Harrison, E. D., 25
Hartley, A., 99
Hartley, A. A., 96
Hastie, R., 91
Hatfield, E., 132
Hawkes, K., 148
Hawkins, D. N., 138
Hawkley, L. C., 121, 235, 285
Hayes, S. C., 27
Hayflick, L., 24
Hays, J. C., 208
Hayslip, B., Jr., 147
Hayward, M. D., 124
Hazan, C., 135
Hazell, L. V., 258
He, W., 54
Healey, M. K., 93
Hearing Loss Association of
    America, 33, 34
Heath, C. W., 200
Heck, N. C., 235
Heckhausen, J., 105
Heckman, G., 35
Hedden, T., 80, 81
Heggestad, E. D., 165
Hekler, E. B., 42
Hellerstein, J., 160
Helms M. J., 165
Helson, R., 186, 188, 236
Henderson, C. E., 147
Henkens K., 173
Henn, P., 33

Henninger, W., 249
Henry, J. D., 83
Henry, W. E., 104, 272
Hequembourg, A., 19
Herd, P., 69
Herman, C. P., 25
Herman, W. H., 57
Hernández Ramos, J. G., 82
Heron, M., 66
Hershey, D. A., 91
Hertwig, R., 148
Hertzog, C., 81
Hess, R., 44
Hess, T. M., 85
Hevey, D., 72
Hewitt, B., 139
Higgins, C. A., 188
Hill, P. L., 189
Hinds, P., 235
Hinson, J. T., 85
Hirai, R., 242
Ho, K. K., 40
Hobbs, M., 241
Hochwarter, W. A., 165
Hoerger, M., 189
Hofer, J., 193
Hofer, S. M., 45, 89
Hoffman, H. J., 33
Hoge, C. W., 241
Hogeboom, D. L., 98
Holden, C., 66
Holland, J. L., 157, 158
Holloszy, J. O., 25
Holmes, T. H., 228
Holt-Lunstad, J., 149, 239
Holtzman, S., 240
Hommel, B., 89
Hood, K. E., 9
Hooker, S. A., 210
Hope, C. W., 59
Horgan, J. H., 72
Horn, J., 96
Horn, J. L., 88, 89
Horn, M. C., 229
Hornsby, A. K., 24
Hornsby, P. J., 24
Horowitz, L. M., 135
Hosemann, J., 25
House, J. S., 69
Howard, V. J., 96

Hoyer, W. J., 82
Hoyert, D. L., 55, 66
Hoyt, W. T., 210
Hrdy, S. B., 148
Hua, J., 166
Huang, B., 210
Huang, J., 118, 122
Huang, Y., 166
Hulme, C., 90
Hultsch, D. F., 81
Hung, T.-M., 90
Hunkin, J. L., 24
Hunt, R. R., 83
Hunte, H. E. R., 235
Hunter, W. J, 215
Huppert, F. A., 95
Hurd, M. D., 189
Huth, C., 166
Huybrechts, K. F., 97
Huynh, J. Y., 166
Hy, L. X., 198
Hybels, C. F., 274

I

Iacono, W. G., 94
Idler, E. L., 208
Ilies, R., 169
Inagaki T. K., 150
Indian Health Services, 70
Infurna, F. J., 166, 241, 242
Insurance Institute for Highway
    Safety, 99, 100
Ioannou, M., 153
Isaacowitz, D. M., 93
Isfahani, N. S., 35

J

Jackson, J. S., 71, 146
Jacob, J. A., 39, 152
Jacobs, D. M., 96
Jacques, E., 269
Jäger, T., 83
James, W., 78, 221
Janicki-Deverts, D., 72
Jankowiak, W. R., 132
Jaspers, L., 44
Jenal, A., 56
Jennings, J. M., 84
Jensen, A. R., 86
Jeste, D., 284

Johansson, B., 94, 95
John, O. P., 188, 192
Johnson, M. L., 249
Johnson, M. M. S., 91, 92
Johnson, R. A., 64
Johnson, S. C., 25
Johnson, W., 88
Jokela, M., 189
Jolles, J., 97
Jones, E., 132
Jones, J. M., 250
Jones, L. B., 81
Jonson, J. L., 15
Jonsson, T., 65
Joyner, K., 133
Judge, T. A., 188
Jung, C. G., 116, 207, 220
Jung, C. G., 116
Juon, H.-S., 235
Jürges, H., 274

K

Kahn, R. L., 129, 284
Kalil, A., 73
Kalish, R. A., 247
Kalmijn, M, 173
Kaltman, S., 258
Kang, T., 122
Kanter, M., 152
Kapahi, P., 25
Kaprio, J., 230
Kaptin, R., 148
Karantzas, G. C., 150
Kardatzke, K. N., 145
Karpiak, C. P., 212
Karpinski, A. C., 34, 40, 151
Karter, A. J., 71
Kasl, S. V., 208
Kasser, T., 196
Kato, B. S., 24
Katsuma, R., 73
Katzel, L. I., 94
Kaus, C. R., 215
Keen, S., 223
Kegan, R., 216, 219
Kellehear, A., 251
Kelly, J., 114
Kelly, S., 64
Keltner, D., 258
Kemp, C. L., 146

Kendig, N., 34
Kennedy, B. K., 23
Kennedy, G., 286
Kennedy, K. M., 90
Kenrick, D.T., 130
Kersten, A. W., 82
Kersten, M., 166
Kessler, R. C., 60, 61, 69, 70, 135, 232
Kiely, K. M., 94
Kiernan, P. T., 59
Kiley, J., 141
Kim, K., 143
Kim, S., 93
Kinderman, S. S., 94
King, L. A., 239
Kira, I., 236
Kirkland, J. L., 27
Kirschner, P. A., 34, 40, 151
Klein, L. C., 233
Kleykamp, B. A., 84
Kliegel, M., 83
Kliegel, R., 84
Kline, G. H., 139
Knight, J. M., 236
Knight, K. M., 71
Knott, V., 236
Knudsen, K., 146
Kobor, M. S., 236
Kochanek, K., 62
Kockel, L., 25
Koenig, C. S., 248
Kohlberg, L., 212, 213, 214, 215
Kokovay, E., 25, 38
Köpetz, C., 85
Koslowsky, M., 237
Koster, E. H. W., 248
Kozak, A., 166
Krahn, H. J., 13, 14
Kramer, A. F., 83, 90, 96
Kraus, L., 53
Krause, N., 150, 240
Kreider, R. M., 110, 124
Kremen, W. S., 9
Kretzschmar, F., 25
Kretzschmar, K., 25
Kritchevsky, S. B., 46
Krogstad, J. M., 117
Krohn, S., 39
Krol-Zielinska, M., 40

Kropnik, V. S., 8
Kruk, E., 274
Kryla-Lighthall, N., 130
Kübler-Ross, E., 250
Kuehne, V. S., 277
Kugelmass, H., 70, 71
Kuh, D., 73
Kujala, U. M., 45
Kumar, R., 66
Kurdek, L. A., 141
Kusy, K., 40
Kwan, V. S. Y., 186, 192
Kwon, Y., 239

L

La Guardia, J. G., 202
Lachman, M. E., 84, 270
Lachs, M. S., 122
Lamond, A. J., 72
Lampkin, C. L., 116
Lancioni, G. E., 250
Lane, C. J., 79
Lane, M., 63, 70
Lapp, D., 84
Larkin, G. R., 93
Larson, D. B., 210
Lau, R. W. I., 119
Laukka, E. J., 12, 13, 17
Laumann, E. O., 44
Laursen, P., 95
Lautenschlager, G., 80, 81
Layton, J. B., 149, 239
Leary, M. R., 131
Leclerc, J., 72, 210
Ledreux, A., 84
Lee, C., 53
Lee, H., 236
Lee I.-M., 39
Lee, K. S., 39, 119, 140
Lee, M., 239
Legato, M. J., 66
Lehman, D. R., 259
Leifheit-Limson, E., 85
Leiter, M. P., 166
Lemaster, P., 116
Lemasters, E. E., 114
Lemogne, C., 72
Lent, R. W., 158
Leong, F. T. L., 193
Leopold, T., 109

Lerner, M. R., 55
Lerner, R. M., 10
Lester, P. B., 243
Levenstein, S., 72
Levert, E., 193
Levin, L. A., 128
Levin, M. E., 27
Levinson, D. J., 219
Levy, B. R., 85
Levy, J. A., 256
Lewin, T., 251
Lewis, J. M., 110
Lewis, L. L., 106
Li, S. C., 89
Lieberman, M., 2366
Light, L. L., 82
Lightfoot, S. A., 55
Lillberg, K., 230
Lillis, J., 27
Lin, F. R., 94
Lin, J., 24
Lincoln, K. D., 240
Linden, W., 73
Lindenberger, U., 82, 89, 94, 95
Lindström, M., 73
Lingo, E. L., 162
Linn, S., 234
Lipka, M., 250
Lipsitt, L. P., 10, 284
Liu, D., 34, 40, 151
Liu, H., 40
Liu, S. W., 34
Liu, X.-Y., 169
Liu, Y., 169
Liu-Ambrose, T., 79
Livingston, G., 123, 170
Livingston, N. A., 235
Livson, F. B., 275, 276, 281
Livson, N., 275, 276
Lloyd, S. A., 132
Lobar, S. L., 258
Lockley, S. W., 41, 42
Loevinger, J., 198
Loew, B., 138
Lofaro, N., 106
Logan, B. R., 236
Long Lingo, E., 114
Lonky, E., 215
Looker, A. C., 35
Lopez, S. J., 72

Loprinzi, P. D., 96
Losonsky, K. G., 33
Lougheed, E., 151
Loveland, A. D., 90
Loving, T. J., 140
Lowe, J. C., 105
Lowe, S. R., 236
Lucas, G. M., 243
Lucas, J. W., 53, 66
Luecken, L. J., 210, 211
Luhmann, M., 121
Luscombe, B., 123
Lustig, C., 84
Lyles, C. R., 71
Lynn, J., 256
Lyons, M., 172, 173
Lyons, M. J., 9
Lyons, N. P., 216

M
Maciosek, M. V., 63
Mackinlay, R., 83
MacLeod, M. S., 83
Maddi, S. R., 210
Magdol, L., 139
Magidson, J. F., 252
Mahieu, L., 44
Maillot, P., 99
Maitland, S. B., 83
Majerus, S., 80
Mak, E. P. M., 119
Manago, A. M., 107, 109
Mancini, A. D., 241, 242
Manly, J. J., 96
Manove, E. E., 236
Mansson, D. H., 146
Marenco, A., 116
Markides, K. S., 69
Markman, H., 138
Markman, H. J., 137, 138, 139
Marshall, V. W., 256
Marsiske, M., 86, 90
Martin, C. L., 161
Martin, J. A., 112
Martinez, M. L., 107
Martin-Villalba, A., 38
Martire, L. M., 118
Martires, K. J., 45
Maschino, A. C., 36
Masci, D., 141

Mashek, D., 132
Masi, C. M., 285
Maslach, C., 166
Masoro, E. J., 27
Masters, K. S., 210
Mastorci, F., 73
Masunaga, H., 96
Mather, M., 92, 93, 130
Maticka-Tyndale, E., 42
Matthews, K. A., 231
Matthews, M. D., 243
Maughan, B., 283
Mayer, K. U., 13
Mayeux, R., 285
Maylor, E. A., 83
Maynard, L. A., 25
Mayou, R. A., 241
Mays, V. M., 196
Mazerolle, M., 85, 86
Mazza, O., 231
Mazzocco, M., 168
McAdams, D. P., 104, 199
McCarthy, E. P., 69
McCarthy, J., 98
McCay, C. M., 25
McClain, L., 140
McClearn, G. E., 45, 94, 95
McCoy, S. L., 94
McCrae, R. R., 182, 184, 283
McCullough, M. E., 210
McDaniel, M. A., 83, 164
McDermott, R. J., 98
McDonough, I., 38, 78
McFadden, S. H., 249
McGee, E., 133
McGee, H. M., 72
McGee, M., 95
McGinn, K. L., 114, 162
McGowan, P. O., 9
McGue, M., 94
McGurk, D., 59
McGwin, G., Jr., 99
McKee-Ryan, F. M., 167
Medina, J. J., 42, 43
Meevissen, Y. M., 252
Melby-Lervåg, M., 90
Mendelsohn, G. A., 134
Merrick, S. K., 129
Messer, S. C., 241
Messerli-Bürgy, N., 252

Metter, E. J., 94
Meuwly, N., 135
Meyer, B. J. F., 91
Meyer, J. S., 96
Mez, J., 59
Michelson, K. D., 135
Mickels, J. A., 130
Micocci, F., 107
Middeldorp, J., 38
Mienaltowski, A., 92
Mika, E., 286
Mikels, J. A., 93
Mikels, J. S., 93
Mikulincer, M., 128, 135
Milevsky, A., 148, 149
Miller, A. S., 208
Miller, B. A., 69
Miller, G. E., 72, 227, 236
Miller, K. D., 56
Miller, L., 223
Miller, R. A., 25
Millsap, R. E., 185
Miyake, A., 81
Moen, P., 274
Moffitt, T. E., 139, 188
Mogle, J., 231
Moliver, N., 286
Molloy, G., 252
Montesanto, A., 25
Moon, M., 173
Moore, J. W., 105
Moore, S. Y., 167
Moorman, S. M., 42
Morgan, G. S., 236
Morisset, P., 85, 86
Morman, M. T., 144
Morris, P. A., 10
Morris, T., 252
Mortel, K. F., 96
Mosher, W. D., 110
Moskowitz, J. T., 237, 239, 259
Mroczek, D. K., 230
Mudrazija, S., 69, 70
Muenchrath, M. N., 54
Mulcahy, J., 118, 122
Müller, V., 84
Muoio, D., 64
Murphy, M. L. M., 236
Murphy, S. L., 66
Murray, C. E., 145

Musick, M. A., 208
Mustelin, L., 45
Myerson, J., 80, 81

N

Nadash, P., 122
Nair, K. S., 40
National Alliance of Caregiving, 118
National Center for Education Statistics, 164
National Center for Veterans Affairs, 243
National Center of Addiction and Substance Abuse, 63
National Center on Elder Abuse, 122
National Eye Institute, 32
National Highway Traffic Safety Administration, 99
National Institute of Diabetes and Digestive and Kidney Disorders, 43
National Institute of Mental Health, 61
National Institute on Aging, 36, 54
National Institute on Drug Abuse, 61
National Institutes of Health, 23
National Jewish Health Centers, 65
National Osteoporosis Foundation, 35
National Senior Service Corps, 177
National Women's Law Center, 160
Naveh-Benjamin, M., 82
Neergaard, M. A., 253
Nehrke, M. F., 196
Neiderhiser, J. M., 18
Nelson, A. E., 40
Nelson, D. L., 167, 229
Nelson, L. J., 107
Nepple, J. J., 36
Neria, Y., 241
Neugarten, B., 8
Neugarten, B. L., 104, 109, 247, 283

Neumark, D., 160
Newcomer, R. J., 122
Neyer, F. J., 149
Ng, T. W. H., 164, 165
Nilsson, L. G., 82
Nisan, M., 214, 215
Nisbett, R. E., 86
Nitsche, N., 112–114
Noller, P., 135
Noone, R. J., 228
Norris, F. H., 232
North, M. S., 17
Notarius, C. I., 137
Nyberg, L., 82, 83
Nyberg, S. T., 189

O

Oates, G., 96
O'Brien, P., 40
O'Connell, J. F., 148
Oertelt-Prigione, S., 39
Office of Disease Prevention and Health Promotion, 74
Ogden, C. L., 27, 29
Old, S. R., 82
O'Leary, K. D., 138
Olfson, M., 63, 66, 70
Olkin, I., 40
Olshansky, S. J., 46, 274
Omalu, B., 59
Ono, H., 39, 119, 140
Orchek, E., 150
O'Reilly, M. F., 250
Organisation for Economic Cooperation and Development, 112
Ornstein. P. A., 82
Ortega-Alonso, A., 45
Orth-Gomér, K., 239
Osipow, S. H., 160
Osmond, C., 73
Ostrosky-Solis, F., 96
Oswald, A. J., 270
O'Tuathaigh, C. M. P., 33
Owen, D., 34

P

Pacheco, J. L., 101
Packard, K. C., 239
Papa, A., 259

Paradies, Y. C., 234
Parisi, J. M., 86
Park, D. C., 38, 78, 80, 81
Park J. H., 38, 78
Park, N., 243
Parker, S. K., 158
Parol, R., 39
Parrish, M. S., 210
Parsons, E., 157
Pascoe. E., 235
Passarino, G., 25
Pastore, M., 84
Pattie, A., 88, 89
Paulus, M., 258
Pearlin, L. I., 228
Pedersen, N. L., 72, 94, 165
Peeters, M. C. W., 166
Pereira, A., 250
Perez, M., 160
Perkins, M., 118
Perls, F., 221
Perrewe, P. L., 165
Perrin, A., 151
Perrin, K. M., 98
Perrot, A., 99
Perry-Jenkins, M., 114
Persson, J., 81
Peskin, H., 275, 276
Pesta, B. J., 164
Peters, A., 38
Peters, M. L., 252
Peterson, C., 243
Pettingale, K. W., 252
Pew Research Center, 151, 206, 208
Phelan, K., 121
Phillips, L. H., 83
Phillips, M. J., 73
Phillips, R. S., 69
Piazza, J. R., 231, 233
Pickles, A., 283
Pietilainen, K., 45
Pillemer, K., 148
Pillemer, K. A., 122
Plambeck, K. E., 38
Plassman, B. L., 165
Pleimling, D., 25
Pless, A. P., 239
Plikuhn, M., 148
Plomin, R., 8, 94

Polivy, J., 25
Pollatsek, A., 100
Polster, A. M., 45
Ponds, R. W. H. M., 97
Poole, L., 252
Porter, R. S., 29, 31, 38
Positive Psychology Center, 243
Posner, M. I., 81
Postmes, T., 235
Potter, G. G., 165
Poulin, M. J., 234
Poushter, J., 152
Powell, L. H., 210
Prakash, R., 286
Pratt, M. W., 215
Pressman, S. D., 72
Price-Glynn, K., 162
Proctor, D. N., 284
Purnell, J. Q., 57

Q

Quick, J. C., 167
Quinn, J. F., 176
Quinton, D., 283

R

Racco, N., 122
Radloff, L. S., 15
Rafferty, J. A., 71
Rahe, R. H., 228
Rainie, L., 151
Rakovski, C., 162
Rando, T. A., 258
Rastogi, P., 286
Raus, K., 251
Raz, N., 90, 96
Rebok, G. W., 84, 90
Redhead, Y. T., 24
Redick, T. S., 90
Reed, D., 34
Reed, N. S., 34
Rees, D. J., 24
Reese, H. W., 10, 284
Régner, I., 85, 86
Reider, B., 36
Reijnders, J., 285
Reimer, J., 214, 215
Reinhold, S., 274
Reis, H. T., 149
Reker, G. T., 217

Rendell, P. G., 83
Renner, F., 252
Resett, S., 107
Rest, J. R., 215, 221
Reuter-Lorenz, P. A., 81, 93
Revelle, W., 183
Reyes, M. E. S., 249
Rhoades, G., 138
Rhoades, G. K., 137, 138, 139
Rhodes, J. E., 236
Richardson, L. J., 67, 234
Richmond, L. S., 128
Richter, D., 131
Rickwood, D. J., 151
Riegel, K., 207
Rigt-Poortman, A., 144, 146
Riley, K. P., 20
Ritchie, 51
Rix, S. E., 176, 177
Rizza, R. A., 40
Rizzo, A., 243
Rizzo, J. D., 236
Rizzuto, D., 12, 13, 17
Robbins, S., 152
Robert, S. A., 69
Roberto, K. A, 121
Roberts, A. H., 59
Roberts, B. W., 189, 192, 236, 252
Robinaugh, D., 241, 242
Robinson, J. K., 45
Robison, L., 240
Rodrigue, K. M., 90
Roenker, D. L., 100
Rogers, C., 221
Rogers, R. L, 96
Rohleder, N., 236
Rohwedder, S., 274
Roisman, G. I., 136, 141
Romoser, M. R. E., 100
Rönnlund, M., 82, 83
Roodin, P. A., 215
Rose, N. S., 80, 81
Rosenberger, N., 107
Rosenbloom, C., 46
Rosenfeld, I., 29
Rosengren, A., 239
Rosenman, R. H., 72
Roser, 51
RoserRoser, 51
Rosin, A., 66

Ross, M., 93
Rosselli, M., 96
Rossi, A. S., 116
Roth, D. L., 118
Rothbart, M. K., 81
Rothberg, A. E., 57
Rothblum, E. D., 142
Rounds, J., 160
Rovine, M., 114
Rowe, J. W., 284
Rubin, O., 143
Ruble, D. N., 161
Rudolph, C. W., 164
Ruiz, C., 168
Ruiz Castro, M., 114, 162
Ruiz, S. A, 147
Russo, C., 91
Ruthig, J. C., 72
Rutsohn, J. P., 189
Ryan, R. M., 202
Ryckewaert, R., 248

S

Sabaté, E., 97
Sagi-Schwartz, A., 234
Salkind, N. J., 19
Salmela-Aro, K., 107, 162
Salmon, C., 138
Salthouse, T. A., 82, 89, 95, 96, 164
Salvatore, J. E., 135, 136
Sameroff, A. J., 10, 107
Sampson, N., 63
Samrani, G., 81
Sander, J., 131
Sanders, L. M., 147
Sandstrom, A., 247
Sanfey, A. C., 91
Sano, M., 96
Santillanes, G., 258
Sasaki, A., 9
Sauceda, J. A., 97
Sayed, K., 38, 78
Sayer, A., 196
Sayer, L. C., 125
Sbarra, D. A., 138
Scarmeas, N., 285
Schacter, D. L., 83
Schaefer, H. M., 38
Schafer, M. H., 71, 150, 152
Schaie, K. W., 87, 90, 96

Scharlach, A. E., 236
Schaufeli, W., 274
Schaufeli, W. B., 166
Scheier, L. M., 243
Scheier, M. F., 189, 242
Schillmöller, Z., 166
Schmeidler, J., 232
Schmitt, D. P., 106, 134
Schmitt, M. T., 235
Schmukle, S. C., 187
Schneider-Graces, N. J., 81
Schoebi, D., 135
Schooler, C., 96
Schrader, S. S., 143
Schryer, E., 93
Schulenberg, J. E., 107
Schultheiss, D. E. P., 161
Schupp, J., 131
Schuster, J.-P., 72
Schuth, M., 274
Schwartz, L. M., 44
Schwartz, P., 252
Scott, J., 248
Scott, S. B., 234
Seale, C., 251
Seay, R. B., 92
Sechrist, J., 148
Seeman, M., 210
Seeman, T. E., 210
Segerstrom, S. C., 227
Segrin, C., 210
Seib, D., 38
Selcuk, E., 150
Seligman, M. E. P., 72, 202, 243
Selye, H., 227
Selzer, F., 57
Semuels, A., 162
Settersten, R. A., Jr., 23
Seubert, J., 12, 13, 17
Shackelford, T. K., 134, 146
Shafto, M. A., 82, 83
Shanahan, M. J., 107
Shankar, A., 235
Shapiro, A. F., 114
Sharp, Z. D., 25
Shaver, P., 135
Shaver, P. R, 135
Shear, K., 241, 242
Sheehy, G., 269
Sheikh, J. A, 84

Sheldon, K. M., 196
Shen, D., 56
Sherman, C. W., 274, 275
Shevlin, M., 133
Shifren, J. L., 42–44
Shiner, R. L., 189
Shippee, T. P., 71
Shneidman, E. S., 271
Shriver Center on Poverty Law, 174
Shuchter, S. R., 258
Siegel, R. L., 56
Silventoinen, K., 45
Silver, R. C., 234
Silverstein, M., 116, 124, 147
Simmons, B. L., 167
Simon, S., 56
Simpson, J. A., 135, 136
Sims, R. V., 99
Singh, N. N., 250
Sinnott, J. D., 101, 207
Sipilä, S., 45
Skitka, L. J., 236
Skovronek, E., 95
Slavich, G. M., 235, 236
Small, B. J., 80, 94, 95
Smart, E. L., 165
Smart Richman, L., 235
Smetana, J. G, 215
Smith, A., 98, 134, 151
Smith, B. J., 55
Smith, C. D., 90
Smith, J., 84, 95
Smith, J. Z., 114
Smith, K. P., 150
Smith, M. J., 81
Smith R. E., 83
Smith, T. B., 149, 239
Smith, T. W., 72
Smylie, L., 42
Snarey, J. R., 214, 215, 277
Sneed, J. R., 196
Snowdon, D, 20
Snowdon, D. A., 20, 189
Social Security Administration, 175
Sokolowski, T., 253
Solano-Fonseca, R., 25, 38
Solberg, Ø., 242
Soldz, S., 200

Solomon, Z., 236
Son, L., 277
Song, A., 167
Spanier, G. B., 114
Spearman, C., 86
Specht, J., 187
Spotts, E. L., 18
Spradlin, A., 151
Spry, N., 38, 229, 234
Stamatakis, E. A., 83
Stanley, S. M., 137, 139
Stark, R., 208
Starr, J. M., 89, 185
Statham, J. A., 85
Staudinger, U. M., 101
Stawski, R. S., 233
Steinberg, S., 65
Steindl-Rast, B. D., 260
Stephan, Y., 191, 192
Stepler, R., 120, 121, 139, 140, 144
Steptoe, A., 210
Stern, Y., 285
Sternberg, R. J., 80, 88, 132
Stone, A. J., 160
Stöppler, M. C., 66
Storandt, M., 59
Stringer, H., 124
Strong, R., 25
Strough, J., 116
Su, R., 160
Substance Abuse and Mental Health Services Administration, 62
Sugimoto, K., 9
Suitor, J. J., 148
Super, D. E., 157, 168
Sutin, A. R., 191, 192

T

Takahashi, K., 129
Talbot, A., 91
Tan, J.-P., 147
Tartaro, J., 210, 211
Tatsuoka, M. M., 183
Taylor, A. C., 146
Taylor, R. J., 240
Taylor, S. E., 233
Tchkonia, T., 27
Tennov, D., 132

Tennstedt, S. L, 90
Teno, J. M., 253
Teresa of Ávila, St., 220, 225
Terracciano, A., 191, 192
Teshale, S., 270
Thoits, P. A., 66, 71
Thomas, H. N., 44
Thomas, J. L., 24
Thomese, F., 148
Thompson, D., 255
Thompson, S. H., 151
Thorand, B., 166
Thoreson, C. J., 188
Thurston, R. C., 44
Tighe, L. A., 130
Tolvanen, A., 107, 162
Toma, C. L., 134
Tomasetto, C., 162
Tomer, A., 249
Tomic, D., 43
Tooby, J., 193
Tornstam, L., 207
Torpy, J. M., 254
Toterdell, P., 158
Towers, H., 18
Trappler, B., 234
Trella, P., 72
Trivers, R. L., 112
Truluck, J. E., 199
Trzesniewski, K., 186
Tulloo, R., 234
Tulving, E., 81, 83
Tun, P. A., 94
Turiano, N. A., 189, 230, 241, 242
Tynkkynen, L., 107, 162

U

U.S. Department of Health and
    Human Services, 70
Uchida, K., 73
Uchino, B. N., 239
Uematsu, H., 34
Underhill, E., 220
Underwood, L., 211
Unson, C., 72
U.S. Bureau of Labor Statistics,
    159, 161, 163, 164, 166, 168,
    169, 172, 176, 177
U.S. Census Bureau, 99, 117,
    168, 176

U.S. Department of Health and
    Human Services, 70
U.S. Department of Labor, 34
U.S. Government Accountability
    Office, 177
Uttl, B., 88

V

Vaillant, C. O., 275
Vaillant, G. E., 9, 199, 200, 204,
    275, 276
Valente, M., 34
Valleda, S. A., 38
Van Alstine, C. L., 88
Van Alstine Makomenaw, M.,
    107, 109
van Boxtel, M., 285
van Boxtel, M. P. J., 97
van de Vijver, F. J. R., 193
Van der Linden, M., 80
van Heugten, C., 285
van IJzendoorn, M., 129
van Tilburg, T. G., 144, 146, 148,
    285
Vargas Lascano, D. I., 13, 14
Varner, K. E., 36
Ventura, S. J, 112
Verhaegen, C., 80
Verhaeghen, P., 82
Verkasalo, P. K., 230
Verma, J., 193
Vernon, L. L., 82, 232
Vespa, J., 108, 110
Vicentini, M., 73
Vickers, A. J., 36
Vie, L. L., 243
Vigdorchik, J. M., 36
Viltart, O., 73
Vogler, G. P., 45
Vogt, D. S., 239
von Bastian, C. C., 84
von Schrader, S., 53

W

Waddington, C. H., 279
Wadley, V. G., 96, 118
Wahed, A. S., 57
Wahlin, Å., 80, 94, 95
Waite, L. J., 44
Walaskay, M., 196

Waldstein, S. R., 94
Walker, E. J., 285
Walker, L. J., 215
Walton, A., 90
Walton, G. M., 186, 187
Wanberg, C. R., 144, 157, 167,
    174, 176, 177
Wang, M., 144, 157, 174,
    176, 177
Wang, P. S., 63, 66, 70
Wang, Q., 165
Wang, T. R., 144, 145
Ward, C. V., 228
Wascher, E., 78
Waterreus, A., 38, 229, 234
Waters, E., 128, 129
Watson, D. P., 240
Watson. P. J., 232
Weatherbee, S. R., 89
Weaver, A. J., 249
Weaver, S. E., 125
Weber, K. V., 250
Webster, L. M., 84
Webster, N. J., 274, 275
Wechsler, D., 86
Wedel, H., 239
Weiss, R. S., 128, 143
Wen, T., 250
Westerhof, G. J., 272, 273
Weststrate, N. M., 222
Wethington, E., 270
Whisman, M. A., 138
Whitbourne, S. K., 15,
    16, 196
Whiteman, M. K., 43
Wickramaratne, P., 223
Wiederhold, B. K., 152
Wight, R. G., 121
Wight, V. R., 160
Wilbur, K. H., 124
Wilkinson, A. M., 256
Williams, D. R., 235
Williams, G. C., 66
Williams, J. E., 106
Williams, L., 239
Willis, R. J., 274
Willis, S. L., 90, 96, 285
Wilson, J. A., 91
Wilson, R. S., 96
Wiltz, T., 117

Winefield, A. H., 166
Wingbermuehle, C., 250
Wingfield, A., 94
Wink, P., 206, 209, 210, 248
Winter, P. D., 73
Wisneski, D. C., 236
Wolf, D. A., 118
Wolff, J. L., 118, 122
Woloshin, S., 44
Wood, A. M., 167
Wood, W., 160
Woodnutt, T., 151
Woods, L. N., 139
Woods, S. P., 97
World Health Organization, 32, 33, 51
World Health Organization, 3, 32, 51
Worthy, D. A., 101

Wortman, C. B., 259
Wright, M. R., 140

X
Xanthopoulou, D., 166
Xu, J., 55
Xu, S., 166
Xu, X., 132

Y
Yamaguchi, S., 168
Yamanski, K., 73
Yang, K. S., 194
Yee, A., 141
Yehuda, R., 232, 233
Yesavage, J., 84
Yetz, J. P., 232
Yi, Y., 81
Young, B. A., 71

Ysasi, N. S, 141
Yu, J. W., 63

Z
Zanjani, F., 87
Zarit, S., 145
Zelinski, E. M., 79
Zhang, J. X., 193
Zhang, R., 239
Zhang, Y., 140
Zhang, Z., 124
Zhou, N., 169
Zhu, W., 96
Ziol-Guest, K. M., 73
Zisook, S., 258
Zissimopoulos, J., 275
Zivotofsky, A. Z., 237
Zogg, J. B., 97
Zuschlag, M. K., 15, 16, 196

Subject Index

A

Ability/expertise trade-off, 164
Acceptance, as reaction to death, 250, 251
Accommodate, lens and, 31
Achievement, personality traits and, 188–189
Acute conditions, 52
Adaptive/maladaptive outcomes vs. happiness, 283
Adaptive nature of cognition, 85
ADLs (activities of daily living), 53
Adult development. See also Model of adult growth and development
   age and, 5
   bioecological model of development, 10–11
   change, sources of, 5–9
   concepts in, 2–5
   defined, 2
   developmental research, 11–20
   introduction to, 1–21
   life-span developmental psychology approach, 10
   perspectives on, guiding, 9–11
   stability, 3–4
Adult development, themes of, 263–273
   emerging adulthood (age 18–24), 265–266
   late adulthood (age 75 and older), 271–273
   middle adulthood (age 40–64), 268–269
   older adulthood (age 65–74), 269–271
   review of, 264–265 (See also Adult functioning, changes in domains of)
   young adulthood (age 25–39), 266–268
Adult development, variations in successful, 273–278
Adult functioning, changes in domains of, 264–265
   cognitive change, 264

family and gender roles, 264
major tasks, 265
meaning, 265
personality, 265
physical change, 264
relationships, 264
work roles, 265
Affectional solidarity, 143
Affection in family relationships, 143–144
African Americans. See also Racial and ethnic groups
   perceived discrimination and, health-related effects of, 235
Age
   biological, 5
   chronological, 5
   death anxiety and, 248
   functional, 5
   psychological, 5
   social, 5
   stress-related disorders and, 233–234
Ageism, 6
Age-related macular degeneration, 32
Age trends in work experience, 162–165
   job performance, 164
   job satisfaction, 165
   job training and retraining, 164–165
Aging in place, 121
Aging parents, caring for, 118–119
Agreeableness, 183
AIDS, 58, 259
Alarm reaction, 228
Alaskan Natives, health of, 70. See also Racial and ethnic groups
Aldosterone, 38
Alternative medicine, 286
Alzheimer's disease, 58–59
Ambivalence, 150
American Indians, health of, 70. See also Racial and ethnic groups
Anger, as reaction to death, 251
Antibodies, 38

Antioxidants, 24
Anxiety disorders, 60
Anxious preoccupation, as response to imminent death, 252
APOE E4 gene, 58
APP gene, 58
Asian Americans, health of, 69
Asset income, 174
Assistance animals, 64
Assistance solutions, 63–64
Assistive technology, 64
Associated solidarity, 143
Atherosclerosis, 55
Athletic abilities, changes in, 40
Attachment
   concept of, 128–129
   in intimate partnerships, 135–137
Attachment behaviors, 128
Attachment orientation, 129
Attachment theory, 128–129
Attention, 78–79
   divided, 78–79
   visual search, 79
Attraction, 132–135
Attraction system, 132
Attrition, 13
Atypical families, social roles in, 122–125
   childless, 123–124
   divorced (and remarried) adults, 124–125
   lifelong singles, 122–123
Atypical stages of life, 4
Auditory acuity, 94
Autonomy
   in ego development, 198
   in self-determination theory, 202–203
Average lifespan, 25
Avoidant-denial strategy, 92
Awakening stage of mystical experience, 220

B

Balance, changes in, 40–41
Bargaining, as reaction to death, 250, 251

B cells, 38
Behavioral genetics, 8
Behavior patterns
    individual differences in
        health, 72–73
Being motives, 201
Bereavement. *See* Death and
    bereavement
Berlin Study of Aging, 13, 94
"Big Five Model," 183
Bioecological model of
    development, 10, 11
Biological age, 5
Biological clock, 6, 104, 268
Biology, 6
Body composition, changes
    in, 27–29
Body mass index (BMI), 27, 28
Bone mass density (BMD), 35
Bones, changes in, 35–37
    osteoarthritis, 36
    osteoporosis, 35–36
    patient adherence to treatment
        for bone loss, 36
Botox, 29, 30
Brain aging, 78
Brain, changes in, 37–38
Breast cancer
    individual variations/
        adaptations to dying, 252
    stress and, 230, 236
Bridge employment, 176–177
Brief COPE Inventory, 237
Brief Multidimensional Measure
    of Religiousness/Spirituality
    (BMMRS), 211
Buffering effect, 239

C

California Psychological Inventory
    (CPI), 183
Caloric restriction (CR), 24–25
Cancer, 55–57. *See also*
    Breast cancer
    cervical, HPV vaccine and, 56
    death from, 55
    individual adaptations to
        dying, 252
    survival rates, 252
Cardiovascular disease, 55
Cardiovascular system,
    changes in, 37

Career
    commitment, retirement and,
        173–174
    defined, 157
    development, theory of, 157–158
    patterns, gender differences in,
        158–159
Career consolidation, 199
Career recycling, 164
Career selection, 160–162
    changes over adulthood, review
        of, 178
    family influences, 162
    gender and, 160–162
Caregiver burden, 126
Caregiving
    gender and, 118
    impact of, 118
Caregiving orientation, 129
Care receiver, becoming, 121–122
Cataracts, 32
Change
    defined, 3
    external, 4
    internal, 4
Change, sources of, 5–9
    nonnormative life events, 8
    normative age-graded
        influences, 6
    normative history-graded
        influences, 6–7
Chemical peels, 29
Child-free adults, 124
Childless families, 123–124
Children
    cohabitation and, 140
    cultural acceptance of, 139–140
    departure of (empty nest),
        115–116
    gender roles in couples
        with, 112
    problem, in adulthood, 145
Choice board, 91
Chronic conditions, 52
    individual differences in
        cognitive change, 94
Chronic life strains, stress and, 229
Chronic traumatic encephalopathy
    (CTE), 59
Chronological age, 5
Chronosystem, 10, 11
Cialis, 43

Climacteric
    in men, 38
    in women, 39
Cochlea, 33
Cognitive assistance, 96–100
    driving, 99–100
    electronic games, 98–99
    e-readers, 98–99
    medication adherence, 97
    social networking, 98
Cognitive change, 77–102
    attention, 78–79
    cognitive assistance, 96–100
    decision making and problem
        solving, 91–93
    individual differences in, 93–97
    intelligence, 86–90
    memory, 79–86
    review of, 101–102, 264
Cognitive complexity, 165
Cohabitation, 109–110, 138–140
    children and, 140
    marriages and, 138–140
    selection effect, 139
Cohort, 7
    quality of life and, 274
Collectivism, 218
Commonalities, 3
Communal qualities, 106, 125
Community dwelling, 54
Comparison of means, 17
Competence, in self-determination
    theory, 202
Complementary and alternative
    medicine providers, 63
Complementary
    medicine, 286
Conformist stage of ego
    development, 198
Conjunctive faith, 217
Conscientiousness, 183–193
Conscientious stage of ego
    development, 198
Consensual solidarity, 143
Contextual perspective, 85
Continuity of change
    differential, 183, 187
    environmental influences,
        191–192
    evolutionary influences, 193
    explanations of, 190–194
    genetics, 190–191

Conventional level of Kohlberg's stages of moral reasoning, 212, 213
Convoy, 129
Convoy model, 129–130
Coping
  behaviors, 237–239
  Brief COPE Inventory, 237
  defined, 227
  drugs and alcohol as coping mechanism, 237
  effectiveness of, 238–239
  emotion-focused, 237–238
  meaning-focused, 238
  personality traits and, 241–242
  problem-focused coping, 237
  social-focused coping, 238
  social support and, 239–240
Coping flexibility, 239
Correlational analysis, 17
Cortisol levels, 211
Country of residence, quality of life and, 275
Crossover of gender roles, 116
Cross-sectional study, 12–13
Crystallized intelligence, 88
Cultures, 6
Cyclic GMP, 43

D

Daily stressors, 229
Dark adaptation, 31
Dark night of the soul stage of mystical experience, 220
Data analyses in developmental research, 15–17
  comparison of means, 15, 17
  correlational analysis, 17
  meta-analysis, 17
Death
  from cancer, 55
  from cardiovascular disease, 55
  rates, 52
Death and bereavement, 247–260
  adaptations to dying, individual, 252
  choosing when to die, 254–256
  choosing where to die, 252–254
  farewells, importance of, 251–252
  finitude, 249
  funerals and ceremonies, 256
  a good death, importance of, 254
  grieving process, 256–260

process of, 250–256
  reactions to death, stages of, 250–251
  rituals and grieving, 256–260
  understanding of, achieving, 247–250
Death anxiety, 248–249
  age and, 248
  defined, 248
  gender and, 249
  personality traits and, 249
  religiosity and, 248–249
Death, meanings of, 247
  as an organizer of time, 247
  as loss, 247
  as punishment, 247
  as transition, 247
Decentering, 214
Decision making and problem solving, 91–93
  avoidant-denial strategy, 92
  choice board, 91
  positivity bias, 92–93
  problem-focused approach, 92
  socioemotional selectivity theory, 93
Declarative memory, 81
Defense mechanism, 199
Deficiency motives, 201
Dementia, 54, 58
Demographics, 95
Denial, as reaction to death, 250, 251
Departure of children (empty nest), 115–116
Depression, as reaction to death, 250, 251
Depressive symptoms, 61, 66
Descriptive research, 19–20
Designs in developmental research, 17–20
  descriptive research, 19–20
  experimental, 17, 19
  qualitative research, 19–20
  quantitative research, 19
  questions in, 11–12
Desire, sexual, 43–44
Despair, ego integrity vs., 195, 272
Detribalization, 219, 268
Developmental origins, 73–74
Developmental origins hypothesis, 73

Developmental patterns, asynchrony of, 281
Developmental psychology, 2
Developmental research, 11–20
  data analyses, 15–17
  designs, 17–20
  measures, 15
  questions, 11–12
Developmental research methods, 12–15
  attrition, 13
  cross-sectional study, 12–13
  longitudinal study, 13–14
  sequential study, 15
Dexterity, changes in, 40–41
DHEA (dehydroepiandrosterone), 40
Diabetes, 57–58
Diagnostic and Statistical Manual (DSM) 3rd edition (DSM-III), 60
Diet, 285
Differential continuity, 183–184
Digit-span task, 80
Disability, 53–54
Discrimination, 70–72
Diseases, 54–59
  Alzheimer's disease, 58–59
  cancer, 55–57
  cardiovascular disease, 55
  diabetes, 57–58
Disengagement, 271–272
Disequilibrium, 282
  adaptive/maladaptive outcomes vs. happiness, 283
  asynchrony of developmental patterns, 281
  cumulative effects of, 283
  flowchart of, 281
  major life changes, 282
  outcome of, 282, 283
  periods of, 280
  personality and role requirements, poor match between, 281
  personality or spiritual development, 282
  role transitions, 281
  stability and age, 280
Distal causes, 106
Distress, 227. See also Stress
Divided attention, 78–79
Divorced (and remarried) adults
  late-life, 144–145
  social roles, 124–125

Dizygotic twins, 8, 18–19
DNA methylation, 9
Dopamine, 132
Downregulate (or silence), 56
Driving, 99–100
Drugs, coping and, 237
DXA scan, 35

E
Earnings
   retirement and, 174–176
   of women, 160
Ecological systems approach, 284
Economic exchange theory, 112
Education
   quality of life and, 274
Egalitarian roles, 110
Ego development, 198–199
   autonomous stage of, 198
   conformist stage of, 198
   conscientious stage of, 198
   impulsive stage of, 198
   individualistic stage of, 198
   integrated stage of, 198
   integrative themes in, 199
   self-aware stage of, 198
   self-protective stage of, 198
Ego integrity, 195
   vs. despair, 195, 272
Elder abuse, 121
Electronic games, 98–99
Emerging adulthood, 107
Emerging adulthood (age 18–24),
   265–266
   review of, 264–265
Emotion-focused coping, 237–238
Empty nest (departure of),
   115–116
Engaged cohabitation, 139
Environment, 8–9
Epigenetic inheritance, 9, 56
Episodic memory, 81–83
E-readers, 98–99
Erectile dysfunction (ED), 42, 43, 45
Erikson's stages of psychosocial
   development, 194–197
Estrogen, 39
Ethical principles of moral
   reasoning, 213
Ethnicity. *See* Racial and ethnic
   groups
Eudaimonia, 202
Evocative transactions, 192

Evolutionary psychology, 106,
   130–131
Evolutionary truce, 219
Exchange theory, 133
Executive function, 81
Exhaustion in general adaptation
   syndrome, 228
Exosystem, 10, 11
Experimental design, 17
Expertise, 96
Explicit memory, 81
Extended families, 142
External change, 4
Extraversion, 183–187, 189,
   191–193, 200
Extrinsic religiosity, 249
Eye, 31–32. *See also* Vision,
   changes in

F
Face-to-face meeting, 131, 153
Factor analysis, 183, 193
Faith, 216–218
   defined, 216
   stages of, 216–217 (*See also*
      Fowler's stages of faith
      development)
Family
   career selection and, influences
      on, 162
   interaction, patterns of, 142–143
   quality of life and, 274
   retirement and, 173
Family and Medical Leave Act
   (FMLA), 170
Family life and work, 168–170
Family members, social
   relationships with, 142–149
   family interaction, patterns of,
      142–143
   grandparent-grandchild
      relationships, 146–148
   intergenerational solidarity
      theory, 142
   parent-child relationships in
      adulthood, 143–145
   siblings, 148–149
Family roles, review of changes
   in, 264
Family–work spillover, 169–170
Fantasies, sexual, 43
Farewells, importance of,
   251–252

Fatalism (stoic acceptance), as
   response to imminent death, 252
Feeling in-between, 266
Feminization of poverty, 174–176
Fictive families, 274
Fighting spirit, as response to
   imminent death, 252
Fight or flight responds, 227, 228
Filter theory, 132
Finances, retirement and, 173
Finitude, 249
Five-Factor Model (FFM), 183
Fluid intelligence, 88–89
Flynn effect, 88
Food deserts, 46
Foster Grandparents
   Program, 177
Fowler's stages of faith develop-
   ment, 216–218
   conjunctive faith, 217
   individuative-reflective
      faith, 216
   points about, 217
   research findings, 217–218
   synthetic-conventional faith, 216
   universalizing faith, 217
Free radicals, 24
Friendship
   in adulthood, 149–153
   defined, 149
   networks, 149–150
   social media friends, 150–153
Functional age, 5
Functional solidarity, 143
Funerals and ceremonies, 256

G
G, 88
Gay partnerships, 140–142
Gender
   career patterns and, 158–159
   career selection and, 160–162
   death anxiety and, 249
   grandparent-grandchild relation-
      ships, 146–148
   individual differences in health,
      65–66
   posttraumatic stress disorder
      and, 233
   stress-related disorders
      and, 233
Gender crossover, 200–201
Gender ideology, 114

Gender roles
  in couples with children, 112
  crossover of, 116
  defined, 106
  in early partnerships, 110
  at midlife, 116
  review of changes in, 264
  stereotypes compared to, 106–107
Gender schema theory, 106
Gender stereotypes, 106–107
General adaptation syndrome, 227
General Assessment Tool
    (GAT), 243
Generation, 7. *See also* Cohort
Generativity, 195–197
  defined, 195
  Loyola Generativity Scale for
    measuring, 197
  in midlife, 197
  vs. self-absorption, 195
  vs. stagnation, 195, 196
Genetic limits, 24
Genetics, 8–9
  cognitive change and, individual
    differences in, 94–95
  continuity of change and,
    explanations of, 190–191
  health and, individual differences
    in, 65
  primary aging and, 45
Genotype, 65
Gerotranscendence, 207
GH (growth hormone), 40
Glaucoma, 32
Good-boy or good-girl
    orientation, 212
Good death, 254
Goodness of fit, 239
Grandfamilies, 117
Grandmother effect, 148
Grandparent-grandchild relation-
    ships, 146–148
  grandmother effect, 148
  informal care, 147
  in time of family crisis, 147
Grandparents
  becoming, 116–117
  raising grandchildren, 117
Grant Study of Harvard Men, 9
Great Depression, 7
Grief work, 245
Grieving process, 256–260
Guilt, initiative *vs.*, 195

H
Hair, changes in, 30–31
Happiness *vs.* adaptive/maladap-
    tive outcomes, 283
Happy marriages, 137–138
Hardiness, resilience and, 210
"Having a choice over challenges"
    strategy, 202
Hayflick limit, 24
Health and health disorders, 50–76.
    See also Diseases
  assistance solutions, 63–64
  disability, 53–54
  individual differences in health,
    65–74
  intelligence used to predict, 89
  morbidity rates, 52
  mortality and morbidity, 52
  personality traits and, 189–190
  psychological disorders, 59–63
  quest for meaning and, 210–211
  retirement and, 173
  review of, 75–76
Health, individual differences in
    cognitive change, 94
  chronic disease, 94
  hearing, 94
  medication, 94
  vision, 94
Hearing aids, 34
Hearing, changes in, 33–34
  individual differences in cogni-
    tive changes, 94
Heart disease, stress and, 230, 231
Hedonia, 202
Helplessness/hopelessness, as
    response to imminent death, 252
Heritability of cognitive abilities, 94
Heritability scores, 94
Hierarchy of needs, Maslow's,
    201–202
Hippocampus, 96
Hispanic Americans. *See also* Racial
    and ethnic groups
Hispanic/Latinx Americans
  health risks of, 69
  life expectancy of, 69
  racial discrimination in health
    care, 69–70
HIV, 70
Holland's theory of vocational
    interests, 157, 158

Hormonal system, changes in,
    38–40
  climacteric in men, 38
  climacteric in women, 39
  DHEA (dehydroepiandroster-
    one), 40
  estrogen, 39
  GH (growth hormone), 40
  menopause and, 39
  progesterone, 39
Hormone replacement, 39
  DHEA replacement, 40
  growth hormone
    replacement, 40
  hormone replacement therapy, 39
  for menopause, 39
  testosterone replacement
    therapy, 39
Hormone replacement therapy, 39
Hospice approach, 254
Hospice care, 254
Hostility, 72
Hot flash, 39
Human papillomavirus (HPV)
    vaccine, 56
Human social genomics, 235
Hyaluranic acid, 36

I
IADLs (instrumental activities of
    daily living), 53
Identity, 194
  vs. role confusion, 194–196, 198
Identity exploration, 266
Illumination stage of mystical expe-
    rience, 220
Imaging techniques, 59
Immune response to stress, 227
Immune system
  changes in, 38
Improvised explosive devices
    (IEDs), 59
Impulsive stage of ego develop-
    ment, 198
Income
  quality of life and, 274
  retirement and, 174–176
Individual differences, defined, 3
Individual differences, in cognitive
    change, 93–97
  decline, subjective evaluation
    of, 97

demographics and sociobiographical history, 95
education and intellectual activity, 95–96
genetics, 94–95
health, 94
physical exercise, 96
schooling, 95, 96
subjective evaluation of decline, 97
Individual differences, in health, 65–74
developmental origins, 73–74
discrimination, 70–72
genetics, 65
lifestyle, 74
personality and behavior patterns, 72–73
race and ethnicity, 69–70
sex and gender, 65–66
socioeconomic class, 66–69
Individual differences, in primary aging, 45–49
genetics, 45
lifestyle, 45–46
race and ethnicity, 46–47
socioeconomic factors, 46–47
Individual differences, in quality of life, 274–275
cohort, 274
country of residence, 275
education and income, 274
family, 274–275
social comparisons, 275
work satisfaction, 274
Individual differences, in stress-related disorders, 233–236
age, 233–234
discrimination, 234–235
environment-gene interactions and, 235–236
gender, 233
Individualism, 216
Individualistic stage of ego development, 198
Individual principles of conscience orientation, 212
Individuative-reflective faith, 216
Industry *vs.* inferiority, 195
Inferiority, industry *vs.*, 195
Infertility, 123–124
Initiative *vs.* guilt, 195

Insomnia, 42
Instability, positive, 266
Institute for Human Development longitudinal study, 209
Instrumental qualities, 106
Integrated stage of ego development, 198
Integrative themes in ego development, 199
Intellectual activity, 96
Intelligence, 86–90
age changes in, 87–88
components of, 88–90
crystallized, 88
defined, 86
expertise, 96
fluid, 88–89
Flynn effect, 88
health and longevity predicted by, 89
psychometrics, 86
reversing declines in, 90
Interactionist view, 9
Intergenerational effects, 73
Intergenerational family structure, 143
Intergenerational solidarity theory, 143–144
Internal change, 4
Internal working model, 129, 207
Internet, 102
Intimacy, 194, 195
vs. isolation, 195
Intimate partnership, 131–142
establishing, 131–137
libido, 132
living in, 137–142
lust, 132–135
mate selection, 132
Intimate relationships
attachment, 135–137
attraction, 132–135
cohabitation and marriage, 138–140
exchange theory, 133
filter theory, 132
happy marriages, 137–138
personality traits and, 188
same-sex marriages and partnerships, 140–142
same-sex partnerships, 140–142
successful marriages, 139
Intra-individual variability, 185–187

Intrinsic religiosity, 248–249
Inventory of Psychosocial Development (IPD), 196
IQ (intelligence quotient), 86–89. *See also* Intelligence
measures, 15
scores, 86–88, 94, 101
tests, 86, 88
Isolation, intimacy *vs.*, 194, 195

J

Job burnout, 166
Job expertise, 164
Job insecurity, 167
Job loss, 167
Job performance, 164
Job satisfaction, 165
Job strain, 165
Job training and retraining, 164–165

K

Kohlberg's stages of moral reasoning, 212–215
conventional level, 212
data, 214–215
decentering, 214
ethical principles, 213
evaluation and comment, 215–216
good-boy or good-girl orientation, 212
individual principles of conscience orientation, 212, 213
naive hedonism orientation, 212
postconventional level, 212, 213
preconventional level, 212
punishment-and-obedience orientation, 212
social contract orientation, 212, 213
social order maintaining orientation, 212
unity orientation, 214

L

Labor force, 172
Late adulthood (age 75 and older), 271–273
disengagement in, 271–272
life review in, 272–273
review of, 272–273
selective optimization with compensation in, 272

Late adulthood, social roles in, 119–122
  care receiver, becoming, 121–122
  living alone, 120–121
Learning-schema theory, 125
Leaving (and returning) home, 107–109
Leisure-time interests, retirement and, 174
Lens, 31
Lesbian, gay, bisexual, and transgendered (LGBT+) people, 140–142
Levitra, 43
LGBT people. *See* Lesbian, gay, bisexual, and transgendered (LGBT+) people
Libido, 132
Life as a journey, 222–223
Life-change events, 228
Lifelong singles, 122–123
Life review, 272
Life-span developmental psychology approach, 10, 284
Life-span/life-space theory, 157
Lifestyle
  individual differences in health, 74
  primary aging and, 45–46
Limerance, 132
Living alone, in late adulthood, 120–121
Living will, 250
Longevity
  caloric restriction, 25
  genetics, 25, 48
  intelligence used to predict, 89
Longitudinal study, 13–14
Long-term marriages, 138
Loudness scale, 33
Loyola Generativity Scale (LGS), 197

M

Macrosystem, 10, 11
Macular degeneration, 32
Major depression, 61, 66
Major life changes, disequilibrium in, 282
Major life events, stress and, 229, 230, 234
Major tasks, review of changes in, 265

Manipulative transactions, 192
Marital friendship, 124
Marital happiness
  health and, 114–115
  parenthood and, 114–115
Marriage
  cohabitation and, 138–140
  happy, intimate partnerships and, 137–138
  negative patterns in, 138
Maslow's hierarchy of needs, 201–202
Masturbation, 42
Mate selection, 132
Mature adaptation, 199–200
Maximum lifespan, 25
Meaning
  quest for (*See* Quest for meaning)
  review of changes in, 265
Meaning-focused coping, 238
Meaning systems, study of age-related changes in, 207–211
  approaches to, 207–208
  quest for meaning, changes in, 208–210
  religion, spirituality, and health, 210–211
Mean-level change, 184–185
Measures in developmental research, 15
  personal interview, 15
  standardized tests, 15
  survey questionnaire, 15
Medication
  adherence, 97
  individual differences in cognitive change, 94
Memory, 79–86
  adaptive nature of cognition, 85
  in context, 85–86
  contextual perspective, 85
  declarative memory, 81
  defined, 79
  digit-span task, 80
  episodic, 81–83
  executive function, 81
  long-term store, 79
  name-retrieval failures, 83
  nondeclarative (procedural) memory, 83
  prospective, 83–84
  semantic, 82–83
  short-term (primary), 80

  short-term and working, 80–81
  short-term store, 79
  slowing declines in, 84–85
  stereotype threat, 85–86
  tip-of-the-tongue phenomenon, 83
  word-finding failures, 83
Menopause, 39
Mental exercise, 284–285
Mental health disorders, 231–232
Mental Measurements Yearbook, 15
Mesosystem, 10, 11
Meta-analysis, 17
Metaphor, 223
Microdermabrasion, 29
Microsystem, 10
Microvascular disease (MVD), 55
Middle adulthood (age 40–64), 268–269
  biological clock in, 268
  marriage and, 269
  midlife crisis and, 269
  review of, 264–265
  social clock in, 268
  work and, 269
Middle adulthood, social roles in, 115–119
  aging parents, caregiving for, 118–119
  departure of children (empty nest), 115–116
  gender roles, 116
  grandparent, becoming, 116–117
Midlife crisis, 269
Mild cognitive impairment (MCI), 59
Minnesota Multiphasic Personality Inventory (MMPI), 183
MMPI, 15, 183
Model of adult growth and development, 278–283
  adaptive/maladaptive outcomes *vs.* happiness, 283
  age-linked shared, physical and psychological developments, 278–279
  episodes of stable life structure and disequilibrium, 280–282
  influences on adult development, 279
  outcome of disequilibrium, 282, 283

stable periods and age, relationship of, 280
transitions, cumulative effects of, 283
turning points, 280, 282 (*See also* Disequilibrium*)*
Modern Maturity Sexuality Survey, 42
Monozygotic twins, 8, 18–19
Mood disorders, 69
Moral reasoning, 212–216. *See also* Kohlberg's stages of moral reasoning
data, 214–215
defined, 212
evaluation and comment, 215–216
measurement of, 212
Morbidity rates, 52
Mortality rates, 52
Mouth, taste and, 34
Muscles, changes in, 35–37
Myers-Briggs Type Indicator, 15
Mystical experience, 220
awakening stage of, 220
dark night of the soul stage of, 220
illumination stage of, 220
purification stage of, 220
unity stage of, 220
Mysticism, 220
Mysticism (Underhill), 208

N

Naive hedonism orientation, 212
Name-retrieval failures, 83
National Center for Veterans Affairs (2016), 243
National Comorbidity Survey, 60
National Health and Nutrition Examination Survey, 66
National Senior Services Corps, 177
National Study of Daily Experiences (NSDE), 229
National Survey of Sexual Health and Behavior, 44
Native Americans, health and. *See also* Racial and ethnic groups
Natural immunity, 227
NEO Personality Inventory, 183, 194
Nervous system, changes in, 37–38

Networks, friendship, 149–150
Neurofibrillary tangles, 58
Neurogenesis, 38
Neurons, 37
Neuroticism, 184–186, 188, 189, 191–193, 200, 282
Neurotransmitters, 132
Noise exposure, 34
Nondeclarative (procedural) memory, 83
Non-hispanic black Americans, health of, 70
Non-hispanic white, health of, 70
Nonnormative life events, 8
Nontraditional student, 164
Norepinephrine, 132
Normative age-graded influences, 6
biology, 6
defined, 6
shared experiences, 6
Normative history-graded influences, 6–7
Normative solidarity, 143
Nose, taste/smell and, 34–35
Nuclear families, 142
Nun Study of the School Sisters of Notre Dame, 19
Nursing home, 121
Nutrition, 285
Nutritional supplements, 38

O

Obesity
Alzheimer's disease and, 59
body mass index, 27–29
cancer risk and, 57
cardiovascular disease and, 55
defined, 27
developmental origins, 73
diabetes and, 57
lifestyle and, 74
in older adults, proportion of, 26
in racial and ethnic groups, 70
risk factors for, 27
Obsessive love, 132
Occupational gender segregation, 160–162
Odor receptors, 34
Older adulthood (age 65–74), 269–271
review of, 264–265

Olfactory membrane, 34
On Death and Dying (Kübler-Ross), 250
Onset, 61
Open ended personal interview, 15
Openness, 183–187, 189, 191, 193, 200, 201, 203, 204
Optimism, 72
Optimism, resilience and, 242
Organ transplant donor, 250
Osteoarthritis, 36
Osteoporosis, 35–36
Outward appearance, changes in, 26–31
body composition, 27–29
skin, 29–30
weight, 27–29
Oxidative damage, 23–24

P

Pacific Islanders, health of, 69
Paid parental leave policy, 169
Palliative care, 254
Parental investment theory, 112
Parental leave, 169–170
Parent-child relationships in adulthood, 143–145
intergenerational solidarity theory, 143–144
late-life divorce, effects of, 144–145
problem children in adulthood, 145
Parents
aging parents, caring for, 118–119
becoming, 111–115
departure of children (empty nest), 115–116
gender roles in couples with children, 112
marital happiness and, 114–115
in young adulthood, 111–115
Partners. *See also* Intimate relationships
becoming, 111–115
gender roles in early partnerships, 110
sexual, 44
Passion, 132
Passionate love, 132
Patient adherence to treatment for bone loss, 36

Peak experiences, 202
Pensions, 174
Perceived control, 241–242
Perceived discrimination
   posttraumatic stress disorder
      and, 235
   stress-related disorders and,
      234–235
Perimenopause, 39
Personal computers, 98
Personal interview, 15
Personality, 181–203
   continuity of change,
      explanations of, 190–194
   defined, 182
   development, disequilibrium
      in, 282
   individual differences in health,
      72–73
   measures (*See* Measures in
      developmental research)
   quest for meaning and,
      integrating, 218–220
   review of changes in, 265
   role requirements and, poor
      match between, 281
   structures (*See* Personality traits)
Personality development, theories
   of, 194–203
   ego development, 198–199
   gender crossover, 200–201
   mature adaptation, 199–200
   positive well-being, 201–203
   psychosocial development,
      194–197
Personality factors, 183
Personality states, 182
Personality structures. *See*
   Personality traits
Personality traits, 182–183
   achievement and, 188–189
   coping with stress, 247
   death anxiety and, 249
   defined, 182
   differential continuity, 183–184
   factors and, 182–183
   Five-Factor Model (FFM) of
      personality and, 183
   functions of, 188–190
   health and, 189–190
   intra-individual variability,
      185–187
   mean-level change, 184–185

   relationships and, 188
   resilience, 241–242
Personal life and work, 165–170
   the individual, 165–167
   marriage, 168–170
Person-environment
   transactions, 192
Phased retirement, 177
Phobias, 60
Physical behavior, changes in,
   40–45
   athletic abilities, 40
   balance, 40–41
   dexterity, 40–41
   sexual activity, 42–45
   sleep, 41–42
   stamina, 40–41
Physical change, review of, 264
Physical changes during
   adulthood, 22–49. *See also*
   Physical behavior, changes in;
   Primary aging
   bones, 35–37
   brain, 37–38
   cardiovascular system, 37
   hormonal system, 38–40
   immune system, 38
   muscles, 35–37
   nervous system, 37–38
   outward appearance, 26–31
   overview of, 48–49
   respiratory system, 37
   senses, 31–35
Physical disease, stress-related,
   230–231
Physical exercise, 284–285
Physician-assisted suicide, 255
Plaques, 55
Plasticity, 38
Plastic surgery, 29, 30
Polystrengths, resilience and, 242
Positive avoidance (denial),
   as response to imminent
   death, 252
Positive emotion, resilience and, 242
Positive instability, 266
Positive psychology, 202
Positive well-being, 201–203
Positivity bias, 92–93
Possibilities, imagining, 266
Postconventional level of
   Kohlberg's stages of moral
   reasoning, 212

Post-Deployment Health
   Assessment (PDHA), 243
Postformal stages, 207
Postparental stage, 115. *See also*
   Middle adulthood, social
   roles in
Posttraumatic stress disorder (PTSD)
   age differences in, 233–234
   defined, 231
   gender differences in, 233
   perceived discrimination and,
      234–235
   resilience and, 241
   symptom reporting, 243
Posttraumatic stress syndrome
   (PTSD), 59
Poverty, feminization of, 174–176
Preconventional level of Kohlberg's
   stages of moral reasoning, 212
Preengaged cohabitation, 139
Presbyopia, 31
Prevalence, 60
Primary aging
   defined, 23
   individual differences in, 45–49
Primary aging, theories of, 23–26
   caloric restriction (CR), 24–25
   genetic limits, 24
   oxidative damage, 23–24
Primary memory, 80–81
Privacy, in sexual activity, 44
Private beliefs and practices,
   changes in, 208
Proactive transactions, 192
Problem-focused approach, 92
Problem-focused coping, 237
Problem solving. *See* Decision
   making and problem solving
Procedural (nondeclarative)
   memory, 83
Progesterone, 39
Propecia, 31
Prospective memory, 83–84, 97
Proximal causes, 106
PSEN1 gene, 58
PSEN2 gene, 58
Psychological age, 5
Psychological disorders, 59–63
   anxiety disorders, 60
   depressive disorders, 60–61
   substance-related and addictive
      disorders, 61–63
   treatment of, 63

Psychological health, 275, 276
  psychosocial adjustment, 275
  quality of life, 275–277
Psychometrics, 86
Psychosocial adjustment, 275
Psychosocial development, 194–197
  Erikson's stages of, 194–197
Punishment-and-obedience orientation, 212
Pupils, 31
Purification stage of mystical experience, 220

Q

Qualitative research, 19–20
Quality of life, individual differences in. *See* individual differences, in quality of life
Quantitative research, 19
Quest for meaning, 206–223
  defined, 206
  importance of, 206
  meaning systems, study of age-related changes in, 207–211
  personality and, integrating, 218–220
  shapes of, 222–223
  spiritual development, theories of, 212–218
  transition, process of, 220–222
Questions, in developmental research, 11–12

R

Race and ethnicity
  individual differences, in health, 69–70
Racial and ethnic groups
  primary aging and, 46–47
Racial discrimination in health care, 69–70
Random mutations explanation, 56
Rapamycin, 25
Reactive heritability, 193
Reactive transactions, 192
Relatedness, in self-determination theory, 203
Relationships, review of changes in, 264
Reliability of standardized tests, 15
Religion, quest for meaning and, 210–211

Religiosity
  death anxiety and, 248–249
  defined, 207, 248
  meaning systems and, 207
Reminiscence, 250
Replicative senescence, 24
Research. *See* Developmental research
Research methods. *See* Developmental research methods
Residence, retirement and, 176
Resilience, 240–243. *See also* individual differences, in resilience
  defined, 240
  in military deployment, 243
  personality traits, 241–242
  trauma and, reactions to, 241
Resistance, 228
Resistance resources, 236
Resistance training, 37
Respiratory system, 37
Response-oriented viewpoint, 228
Restylane, 30
Resveratrol, 25
Retinas, 31
Retired and Senior Volunteer Program (RSVP), 177
Retirement, 171–178
  alternatives to, 176–177
  bridge employment, 176–177
  career commitment and, 173–174
  defined, 171
  effects of, 174–176
  family and, 173
  health and, 173
  leisure-time interests, 174
  phased, 177
  preparation for, 171–172
  reasons for, 173–174
  returning to the workforce, 176
  shunning, 176
  timing of, 172
  volunteer work, 177
  and well-being, 177–178
Retirement-related value, 173
Returning (and leaving) home, 107–109
Revised NEO Personality Inventory, 183
Ritual mourning, 256
Rogaine, 31
Role confusion, identity *vs.*, 194–196, 198

Role requirements, personality and, 281
Role transitions, 104
  disequilibrium in, 281
Romantic love, 132

S

Saliva, 35
Same-sex couples, sexual activity in, 44, 45
Same-sex partnerships, 140–142
Schooling, 95, 96
Seattle Longitudinal Study, 87, 96
Secondary aging, 23, 51. *See also* Health and health disorders
Selection effect, 139
Selective optimization with compensation, 272
Self-absorption, generativity *vs.*, 195
Self-actualization, 201–202, 206, 208, 218
Self-aware stage of ego development, 198
Self-determination theory, 202
Self-efficacy, 158
Self, focusing on, 266
Self-identity, resilience and, 242
Self-preoccupation, 218
Self-protective stage of ego development, 198
Self-transcendence, 206
Semantic memory, 82–83
Senile plaque, 58
Senior Companion Program, 177
Sense of purpose in life, 249
Senses, changes in, 31–35
  hearing, 33–34
  smell, 34–35
  taste, 34–35
  vision, 31–33
Sensorineural hearing loss, 33
Sequential study, 15
Serotonin, 132
Sexual activity, changes in, 42–45
  cyclic GMP, 43
  masturbation, 44
  physical ability, 42–43
  privacy, 44
  response in older adults *vs.* younger adults, 42–43
  same-sex couples, 44
  sexual desire, 43–44
  sexual partner, 44

Sexual orientation, 196
Sexual problems
  erectile dysfunction (ED), 43, 45
  treatment for, 44, 45
  vaginal dryness, 43
Short-term life events, stress and, 228
Short-term memory, 80–81
Short-term store, 79
Sibling relationships, 148–149
SIREAC types of vocational interests, 157, 158
Sixteen Personality Factor Questionnaire (16PF), 183
Skin, changes in, 29–30
Sleep apnea, 42
Sleep, changes in, 41–42
Smell, changes in, 34–35
Social age, 5
Social anxiety, 60
Social clock, 6, 104
  in emerging adulthood (age 18–24), 266
  in middle adulthood (age 40–64), 268
  in older adulthood (age 65–74), 269
  in young adulthood (age 25–39), 267
Social-cognitive theory, 158
Social comparisons, quality of life and, 275
Social contract orientation, 212, 213
Social engagement, 285
Social-focused coping, 238
Social media friends, 150–153
Social networks
  cognitive assistance and, 98
  convoy model and, 129–130
  negative effects of, 240
  social media friends, 150–153
  theories of social relationships and, 129, 130
Social order maintaining orientation, 212
Social relationships, 127–155
  defined, 128
  friendships in adulthood, 149–153
  intimate partnerships, 131–142
  review of changes in, 153
  with other family members, 142–149

Social relationship theories, 128–131
  attachment theory, 128–129
  convoy model, 129–130
  evolutionary psychology, 130–131
  similarities in, 131
  socioemotional selectivity theory, 130
Social roles, 103–126
  in atypical families, 122–125
  defined, 104
  gender roles, 106–107
  in late adulthood, 119–122
  in middle adulthood, 115–119
  review of, 125–126
  social timing, 104–105
  transitions and, 104–105
  in young adulthood, 107–115
Social role theory, 106
Social Security benefits, 172–174
Social support, 239–240
  buffering effect of, 239–240
  coping and, 239
  defined, 239
  in social networks, 240
Social timing, 104–105
Sociobiographical history, 95
Socioeconomic class
  individual differences in health, 66–69
Socioeconomic status (SES)
  factors in primary aging, 46–47
  quality of life and, 274
Socioemotional selectivity theory, 93, 130
Specific immunity, 227
Spillover, 168, 169
Spiritual development, theories of, 212–218. See also Quest for meaning
  faith, development of, 212–216
  moral reasoning, development of, 212–216
Spirituality
  changes in, 210–211
  defined, 208
  development, disequilibrium in, 282
Spouse, becoming, 109–115
Stability, defined, 3
Stages
  defined, 4
  typical and atypical, 4

Stagnation, generativity vs., 195, 196
Stamina, changes in, 40–41
Standardized tests, 15
Stem cells, 38
Stepfathers, 125
Stepmothers, 125
Stereotype threat, 85–86
Stimulus-oriented viewpoint, 228
Stoic acceptance (fatalism), as response to imminent death, 252
Stress, 227–243
  coping with, 236–240 (See also Coping)
  defined, 227
  general adaptation syndrome, 227
  immune response to, 227
  resilience, 240–243
  response-oriented viewpoint, 228
  stimulus-oriented viewpoint, 228
  types of, 228–229
Stress, effects of, 229–236. See also individual differences, in stress-related disorders
  mental health disorders, 231–232
  physical disease, 230–231
  stress-related growth and, 236
Stressors, 227
Stress-related growth, 236
Stretching, 37
Structured personal interview, 15
Subjective well-being, 274 See also individual differences, in quality of life
Substance-related and addictive disorders, 61–63
Successful adult development, variations in, 275, 277–278
  psychological health, 275, 276
  psychosocial adjustment, 275
  quality of life, 274–275
Successful aging, 274–275. See also individual differences, in quality of life
  complementary and alternative medicine, 286
  diet and nutrition, 285
  physical and mental exercise, 284–285
  social engagement, 285
Survey questionnaire, 15

Swedish Twin Study database, 18–19
Synthesizing model, 213–214
Synthetic-conventional faith, 216

T

Taste buds, 34
Taste, changes in, 34–35
T cells, 38
Telomeres, 24
Testosterone, 38
Testosterone replacement therapy, 39
Theory of career development, 157–158
The Varieties of Religious Experience (James), 208
Throat, taste and, 34
Tip-of-the-tongue phenomenon, 83
Tongue, taste and, 34
Transition
    to adulthood, 107
    social roles and, 104–105
Transition, process of, 220–222
    impact of life changes, 222
    transition theory, 221
    trigger, 221–222
Transition theory, 221
Trauma, reactions to, 241. *See also* Posttraumatic stress disorder (PTSD)
    grief work, 245
Traumatic brain injury (TBI), 59
Tribalization, 267, 268
Trigger transition, 221–222
Trust *vs.* mistrust, 195
Twin studies, 8
Type A behavior pattern, 72
Type B behavior pattern, 72

U

Unemployment, 166
Unity orientation, 214
Unity stage of mystical experience, 220
Universalizing faith, 217
Useful field of view (UFOV), 99–100
U.S. National Health Interview Survey, 53

V

Vaginal dryness, 39, 43
Validity of standardized tests, 15
Variability, intra-individual, 185–187
Viagra, 43
Victoria Longitudinal Study, 81
Vision, changes in, 31–33
    cataracts, 32
    dark adaptation, 31
    eyes, parts of, 31
    glaucoma, 32
    individual differences in cognitive change, 94
    macular degeneration, 32
    presbyopia, 31
    risk factors for age-related visual conditions, 32
Visual acuity, 31, 32
Visual search, 79
Vocational interests, 157
Volunteer work, 177

W

Waddington's image of epigenetic landscape, 279
Wechsler Adult Intelligence Scale (WAIS-IV), 87

Wechsler Scales, 15
Weight, changes in, 27–29
Well-being, positive, 201–203
Women
    cardiovascular disease and, death from, 55
    climacteric in, 39
    earnings of, 160
Women's Health Study (WHS), 39
Word-finding failures, 83
Work, 157–170. *See also* Retirement
    age trends in work experience, 162–165
    careers, selecting (*See* Career selection)
    changes in careers over adulthood, review of, 178
    importance of, in adulthood, 157–159
    personal life and, 165–170
Work engagement, 166
Work–family spillover, 169
Working memory, 80–81
Work-related value, 173
Work roles, review of changes in, 265
Work satisfaction
    quality of life and, 274
Work strain, 229

Y

Young adulthood (age 25–39), 266–268
    review of, 264–265
Young adulthood, social roles in, 107–115
    becoming a parent, 111–115
    leaving (and returning) home, 107–109
    spouse or partner, becoming, 107–109